P9-AGS-495

Money for Graduate Students in the Health Sciences 2007-2009

Gail Ann Schlachter
R. David Weber

A List of Fellowships, Grants, Awards, Traineeships, and Other Funding Programs Set Aside to Support Graduate Study, Training, Research, and Creative Activities in the Health Sciences and a Set of Five Indexes: Sponsor, Residency, Tenability, Subject, and Deadline.

Reference Service Press
El Dorado Hills, California
2007

ISBN 1588411753
ISBN 13: 9781588411754

10 9 8 7 6 5 4 3 2 1

Reference Service Press (RSP) began in 1977 with a single financial aid publication *(The Directory of Financial Aids for Women)* and now specializes in the development of financial aid resources in multiple formats, including books, large print books, disks, CD-ROMs, print-on-demand reports, eBooks, and online sources. Long recognized as a leader in the field, RSP has been called, by the *Simba Report on Directory Publishing* "a true success in the world of independent directory publishers." Both Kaplan Educational Centers and Military.com have hailed RSP as "the leading authority on scholarships."

Reference Service Press
El Dorado Hills Business Park
5000 Windplay Drive, Suite 4
El Dorado Hills, CA 95762
    (916) 939-9620
    Fax: (916) 939-9626
    E-mail: info@rspfunding.com
Visit our web site: www.rspfunding.com

Manufactured in the United States of America
Price: $40.00, plus $6 shipping.

ACADEMIC INSTITUTIONS, LIBRARIES, ORGANIZATIONS AND OTHER QUANTITY BUYERS:
Discounts on this book are available for bulk purchases. Write or call for information on our discount programs.

This is one of five volumes that make up
Reference Service Press's *Graduate Funding Set.*
The other four titles in the set are:
    1) *Money for Graduate Students in the Arts & Humanities*
    2) *Money for Graduate Students in the Biological Sciences*
    3) *Money for Graduate Students in the Physical & Earth Sciences*
    4) *Money for Graduate Students in the Social & Behavioral Sciences*

Contents

Introduction **5**

    Why this directory is needed 5
    What's included 5
    What's excluded 6
    Sample entry 7
    How the information is compiled 8
    How the directory is organized 8
    How to use the directory 10
    Plans to update the directory 10
    Other related publications 11
    Acknowledgements 11

About the Authors **12**

**Money for Graduate Study or Research
in the Biological & Health Sciences** **13**

    Study and Training 15
    Research and Creative Activities 193

Indexes **271**

    Sponsoring Organization 271
    Residency 279
    Tenability 283
    Subject 287
    Calendar 297

Introduction

WHY THIS DIRECTORY IS NEEDED

Have you decided to get a graduate degree in the health sciences? Congratulations. You have made a wise decision. According to the U.S. Bureau of the Census, the average salary for a college graduate is around $40,000. But, this figure rises to more than $52,000 for master's degree recipients and to $75,000 or more for those with doctoral or professional degrees.

Getting a graduate education, however, is expensive. It can cost more than $20,000 to complete a master's degree and $100,000 or more to finish some doctoral or professional degrees. That's more than most students can afford to pay on their own.

Fortunately, there are billions of dollars available to support graduate study, training, research, and creative activities (writing, projects, etc.) in dentistry, genetics, medicine, nursing, nutrition, pharmacology, rehabilitation, and the other health-related fields. The challenge, of course, is to identify those opportunities.

For many years, the only way to find out about these resources was to use Reference Service Press's award-winning directory, *Money for Graduate Students in the Biological & Health Sciences.* Over time, however, the number of funding opportunities offered in these two disciplines has been steadily increasing, and it has now become impossible to try to cover both fields comprehensively in a single volume. Consequently, beginning with this edition, Reference Service Press has permanently split *Money for Graduate Students in the Biological & Health Sciences* into two separate titles: *Money for Graduate Students in the Health Sciences* and *Money for Graduate Students in the Biological Sciences.* Dividing the previously-combined publication in this way will make it possible to continue our twin goals of 1) providing the most comprehensive and current coverage of available funding in each of these fields and 2) making it easier for graduate students in the both fields (along with the counselors and librarians working with them) to become aware of the wide array of fellowships, awards, and grants currently available to support their graduate study, training, research, and creative activities.

The first edition of *Money for Graduate Students in the Health Sciences* mirrors the organization, scope, depth, and attention to detail that has characterized the other *Money for Graduate Students* directories issued by Reference Service Press during the past decade, including *Money for Graduate Students in the Arts & Humanities, Money for Graduate Students in the Physical & Earth Sciences,* and *Money for Graduate Students in the Social & Behavioral Sciences.* Each of these titles has been highly praised by the reviewers. *American Reference Books Annual* called the titles "invaluable;" Wisconsin Bookwatch labeled them "a fine reference for advanced studies;" and *Choice* concluded that the *Money* books are not only "reasonably priced" and "highly recommended," but "a welcome addition" as well.

WHAT'S INCLUDED?

Money for Graduate Students in the Health Sciences, is unique in many ways. First of all, only funding that students in health-related fields can use is included. If a program doesn't support study, training, research, or creative activities in one or more of these areas, it's not listed here. Now you can turn to just one place to find out about the more than 900 funding opportunities available to support graduate-level activities in dentistry, genetics, medicine, nursing, nutrition, pharmacology, rehabilitation, and the rest of the health sciences.

Second, the directory only lists programs open to graduate students. Most other directories mix together programs for a number of groups—high school students, college students, graduate students, or even postdoctorates. Now, you won't have to spend your time sifting through programs that aren't aimed at you.

Third, only "free" money is identified. If a program requires repayment, charges interest, or requires service to avoid loan repayment, it is not listed. Here's your chance to find out about billions of dollars in aid, knowing that not one dollar of that will ever need to be repaid (provided, of course, that stated requirements are met).

Next, only the biggest and best funding programs are covered in this book. To be listed here, a program has to offer at least $1,000 per year. Many go way beyond that, paying $20,000 or more each year, or covering the full cost of graduate school attendance.

In addition, many of the programs listed here have never been included in the other financial aid directories. So, even if you have checked elsewhere, you will want to look at *Money for Graduate Students in the Health Sciences* for additional leads.

Plus, you can take the money awarded by these fellowships to any number of schools. Unlike other financial aid directories that often list large number of awards available only to students enrolled at one specific school, all of the entries in this book are "portable."

Finally, the directory has been designed to make your search as easy as possible. You can identify programs by purpose (study/training or research/creative activities), specific subject, sponsoring organization, program title, where you live, where you want to study or conduct your research, and deadline date. Plus, you'll find all the information you need to decide if a program is right for you: purpose, eligibility requirements, financial data, duration, special features, limitations, number awarded, and application date. You even get fax numbers, toll-free numbers, e-mail addresses, and web sites (when available), along with complete contact information.

In all, the directory identifies the 934 biggest and best sources of free money available to graduate students interested in study, training, research, or creative activities in health-related fields. All types of funding are covered, including:

- *Fellowships.* Programs that support study, training, and related activities at the graduate level in the United States.

- *Grants.* Programs that provide funding to support innovative efforts, travel, projects, creative activities, or research in the United States.

- *Awards.* Competitions, prizes, and honoraria granted in recognition of personal accomplishments, research results, creative writing, artistic activities, or other achievements. Prizes received solely as the result of entering contests are excluded.

WHAT'S EXCLUDED?

The focus of *Money for Graduate Students in the Health Sciences* is on "portable" funding that can be used to support study, training, research, or creative activities in the health-related fields at practically any graduate school in the United States. Excluded from this listing are:

- *Programs in other areas:* Only funding for the health sciences is covered here. If you are looking for money to support graduate study, training, research, or creative activities in other areas, use one of the other books in Reference Service Press's Graduate Funding Set: *Money for Graduate Students in the Arts & Humanities, Money for Graduate Students in the Biological Sciences, Money*

SAMPLE ENTRY

(1) **[35]**

(2) **AMBUCS SCHOLARSHIPS FOR THERAPISTS**

(3) National AMBUCS, Inc.
P.O. Box 5127
High Point, NC 27262
(336) 852-0052   Fax: (336) 852-6830
E-mail: ambucs@ambucs.org
Web: www.ambucs.org

(4) **Summary** To provide financial assistance to undergraduate and graduate students who are interested in preparing for a career serving disabled citizens in various fields of clinical therapy.

(5) **Eligibility** This program is open to U.S. citizens who have been accepted at the upper-division or graduate level in an accredited program that qualifies the students for clinical practice in occupational therapy, physical therapy, speech language pathology, or hearing audiology. Programs for therapy assistants are not included. Applicants must submit college transcripts for the last 3 semesters, a 500-word essay on their interest in therapy as a career, and a statement of family financial circumstances. Selection is based on financial need, commitment to local community, demonstrated academic accomplishment, character for compassion and integrity, and career objectives.

(6) **Financial data** Most of these awards range from $500 to $1,500 per year; 1 scholarship of $6,000 for 2 years is also awarded. Funds are paid directly to the recipient's school.

(7) **Duration** 1 year.

(8) **Additional information** This program was established in 1955; since then, the association has awarded more than $5 million for more than 9,900 scholarships.

(9) **Number awarded** Approximately 400 each year, with a total value of $225,000.

(10) **Deadline** April of each year.

DEFINITION

(1) **Entry number:** Consecutive number assigned to the references and used to index the entry.

(2) **Program title:** Title of fellowship, grant, award, or traineeship.

(3) **Sponsoring organization:** Name, address, telephone number, toll-free number, fax number, e-mail address, and web site (when information was supplied) for organization sponsoring the program.

(4) **Summary:** Identifies the major program requirements; read the rest of the entry for additional detail.

(5) **Eligibility:** Qualifications required of applicants and factors used in the selection process.

(6) **Financial data:** Financial details of the program, including fixed sum, average amount, or range of funds offered, expenses for which funds may and may not be applied, and cash-related benefits supplied (e.g., room and board).

(7) **Duration:** Time period for which support is provided; renewal prospects.

(8) **Additional information:** Any unusual (generally nonmonetary) benefits, features, restrictions, or limitations associated with the program.

(9) **Number of awards:** Total number of recipients each year or other specified period.

(10) **Deadline:** The month by which applications must be submitted.

for Graduate Students in the Physical & Earth Sciences, or *Money for Graduate Students in the Social & Behavioral Sciences.*

- *Programs not aimed at graduate students:* Even if a program focuses on the health sciences, it's not listed here if it is open only to a different category of student (e.g., undergraduates, postdoctorates) or if it is not specifically for graduate students (e.g., an essay contest on dentistry open to any adult).

- *School-based programs:* The directory identifies "portable" programs—ones that can be used at any number of schools. Financial aid administered by a single school solely for the benefit of its own graduate students is not covered. Write directly to the schools you are considering to get information on their offerings.

- *Money for study or research outside the United States:* Since there are comprehensive and up-to-date directories that describe all available funding for study and research abroad (see the titles listed on the inside of the front cover), only programs that support study or research in the United States are covered here.

- *Programs that exclude U.S. citizens or residents:* If a program is open only to foreign nationals or excludes Americans from applying, it is not included.

- *Very restrictive programs:* In general, programs are excluded if they are open only to a limited geographic area (less than a state) or available to a limited membership group (e.g., a local union or a tightly targeted organization).

- *Programs offering limited financial support:* The focus is on programs that can reduce substantively the cost of graduate education. Fellowships, grants, and awards must offer at least $1,000 per year or they are not covered here.

- *Programs that did not respond to our research inquiries:* Programs are included only if the sponsors responded to our research requests for up-to-date information (we never write program descriptions from secondary sources). Despite our best efforts (described below), some organizations did not supply information and, consequently, are not described in this edition of *Money for Graduate Students in the Health Sciences.*

HOW THE INFORMATION IS COMPILED

The preparation of the first edition of *Money for Graduate Students in the Health Sciences* involved extensive research and revision. To make sure that the information included here is both reliable and current, the editors at Reference Service Press 1) reviewed and updated all relevant programs currently in our funding database and 2) searched exhaustively for new program leads in a variety of sources, including directories, news reports, newsletters, annual reports, and sites on the Internet. Since we only include program descriptions that are written directly from information supplied by the sponsoring organization, we check the sponsor's Internet site and/or send up to four collection letters (followed by up to three telephone inquiries, if necessary) to each sponsor identified in this process. Despite our best efforts, however, some sponsoring organizations still failed to respond and, as a result, their programs are not included in this edition.

HOW THE DIRECTORY IS ORGANIZED

The directory is divided into two sections: 1) a detailed list of funding opportunities open to graduate students in the health sciences and 2) a set of indexes to help you pinpoint appropriate funding programs.

Money for Graduate Study or Research in the Health Sciences. The first section of the directory describes 934 fellowships, grants, and awards open to graduate students in health-related fields. The programs listed are sponsored by federal and state government agencies, professional organizations, foundations, educational associations, social and religious groups, corporations, and military/veterans organizations. Programs for master's, doctoral, professional, and other graduate-level degrees are covered.

To help you tailor your search, the entries in this section are grouped into two main categories:

- **Study and Training.** Described here are 663 fellowships, traineeships, and other awards that support structured and unstructured study or training in the health sciences on the graduate school level, including formal academic classes, courses of study, research training, degree-granting programs, and other educational activities. Funding is available for all graduate-level degrees: master's, doctoral, and professional.

- **Research and Creative Activities.** Described here are 271 grants, awards, and traineeships that support graduate-level research and creative activities in the health sciences.

Each program entry in the first section of the guide has been prepared to give you a concise but clear picture of the available funding. Information (when available) is provided on organization address, telephone numbers (including fax and toll-free), e-mail address, web site, purpose, eligibility, money awarded, duration, special features, limitations, number of awards, and application deadline. The sample entry on page 7 illustrates and explains the program entry structure.

The information provided for each of the programs covered in this section was supplied by sponsoring organizations in response to questionnaires we sent through the first half of 2007. While *Money for Graduate Students in the Health Sciences* is intended to cover as comprehensively as possible the funding available in these areas, some sponsoring organizations did not respond to our research inquiries and, consequently, are not included in this edition of the directory.

Indexes. To help you find the aid you need, we have included five indexes; these will let you access the listings by sponsoring organization, residency, tenability, subject, and deadline. These indexes use a word-by-word alphabetical arrangement. Note: numbers in the index refer to entry numbers, not to page numbers in the book.

Sponsoring Organization Index. This index makes it easy to identify the more than 700 agencies that offer funding for graduate-level study, training, research, or creative activities in the health sciences. Sponsoring organizations are listed alphabetically, word by word. In addition, we've used a code to help you identify the focus of the funding programs sponsored by these organizations: study/training or research/creative activities.

Residency Index. Some programs listed in this book are restricted to residents of a particular location. Others are open to students wherever they live. This index helps you identify programs available only to residents in your area as well as programs that have no residency restrictions.

Tenability Index. Some programs in this book can be used only in specific cities, counties, states, or regions. Others may be used anywhere in the United States (or even abroad). Use this index to find out what programs are available to support your activities in a particular geographic area.

Subject Index. Use this index when you want to identify graduate funding in the health sciences by specific subject (over 200 are included in this index). To help you pinpoint your search, we've also included hundreds of "see" and "see also" references.

Calendar Index. Since most financial aid programs have specific deadline dates, some may have closed by the time you begin to look for funding. You can use the Calendar Index to identify which programs are still open. This index is arranged by purpose (study or research) and divided by month during which the deadline falls. Filing dates can and quite often do vary from year to year; consequently, the dates in this index should be viewed as only approximations after the year 2009.

HOW TO USE THE DIRECTORY

Here are some tips to help you get the most out of the financial aid listings in *Money for Graduate Students in the Health Sciences:*

To Locate Funding by Purpose. If you want to get an overall picture of what kind of graduate funding is available to support either study/training or research/creative activities in the health sciences, turn to the appropriate category in the first section of the guide and browse through the listings there. Originally, we also intended to subdivide these two chapters by degree level. Once the compilation was complete, however, it became clear that few programs limited funding to either master's degree or doctoral degree students exclusively. Thus, further subdivision beyond 1) study or training and 2) research or creative activities would have been unnecessarily repetitious.

To Find Information on a Particular Financial Aid Program. If you know the name and primary purpose of a particular financial aid program, you can go directly to the appropriate category in the first section of the directory, where you'll find program profiles listed alphabetically by title.

To Browse Quickly Through the Listings. Turn to the section that matches your funding needs (study/training or research/creative activities) and read the "Summary" field in each entry. In seconds, you'll know if this is an opportunity that you might want to pursue. If it is, be sure to read the rest of the information in the entry, to see if you are able to meet all of the program requirements before contacting the sponsor for an application form.

To Locate Financial Aid Programs Sponsored by a Particular Organization. The Sponsoring Organization Index makes it easy to determine which groups are providing graduate funding (more than 700 are listed here) and to identify specific financial aid programs offered by a particular sponsor. Each entry number in the index is coded to indicate purpose (study/training or research/creative activities), to help you target appropriate entries.

To Locate Financial Aid Based on Residency or Where You Want to Study/Conduct Your Research. Use the Residency Index to identify funding that has been set aside to support applicants from your area. If you are looking for funding to support activities in a particular city, county, state, or region, turn to the Tenability Index. Both of these indexes are subdivided by broad purpose (study/training and research/creative activities), to help you identify the funding that's right for you. When using these indexes, always check the listings under the term "United States," since the programs indexed there have no geographic restrictions and can be used in any area.

To Locate Financial Aid for Study or Research in a Particular Subject Area. Turn to the subject index first if you are interested in identifying available funding in a specific subject area (more than 200 different subject areas are indexed there). As part of your search, be sure to check the listings in the index under the heading "General programs." That term identifies programs supporting activities in any subject area (although they may be restricted in other ways). Each index entry indicates whether the funding is available for study/training or for research/creative activities.

To Locate Financial Aid by Deadline Date. If you are working with specific time constraints and want to weed out financial aid programs whose filing dates you won't be able to meet, turn first to the Calendar Index and check the program references listed under the appropriate purpose (study/training or research/activities). Note: not all sponsoring organizations supplied deadline information, so not all programs are covered in this index. To identify every relevant financial aid program, regardless of filing dates, go to the first section and read through all the entries in the chapter that represents your interest (study/training or research/creative activities).

PLANS TO UPDATE THE DIRECTORY

This is the first edition of volume *Money for Graduate Students in the Health Sciences.* The next biennial edition will cover 2009-2011 and will be released in the first half of 2009.

OTHER RELATED PUBLICATIONS

In addition to *Money for Graduate Students in the Health Sciences,* Reference Service Press publishes several other titles dealing with fundseeking, including the companion volumes, *Money for Graduate Students in the Biological Sciences, Money for Students in the Social & Behavioral Sciences, Money for Graduate Students in the Physical & Earth Sciences,* and *Money for Graduate Students in the Arts & Humanities.* For more information on these and other related publications, you can 1) write to Reference Service Press' marketing department at 5000 Windplay Drive, Suite 4, El Dorado Hills, CA 95762; 2) give us a call at (916) 939-9620; 3) fax us at (916) 939-9626; 4) send us an e-mail message at info@rspfunding.com; or 5) visit our site on the web: www.rspfunding.com.

ACKNOWLEDGEMENTS

A debt of gratitude is owed all the organizations that contributed information to this edition of *Money for Graduate Students in the Health Sciences.* Their generous cooperation has helped to make this first edition a current and comprehensive survey of graduate funding for students in heath-related fields.

ABOUT THE AUTHORS

Dr. Gail Schlachter has worked for more than three decades as a library educator, a library manager, and an administrator of library-related publishing companies. Among the reference books to her credit are the biennially-issued *Directory of Financial Aids for Women* and two award-winning bibliographic guides: *Minorities and Women: A Guide to Reference Literature in the Social Sciences* (which was chosen as an "Outstanding Reference Book of the Year" by *Choice)* and *Reference Sources in Library and Information Services* (which won the first Knowledge Industry Publications "Award for Library Literature"). She is the former editor of *Reference and User Services Quarterly,* was the reference book review editor of *RQ* for 10 years, is a past president of the American Library Association's Reference and User Services Association, and is currently serving her fourth term on the American Library Association's governing council. In recognition of her outstanding contributions to reference service, Dr. Schlachter has been named the University of Wisconsin School of Library and Information Studies' "Distinguished Alumna of the Year" and awarded both the prestigious Isadore Gilbert Mudge Citation and the Louis Shores–Oryx Press Award.

Dr. R. David Weber teaches both economics and history at Los Angeles Harbor College (Wilmington, California), where he directed the Honors Program for many years. He is the author of a number of critically-acclaimed reference works, including *Dissertations in Urban History* and the three-volume *Energy Information Guide.* With Gail Schlachter, he compiled Reference Service Press' award-winning *Financial Aid for the Disabled and Their Families* and a number of other financial aid titles, including *Financial Aid for Veterans, Military Personnel, and Their Dependents.*

Money for Graduate Students in the Health Sciences

Study and Training ●
Research and Creative Activities ●

Study and Training

Listed alphabetically by program title are 663 fellowships, traineeships, and awards that support structured and unstructured study or training in the health sciences on the graduate level in the United States. Check here if you need funding for formal academic classes, training courses, degree-granting programs, independent study opportunities, or other educational activities in any health-related field, including dentistry, genetics, medicine, nursing, nutrition, pharmacology, rehabilitation, etc.

[1]
ABBOTT/PAMELA BALZER CAREER MOBILITY SCHOLARSHIP

American Nephrology Nurses' Association
Attn: ANNA National Office
200 East Holly Avenue
P.O. Box 56
Pitman, NJ 08071-0056
(856) 256-2320   Toll-free: (888) 600-2662
Fax: (856) 589-7463   E-mail: annascholarships@ajj.com
Web: www.annanurse.org

Summary To provide financial assistance to members of the American Nephrology Nurses' Association (ANNA) who are interested in working on a baccalaureate or advanced degree in nursing.

Eligibility Applicants must be current association members, have been members for at least 2 years, be currently employed in nephrology nursing, and be accepted or enrolled in a baccalaureate or higher degree program in nursing. Along with their application, they must submit a 250-word essay on their career and education goals that includes how their degree will apply to nephrology nursing, provides a time frame for completing their program, and indicates how the funds will meet their educational needs.

Financial data The stipend is $2,500.

Duration 1 year.

Additional information Funds for this program, established in 2002, are supplied by Abbott Renal Care Group. Information is also available from Sharon Longton, Awards and Scholarships Chair, (313) 966-2674, E-mail: slongton@dmc.org.

Number awarded 1 each year.

Deadline October of each year.

[2]
ABE AND ESTHER HAGIWARA STUDENT AID AWARD

Japanese American Citizens League
Attn: National Scholarship Awards
1765 Sutter Street
San Francisco, CA 94115
(415) 921-5225   Fax: (415) 931-4671
E-mail: jacl@jacl.org
Web: www.jacl.org/leadership_development_5.php

Summary To provide financial assistance for college or graduate school to student members of the Japanese American Citizens League (JACL) who can demonstrate severe financial need.

Eligibility This program is open to JACL members who are enrolled or planning to enroll in a college, university, trade school, or business college. Applicants must be undergraduate or graduate students who are able to demonstrate that, without this aid, they will have to delay or terminate their education. They must submit a statement describing their current level of involvement in the Japanese American community or Asian Pacific community and how they will continue their involvement in future years. Selection is based on financial need, academic record, extracurricular activities, and community involvement.

Financial data The stipend depends on the availability of funds but usually ranges from $1,000 to $5,000.

Duration 1 year; nonrenewable.

Additional information Applications must be submitted to the JACL National Scholarship Program, c/o San Diego JACL Chapter, 1031 25th Street, San Diego, CA 92102.

Number awarded At least 1 each year.

Deadline March of each year.

[3]
ABILIO REIS MEMORIAL SCHOLARSHIP AWARD

Luso-American Education Foundation
Attn: Administrative Director
7080 Donlon Way, Suite 202
P.O. Box 2967
Dublin, CA 94568
(925) 828-3883   Fax: (925) 828-3883
Web: www.luso-american.org/laef/html/reis.html

Summary To provide financial assistance to medical students of Portuguese descent in California.

Eligibility This program is open to California residents of Portuguese descent who have completed a bachelor's degree. Applicants must be interested in studying medicine. Selection is based on promise of success in the field of medicine, financial need, and sincerity of purpose.

Financial data The stipend is $2,500.

Duration 1 year; nonrenewable.

Number awarded 1 each year.

Deadline February of each year.

[4]
ACADEMY OF NEONATAL NURSING SCHOLARSHIP AWARD

Academy of Neonatal Nursing
2270 Northpoint Parkway
Santa Rosa, CA 95407-7398
(707) 568-2168   Fax: (707) 569-0786
Web: www.academyonline.org/awards_scholarships.html

Summary To provide financial assistance to members of the Academy of Neonatal Nursing (ANN) who are working on an undergraduate or graduate degree in neonatal nursing or a related nursing major.

Eligibility This program is open to ANN members who have been in good standing for at least 2 years. Applicants must have at least 2 years of neonatal practice experience with at least 1 of those years completed in the past 18 months. They must be enrolled in a nursing academic degree program or a neonatal graduate program in which they have completed at least 2 degree-required courses with a GPA of 3.0 or higher. Only professionally-active neonatal nurses are eligible, i.e., currently engaged in a clinical, research, or educational role that contributes directly to the health care of neonates or to the nursing profession and taking 15 contact hours of continuing education a year. Along with their application, they must submit a 200-word essay on why they are pursuing their education and how attainment of this degree will benefit them in their professional role. Financial need is not considered in the selection process.

Financial data The stipend is $1,000. Funds are paid directly to the recipient and the educational program.

Duration 1 year; recipients are not eligible for another scholarship for 5 years.

Number awarded 1 or more each year.

Deadline April of each year.

[5]
ACMPE LEADERS SCHOLARSHIPS

American College of Medical Practice Executives
Attn: ACMPE Scholarship Fund Inc.
104 Inverness Terrace East
Englewood, CO 80112-5306
(303) 799-1111, ext. 232   Toll-free: (877) ASK-MGMA
Fax: (303) 643-4439   E-mail: acmpe@mgma.com
Web: www.mgma.com/academics/scholar.cfm

Summary To provide financial assistance to practitioners in medical practice management interested in pursuing professional development on the undergraduate or graduate school level.

Eligibility This program is open to professionals working on an undergraduate or graduate degree in a program relevant to medical practice management, including public health, business administration, health care administration, or other related areas. Students working on a degree in medicine, physical therapy, nursing, or other clinically-related professions are not eligible. Applicants must submit a letter describing their career goals and objectives relevant to medical practice management; a resume; 2 reference letters commenting on their performance, character, potential to succeed, and need for scholarship support; and either documentation indicating acceptance into an undergraduate or graduate program or academic transcripts indicating undergraduate or graduate work completed to date.

Financial data The stipend is $3,000. Funds are paid directly to the recipient's college or university.

Duration 1 year.

Additional information This program is managed by Scholarship Program Administrators, Inc. 1201 Eighth Avenue South, P.O. Box 23737, Nashville, TN 27202-3737, (615) 320-3149, (800) 310-4053, Fax: (615) 320-3151, E-mail: info@spaprog.com. It was established to honor past presidents of the American College of Medical Practice Executives (ACMPE), Ernest S. Moscatello, Edgar J. Saux, Charles Wallace, Robert W. "Win" Baker, the Medical Group Management Association (MGMA) Academic Practice Assembly (APA), the MGMA Anesthesia Administration Assembly (AAA), and the MGMA Integrated Health Care Organizations Society (IHOS).

Number awarded 4 each year.

Deadline April of each year.

[6]
ADA DENTAL STUDENT SCHOLARSHIPS

American Dental Association
Attn: ADA Foundation
211 East Chicago Avenue
Chicago, IL 60611
(312) 440-2547   Fax: (312) 440-3526
E-mail: adaf@ada.org
Web: www.ada.org

Summary To provide financial assistance to currently-enrolled dental school students.

Eligibility Applicants must be entering their second year of full-time study at a dental school accredited by the Commission on Dental Accreditation. They must have a GPA of 3.0 or higher and be able to demonstrate financial need of at least $2,500. U.S. citizenship is required. Selection is based on academic achievement, a written summary of personal and professional goals, letters of reference, and financial need.

Financial data Stipends range up to $2,500 per year. Funds are to be used to cover school expenses (tuition, fees, books, supplies, living expenses) and are paid in 2 equal installments to the recipient's school.

Duration 1 year.

Additional information This program was established in 1991.

Number awarded 25 each year.

Deadline October of each year.

[7]
ADELAINE DUNN SCHOLARSHIP

National Association of University Women-Southwest Section
c/o Sallie Gibson, Scholarship Chairperson
5576 Village Green
Los Angeles, CA 90016
(323) 292-4882

Summary To provide financial assistance to graduate students in selected states.

Eligibility Eligible to apply for this scholarship are full-time graduate students who have permanent residency in 1 of the following states: California, Arizona, New Mexico, Colorado, Nevada, or Hawaii. Finalists are interviewed (applicants must provide their own transportation to the interview). Selection is based on academic record (must have at least a 3.0 to apply), honors or awards, extracurricular activities, an essay on future plans, the interview, and financial need. Students who have previously received a scholarship from a branch of the National Association of University Women are not eligible to apply for this support.

Financial data The stipend is $1,000.

Duration 1 year; nonrenewable.

Additional information The National Association of University Women is an organization of African American women.

Number awarded 1 each year.

Deadline November of each year.

[8]
ADELE RYERSON SMITH MEMORIAL AWARD

American Occupational Therapy Foundation
Attn: Scholarship Coordinator
4720 Montgomery Lane
P.O. Box 31220
Bethesda, MD 20824-1220
(301) 652-2682   Fax: (301) 656-3620
TDD: (800) 377-8555   E-mail: aotf@aotf.org
Web: www.aotf.org

Summary To provide financial assistance to students in Arizona who are working on a degree in occupational therapy.

Eligibility This program is open to Arizona residents who are enrolled in an accredited occupational therapy educational program in the state at the associate or professional master's degree level. Applicants must demonstrate a need for financial assistance and have a sustained record of outstanding scholastic performance. As part of the application process, they must submit transcripts, 2 personal references, and a statement from their curriculum director.

Financial data The stipend is $1,000.

Duration 1 year.

Number awarded 1 each year.

Deadline January of each year.

[9]
ADHA INSTITUTE PART-TIME SCHOLARSHIP

American Dental Hygienists' Association
Attn: Institute for Oral Health
444 North Michigan Avenue, Suite 3400
Chicago, IL 60611
(312) 440-8918   Toll-free: (800) 735-4916
Fax: (312) 440-8929   E-mail: institute@adha.net
Web: www.adha.org/institute/Scholarship/index.htm

Summary To provide financial assistance to students enrolled part time in doctoral, master's, baccalaureate, or certificate/associate programs in dental hygiene.

Eligibility This program is open to part-time undergraduate and graduate students who are active members of the Student American Dental Hygienists' Association (SADHA) or the American Dental Hygienists' Association (ADHA). Applicants must have a GPA of 3.0 or higher, be able to document financial need of at least $1,500, and have completed at least 1 year in an accredited dental hygiene program in the United States. Along with their application, they must submit a statement that covers their long-term career goals, their intended contribution to the dental hygiene profession, their professional interests, a list of past and/or present involvement in professional and/or community activities, and the manner in which their degree will enhance their professional capacity.

Financial data Stipends range from $1,000 to $2,000.

Duration 1 year.

Number awarded 1 each year.

Deadline June of each year.

[10]
AFPE PRE-DOCTORAL FELLOWSHIPS IN THE PHARMACEUTICAL SCIENCES

American Foundation for Pharmaceutical Education
Attn: Grants Manager
One Church Street, Suite 202
Rockville, MD 20850-4158
(301) 738-2160   Fax: (301) 738-2161
E-mail: info@afpenet.org
Web: www.afpenet.org/pro_doc_grad_fellow.htm

Summary To provide financial assistance to graduate students working on a Ph.D. in clinical pharmacy sciences.

Eligibility This program is open to students who have completed at least 3 semesters of graduate study and have no more than 3 years remaining to complete a Ph.D. degree at a U.S. college of pharmacy. Preference is given to students who have a Pharm.D. degree and are working on a Ph.D. or who are enrolled in a combined Pharm.D./Ph.D. program. Applicants must be U.S. citizens or permanent residents. Students with the following majors are encouraged to apply: medicinal/pharmaceutical chemistry, pharmaceutics, pharmacology/toxicology, pharmacy administration, pharmacognosy, pharmacokinetics/metabolism, and the pharmaceutical sciences.

Financial data The stipend is $6,000 per year. Funds must be used to enable the students to make progress on their Ph.D. (e.g., student stipend, laboratory supplies, books, materials, travel) but not for indirect costs for the institution.

Duration 1 year; may be renewed up to 2 additional years.

Additional information This program includes the following named Memorial and Citation Fellowships: the W. Paul Briggs Fellowship, the Donald and Frances Brodie Fellowship, the Albert H. Diebold Fellowship, the George V. Doerr Fellowship, the H.A.B. Dunning Fellowship, the Richard E. Faust Fellowship, the Albert B. Fisher, Jr. Fellowship, the James E. Hoge Fellowship, the Robert Wood Johnson Fellowship, the Josiah Kirby Lilly Sr. Fellowship, the Charles J. Lynn Fellowship, the Robert Lincoln McNeil Fellowship, the E. Mead Johnson Fellowship, the E.I. Newcomb Fellowship, the Sydnor Barksdale Penick Fellowship, the Abe Plough Fellowship, the Paul M. Scott Fellowship, the Charles R. Walgreen Fellowship, the William E. Weiss Fellowship, and the Sir Henry S. Wellcome Fellowship. Support for this program is provided by a number of corporate and association sponsors, including (but not limited to) Abbott Laboratories, the American Association of Colleges of Pharmacy, the American Association of Pharmaceutical Scientists, the American Council of Pharmaceutical Education, the American Pharmaceutical Association, the American Society of Health-System Pharmacists, AstraZeneca Pharmaceuticals, L.P., Aventis Pharmaceuticals, Inc., Blistex, Inc., Bristol-Myers Squibb Company, the Burroughs Wellcome Fund, Fujisawa Healthcare, Inc., GlaxoSmithKline, Janssen Pharmaceutica Products, L.P., Johnson & Johnson Medical, Inc., Kappa Epsilon Pharmacy Fraternity, the Merck Company Foundation, the National Association of Chain Drug Stores, the National Community Pharmacists Association, Novartis Pharmaceuticals Corporation, Novo Nordisk Pharmaceuticals, Inc., Ortho Biotech, Ortho-McNeil Pharmaceutical Corporation, Pfizer Inc., the Pharmaceutical Research and Manufacturers of America Foundation, Pharmacia Corporation, Procter & Gamble Company, Schering Laboratories, Schering-Plough Foundation, Inc., Sanofi-Synthelabo, Inc., and Wyeth Pharmaceuticals.

Number awarded Up to 70 each year.

Deadline February of each year.

[11]
AGNES JONES JACKSON SCHOLARSHIPS

National Association for the Advancement of Colored People
Attn: Education Department
4805 Mt. Hope Drive
Baltimore, MD 21215-3297
(410) 580-5760   Toll-free: (877) NAACP-98
E-mail: youth@naacpnet.org
Web: www.naacp.org/rat/education/education_scholar.html

Summary To provide financial assistance to members of the National Association for the Advancement of Colored People (NAACP) who are attending or planning to attend college or graduate school.

Eligibility This program is open to members of the NAACP who are younger than 25 years of age and full-time undergraduates or full- or part-time graduate students. The minimum GPA is 2.5 for graduating high school seniors and undergraduate students or 3.0 for graduate students. All applicants must be able to demonstrate financial need (family income must be less than $14,355 for a family of 1, ranging up to $48,585 for a family of 8) and U.S. citizenship. Along with their application, they must submit a 1-page essay on their interest in their major and a career, their life's ambition, what they hope to accomplish in their lifetime, and what position they hope to attain.

Financial data The stipend is $1,500 per year for undergraduate students or $2,500 per year for graduate students.

Duration 1 year; recipients may apply for renewal.

Additional information Information is also available from the United Negro College Fund, Scholarships and Grants Administration, 8260 Willow Oaks Corporate Drive, Fairfax, VA 22031, (703) 205-3400. Renewal awards may be reduced or denied based on insufficient NAACP activities.

Number awarded Varies each year; recently, 17 of these scholarships were awarded.

Deadline   March of each year.

[12]
AGNES MISSIRIAN SCHOLARSHIP

Armenian International Women's Association
65 Main Street, Room 3A
Watertown, MA 02472
(617) 926-0171   E-mail: aiwainc@aol.com
Web: www.aiwa-net.org/scholarshipinfo.html

Summary   To provide financial assistance to Armenian women who are upper-division and graduate students.

Eligibility   This program is open to full-time women students of Armenian descent attending an accredited college or university. Applicants must be full-time juniors, seniors, or graduate students with a GPA of 3.2 or higher. They must submit an essay, up to 500 words, describing their planned academic program, their career goals, and the reasons why they believe they should be awarded this scholarship. Selection is based on financial need and merit.

Financial data   The stipend is $2,000.

Duration   1 year.

Number awarded   1 or more each year.

Deadline   April of each year.

[13]
AIR FORCE HEALTH PROFESSIONS SCHOLARSHIP PROGRAM

U.S. Air Force
Attn: AFIT/CIMJ
Building 16, Room 120
2275 D Street
Wright-Patterson AFB, OH 45433-7221
(937) 255-5824, ext. 3036
Toll-free: (800) 543-3490, ext. 3036   Fax: (937) 656-7156
E-mail: afit.cimj3@afit.edu
Web: www.airforce.com

Summary   To provide financial assistance for education in a medical or scientific field to future Air Force medical officers.

Eligibility   This program is open to U.S. citizens who are accepted to or already attending a school of medicine (allopathic or osteopathic), dentistry, optometry, nursing, or pharmacy. They must be working on a degree as a doctor of medicine (M.D.), doctor of osteopathic medicine (D.O.), dentist (D.D.S. or D.M.D.), doctor of pharmacy (Pharm.D.), doctor of optometry (O.D.), nurse practitioner (M.S.N.), nurse anesthetist or CRNA (M.S.N.), or doctor or master's of science in bioenvironmental engineering. Upon acceptance into the program, applicants are commissioned as officers in the U.S. Air Force; after completion of medical school, they must perform at least 3 years of active-duty service in the U.S. Air Force.

Financial data   This program pays full tuition at any school of medicine or osteopathy located in the United States or Puerto Rico, and it also covers the cost of fees, books, and other required equipment. In addition, recipients are awarded a stipend of $1,279 per month for 10 1/2 months of the year; for the other 1 1/2 months of each year, they perform active-duty service, usually at an Air Force medical facility, and receive the normal pay of a Second Lieutenant.

Duration   Assistance under this program continues until the student completes work for the appropriate advanced degree.

Additional information   Following receipt of the degree, students serve an internship and residency either in an Air Force hospital (in which case they receive Air Force active-duty pay) or, if not selected for Air Force graduate medical education, in a civilian hospital (where they receive only the regular salary paid by the civilian institution). Only after completion of the residency, in either an Air Force or a civilian hospital, do the students begin the active-duty service obligation. That obligation is 2 years for the first 2 years of participation in the program, plus half a year of service for each additional half year of program participation; in any case, the minimum service obligation is 3 years regardless of years of participation. Information on this program is also available from the Air Force Personnel Center, HQ AFPC/DPAME, Attn: Graduate Medical Education Programs, 550 C Street West, Suite 25, Randolph AFB, TX 79150-4727, (210) 565-2638, (800) 531-5800, Fax: (210) 565-2830.

Number awarded   Approximately 325 each year.

[14]
AIR FORCE OFFICERS' WIVES' CLUB OF WASHINGTON, D.C. CONTINUING EDUCATION SCHOLARSHIPS FOR AIR FORCE DEPENDENTS

Air Force Officers' Wives' Club of Washington, D.C.
Attn: AFOWC Scholarship Committee
50 Theisen Street
Bolling Air Force Base
Washington, DC 20032-5411

Summary   To provide financial assistance for undergraduate or graduate education to the dependents of Air Force members in the Washington, D.C. area.

Eligibility   This program is open to the dependents of Air Force members residing in the Washington, D.C. metropolitan area in the following categories: active duty, retired, MIA/POW, or deceased. Dependents are eligible if their Air Force sponsor is assigned remote from the area or reassigned during the current school year and the student has remained behind to continue school. Applicants must be currently enrolled full time at an accredited college or university with a GPA of 3.0 or higher. Along with their application, they must submit a 500-word essay on their interests, goals, and how being an Air Force dependent has affected their life. Selection is based on academic and citizenship achievements; financial need is not considered. Applicants who receive an appointment to a service academy are not eligible.

Financial data   A stipend is awarded (amount not specified). Funds may be used only for payment of tuition or academic fees.

Duration   1 year.

Number awarded   Varies each year.

Deadline   February of each year.

[15]
AIR FORCE ROTC PROFESSIONAL OFFICER CORPS INCENTIVE

U.S. Air Force
Attn: Headquarters AFROTC/RRUC
551 East Maxwell Boulevard
Maxwell AFB, AL 36112-5917
(334) 953-2091   Toll-free: (866) 423-7682
Fax: (334) 953-6167
Web: www.afrotc.com/overview/programs.php

Summary   To provide financial assistance for undergraduate and graduate education to individuals who have completed 2 years of college and who are willing to join Air Force ROTC and serve as Air Force officers following completion of their degree.

Eligibility   Applicants must be U.S. citizens who have completed 2 years of the general military course at a college or university with an Air Force ROTC unit on campus or a college with a cross-enrollment agreement with such a college. They must be full-time students, have a GPA of 2.0 or higher both cumulatively and for the prior term, be enrolled in both Aerospace Studies class and Leadership Laboratory, pass the Air Force Officer Qualifying Test, meet Air Force physical fitness and weight requirements, and be able to be commissioned before they become 31 years of age. They must agree to serve for at least 4 years as active-duty Air Force officers following graduation from college with either a bachelor's or graduate degree.

Financial data This scholarship provides $3,000 per year for tuition and a monthly subsistence allowance of $350 as a junior or $400 as a senior.

Duration Until completion of a graduate degree.

Additional information Scholarship recipients must complete 4 years of aerospace studies courses at 1 of the 144 colleges and universities that have an Air Force ROTC unit on campus; students may also attend other colleges that have cross-enrollment agreements with the institutions that have an Air Force ROTC unit on campus. Recipients must also attend a 4-week summer training camp at an Air Force base between their junior and senior year.

Number awarded Varies each year.

[16]
ALABAMA G.I. DEPENDENTS' SCHOLARSHIP PROGRAM

Alabama Department of Veterans Affairs
770 Washington Avenue, Suite 530
P.O. Box 1509
Montgomery, AL 36102-1509
(334) 242-5077   Fax: (334) 242-5102
E-mail: willie.moore@va.state.al.us
Web: www.va.state.al.us/scholarship.htm

Summary To provide educational benefits to the dependents of disabled, deceased, and other Alabama veterans.

Eligibility Eligible are spouses, children, stepchildren, and unremarried widow(er)s of veterans who served honorably for 90 days or more and 1) are currently rated as 20% or more service-connected disabled or were so rated at time of death; 2) were a former prisoner of war; 3) have been declared missing in action; 4) died as the result of a service-connected disability; or 5) died while on active military duty in the line of duty. The veteran must have been a permanent civilian resident of Alabama for at least 1 year prior to entering active military service; veterans who were not Alabama residents at the time of entering active military service may also qualify if they have a 100% disability and were permanent residents of Alabama for at least 5 years prior to filing the application for this program or prior to death, if deceased. Children and stepchildren must be under the age of 26, but spouses and unremarried widow(er)s may be of any age.

Financial data Eligible dependents may attend any state-supported Alabama institution of higher learning or enroll in a prescribed course of study at any Alabama state-supported trade school without payment of any tuition, book fees, or laboratory charges.

Duration This is an entitlement program for 4 years of full-time undergraduate or graduate study or part-time equivalent. Spouses and unremarried widow(er)s whose veteran spouse is rated between 20 and 90% disabled, or 100% disabled but not permanently so, may attend only 2 standard academic years.

Additional information Benefits for children, spouses, and unremarried widow(er)s are available in addition to federal government benefits. Assistance is not provided for noncredit courses, placement testing, GED preparation, continuing educa-

tional courses, pre-technical courses, or state board examinations.

Number awarded Varies each year.

Deadline Applications may be submitted at any time.

[17]
ALBERT W. DENT STUDENT SCHOLARSHIP

American College of Healthcare Executives
One North Franklin Street, Suite 1700
Chicago, IL 60606-3529
(312) 424-2800   Fax: (312) 424-0023
E-mail: ache@ache.org
Web: www.ache.org

Summary To provide financial assistance to minority graduate student members of the American College of Healthcare Executives (ACHE).

Eligibility This program is open to ACHE student associates entering their final year of didactic work in a health care management graduate program. Applicants must be minority students, enrolled full time, able to demonstrate financial need, and U.S. or Canadian citizens. Along with their application, they must submit an 800-word essay describing their leadership abilities and experiences, their community and volunteer involvement, their goals as a health care executive, and how this scholarship can help them achieve their career goals.

Financial data The stipend is $3,500.

Duration 1 year.

Additional information The program was established and named in honor of Dr. Albert W. Dent, the foundation's first Black fellow and president emeritus of Dillard University.

Number awarded Varies each year.

Deadline March of each year.

[18]
ALCAVIS INTERNATIONAL CAREER MOBILITY SCHOLARSHIP

American Nephrology Nurses' Association
Attn: ANNA National Office
200 East Holly Avenue
P.O. Box 56
Pitman, NJ 08071-0056
(856) 256-2320   Toll-free: (888) 600-2662
Fax: (856) 589-7463   E-mail: annascholarships@ajj.com
Web: www.annanurse.org

Summary To provide financial assistance to members of the American Nephrology Nurses' Association (ANNA) who are interested in working on a baccalaureate or advanced degree in nursing.

Eligibility Applicants must be current association members, have been members for at least 2 years, be currently employed in nephrology nursing, and be accepted or enrolled in a baccalaureate or higher degree program in nursing. Along with their application, they must submit a 250-word essay on their career and education goals that includes how their degree will apply to nephrology nursing, provides a time frame for completing their program, and indicates how the funds will meet their educational needs.

Financial data The stipend is $2,500.

Duration 1 year.

Additional information Funds for this scholarship, first awarded in 2006, are supplied by Alcavis International, Inc. Information is also available from Sharon Longton, Awards and Scholarships Chair, (313) 966-2674, E-mail: slongton@dmc.org.

Number awarded 1 each year.

Deadline October of each year.

[19]
ALCOA FOUNDATION ACADEMIC SCHOLARSHIP

American Association of Occupational Health Nurses, Inc.
Attn: AAOHN Foundation
2920 Brandywine Road, Suite 100
Atlanta, GA 30341-4146
(770) 455-7757   Fax: (770) 455-7271
E-mail: foundation@aaohn.org
Web: www.aaohn.org/foundation/scholarships/index.cfm

Summary To provide financial assistance to registered nurses who are working on a bachelor's or graduate degree to prepare for a career in occupational and environmental health.

Eligibility This program is open to registered nurses who are enrolled in a baccalaureate or graduate degree program. Applicants must demonstrate an interest in, and commitment to, occupational and environmental health. Along with their application, they must submit a 500-word narrative on their professional goals as they relate to the academic activity and the field of occupational and environmental health. Selection is based on that essay (50%), impact of education on applicant's career (20%), and 2 letters of recommendation (30%).

Financial data The stipend is $3,000.

Duration 1 year; may be renewed up to 2 additional years.

Additional information Funding for this program is provided by the Alcoa Foundation.

Number awarded 2 each year.

Deadline November of each year.

[20]
ALICE HINCHCLIFFE WILLIAMS GRADUATE SCHOLARSHIP

American Dental Hygienists' Association
Attn: Institute for Oral Health
444 North Michigan Avenue, Suite 3400
Chicago, IL 60611
(312) 440-8918   Toll-free: (800) 735-4916
Fax: (312) 440-8929   E-mail: institute@adha.net
Web: www.adha.org/institute/Scholarship/index.htm

Summary To provide financial assistance to licensed dental hygienists from Virginia who are enrolled as full-time graduate students at a university.

Eligibility This program is open to licensed dental hygienists who have a baccalaureate degree and have completed at least 1 year of work as a full-time master's or doctoral degree student in a university graduate program. Applicants must be residents of Virginia, be active members of the Student American Dental Hygienists' Association (SADHA) or the American Dental Hygienists' Association (ADHA), have a GPA of at least 3.0, and be able to document financial need of at least $1,500. Along with their application, they must submit a statement that covers their long-term career goals, their intended contribution to the dental hygiene profession, their professional interests, the manner in which their degree will enhance their professional capacity, a description of the research in which they are involved or would like to become involved, and a list of past and/or present involvement in professional and/or community activities.

Financial data Stipends range from $1,000 to $2,000.

Duration 1 year.

Additional information This program, established in 2006, is funded by the Virginia Dental Hygienists' Association Foundation.

Number awarded 1 or more each year.

Deadline June of each year.

[21]
ALICE W. ROOKE SCHOLARSHIP

National Society Daughters of the American Revolution
Attn: Committee Services Office, Scholarships
1776 D Street, N.W.
Washington, DC 20006-5303
(202) 628-1776
Web: www.dar.org/natsociety/edout_scholar.cfm

Summary To provide financial assistance to medical school students.

Eligibility Eligible to apply for these scholarships are students who have been accepted into or are pursuing an approved course of study at an accredited medical school. Applicants must be sponsored by a local chapter of the Daughters of the American Revolution (DAR). Selection is based on academic excellence, commitment to the field of study, and financial need. U.S. citizenship is required.

Financial data The stipend is $5,000 per year.

Duration 1 year; may be renewed up to 3 additional years.

Additional information Requests for applications must be accompanied by a self-addressed stamped envelope.

Number awarded 1 or more each year.

Deadline April of each year.

[22]
ALL-INK COLLEGE SCHOLARSHIPS

All-Ink.com
P.O. Box 50868
Provo, UT 84606
(801) 794-0123   Toll-free: (888) 567-6511
Fax: (801) 794-0124   E-mail: Scholarship2006@all-ink.com
Web: www.all-ink.com/scholarship.aspx

Summary To provide financial assistance for college or graduate school to students who submit a scholarship application online.

Eligibility This program is open to U.S. citizens and permanent residents who are enrolled or planning to enroll at an accredited college or university at any academic level from freshman through graduate student. Applicants must have a GPA of 2.5 or higher. They must submit, through an online process, an essay of 50 to 200 words on a person who has had the greatest impact on their life and another essay of the same length on what they hope to achieve in their personal and professional life after graduation. Applications are not accepted through the mail.

Financial data Stipends range up to $5,000.

Duration 1 year.

Number awarded Varies each year; recently 5 of these scholarships were awarded.

Deadline December of each year.

[23]
ALLIANCE MEDICAL EDUCATION SCHOLARSHIP FUND

Pennsylvania Medical Society
Attn: Foundation
777 East Park Drive
P.O. Box 8820
Harrisburg, PA 17105-8820
(717) 558-7854   Toll-free: (800) 228-7823 (within PA)
Fax: (717) 558-7818
E-mail: studentservices-foundation@pamedsoc.org
Web: www.foundationpamedsoc.org

Summary To provide financial assistance to residents of Pennsylvania who are enrolled in medical school in the state.

Eligibility This program is open to residents of Pennsylvania who are enrolled full time in the second or third year at an accredited allopathic or osteopathic medical school in Pennsylvania. Applicants must submit a 1-page essay explaining why they chose to become a physician. Selection is based on merit, leadership, service, and financial need.

Financial data The stipend is $2,500. Funds are paid directly to the recipient's medical school through the appropriate channels.

Duration 1 year.

Additional information These scholarships, first awarded in 2003, are supported by the Pennsylvania Medical Society Alliance, an organization of spouses of physicians. The program includes the Robert and Arlene Oyler Award.

Number awarded Several each year.

Deadline March of each year.

[24]
ALLIE RANEY HUNT SCHOLARSHIP

Alexander Graham Bell Association for the Deaf
Attn: Financial Aid Coordinator
3417 Volta Place, N.W.
Washington, DC 20007-2778
(202) 337-5220   Fax: (202) 337-8314
TTY: (202) 337-5221   E-mail: financialaid@agbell.org
Web: www.agbell.org

Summary To provide financial assistance to undergraduate and graduate students with moderate to profound hearing loss.

Eligibility This program is open to undergraduate and graduate students who have been diagnosed with a moderate to profound hearing loss prior to acquiring spoken language (hearing loss averages 60dB or greater in the better ear in the speech frequencies of 500, 1000, and 2000 Hz). Applicants must be committed to using spoken language as their primary mode of communication. They must be accepted or enrolled at a mainstream college or university as a full-time student. Along with their application, they must submit a 1-page essay discussing their career goals and how spoken communication is helping them to reach those goals as a person with a hearing loss. Financial need is considered in the selection process. This scholarship is reserved for students who are oral deaf.

Financial data The stipend is $2,000 per year.

Duration 1 year; may be renewed 1 additional year.

Number awarded 1 each year.

Deadline April of each year.

[25]
ALMA WELLS GIVENS SCHOLARSHIP

Auxiliary to the National Medical Association
1012 10th Street, N.W.
Washington, DC 20001
(202) 371-1674   Fax: (202) 289-2662
E-mail: anmanationaloffice@earthlink.net
Web: www.anma-online.org

Summary To provide financial assistance to African American medical students attending selected schools.

Eligibility This program is open to African American medical school students who have completed their sophomore year at 1 of the following medical schools: Howard University College of Medicine (Washington, D.C.), Meharry Medical College (Nashville, Tennessee), Morehouse School of Medicine (Atlanta, Georgia), or Charles R. Drew University (Los Angeles, California). Selection is based on medical aptitude, academic record, personal record, and need.

Financial data A stipend is awarded (amount not specified).

Duration 1 year.

Additional information This program was originally established in 1942. The first scholarships were presented to students at Howard University and Meharry Medical College in 1948-49, at Morehouse College in 1980, and at Charles R. Drew University in 1983.

Number awarded 1 each year.

[26]
ALPHA EPSILON IOTA SCHOLARSHIP FUND

Alpha Epsilon Iota
c/o McDonald Financial Group
Attn: Key Trust Financial Services
Mail code OH-01-27-1614
P.O. Box 89464
Cleveland, OH 44101-6464
Toll-free: (800) 999-9658

Summary To provide financial assistance to women enrolled or accepted at an accredited school or college of medicine in the United States.

Eligibility Applicants must be candidates for degrees in accredited schools or colleges of medicine or osteopathy in the United States. Only women may apply. Selection is based on scholastic merit, work experience, scholarly publication, research experience, and financial need (last year's income cannot exceed $15,000 and assets cannot exceed $10,000). Race, age, religion, political affiliation, or national origin are not considered in awarding the fellowships. Priority is given to applicants in their first year of medical school. An interview may be required.

Financial data Awards range from $3,000 to $4,000 each year. Funds may be used for tuition-related fees, books, materials, food, clothing, housing, transportation, medical and dental expenses, insurance, and child care.

Duration 1 year; renewal is possible.

Number awarded 2 each year.

Deadline April of each year.

[27]
ALPHA KAPPA ALPHA FINANCIAL NEED SCHOLARSHIPS
Alpha Kappa Alpha Sorority, Inc.
Attn: Educational Advancement Foundation
5656 South Stony Island Avenue
Chicago, IL 60637
(773) 947-0026   Toll-free: (800) 653-6528
Fax: (773) 947-0277   E-mail: akaeaf@aol.com
Web: www.akaeaf.org/scholarships.htm

Summary To provide financial assistance to undergraduate and graduate students (especially African American women) who demonstrate financial need.

Eligibility This program is open to undergraduate or graduate students who have completed at least 1 year in an accredited degree-granting institution or a work-in-progress program in a noninstitutional setting, are planning to continue their program of education, and can demonstrate unmet financial need. Applicants must have a GPA of 2.5 or higher. Men and women of all ethnic groups are eligible for these scholarships, but the sponsor is a traditionally African American women's sorority.

Financial data Awards range from $750 to $1,500 per year.

Duration 1 year; nonrenewable.

Number awarded Varies each year. Recently, 38 of these scholarships were awarded: 26 to undergraduates and 12 to graduate students.

Deadline January of each year.

[28]
ALPHA KAPPA ALPHA MERIT SCHOLARSHIPS
Alpha Kappa Alpha Sorority, Inc.
Attn: Educational Advancement Foundation
5656 South Stony Island Avenue
Chicago, IL 60637
(773) 947-0026   Toll-free: (800) 653-6528
Fax: (773) 947-0277   E-mail: akaeaf@aol.com
Web: www.akaeaf.org/scholarships.htm

Summary To provide financial assistance to undergraduate and graduate students (especially African American women) who have excelled academically.

Eligibility This program is open to undergraduate and graduate students who have completed at least 1 year in an accredited degree-granting institution and are planning to continue their program of education. Applicants must have demonstrated exceptional academic achievement (GPA of 3.0 or higher) and present evidence of leadership through community service and involvement. Men and women of all ethnic groups are eligible for these scholarships, but the sponsor is a traditionally African American women's sorority.

Financial data The stipend is $1,000 per year.

Duration 1 year; nonrenewable.

Number awarded Varies each year. Recently, 27 of these scholarships were awarded: 20 to undergraduates and 7 to graduate students.

Deadline January of each year.

[29]
ALPHA MU TAU GRADUATE SCHOLARSHIP
Alpha Mu Tau Fraternity
c/o American Society for Clinical Laboratory Science
6701 Democracy Boulevard, Suite 300
Bethesda, MD 20817
(301) 657-2768   Fax: (301) 657-2909
E-mail: ascls@ascls.org
Web: www.ascls.org/leadership/awards/amt.asp

Summary To provide financial assistance for graduate school to members of Alpha Mu Tau, a national fraternity for professionals in the clinical laboratory sciences.

Eligibility Applicants must be U.S. citizens or permanent residents, accepted into or currently enrolled in a graduate program in clinical laboratory science (including clinical laboratory education or management programs), and members of Alpha Mu Tau. Along with their application, they must submit a 500-word statement describing their interest and reasons for working on an advanced degree in clinical laboratory science. Financial need is also considered in the selection process.

Financial data The maximum stipend is $2,000 for a full-time student or $1,000 for a part-time student.

Duration 1 year.

Additional information Information is also available from Joe Briden, Alpha Mu Tau Fraternity Scholarship Coordinator, 7809 South 21st Drive, Phoenix, AZ 85041-7736.

Number awarded 1 each year.

Deadline March of each year.

[30]
ALPHA SIGMA PI FRATERNITY FELLOWSHIP
Gallaudet University Alumni Association
Attn: Graduate Fellowship Fund Committee
Peikoff Alumni House
Gallaudet University
800 Florida Avenue, N.E.
Washington, DC 20002-3695
(202) 651-5060   Fax: (202) 651-5062
TTY: (202) 651-5061
E-mail: alumni.relations@gallaudet.edu
Web: www.gallaudet.edu

Summary To provide financial assistance to deaf students who wish to work on a doctoral degree at universities for people who hear normally.

Eligibility This program is open to deaf and hard of hearing graduates of Gallaudet University or other accredited colleges or universities who have been accepted for graduate study at academic institutions for people who hear normally. Applicants must be working on a doctorate or other terminal degree. Preference is given to alumni members of Alpha Sigma Pi Fraternity. Financial need is considered in the selection process.

Financial data The amount awarded varies, depending upon the needs of the recipient and the availability of funds.

Duration 1 year; may be renewed.

Additional information This program was established in 2001 as 1 of 11 designated funds within the Graduate Fellowship Fund of the Gallaudet University Alumni Association. Recipients must carry a full-time load.

Number awarded Up to 1 each year.

Deadline April of each year.

[31]
ALUMNI PRN GRANT
Alpha Tau Delta
Attn: Central Office
11252 Camarillo Street
Toluca Lake, CA 91602
E-mail: info@atdnursing.org
Web: www.atdnursing.org/awards.html

Summary To provide financial assistance for graduate education in nursing to members of Alpha Tau Delta (the national fraternity for professional nurses).

Eligibility This program is open to members in good standing who have been accepted into a graduate or doctoral program in a course of study to "enhance and further nursing service." Selection is based on involvement in the organization, community involvement, professional accomplishments, and financial need.

Financial data Stipends range from $100 to $1,000.

Duration 1 year.

Number awarded 1 each year.

Deadline May of each year.

[32]
ALVA S. APPLEBY SCHOLARSHIP
Maine Dental Association
Attn: Executive Director
28 Association Drive
P.O. Box 215
Manchester, ME 04351-0215
(207) 622-7900   Toll-free: (800) 369-8217
Fax: (207) 622-6210   E-mail: info@medental.org
Web: www.medental.org/resources/student_resources.html

Summary To provide financial assistance to dental school students from Maine.

Eligibility This program is open to residents of Maine who are enrolled in a dental school accredited by the American Dental Association. Selection is based on academic performance and an essay on the applicant's choice of dentistry as a career and future goals.

Financial data Stipends range from $500 to $1,000.

Duration 1 year; may be renewed.

Additional information This scholarship was first awarded for the 1997-98 academic year.

Number awarded 1 or 2 each year.

Deadline October of each year.

[33]
AMA FOUNDATION MINORITY SCHOLARS AWARDS
American Medical Association
Attn: AMA Foundation
515 North State Street
Chicago, IL 60610
(312) 464-4193   Fax: (312) 464-4142
E-mail: dina.lindenberg@ama-assn.org
Web: www.ama-assn.org/ama/pub/category/14772.html

Summary To provide financial assistance to medical school students who are members of underrepresented minority groups.

Eligibility This program is open to members of the following minority groups: African American/Black, Native American, Native Hawaiian, Alaska Native, and Hispanic/Latino. Only nominations are accepted. Nominees must be entering their second or third year of medical school. Each medical school is invited to submit 2 nominees.

Financial data The stipend is $10,000.

Duration 1 year.

Number awarded 10 each year.

Deadline April of each year.

[34]
AMA FOUNDATION PHYSICIANS OF TOMORROW SCHOLARSHIPS
American Medical Association
Attn: AMA Foundation
515 North State Street
Chicago, IL 60610
(312) 464-4193   Fax: (312) 464-4142
E-mail: dina.lindenberg@ama-assn.org
Web: www.ama-assn.org/ama/pub/category/14772.html

Summary To provide financial assistance to medical school students.

Eligibility This program is open to U.S. citizens enrolled in accredited U.S. or Canadian medical schools that grant the M.D. degree. Only nominations are accepted. Nominees must be entering their fourth year of medical school. The number of students who can be nominated per school depends upon the size of the third-year class: 1 nominee for a class size up to 150 students; 2 nominees for a class size between 151 and 250 students; 3 nominees for a class size of 251 students or more. Selection is based on demonstrated interest in communication of academic achievement and/or financial need.

Financial data The stipend is $10,000.

Duration 1 year.

Additional information This program was established in 2003 as the AMA Foundation National Scholarships and given its current name in 2006.

Number awarded Varies each year; recently, 2 of these scholarships were awarded.

Deadline May of each year.

[35]
AMBUCS SCHOLARSHIPS FOR THERAPISTS
National AMBUCS, Inc.
Attn: Scholarship Coordinator
P.O. Box 5127
High Point, NC 27262
(336) 852-0052   Fax: (336) 852-6830
E-mail: ambucs@ambucs.org
Web: www.ambucs.org

Summary To provide financial assistance to undergraduate and graduate students who are interested in preparing for a career serving disabled citizens in various fields of clinical therapy.

Eligibility This program is open to U.S. citizens who have been accepted at the upper-division or graduate level in an accredited program that qualifies the students for clinical practice in occupational therapy, physical therapy, speech language pathology, or hearing audiology. Programs for therapy assistants are not included. Applicants must submit college transcripts for the last 3 semesters, a 500-word essay on their interest in therapy as a career, and a statement of family financial circumstances. Selection is based on financial need, commitment to local community, demonstrated academic accomplishment, character for compassion and integrity, and career objectives.

Financial data Most of these awards range from $500 to $1,500 per year; 1 scholarship of $6,000 for 2 years is also awarded. Funds are paid directly to the recipient's school.

Duration 1 year.

Additional information This program was established in 1955; since then, the association has awarded more than $5 million for more than 9,900 scholarships.

Number awarded Approximately 400 each year, with a total value of $225,000.

Deadline April of each year.

[36]
AMERICAN ACADEMY OF AMBULATORY CARE NURSING SCHOLARSHIP

American Academy of Ambulatory Care Nursing
Attn: Scholarships
200 East Holly Avenue
P.O. Box 56
Pitman, NJ 08071-0056
(856) 256-2350   Toll-free: (800) AMN-NURS
Fax: (856) 589-7463   E-mail: aaacn@ajj.com
Web: www.aaacn.org

Summary To provide financial assistance to members of the American Academy of Ambulatory Care Nursing (AAACN) who are interested in working on an academic degree.

Eligibility This program is open to nurses who have been AAACN members for at least 2 years. Applicants must be enrolled in an accredited school of nursing or a program that the sponsor regards as advancing the profession of nursing. They may be working on a B.S.N., master's, doctoral, or other degree in nursing, business, health, or other related field. Along with their application, they must submit a brief paragraph describing why they are applying for this scholarship.

Financial data Stipends range from $100 to $1,000.

Duration 1 year.

Additional information Recipients must write an article for *Viewpoint* describing the professional benefits they have derived from this award.

Number awarded 1 or more each year.

Deadline January of each year.

[37]
AMERICAN ACADEMY OF NURSE PRACTITIONERS FOUNDATION DOCTORAL EDUCATION NP SCHOLARSHIPS

American Academy of Nurse Practitioners
Attn: AANP Foundation
P.O. Box 10729
Glendale, AZ 85318-0729
(623) 376-9467   Fax: (623) 376-0369
E-mail: foundation@aanp.org
Web: www.aanpfoundation.org

Summary To provide financial assistance to members of the American Academy of Nurse Practitioners (AANP) who are working on a doctoral degree.

Eligibility This program is open to student and full members of the academy who are working on a doctoral degree and have a GPA of 3.75 or higher. Applicants must be currently licensed practicing nurse practitioners (NPs) in the United States. They must have completed at least 25% but no more than 75% of their doctoral program requirements.

Financial data The stipend is $1,500. Funds may be used only for educational expenses (tuition, books, equipment, etc.), not for expenses related to dissertation and/or general research projects.

Duration 1 year.

Additional information The AANP Foundation was established in 1998. Recent corporate sponsors of these scholarships have included Daiichi Pharmaceutical Corporation, Novo Nordisk Pharmaceuticals, Inc., and Ross Products Division of Abbott Laboratories. There is a $10 application fee.

Number awarded Varies each year. In a recent semi-annual funding cycle, 3 of these scholarships were available.

Deadline April or October of each year.

[38]
AMERICAN ACADEMY OF NURSE PRACTITIONERS FOUNDATION NP STUDENT SCHOLARSHIPS

American Academy of Nurse Practitioners
Attn: AANP Foundation
P.O. Box 10729
Glendale, AZ 85318-0729
(623) 376-9467   Fax: (623) 376-0369
E-mail: foundation@aanp.org
Web: www.aanpfoundation.org

Summary To provide financial assistance to members of the American Academy of Nurse Practitioners (AANP) who are working on a master's degree.

Eligibility This program is open to current student and full members of the academy who are enrolled in a M.S.N. degree program as a nurse practitioner (NP). Applicants must have a GPA of 3.5 or higher. They must have completed at least 25% but no more than 75% of their program requirements.

Financial data The stipend is $1,000. Funds may be used only for educational expenses (tuition, books, equipment, etc.), not for expenses related to master's thesis and/or general research projects.

Duration 1 year.

Additional information The AANP Foundation was established in 1998. Recent corporate sponsors included Aventis Pharmaceuticals (sponsor of the Allegra Fexofenadine HCl Student Scholarships), the CFIDS Association of America, Daiichi Pharmaceutical Corporation, Exact Sciences, Fitzgerald Health Education Associates, Health Monitor Network, Organon Pharmaceuticals USA, and the Ross Products Division of Abbott Laboratories. There is a $10 application fee.

Number awarded Varies each year. In a recent semi-annual funding cycle, 12 of these scholarships were available.

Deadline April or October of each year.

[39]
AMERICAN ACADEMY OF NURSE PRACTITIONERS FOUNDATION POST-MS NP STUDENT SCHOLARSHIP

American Academy of Nurse Practitioners
Attn: AANP Foundation
P.O. Box 10729
Glendale, AZ 85318-0729
(623) 376-9467   Fax: (623) 376-0369
E-mail: foundation@aanp.org
Web: www.aanpfoundation.org

Summary To provide financial assistance to members of the American Academy of Nurse Practitioners (AANP) who are pursuing post-master's degree study.

Eligibility This program is open to student and full members of the academy who have a master's degree in nursing and are pursuing nurse practitioner (NP) education in an accredited post-M.S. program. Applicants must have at least a 3.5 GPA in their post-master's program. They must have completed at least 25% but no more than 75% of their program requirements.

Financial data The stipend is $1,500. Funds may be used only for educational expenses (tuition, books, equipment, etc.), not for expenses related to thesis and/or general research projects.

Duration 1 year.

Additional information The AANP Foundation was established in 1998. Recent corporate sponsors of these scholarships have included Daiichi Pharmaceutical Corporation and Ross Products Division of Abbott Laboratories. There is a $10 application fee.

Number awarded Varies each year. In a recent semi-annual funding cycle, 2 of these scholarships were available.

Deadline April or October of each year.

[40]
AMERICAN ARAB NURSES ASSOCIATION SCHOLARSHIPS

American Arab Nurses Association
P.O. Box 43
Dearborn Heights, MI 48127
(313) 982-4070
Web: www.americanarabnurses.org/aana/scholarship.asp

Summary To provide financial assistance to nursing students, nurses, and students interested in preparing for a career in nursing.

Eligibility This program is open to 5 categories of students: 1) freshman scholarships, for students newly admitted to a school of nursing; 2) R.N. scholarships, for registered nurses who have completed at least 8 units of a baccalaureate degree in nursing program with a GPA of 3.0 or higher; 3) minority student scholarships, for minority students working on an undergraduate degree in nursing; 4) M.S.N. scholarships, for registered nurses who have a baccalaureate degree, have completed at least 6 nursing credits for a master's degree, and have a GPA of 3.0 or higher; and 5) nursing as a second degree scholarships, for people working on an undergraduate degree in nursing as a second degree and have completed at least 8 nursing credits with a GPA of 3.0 or higher. Applicants must submit essays on why they have chosen nursing as their professional career and why they should be chosen to receive this scholarship; a list of their volunteer and/or community activities; and information on their financial need.

Financial data The stipend is $1,000.

Duration 1 year.

Additional information This program is sponsored by Allegiance Home Health Care.

Number awarded 5 each year: 1 in each of the categories.

Deadline June of each year.

[41]
AMERICAN ART THERAPY ASSOCIATION ANNIVERSARY SCHOLARSHIP FUND

American Art Therapy Association, Inc.
Attn: Scholarships and Grants Committee
5999 Stevenson Avenue
Alexandria, VA 22304
(703) 212-2238   Toll-free: (888) 290-0878
E-mail: info@arttherapy.org
Web: www.arttherapy.org/stscholarships.html

Summary To provide financial assistance for graduate study to members of the American Art Therapy Association (AATA).

Eligibility This program is open to graduate student AATA members accepted or enrolled in an art therapy program approved by the association. Applicants must be able to demonstrate financial need and a GPA of 3.25 or higher. Along with their application, they must submit transcripts, 2 letters of reference, a student financial information form, and a 2-page essay that contains a brief biography and a statement of how they see their role in the future of art therapy.

Financial data A stipend is awarded (amount not specified).

Duration 1 year.

Number awarded 1 each year.

Deadline June of each year.

[42]
AMERICAN ASSOCIATION OF JAPANESE UNIVERSITY WOMEN SCHOLARSHIP PROGRAM

American Association of Japanese University Women
c/o Akiko Agishi, Scholarship Committee Co-Chair
Creative International, Inc.
3127 Nicholas Canyon Road
Los Angeles, CA 90046
E-mail: scholarship@aajuw.org
Web: www.aajuw.org/Scholarship.htm

Summary To provide financial assistance to female students currently enrolled in upper-division or graduate classes in California.

Eligibility This program is open to female students enrolled in accredited colleges or universities in California. They must have junior, senior, or graduate standing. Applicants must be a contributor to U.S.-Japan relations, cultural exchanges, and leadership development in the areas of their designated field of study. To apply, they must submit a current resume, an official transcript of the past 2 years of college work, 2 letters of recommendation, and an essay (up to 2 pages in English or 1,200 characters in Japanese) on either 1) what they hope to accomplish in their field of study to develop leadership and role model qualities, or 2) thoughts on how their field of study can contribute to U.S.-Japan relations and benefit international relations.

Financial data The stipend is $1,500.

Duration 1 year.

Additional information The association was founded in 1970 to promote the education of women as well as to contribute to U.S.-Japan relations, cultural exchanges, and leadership development.

Number awarded 2 or 3 each year.

Deadline October of each year.

[43]
AMERICAN ASSOCIATION OF NURSE ANESTHETISTS FOUNDATION SCHOLARSHIPS

American Association of Nurse Anesthetists
Attn: AANA Foundation
222 South Prospect Avenue
Park Ridge, IL 60068-4001
(847) 692-7050, ext. 1171   Fax: (847) 692-7137
E-mail: foundation@aana.com
Web: www.aana.com/foundation/default.asp

Summary To provide financial assistance to African and African American members of the American Association of Nurse Anesthetists (AANA) who are interested in obtaining further education.

Eligibility This program is open to African and African American members of the association who are currently enrolled in an accredited nurse anesthesia education program. First-year students must have completed 6 months of nurse anesthesia classes; second-year students must have completed 12 months of nurse anesthesia classes. Along with their application, they must submit a 200-word essay describing why they have chosen nurse anesthesia as a professional and their professional goals for the future. Financial need is also considered in the selection process.

Financial data The stipend is $1,000 per year.

Duration 1 academic year.

Additional information The application processing fee is $25.

Number awarded 2 each year.

Deadline March of each year.

[44]
AMERICAN ASSOCIATION OF OCCUPATIONAL HEALTH NURSES FOUNDATION ACADEMIC SCHOLARSHIP

American Association of Occupational Health Nurses, Inc.
Attn: AAOHN Foundation
2920 Brandywine Road, Suite 100
Atlanta, GA 30341-4146
(770) 455-7757   Fax: (770) 455-7271
E-mail: foundation@aaohn.org
Web: www.aaohn.org/foundation/scholarships/index.cfm

Summary To provide financial assistance to registered nurses who are working on a bachelor's or graduate degree to prepare for a career in occupational and environmental health.

Eligibility This program is open to registered nurses who are enrolled in a baccalaureate or graduate degree program. Applicants must demonstrate an interest in, and commitment to, occupational and environmental health. Along with their application, they must submit a 500-word narrative on their professional goals as they relate to the academic activity and the field of occupational and environmental health. Selection is based on that essay (50%), impact of education on applicant's career (20%), and 2 letters of recommendation (30%).

Financial data The stipend is $3,000.

Duration 1 year; may be renewed up to 2 additional years.

Number awarded 1 each year.

Deadline November of each year.

[45]
AMERICAN ASSOCIATION OF UNIVERSITY WOMEN CAREER DEVELOPMENT GRANTS

American Association of University Women
Attn: AAUW Educational Foundation
301 ACT Drive, Department 60
P.O. Box 4030
Iowa City, IA 52243-4030
(319) 337-1716   Fax: (319) 337-1204
E-mail: aauw@act.org
Web: www.aauw.org

Summary To provide financial assistance to women who are seeking career advancement, career change, or reentry into the workforce.

Eligibility This program is open to women who are U.S. citizens or permanent residents, have earned a bachelor's degree, received their most recent degree more than 4 years ago, and plan to work toward a master's degree, second bachelor's degree, or specialized training in technical or professional fields. Applicants must be planning to undertake course work at an accredited 2- or 4-year college or university (or a technical school that is licensed, accredited, or approved by the U.S. Department of Education). Special consideration is given to qualified members of the American Association of University Women (AAUW), women of color, women working on their first advanced degree, and women working on degrees in nontraditional fields. Doctoral students and candidates eligible for other fellowship programs of the AAUW may not apply for these grants. Selection is based on demonstrated commitment to education and equity for women and girls, reason for seeking higher education or technical training, degree to which study plan is consistent with career objectives, potential for success in chosen field, documentation of opportunities in chosen field, feasibility of study plans and proposed time schedule, validity of proposed budget and budget narrative (including sufficient outside support), and quality of written proposal.

Financial data Grants range from $2,000 to $8,000. The funds are to be used for tuition, fees, books, supplies, local transportation, and dependent care.

Duration 1 year, beginning in July; nonrenewable.

Additional information The filing fee is $25 for AAUW members or $35 for nonmembers.

Number awarded Varies each year; recently, 34 of these grants were awarded.

Deadline December of each year.

[46]
AMERICAN COLLEGE OF NURSE PRACTITIONERS STUDENT SCHOLARSHIP

American College of Nurse Practitioners
Attn: Student Scholarship Committee
1111 19th Street, N.W., Suite 404
Washington, DC 20036
(202) 659-2190   Fax: (202) 659-2191
E-mail: acnp@acnpweb.org
Web: www.nurse.org/acnp/awards/acnp.scholar.shtml

Summary To provide financial assistance to members of the American College of Nurse Practitioners (ACNP) who are working on an advanced degree.

Eligibility Applicants must have been student members of ACNP for more than 3 months and have a current GPA of 3.4 or higher. Along with their application, they must submit a current curriculum vitae; 2 letters of recommendation from professional colleagues that indicate their leadership roles and involvement in public, student, or organizational policy development; and a 200-word statement on their personal goals as related to the ACNP mission statement.

Financial data The stipend is $1,000. The award also includes 1-year's membership in ACNP, complimentary registration to the ACNP annual national clinical symposium where the award is presented, and up to $750 to pay travel and lodging expenses.

Duration 1 year.

Additional information Only the first 20 applications received are considered.

Number awarded 1 each year.

Deadline June of each year.

[47]
AMERICAN COLLEGE OF NURSE-MIDWIVES FOUNDATION FELLOWSHIP FOR GRADUATE EDUCATION

American College of Nurse-Midwives
Attn: ACNM Foundation, Inc.
8403 Coleville Road, Suite 1550
Silver Spring, MD 20915
(240) 485-1850   Fax: (240) 485-1818
Web: www.midwife.org

Summary To provide financial assistance for midwifery education to graduate student members of the American College of Nurse-Midwives (ACNM).

Eligibility This program is open to ACNM members who are currently enrolled in a doctoral or postdoctoral midwife education program. Applicants must be a certified nurse midwife (CNM) or a certified midwife (CM). Along with their application, they must submit a curriculum vitae; a sample of up to 30 pages of scholarly work; and brief essays on their 5-year academic career plans, intended use of the fellowship money, and intended future participation in the local, regional, and/or national activities of ACNM or other activities that contribute to midwifery research, education, or practice.

Financial data A stipend is awarded (amount not specified).

Duration 1 year.

Additional information This program was established in 1997 with a grant from Ortho-McNeil Pharmaceutical Corporation.

Number awarded 1 each year.

Deadline March of each year.

[48]
AMERICAN COLLEGE OF SPORTS MEDICINE GRADUATE TRAINING SCHOLARSHIPS FOR MINORITY STUDENTS

American College of Sports Medicine
Attn: Director of Membership and Chapter Services
401 West Michigan Street
P.O. Box 1440
Indianapolis, IN 46206-1440
(317) 637-9200, ext. 104   Fax: (317) 637-7817
E-mail: csawyer@acsm.org
Web: www.acsm.org

Summary To provide financial assistance to minority graduate students who are interested in preparing for a career in sports medicine or exercise science.

Eligibility This program is open to minorities who have been accepted in a full-time master's or doctoral program in sports medicine, exercise science, kinesiology, or other related field.

Minorities are defined as American Indians, Alaskan Natives, Asians, Native Hawaiians and other Pacific Islanders, Blacks or African Americans, and Latinos or Hispanics. Applicants must submit 2 letters of professional recommendation (including at least 1 from a current member of the American College of Sports Medicine), a summary of participation in scholarly activities associated with sports medicine, exercise science, kinesiology, or a related field (including documentation of research and scholarly activities), transcripts, GRE or MCAT scores, and a 300-word description of short- and long-term academic and career goals in sports medicine, exercise science, kinesiology, or a related field. U.S. or Canadian citizenship is required.

Financial data The stipend is $3,000 per year.

Duration 1 year.

Additional information Recipients are given a 1 year's free membership in the American College of Sports Medicine.

Number awarded 1 or more each year.

Deadline January of each year.

[49]
AMERICAN DIETETIC ASSOCIATION GRADUATE SCHOLARSHIPS

American Dietetic Association
Attn: Accreditation, Education Programs, and Student
    Operations
120 South Riverside Plaza, Suite 2000
Chicago, IL 60606-6995
(312) 899-0040   Toll-free: (800) 877-1600, ext. 5400
Fax: (312) 899-4817   E-mail: education@eatright.org
Web: www.eatright.org

Summary To provide financial assistance to graduate student members of the American Dietetic Association (ADA).

Eligibility This program is open to ADA members who are enrolled or planning to enroll in a master's or doctoral degree program in dietetics. Applicants who are currently completing a dietetic internship or preprofessional practice program that is combined with a graduate program may also apply. The graduate scholarships are available only to U.S. citizens and permanent residents. Applicants should intend to practice in the field of dietetics. Some scholarships require specific areas of study (e.g., public health nutrition, food service administration) and status as a registered dietitian. Others may require membership in a specific dietetic practice group, residency in a specific state, or underrepresented minority group status. The same application form can be used for all categories.

Financial data Stipends range from $500 to $3,000; most are for $1,000.

Duration 1 year.

Number awarded Varies each year, depending upon the funds available. Recently, the sponsoring organization awarded 211 scholarships for all its programs.

Deadline February of each year.

[50]
AMERICAN INDIAN GRADUATE CENTER FELLOWSHIPS

American Indian Graduate Center
Attn: Executive Director
4520 Montgomery Boulevard, N.E., Suite 1-B
Albuquerque, NM 87109-1291
(505) 881-4584   Toll-free: (800) 628-1920
Fax: (505) 884-0427   E-mail: aigc@aigc.com
Web: www.aigc.com

Summary To provide financial assistance to Native American students interested in attending graduate school.

Eligibility This program is open to enrolled members of U.S. federally-recognized American Indian tribes and Alaska Native groups and other students who can document one-fourth degree federally-recognized Indian blood. Applicants must be enrolled as full-time students in a graduate or professional school in the United States working on a master's, doctoral, or professional degree in any field. Selection is based on academic achievement, financial need, and an essay on the meaning of their graduate education to the Indian community.

Financial data Awards are based on each applicant's unmet financial need and range from $250 to $4,000 per year.

Duration 1 year; may be renewed up to 1 additional year for master's degree students; up to 2 additional years for M.F.A. students; up to 3 additional years for doctoral degree students; up to 3 additional years for medicine, osteopathic medicine, dentistry, chiropractic, and veterinary degree students; or up to 2 additional years for law degree students.

Additional information The application fee is $15. Since this a supplemental program, students must apply in a timely manner for federal financial aid and campus-based aid at the college they are attending to be considered for this program. Failure to apply will disqualify an applicant.

Number awarded Varies each year; recently, 34 of these fellowships were awarded.

Deadline May of each year.

[51]
AMERICAN SOCIETY OF CRIME LABORATORY DIRECTORS SCHOLARSHIP PROGRAM

American Society of Crime Laboratory Directors
Scholarship Application
139K Technology Drive
Garner, NC 27529
(919) 773-2044   Fax: (919) 773-2602
Web: www.ascld.org/visitors/resources.php

Summary To provide financial assistance to students preparing for careers in forensic science.

Eligibility This program is open to juniors, seniors, and graduate students who are working on a degree in forensic science, forensic chemistry, or physical or natural science. Current forensic science laboratory employees working on a graduate degree are not eligible. Applicants must submit a statement describing their motivation for applying for this award, including their interest in specific forensic disciplines, career goals, past projects, financial need, or any other topic that will help explain their situation. Selection is based on that statement, overall scholastic record, scholastic record in forensic science course work, motivation or commitment to a forensic science career, and recommendations.

Financial data The stipend is $1,000.

Duration 1 year.

Number awarded 1 or more each year.

Deadline April of each year.

[52]
AMERICAN SOCIETY OF HEMATOLOGY TRAINEE RESEARCH AWARDS

American Society of Hematology
Attn: Award Program Coordinator
1900 M Street, N.W., Suite 200
Washington, DC 20036
(202) 776-0544, ext. 1168   Fax: (202) 776-0545
E-mail: ASH@hematology.org
Web: www.hematology.org/education/awards/trainee.cfm

Summary To provide an opportunity for medical students, residents, and selected undergraduates to work on a research training project in hematology.

Eligibility This program is open to medical students and residents who are interested in working on a research project in hematology under the supervision of a mentor or training director who is a member of the American Society of Hematology (ASH). Undergraduates may participate at the discretion of the mentor or training director. Applications must be submitted by the institution, which must have an accredited training program with a director in hematology or a hematology-related area. The institution must be in the United States, Canada, or Mexico. The mentor and the student should work collaboratively to complete the application. It should include a 500-word research outline covering the scientific question, background, proposed method, proposed results, and impact. Both laboratory research and clinical investigation are eligible.

Financial data The grant includes $4,000 for research support and an additional $1,000 to support travel to the annual meeting of the ASH. Research stipends are paid directly to the institution, not the student.

Duration 3 months any time during the year.

Additional information Trainees are required to submit a final summary of their work at the end of their research.

Number awarded Varies each year; each training program may support only 1 student unless there are unclaimed funds available.

Deadline March of each year.

[53]
AMERICAN SOCIETY OF PERIANESTHESIA NURSES DEGREE SCHOLARSHIPS

American Society of PeriAnesthesia Nurses
Attn: Scholarship Program
10 Melrose Avenue, Suite 110
Cherry Hill, NJ 08003-3696
(856) 616-9600   Toll-free: (877) 737-9696, ext. 13
Fax: (856) 616-9601   E-mail: aspan@aspan.org
Web: www.aspan.org/ScholarshipProgram.htm

Summary To provide financial assistance for additional education to members of the American Society of PeriAnesthesia Nurses (ASPAN).

Eligibility This program is open to registered nurses who have been members of the society for at least 2 years and have been employed for at least 2 years in any phase of the perianesthesia setting (preanesthesia, postanesthesia, ambulatory surgery, management, research, or education). Applicants must be interested in working on a bachelor of science in nursing, a master of science in nursing, or a doctorate in nursing. Along with their application, they must submit a statement of financial need; 2 letters of recommendation; and a narrative statement describing their level of activity or involvement in a phase of perianesthesia nursing, ASPAN and/or a component, or their community. Their statement should explain how they see their perianesthesia practice changing and benefiting as a result of their degree and how receiving this scholarship will help them obtain their professional goals and contribute to the perianesthesia community.

Financial data The stipend is $1,000 per year; funds are sent directly to the recipient's university.

Duration 1 year; recipients may not reapply for additional funding until 3 years have elapsed.

Number awarded At least 2 each year.

Deadline June of each year.

[54]
AMERICAN SPEECH-LANGUAGE-HEARING FOUNDATION GENERAL GRADUATE STUDENT SCHOLARSHIPS

American Speech-Language-Hearing Foundation
Attn: Graduate Student Scholarship Competition
10801 Rockville Pike
Rockville, MD 20852-3279
(301) 897-5700   Toll-free: (800) 498-2071
Fax: (301) 571-0457   TTY: (800) 498-2071
E-mail: foundation@asha.org
Web: www.ashfoundation.org

Summary To provide financial assistance to graduate students in communication sciences and disorders programs.

Eligibility This program is open to full-time graduate students who are enrolled in or accepted to a communication sciences and disorders program. Master's (but not doctoral) candidates must be enrolled in an ASHA Educational Standards Board (ESB) accredited program. Selection is based on academic promise and outstanding academic achievement.

Financial data The stipend is $4,000. Funds must be used for educational support (e.g., tuition, books, school living expenses), not for personal or conference travel.

Duration 1 year.

Additional information This program is sponsored in part by the Marni Riesberg Memorial Fund and Psi Iota Xi National Philanthropic Organization.

Number awarded Varies each year; recently, 9 of these scholarships were awarded.

Deadline June of each year.

[55]
AMERICAN SPEECH-LANGUAGE-HEARING FOUNDATION SCHOLARSHIP FOR MINORITY STUDENTS

American Speech-Language-Hearing Foundation
Attn: Graduate Student Scholarship Competition
10801 Rockville Pike
Rockville, MD 20852-3279
(301) 897-5700   Toll-free: (800) 498-2071
Fax: (301) 571-0457   TTY: (800) 498-2071
E-mail: foundation@asha.org
Web: www.ashfoundation.org

Summary To provide financial assistance to minority graduate students in communication sciences and disorders programs.

Eligibility This program is open to full-time graduate students who are enrolled in communication sciences and disorders programs, with preference given to U.S. citizens who are members of a racial or ethnic minority group. Selection is based on aca-

demic promise and outstanding academic achievement. Master's (but not doctoral) candidates must be enrolled in an ASHA Educational Standards Board (ESB) accredited program.

Financial data The stipend ranges from $2,000 to $4,000. Funds must be used for educational support (e.g., tuition, books, school living expenses), not for personal or conference travel.

Duration 1 year.

Number awarded 1 each year.

Deadline June of each year.

[56]
AMERICORPS STATE AND NATIONAL PROGRAM

Corporation for National and Community Service
1201 New York Avenue, N.W.
Washington, DC 20525
(202) 606-5000   Toll-free: (800) 942-2677
Fax: (202) 565-2784   TTY: (202) 606-3472
TTY: (800) 833-3722   E-mail: questions@americorps.org
Web: www.americorps.gov

Summary To enable Americans to earn money for college or graduate school while serving as volunteers for public or nonprofit organizations that work to meet the nation's education, public safety, human, or environmental needs.

Eligibility Applicants must be at least 17 years old, be U.S. citizens or permanent residents, and have completed at least their high school diploma or agree to obtain the diploma before using the education award. They must be interested in working on community projects in 1 of 4 areas: education, public safety, health, and the environment. Additional qualifications are set by participating agencies.

Financial data Full-time participants (at least 1,700 service hours) receive a modest living allowance of approximately $9,300, limited health care, and a post-service education award of $4,725 to pay for college, graduate school, or repayment of student loans. Half-time members (900 service hours) receive a post-service education award of $2,362 per term. Other education awards are $1,800 for reduced half time (675 service hours), $1,250 for quarter time (450 service hours), or $1,000 for minimum time (300 service hours). In lieu of the education award, participants may elect to receive an end-of-service stipend of $1,200.

Duration The length of the term is established by each participating agency but ranges from 9 to 12 months.

Additional information More than 900 programs throughout the country participate in this network. Most programs are administered by nonprofit organizations, Native American nations, institutions of higher education, or government agencies. Applications are obtained from and submitted to the particular agency where the applicant wishes to serve; for a directory of participating agencies, contact the sponsor.

Number awarded Varies each year; recently, approximately 44,000 members served in this program.

Deadline Each participating organization sets its own deadline.

[57]
AMERICORPS VISTA

Corporation for National and Community Service
1201 New York Avenue, N.W.
Washington, DC 20525
(202) 606-5000   Toll-free: (800) 942-2677
Fax: (202) 565-2784   TTY: (202) 606-3472
TTY: (800) 833-3722   E-mail: questions@americorps.org
Web: www.americorps.gov

Summary To enable Americans to earn money for higher education or other purposes while working as volunteers for public or nonprofit organizations that serve low-income communities.

Eligibility This program is open to U.S. citizens or permanent residents 18 years of age or older who either have a baccalaureate degree or at least 3 years of related volunteer/job experience and skills. Participants serve at approved public or nonprofit sponsoring organizations in low-income communities located in the United States, Virgin Islands, or Puerto Rico. Assignments may include working to fight illiteracy, improve health services, create businesses, increase housing opportunities, or bridge the digital divide. Sponsors may also establish particular skill, education, or experience requirements; Spanish language skills are desirable for some assignments.

Financial data Participants receive a monthly living allowance for housing, food, and incidentals; the allowance does not affect Social Security, veterans', or public assistance benefits but is subject to taxation. Health insurance is also provided for participants, but not for family members. Upon completion of service, participants also receive a stipend of $100 per month or an educational award of $4,725 per year of service which may be used to pay for educational expenses, repay student loans, or pay the expenses of participating in a school-to-work program. Up to $9,450 in educational benefits may be earned.

Duration Full-time service of at least 1 year is required to earn educational benefits; up to 2 years of service may be performed.

Additional information This program has operated since 1965 as Volunteers in Service to America (VISTA). It recently became 1 of the programs directly administered by the Corporation for National and Community Service. Stafford and Perkins student loans may be deferred during AmeriCorps VISTA service.

Number awarded Varies each year; recently, approximately 6,000 volunteers served in this program.

Deadline March of each year for first consideration; October of each year for fall replacements.

[58]
AMGEN CAREER MOBILITY SCHOLARSHIP

American Nephrology Nurses' Association
Attn: ANNA National Office
200 East Holly Avenue
P.O. Box 56
Pitman, NJ 08071-0056
(856) 256-2320   Toll-free: (888) 600-2662
Fax: (856) 589-7463   E-mail: annascholarships@ajj.com
Web: www.annanurse.org

Summary To provide financial assistance to members of the American Nephrology Nurses' Association (ANNA) who are interested in working on a baccalaureate or advanced degree in nursing.

Eligibility Applicants must be current association members, have been members for at least 2 years, be currently employed in nephrology nursing, and be accepted or enrolled in a baccalaureate or higher degree program in nursing. Along with their application, they must submit a 250-word essay on their career and

education goals that includes how their degree will apply to nephrology nursing, provides a time frame for completing their program, and indicates how the funds will meet their educational needs.

Financial data The stipend is $2,500.

Duration 1 year.

Additional information Funds for this scholarship, first awarded in 1993, are supplied by Amgen Inc. Information is also available from Sharon Longton, Awards and Scholarships Chair, (313) 966-2674, E-mail: slongton@dmc.org.

Number awarded 1 each year.

Deadline October of each year.

[59]
AMY LOUISE HUNTER-WILSON, M.D. MEMORIAL SCHOLARSHIP

Wisconsin Medical Society
Attn: Executive Director, Wisconsin Medical Society
   Foundation
330 East Lakeside Street
P.O. Box 1109
Madison, WI 53701-1109
(608) 442-3722   Toll-free: (866) 442-3800, ext. 3722
Fax: (608) 442-3802   E-mail: eileenw@wismed.org
Web: www.wisconsinmedicalsociety.org

Summary To provide financial assistance to American Indians (especially those from Wisconsin) interested in working on a degree in medicine, nursing, or allied health care.

Eligibility This program is open to members of federally-recognized American Indian tribes who are 1) full-time students enrolled in a health career program at an accredited institution, 2) adults returning to school in an allied health field, and 3) adults working in a non-professional health-related field returning for a professional license or degree. Applicants must be working on a degree or advanced training as a doctor of medicine, nurse, or technician. Preference is given to residents of Wisconsin who are students at educational institutions in the state and applicants close to completing their degree. U.S. citizenship is required. Selection is based on financial need, academic achievement, personal qualities and strengths, and letters of recommendation.

Financial data The stipend is at least $1,000.

Duration 1 year.

Number awarded 1 or more each year.

Deadline January of each year.

[60]
ANAC STUDENT DIVERSITY MENTORSHIP SCHOLARSHIP

Association of Nurses in AIDS Care
3538 Ridgewood Road
Akron, OH 44333
(330) 670-0101   Toll-free: (800) 260-6780
Fax: (330) 670-0109   E-mail: anac@anacnet.org
Web: www.anacnet.org/programs_pubs-awards.php

Summary To provide financial assistance to students nurses from minority groups who are interested in HIV/AIDS nursing and in attending the national conference of the Association of Nurses in AIDS Care (ANAC).

Eligibility This program is open to student nurses from a diverse racial or ethnic background, defined to include African Americans, Hispanics/Latinos, Asians/Pacific Islanders, and American Indians/Alaskan Natives. Candidates must have a genuine interest in HIV/AIDS nursing, be interested in attending the ANAC national conference, and desire to develop a mentorship relationship with a member of the ANAC Diversity Specialty Committee. They must be currently enrolled in an accredited nursing program at any level (e.g., L.P.N., A.D.N., diploma, B.S.N., or graduate nursing). Nominees may be recommended by themselves, nursing faculty member, or ANAC member, but their nomination must be supported by an ANAC member. Along with their nomination form, they must submit a 500-word personal statement describing their interest or experience in HIV/AIDS care and why they want to attend the ANAC conference.

Financial data Recipients are awarded a $1,000 scholarship (paid directly to the school), up to $599 in reimbursement of travel expenses to attend the ANAC annual conference, free conference registration, an award plaque, a free ticket to the awards ceremony at the conference, and a 1-year ANAC membership.

Duration 1 year.

Additional information The mentor will be assigned at the conference and will maintain contact during the period of study.

Number awarded 1 each year.

Deadline May of each year.

[61]
ANDREW CMELKO CRNA MEMORIAL SCHOLARSHIPS

American Association of Nurse Anesthetists
Attn: AANA Foundation
222 South Prospect Avenue
Park Ridge, IL 60068-4001
(847) 692-7050, ext. 1171   Fax: (847) 692-7137
E-mail: foundation@aana.com
Web: www.aana.com/foundation/default.asp

Summary To provide financial assistance to members of the American Association of Nurse Anesthetists (AANA), especially married males, who are interested in obtaining further education.

Eligibility This program is open to members of the association who are currently enrolled in an accredited nurse anesthesia education program. Preference is given to married male nurse anesthesia students. First-year students must have completed 6 months of nurse anesthesia classes; second-year students must have completed 12 months of nurse anesthesia classes. Along with their application, they must submit a 200-word essay describing why they have chosen nurse anesthesia as a profession and their professional goals for the future. Financial need is also considered in the selection process.

Financial data The stipend is $1,000 per year.

Duration 1 academic year.

Additional information The application processing fee is $25.

Number awarded 2 each year.

Deadline March of each year.

[62]
ANN OLSON MEMORIAL DOCTORAL SCHOLARSHIP

Oncology Nursing Society
Attn: ONS Foundation
125 Enterprise Drive
Pittsburgh, PA 15275-1214
(412) 859-6100, ext. 8503   Toll-free: (866) 257-4ONS
Fax: (412) 859-6160   E-mail: foundation@ons.org
Web: www.ons.org/awards/foundawards/doctoral.shtml

Summary To provide financial assistance to registered nurses interested in working on a doctoral degree in oncology nursing.

Eligibility Candidates must be registered nurses with a demonstrated interest in and commitment to oncology nursing; be enrolled in or applying to a doctoral nursing degree program or related program; and never have received a doctoral scholarship from this sponsor. Along with their application, they must submit brief essays on why they chose their doctoral program; the courses and clinical experience of the program that are related to cancer nursing; their research area of interest and plans for a dissertation; their professional goals and their relationship to the advancement of oncology nursing; and how the doctoral program will assist them in achieving their goals.

Financial data The stipend is $3,000.

Duration 1 year; nonrenewable.

Additional information This program, established in 1991, is currently sponsored by Pfizer Inc. At the end of each year of scholarship participation, recipients must submit a summary of their educational activities. Applications must be accompanied by a $5 fee.

Number awarded 1 each year.

Deadline January of each year.

[63]
ANNA CAREER MOBILITY SCHOLARSHIPS

American Nephrology Nurses' Association
Attn: ANNA National Office
200 East Holly Avenue
P.O. Box 56
Pitman, NJ 08071-0056
(856) 256-2320   Toll-free: (888) 600-2662
Fax: (856) 589-7463   E-mail: annascholarships@ajj.com
Web: www.annanurse.org

Summary To provide financial assistance to members of the American Nephrology Nurses' Association (ANNA) who are interested in working on a baccalaureate or advanced degree in nursing.

Eligibility Applicants must be current association members, have been members for at least 2 years, be currently employed in nephrology nursing, and be accepted or enrolled in a baccalaureate or higher degree program in nursing. Along with their application, they must submit a 250-word essay on their career and education goals that includes how their degree will apply to nephrology nursing, provides a time frame for completing their program, and indicates how the funds will meet their educational needs.

Financial data The stipend is $2,000.

Duration 1 year.

Additional information These scholarships were first awarded in 1993. Information is also available from Sharon Longton, Awards and Scholarships Chair, (313) 966-2674.

Number awarded 5 each year.

Deadline October of each year.

[64]
ANTOINETTE M. MOLINARI MEMORIAL SCHOLARSHIP

American Academy of Optometry
Attn: American Optometric Foundation
6110 Executive Boulevard, Suite 506
Rockville, MD 20852
(301) 984-4734, ext. 3007   Fax: (301) 984-4737
E-mail: laraf@aaoptom.org
Web: www.aaopt.org/aof/scholarship/molinari/index.asp

Summary To provide financial assistance to students working on a doctorate of optometry degree.

Eligibility This program is open to students working on a doctorate of optometry degree on a full-time basis. Applicants must have a GPA of 3.5 or higher. Selection is based primarily on financial need, although academic and leadership potential are also considered.

Financial data The stipend is $5,000.

Duration 1 year.

Additional information This scholarship rotates annually among optometry schools; for a list of the schools at which it is available in the current year, contact the foundation.

Number awarded 1 each year.

Deadline April of each year.

[65]
AORN FOUNDATION DOCTORAL DEGREE SCHOLARSHIP

Association of periOperative Registered Nurses
Attn: AORN Foundation
2170 South Parker Road, Suite 300
Denver, CO 80231-5711
(303) 755-6300, ext. 328
Toll-free: (800) 755-2676, ext. 328   Fax: (303) 755-4219
E-mail: ibendzsa@aorn.org
Web: www.aorn.org/foundation/scholarships.asp

Summary To provide financial assistance to members of the Association of periOperative Registered Nurses (AORN) who wish to work on a doctoral degree.

Eligibility This program is open to registered nurses who are committed to perioperative nursing, have been members of the association for at least 1 year, and are currently enrolled in a doctoral program at an accredited university with a GPA of 3.0 or higher. Along with their application, they must submit a personal statement describing their role as a perioperative nurse; current and past contributions to AORN on a local, state, and national level; their financial need; their professional goals and how this degree will help them achieve those goals; their knowledge of and commitment to the AORN Foundation; and volunteer community activities or other community services.

Financial data Stipends range from $1,000 to $4,000. Funds are paid directly to the recipient.

Duration 1 year.

Additional information This program was established in 1991.

Number awarded 1 or more each year.

Deadline May of each year.

[66]
AORN FOUNDATION MASTER'S DEGREE SCHOLARSHIP

Association of periOperative Registered Nurses
Attn: AORN Foundation
2170 South Parker Road, Suite 300
Denver, CO 80231-5711
(303) 755-6300, ext. 328
Toll-free: (800) 755-2676, ext. 328   Fax: (303) 755-4219
E-mail: ibendzsa@aorn.org
Web: www.aorn.org/foundation/scholarships.asp

Summary To provide financial assistance to members of the Association of periOperative Registered Nurses (AORN) who wish to work on a master's degree.

Eligibility This program is open to registered nurses who are committed to perioperative nursing, have been members of the association for at least 1 year, and are currently enrolled in an accredited master's degree program with a GPA of 3.0 or higher. Along with their application, they must submit a personal statement describing their role as a perioperative nurse; current and past contributions to AORN on a local, state, and national level; their financial need; their professional goals and how this degree will help them achieve those goals; their knowledge of and commitment to the AORN Foundation; and volunteer community activities or other community services.

Financial data Stipends range from $1,000 to $4,000. Funds are paid directly to the recipient.

Duration 1 year.

Additional information This program was established in 1991.

Number awarded 1 or more each year.

Deadline May of each year.

[67]
APMA EDUCATIONAL FOUNDATION SCHOLARSHIP FUND

American Podiatric Medical Association
Attn: APMA Educational Foundation
9312 Old Georgetown Road
Bethesda, MD 20814-1621
(301) 571-9200   Fax: (301) 530-2752
Web: www.apma.org

Summary To provide financial assistance to students at podiatry schools.

Eligibility This program is open to third- and fourth-year students at the 8 colleges of podiatric medicine. Applicants must submit a 1-page statement on their involvement in school, community, and podiatric medical-related activities. They must have a GPA of 2.5 or higher. Selection is based on financial need (33%), GPA (33%), and participation in extracurricular activities (33%).

Financial data The stipend is $1,000 per year.

Duration 1 year; may be renewed.

Number awarded Approximately 190 each year.

Deadline May of each year.

[68]
APPLIED EPIDEMIOLOGY FELLOWSHIP

CDC Foundation
Attn: CDC Experience Program
50 Hurt Plaza, Suite 765
Atlanta, GA 30303
(404) 653-0790   Toll-free: (888) 880-4CDC
Fax: (404) 653-0330   E-mail: cdcexperience@cdc.gov
Web: www.cdcfoundation.org

Summary To provide medical students with a training experience in epidemiology and public health at the Centers for Disease Control and Prevention (CDC) in Atlanta, Georgia.

Eligibility This program is open to third- and fourth-year medical students who are preparing for a career in clinical medicine, clinical epidemiology, health services research, the Epidemic Intelligence Service (EIS) of the CDC, and public health. Areas of concentration include birth defects, injury, chronic diseases, infectious disease, environmental health, reproductive health, and minority health. Applicants must submit a curriculum vitae; a 2-page personal statement on why this experience is worthwhile for them to take a year off from medical school, how it would advance their career and personal goals, their career plans, and how their previous experiences have shaped their future direction and motivations; 3 letters of recommendation; and transcripts. U.S. citizenship is required.

Financial data A stipend is provided (amount not specified).

Duration 10 to 12 months.

Additional information This program, which began in 2004, is sponsored by Pfizer Inc. Information is also available from Catherine Piper, Centers for Disease Control and Prevention, Office of Workforce and Career Development, 1600 Clifton Road, N.E., Mailstop E-92, Atlanta, GA 30333. (404) 498-6151.

Number awarded 8 each year.

Deadline December of each year.

[69]
ARC OF WASHINGTON TRUST FUND STIPEND AWARD PROGRAM

ARC of Washington Trust Fund
c/o Neal Lessenger, Secretary
P.O. Box 27028
Seattle, WA 98125-1428
(206) 363-2206   E-mail: arcwatrust@charter.net
Web: www.arcwa.org/student_grants.htm

Summary To provide financial assistance to undergraduate and graduate students in northwestern states who have a career interest in work relating to mental retardation.

Eligibility This program is open to upper-division and graduate students in schools in Washington, Oregon, Alaska, and Idaho who have a demonstrated interest in the field of mental retardation or other developmental or intellectual disabilities. Applicants must submit a statement of interest in the field of mental retardation or closely-related field, academic and other qualifications, achievements, immediate and long-term goals, and letters of endorsement from at least 2 faculty sponsors. Financial need is not considered in the selection process.

Financial data The stipend is $5,000 per year, paid in 4 equal installments. Funds are sent to the recipient's school and must be used for tuition, books, and general living expenses.

Duration 1 year.

Number awarded Several each year.

Deadline February of each year.

[70]
ARFORA–MARTHA GAVRILA SCHOLARSHIP FOR WOMEN

Romanian Orthodox Episcopate of America
Attn: Scholarship Committee
1920 King James Parkway, Apartment 18
Westlake, OH 44145-3466
E-mail: roeasolia@aol.com
Web: www.roea.org/schol/schol-gavrila.htm

Summary To provide financial assistance to women who are members of a parish of the Romanian Orthodox Episcopate of America and interested in working on a graduate degree.

Eligibility Applicants must be women, voting members of a parish of the Romanian Orthodox Episcopate of America, graduates of an accredited university or college, and accepted by a graduate school. As part of the application process, students must submit a formal letter describing their personal goals, projected use of the degree, church and community involvement, and honors and awards.

Financial data The stipend is $1,000.

Duration 1 year.

Additional information The first scholarship was awarded in 1985. This program is offered by the Association of Romanian Orthodox Ladies Auxiliaries (ARFORA).

Number awarded 1 each year.

Deadline April of each year.

[71]
ARIZONA CHAPTER ASSE SCHOLARSHIP

American Society of Safety Engineers
Attn: ASSE Foundation
1800 East Oakton Street
Des Plaines, IL 60018
(847) 768-3435   Fax: (847) 768-3434
E-mail: agabanski@asse.org
Web: www.asse.org/foundation

Summary To provide financial assistance to upper-division and graduate student members of the American Society of Safety Engineers (ASSE) from designated western states who are working on a degree in occupational health and related fields.

Eligibility This program is open to ASSE student members who are working on an undergraduate or graduate degree in occupational safety, health, and environment or a closely-related field (e.g., industrial or environmental engineering, environmental science, industrial hygiene, occupational health nursing). Priority is given first to residents of Arizona, then to residents of other states in ASSE Region II (Colorado, Idaho, Montana, Nevada, New Mexico, Utah, and Wyoming). Undergraduates must be full-time students who have completed at least 60 semester hours with a GPA of 3.0 or higher. Graduate students must also be enrolled full time, have completed at least 9 semester hours with a GPA of 3.5 or higher, and have had a GPA of 3.0 or higher as an undergraduate. Along with their application, they must submit 2 essays of 300 words or less: 1) why they are seeking a degree in occupational safety and health or a closely-related field, a brief description of their current activities, and how those relate to their career goals and objectives; and 2) why they should be awarded this scholarship (including career goals and financial need).

Financial data The stipend is $1,000.

Duration 1 year; nonrenewable.

Additional information This program, established in 2005, is supported by the Arizona Chapter of ASSE.

Number awarded 1 each year.

Deadline   November of each year.

[72]
ARIZONA LEVERAGING EDUCATIONAL ASSISTANCE PARTNERSHIP GRANTS

Arizona Commission for Postsecondary Education
2020 North Central Avenue, Suite 550
Phoenix, AZ 85004-4503
(602) 258-2435   Fax: (602) 258-2483
E-mail: toni@azhighered.org
Web: www.azhighered.org

Summary   To provide financial assistance to undergraduate and graduate students in Arizona who can demonstrate financial need.

Eligibility   This program is open to Arizona residents who are attending or planning to attend a participating Arizona postsecondary educational institution as either a full-time or part-time undergraduate or graduate student. Applicants must be able to demonstrate financial need.

Financial data   Awards range from $100 to $2,500 per year.

Duration   1 year; may be renewed.

Additional information   This program was formerly known as the Arizona State Student Incentive Grant Program.

Number awarded   Varies each year.

Deadline   Each participating institution in Arizona sets its own deadline.

[73]
ARKANSAS HEALTH EDUCATION GRANT PROGRAM

Arkansas Department of Higher Education
Attn: Financial Aid Division
114 East Capitol Avenue
Little Rock, AR 72201-3818
(501) 371-2050   Toll-free: (800) 54-STUDY
Fax: (501) 371-2001   E-mail: finaid@adhe.arknet.edu
Web: www.arkansashighered.com/arheg.html

Summary   To provide financial assistants to residents of Arkansas interested in attending out-of-state institutions that offer health-related programs not available in Arkansas.

Eligibility   This program is open to residents of Arkansas interested in studying dentistry, optometry, osteopathy, chiropractic, podiatry, or veterinary medicine at designated institutions in near-by states. Applicants must have been accepted as a full-time student at a participating institution. U.S. citizenship is required.

Financial data   The amount and form of this assistance depends on the institution that the Arkansas recipient attends. If the school participates in the contract program of the Board of Control for Southern Regional Education (SREB), this program pays a set fee per student to the SREB which negotiates a contract with the school to have a certain number of slots open for Arkansas students and to charge those students in-state tuition. Recently, the fees were $14,000 for dentistry, $12,200 for optometry, $12,200 for osteopathy, $8,600 for podiatry, and $20,400 for veterinary medicine. Schools that do not have a differential for in-state and out-of-state students agree to have a number of slots open for Arkansas students and reduce tuition for each student by $500 per year. Schools that do not participate in the SREB program contract directly with the Arkansas Department of Higher Education. If the school charges different tuition for in-state and out-of-state students, this program pays them the difference so the Arkansas student can attend at the in-state rate.

If the school does not charge different tuition to in-state and out-of-state students, this program will pay at least $5,000 per year. Students who complete a degree in dentistry are eligible for loan forgiveness at the rate of 1 academic year's loan for each year of dental practice in Arkansas.

Duration   Recipients are eligible to utilize this assistance until they complete their course of study.

Additional information   The following institutions have been accepted for participation in this program: for dentistry, Texas A&M University System HSC (Dallas, Texas), University of Alabama (Birmingham), Louisiana State University (New Orleans), Meharry Medical College (Nashville, Tennessee), University of Louisville (Kentucky), University of Missouri (Kansas City), University of Oklahoma (Oklahoma City), and University of Tennessee (Memphis); for optometry, Southern College of Optometry (Memphis), Northeastern State University (Tahlequah, Oklahoma), and University of Missouri (St. Louis); for osteopathy, Oklahoma State University (Tulsa), Pikeville College (Pikeville, Kentucky), Des Moines University of Osteopathic Medicine and Health Sciences (Des Moines, Iowa), and the University of Health Sciences (Kansas City, Missouri); for chiropractic, Cleveland Chiropractic College (Kansas City, Missouri), Logan College of Chiropractic (Chesterfield, Missouri), Palmer College of Chiropractic (Davenport, Iowa), Parker College of Chiropractic (Irving, Texas), and Texas Chiropractic College (Pasadena, Texas); for podiatry, Finch University of Health Sciences (Chicago), Ohio College of Podiatric Medicine (Cleveland), Barry University (Miami Shores, Florida), Des Moines University of Osteopathic Medicine and Health Sciences (Des Moines, Iowa); for veterinary medicine, Louisiana State University (Baton Rouge), Mississippi State University (Starkville), Tuskegee University (Alabama), University of Missouri (Columbia), and Oklahoma State University (Stillwater).

Number awarded   Varies each year; recently, 72 students were admitted to this program: 30 in dentistry, 7 in optometry, 6 in osteopathy, 4 in podiatry, 13 in chiropractic, and 12 in veterinary medicine.

[74]
ARKANSAS MISSING IN ACTION/KILLED IN ACTION DEPENDENTS' SCHOLARSHIP PROGRAM

Arkansas Department of Higher Education
Attn: Financial Aid Division
114 East Capitol Avenue
Little Rock, AR 72201-3818
(501) 371-2050   Toll-free: (800) 54-STUDY
Fax: (501) 371-2001   E-mail: finaid@adhe.arknet.edu
Web: www.arkansashighered.com/miakia.html

Summary   To provide financial assistance for educational purposes to dependents of Arkansas veterans who were killed in action or became POWs or MIAs after January 1, 1960.

Eligibility   This program is open to the natural children, adopted children, stepchildren, and spouses of Arkansas residents who became a prisoner of war, killed in action, missing in action, or killed on ordnance delivery after January 1, 1960. Applicants may be working or planning to work 1) on an undergraduate degree in Arkansas or 2) on a graduate or professional degree in Arkansas if their undergraduate degree was not received in Arkansas. Applicants need not be current Arkansas residents, but their parents or spouses must have been an Arkansas resident at the time of entering military service or at the time they were declared a prisoner of war, killed in action, or missing in action.

Financial data   The program pays for tuition, general registration fees, special course fees, activity fees, room and board (if provided in campus facilities), and other charges associated with earning a degree or certificate.

Duration 1 year; undergraduates may obtain renewal as long as they make satisfactory progress toward a baccalaureate degree; graduate students may obtain renewal as long as they maintain a minimum GPA of 2.5 and make satisfactory progress toward a degree.

Additional information Return or reported death of the veteran will not alter benefits. Applications must be submitted to the financial aid director at an Arkansas state-supported institution of higher education or state-supported technical/vocational school.

Number awarded Varies each year; recently, 4 of these scholarships were awarded.

Deadline July of each year for the fall term; November of each year for the spring term; April of each year for summer term I; June of each year for summer term II.

[75]
ARMED FORCES HEALTH PROFESSIONS SCHOLARSHIPS

U.S. Navy
Attn: Naval Medical Education and Training Command
Code OH
8901 Wisconsin Avenue
Bethesda, MD 20889-5611
(301) 295-2373   Toll-free: (800) USA-NAVY
Fax: (301) 295-6014   E-mail: OH@nmetc.med.navy.mil
Web: nshs.med.navy.mil/hpsp/Pages/HPSPHome.htm

Summary To provide financial assistance for education in a medical field to future Navy medical officers.

Eligibility Applicants for this assistance must be U.S. citizens, under 36 years of age, who are enrolled in or accepted at an accredited medical, osteopathic, dental, or optometry school located in the United States or Puerto Rico. Upon acceptance into the program, applicants are commissioned as officers in the U.S. Navy Medical Corps Reserve; after completion of medical school, they must perform at least 3 years of active-duty service in the U.S. Navy.

Financial data This program pays full tuition at any school of medicine, osteopathy, dentistry, or optometry located in the United States or Puerto Rico, and also covers the cost of fees, books, and required equipment. In addition, recipients are awarded a stipend of $1,279 per month for 10 1/2 months of the year; for the other 1 1/2 months of each year, they perform active-duty service, usually at a Navy medical facility, and receive the normal pay of an Ensign.

Duration Assistance under this program continues until the student completes work for a doctorate degree.

Additional information Following receipt of the doctorate degree, recipients serve an internship and residency either in a naval hospital (in which case they receive Navy active-duty pay) or, if not selected for naval graduate medical education, in a civilian hospital (where they receive only the regular salary of the civilian institution). After completion of the residency, the students must begin the active-duty service obligation. That obligation is 2 years for the first 2 years of participation in the program, plus half a year of service for each additional half-year of program participation; in any case, the minimum service obligation is 3 years regardless of years of participation.

Number awarded Varies each year.

Deadline August of each year.

[76]
ARMENIAN PROFESSIONAL SOCIETY GRADUATE STUDENT SCHOLARSHIP

Armenian Professional Society
Attn: Scholarship Chair
P.O. Box 1944
Glendale, CA 91209-1944
(818) 685-9946   E-mail: apsla@apsla.org
Web: www.apsla.org

Summary To provide financial assistance to graduate students of Armenian ancestry.

Eligibility This program is open to graduate students of Armenian ancestry. Applicants should submit official transcripts for the past 4 years; a brief essay about themselves, including their involvement in the Armenian community and why they should be a scholarship recipient; tax returns for themselves and their parents; and 2 letters of recommendation. U.S. citizenship or permanent resident status is not required. Selection is based on academic achievement, faculty recommendations, involvement in the Armenian community, and financial need.

Financial data A stipend is awarded (amount not specified).

Duration 1 year; may be renewed 1 additional year.

Number awarded Varies each year.

Deadline August of each year.

[77]
ARMENIAN STUDENTS' ASSOCIATION SCHOLARSHIPS

Armenian Students' Association
Attn: Scholarship Committee
333 Atlantic Avenue
Warwick, RI 02888
(401) 461-6114   Fax: (401) 461-6112
E-mail: asa@asainc.org
Web: www.asainc.org/national/scholarships.shtml

Summary To provide financial assistance for undergraduate and graduate education to students of Armenian ancestry.

Eligibility This program is open to undergraduate and graduate students of Armenian descent who have completed at least the first year of college (including graduate, medical, and law school). Applicants must be enrolled full time at a 4-year college or university or a 2-year college and planning to transfer to a 4-year institution in the following fall. They must be a U.S. citizen or have appropriate Visa status to study in the United States. Along with their application, they must submit a 300-word essay about themselves, including their future plans. Financial need is considered in the selection process.

Financial data The stipends range from $500 to $2,500.

Duration 1 year.

Additional information There is a $15 application fee.

Number awarded Varies each year; recently, 21 of these scholarships, worth $48,000, were awarded.

Deadline March of each year.

[78]
ARMY HEALTH PROFESSIONS SCHOLARSHIP PROGRAM

U.S. Army
Human Resources Command, Health Services Division
Attn: AHRC-OPH-AN
200 Stovall Street, Room 9N47
Alexandria, VA 22332-0417
(703) 325-2330   Fax: (703) 325-2358
Web: www.hrc.army.mil

Summary To provide financial assistance to future Army officers who are interested in preparing for a career in medically-related fields.

Eligibility This program is open to U.S. citizens under 35 years of age. Applicants must be enrolled in or accepted at an accredited professional school located in the United States or Puerto Rico in 1 of the following areas: allopathic or osteopathic medicine, dentistry, clinical psychology, optometry, veterinary science, or nurse anesthesia. They must have an undergraduate GPA of 3.5 or higher and minimum scores of 29 on the MCAT or 19 on the DAT. Upon acceptance into the program, applicants are commissioned as officers in the U.S. Army Reserve; after completion of school, they must perform active-duty service in the U.S. Army Medical Corps, Dental Corps, Medical Service Corps (for clinical psychology and optometry), Veterinary Corps, or Nurse Corps.

Financial data This program pays full tuition at any school or college granting a doctoral or other relevant professional degree located in the United States or Puerto Rico and covers the cost of fees, books, and other required equipment. Recipients are also awarded a stipend of $1,279 per month for 10 1/2 months of the year (or a total of $13,429.50). During the other 1 1/2 months of each year, they perform active-duty service, usually at an Army medical facility, and receive the normal pay of a Second Lieutenant.

Duration 1 to 4 years for the medical program; 1 to 4 years for the dental program; 2 or 3 years for the clinical or counseling psychology program; 2 to 4 years for the optometry program; 1 to 3 years for the veterinary program; 1 to 4 years for the nurse anesthesia program.

Additional information Participants incur an active-duty obligation based on existing Department of Defense and Army Directives in effect at the time they sign their contract accepting support through this program. Recently, the obligation has been 1 year for each year of support and a minimum of 2 years for the medical program, 1 year for each year of support and a minimum of 3 years for the dental program, 3 years for the clinical or counseling psychology program, 3 years for the optometry program, 3 years for the veterinary program, and 1 year for each year of support and a minimum of 3 years for the nurse anesthesia program.

Number awarded Varies each year.

Deadline Applications may be submitted at any time.

[79]
ARNOLD SADLER MEMORIAL SCHOLARSHIP

American Council of the Blind
Attn: Coordinator, Scholarship Program
1155 15th Street, N.W., Suite 1004
Washington, DC 20005
(202) 467-5081   Toll-free: (800) 424-8666
Fax: (202) 467-5085   E-mail: info@acb.org
Web: www.acb.org

Summary To provide financial assistance to undergraduate or graduate students who are blind and are interested in studying in a field of service to persons with disabilities.

Eligibility This program is open to students in rehabilitation, education, law, or other fields of service to persons with disabilities. Applicants must be legally blind and U.S. citizens. In addition to letters of recommendation and copies of academic transcripts, applications must include an autobiographical sketch. A cumulative GPA of 3.3 or higher is generally required. Selection is based on demonstrated academic record, involvement in extracurricular and civic activities, and academic objectives. The severity of the applicant's visual impairment and his/her study methods are also taken into account.

Financial data The stipend is $2,000. In addition, the winner receives a Kurzweil-1000 Reading System.

Duration 1 year.

Additional information This scholarship is funded by the Arnold Sadler Memorial Scholarship Fund. Scholarship winners are expected to be present at the council's annual conference; the council will cover all reasonable expenses connected with convention attendance.

Number awarded 1 each year.

Deadline February of each year.

[80]
ASCLS EDUCATION AND RESEARCH FUND GRADUATE SCHOLARSHIPS

Alpha Mu Tau Fraternity
c/o American Society for Clinical Laboratory Science
6701 Democracy Boulevard, Suite 300
Bethesda, MD 20817
(301) 657-2768   Fax: (301) 657-2909
E-mail: ascls@ascls.org
Web: www.ascls.org/leadership/awards/e_and_r.asp

Summary To provide financial assistance for graduate studies to members of Alpha Mu Tau, a national laboratory fraternity.

Eligibility Applicants must be U.S. citizens or permanent residents, members of Alpha Mu Tau, and accepted into or currently enrolled in an approved master's or doctoral program in an area related to clinical laboratory science, including clinical laboratory education or management.

Financial data The stipend is $3,000.

Duration 1 year.

Additional information Funding for this program is provided by the Education and Research Fund of the American Society for Clinical Laboratory Science (ASCLS). Information is also available from Carol Lee Shearer, 3024 Tamarak Drive, Manhattan, KS 66503, E-mail: Carol_Shearer@dadebehring.com.

Number awarded 1 or more each year.

Deadline February of each year.

[81]
ASSOCIATION OF PERIOPERATIVE REGISTERED NURSES (AORN) FOUNDATION NURSING STUDENT SCHOLARSHIPS

Association of periOperative Registered Nurses
Attn: AORN Foundation
2170 South Parker Road, Suite 300
Denver, CO 80231-5711
(303) 755-6300, ext. 328
Toll-free: (800) 755-2676, ext. 328   Fax: (303) 755-4219
E-mail: ibendzsa@aorn.org
Web: www.aorn.org/foundation/scholarships.asp

Summary To provide financial assistance to students interested in preparing for a career in nursing, especially perioperative nursing.

Eligibility This program is open to students currently enrolled in an accredited nursing program leading to initial licensure as an R.N. The program may be for a diploma or an A.D.N., B.S.N., master's entry, or accelerated second B.S.N. degree. Applicants must have a GPA of 3.0 or higher. Along with their application, they must submit a personal statement describing why they have chosen to prepare for a career in nursing, their financial need, their career goals, their volunteer community activities, their academic and/or clinical experience or exposure to the operating room/surgical field, and how they believe the Association of periOperative Registered Nurses (AORN) promotes the specialty of perioperative nursing.

Financial data Stipends range from $500 to $2,500. Funds are paid directly to the recipient.

Duration 1 year; may be renewed if the recipient maintains a GPA of 3.0 or higher.

Additional information This program was established in 2001.

Number awarded 1 or more each year.

Deadline May of each year.

[82]
ASSOCIATION OF UNITED NURSES SCHOLARSHIPS

Scholarship Administrative Services, Inc.
Attn: AUN Program
457 Ives Terrace
Sunnyvale, CA 94087

Summary To provide financial assistance to undergraduate and graduate students working on a degree in nursing.

Eligibility This program is open to full-time students working on or planning to work on an undergraduate or graduate degree in nursing. Applicants must have a GPA of 3.0 or higher and be able to demonstrate a record of involvement in extracurricular and work activities related to nursing. Along with their application, they must submit a 1,000-word essay on their educational and career goals, why they believe nursing is essential to America, and why they have decided to prepare for a career in nursing. Financial need is not considered in the selection process.

Financial data The stipend is $5,000 per year.

Duration 1 year; may be renewed 1 additional year if the recipient maintains full-time enrollment and a GPA of 3.0 or higher.

Additional information This program is sponsored by the Association of United Nurses (AUN) and administered by Scholarship Administrative Services, Inc. AUN was established in 2005 to encourage more American students to consider a career as a nurse. Requests for applications should be accompanied by a self-addressed stamped envelope, the student's e-mail address, and the source where they found the scholarship information.

Number awarded Up to 20 each year.

Deadline April of each year.

[83]
A.T. ANDERSON MEMORIAL SCHOLARSHIP PROGRAM

American Indian Science and Engineering Society
Attn: Scholarship Coordinator
2305 Renard, S.E., Suite 200
P.O. Box 9828
Albuquerque, NM 87119-9828
(505) 765-1052, ext. 106   Fax: (505) 765-5608
E-mail: shirley@aises.org
Web: www.aises.org/highered/scholarships

Summary To provide financial assistance to members of the American Indian Science and Engineering Society who are majoring in designated fields as undergraduate or graduate students.

Eligibility This program is open to members of the society who can furnish proof of tribal enrollment or Certificate of Degree of Indian Blood. Applicants must be full-time students at the undergraduate or graduate school level attending an accredited 4-year college or university or a 2-year college leading to an academic degree in engineering, mathematics, medicine, natural resources, physical science, or the sciences. They must submit a 500-word essay that demonstrates their interest in and motivation to continue higher education, an understanding of the importance of college and a commitment to completion, their educational and/or career goals, and a commitment to learning and giving back to the community. Selection is based on the essay, academic achievement (GPA of 2.7 or higher), leadership potential, and commitment to helping other American Indians. Financial need is not considered.

Financial data The annual stipend is $1,000 for undergraduates or $2,000 for graduate students.

Duration 1 year; nonrenewable.

Additional information This program was launched in 1983 in memory of A.T. Anderson, a Mohawk and a chemical engineer who worked with Albert Einstein. Anderson was 1 of the society's founders and was the society's first executive director. The program includes the following named awards: the Al Qöyawayma Award for an applicant who is majoring in science or engineering and also has a strong interest in the arts, the Norbert S. Hill, Jr. Leadership Award, the Polingaysi Qöyawayma Award for an applicant who is working on a teaching degree in order to teach mathematics or science in a Native community or an advanced degree for personal improvement or teaching at the college level, and the Robert W. Brocksbank Scholarship.

Number awarded Varies; generally, 200 or more each year, depending upon the availability of funds from corporate and other sponsors.

Deadline June of each year.

[84]
AUDIO-DIGEST FOUNDATION SCHOLARSHIP

American Medical Association
Attn: AMA Foundation
515 North State Street
Chicago, IL 60610
(312) 464-4193   Fax: (312) 464-4142
E-mail: dina.lindenberg@ama-assn.org
Web: www.ama-assn.org/ama/pub/category/14772.html

Summary To provide financial assistance to medical school students interested in communication of science.

Eligibility This program is open to U.S. citizens enrolled in accredited U.S. or Canadian medical schools that grant the M.D. degree. Only nominations are accepted. Nominees must be rising seniors and plan to specialize in communication of science, through such activities as mentoring or teaching. The number of students who can be nominated per school depends upon the size of the third-year class: 1 nominee for a class size up to 150 students; 2 nominees for a class size between 151 and 250 students; 3 nominees for a class size of 251 students or more. Selection is based on demonstrated interest in communication of science, academic record, and financial need.
Financial data The stipend is $10,000.
Duration 1 year.
Additional information This program is funded by the Audio-Digest Foundation. It was formerly named the Jerry L. Pettis Memorial Scholarship.
Number awarded 1 each year.
Deadline May of each year.

[85]
AWARDS FOR STUDENT RESEARCH TRAINING IN ALTERNATIVE METHODS
Society of Toxicology
Attn: Education Committee
1821 Michael Faraday Drive, Suite 300
Reston, VA 20190-5348
(703) 438-3115   Fax: (703) 438-3113
E-mail: sothq@toxicology.org
Web: www.toxicology.org/ai/af/awards.aspx
Summary To provide funding to graduate student members of the Society of Toxicology (SOT) interested in research training in alternative methods for the use of animals in toxicological research.
Eligibility This program is open to society members who are enrolled in Ph.D. or master's degree study in toxicology. Applicants must be interested in developing expertise in the use of alternative methods that involve the use of the "3 R's": replacement (methods that do not employ animals), reduction (methods that result in the use of fewer animals than existing methods), or refinement (methods or techniques that reduce pain, distress, or discomfort to the animal). The proposed research training may take place at 1) a laboratory away from their home institution, 2) a laboratory at their home institution that would not be available to them otherwise, or 3) approved workshops, symposia, or continuing education programs where hands-on training is provided. The training should help them enhance their thesis or dissertation research and gain appreciation of the use of alternatives in toxicology. work planned for the future, relevance of graduate work to toxicology, and description of the techniques the applicant proposes to learn and how those would enhance the research program. Letters of support from the applicant's research advisor and director of the hosting laboratory are also required. The research director must also be an SOT member.
Financial data The grant is $3,500. Funds may be used for travel, per diem, and training expenses (including research costs at the home and host institutions).
Additional information This program, first offered in 2000, is funded by Colgate-Palmolive Company.
Number awarded 2 each year.
Deadline February, June, or October of each year.

[86]
BACHRACH FAMILY SCHOLARSHIP FOR EXCELLENCE IN HEALTH CARE ADMINISTRATION
American College of Medical Practice Executives
Attn: ACMPE Scholarship Fund Inc.
104 Inverness Terrace East
Englewood, CO 80112-5306
(303) 799-1111, ext. 232   Toll-free: (877) ASK-MGMA
Fax: (303) 643-4439   E-mail: acmpe@mgma.com
Web: www.mgma.com/academics/scholar.cfm
Summary To provide financial assistance to graduate students working on a degree in health care administration.
Eligibility This program is open to graduate students enrolled in a program in health care administration whose career interests may lead them to a position in medical practice administration. Applicants must have a GPA of 3.0 or higher. Preference is given to applicants who are from a disadvantaged background and/or the first person in their family to pursue a graduate degree. Students working on a degree in medicine, physical therapy, nursing, or other clinically-related professions are not eligible. Applicants must submit a letter describing their career goals and objectives relevant to medical practice management; a resume; 3 reference letters commenting on their performance, character, potential to succeed, and need for scholarship support; and either documentation indicating acceptance into an undergraduate or graduate college or university or academic transcripts indicating undergraduate or graduate work completed to date.
Financial data The stipend is at least $1,000. Funds are paid directly to the recipient's college or university.
Duration 1 year.
Additional information This program is managed by Scholarship Program Administrators, Inc. 1201 Eighth Avenue South, P.O. Box 23737, Nashville, TN 27202-3737, (615) 320-3149, (800) 310-4053, Fax: (615) 320-3151, E-mail: info@spaprog.com.
Number awarded 1 each year.
Deadline April of each year.

[87]
BAMFORD-LAHEY SCHOLARSHIPS
Bamford-Lahey Children's Foundation
2995 Woodside Road, Suite 400
Woodside, CA 94062
E-mail: info@bamford-lahey.org
Web: bamford-lahey.org/scholarships.html
Summary To provide financial assistance to doctoral students interested in a program of study and research in children's language disorders.
Eligibility This program is open to doctoral students who have been accepted at an accredited university that provides sufficient course work and faculty advisement for study and research in children's language disorders and that has an emphasis on research skills. Applicants must be able to demonstrate an ability to complete a doctoral program and a commitment to become a teacher-investigator with an emphasis on children's language disorders at a college or university. Selection is based on motivation to complete the doctoral program, academic skills necessary to complete the program successfully, promise as a teacher who will educate future clinicians about children's language disorders, promise as a researcher who will contribute to the body of knowledge about children's language disorders, commitment to the field of children's language disorders, and responsibility for appropriate use of the funds. The ability of the institution to provide the applicant with mentors and course work in children's language disorders and related fields is also considered.

Financial data The stipend is $10,000.
Duration 1 year.
Additional information This foundation was established in 2000.
Number awarded Varies each year; recently, 3 of these fellowships were awarded.
Deadline March of each year.

[88]
BARBARA A. COOLEY SCHOLARSHIP

American Association for Health Education
Attn: Scholarship Committee
1900 Association Drive
Reston, VA 20191-1599
(703) 476-3437   Toll-free: (800) 213-7193, ext. 437
Fax: (703) 476-6638   E-mail: aahe@aahperd.org
Web: www.aahperd.org/aahe/heawards/Cooley.html
Summary To provide financial assistance to master's degree students who are currently enrolled in a health education program.
Eligibility Eligible to apply for this support are master's degree students who are enrolled in a health education program, have a GPA of 3.0 or higher, and have never won an award from the association. All applications must be accompanied by a current resume, an official transcript, 3 letters of recommendation, and a 3-part narrative (up to 3 pages), indicating their philosophy of health education, professional goals, and assessment of current and future issues in health education. Selection is based on evidence of leadership potential, academic talent, and activity in health education profession-related activities or organizations at the college, university, and/or community level.
Financial data The stipend is $1,000 plus a 1-year complimentary student membership in the association.
Duration 1 year; nonrenewable.
Number awarded 1 each year.
Deadline November of each year.

[89]
BASIC MIDWIFERY SCHOLARSHIPS

American College of Nurse-Midwives
Attn: ACNM Foundation, Inc.
8403 Coleville Road, Suite 1550
Silver Spring, MD 20915
(240) 485-1850   Fax: (240) 485-1818
Web: www.midwife.org
Summary To provide financial assistance for midwifery education to student members of the American College of Nurse-Midwives (ACNM).
Eligibility This program is open to ACNM members who are currently enrolled in an accredited basic midwife education program and have successfully completed 1 academic or clinical semester/quarter or clinical module. Applicants must submit a 150-word essay on their midwifery career plans and a 100-word essay on their intended future participation in the local, regional, and/or national activities of the ACNM. Selection is based on leadership potential, financial need, academic history, and potential for future professional contribution to the organization.
Financial data The stipend is $3,000.
Duration 1 year.
Additional information This program includes the following named scholarships: the A.C.N.M. Foundation Memorial Scholarship, the TUMS Calcium for Life Scholarship (presented by Glax-

oSmithKline), the Edith B. Wonnell CNM Scholarship, and the Margaret Edmundson Scholarship.
Number awarded Varies each year; recently, 4 of these scholarships were awarded.
Deadline March of each year.

[90]
BEALE FAMILY MEMORIAL SCHOLARSHIP

Maine Osteopathic Association
Attn: Executive Director
693 Western Avenue, Suite 1
Manchester, ME 04351
(207) 623-1101   Fax: (207) 623-4228
E-mail: info@mainedo.org
Web: www.mainedo.org
Summary To provide financial assistance to Maine residents who are attending osteopathic medical school.
Eligibility This program is open to continuing students who have been Maine residents for at least 3 years, are able to present proof of enrollment at an approved college of osteopathic medicine, are in their second through fourth year of study, and are interested in practicing primary care in Maine. Residency in Maine for the sole purpose of postsecondary education is not considered evidence of Maine residence for the purpose of this scholarship. Applicants who are graduates of a public or private secondary school in Maine are considered eligible, whether or not they have resided elsewhere in the interim between high school graduation and application. Preference is given to applicants from the Bangor, Maine area.
Financial data The stipend is $1,000.
Duration 1 year.
Number awarded 1 each year.
Deadline April of each year.

[91]
BETTY HANSEN NATIONAL SCHOLARSHIPS

Danish Sisterhood of America
Attn: Lizette Burtis, Scholarship Chair
3020 Santa Juanita Court
Santa Rosa, CA 95405-8219
(707) 539-1884   E-mail: lburtis@sbcglobal.net
Web: www.danishsisterhood.org/rschol.asp
Summary To provide financial assistance for educational purposes in the United States or Denmark to members or relatives of members of the Danish Sisterhood of America.
Eligibility This program is open to members or the family of members of the sisterhood who are interested in attending an accredited 4-year college or university as a full-time undergraduate or graduate student. Members must have belonged to the sisterhood for at least 1 year. Selection is based on academic excellence (at least a 2.5 GPA). Upon written request, the scholarship may be used for study in Denmark.
Financial data The stipend is $1,000.
Duration 1 year; nonrenewable.
Number awarded Up to 8 each year.
Deadline February of each year.

[92]
BIG FIVE SCHOLARSHIP

Daughters of Penelope
Attn: Daughters of Penelope Foundation, Inc.
1909 Q Street, N.W., Suite 500
Washington, DC 20009-1007
(202) 234-9741   Fax: (202) 483-6983
E-mail: daughters@ahepa.org
Web: www.ahepa.org

Summary To provide financial assistance for graduate study to women of Greek descent.

Eligibility This program is open to women who have been members of the Daughters of Penelope or the Maids of Athena for at least 2 years, or whose parents or grandparents have been members of the Daughters of Penelope or the Order of Ahepa for at least 2 years. Applicants must be accepted or currently enrolled for a minimum of 9 units per academic year in an M.A., M.S., M.B.A., J.D., Ph.D., D.D.S., M.D., or other university graduate degree program. They must have taken the GRE or other entrance examination (or Canadian, Greek, or Cypriot equivalent) and must write an essay (in English) about their educational and vocational goals. Selection is based on academic merit.

Financial data The stipend is $1,000 per year.

Duration 1 year; nonrenewable.

Additional information Information is also available from Helen Santire, National Scholarship Chair, P.O. Box 19709, Houston, TX 77242-9709, (713) 468-6531.

Number awarded 1 each year.

Deadline May of each year.

[93]
BOARD OF GOVERNORS MEDICAL SCHOLARSHIP PROGRAM

North Carolina State Education Assistance Authority
Attn: Scholarship and Grant Services
10 T.W. Alexander Drive
P.O. Box 14103
Research Triangle Park, NC 27709-4103
(919) 549-8614   Toll-free: (800) 700-1775
Fax: (919) 549-8481   E-mail: information@ncseaa.edu
Web: www.ncseaa.edu

Summary To provide financial assistance to residents of North Carolina who have been admitted to a medical school in the state.

Eligibility Students must be nominated for this program. Nominees must be residents of North Carolina, be able to demonstrate financial need, express an intent to practice medicine in North Carolina, and have been accepted for admission to 1 of the 4 medical schools in North Carolina: Bowman Gray School of Medicine at Wake Forest University, Duke University School of Medicine, Brody School of Medicine at East Carolina University School, and the University of North Carolina at Chapel Hill School of Medicine. Minorities are especially encouraged to apply.

Financial data Each scholarship provides a stipend of $5,000 a year, plus tuition, mandatory fees, medical insurance, and a laptop computer.

Duration 1 year; renewable up to 3 additional years, provided the recipient makes satisfactory academic progress, continues to have financial need, and remains interested in medical practice in North Carolina.

Number awarded 20 new awards are granted each year. Recently, a total of 81 students were receiving $1,637,085 in support through this program.

Deadline April of each year.

[94]
BOBBIE ANDERSON FACULTY SCHOLARSHIP

National Organization for Associate Degree Nursing
Attn: Foundation
7794 Grow Drive
Pensacola, FL 32514
(850) 484-6948   Toll-free: (877) 966-6236
Fax: (850) 484-8762   E-mail: noadn@puetzamc.com
Web: www.noadn.org/noadnfoundation.htm

Summary To provide financial assistance to nurses interested in earning a master's degree in order to teach associate degree nursing.

Eligibility This program is open to R.N.s who have been accepted into a master's program in a school of nursing. Applicants must submit 1) an essay of approximately 200 words describing their interest in teaching in associate degree nursing and their willingness to teach at least 2 years in an A.D.N. program; 2) a list of their professional and community organizational activities; 3) 2 letters of reference regarding their professional work, commitment to nursing, and potential as a teacher; 4) a letter of support from an agency member of the sponsoring organization; and 5) a graduate and/or undergraduate transcript.

Financial data The stipend is $1,000.

Duration 1 year.

Number awarded 1 each year.

Deadline June of each year.

[95]
BOOMER ESIASON FOUNDATION SCHOLARSHIP PROGRAM

Boomer Esiason Foundation
c/o Jerry Cahill
417 Fifth Avenue, Second Floor
New York, NY 10016
(646) 344-3765   Fax: (646) 344-3757
E-mail: jcahill@esiason.org
Web: www.esiason.org

Summary To provide financial assistance to undergraduate and graduate students who have cystic fibrosis (CF).

Eligibility This program is open to CF patients who are working on an undergraduate or graduate degree. Applicants must submit a letter from a social worker describing their needs, a detailed breakdown of tuition costs from their academic institution, transcripts, and a 1-page essay on their post-graduation goals. Selection is based on academic ability, character, leadership potential, service to the community, and financial need. Finalists are interviewed by telephone.

Financial data Stipends range from $500 to $2,000. Funds are paid directly to the academic institution to assist in covering the cost of tuition and fees.

Duration 1 year; nonrenewable.

Additional information Recipients must be willing to participate in the sponsor's CF Ambassador Program by speaking once a year at a designated CF event to help educate the general public about CF.

Number awarded 10 to 15 each year.

[96]
BOSTONWORKS NURSING FACULTY SCHOLARSHIP

Massachusetts Hospital Association
Attn: Education
5 New England Executive Park
Burlington, MA 01803
(781) 272-8000, ext. 177 E-mail: education@mhalink.org
Web: www.mhalink.org/public/education/scholarship.cfm

Summary To provide financial assistance to registered nurses interested in working on a graduate degree to prepare for a career as a faculty member.

Eligibility This program is open to registered nurses who are enrolled or accepted for enrollment in a graduate nursing program (M.S.N. or Ph.D.) on at least a half-time basis. Applicants must be able to document a commitment to nursing faculty role preparation and plans to serve as academic faculty after graduation. Selection is based on academic excellence. U.S. citizenship is required.

Financial data The stipend is $20,000.

Duration 1 year.

Additional information This program was established in 2006 with a donation from BostonWorks.

Number awarded 1 each year.

Deadline April of each year.

[97]
BUDWEISER CONSERVATION SCHOLARSHIP

National Fish and Wildlife Foundation
1120 Connecticut Avenue, N.W., Suite 900
Washington, DC 20036
(202) 857-0166 Fax: (202) 857-0162
E-mail: Alison.Bolz@nfwf.org
Web: www.nfwf.org/programs/budscholarship

Summary To provide financial assistance to undergraduate and graduate students who are interested in studying or conducting research related to the field of conservation.

Eligibility This program is open to U.S. citizens at least 21 years of age and enrolled in an accredited institution of higher education in the United States. Applicants must be working on a graduate or undergraduate degree (sophomores and juniors in the current academic year only) in environmental science, natural resource management, biology, public policy, geography, political science, or a related discipline. They must submit transcripts, 3 letters of recommendation, and an essay (up to 1,500 words) describing their academic objectives and focusing on a specific issue affecting the conservation of fish, wildlife, or plant species in the United States and the research or study they propose to address the issue. Selection is based on the merits of the proposed research or study, its significance to the field of conservation, its feasibility and overall quality, the innovativeness of the proposed research or study, the student's academic achievements, and their commitment to leadership in the conservation field.

Financial data Stipends range up to $10,000. Funds must be used to cover expenses related to the recipients' studies, including tuition, fees, books, room, and board. Payments may supplement but not duplicate benefits from their educational institution or from other foundations, institutions, or organizations. The combined benefits from all sources may not exceed the recipient's educational expenses.

Duration 1 year.

Additional information This program, established in 2001, is jointly sponsored by Anheuser-Busch and the National Fish and Wildlife Foundation.

Number awarded At least 10 each year.

Deadline April of each year.

[98]
BUENA M. CHESSHIR MEMORIAL WOMEN'S EDUCATIONAL SCHOLARSHIP

Business and Professional Women of Virginia
Attn: Virginia BPW Foundation
P.O. Box 4842
McLean, VA 22103-4842
Web: www.bpwva.org/scholarships.shtml

Summary To provide financial assistance to mature women in Virginia who are interested in upgrading their skills or education at a college, law school, or medical school in the state.

Eligibility This program is open to women who are residents of Virginia, U.S. citizens, and at least 25 years of age. Applicants must have been accepted into an accredited program or course of study at a Virginia institution, have a definite plan to use their training to improve their chances for upward mobility in the workforce, and be graduating within 2 years. Undergraduate applicants may be majoring in any field, but doctoral students must be working on a degree in law or medicine. Selection is based on academic achievement, demonstrated financial need, and defined career goals.

Financial data Stipends range from $100 to $1,000 per year; funds may be used for tuition, fees, books, transportation, living expenses, and dependent care.

Duration Recipients must complete their course of study within 2 years.

Number awarded 1 or more each year.

Deadline March of each year.

[99]
BUSH LEADERSHIP FELLOWS PROGRAM

Bush Foundation
Attn: Program Assistant
332 Minnesota Street, Suite E-990
St. Paul, MN 55101-1315
(651) 227-0891 Toll-free: (800) 605-7315
Fax: (651) 297-6485 E-mail: info@bushfoundation.org
Web: www.bushfoundation.org

Summary To provide funding to mid-career professionals interested in obtaining further education to prepare themselves for higher-level responsibilities.

Eligibility This program is open to U.S. citizens or permanent residents who are at least 28 years of age. Applicants must have lived or worked for at least 1 year immediately before the application deadline in Minnesota, North Dakota, South Dakota, or northwestern Wisconsin (Ashland, Barron, Bayfield, Buffalo, Burnett, Chippewa, Douglas, Dunn, Eau Claire, Florence, Forest, Iron, La Crosse, Lincoln, Oneida, Pepin, Pierce, Polk, Price, Rusk, St. Croix, Sawyer, Taylor, Trempealeau, Vilas, and Washburn counties). They should be employed full time and have at least 5 years of work experience. Some experience in a policy-making or administrative capacity is desirable. Work experience may include part-time and volunteer work. Most successful applicants have baccalaureate degrees or their equivalent. Fields of work have included public service, education, government, health, business, community development, engineering, architecture, science, farming, forestry, law, trade unions, law enforcement, journalism, and social work. They must be interested in pursuing full-time involvement in a learning experience that may include academic course work, internships, self-designed study programs, or various combinations of those and other kinds of learning experiences. Fellowships are not granted for applicants currently enrolled as full-time students, part-time study combined with full- or part-time employment, academic research, publications, or design and implementation of service programs or projects. Fellowships are unlikely to be awarded for full-time study plans built on academic programs designed primarily for part-time students, programs intended to meet the continuing education requirements for professional certification, completion of basic educational requirements for entry level jobs, segments of degree programs that cannot be completed within or near the end of the fellowship period, or projects that might more properly be the subjects of grant proposals from organizations. Selection is based on the applicants' personal integrity, adaptability, intelligence, and energy; work experience and community service record; fellowship plans; and goals.

Financial data Fellows receive a stipend of $3,800 per month for living expenses; an allowance for instructional expenses (50% of the first $8,000 plus 80% of expenses after $8,000) to a maximum of $18,000; and reimbursements up to $6,000 for travel expenses.

Duration From 2 to 18 months.

Additional information Awards are for full-time study and internships anywhere in the United States. This program began in 1965.

Number awarded Approximately 25 each year.

Deadline October of each year.

[100]
CALIFORNIA BREAST CANCER DISSERTATION FELLOWSHIPS

California Breast Cancer Research Program
c/o University of California, Office of the President
300 Lakeside Drive, Sixth Floor
Oakland, CA 94612-3550
(510) 987-9884   Toll-free: (888) 313-BCRD
Fax: (510) 987-6325   E-mail: CBCRP2ucop.edu
Web: www.cbcrp.org

Summary To provide funding for research training related to breast cancer to graduate students at universities in California.

Eligibility This program is open to students who have advanced to candidacy for a master's or doctoral degree at a California university. The proposed research training should relate to 1 of the current priorities of the sponsor: 1) the community impact of breast cancer, especially studies of the factors that contribute to the unequal burden of the disease among diverse communities; 2) etiology and prevention; 3) the basic science of the disease; or 4) detection, prognosis, and treatment. The student must act as the principal investigator and must prepare the application. A full-time faculty member at the institution must serve as mentor; the mentor should either be experienced and have published in breast cancer or collaborate with a breast cancer researcher. Applications must include a training plan focused on breast cancer.

Financial data The grant is $38,000 per year. Funds may be used for stipend, fringe benefits, tuition and fee remission, supplies, and travel; no indirect costs are allowed.

Duration 1 year for master's students or 2 years for doctoral students.

Number awarded Varies each year; recently, 17 of these fellowships were awarded.

Deadline January of each year.

[101]
CALIFORNIA SCOTTISH RITE FOUNDATION SPEECH LANGUAGE PATHOLOGY FELLOWSHIPS

California Scottish Rite Foundation
Attn: Secretary
855 Elm Avenue
Long Beach, CA 90813-4491
(562) 435-6061
Web: www.scottishritecalifornia.org/foundation_history.htm

Summary To provide financial assistance to California residents working on a degree in speech language pathology.

Eligibility This program is open to California residents who are preparing for a career in speech language pathology at a graduate school providing such programs in the state.

Financial data The stipend is $6,000 per year.

Duration 1 year.

Additional information Requests for applications must be submitted in writing; telephone requests will not be honored.

Number awarded Varies each year, depending on the availability of funds.

Deadline March of each year.

[102]
CAMPUSRN/AACN NURSING SCHOLARSHIP FUND

American Association of Colleges of Nursing
One Dupont Circle, N.W., Suite 530
Washington, DC 20036
(202) 463-6930   Fax: (202) 785-8320
E-mail: scholarships@campuscareercenter.com
Web: aacn.campusrn.com/scholarships/scholarship_m.asp

Summary To provide financial assistance to students at institutions that are members of the American Association of Colleges of Nursing (AACN).

Eligibility This program is open to students working on a baccalaureate, master's, or doctoral degree at an AACN member school. Preference is given to applicants who are 1) enrolled in a master's or doctoral program to prepare for a nursing faculty career; 2) completing an R.N. to baccalaureate (B.S.N.) program; or 3) enrolled in an accelerated baccalaureate or master's degree nursing program. Applicants must have a GPA of 3.25 or higher. Along with their application, they must submit an essay of 200 to 250 words on their goals and aspirations as related to their education, career, and future plans. They must also register and submit their resume to CampusRN.com.

Financial data The stipend is $2,500.

Duration 1 year.

Additional information This program, established in 2003, is sponsored by CampusRN, an employment web site for nursing and allied health care students.

Number awarded 6 each year.

Deadline February, April, June, August, October, or December of each year.

[103]
CANFIT PROGRAM SCHOLARSHIPS

California Adolescent Nutrition, Physical Education, and
   Culinary Arts Scholarships
2140 Shattuck Avenue, Suite 610
Berkeley, CA 94704
(510) 644-1533   Toll-free: (800) 200-3131
Fax: (510) 644-1535   E-mail: info@canfit.org
Web: www.canfit.org/scholarships.html

Summary To provide financial assistance to minority undergraduate and graduate students who are studying nutrition, physical education or culinary arts in California.

Eligibility Eligible to apply are American Indians/Alaska Natives, African Americans, Asians/Pacific Islanders, and Latinos/Hispanics who are enrolled in either: 1) an approved master's or doctoral program in nutrition, public health nutrition, or physical education or in a preprofessional practice program approved by the American Dietetic Association at an accredited university in California; or, 2) an approved bachelor's or professional certificate program in culinary arts, nutrition, or physical education at an accredited university or college in California. Graduate student applicants must have completed at least 12 units of graduate course work and have a cumulative GPA of 3.0 or higher; undergraduate applicants must have completed 50 semester units or the equivalent of college credits and have a cumulative GPA of 2.5 or higher. Selection is based on financial need, academic goals, and community nutrition or physical education activities.

Financial data Graduate stipends are $1,000 each and undergraduate stipends are $500 per year.

Additional information A goal of the California Adolescent Nutrition and Fitness (CANFit) program is to improve the nutritional status and physical fitness of California's low-income multiethnic youth aged 10 to 14. By offering these scholarships, the program hopes to encourage more students to consider careers in adolescent nutrition and fitness.

Number awarded 5 graduate scholarships and 10 undergraduate scholarships are available each year.

Deadline March of each year.

[104]
CAPS SCHOLARSHIPS

Chinese American Physicians Society
c/o Lawrence Ng, Award Committee Chair
345 Ninth Street, Suite 204
Oakland, CA 94607-4206
(510) 895-5539   Fax: (510) 839-0988
E-mail: scholarship@caps-ca.org
Web: www.caps-ca.org/scholarship.html

Summary To provide financial assistance to medical students in the United States.

Eligibility This program is open to students attending or planning to attend a U.S. medical school. Applicants may be from any location and of any sex, race, or color. Preference is given to those willing to serve Chinese communities after graduation. Along with their application, they must submit a 500-word essay on the cause of the mental health crisis facing Asian American communities and possible solutions. Selection is based on the essay, academic achievement, financial need, and Asian American community service.

Financial data Stipends range from $1,000 to $5,000 per year.

Duration 1 year; may be renewed.

Number awarded Varies each year; recently, 5 of these fellowships were awarded.

Deadline March of each year.

[105]
CAREER ADVANCEMENT SCHOLARSHIPS

Business and Professional Women's Foundation
Attn: Scholarship Program
301 ACT Drive
P.O. Box 4030
Iowa City, IA 52243-4030
Toll-free: (800) 525-3729   E-mail: bpwfoundation@act.org
Web: www.bpwfoundation.org

Summary To provide financial assistance for college or graduate school to mature women who are employed or seeking employment in selected fields.

Eligibility This program is open to women who are at least 25 years of age, citizens of the United States, within 2 years of completing their course of study, officially accepted into an accredited program or course of study at an American institution (including those in American Samoa, Puerto Rico, and the Virgin Islands), able to demonstrate critical financial need, and planning to use the desired training to improve their chances for advancement, train for a new career field, or enter/reenter the job market. Applicants must be interested in working on an associate degree, bachelor's degree, master's degree, certificate program for a person with a degree (e.g., teacher's certificate), or certificate program that does not require a degree (e.g., nurse practitioner). Along with their application, they must submit a 1-page essay on their specific, short-term goals and how the proposed training and award will help them accomplish their goals and make a difference in their professional career. Study for a doctoral-level or terminal degree (e.g., Ph.D., M.D., D.D.S., D.V.M., J.D.) is not eligible.

Financial data Stipends range from $1,000 to $2,500 per year.

Duration 1 year; recipients may reapply.

Additional information The scholarship may be used to support part-time study as well as academic or vocational/paraprofessional/office skills training. The program was established in 1969. Scholarships cannot be used to pay for classes already in progress. The program does not cover study at the doctoral level, correspondence courses, postdoctoral studies, or studies in foreign countries. Training must be completed within 24 months.

Number awarded Varies each year; recently, 75 of these scholarships were awarded.

Deadline April of each year.

[106]
CARING SCHOLARSHIP

National Association Directors of Nursing Administration in
   Long Term Care
Attn: Education/Scholarship Committee
10101 Alliance Road, Suite 140
Cincinnati, OH 45242
(513) 791-3679   Toll-free: (800) 222-0539
Fax: (513) 791-3699   E-mail: info@nadona.org
Web: www.nadona.org

Summary To provide financial assistance to students who are working on a nursing degree and who are members of the National Association of Directors of Nursing Administration in Long Term Care (NADONA/LTC).

Eligibility This program is open to members of the association who are currently employed in long-term care (for at least 1 year) and plan to remain employed in long-term care for at least 2 years after graduation. Applicants must be currently accepted or enrolled in a National League for Nursing (NLN) accredited B.S.N., master's, or higher degree program (proof of acceptance and NLN accreditation must accompany the application). Along with their application, they must submit an essay (up to 250 words) that describes why they are seeking this degree and how the education will be used in the future. Students who received funds/awards from a NADONA/LTC scholarship within the last 4 years are ineligible to apply for this award.

Financial data A stipend is awarded (amount not specified); a total of $5,000 is currently available for this program each year.

Duration 1 year.

Additional information Funds for this scholarship are provided by the Parke-Davis Division of Warner-Lambert.

Number awarded At least 1 each year.

Deadline February of each year.

[107]
CARL FOLEY GRADUATE SCHOLARSHIP PROGRAM

Council of Citizens with Low Vision International
c/o Pat Beattie, President
906 North Chambliss Street
Alexandria, VA 22312-3005
(703) 578-6513   Toll-free: (800) 733-2258
Fax: (703) 671-9053   E-mail: pbeattie@nib.org
Web: www.cclvi.org/scholarship.html

Summary To provide financial assistance to graduate students in the field of vision rehabilitation.

Eligibility Eligible are graduate students in the field of vision rehabilitation at academic institutions identified as having programs or special study targeting the needs of people with low vision. Applicants do not need to be visually impaired.

Financial data The stipend is $1,000.

Duration 1 year.

Additional information Recently, the participating schools were Northern Illinois University, Pennsylvania College of Optometry, University of Texas at Austin, Western Michigan University, and Peabody College at Vanderbilt University.

Number awarded Varies each year.

Deadline April of each year.

[108]
CAROLINA PANTHERS SCHOLARSHIP

Foundation for the Carolinas
Attn: Senior Vice President, Scholarships
217 South Tryon Street
P.O. Box 34769
Charlotte, NC 28234-4769
(704) 973-4535   Toll-free: (800) 973-7244
Fax: (704) 973-4935   E-mail: jseymour@fftc.org
Web: www.fftc.org/scholarships

Summary To provide financial assistance for graduate school to seniors at colleges and universities in South Carolina or North Carolina who have participated in athletics.

Eligibility This program is open to graduating seniors at colleges and universities in South Carolina and North Carolina who have earned an intercollegiate varsity letter in college. Female athletes may letter in any sport; male athletes must letter in football. Applicants must have a GPA of 3.0 or higher. They must be

planning to enroll in graduate school as a full-time student. Along with their application, they must submit a 1,000-word essay on why they are applying for the scholarship, their involvement in athletics, and their educational and career goals. Selection is based on leadership, citizenship, and academic merit.

Financial data The stipend is $5,000. Funds are paid directly to the recipient's school to be used for tuition, required fees, books, and supplies.

Duration 1 year.

Number awarded 1 or more each year.

Deadline March of each year.

[109]
CELEBRATION OF EXCELLENCE SCHOLARSHIP

Georgia Association of Homes and Services for Children
Attn: Celebration of Excellence
34 Peachtree Street, N.W., Suite 1710
Atlanta, GA 30303
(404) 572-6170   Fax: (404) 572-6171
E-mail: cara@gahsc.org
Web: www.celebrationofexcellence.org

Summary To provide financial assistance for college or graduate school to residents of Georgia who have been in foster care.

Eligibility This program is open to Georgia residents who were in the custody of the Georgia Department of Family and Children Services or placed at a licensed private residential program at the time of their 18th birthday. Applicants must be attending or planning to attend an approved college, university, vocational program, or graduate school. They must submit an essay of 3 to 5 pages that discusses their educational and career goals, their extracurricular activities and community involvement, and why they think this scholarship will help them reach their goals. Selection is based on that essay, transcripts, SAT/ACT scores, 2 letters of reference, and financial need.

Financial data The stipend is $1,000 per year.

Duration 1 year; may be renewed for a total of 4 years of undergraduate and/or graduate study.

Number awarded 1 or more each year.

Deadline April of each year.

[110]
CERT SCHOLARSHIPS

Council of Energy Resource Tribes
Attn: Education Program Director
695 South Colorado Boulevard, Suite 10
Denver, CO 80246-8008
(303) 282-7576   Fax: (303) 282-7584
E-mail: info@CERTRedEarth.com
Web: www.certredearth.com

Summary To provide financial assistance to American Indians who are interested in studying fields related to mathematics, business, science, engineering, or other technical fields on the undergraduate or graduate school level.

Eligibility This program is open to Indian high school seniors, college students, and graduate students who have participated in the Tribal Resource Institute in Business, Engineering, and Science (TRIBES) program, an intensive 7-week summer college-level program. CERT internship participants are also eligible. Applicants must be planning to enroll full time at an accredited 2- or 4-year tribal, public, or private college or university and major in business, engineering, science, mathematics, computer technology, or a related field. Along with their application, they must submit official tribal affiliation documents, university or college enrollment verification, and their most recent academic transcripts. Financial need is also considered in the selection process.

Financial data Costs of instruction, activities, and room and board for the summer institute are paid by the TRIBES program. The amount of the college scholarship is $1,000 per year.

Duration 1 year; may be renewed up to 4 additional years, provided the recipient maintains a GPA of 2.5 or higher.

Additional information The TRIBES program runs for 7 weeks during the summer at the University of New Mexico, Native American Studies, MSCO6 3740, Albuquerque, NM 87131-0001, (505) 277-1812, Fax: (505) 277-1818.

Deadline Applications for the TRIBES program must be submitted by January of each year. Other students may apply by the end of August for the fall semester or January for the spring semester.

[111]
CHALLENGE SCHOLARSHIPS

National Strength and Conditioning Association
Attn: Grants and Scholarships
1885 Bob Johnson Drive
Colorado Springs, CO 80906
(719) 632-6722, ext. 105   Toll-free: (800) 815-6826
Fax: (719) 632-6367   E-mail: nsca@nsca-lift.org
Web: www.nsca-lift.org/Foundation

Summary To provide financial assistance for undergraduate or graduate study in strength training and conditioning to members of the National Strength and Conditioning Association (NSCA).

Eligibility This program is open to undergraduate and graduate students working on a degree in a strength and conditioning-related field. Applicants must have been members of the association for at least 1 year prior to the application deadline. Along with their application, they must submit a 500-word essay describing their course of study, career goals, and financial need. Selection is based on scholarship (25 points), strength and conditioning experience (15 points), the essay (15 points), recommendations (5 points), honors and awards (10 points), community involvement (10 points), and NSCA involvement (20 points).

Financial data The stipend is $1,000; funds must be applied toward tuition.

Duration 1 year.

Additional information The NSCA is a nonprofit organization of strength and conditioning professionals, including coaches, athletic trainers, physical therapists, educators, researchers, and physicians.

Number awarded 1 or more each year.

Deadline March of each year.

[112]
CHANCELLOR'S LIST SCHOLARSHIPS

Educational Communications Scholarship Foundation
Attn: Scholarship Coordinator
7211 Circle S Road
P.O. Box 149319
Austin, TX 78714-9319
(512) 440-2300   Fax: (512) 447-1687
Web: www.ecisf.org/cl_main.aspx

Summary To provide financial assistance to graduate students who are listed in *The Chancellor's List*.

Eligibility This program is open to graduate students who are U.S. citizens and have been nominated by their dean, honor soci-

ety advisor, or other college official to have their name appear in *The Chancellor's List*. All students listed in that publication automatically receive an application for these scholarships in the mail. Selection is based on GPA, achievement test scores, leadership qualifications, work experience, evaluation of an essay, and some consideration for financial need.

Financial data Stipends are $1,000; payments are issued directly to the financial aid office at the institution the student attends.

Duration 1 year.

Additional information The Educational Communications Scholarship Foundation was established in 1968 by Educational Communications Inc., publisher of *The National Dean's List*. Applications must be accompanied by a $4 processing fee.

Number awarded 10 each year.

Deadline May of each year.

[113]
CHARLES AND MELVA T. OWEN MEMORIAL SCHOLARSHIPS

National Federation of the Blind
c/o Peggy Elliott, Scholarship Committee Chair
805 Fifth Avenue
Grinnell, IA 50112
(641) 236-3366
Web: www.nfb.org/sch_intro.htm

Summary To provide financial assistance to blind undergraduate or graduate students.

Eligibility This program is open to legally blind students who are working on or planning to work full time on an undergraduate or graduate degree. Scholarships, however, will not be awarded for the study of religion or solely to further general or cultural education; the academic program should be directed towards attaining financial independence. Selection is based on academic excellence, service to the community, and financial need.

Financial data Stipends are $10,000 or $3,000.

Duration 1 year; recipients may resubmit applications up to 2 additional years.

Additional information Scholarships are awarded at the federation convention in July. Recipients attend the convention at federation expense; that funding is in addition to the scholarship grant.

Number awarded 2 each year: 1 at $10,000 and 1 at $3,000.

Deadline March of each year.

[114]
CHARLOTTE MCGUIRE SCHOLARSHIP PROGRAM

American Holistic Nurses' Association
2733 East Lakin Drive
P.O. Box 2130
Flagstaff, AZ 86003-2130
(928) 526-2196   Toll-free: (800) 278-AHNA, ext. 12
Fax: (928) 526-2752   E-mail: info@ahna.org
Web: www.ahna.org/edu/assist.html

Summary To provide financial assistance to nurses working on an undergraduate or graduate degree in holistic nursing.

Eligibility This program is open to students who are working on an undergraduate (A.D.N., B.S.N.) or graduate (M.S.N., Ph.D., D.N.Sc.) degree in holistic nursing education. Applicants must have a GPA of 3.0 or higher, have been a member of the American Holistic Nurses' Association (AHNA) for at least 6 months if an undergraduate or 1 year if a graduate student, and have experience in healing and holistic nursing practice. Along with their application, they must submit 1) information on their educational and employment history; 2) a description of their personal interests, hobbies, and activities; 3) documentation of financial need; 4) official transcripts; 5) an essay on how they will integrate the AHNA Philosophy, the Standards of Holistic Nursing Practice, and Core Values of Holistic Nursing into their professional nursing career; and 6) letters from 2 nurses, including 1 AHNA member, who agree to serve as a sponsor.

Financial data The amount awarded varies, depending upon the availability of funds.

Duration 1 year.

Additional information These scholarships were first offered in 1987.

Number awarded 2 each year: 1 to an undergraduate and 1 to a graduate student.

Deadline March of each year.

[115]
CHEERIOS BRAND HEALTH INITIATIVE SCHOLARSHIP

Congressional Black Caucus Foundation, Inc.
Attn: Director, Educational Programs
1720 Massachusetts Avenue, N.W.
Washington, DC 20036
(202) 263-2836   Toll-free: (800) 784-2577
Fax: (202) 775-0773   E-mail: spouses@cbcfinc.org
Web: www.cbcfinc.org

Summary To provide financial assistance to minority and other undergraduate and graduate students who reside in a Congressional district represented by an African American and are interested in preparing for a health-related career.

Eligibility This program is open to 1) minority and other graduating high school seniors planning to attend an accredited institution of higher education and 2) currently-enrolled full-time undergraduate, graduate, and doctoral students in good academic standing with a GPA of 2.5 or higher. Applicants must reside or attend school in a Congressional district represented by a member of the Congressional Black Caucus. They must be interested in preparing for a career in a medical, food services, or other health-related field, including pre-medicine, nursing, chemistry, biology, physical education, and engineering. Along with their application, they must submit a 500-word personal statement on 1) the field of study they intend to pursue and why they have chosen that field; 2) their interests, involvement in school activities, community and public service, hobbies, special talents, sports, and other highlight areas; and 3) any other experiences, skills, or qualifications they feel should be considered. They must also be able to document financial need.

Financial data A stipend is awarded (amount not specified).

Duration 1 year.

Additional information The program was established in 1998 with support from General Mills, Inc.

Number awarded Varies each year.

Deadline April of each year.

[116]
CHIMSS SCHOLARSHIP

Healthcare Information and Management Systems Society-Colorado Chapter
c/o Fred Lunger, Treasurer
5653 North Quinlin Court
Parker, CO 80134
(303) 403-7731   E-mail: LungerF@Exempla.org
Web: www.chimss.org/scholarship/scholarship.html

Summary To provide financial assistance to residents of Colorado working on a graduate degree in health care informatics.

Eligibility This program is open to Colorado residents currently enrolled in a master's or Ph.D. program in health care informatics or a sub-specialty, such as nursing informatics. Applicants must submit a 500-word essay on how they will impact the field of health care informatics and 2 letters of recommendation.

Financial data The stipend is $5,000. The winner also receives a 1-year complimentary membership in the Colorado Healthcare Information and Management Systems Society (CHIMSS).

Duration 1 year.

Number awarded 1 each year.

[117]
CHIYOKO AND THOMAS SHIMAZAKI SCHOLARSHIP

Japanese American Citizens League
Attn: National Scholarship Awards
1765 Sutter Street
San Francisco, CA 94115
(415) 921-5225   Fax: (415) 931-4671
E-mail: jacl@jacl.org
Web: www.jacl.org/leadership_development_5.php

Summary To provide financial assistance to student members of the Japanese American Citizens League (JACL) who are interested in preparing for a career in medicine.

Eligibility This program is open to JACL members who are interested in preparing for a career in the medical field. Applicants must submit a statement describing their current level of involvement in the Japanese American community or Asian Pacific community and how they will continue their involvement in future years. Selection is based on academic record, extracurricular activities, financial need, and community involvement.

Financial data The stipend depends on the availability of funds but usually ranges from $1,000 to $5,000.

Duration 1 year; nonrenewable.

Additional information Applications must be submitted to the JACL National Scholarship Program, c/o San Diego JACL Chapter, 1031 25th Street, San Diego, CA 92102.

Number awarded At least 1 each year.

Deadline March of each year.

[118]
CHRISTIAN CONNECTOR SEMINARY/CHRISTIAN GRADUATE SCHOOL SCHOLARSHIP

Christian Connector, Inc.
627 24 1/2 Road, Suite D
Grand Junction, CO 81501
(970) 256-1610   Toll-free: (800) 667-0600
Web: www.christianconnector.com

Summary To provide financial assistance to students interested in attending a Christian-affiliated graduate school.

Eligibility This competition is open to students planning to enroll for the first time at a Christ-centered seminary or Christian graduate school. Schools that are members of the CCCU, NAC-CAP, or AABC automatically qualify. Students currently enrolled at a seminary or Christian graduate school are not eligible. Applicants enter the competition by registering online with the sponsoring organization, indicating their gender, ethnic background, undergraduate college, intended enrollment year, undergraduate GPA, degree or program of interest, and level of degree sought. The recipient of the scholarship is selected in a random drawing.

Financial data The award is $1,000. Funds are sent directly to the winner's school.

Duration The competition is held annually.

Number awarded 1 each year.

Deadline May of each year.

[119]
CLAIRE M. FAGIN PREDOCTORAL FELLOWS PROGRAM

American Academy of Nursing
Attn: Building Academic Geriatric Nursing Capacity Program
1030 15th Street, N.W., Suite 250
Washington, DC 20005-1503
(202) 682-2850   Fax: (202) 842-1150
E-mail: parchbold@aannet.org
Web: www.geriatricnursing.org

Summary To provide funding to nurses interested in working on a doctoral degree in gerontological nursing.

Eligibility This program is open to registered nurses who hold a degree in nursing and have been admitted to a doctoral program. The school must have strong gerontological offerings and should have postdoctoral programs available in gerontological nursing. Applicants must show a commitment to gerontology and a plan for their future careers. They must identify a mentor/advisor with whom they will work and who has a program of research in gerontological nursing. Selection is based on potential to contribute to the knowledge base in gerontological nursing in significant ways; leadership potential; evidence of commitment to a career in research and education; and nature and extent of involvement in educational, research, and professional activities. U.S. citizenship or permanent resident status is required. Members of underrepresented minority groups are especially encouraged to apply.

Financial data The stipend is $50,000 per year. An additional $5,000 is available to fellows whose research includes the study of pain in the elderly.

Duration 2 years.

Additional information This program began in 2001 with funding from the John A. Hartford Foundation. In 2004, the Mayday Fund added support to scholars who focus on the study of pain in the elderly. Recipients must enroll full time.

Number awarded Varies each year; recently, 13 of these fellowships were awarded.

Deadline January of each year.

[120]
CLIFFORD JORDAN SCHOLARSHIP

Florida Council of periOperative Registered Nurses
c/o Connie L. Hammond, Scholarship Chair
5207 East Whiteway Drive
Temple Terrace, FL 33617
(813) 988-7558   E-mail: hamco@gate.net
Web: www.afn.org/~fcorn/scholar.htm

Summary To provide financial assistance to nursing students

and registered nurses in Florida who are working on a degree to advance their career as a perioperative nurse.

Eligibility This program is open to residents of Florida who are 1) students in the final year of an accredited nursing program, or 2) perioperative nurses. Students must have a GPA of 3.0 or higher and be planning to work in a perioperative setting after graduation. Current perioperative nurses must be interested in working on an R.N. to B.S.N. or B.S.N. to M.S.N. degree in hospital administration or health care. Applicants must submit information on their educational history, professional activities, civic and school activities, work experience, personal philosophy of perioperative nursing, and reasons for applying. Financial need is not considered.

Financial data A stipend is awarded (amount not specified).

Duration 1 year.

Number awarded 1 or more each year.

Deadline January of each year.

[121]
CLINICAL RESEARCH PRE-DOCTORAL FELLOWSHIP PROGRAM

American Nurses Association
Attn: SAMHSA Minority Fellowship Programs
8515 Georgia Avenue, Suite 400
Silver Spring, MD 20910-3492
(301) 628-5247   Fax: (301) 628-5339
E-mail: jjackson@ana.org
Web: www.nursingworld.org/emfp/fellowships/pre.htm

Summary To provide financial assistance to minority nurses who are doctoral candidates interested in psychiatric, mental health, and substance abuse issues that impact the lives of ethnic minority people.

Eligibility This program is open to nurses who have a master's degree and are members of an ethnic or racial minority group, including but not limited to Blacks or African Americans, Hispanics or Latinos, American Indians and Alaska Natives, Asian Americans, and Native Hawaiians and other Pacific Islanders. Applicants must be able to demonstrate a commitment to a research career in nursing and psychiatric/mental health issues affecting ethnic minority populations. They must be interested in a program of full-time doctoral study, with a research focus on such issues of concern to minority populations as child abuse, violence in intimate relationships, mental health disorders, substance abuse, mental health service utilization, and stigma as a barrier to mental health care and personal resilience. U.S. citizenship or permanent resident status and membership in the American Nurses Association are required. Selection is based on research potential, scholarship, writing ability, knowledge of broad issues in mental health nursing, and professional commitment to ethnic minority concerns.

Financial data The program provides an annual stipend (amount not specified) and tuition assistance.

Duration 3 to 5 years.

Additional information Funds for this program are provided by the Substance Abuse and Mental Health Services Administration (SAMHSA).

Number awarded 1 or more each year.

Deadline February of each year.

[122]
CNA FOUNDATION SCHOLARSHIP
American Society of Safety Engineers
Attn: ASSE Foundation
1800 East Oakton Street
Des Plaines, IL 60018
(847) 768-3435   Fax: (847) 768-3434
E-mail: agabanski@asse.org
Web: www.asse.org/foundation

Summary To provide financial assistance to upper-division and graduate student members of the American Society of Safety Engineers (ASSE) who are working on a degree in occupational health and related fields.

Eligibility This program is open to ASSE student members who are working on an undergraduate or graduate degree in occupational safety, health, and environment or a closely-related field (e.g., industrial or environmental engineering, environmental science, industrial hygiene, occupational health nursing). Undergraduates must be full-time students who have completed at least 60 semester hours with a GPA of 3.0 or higher. Graduate students must also be enrolled full time, have completed at least 9 semester hours with a GPA of 3.5 or higher, and have had a GPA of 3.0 or higher as an undergraduate. Along with their application, they must submit 2 essays of 300 words or less: 1) why they are seeking a degree in occupational safety and health or a closely-related field, a brief description of their current activities, and how those relate to their career goals and objectives; and 2) why they should be awarded this scholarship (including career goals and financial need).

Financial data The stipend is $4,000.
Duration 1 year; nonrenewable.
Additional information This program, established in 2006, is supported by the CNA Foundation.
Number awarded 2 each year.
Deadline November of each year.

[123]
CNF PROFESSIONAL GROWTH SCHOLARSHIPS
School Nutrition Association
Attn: Child Nutrition Foundation Scholarship Committee
700 South Washington Street, Suite 300
Alexandria, VA 22314-4287
(703) 739-3900   Toll-free: (800) 877-8822
Fax: (703) 739-3915   E-mail: cnf@schoolnutrition.org
Web: www.schoolnutrition.org/Index.aspx?ID=1043

Summary To provide financial assistance to members of the School Nutrition Association (SNA) who are interested in additional undergraduate or graduate study.

Eligibility This program is open to active SNA members who meet all 4 of the following criteria: 1) plan to work on an undergraduate or graduate degree at a college or vocational/technical institution that has a program designed to improve school food service (e.g., nutrition, food service management, business administration); 2) have a history of employment in school food service and at least 1 year's SNA membership; 3) have a satisfactory academic record; and 4) express a desire to make school food service a career. Applicants must submit a 1-page personal essay (up to 500 words) stating the reason for selecting school food service as a profession; what they expect to gain from continuing their education; and their long-term professional goals/plans. Selection is based on the essay (35 points), letters of recommendation (20 points), SNA state and local chapter activity participation (15 points), organization and neatness (10 points), program of study (15 points), and GPA (5 points).

Financial data Stipends up to $1,000 are available.
Duration 1 year; may be renewed up to 3 additional years.
Additional information The SNA was formerly the American School Food Service Administration.
Number awarded Varies each year; recently, 21 of these scholarships were awarded.
Deadline April of each year.

[124]
COLGATE-PALMOLIVE/HDA FOUNDATION SCHOLARSHIPS
Hispanic Dental Association
Attn: HDA Foundation
3085 Stevenson Drive, Suite 200
Springfield, IL 62703
(217) 529-6517   Toll-free: (800) 852-7921
Fax: (217) 529-9120   E-mail: HispanicDental@hdassoc.org
Web: www.hdassoc.org/site/epage/8351_351.htm

Summary To provide financial assistance to Hispanic students interested in preparing for a career in dental public health.

Eligibility This program is open to Hispanics who are entering or enrolled in an accredited master's in public health/dental public health program. Applicants must have a GPA of 3.0 or higher. Along with their application, they must submit an essay on their career goals. Selection is based on scholastic achievement, community service, leadership skill, and commitment to improving health in the Hispanic community.

Financial data The stipend is $10,000.
Duration 1 year.
Additional information This program, which began in 2005, is sponsored by the Colgate-Palmolive Company
Number awarded Varies each year; recently, 3 of these scholarships were awarded.
Deadline June of each year.

[125]
COLLEGE SCHOLARSHIP PROGRAM OF THE HISPANIC SCHOLARSHIP FUND
Hispanic Scholarship Fund
Attn: Selection Committee
55 Second Street, Suite 1500
San Francisco, CA 94105
(415) 808-2366   Toll-free: (877) HSF-INFO
Fax: (415) 808-2302   E-mail: scholar1@hsf.net
Web: www.hsf.net/scholarship/programs/college.php

Summary To provide financial assistance for college or graduate school to Hispanic American students.

Eligibility This program is open to U.S. citizens, permanent residents, and visitors with a passport stamped I-551. Applicants must be of Hispanic heritage and enrolled full time in a degree-seeking program at an accredited community college, 4-year university, or graduate school in the United States, Puerto Rico, or the U.S. Virgin Islands. They must have completed at least 12 undergraduate units with a GPA of 3.0 or higher and have applied for federal financial aid. Along with their application, they must submit 600-word essays on 1) how their Hispanic heritage has influenced their academic and personal long-term goals; 2) how they contribute to their community and what they have learned from their experiences; and 3) an academic challenge they have faced and how they have overcome it. Selection is based on academic record, personal qualities, community service, and financial need.

Financial data Stipends normally range from $1,000 to $5,000 per year.

Duration 1 year; recipients may reapply.

Additional information Since this program began in 1975, more than $195 million has been awarded to more than 78,000 Hispanic students.

Number awarded More than 4,000 each year.

Deadline October of each year.

[126]
COLORADO GRADUATE FELLOWSHIP PROGRAM

Colorado Commission on Higher Education
1380 Lawrence Street, Suite 1200
Denver, CO 80204
(303) 866-2723   Fax: (303) 866-4266
E-mail: cche@state.co.us
Web: www.state.co.us

Summary To provide financial assistance for graduate education to residents of Colorado.

Eligibility Eligible for the program are residents of Colorado (as well as a limited number of nonresidents) who are enrolled or accepted for enrollment full time in master's and doctoral programs at state-supported and private colleges and universities in Colorado. Selection is based on merit.

Financial data The amount of assistance varies (up to the actual cost of tuition plus $5,000 per year).

Duration 1 year; renewable.

Additional information Applications are available either from the Colorado Commission on Higher Education or from the financial aid office of eligible Colorado institutions.

Number awarded Varies each year.

Deadline Each participating institution sets its own deadlines.

[127]
COLORADO GRADUATE GRANTS

Colorado Commission on Higher Education
1380 Lawrence Street, Suite 1200
Denver, CO 80204
(303) 866-2723   Fax: (303) 866-4266
E-mail: cche@state.co.us
Web: www.state.co.us

Summary To provide financial assistance for graduate education to residents of Colorado who can demonstrate financial need.

Eligibility Eligible for the program are residents of Colorado who are enrolled or accepted for enrollment on at least a half-time basis in master's and doctoral programs at state-supported and private colleges and universities in Colorado. Selection is based on financial need, as indicated by the student's expected family contribution (EFC) and the amount required for a federal Pell Grant. Students whose EFC is between zero and 150% of that required for a Pell Grant are in level 1, students whose EFC is between 150% and 200% of that required for the minimum Pell Grant are in level 2, and all other students who demonstrate financial need are in level 3.

Financial data The amount of assistance varies. Students in level 1 receive grants from $1,000 to $5,000; students in level 2 receive up to $2,500 or the maximum amount of unmet need, whichever is less; students in level 3 receive up to $500.

Duration 1 year; renewable.

Additional information Applications are available either from the Colorado Commission on Higher Education or from the financial aid office of eligible Colorado institutions.

Number awarded Varies each year.

Deadline Each participating institution sets its own deadlines.

[128]
COMMUNICATIVE DISORDERS SCHOLARSHIPS

Sertoma International
Attn: Director of Finance and Administration
1912 East Meyer Boulevard
Kansas City, MO 64132-1174
(816) 333-8300, ext. 214   Fax: (816) 333-4320
TTY: (816) 333-8300   E-mail: aellington@sertoma.org
Web: www.sertoma.org

Summary To provide financial assistance to students working on a graduate degree in communication disorders.

Eligibility This program is open to students who are working on a master's degree in speech-language pathology or audiology at a college or university in the United States. Applicants must have a GPA of 3.2 or higher. Along with their application, they must submit a statement of purpose on how this scholarship will help them achieve their goals. U.S. citizenship is required. Selection is based on academic achievement, honors and awards received, community volunteer activities, school-related activities, extracurricular activities, internships or experience in speech language pathology and audiology, 2 letters of recommendation, and financial need.

Financial data The stipend is $1,000. Funds may be used only for such direct educational expenses as tuition, fees, and books.

Duration 1 year; may be renewed 1 additional year.

Additional information Sertoma, which stands for SERvice TO MAnkind, is a volunteer service organization with 25,000 members in 800 clubs across North America. This program began in the academic year 1992-93. Recipients must be enrolled full time.

Number awarded 30 each year.

Deadline March of each year.

[129]
CONGRESSIONAL BLACK CAUCUS SPOUSES EDUCATION SCHOLARSHIP

Congressional Black Caucus Foundation, Inc.
Attn: Director, Educational Programs
1720 Massachusetts Avenue, N.W.
Washington, DC 20036
(202) 263-2836   Toll-free: (800) 784-2577
Fax: (202) 775-0773   E-mail: spouses@cbcfinc.org
Web: www.cbcfinc.org

Summary To provide financial assistance to minority and other undergraduate and graduate students who reside in a Congressional district represented by an African American.

Eligibility This program is open to 1) minority and other graduating high school seniors planning to attend an accredited institution of higher education and 2) currently-enrolled full-time undergraduate, graduate, and doctoral students in good academic standing with a GPA of 2.5 or higher. Applicants must reside or attend school in a Congressional district represented by a member of the Congressional Black Caucus. Along with their application, they must submit a 500-word personal statement on 1) the field of study they intend to pursue and why they have chosen that field; 2) their interests, involvement in school activities, community and public service, hobbies, special talents, sports, and other highlight areas; and 3) any other experiences, skills, or qualifications they feel should be considered. They must also be able to document financial need.

Financial data A stipend is awarded (amount not specified).

Duration 1 year.

Additional information The program was established in 1988.

Number awarded Varies each year.

Deadline April of each year.

[130]
CONNECTICUT COMMUNITY COLLEGE MINORITY FELLOWSHIP PROGRAM

Connecticut Community College System
Attn: System Officer for Diversity Awareness
61 Woodland Street
Hartford, CT 06105-9949
(860) 244-7606   Fax: (860) 566-6624
E-mail: karmstrong@commnet.edu
Web: www.commnet.edu/minority_fellowship.asp

Summary To provide financial assistance and work experience to graduate students, especially minorities, in Connecticut who are interested in preparing for a career in community college teaching (any field) or administration.

Eligibility This program is open to graduate students who have completed at least 6 credits of graduate work and have indicated an interest in a career in community colleges. Current employees of the Connecticut Community Colleges are also eligible. Applicants must be willing to commit to at least 1 year of employment in the Connecticut Community College System. Although all qualified graduate students are eligible, the program encourages applicants to register who strengthen the racial and cultural diversity of the minority fellow registry. That includes, in particular, making all possible efforts to recruit from historically underrepresented people (Asians, Blacks, and Hispanics).

Financial data Non-employee fellows receive a stipend of $3,500 per semester. Fellows who are current employees are reassigned time from their responsibilities.

Duration 1 year; may be renewed.

Additional information Fellows are expected to dedicate 9 hours per week to the program. They spend 6 hours per week in teaching or administrative activities under the supervision of a mentor. During the second semester, they assist the mentor in teaching a course or engaging in structured administrative activities. The remaining time is spent on program and campus orientation activities, attendance at relevant faculty or staff meetings, and participation in other college meetings or professional development activities.

Number awarded Up to 13 each year: 1 at each of the 12 colleges in the system and 1 in the chancellor's office.

[131]
CONSTANCE L. LLOYD SCHOLARSHIP

American College of Medical Practice Executives
Attn: ACMPE Scholarship Fund Inc.
104 Inverness Terrace East
Englewood, CO 80112-5306
(303) 799-1111, ext. 232   Toll-free: (877) ASK-MGMA
Fax: (303) 643-4439   E-mail: acmpe@mgma.com
Web: www.mgma.com/academics/scholar.cfm

Summary To provide financial assistance to undergraduate or graduate women in Georgia who are working on a degree in health care or health care administration.

Eligibility This program is open to women enrolled at the undergraduate or graduate level at an accredited college or university in Georgia who are working on either an administrative or clinically-related degree in the health care field. Students working on a degree in medicine, physical therapy, nursing, or other clinically-related professions are not eligible. Applicants must submit a letter describing their career goals and objectives relevant to medical practice management; a resume; 3 reference letters commenting on their performance, character, potential to succeed, and need for scholarship support; and either documentation indicating acceptance into an undergraduate or graduate program or academic transcripts indicating undergraduate or graduate work completed to date.

Financial data The stipend is $2,500. Funds are paid directly to the recipient's college or university.

Duration 1 year.

Additional information This program, established in 1993, is managed by Scholarship Program Administrators, Inc. 1201 Eighth Avenue South, P.O. Box 23737, Nashville, TN 27202-3737, (615) 320-3149, (800) 310-4053, Fax: (615) 320-3151, E-mail: info@spaprog.com.

Number awarded 1 each year.

Deadline April of each year.

[132]
CORA AGUDA MANAYAN FUND

Hawai'i Community Foundation
Attn: Scholarship Department
1164 Bishop Street, Suite 800
Honolulu, HI 96813
(808) 566-5570   Toll-free: (888) 731-3863
Fax: (808) 521-6286   E-mail: scholarships@hcf-hawaii.org
Web: www.hawaiicommunityfoundation.org

Summary To provide financial assistance to Hawaii residents of Filipino ancestry who are interested in preparing for a career in the health field.

Eligibility This program is open to Hawaii residents of Filipino ancestry who are interested in enrolling as full-time students in a health-related field (on the undergraduate or graduate school level). Applicants must be able to demonstrate academic achievement (GPA of 2.7 or higher), good moral character, and financial need. Along with their application, they must submit a short statement indicating their reasons for attending college, their planned course of study, and their career goals. Preference may be given to applicants studying at a college or university in Hawaii.

Financial data The amounts of the awards depend on the availability of funds and the need of the recipient; recently, stipends averaged $1,000.

Duration 1 year.

Number awarded Varies each year; recently, 8 of these scholarships were awarded.

Deadline February of each year.

[133]
COSTCO PHARMACY SCHOLAR PROGRAM
Hispanic College Fund
Attn: Scholarship Processing
1301 K Street, N.W., Suite 450-A West
Washington, D.C. 20005
(202) 296-5400   Toll-free: (800) 644-4223
Fax: (202) 296-3774   E-mail: hcf-info@hispanicfund.org
Web: www.hispanicfund.org/scholarships.php

Summary To provide financial assistance to Hispanic American students who are preparing for a career as a pharmacist.

Eligibility This program is open to U.S. citizens and permanent residents of Hispanic background (at least 1 grandparent must be 100% Hispanic) who are enrolled full time at a pharmacy school in the 50 states or Puerto Rico. Applicants must have completed 1 year of pharmacy school or be in their second year of their pharmacy education. They must have a GPA of 3.0 or higher and be able to demonstrate financial need.

Financial data Stipends range up to $9,500 per year. Students who are selected for this program are required to work at a Costco pharmacy store for at least 1 year. They receive $500 towards their licensure examination.

Duration 1 year; may be renewed.

Additional information This program is sponsored by Costco Wholesale. All applications must be submitted online; no paper applications are available.

Number awarded Varies each year. Recently, a total of $51,000 was available for these scholarships.

Deadline March of each year.

[134]
CREST ORAL-B SCHOLARSHIPS FOR DENTAL HYGIENE STUDENTS PURSUING ACADEMIC CAREERS
American Dental Education Association
Attn: Awards Program Coordinator
1400 K Street, N.W., Suite 1100
Washington, DC 20005
(202) 289-7201   Fax: (202) 289-7204
E-mail: morganm@adea.org
Web: www.adea.org/Awards/default.htm

Summary To provide financial assistance to dental hygiene students who are interested in an academic career.

Eligibility This program is open to students who have graduated from an accredited dental hygiene program with an associate degree or certificate to practice dental hygiene and are currently enrolled in a degree completion program for a bachelor's or graduate degree at an institution that is a member of the American Dental Education Association (ADEA). Applicants must show a commitment to pursuing an academic degree in dental hygiene and be individual ADEA members. Along with their application, they must submit a personal statement that details their experiences, influences, decision-making, and commitment to become an allied dental faculty member. Priority is given to qualified candidates enrolled in bachelor's degree completion programs.

Financial data The stipend is $2,000. Funds are applied to tuition and fees.

Duration 1 year; nonrenewable.

Additional information Funding for this program, which began in 2000, is provided by the Procter & Gamble Company.

Number awarded 2 each year.

Deadline November of each year.

[135]
CWG SCHOLARSHIP FUND
Maine Community Foundation
Attn: Program Director
245 Main Street
Ellsworth, ME 04605
(207) 667-9735   Toll-free: (877) 700-6800
Fax: (207) 667-0447   E-mail: info@mainecf.org
Web: www.mainecf.org/html/scholarships/index.html

Summary To provide financial assistance to Maine residents who are registered nurses or college graduates interested in graduate training in mental health services.

Eligibility This program is open to 2 categories of Maine residents: 1) college graduates employed by providers of mental health service in the state who are interested in continuing their professional education by obtaining an M.S.W. or other degree related to work in the mental health field; and 2) registered nurses working for hospitals or outpatient providers of social and mental health services who are interested in obtaining specialized, post-R.N. training in order to work more effectively with patients who have mental health problems. Special consideration is given to applicants whose career goals include work with adolescents and adults and who wish to continue to work in Maine. Financial need is considered in the selection process.

Financial data A stipend is paid (amount not specified).

Duration 1 year.

Additional information This program was established in 1999.

Number awarded 1 or more each year.

Deadline April of each year.

[136]
DAIMLERCHRYSLER CORPORATION FUND ASSE SCHOLARSHIP
American Society of Safety Engineers
Attn: ASSE Foundation
1800 East Oakton Street
Des Plaines, IL 60018
(847) 768-3435   Fax: (847) 768-3434
E-mail: agabanski@asse.org
Web: www.asse.org/foundation

Summary To provide financial assistance to upper-division and graduate student members of the American Society of Safety Engineers (ASSE) who are working on a degree in occupational health and related fields.

Eligibility This program is open to ASSE student members who are working on an undergraduate or graduate degree in occupational safety, health, and environment or a closely-related field (e.g., industrial or environmental engineering, environmental science, industrial hygiene, occupational health nursing). Undergraduates must be full-time students who have completed at least 60 semester hours with a GPA of 3.0 or higher. Graduate students must also be enrolled full time, have completed at least 9 semester hours with a GPA of 3.5 or higher, and have had a GPA of 3.0 or higher as an undergraduate. Along with their application, they must submit 2 essays of 300 words or less: 1) why they are seeking a degree in occupational safety and health or a closely-related field, a brief description of their current activities, and how those relate to their career goals and objectives; and 2) why they should be awarded this scholarship (including career goals and financial need).

Financial data The stipend is $2,500.

Duration 1 year; nonrenewable.

Additional information This program is supported by the DaimlerChrysler Corporation.
Number awarded 1 each year.
Deadline November of each year.

[137]
DARREL PERRY, RN MEMORIAL SCHOLARSHIP
American Association of Nurse Anesthetists
Attn: AANA Foundation
222 South Prospect Avenue
Park Ridge, IL 60068-4001
(847) 692-7050, ext. 1171   Fax: (847) 692-7137
E-mail: foundation@aana.com
Web: www.aana.com/foundation/default.asp

Summary To provide financial assistance to members of the American Association of Nurse Anesthetists (AANA) who are serving in the Army and interested in obtaining further education.
Eligibility This program is open to members of the association who are currently enrolled in an accredited nurse anesthesia education program. Applicants must be members of the U.S. Army (Active or Reserves). First-year students must have completed 6 months of nurse anesthesia classes; second-year students must have completed 12 months of nurse anesthesia classes. Along with their application, they must submit a 200-word essay describing why they have chosen nurse anesthesia as a profession and their professional goals for the future. Financial need is also considered in the selection process.
Financial data The stipend is $1,000 per year.
Duration 1 academic year.
Additional information The application processing fee is $25.
Number awarded 1 each year.
Deadline March of each year.

[138]
DAVID L. BOREN GRADUATE FELLOWSHIPS
Academy for Educational Development
Attn: National Security Education Program
1825 Connecticut Avenue, N.W.
Washington, DC 20009-5721
(202) 884-8285   Toll-free: (800) 498-9360
Fax: (202) 884-8407   E-mail: nsep@aed.org
Web: nsep.aed.org

Summary To provide financial assistance to students who are working on a graduate degree and are interested in developing expertise in languages, cultures, and area studies of countries less commonly studied by Americans.
Eligibility This program is open to graduate students in professional and other disciplines who are interested in introducing an international component to their degree studies by focusing on an area of the world that is critical to national security and economic competitiveness. Fields of study include agriculture, anthropology, biology, business, economics, engineering and applied sciences, environmental sciences, history, law, public health, and sociology. Applicants in international affairs, policy studies, and political science often specialize in such subfields as democracy and governance and nonproliferation studies. Support is also provided for the study of the following languages: Albanian, Amharic, Arabic (and dialects), Armenian, Azeri, Belarusian, Bulgarian, Burmese, Cantonese, Czech, Farsi, Georgian, Hebrew, Hindi, Hungarian, Indonesian, Japanese, Kazakh, Khmer, Korean, Kurdish, Kyrgyz, Lingala, Macedonian, Malay, Mandarin, Mongolian, Polish, Portuguese, Romanian, Russian, Serbo-Croatian, Sinhala, Slovak, Slovene, Swahili, Tagalog, Tajik, Tamil, Thai,

Turkish, Turkmen, Uighar, Ukrainian, Urdu, Uzbek, or Vietnamese. The study of French or Spanish is not supported unless the language instruction is at the advanced level or is combined with the study of business, the applied sciences, or engineering. Applicants must be U.S. citizens, enrolled in or applying to an accredited graduate school in the United States, and interested in internationalizing their educational experience or in enhancing an existing internationally-focused program. Part-time students are eligible to be considered for the fellowship, but they must be enrolled in a degree program. Selection is based on demonstrated academic excellence; a comprehensive, clear, and feasible proposal for study; a plan to develop, maintain, or advance language competence; evidence of ability to adapt to a different cultural environment; and the integration of the proposed program into the applicant's academic field and career goals.
Financial data Fellowships provide support for overseas or domestic study, or a combination of both. The maximum award for overseas study is $12,000 per semester for up to two semesters ($24,000 total). A maximum of $12,000 is available for a program of domestic study only. Support for domestic study is limited to language or area studies which enhance a degree program. The maximum level of support for a combined overseas and domestic program is $30,000.
Duration From 1 to 6 academic semesters.
Additional information Study outside the United States is strongly encouraged. This program is part of the National Security Education Program (NSEP), funded by the National Security Education Act, and administered by the Academy for Educational Development. All fellowships must include study of a language other than English and the corresponding culture that is appropriate for the degree program in which the student is enrolled. The program supports study abroad in areas of the world critical to national security; study will not be supported in most cases in western Europe, Canada, Australia, or New Zealand. Fellowship recipients incur a service obligation and must agree to work for the federal government or in the field of higher education subsequent to the fellowship period.
Number awarded Varies; generally, at least 300 per year.
Deadline January of each year.

[139]
DAVIS-PUTTER SCHOLARSHIPS
Davis-Putter Scholarship Fund
P.O. Box 7307
New York, NY 10116-7307
E-mail: information@davisputter.org
Web: www.davisputter.org

Summary To provide financial assistance to undergraduate and graduate student activists.
Eligibility This program is open to undergraduate and graduate students who are involved in "struggles for civil rights, economic justice, international solidarity or other progressive issues." While U.S. citizenship is not required, applicants must be living in the United States and planning to enroll in school here. They must submit a completed application, a personal statement, financial need reports, recommendation letters, transcripts, and a photograph.
Financial data Grants range up to $6,000, depending upon need.
Duration 1 year.
Additional information This fund was established in 1961. Early recipients fought for civil rights, against McCarthyism, and to stop the war in Vietnam. More recently, grantees have included students active in the struggle against racism, sexism, homopho-

bia, and other forms of oppression. This program includes the Jessie Lloyd O'Connor Scholarship.

Number awarded Varies each year; recently, a total of 28 of these scholarships were awarded.

Deadline March of each year.

[140]
DEAN AND FRED HAYDEN MEMORIAL NATIONAL SCHOLARSHIP

American Association of Nurse Anesthetists
Attn: AANA Foundation
222 South Prospect Avenue
Park Ridge, IL 60068-4001
(847) 692-7050, ext. 1171   Fax: (847) 692-7137
E-mail: foundation@aana.com
Web: www.aana.com/foundation/default.asp

Summary To provide financial assistance to members of the American Association of Nurse Anesthetists (AANA) who are interested in obtaining further education.

Eligibility This program is open to members of the association who are currently enrolled in an accredited nurse anesthesia education program. Applicants must be second-year students who have completed 12 months of nurse anesthesia classes. Along with their application, they must submit a 200-word essay describing why they have chosen nurse anesthesia as a profession and their professional goals for the future. Financial need is also considered in the selection process.

Financial data The stipend is $1,000 per year.

Duration 1 academic year.

Additional information The application processing fee is $25.

Number awarded 1 each year.

Deadline March of each year.

[141]
DEAN M. COX MEMORIAL SCHOLARSHIPS

American Association of Nurse Anesthetists
Attn: AANA Foundation
222 South Prospect Avenue
Park Ridge, IL 60068-4001
(847) 692-7050, ext. 1171   Fax: (847) 692-7137
E-mail: foundation@aana.com
Web: www.aana.com/foundation/default.asp

Summary To provide financial assistance to members of the American Association of Nurse Anesthetists (AANA) who are interested in obtaining further education.

Eligibility This program is open to members of the association who are currently enrolled in an accredited nurse anesthesia education program. Applicants must have a record of promoting education in the CRNA profession. First-year students must have completed 6 months of nurse anesthesia classes; second-year students must have completed 12 months of nurse anesthesia classes. Along with their application, they must submit a 200-word essay describing why they have chosen nurse anesthesia as a profession and their professional goals for the future. Financial need is also considered in the selection process.

Financial data The stipend is $1,000 per year.

Duration 1 academic year.

Additional information The application processing fee is $25.

Number awarded 2 each year.

Deadline March of each year.

[142]
DEDICATED ARMY NATIONAL GUARD (DEDARNG) SCHOLARSHIPS

U.S. Army
ROTC Cadet Command
Attn: ATCC-OP-I-S
55 Patch Road, Building 56
Fort Monroe, VA 23651-1052
(757) 727-4558   Toll-free: (800) USA-ROTC
E-mail: atccps@usaac.army.mil
Web: www.rotc.usaac.army.mil

Summary To provide financial assistance to college and graduate students who are interested in enrolling in Army ROTC and serving in the Army National Guard following graduation.

Eligibility This program is open to full-time students entering their junior year of college with a GPA of 2.5 or higher. Graduate students are also eligible if they have only 2 years remaining for completion of their graduate degree. Students who have been awarded an ROTC campus-based scholarship may apply to convert to this program during their freshman year. Applicants must meet all medical and moral character requirements for enrollment in Army ROTC. They must be willing to enroll in the Simultaneous Membership Program (SMP) of an ROTC unit on their campus; the SMP requires simultaneous membership in Army ROTC and the Army National Guard.

Financial data Participants receive reimbursement of tuition (up to $28,000 per year), a grant of $600 per year for books, plus an ROTC stipend for 10 months of the year at $350 per month during their junior year and $400 per month during their senior year. As a member of the Army National Guard, they also receive weekend drill pay at the pay grade of E-5 during their junior year or E-6 during their senior year.

Duration Normally 2 years. Students who convert to this program may be eligible for support up to 4 years.

Additional information After graduation, participants serve 3 to 6 months on active duty in the Officer Basic Course (OBC). Following completion of OBC, they are released from active duty and are obligated to serve 8 years in the Army National Guard.

Number awarded 594 each year (11 in each state or U.S. territory).

[143]
DEETS-LAINE GERIATRIC NP STUDENT SCHOLARSHIPS

American Academy of Nurse Practitioners
Attn: AANP Foundation
P.O. Box 10729
Glendale, AZ 85318-0729
(623) 376-9467   Fax: (623) 376-0369
E-mail: foundation@aanp.org
Web: www.aanpfoundation.org

Summary To provide financial assistance to members of the American Academy of Nurse Practitioners (AANP) who are working on a master's degree or enrolled in a post-M.S. program in geriatric nursing.

Eligibility This program is open to current student and full members of the academy who 1) are enrolled in a M.S.N. degree program as a geriatric nurse practitioner (GNP); 2) are practicing family nurse practitioners (FNPs) or adult nurse practitioners (ANPs) with an M.S.N. degree enrolled in an accredited post-M.S. GNP program; or 3) are not a current nurse practitioner but have an M.S.N. degree and are enrolled in an accredited post-M.S. GNP program. Applicants must have a GPA of 3.5 or higher. They must have completed at least 25% but no more than 75% of their program requirements.

Financial data   The stipend is $1,000. Funds may be used only for educational expenses (tuition, books, equipment, etc.), not for expenses related to master's thesis and/or general research projects.

Duration   1 year.

Additional information   This program was established in 2002. There is a $10 application fee.

Number awarded   1 each year.

Deadline   April of each year.

[144]
DELA CRUZ-MILLMAN FILIPINO-AMERICAN NP STUDENT SCHOLARSHIP

American Academy of Nurse Practitioners
Attn: AANP Foundation
P.O. Box 10729
Glendale, AZ 85318-0729
(623) 376-9467   Fax: (623) 376-0369
E-mail: foundation@aanp.org
Web: www.aanpfoundation.org

Summary   To provide financial assistance to members of the American Academy of Nurse Practitioners (AANP) from designated states who are of Filipino heritage and working on a master's degree.

Eligibility   This program is open to current student and full members of the academy who are enrolled in a M.S.N. degree program as a nurse practitioner (NP). Applicants must be of Filipino or Filipino American heritage and residents of California, Florida, Hawaii, Illinois, Maryland, New Jersey, New York, Texas, Virginia, or Washington. They must have a GPA of 3.2 or higher and have completed at least 25% but no more than 75% of their program requirements.

Financial data   The stipend is $1,000. Funds may be used only for educational expenses (tuition, books, equipment, etc.), not for expenses related to master's thesis and/or general research projects.

Duration   1 year.

Additional information   This program was established in 1999. There is a $10 application fee.

Number awarded   1 each year.

Deadline   April or October of each year.

[145]
DELAWARE SCHOLARSHIP INCENTIVE PROGRAM

Delaware Higher Education Commission
Carvel State Office Building
820 North French Street
Wilmington, DE 19801
(302) 577-3240   Toll-free: (800) 292-7935
Fax: (302) 577-6765   E-mail: dhec@doe.k12.de.us
Web: www.doe.state.de.us/high-ed/scip.htm

Summary   To provide financial assistance for undergraduate or graduate study to Delaware residents with financial need.

Eligibility   This program is open to Delaware residents who are 1) enrolled full time in an undergraduate degree program at a Delaware or Pennsylvania college or university, or 2) enrolled full time in a graduate degree program at an accredited out-of-state institution or at a private institution in Delaware if their major is not offered at the University of Delaware or Delaware State University. All applicants must be able to demonstrate financial need and

have a GPA of 2.5 or higher. U.S. citizenship or permanent resident status is required.

Financial data   The amount awarded depends on the need of the recipient but does not exceed the cost of tuition, fees, and books. Currently, the maximum for undergraduates ranges from $700 to $2,200 per year, depending on GPA; the maximum for graduate students is $1,000 per year.

Duration   1 year; renewable.

Number awarded   Approximately 1,500 each year.

Deadline   April of each year.

[146]
DELBERT OBERTEUFFER SCHOLARSHIP

American Association for Health Education
Attn: Scholarship Committee
1900 Association Drive
Reston, VA 20191-1599
(703) 476-3437   Toll-free: (800) 213-7193, ext. 437
Fax: (703) 476-6638   E-mail: aahe@aahperd.org
Web: www.aahperd.org/aahe/heawards/Oberteuffer.html

Summary   To provide financial assistance to members of the American Association for Health Education (AAHE) who are working on a doctoral degree.

Eligibility   This program is open to AAHE members who are enrolled full time as a doctoral student in a program designed to prepare them to develop, implement, and/or evaluate health education programs for children and youth. Applicants must have a cumulative graduate GPA of 3.5 or higher. They must submit a resume or curriculum vitae, a transcript from the institution granting the most recent degree, 2 letters of recommendation, and a 5-page essay that includes their professional goals and explains how their dissertation topic will contribute to the health of children and youth. Selection is based on academic achievement, potential for advancing the health of children and youth, professional goals, and caliber of documents.

Financial data   The stipend is $1,500.

Duration   1 year; nonrenewable.

Number awarded   1 each year.

Deadline   November of each year.

[147]
DELORES A. AUZENNE FELLOWSHIP FOR GRADUATE STUDY

State University System of Florida
Attn: Office of Academic and Student Affairs
325 West Gaines Street, Suite 1501
Tallahassee, FL 32399-1950
(850) 245-0467   Fax: (850) 245-9667
Web: www.flbog.org/asa

Summary   To provide financial assistance to minority students in Florida working on a graduate degree in an underrepresented discipline.

Eligibility   Eligible to be nominated are minority students working on a graduate degree at a public university in Florida. Nominees must be enrolled in full-time studies in a discipline in which there is an underrepresentation of the minority group to which they belong. A GPA of 3.0 or higher and U.S. citizenship or permanent resident status are required.

Financial data   The stipend is $5,000 per year.

Duration   1 year; may be renewed if the recipient maintains full-time enrollment and at least a 3.0 GPA.

Additional information This program is administered by the equal opportunity program at each of the 11 State University System of Florida 4-year institutions. Contact that office for further information.

Number awarded 5 each year.

[148]
DELTA GAMMA FOUNDATION FLORENCE MARGARET HARVEY MEMORIAL SCHOLARSHIP

American Foundation for the Blind
Attn: Scholarship Committee
11 Penn Plaza, Suite 300
New York, NY 10001
(212) 502-7661   Toll-free: (800) AFB-LINE
Fax: (212) 502-7771   TDD: (212) 502-7662
E-mail: afbinfo@afb.net
Web: www.afb.org/scholarships.asp

Summary To provide financial assistance to blind undergraduate and graduate students who wish to study in the field of rehabilitation and/or education of the blind.

Eligibility This program is open to legally blind juniors, seniors, or graduate students. U.S. citizenship is required. Applicants must be studying in the field of rehabilitation and/or education of visually impaired and blind persons. Along with their application, they must submit an essay that includes the field of study they are pursuing and why they have chosen it; their educational and personal goals; their work experience; any extracurricular activities with which they have been involved, including those in school, religious organizations, and the community; and how they intend to use scholarship monies that may be awarded.

Financial data The stipend is $1,000.

Duration 1 year.

Additional information This scholarship is supported by the Delta Gamma Foundation and administered by the American Foundation for the Blind.

Number awarded 1 each year.

Deadline April of each year.

[149]
DENNIS WONG AND ASSOCIATES SCHOLARSHIP

Ke Ali'i Pauahi Foundation
Attn: Financial Aid & Scholarship Services
567 South King Street, Suite 160
Honolulu, HI 96813
(808) 534-3966   Toll-free: (800) 842-4682, ext. 43966
Fax: (808) 534-3890   E-mail: giving@pauahi.org
Web: www.pauahi.org

Summary To provide financial assistance to undergraduate or graduate students of Hawaiian descent.

Eligibility This program is open to Native Hawaiians (descendants of the aboriginal inhabitants of the Hawaiian Islands prior to 1778). Applicants must be working on an undergraduate degree in liberal arts or science or a graduate degree in a professional field. They must have a well-rounded and balanced record of achievement in preparation for career objectives. Residency in Hawaii is not required.

Financial data The stipend is $1,100.

Duration 1 year.

Number awarded 2 each year.

Deadline May of each year.

[150]
DEPARTMENT OF HOMELAND SECURITY GRADUATE FELLOWSHIPS

Oak Ridge Institute for Science and Education
Attn: Science and Engineering Education
P.O. Box 117
Oak Ridge, TN 37831-0117
(865) 576-8239   Fax: (865) 241-5219
E-mail: igrid.gregory@orau.gov
Web: www.orau.gov/orise.htm

Summary To provide financial assistance and summer research experience to graduate students who are working on a degree in a field of interest to the Department of Homeland Security (DHS).

Eligibility This program is open to students working on a master's or doctoral degree in a program that includes a thesis requirement. Applicants must have a GPA of 3.3 or higher. Their field of study must be in the agricultural sciences, biological and life sciences, computer and information sciences, engineering, mathematics, physical sciences, psychology, social sciences, selected humanities (religious studies, cultural studies, public policy, advocacy, communications, or science writing), or selected fields limited to D.V.M. or Ph.D. programs (basic biomedical sciences, infectious diseases and zoonoses, animal health and food safety, comparative medicine and laboratory animal medicine, population medicine, public health, and epidemiology). Along with their application, they must submit 2 statements on 1) their educational and professional goals, the kinds of research they are interested in conducting, specific questions that interest them, and how they became interested in them; and 2) how they think their interests, talents, and initiative would contribute to make the homeland safer and secure. Selection is based on those statements, academic record, references, and GRE scores, As part of their program, they must be interested in participating in summer research activities at a DHS-designated facility. U.S. citizenship is required.

Financial data This program provides a stipend of $2,300 per month for 12 months plus full payment of tuition and mandatory fees.

Duration 3 academic years plus 10 weeks during the summer after the first year.

Additional information This program, established in 2003, is funded by DHS and administered by Oak Ridge Institute for Science and Education (ORISE). Recipients must enroll full time.

Number awarded Approximately 50 each year.

Deadline January of each year.

[151]
DERMIK LABORATORIES CAREER MOBILITY SCHOLARSHIPS

Dermatology Nurses' Association
c/o A.J. Jannetti, Inc.
200 East Holly Avenue
P.O. Box 56
Pitman, NJ 08071-0056
(856) 256-2330   Toll-free: (800) 454-4DNA
Fax: (856) 589-7463   E-mail: dna@ajj.com
Web: www.dnanurse.org

Summary To provide financial assistance to members of the Dermatology Nurses' Association (DNA) who are working on an undergraduate or graduate degree.

Eligibility Applicants for these scholarships must 1) have been members of the association for at least 2 years, 2) be employed in the specialty of dermatology, and 3) be working on a degree or advanced degree in nursing. Selection is based on a letter in which applicants describe their professional goals, proposed course of study, time frame for completion of study, funds necessary to meet their educational needs, and financial need.

Financial data　The stipend is $2,500.

Duration　1 year.

Additional information　Funding for this program is provided by Dermik Laboratories.

Number awarded　2 each year.

Deadline　September of each year.

[152]
DHHS SCHOLARSHIP FUND

Alexander Graham Bell Association for the Deaf
Attn: Financial Aid Coordinator
3417 Volta Place, N.W.
Washington, DC 20007-2778
(202) 337-5220　　　　　　　　　Fax: (202) 337-8314
TTY: (202) 337-5221　　　　E-mail: financialaid@agbell.org
Web: www.agbell.org

Summary　To provide financial assistance to undergraduate and graduate students who are members of the Alexander Graham Bell Association for the Deaf (AG Bell).

Eligibility　This program is open to undergraduate and graduate students who have been diagnosed with a moderate to profound hearing loss prior to acquiring spoken language (hearing loss averages 60dB or greater in the better ear in the speech frequencies of 500, 1000, and 2000 Hz). Applicants must be committed to using spoken language as their primary mode of communication. They must be accepted or enrolled at a mainstream college or university as a full-time student. Along with their application, they must submit a 1-page essay discussing their career goals and how spoken communication is helping them to reach those goals as a person with a hearing loss. Financial need is considered in the selection process. This scholarship is reserved for students who are members of AG Bell and its Deaf and Hard of Hearing Section (DHHS).

Financial data　The stipend is $1,000 per year.

Duration　1 year; may be renewed 1 additional year.

Number awarded　2 each year.

Deadline　April of each year.

[153]
DOCTORAL DEGREE SCHOLARSHIPS IN CANCER NURSING

American Cancer Society
Attn: Extramural Grants Department
1599 Clifton Road, N.E.
Atlanta, GA 30329-4251
(404) 329-7558　　　　　　　　Toll-free: (800) ACS-2345
Fax: (404) 321-4669　　　　　　E-mail: grants@cancer.org
Web: www.cancer.org

Summary　To provide financial assistance to graduate students working on a doctoral degree in cancer nursing.

Eligibility　This program is open to registered nurses with a current license to practice who are enrolled in or applying to a doctoral degree program in cancer nursing at an academic institution within the United States. The institution must offer an organized multidisciplinary program in cancer control or cancer care that allows a student the flexibility to develop educational and research activities related to cancer nursing. Applicants must be

U.S. citizens or permanent residents; be committed to preparing for a career full time; have had experience in professional nursing (as well as cancer nursing); be involved in professional organizations; be involved in the American Cancer Society and other volunteer organizations; have published or contributed to publications and creative works; have received professional and personal awards and honors; have clear, explicit, and realistic professional goals; have considered geographic location and financial needs as well as program components in selecting a doctoral program; have conducted or plan to conduct research that is meritorious, methodologically sound, and relevant to cancer nursing; have identified a faculty sponsor who is experienced in their area of study and will provide guidance in academic and research activities; have selected a doctoral program that will support their professional goals and research; and have made a career commitment to cancer nursing. They must be preparing to work in the following fields of cancer nursing: research, education, administration, or clinical practice.

Financial data　The stipend is $15,000 per year. Payments are made to the institution at the beginning of each semester.

Duration　2 years; may be renewed for an additional 2-year period.

Number awarded　Varies each year.

Deadline　October of each year.

[154]
DOCTORAL TRAINING GRANTS IN ONCOLOGY SOCIAL WORK

American Cancer Society
Attn: Extramural Grants Department
1599 Clifton Road, N.E.
Atlanta, GA 30329-4251
(404) 329-7558　　　　　　　　Toll-free: (800) ACS-2345
Fax: (404) 321-4669　　　　　　E-mail: grants@cancer.org
Web: www.cancer.org

Summary　To provide financial assistance to doctoral candidates at schools of social work or medical institutions who plan to conduct research related to psychosocial needs of people with cancer and their families.

Eligibility　This program is open to doctoral candidates who have a master's degree in social work and at least 1 year of clinical experience in a health care setting (oncology experience is not required). Applicants must have a demonstrated commitment to a career in oncology social work. They must be nominated by an accredited academic institution in the United States that can award a doctoral degree in social work. The program must offer an affiliation with an institution that has an active program in psychosocial oncology research, an organized multidisciplinary program in cancer control or cancer care, or access to other resources that allow the applicant to participate in educational and research activities related to oncology social work. The institution must designate a mentor who is qualified to serve as the chair of the applicant's doctoral dissertation committee and who has a record of psychosocial oncology research experience.

Financial data　The grant is $20,000 per year. Up to $5,000 of the grant may be used to allow the student and faculty mentor to attend the Society of Social Work Research annual conference and other professional conferences of their choosing.

Duration　2 years; may be renewed for 2 additional years.

Number awarded　Varies each year.

Deadline　October of each year.

[155]
DOLORES ZOHRAB LIEBMANN FELLOWSHIPS

Dolores Zohrab Liebmann Fund
c/o JPMorgan Private Bank
Philanthropic Services
345 Park Avenue, Fourth Floor
New York, NY 10154
(212) 464-2443   E-mail: sara.j.rosen@jpmchase.com

Summary To provide financial assistance for graduate study or research in any field.

Eligibility Candidates for this fellowship must have received a baccalaureate degree and have an outstanding academic record. They must be U.S. citizens, be currently enrolled in an academic institution in the United States, be able to show promise for achievement and distinction in their chosen field of study, and be able to document financial need. They may request funds for degree work or for independent research or study projects. All applications must be submitted through the dean of their university (each university is permitted to submit only 3 candidates for review each year). Candidates may be working on a degree in any field in the humanities, social sciences, or natural sciences, including law, medicine, engineering, architecture, or other formal professional training. They may be of any national descent or background.

Financial data Fellowships provide a stipend of $18,000 plus full payment of tuition.

Duration 1 year; may be renewed for 2 additional years.

Additional information Recipients must submit periodic progress reports. They must study or conduct their independent research projects in the United States. For a list of the 81 universities at which the fellowship is current tenable, contact the sponsor.

Number awarded Varies each year; recently, this program awarded $909,377 for fellowships and $43,075 for independent research projects.

Deadline January of each year.

[156]
DORA AMES LEE LEADERSHIP DEVELOPMENT FUND

United Methodist Church
General Board of Global Ministries
Attn: Health and Welfare Program
475 Riverside Drive, Room 330
New York, NY 10115
(212) 870-3871   Toll-free: (800) UMC-GBGM
E-mail: jyoung@gbgm-umc.org
Web: hbs.gbgm-umc.org/umcor/work/health/scholarships

Summary To provide financial assistance to Methodists and other Christians of Asian or Native American descent who are preparing for a career in a health-related field.

Eligibility This program is open to U.S. citizens who are of Asian American, Pacific Islander, or Native American descent. Applicants must be professed Christians, preferably United Methodists. They must be attending a college or university to enter or continue in a health-related field. Financial need is considered in the selection process.

Financial data The stipend is $2,000.

Duration 1 year.

Additional information This program was established in 1980.

Number awarded 6 each year.

Deadline June of each year.

[157]
DOUBLE YOUR DOLLARS FOR SCHOLARS PROGRAM

United Methodist Higher Education Foundation
Attn: Scholarship Office
1001 19th Avenue South
P.O. Box 340005
Nashville, TN 37203-0005
(615) 340-7385   Toll-free: (800) 811-8110
Fax: (615) 340-7330
E-mail: umhefscholarships@gbhem.org
Web: www.umhef.org/DOUBLE.HTML

Summary To provide financial assistance to students at Methodist colleges, universities, and seminaries whose home churches agree to contribute to their support.

Eligibility This program is open to students attending or planning to attend a United United Methodist-related college, university, or seminary as a full-time student. Applicants must have been an active, full member of a United Methodist church for at least 1 year prior to applying. Their home church must nominate them and agree to contribute to their support. Many of the United Methodist colleges and universities have also agreed to contribute matching funds for a Triple Your Dollars for Scholars Program and a few United Methodist conference foundations have agreed to contribute additional matching funds for a Quadruple Your Dollars for Scholars Program. Awards are granted on a first-come, first-served basis.

Financial data The sponsoring church contributes $1,000 and the United Methodist Higher Education Foundation (UMHEF) contributes a matching $1,000. Students who attend a participating United Methodist college or university receive an additional $1,000 for the Triple Your Dollars for Scholars Program and those from a participating conference receive a fourth $1,000 increment for the Quadruple Your Dollars for Scholars Program.

Duration 1 year; may be renewed as long as the recipients maintain satisfactory academic progress as defined by their institution.

Additional information Currently, participants in the Triple Your Dollars for Scholars program include 10 United Methodist seminaries and theological schools, 68 senior colleges and universities, and 6 2-year colleges (for a complete list, consult the UMHEF). The participating conference foundations are limited to the California-Pacific United Methodist Foundation (for students attending Triple Your Dollars institutions only), the North Georgia United Methodist Foundation, and the Oklahoma United Methodist Foundation (for students attending Oklahoma City University only).

Number awarded 325 each year.

Deadline Local churches must submit applications in March of each year or June of each year for 2-year colleges.

[158]
DOYNE M. GREEN SCHOLARSHIP

Seattle Foundation
Attn: Scholarship Administrator
1200 Fifth Avenue, Suite 1300
Seattle, WA 98101-3151
(206) 622-2294   Fax: (206) 622-7673
E-mail: info@seattlefoundation.org
Web: www.seafound.org

Summary To provide financial assistance to women in Washington working on a graduate degree in law, medicine, or social and public services.

Eligibility This program is open to female residents of Washington who have completed the first year of graduate study of law, medicine, or social and public services. Applicants must be able to demonstrate financial need. Along with their application, they must submit a 150-word statement on themselves, their educational and professional goals, the challenges they foresee, how they plan to accomplish their goals, and how this scholarship will assist them in achieving their goals.

Financial data The stipend is $4,000 per year.

Duration 1 year; may be renewed.

Number awarded At least 3 each year.

Deadline April of each year.

[159]
DR. ALFRED C. FONES SCHOLARSHIP

American Dental Hygienists' Association
Attn: Institute for Oral Health
444 North Michigan Avenue, Suite 3400
Chicago, IL 60611
(312) 440-8918   Toll-free: (800) 735-4916
Fax: (312) 440-8929   E-mail: institute@adha.net
Web: www.adha.org/institute/Scholarship/index.htm

Summary To provide financial assistance to dental hygiene students who are in a bachelor's or graduate degree program and intend to become teachers or educators.

Eligibility This program is open to dental hygiene students at the baccalaureate, master's, and doctoral level who have completed at least 1 year of study with a GPA of at least 3.0. Applicants must intend to prepare for a career as a dental hygiene teacher or educator. They must be active members of the Student American Dental Hygienists' Association (SADHA) or the American Dental Hygienists' Association (ADHA) and be able to document financial need of at least $1,500. Along with their application, they must submit a statement that covers their long-term career goals, their intended contribution to the dental hygiene profession, their professional interests, a list of past and/or present involvement in professional and/or community activities, and the manner in which their degree will enhance their professional capacity.

Financial data Stipends range from $1,000 to $2,000.

Duration 1 year.

Number awarded 1 each year.

Deadline June of each year.

[160]
DR. ALVIN AND MONICA SAAKE FOUNDATION SCHOLARSHIPS

Hawai'i Community Foundation
Attn: Scholarship Department
1164 Bishop Street, Suite 800
Honolulu, HI 96813
(808) 566-5570   Toll-free: (888) 731-3863
Fax: (808) 521-6286   E-mail: scholarships@hcf-hawaii.org
Web: www.hawaiicommunityfoundation.org

Summary To provide financial assistance to Hawaii residents who are interested in preparing for a career in designated health fields.

Eligibility This program is open to Hawaii residents who are enrolled as full-time juniors, seniors, or graduate students. Applicants must be majoring in kinesiology, leisure science, physical education, athletic training, exercise science, sports medicine, physical therapy, or occupational therapy. They must be able to

demonstrate academic achievement (GPA of 2.7 or higher), good moral character, and financial need. Along with their application, they must submit a short statement indicating their reasons for attending college, their planned course of study, and their career goals.

Financial data The amounts of the awards depend on the availability of funds and the need of the recipient; recently, stipends averaged $2,200.

Duration 1 year.

Additional information Recipients may attend college in Hawaii or on the mainland.

Number awarded Varies each year; recently, 21 of these scholarships were awarded.

Deadline February of each year.

[161]
DR. AND MRS. DAVID B. ALLMAN MEDICAL SCHOLARSHIPS

Miss America Pageant
Attn: Scholarship Department
Two Miss America Way, Suite 1000
Atlantic City, NJ 08401
(609) 345-7571, ext. 27   Toll-free: (800) 282-MISS
Fax: (609) 347-6079   E-mail: info@missamerica.org
Web: www.missamerica.org

Summary To provide financial assistance to medical students who have competed or are competing in the Miss America contest at any level.

Eligibility This program is open to women who have competed in the Miss America competition at least once, at any level of competition, within the past 10 years. Applicants do not have to apply during the year they competed; they may apply any year following as long as they are attending or accepted by a medical school and plan to become a medical doctor. They must submit an essay, up to 500 words, on why they wish to become a medical doctor and how this scholarship can help them attain that goal. Selection is based on GPA, class rank, MCAT score, extracurricular activities, financial need, and level of participation within the system.

Financial data Stipends are $2,100 or $1,500.

Duration 1 year.

Additional information This scholarship was established in 1974.

Number awarded Varies each year. Recently, 4 of these scholarships were awarded: 2 at $2,100 and 2 at $1,500.

Deadline June of each year.

[162]
DR. BESSIE ELIZABETH DELANEY FELLOWSHIP

National Dental Association
Attn: National Dental Association Foundation, Inc.
3517 16th Street, N.W.
Washington, DC 20010
(202) 588-1697   Fax: (202) 588-1242
E-mail: admin@ndaonline.org
Web: www.nadonline.org/ndafoundation.asp

Summary To provide financial assistance to female dental postdoctoral students who are members of underrepresented minority groups.

Eligibility This program is open to members of underrepresented minority groups who are women dentists working on a degree in subspecialty areas of dentistry, public health, administration, research, or law. Students working on a master's degree beyond their residency may be considered. Applicants must be members of the National Dental Association (NDA) and U.S. citizens or permanent residents. Along with their application, they must submit a letter explaining why they should be considered for this scholarship, 2 letters of recommendation, a curriculum vitae, a description of the program, nomination by their program director, and documentation of financial need.

Financial data   The stipend is $10,000.

Duration   1 year.

Additional information   This program, established in 1990, is supported by the Colgate-Palmolive Company.

Number awarded   1 each year.

Deadline   May of each year.

[163]
DR. CLIFTON O. DUMMETT AND LOIS DOYLE DUMMETT FELLOWSHIP

National Dental Association
Attn: National Dental Association Foundation, Inc.
3517 16th Street, N.W.
Washington, DC 20010
(202) 588-1697   Fax: (202) 588-1242
E-mail: admin@ndaonline.org
Web: www.nadonline.org/ndafoundation.asp

Summary   To provide financial assistance to underrepresented minority dental postdoctoral students.

Eligibility   This program is open to members of underrepresented minority groups who are dentists working on a degree in subspecialty areas of dentistry, public health, administration, research, or law. Students working on a master's degree beyond their residency may be considered. Applicants must be members of the National Dental Association (NDA) and U.S. citizens or permanent residents. Along with their application, they must submit a letter explaining why they should be considered for this scholarship, 2 letters of recommendation, a curriculum vitae, a description of the program, nomination by their program director, and documentation of financial need.

Financial data   The stipend is $10,000.

Duration   1 year.

Additional information   This program, established in 1990, is supported by the Colgate-Palmolive Company.

Number awarded   1 each year.

Deadline   May of each year.

[164]
DR. FRANCIS ANTHONY BENEVENTI MEDICAL SCHOLARSHIP

National Society Daughters of the American Revolution
Attn: Committee Services Office, Scholarships
1776 D Street, N.W.
Washington, DC 20006-5303
(202) 628-1776
Web: www.dar.org/natsociety/edout_scholar.cfm

Summary   To provide financial assistance to medical school students.

Eligibility   Eligible to apply for these scholarships are students who have been accepted into or are pursuing an approved course of study at an accredited medical school. Applicants must be sponsored by a local chapter of the Daughters of the American Revolution (DAR). They must have a GPA of 3.25 or higher. Selec-

tion is based on academic excellence, commitment to the field of study, and financial need. U.S. citizenship is required.

Financial data   The stipend is $5,000 per year.

Duration   1 year; may be renewed up to 3 additional years, provided the recipient maintains a GPA of 3.25 or higher.

Additional information   Requests for applications must be accompanied by a self-addressed stamped envelope.

Number awarded   1 each year.

Deadline   April of each year.

[165]
DR. GEORGE AND EMMA J. TORRISON SCHOLARSHIP FUND

Evangelical Lutheran Church in America
Attn: Vocation and Education
8765 West Higgins Road
Chicago, IL 60631-4195
(773) 380-2843   Toll-free: (800) 638-3522, ext. 2843
Fax: (773) 380-2750   E-mail: nancy.gruthusen@elca.org
Web: www.elca.org/education/torrison.html

Summary   To provide financial assistance to members of the Evangelical Lutheran Church in America (ELCA) who are working on or planning to work on a medical degree.

Eligibility   This program is open to active members of the ELCA who are either graduating college seniors accepted in a medical school or current medical school students. Students must be nominated for these scholarships. Applicants from ELCA colleges and universities must be nominated by the president of the institution; applicants at public colleges and universities must be nominated by the ELCA campus pastor; applicants at colleges and universities without a Lutheran campus ministry must be nominated by the pastor of the ELCA church in which they hold membership. Selection is based on stated career goals; financial need is not considered. Preference is given to applicants whose careers would lead them toward working to alleviate currently incurable diseases.

Financial data   The stipend is $5,000.

Duration   1 year; nonrenewable.

Additional information   This program was established in 1988.

Number awarded   Up to 4 each year.

Deadline   March of each year.

[166]
DR. GEORGE BLUE SPRUCE FELLOWSHIP

American Indian Graduate Center
Attn: Executive Director
4520 Montgomery Boulevard, N.E., Suite 1-B
Albuquerque, NM 87109-1291
(505) 881-4584   Toll-free: (800) 628-1920
Fax: (505) 884-0427   E-mail: aigc@aigc.com
Web: www.aigc.com

Summary   To provide financial assistance to Native American students interested in working on a degree in dentistry.

Eligibility   This program is open to enrolled members of U.S. federally-recognized American Indian tribes and Alaska Native groups and other students who can document one-fourth degree federally-recognized Indian blood. Applicants must be enrolled as full-time students at a dental school in the United States. Selection is based on academic achievement, financial need, and an essay on the meaning of their graduate education to the Indian community.

Financial data   A stipend is awarded (amount not specified).

Duration 1 year; may be renewed.

Additional information The application fee is $15. Since this a supplemental program, applicants must apply in a timely manner for federal financial aid and campus-based aid at the college they are attending to be considered for this program. Failure to apply will disqualify an applicant.

Number awarded 1 or more each year.

Deadline May of each year.

[167]
DR. HANS AND CLARA ZIMMERMAN FOUNDATION HEALTH SCHOLARSHIPS

Hawai'i Community Foundation
Attn: Scholarship Department
1164 Bishop Street, Suite 800
Honolulu, HI 96813
(808) 566-5570   Toll-free: (888) 731-3863
Fax: (808) 521-6286   E-mail: scholarships@hcf-hawaii.org
Web: www.hawaiicommunityfoundation.org

Summary To provide financial assistance to Hawaii residents who are interested in preparing for a career in the health field.

Eligibility This program is open to Hawaii residents who are interested in majoring in a health-related field as full-time juniors, seniors, or graduate students at a college or university in the United States. Students planning to major in sports medicine, psychology (unless clinical), and social work are not eligible. Applicants must be able to demonstrate academic achievement (GPA of 3.0 or higher), good moral character, and financial need. Along with their application, they must submit a short statement indicating their reasons for attending college, their planned course of study, and their career goals.

Financial data The amounts of the awards depend on the availability of funds and the need of the recipients; recently, stipends averaged $3,600.

Duration 1 year.

Additional information This is 1 of the largest scholarship funds in Hawaii.

Number awarded Varies each year; recently, 181 of these scholarships were awarded.

Deadline February of each year.

[168]
DR. JAMES WATSON FELLOWSHIPS

Golf Course Superintendents Association of America
Attn: Environmental Institute for Golf
1421 Research Park Drive
Lawrence, KS 66049-3859
(785) 832-4424   Toll-free: (800) 472-7878, ext. 4424
Fax: (785) 832-3673   E-mail: ahoward@gcsaa.org
Web: www.gcsaa.org/students/scholarships/default.asp

Summary To provide financial assistance to graduate students who are preparing for a career in golf management.

Eligibility This program is open to graduate students working on a master's or doctoral degree in fields related to turfgrass science and/or golf course management. Applicants must be planning to prepare for a career in research, instruction, or extension in a university setting. Selection is based on academic excellence, peer recommendations, communications skills, commitment to a career as an instructor and/or scientist, accomplishments in research and education, and potential to contribute significantly to the industry. Financial need is not considered.

Financial data The stipend is $5,000.

Duration 1 year; nonrenewable.

Additional information Funding for this program is provided by the Toro Company.

Number awarded Up to 4 each year.

Deadline September of each year.

[169]
DR. JOHN C. YAVIS SCHOLARSHIPS

American Hellenic Educational Progressive Association
Attn: AHEPA Educational Foundation
1909 Q Street, N.W., Suite 500
Washington, DC 20009
(202) 232-6300   Fax: (202) 232-2140
E-mail: ahepa@ahepa.org
Web: www.ahepa.org

Summary To provide financial assistance to undergraduate and graduate students with a connection to the American Hellenic Educational Progressive Association (AHEPA).

Eligibility This program is open to 1) members in good standing of the Order of Ahepa, Daughters of Penelope, Sons of Pericles, or Maids of Athena, and 2) the children of Order of Ahepa or Daughters of Penelope members in good standing. Applicants must be currently enrolled or planning to enroll as undergraduate or graduate students. High school seniors must submit their most recent official transcript as well as SAT or ACT scores; college freshmen and sophomores must submit high school transcripts, SAT or ACT scores, and their most recent college transcript; college juniors and seniors must submit their most recent college transcript; graduate students must submit college transcripts, GRE or MCAT scores (if available), and their most recent graduate school transcript. Along with their application, they must also submit a 500-word biographical essay. Selection is based on academic achievement; extracurricular, personal, and volunteer activities; athletic achievements; and work experience. Financial need is not considered.

Financial data Stipends range from $500 to $2,000 per year.

Duration 1 year.

Additional information A processing fee of $20 must accompany each application.

Number awarded Varies each year; recently, 2 of these scholarships were awarded.

Deadline March of each year.

[170]
DR. JOSEPH L. HENRY SCHOLARSHIPS

National Dental Association
Attn: National Dental Association Foundation, Inc.
3517 16th Street, N.W.
Washington, DC 20010
(202) 588-1697   Fax: (202) 588-1242
E-mail: admin@ndaonline.org
Web: www.nadonline.org/ndafoundation.asp

Summary To provide financial assistance to underrepresented minorities entering their first year of dental school.

Eligibility This program is open to members of underrepresented minority groups who are entering their first year of dental school as full-time students. Applicants must have an undergraduate GPA of 3.5 or higher. Along with their application, they must submit information on their community service, a letter from their school verifying that they are attending, a letter of recommendation from an undergraduate professor, college transcripts, and documentation of financial need. They must be U.S. citizens or permanent residents. Selection is based on academic performance in undergraduate school and service to community and/or country.

Financial data The stipend is $2,000 per year.

Duration 1 year; may be renewed up to 3 additional years.

Additional information This program, established in 1990, is supported by the Colgate-Palmolive Company.

Number awarded 5 each year.

Deadline May of each year.

[171]
DR. KIYOSHI SONODA MEMORIAL SCHOLARSHIP

Japanese American Citizens League
Attn: National Scholarship Awards
1765 Sutter Street
San Francisco, CA 94115
(415) 921-5225   Fax: (415) 931-4671
E-mail: jacl@jacl.org
Web: www.jacl.org/leadership_development_5.php

Summary To provide financial assistance to student members of the Japanese American Citizens League (JACL) who are interested in preparing for a career in dentistry.

Eligibility This program is open to JACL members who are enrolled or planning to enroll in a school of dentistry. Applicants must submit a statement describing their current level of involvement in the Japanese American community or Asian Pacific community and how they will continue their involvement in future years. Selection is based on academic record, extracurricular activities, financial need, and community involvement.

Financial data The stipend depends on the availability of funds but usually ranges from $1,000 to $5,000.

Duration 1 year; nonrenewable.

Additional information Applications must be submitted to the JACL National Scholarship Program, c/o San Diego JACL Chapter, 1031 25th Street, San Diego, CA 92102.

Number awarded At least 1 each year.

Deadline March of each year.

[172]
DR. MARIE E. ZAKRZEWSKI MEDICAL SCHOLARSHIP

Kosciuszko Foundation
Attn: Educational Programs
15 East 65th Street
New York, NY 10021-6595
(212) 734-2130, ext. 210   Fax: (212) 628-4552
E-mail: addy@thekf.org
Web: www.thekf.org/EDScholarships_US_MZMS.html

Summary To provide financial assistance to women of Polish ancestry studying medicine.

Eligibility This program is open to young women of Polish ancestry entering their first, second, or third year of study at an accredited medical school in the United States. Applicants must be U.S. citizens or permanent residents of Polish descent and have a GPA of 3.0 or higher. First preference is given to residents of Massachusetts or former presentees of the Federation Kosciuszko Foundation Ball. If no candidates from the first preference group apply, qualified residents of New England are considered. Selection is based on academic excellence; the applicant's academic achievements, interests, and motivation; the applicant's interest in Polish subjects or involvement in the Polish American community; and financial need.

Financial data The stipend is $3,500.

Duration 1 year; nonrenewable.

Additional information This program is funded by the Massachusetts Federation of Polish Women's Clubs but administered by the Kosciuszko Foundation. There is a nonrefundable application fee of $25.

Number awarded 1 each year.

Deadline January of each year.

[173]
DR. PRENTICE GAUTT POSTGRADUATE SCHOLARSHIPS

Big 12 Conference
2201 Stemmons Freeway, 28th Floor
Dallas, TX 75207
(214) 742-1212   Fax: (214) 753-0145
Web: www.big12sports.com

Summary To provide financial assistance for graduate school to student athletes who complete their undergraduate study at a Big 12 university.

Eligibility This program is open to students graduating from a Big 12 university who have participated in at least 2 years of intercollegiate athletics. Applicants must have a GPA of 3.5 or higher and be planning to enroll in a program of professional or graduate study. Male and female athletes are considered separately.

Financial data The stipend is $6,900.

Duration 1 year.

Additional information This program began with the inception of the league in 1996-97. Members of the Big 12 include Baylor, Colorado, Iowa State, Kansas, Kansas State, Missouri, Nebraska, Oklahoma, Oklahoma State, Texas, Texas A&M, and Texas Tech. Recipients must graduate from their Big 12 university within 15 months of their selection for this scholarship and must enroll in graduate or professional school within 2 years of graduation.

Number awarded 24 each year: 2 (1 male and 1 female) at each member institution.

[174]
DR. RAYMOND K.J. LUOMANEN FUND

Finlandia Foundation-New York Metropolitan Chapter
Attn: Scholarships
P.O. Box 165, Bowling Green Station
New York, NY 10274-0165
E-mail: scholarships@finlandiafoundationny.org
Web: www.finlandiafoundationny.org/scholarships.html

Summary To provide financial assistance to students interested in studying or conducting research on medicine and health care in Finland or the United States.

Eligibility This program is open to students at colleges and universities in the United States who are interested in studying or conducting research on medicine or health care in Finland or the United States. Applicants must submit information on their language proficiency, work experience, memberships (academic, professional, and social), fellowships and scholarships, awards, publications, exhibitions, performances, and future goals and ambitions. Financial need is not considered in the selection process.

Financial data Stipends range from $500 to $5,000 per year.

Duration 1 year.

Additional information Information is also available from Leena Toivonen, (718) 680-1716, E-mail: leenat@hotmail.com.

Number awarded 1 or more each year.

Deadline February of each year.

[175]
DR. RICHARD ALLEN WILLIAMS SCHOLARSHIPS
Association of Black Cardiologists, Inc.
5355 Hunter Road
Atlanta, GA 30349
(404) 201-6600   Toll-free: (800) 753-9222
Fax: (404) 201-6601   E-mail: abcardio@abcardio.org
Web: www.abcardio.org/williams_award.htm
Summary To provide financial assistance to minority medical students interested in preparing for a career as a cardiologist.
Eligibility This program is open to minority students who show promise in medical research, cardiology, and academic medicine. Applicants must 1) demonstrate ability, interest, and participation in the promotion of health for the African American community; 2) participate in research or other extracurricular activities; 3) demonstrate academic pursuits and clinical acumen; and 4) have proven leadership during academic pursuits.
Financial data The stipend is $1,000.
Duration 1 year.
Number awarded 3 each year.
Deadline June of each year.

[176]
DR. SEYMOUR GALINA GRANT
American Optometric Association
Attn: Educational Services
243 North Lindbergh Boulevard
St. Louis, MO 63141-7881
(314) 991-4100   Toll-free: (800) 365-2219, ext. 110
Fax: (314) 991-4101   E-mail: LMBaumstark@aoa.org
Web: www.aoanet.org
Summary To provide financial assistance to members of the American Optometric Student Association (AOSA).
Eligibility This program is open to AOSA members entering their fourth years of study at an accredited school or college of optometry. Applicants must submit an essay, up to 1,500 words in length, on a topic that changes annually; recently, students were invited to write on "The qualities I have developed through my financial planning/work experience during and/or before optometry school which I believe will be most useful to me establishing an ethical/professional optometric practice." They must be able to demonstrate financial need. Each school or college of optometry in the United States and Canada may submit 1 application.
Financial data The stipend is $2,500.
Duration 1 year.
Number awarded 1 each year.
Deadline May of each year.

[177]
DR. SHERI SMITH MEMORIAL GRANT
Wound, Ostomy and Continence Nurses Society
Attn: Scholarship Committee
15000 Commerce Parkway, Suite C
Mt. Laurel, NJ 08054
Toll-free: (888) 224-WOCN   E-mail: info@wocn.org
Web: www.wocn.org/education/scholarship
Summary To provide financial assistance to members of the Would, Ostomy and Continence Nurses (WOCN) Society interested in working on an advanced degree, conducting research, or developing educational materials.

Eligibility This program is open to active members of the society who have a current, unrestricted R.N. license and proof of WOCNCB certification. Applicants must be able to provide evidence of current or previous employment as a wound, ostomy, and/or continence nurse during the last 3 years. They must 1) provide proof of current enrollment or acceptance into an accredited nursing program or other accredited college or university program for non-nursing degrees to work on a master's or doctoral degree or N.P. certificate; 2) be conducting or planning to conduct innovative and theory-driven empirical research in the wound, ostomy, and/or continence specialty; or 3) be interested in developing professional or patient programs and/or materials. Self-nominations and nominations by another WOCN member are accepted.
Financial data The grant is $2,500.
Duration 1 year.
Additional information This program is sponsored by Carrington Laboratories.
Number awarded 2 each year: 1 in the fall and 1 in the spring.
Deadline April or October of each year.

[178]
E. CRAIG BRANDENBURG GRADUATE AWARD
United Methodist Church
Attn: General Board of Higher Education and Ministry
Office of Loans and Scholarships
1001 19th Avenue South
P.O. Box 340007
Nashville, TN 37203-0007
(615) 340-7344   Fax: (615) 340-7367
E-mail: umscholar@gbhem.org
Web: www.gbhem.org/gbhem/loans2.html
Summary To provide financial assistance to Methodist students who are working on an undergraduate or graduate degree to change their profession or continue study after interruption.
Eligibility This program is open to full-time undergraduate and graduate students who are 35 years of age or older. Applicants must have been active, full members of a United Methodist Church for at least 1 year prior to applying. They must 1) be able to demonstrate special need because of a change of profession or vocation, interrupted study, or required continuing education; 2) have a GPA of 3.0 or higher; and 3) be U.S. citizens or permanent residents. Preference is given to applicants attending United Methodist colleges, universities, or seminaries.
Financial data Stipends range from $500 to $2,000.
Duration 1 year; recipients may reapply.
Number awarded Varies each year.
Deadline February of each year.

[179]
EDITH M. ALLEN SCHOLARSHIPS
United Methodist Church
Attn: General Board of Higher Education and Ministry
Office of Loans and Scholarships
1001 19th Avenue South
P.O. Box 340007
Nashville, TN 37203-0007
(615) 340-7344   Fax: (615) 340-7367
E-mail: umscholar@gbhem.org
Web: www.gbhem.org/gbhem/loans2.html
Summary To provide financial assistance to Methodist students who are African American and working on an undergraduate or graduate degree in specified fields.

Eligibility This program is open to full-time undergraduate and graduate students at Methodist colleges and universities (preferably Historically Black United Methodist colleges) who have been active, full members of a United Methodist Church for at least 3 years prior to applying. Applicants must be African Americans working on a degree in education, social work, medicine, and/or other health professions. They must have at least a "B+" average and be recognized as a person whose academic and vocational contributions will help improve the quality of life for others.

Financial data A stipend is awarded (amount not specified).

Duration 1 year; recipients may reapply.

Number awarded Varies each year.

Deadline May of each year.

[180]
EDITH SEVILLE COALE SCHOLARSHIPS

Zonta Club of Washington, D.C.
c/o Yvonne Boggan, President
350 Chaplin Street, S.E.
Washington, DC 20019-4261
(202) 575-4808
Web: www.zontawashingtondc.org

Summary To provide financial assistance to Protestant women in the Washington, D.C. area who have completed the first year of medical school.

Eligibility Protestant women who are in the second, third, or fourth year of medical school in the Washington, D.C. area are eligible to apply. Selection is based on financial need and scholastic achievement.

Financial data The amount awarded varies; recently, stipends averaged $8,500.

Duration 1 year.

Additional information The trust fund contains limited funds. Awards are not made for the first year of medical school. Preference is given to women students nominated by medical school faculty members.

Number awarded Varies each year; recently, 4 of these scholarships were awarded.

Deadline December of each year.

[181]
EDUCATIONAL ADVANCEMENT GRADUATE SCHOLARSHIPS

American Association of Critical-Care Nurses
Attn: Educational Advancement Scholarships
101 Columbia
Aliso Viejo, CA 92656-4109
(949) 362-2000, ext. 338
Toll-free: (800) 899-AACN, ext. 338   Fax: (949) 362-2020
E-mail: info@aacn.org
Web: www.aacn.org

Summary To provide financial assistance to members of the American Association of Critical-Care Nurses (AACN) who are working on a graduate degree in nursing.

Eligibility This program is open to registered nurses who are current members of the association and enrolled in an accredited master's or doctoral degree program in nursing. Applicants must hold an active R.N. license and be currently working in critical care or have 1 year's experience in the last 3 years. They must have a cumulative GPA of 3.0 or higher. Along with their application, they must submit 1) a 1-page essay on how they see their nursing practice changing as a result of their graduate degree;

and 2) a 2-page exemplar (an essay describing a situation in which their intervention made a difference in a patient's outcome). Financial need is not considered in the selection process. Qualified ethnic minority candidates receive at least 20% of these awards.

Financial data The stipend is $1,500. The funds are sent directly to the recipient's college or university and may be used only for tuition, fees, books, and supplies.

Duration 1 year; recipients may reapply.

Number awarded Varies each year; recently, 53 of these scholarships were awarded.

Deadline March of each year.

[182]
EDWARD L. KRUGER MEMORIAL ITTISH AAISHA SCHOLARSHIP

Chickasaw Foundation
110 West 12th Street
P.O. Box 1726
Ada, OK 74821-1726
(580) 421-9030   Fax: (580) 421-9031
E-mail: ChickasawFoundation@chickasaw.net
Web: www.chickasawfoundation.org

Summary To provide financial assistance to members of the Chickasaw Nation who are working on a graduate degree in pharmacy.

Eligibility This program is open to Chickasaw students who are currently enrolled full time in a graduate school of pharmacy. Applicants must have a GPA of 3.0 or higher. Along with their application, they must submit high school or college transcripts, 2 letters of recommendation, a copy of their Certificate of Degree of Indian Blood, a copy of their Chickasaw Nation citizenship card, and a 1-page essay on their long-term goals and plans for achieving them. Financial need is not considered in the selection process.

Financial data The stipend is $1,000 per year.

Duration 1 year.

Number awarded 1 each year.

Deadline May of each year.

[183]
EDWARD P. DOLBEY SCHOLARSHIP

American Society for Clinical Laboratory Science-
   Pennsylvania
P.O. Box 284
Camp Hill, Pa 17001
Toll-free: (800) 484-1002, ext. 4767
E-mail: bsnyderman@msn.com
Web: ascls-pa.org/dolbey_scholarship.htm

Summary To provide financial assistance to members of the American Society for Clinical Laboratory Science (ASCLS) in Pennsylvania who are interested in working on a baccalaureate or graduate degree in a field related to clinical laboratory science.

Eligibility Applicants must have been active members or student members of the ASCLS-Pennsylvania for at least 2 years. They must be enrolled in or planning to enroll in a program or school listed by a nationally-recognized accrediting agency to work on a baccalaureate degree (must already hold certification as MLT, HT, CT and have an associate degree); a master's or doctorate in any field related to clinical laboratory sciences (including but not limited to biochemistry, microbiology, immunology, education, and administration); or a program at a blood bank specialty school. All applicants must be able to document contributions to the clinical laboratory science profession, including publications, community education advancing public awareness of clinical laboratory science, presentations at seminars, workshops, and professional association activities.

Financial data The stipend is $3,000. Funds are paid directly to the recipient.

Duration 1 year.

Additional information The sponsor was formerly the Pennsylvania Society for Clinical Laboratory Science.

Number awarded 1 each year.

Deadline February of each year.

[184]
EDWARD T. CONROY MEMORIAL SCHOLARSHIP PROGRAM

Maryland Higher Education Commission
Attn: Office of Student Financial Assistance
839 Bestgate Road, Suite 400
Annapolis, MD 21401-3013
(410) 260-4563   Toll-free: (800) 974-1024, ext. 4563
Fax: (410) 974-5376   TTY: (800) 735-2258
E-mail: osfamail@mhec.state.md.us
Web: www.mhec.state.md.us

Summary To provide financial assistance for college or graduate school to specified categories of veterans, public safety employees, and their children in Maryland.

Eligibility This program is open to undergraduate and graduate students in the following categories: 1) children and unremarried surviving spouses of state or local public safety employees or volunteers who died in the line of duty; 2) children of armed forces members whose death or 100% disability was directly caused by military service; 3) POW/MIA veterans of the Vietnam Conflict and their children; 4) children and surviving spouses of victims of the September 11, 2001 terrorist attacks who died in the World Trade Center in New York City, the Pentagon in Virginia, or United Airlines Flight 93 in Pennsylvania; 5) veterans who have, as a direct result of military service, a disability of 25% or greater and have exhausted or are no longer eligible for federal veterans' educational benefits; and 6) state or local public safety officers or volunteers who were 100% disabled in the line of duty. The parent, veteran, POW, or public safety officer or volunteer must have been a resident of Maryland at the time of death or when declared disabled. Financial need is not considered.

Financial data The amount of the award is equal to tuition and fees at a Maryland postsecondary institution, to a maximum of $17,800 for children and spouses of the September 11 terrorist attacks or $8,550 for all other recipients.

Duration Up to 5 years of full-time study or 8 years of part-time study.

Additional information Recipients must enroll at a 2-year or 4-year Maryland college or university as a full-time or part-time degree-seeking undergraduate or graduate student or attend a private career school.

Number awarded Varies each year.

Deadline July of each year.

[185]
EIGHT AND FORTY LUNG AND RESPIRATORY DISEASE NURSING SCHOLARSHIP

American Legion
Attn: Americanism and Children & Youth Division
P.O. Box 1055
Indianapolis, IN 46206-1055
(317) 630-1249   Fax: (317) 630-1223
E-mail: acy@legion.org
Web: www.legion.org

Summary To provide financial assistance to registered nurses who wish to prepare for advanced positions in lung and respiratory disease nursing supervision, administration, or teaching.

Eligibility This program is open to registered nurses who are graduates of an accredited school of nursing and who wish to continue their studies in the field of lung and respiratory disease nursing on either a full-time or part-time basis. Awards are based on personal and academic qualifications, especially past experience and future employment prospects as they relate to lung and respiratory disease nursing. U.S. citizenship is required.

Financial data The stipend is $3,000 per year.

Duration 1 year.

Additional information The Eight and Forty was organized by members of the American Legion Auxiliary in 1922; it began awarding these scholarships in 1957.

Number awarded Varies each year.

Deadline May of each year.

[186]
ELA FOUNDATION SCHOLARSHIPS

Ethel Louise Armstrong Foundation
Attn: Executive Director
2460 North Lake Avenue
PMB 128
Altadena, CA 91001
(626) 398-8840   Fax: (626) 398-8843
E-mail: executivedirector@ela.org
Web: www.ela.org/scholarships/scholarships.html

Summary To provide financial assistance for graduate school to women with disabilities.

Eligibility This program is open to women with disabilities who are currently enrolled in or actively applying to a graduate program at an accredited college or university in the United States. Applicants must be active in a local, state, or national disability organization, either in person or electronically, that is providing services or advocacy for people with disabilities. Along with their application, they must submit a 1,000-word essay on "How I will change the face of disability on the planet." Selection is based on academic and leadership merit.

Financial data The stipend ranges from $500 to $2,000 per year.

Duration 1 year.

Additional information The sponsoring foundation was founded in 1994 by Margaret Staton, who was disabled by a spinal cord tumor at 2 years of age. Recipients must agree to 1) network with the sponsor's board of directors and current and alumni scholarship recipients, and 2) update the sponsor on their progress in their academic and working career.

Number awarded Varies each year; recently, 4 of these scholarships were awarded.

Deadline May of each year.

[187]
ELAINE GELMAN SCHOLARSHIP

National Association of Pediatric Nurse Practitioners
Attn: NAPNAP Foundation
20 Brace Road, Suite 200
Cherry Hill, NJ 08034-2633
(856) 857-9700   Toll-free: (877) 662-7627
Fax: (856) 857-1600   E-mail: info@napnap.org
Web: www.napnap.org

Summary To provide financial assistance to students preparing for a career as a nurse practitioner (NP), especially as a pediatric nurse practitioner (PNP).

Eligibility This program is open to students enrolled full or part time in an accredited NP program with an expected graduation date of 2 years or less. Preference is given to applicants in a PNP program or those with interest or experience in health policy or advocacy. Along with their application, they must submit a 200-word statement explaining their reasons for applying and demonstrating their ability to articulate and follow through on an innovative solution to a health care problem.

Financial data The stipend is $1,000.

Duration 1 year.

Number awarded 1 each year.

Deadline June of each year.

[188]
ELEKTA RADIATION THERAPY EDUCATORS SCHOLARSHIP PROGRAM

American Society of Radiologic Technologists
Attn: ASRT Education and Research Foundation
15000 Central Avenue, S.E.
Albuquerque, NM 87123-3909
(505) 298-4500, ext. 2541
Toll-free: (800) 444-2778, ext. 2541   Fax: (505) 298-5063
E-mail: foundation@asrt.org
Web: www.asrt.org

Summary To provide financial assistance to members of the American Society of Radiologic Technologists (ASRT) who are interested in continuing their education to enhance their position in the field.

Eligibility This program is open to licensed radiologic technologists who are current members of ASRT and have worked in the radiologic sciences profession for at least 1 year during the past 5 years in a clinical or didactic setting. Applicants must be employed as a radiation program director, faculty member, clinical coordinator, or clinical instructor. They must have applied to a course of study at the bachelor's, master's, or doctoral level intended to further their career as a radiation therapy educator Along with their application, they must submit a written interview up to 1,000 words on their professional achievements, their career goals, how their degree or certificate will help them to achieve their career goals, their educational goals, and how this scholarship will help them to achieve their educational goals. Financial need is considered in the selection process.

Financial data The stipend is $5,000.

Duration 1 year; may be renewed for 1 additional year.

Additional information This program is supported by Elekta.

Number awarded Varies each year; recently, 4 of these scholarships were awarded.

Deadline January of each year.

[189]
ELIZABETH AND SHERMAN ASCHE MEMORIAL SCHOLARSHIP

Association on American Indian Affairs, Inc.
Attn: Director of Scholarship Programs
966 Hungerford Drive, Suite 12-B
Rockville, MD 20850
(240) 314-7155   Fax: (240) 314-7159
E-mail: lw.aaia@verizon.net
Web: www.indian-affairs.org/scholarships.htm

Summary To provide financial assistance to Native Americans interested in working on an undergraduate or graduate degree in public health.

Eligibility This program is open to American Indian and Alaskan Native full-time undergraduate and graduate students working on a degree in public health. Applicants must submit documentation of financial need, a Certificate of Indian Blood showing at least one-quarter Indian blood, proof of tribal enrollment, an essay on their educational goals, 2 letters of recommendation, and their most recent transcript. Selection is based on merit and need.

Financial data The stipend is $3,000.

Duration 1 year.

Number awarded 1 each year.

Deadline July of each year.

[190]
ELIZABETH J. DAVIS SCHOLARSHIP

Vermont Student Assistance Corporation
Attn: Scholarship Programs
10 East Allen Street
P.O. Box 2000
Winooski, VT 05404-2601
(802) 654-3798   Toll-free: (888) 253-4819
Fax: (802) 654-3765   TDD: (802) 654-3766
TDD: (800) 281-3341 (within VT)   E-mail: info@vsac.org
Web: www.vsac.org

Summary To provide financial assistance to residents of Vermont interested in obtaining an undergraduate degree, graduate degree, or certificate in a field related to home health care.

Eligibility This scholarship is available to the residents of Vermont who are high school seniors, current undergraduate students, and home health care professionals. Applicants must be interested in obtaining a bachelor's degree in a health profession, certification as a home health aide, or (for home health care professionals) an advanced degree. They must be able to demonstrate interest in a career in the home health care field and an intent to work in Vermont for at least 2 years. Selection is based on financial need, required essays, a letter of recommendation, and a personal interview (if necessary).

Financial data Stipends range from $1,000 to $3,000 per year.

Duration 1 year; may be renewed up to 3 additional years.

Number awarded Varies each year; recently, 7 of these scholarships were awarded.

Deadline June of each year.

[191]
ELIZABETH NASH FOUNDATION SCHOLARSHIP PROGRAM

Elizabeth Nash Foundation
P.O. Box 1260
Los Gatos, CA 95031-1260
E-mail: scholarships@elizabethnashfoundation.org
Web: www.elizabethnashfoundation.org

Summary To provide financial assistance for college or graduate school to individuals with cystic fibrosis (CF).

Eligibility This program is open to undergraduate and graduate students who have CF. Applicants must be able to demonstrate clear academic goals and a commitment to participate in activities outside the classroom. Selection is based on academic record, character, demonstrated leadership, service to the community, and financial need.

Financial data Stipends range from $500 to $2,000. Funds are paid directly to the academic institution to be applied to tuition and fees.

Duration 1 year; recipients may reapply.

Additional information This program was established in 2005. Recipients must agree to support the program by speaking at a local event or writing an article for publication by the foundation.

Number awarded 1 or more each year.

Deadline September of each year.

[192]
ELLIS F. HILLNER AWARD

Vasa Order of America
Attn: Vice Grand Master
3236 Berkeley Avenue
Cleveland Heights, OH 44118-2055
(216) 371-5141   E-mail: rolf.bergman@sbcglobal.net
Web: www.vasaorder.com

Summary To provide financial assistance for education in a medical field to members of the Vasa Order of America.

Eligibility Applicants must have belonged to the organization for at least 1 year and be attending or planning to attend an accredited institution on a full-time basis for studies in the medical field. Selection is based on a transcript, letters of recommendation from school and local Vasa lodge officials, and an essay of up to 1,000 words on a topic related to Vasa.

Financial data The stipend is $2,000.

Duration 1 year.

Additional information Vasa Order of America is a Swedish American fraternal organization incorporated in 1899.

Number awarded 1 each year.

Deadline February of each year.

[193]
ELSIE BORCK HEALTH CARE SCHOLARSHIP

Kansas Federation of Business & Professional Women's
  Clubs, Inc.
Attn: Kansas BPW Educational Foundation
c/o Diane Smith, Executive Secretary
10418 Haskins
Lenexa, KS 66215-2162
E-mail: desmith@fcbankonline.com
Web: www.bpwkansas.org/scholarships_and_loans.htm

Summary To provide financial assistance to residents of Kansas who are preparing for a career in a health profession in the state.

Eligibility This program is open to Kansas residents (men and women) who are at least a college junior and preparing to practice in a health profession in the state. Applicants must submit a 3-page personal biography in which they express their career goals, the direction they want to take in the future, their proposed field of study, their reason for selecting that field, the institutions they plan to attend and why, their circumstances for reentering school (if a factor), and what makes them uniquely qualified for this scholarship. They must also be able to document financial need. Applications must be submitted through a local organization of the sponsor.

Financial data A stipend is awarded (amount not specified).

Duration 1 year.

Number awarded 1 or more each year.

Deadline December of each year.

[194]
ELSIE M. BELL GROSVENOR SCHOLARSHIP AWARDS

Alexander Graham Bell Association for the Deaf
Attn: Financial Aid Coordinator
3417 Volta Place, N.W.
Washington, DC 20007-2778
(202) 337-5220   Fax: (202) 337-8314
TTY: (202) 337-5221   E-mail: financialaid@agbell.org
Web: www.agbell.org

Summary To provide financial assistance to undergraduate and graduate students who have moderate to profound hearing loss and attend school in the Washington, D.C. area.

Eligibility This program is open to undergraduate and graduate students who have been diagnosed with a moderate to profound hearing loss prior to acquiring spoken language (hearing loss averages 60dB or greater in the better ear in the speech frequencies of 500, 1000, and 2000 Hz). Applicants must be committed to using spoken language as their primary mode of communication. They must be accepted or enrolled at a mainstream college or university in the Washington, D.C. area as a full-time student. Along with their application, they must submit a 1-page essay discussing their career goals and how spoken communication is helping them to reach those goals as a person with a hearing loss. Financial need is considered in the selection process.

Financial data The stipend is $2,000 per year.

Duration 1 year; may be renewed 1 additional year.

Number awarded 1 each year.

Deadline April of each year.

[195]
ENA FOUNDATION ADVANCED PRACTICE NURSING SCHOLARSHIPS

Emergency Nurses Association
Attn: ENA Foundation
915 Lee Street
Des Plaines, IL 60016-6569
(847) 460-4100   Toll-free: (800) 900-9659, ext. 4100
Fax: (847) 460-4004   E-mail: foundation@ena.org
Web: www.ena.org/foundation/grants

Summary To provide financial assistance to members of the Emergency Nurses Association (ENA) who are working on an advanced clinical practice degree.

Eligibility This program is open to emergency nurses who are working on an advanced practice degree in nursing. Applicants must have been members of the association for at least 12 months. They must submit a 1-page statement on their professional and educational goals and how this scholarship will help them attain those goals. Selection is based on content and clarity of the goal statement (45%), professional involvement (45%), and GPA (10%).

Financial data The stipend is $5,000.

Duration 1 year.

Number awarded 2 each year.

Deadline May of each year.

[196]
ENA FOUNDATION FACULTY MEMORIAL DOCTORAL SCHOLARSHIP

Emergency Nurses Association
Attn: ENA Foundation
915 Lee Street
Des Plaines, IL 60016-6569
(847) 460-4100   Toll-free: (800) 900-9659, ext. 4100
Fax: (847) 460-4004   E-mail: foundation@ena.org
Web: www.ena.org/foundation/grants

Summary To provide financial assistance for doctoral study to nurses who are members of the Emergency Nurses Association (ENA).

Eligibility This program is open to nurses (R.N.) who are working on a doctoral degree to prepare for a career as a faculty member at a college of nursing. Applicants must have been members of the association for at least 12 months. They must submit a 1-page statement on their professional and educational goals and how this scholarship will help them attain those goals. Selection is based on content and clarity of the goal statement (45%), professional association involvement (45%), and GPA (10%).

Financial data The stipend is $6,000.

Duration 1 year; nonrenewable.

Number awarded 1 each year.

Deadline May of each year.

[197]
ENDODONTIC EDUCATOR FELLOWSHIP AWARDS

American Association of Endodontists
Attn: AAE Foundation
211 East Chicago Avenue, Suite 1100
Chicago, IL 60611-2691
(312) 266-7255, ext. 3008   Toll-free: (800) 872-3636
Fax: (312) 266-9867   E-mail: info@aae.org
Web: www.aae.org/foundation/grants_awards/eefa

Summary To provide financial assistance to dental students who are interested in an academic career in endodontics.

Eligibility This program is open to 1) first- and second-year students who have been accepted into or are enrolled in an advanced specialty education program in endodontics at an accredited dental school; and 2) students who have completed an advanced specialty education program in endodontics at an accredited dental school and now wish to further their education through a master's or doctoral degree or postdoctoral training. All applicants must commit to a career in endodontic education on a full-time basis. Along with their application, they must submit an essay on their interest in an academic career and the reasons they are applying for the fellowship.

Financial data Fellows receive tuition plus a stipend of $2,500 per month for living expenses. They must agree to teach full time within 3 months after graduation for at least 5 years at an accredited dental school.

Duration Up to 3 years.

Additional information This program was established in 2000.

Number awarded Up to 4 each year.

Deadline November of each year.

[198]
ENDOWMENT FOR SOUTH ASIAN STUDENTS OF INDIAN DESCENT

Pennsylvania Medical Society
Attn: Foundation
777 East Park Drive
P.O. Box 8820
Harrisburg, PA 17105-8820
(717) 558-7854   Toll-free: (800) 228-7823 (within PA)
Fax: (717) 558-7818
E-mail: studentservices-foundation@pamedsoc.org
Web: www.foundationpamedsoc.org

Summary To provide financial assistance to south Asian residents of Pennsylvania who are enrolled in medical school in the state.

Eligibility This program is open to South Asian Indians or descendants of South Asian Indian immigrants to the United States who have been Pennsylvania residents for at least 12 months. Applicants must be enrolled full time in the second, third, or fourth year at an accredited allopathic or osteopathic medical school in Pennsylvania. They must submit a 1-page essay explaining why they chose to become a physician and what contributions they expect to make to the health profession. Financial need is considered in the selection process.

Financial data The stipend is $1,500. Funds are paid directly to the recipient's medical school through the appropriate channels.

Duration 1 year.

Additional information These scholarships were first awarded in 2003.

Number awarded 1 each year.

Deadline September of each year.

[199]
EPOC SCHOLARSHIP FUND

Environmental Professionals' Organization of Connecticut
Attn: Executive Director
P.O. Box 176
Amston, CT 06231-0176
(860) 228-2492   Fax: (860) 228-4902
E-mail: sjm@epoc.org
Web: www.epoc.org

Summary To provide financial assistance to upper-division and graduate students from Connecticut interested in preparing for a career as an environmental professional.

Eligibility This program is open to Connecticut residents who are preparing for a career as an environmental professional in the state. Applicants must be enrolled as juniors, seniors, or graduate students, but their college or university may be in any state. They must be majoring in a relevant field, including biology, chemistry, earth science, ecology, engineering (agricultural, chemical, civil, environmental, mechanical), environmental science, environmental studies, geology, hydrogeology, hydrology, natural resource management, soil sciences, toxicology, water resources, and wetland science. Along with their application, they must submit an essay of 400 to 500 words on their reasons for choosing their major, what they expect from a career in that field of study, and why this scholarship is important to them. Financial need is not considered in the selection process.

Financial data A stipend is awarded (amount not specified).

Duration 1 year.

Additional information This program was established in 1998. Information is also available from John Figurelli, Scholarship Fund Committee Chair, (860) 513-1473, E-mail: figurelj@wseinc.com.

Number awarded Varies each year; recently, 2 of these scholarships were awarded.

Deadline April of each year.

[200]
ERIC DELSON MEMORIAL SCHOLARSHIP

Caremark Rx, Inc.
Attn: Heather Post
211 Commerce Street. Suite 800
Nashville, TN 37201
Toll-free: (866) 792-2731
Web: www.caremark.com

Summary To provide financial assistance for college or graduate school to students with clinical hemophilia.

Eligibility Students diagnosed with clinical hemophilia are eligible to apply for this program if they are 1) high school seniors, high school graduates, college students, or graduate students currently enrolled or planning to enroll in an accredited 2-year or 4-year college, university, vocational/technical school, or graduate school; or 2) students entering grades 7-12 at a private secondary school in the United States. This program is not open to students with related blood disorders (e.g., von Willebrand Disease). Selection is based on academic record, potential to succeed, leadership, participation in school and community activities, honors, work experience, statement of educational and career goals, recommendations, and unusual personal or family circumstances.

Financial data The stipend is $2,500 or $1,500. Funds are paid in 2 equal installments directly to the recipient.

Duration 1 year; may be renewed for up to 3 additional years, provided the recipient maintains a 3.0 GPA.

Number awarded 4 each year: 3 at $2,500 per year and 1 at $1,500 per year.

Deadline June of each year.

[201]
ESA FOUNDATION GRADUATE STUDY SCHOLARSHIP

Epsilon Sigma Alpha
Attn: ESA Foundation Assistant Scholarship Director
P.O. Box 270517
Fort Collins, CO 80527
(970) 223-2824   Fax: (970) 223-4456
Web: www.esaintl.com/esaf

Summary To provide financial assistance for graduate school to students from any state studying any major.

Eligibility This program is open to students attending an accredited school in the United States with a GPA of 3.5 or higher. Applicants may be majoring in any field. Along with their application, they must submit a 1-page statement on their program of studies and how they will benefit the community in their field. Selection is based on character (20%), leadership (20%), service (20%), financial need (20%), and scholastic ability (20%).

Financial data The stipend is $7,500.

Duration 1 year.

Additional information Epsilon Sigma Alpha (ESA) is a women's service organization, but scholarships are available to both men and women. Information is also available from Lynn Hughes, Scholarship Director, 324 N.E. Mead, Grants Pass, OR 97526, (541) 476-4617, E-mail: orcycler@vsisp.net. Completed applications must be submitted to the ESA State Counselor who verifies the information before forwarding them to the scholarship director. A $5 processing fee is required.

Number awarded 2 each year.

Deadline January of each year.

[202]
ESTELLE MASSEY OSBORNE SCHOLARSHIP

Nurses Educational Funds, Inc.
Attn: Scholarship Coordinator
304 Park Avenue South, 11th Floor
New York, NY 10010
(212) 590-2443   Fax: (212) 590-2446
E-mail: info@n-e-f.org
Web: www.n-e-f.org

Summary To provide financial assistance to African Americans interested in earning a master's degree in nursing.

Eligibility This program is open to African American registered nurses who are members of a national professional nursing organization and enrolled in or applying to an accredited master's degree program in nursing. Applicants must submit a 2-page essay on their professional goals and potential for making a contribution to the nursing profession. They must be U.S. citizens or have declared their official intention of becoming a citizen. Selection is based on academic excellence and potential for contributing to the nursing profession.

Financial data Stipends range from $2,500 to $10,000, depending on the availability of funds.

Duration 1 year; nonrenewable.

Additional information Awards are for full-time study only. There is a $20 application fee.

Number awarded 1 each year.

Deadline February of each year.

[203]
ESTHER MAYO SHERARD SCHOLARSHIP

American Health Information Management Association
Attn: Foundation of Research and Education
233 North Michigan Avenue, Suite 2150
Chicago, IL 60601-5806
(312) 233-1131   Fax: (312) 233-1431
E-mail: fore@ahima.org
Web: www.ahima.org/fore/student/programs.asp

Summary To provide financial assistance to African American members of the American Health Information Management Association (AHIMA) who are interested in working on an undergraduate or graduate degree in health information administration or technology.

Eligibility This program is open to AHIMA members who are African Americans enrolled in a health information administration or health information technology program accredited by the Commission on Accreditation of Allied Health Education Programs. Applicants must be working on an undergraduate or graduate degree on at least a half-time basis and have a GPA of 3.0 or higher. U.S. citizenship is required. Selection is based (in order of importance) on GPA and academic achievement, volunteer and work experience, commitment to the health information management profession, suitability to the health information management profession, quality and suitability of references provided, and clarity of application.

Financial data The stipend ranges from $1,000 to $5,000.

Duration 1 year; nonrenewable.

Additional information This program was established in 2000 by the Esther Mayo Sherard Foundation.

Number awarded 1 each year.

Deadline April of each year.

[204]
E.U. PARKER SCHOLARSHIP

National Federation of the Blind
c/o Peggy Elliott, Scholarship Committee Chair
805 Fifth Avenue
Grinnell, IA 50112
(641) 236-3366
Web: www.nfb.org/sch_intro.htm

Summary To provide financial assistance to blind undergraduate and graduate students.

Eligibility This program is open to legally blind students who are working on or planning to work full time on an undergraduate or graduate degree. Selection is based on academic excellence, service to the community, and financial need.

Financial data The stipend is $3,000.

Duration 1 year; recipients may resubmit applications up to 2 additional years.

Additional information Scholarships are awarded at the federation convention in July. Recipients attend the convention at federation expense; that funding is in addition to the scholarship grant.

Number awarded 1 each year.

Deadline March of each year.

[205]
EUGENE AND ELINOR KOTUR SCHOLARSHIP TRUST FUND

Ukrainian Fraternal Association
Attn: Scholarship Program
371 North Ninth Avenue
Scranton, PA 18504-2005
(570) 342-0937   Fax: (570) 347-5649
Web: members.tripod.com/~ufa_home

Summary To provide financial assistance to currently-enrolled undergraduate and graduate students at selected schools who are of Ukrainian heritage.

Eligibility This program is open to students of Ukrainian ancestry who are currently enrolled in an undergraduate (freshman year excepted) or graduate program of study at 1 of the following colleges or universities: Brown University, California Institute of Technology, Carnegie Mellon, Connecticut University, Cornell University, Dartmouth College, Duke University, George Washington University, Harvard University, Haverford University, Indiana University, John Hopkins University, Massachusetts Institute of Technology, McGill University, Michigan State University, Yale University, Notre Dame University, Oberlin College, Purdue University, Princeton University, Rochester University, Swarthmore College, Tulane University, University of California at Berkeley or Los Angeles, University of Chicago, University of Michigan, University of Pennsylvania, University of Toronto, University of Washington, University of Wisconsin, Vanderbilt University, or Williams College. As part of the application process, students must submit a short autobiography, a photograph, and a copy of their latest transcripts. Selection is based on financial need and academic record.

Financial data The amount of the scholarship varies, depending upon the needs of the recipient. However, each award is at least $1,000. Funds are paid directly to the recipient.

Duration 1 year.

Additional information The Ukrainian Fraternal Association is the first fraternal organization in the United States and Canada to grant outright student stipends.

Number awarded Varies each year.

Deadline May of each year.

[206]
FAR WEST ATHLETIC TRAINERS' ASSOCIATION GRADUATE SCHOLARSHIPS

Far West Athletic Trainers' Association
c/o Jason Bennett, Scholarship Chair
Chapman University
1 University Drive
Orange, CA 92866
(714) 997-6567   E-mail: jbennett@chapman.edu
Web: www.fwata.org/com_scholarships.html

Summary To provide financial assistance to members of the National Athletic Trainers Association (NATA) who are working on a graduate degree in its District 8.

Eligibility This program is open to students enrolled as graduate students at colleges and universities in California, Guam, Hawaii, or Nevada who are preparing for a career as an athletic trainer. Applicants must be student members of NATA and a District 8 member of NATA working on a master's or doctoral degree in athletic training. They must have a GPA of 3.0 or higher and a record of distinction in their athletic training program, academic major, institution, intercollegiate athletics, and higher education. Along with their application, they must submit a statement on their athletic training background, experience, philosophy, and goals. Financial need is not considered in the selection process. Applications are accepted from graduating college seniors as well as students already enrolled in a graduate program.

Financial data The stipend is $1,000.

Duration 1 year.

Additional information FWATA serves as District 8 of NATA. This program includes the following scholarships: the FWATA Hall of Fame Memorial Scholarship and the National Academy of Sports Medicine Scholarship.

Number awarded 2 each year.

Deadline February.

[207]
FEDERATION OF JEWISH WOMEN'S ORGANIZATION SCHOLARSHIP

Alexander Graham Bell Association for the Deaf
Attn: Financial Aid Coordinator
3417 Volta Place, N.W.
Washington, DC 20007-2778
(202) 337-5220   Fax: (202) 337-8314
TTY: (202) 337-5221   E-mail: financialaid@agbell.org
Web: www.agbell.org

Summary To provide financial assistance to undergraduate and graduate students with moderate to profound hearing loss.

Eligibility This program is open to undergraduate and graduate students who have been diagnosed with a moderate to profound hearing loss prior to acquiring spoken language (hearing loss averages 60dB or greater in the better ear in the speech frequencies of 500, 1000, and 2000 Hz). Applicants must be committed to using spoken language as their primary mode of communication. They must be accepted or enrolled at a mainstream college or university as a full-time student. Along with their application, they must submit a 1-page essay discussing their career goals and how spoken communication is helping them to reach those goals as a person with a hearing loss. Financial need is considered in the selection process. This scholarship is reserved for students who are hearing impaired.

Financial data The stipend is $2,000 per year.

Duration 1 year; may be renewed 1 additional year.

Number awarded 1 each year.

Deadline April of each year.

[208]
FELICIA C. BRADY SCHOLARSHIP FUND

Black Nurses' Association of Greater Washington, D.C. Area, Inc.
Attn: Scholarship Committee Chair
P.O. Box 1178
Washington, DC 20013
(202) 291-8866   E-mail: v.myers@bnaofgwdca.org
Web: www.bnaofgwdca.org/scholarships.html

Summary To provide financial assistance to registered nurses from the Washington, D.C. area who are interested in working on an advanced degree.

Eligibility This program is open to registered nurses currently enrolled in a bachelor's, master's, or doctoral program. Applicants must submit a copy of their nursing license, an official transcript from their nursing program, 2 letters of recommendation, and a written essay that describes their personal goals and objectives, reasons they should be selected, and their contributions to nursing and the African American community. Selection is based on that essay, participation in student nurses activities and organizations, involvement in the Washington, D.C. metropolitan community, and financial need.

Financial data A stipend is awarded (amount not specified).

Duration 1 year.

Additional information Information is also available from Verna Myers, 604 Nicholson Street, N.E., Washington, DC 20011. The scholarship is presented at the Annual Salute to a Black Nurse and Awards Ceremony.

Number awarded 1 each year.

Deadline December of each year.

[209]
FILIPINO NURSES' ORGANIZATION OF HAWAII SCHOLARSHIP

Hawai'i Community Foundation
Attn: Scholarship Department
1164 Bishop Street, Suite 800
Honolulu, HI 96813
(808) 566-5570   Toll-free: (888) 731-3863
Fax: (808) 521-6286   E-mail: scholarships@hcf-hawaii.org
Web: www.hawaiicommunityfoundation.org

Summary To provide financial assistance to Hawaii residents of Filipino ancestry who are interested in preparing for a career as a nurse.

Eligibility This program is open to Hawaii residents of Filipino ancestry who are interested in studying in Hawaii or the mainland as full-time undergraduate or graduate students and majoring in

nursing. They must be able to demonstrate academic achievement (GPA of 2.7 or higher), good moral character, and financial need. Along with their application, they must submit a short statement indicating their reasons for attending college, their planned course of study, and their career goals.

Financial data The amounts of the awards depend on the availability of funds and the need of the recipient.

Duration 1 year.

Number awarded Varies each year.

Deadline February of each year.

[210]
FINLANDIA FOUNDATION TRUST SCHOLARSHIPS

Finlandia Foundation National
470 West Walnut Street
Pasadena, CA 91103
(626) 795-2081   Fax: (626) 795-6533
E-mail: ffnoffice@mac.com
Web: www.finlandiafoundation.org

Summary To provide financial assistance to undergraduate and graduate students in the United States and Finland.

Eligibility This program is open to citizens of the United States and Finland who have been accepted to an accredited institution of higher learning. Applicants may be full-time undergraduate (sophomore or higher) or graduate students. They must have a GPA of 3.0 or higher. Students majoring in subjects related to Finnish culture receive special consideration. Selection is based on financial need, course of study, and citizenship.

Financial data Stipends range from $500 to $3,000.

Duration 1 year; nonrenewable.

Number awarded 1 or more each year.

Deadline January of each year.

[211]
FLORENCE L. SMITH MEDICAL SCHOLARSHIP

Norfolk Foundation
Attn: Scholarship Administrator
One Commercial Place, Suite 1410
Norfolk, VA 23510-2103
(757) 622-7951   Fax: (757) 622-1751
E-mail: scholarships@norfolkfoundation.org
Web: www.norfolkfoundation.org

Summary To provide financial assistance to Virginia residents working on a medical degree at a school in the state.

Eligibility This program is open to long-time residents of Virginia who are working on medical degree. Applicants must be attending a medical college in Virginia. Financial need must be demonstrated.

Financial data Stipends awarded by the foundation range from $500 to $6,000 and recently averaged $2,670. Funds are sent to the recipient's school and are to be used for tuition, fees, books, and on-campus housing.

Duration 1 year; may be renewed for 1 additional year.

Additional information This is 1 of more than 50 scholarship funds administered by the Norfolk Foundation, which awards approximately 330 scholarships each year worth more than $860,000.

Number awarded 1 or more each year.

Deadline February of each year.

[212]
FLOYD QUALLS MEMORIAL SCHOLARSHIPS

American Council of the Blind
Attn: Coordinator, Scholarship Program
1155 15th Street, N.W., Suite 1004
Washington, DC 20005
(202) 467-5081   Toll-free: (800) 424-8666
Fax: (202) 467-5085   E-mail: info@acb.org
Web: www.acb.org

Summary To provide financial assistance to undergraduate and graduate students who are blind.

Eligibility Students who are legally blind may apply for these scholarships. Recipients are selected in each of 4 categories: entering freshmen in academic programs, undergraduates (sophomores, juniors, and seniors) in academic programs, graduate students in academic programs, and vocational school students or students working on an associate's degree from a community college. In addition to letters of recommendation and copies of academic transcripts, applications must include an autobiographical sketch. A cumulative GPA of 3.3 or higher is generally required. Selection is based on demonstrated academic record, involvement in extracurricular and civic activities, and academic objectives. The severity of the applicant's visual impairment and his/her study methods are also taken into account.

Financial data The stipend is $2,500. In addition, the winners receive a Kurzweil-1000 Reading System.

Duration 1 year.

Additional information Scholarship winners are expected to be present at the council's annual conference; the council will cover all reasonable expenses connected with convention attendance.

Number awarded Up to 8 each year: 2 in each of the 4 categories.

Deadline February of each year.

[213]
FOCUS PROFESSIONS GROUP FELLOWSHIPS

American Association of University Women
Attn: AAUW Educational Foundation
301 ACT Drive, Department 60
P.O. Box 4030
Iowa City, IA 52243-4030
(319) 337-1716   Fax: (319) 337-1204
E-mail: aauw@act.org
Web: www.aauw.org/fga/fellowships_grants/selected.cfm

Summary To aid women of color who are in their final year of graduate training in the fields of business administration, law, or medicine.

Eligibility This program is open to women of color who are entering their final year of graduate study in these historically underrepresented fields: business administration (M.B.A., E.M.B.A.), law (J.D.), or medicine (M.D., D.O.). Women in medical programs may apply for either their third or final year of study. U.S. citizenship or permanent resident status is required. Special consideration is given to 1) applicants who demonstrate their intent to enter professional practice in disciplines in which women are underrepresented, to serve underserved populations and communities, or to pursue public interest areas; and 2) to applicants who are nontraditional students. Selection is based on professional promise and personal attributes (50%), academic excellence and related academic success indicators (40%), and financial need (10%).

Financial data Stipends range from $5,000 to $12,000 for the academic year.

Duration 1 academic year, beginning in September.

Additional information The filing fee is $35.

Number awarded Varies each year.

Deadline January of each year.

[214]
FORD MOTOR COMPANY ASSE SCHOLARSHIPS

American Society of Safety Engineers
Attn: ASSE Foundation
1800 East Oakton Street
Des Plaines, IL 60018
(847) 768-3435   Fax: (847) 768-3434
E-mail: agabanski@asse.org
Web: www.asse.org/foundation

Summary To provide financial assistance to female upper-division and graduate student members of the American Society of Safety Engineers (ASSE) who are working on a degree in occupational health and related fields.

Eligibility This program is open to female ASSE student members who are working on an undergraduate or graduate degree in occupational safety, health, and environment or a closely-related field (e.g., industrial or environmental engineering, environmental science, industrial hygiene, occupational health nursing). Undergraduates must be full-time students who have completed at least 60 semester hours with a GPA of 3.0 or higher. Graduate students must also be enrolled full time, have completed at least 9 semester hours with a GPA of 3.5 or higher, and have had a GPA of 3.0 or higher as an undergraduate. Along with their application, they must submit 2 essays of 300 words or less: 1) why they are seeking a degree in occupational safety and health or a closely-related field, a brief description of their current activities, and how those relate to their career goals and objectives; and 2) why they should be awarded this scholarship (including career goals and financial need).

Financial data The stipend is $3,450.

Duration 1 year; nonrenewable.

Additional information This program is supported by the Ford Motor Company.

Number awarded 4 each year.

Deadline November of each year.

[215]
FORE DIVERSITY SCHOLARSHIPS

American Health Information Management Association
Attn: Foundation of Research and Education
233 North Michigan Avenue, Suite 2150
Chicago, IL 60601-5806
(312) 233-1131   Fax: (312) 233-1431
E-mail: fore@ahima.org
Web: www.ahima.org/fore/student/programs.asp

Summary To provide financial assistance to minority members of the American Health Information Management Association (AHIMA) who are interested in working on an undergraduate or graduate degree in health information administration or technology.

Eligibility This program is open to AHIMA members who are enrolled in a health information administration or health information technology program accredited by the Commission on Accreditation of Allied Health Education Programs. Applicants must be minorities, be working on an undergraduate or graduate degree on at least a half-time basis, and have a GPA of 3.0 or higher. U.S. citizenship is required. Selection is based (in order of importance) on GPA and academic achievement, volunteer and work experience, commitment to the health information management profession, suitability to the health information management profession, quality and suitability of references provided, and clarity of application.

Financial data Stipends range from $1,000 to $5,000.

Duration 1 year; nonrenewable.

Number awarded Varies each year. Recently, 9 of these scholarships were awarded.

Deadline April of each year.

[216]
FORE GRADUATE MERIT SCHOLARSHIPS

American Health Information Management Association
Attn: Foundation of Research and Education
233 North Michigan Avenue, Suite 2150
Chicago, IL 60601-5806
(312) 233-1131   Fax: (312) 233-1431
E-mail: fore@ahima.org
Web: www.ahima.org/fore/student/programs.asp

Summary To provide financial assistance to graduate student members of the American Health Information Management Association (AHIMA) who are interested in working on a degree in health information management.

Eligibility This program is open to graduate students who are credentialed health information management professionals (RHIA, RHIT, or CCS), hold a bachelor's degree, are enrolled in a college or university accredited by a nationally-recognized accrediting agency, are active or associate members of the association, are full-time students, and are working on at least a master's degree in a program related to health information management (computer science, business management, education, public health, etc.). They must submit a 1-page essay describing how the degree on which they are working will help them to advance the health information management field. U.S. citizenship and a GPA of 3.0 or higher are also required. Selection is based (in order of importance) on GPA and academic achievement, volunteer and work experience, commitment to the health information management profession, suitability to the health information management profession, quality and suitability of references provided, and clarity of application.

Financial data Stipends range from $1,000 to $5,000.

Duration 1 year; nonrenewable.

Additional information This program includes the following named scholarships (not all of which may be offered each year): the David A. Cohen Scholarship (established in 2004), the Jimmy Gamble Memorial Scholarship (established in 2001 and sponsored by 3M Health Information Systems), the Lucretia Spears Scholarship (established in 1998), the Julia LeBlond Memorial Graduate Scholarships (sponsored by Ingenix Companies), the Rita Finnegan Memorial Scholarship (established in 2001 and sponsored by MC Strategies, Inc.), the Connie Marshall Memorial Scholarship (established in 2004 and sponsored by MedQuist Inc.), and the Linda Culp Memorial Scholarship.

Number awarded Varies each year; recently, 17 of these scholarships were awarded.

Deadline April of each year.

[217]
FOSTER G. MCGAW STUDENT SCHOLARSHIP

American College of Healthcare Executives
One North Franklin Street, Suite 1700
Chicago, IL 60606-3529
(312) 424-2800   Fax: (312) 424-0023
E-mail: ache@ache.org
Web: www.ache.org

Summary To provide financial assistance to graduate student members of the American College of Healthcare Executives (ACHE).

Eligibility This program is open to ACHE student associates entering their final year of didactic work in a health care management graduate program. Applicants must be enrolled full time, able to demonstrate financial need, and U.S. or Canadian citizens. Along with their application, they must submit an 800-word essay describing their leadership abilities and experiences, their community and volunteer involvement, their goals as a health care executive, and how this scholarship can help them achieve their career goals.

Financial data The stipend is $3,500.

Duration 1 year; nonrenewable.

Number awarded Varies each year.

Deadline March of each year.

[218]
FOUNDATION FOR NEONATAL RESEARCH AND EDUCATION SCHOLARSHIPS

Academy of Neonatal Nursing
Attn: Foundation for Neonatal Research and Education
200 East Holly Avenue
P.O. Box 56
Pitman, NJ 08071-0056
(856) 256-2343   Fax: (856) 589-7463
E-mail: FNRE@ajj.com
Web: www.inurse.com/fnre/scholarship.htm

Summary To provide financial assistance to neonatal nurses interested in working on a degree.

Eligibility Applicants must be professionally active neonatal nurses, engaged in a service, research, or educational role that contributes directly to the health care of neonates or to the neonatal nursing profession. They must be an active member of a professional association dedicated to enhancing neonatal nursing and the care of neonates. Participation in ongoing professional education in neonatal nursing must be demonstrated by at least 10 contact hours in neonatal content over the past 24 months. Qualified nurses must have been admitted to a college or school of higher education to work on 1 of the following: bachelor of science in nursing, master of science in nursing for advanced practice in neonatal nursing, doctoral degree in nursing, or master's or postmaster's degree in nursing administration or business management. They must have a GPA of 3.0 or higher. Along with their application, they must submit a 250-word statement on how they plan to make a significant difference in neonatal nursing practice. Financial need is not considered in the selection process.

Financial data The stipends are $1,500 or $1,000.

Duration 1 year.

Additional information The Foundation for Neonatal Research and Education was established in 1992 by the National Association of Neonatal Nurses (NANN), 2270 Northpoint Parkway, Santa Rosa, CA 95407, (707) 568-2168. Originally housed at the NANN office, it moved to its current location in 1998. This program includes the Matthew Hester Memorial Scholarship, sponsored by Anthony J. Jannetti, Inc.

Number awarded The Matthew Hester Scholarship of $1,500 and several scholarships at $1,000 (the exact number depending on the availability of funds) are awarded each year.

Deadline April of each year.

[219]
FOUNDATION FOR PHYSICAL THERAPY PROMOTION OF DOCTORAL STUDIES PROGRAM

American Physical Therapy Association
Attn: Foundation for Physical Therapy
1111 North Fairfax Street
Alexandria, VA 22314-1488
(703) 706-8906   Toll-free: (800) 875-1378
Fax: (703) 706-8519   TDD: (703) 683-6748
E-mail: foundation@apta.org
Web: www.apta.org

Summary To provide financial assistance for doctoral training to members of the American Physical Therapy Association.

Eligibility This program is open to members of the association who are 1) licensed physical therapists or eligible for licensure; 2) U.S. citizens, noncitizen nationals, or permanent residents; 3) enrolled in an accredited postprofessional doctoral program with a demonstrated relationship to physical therapy; and 4) able to demonstrate a commitment to further the physical therapy profession through teaching and research in the United States and its territories. Applicants for first-level awards must have completed at least 1 year of graduate study and be seeking funding to continue course work; applicants for second-level awards must have been admitted to candidacy for the Ph.D. and be seeking funding to work on their dissertation. Selection is based on 1) the objectives in the applicant's plan for development of an academically-based research career; 2) the significance of the total experience and its potential impact on teaching and research; and 3) the mentor, facilities, and resources available to the applicant to support the career development plan.

Financial data First-level awards are up to $7,500 per year for support of the course work phase of postprofessional doctoral studies; second-level awards are up to $15,000 per year for support of the postcandidacy phase of postprofessional doctoral studies. Funds are paid directly to the scholarship recipient.

Duration 1 year; first-level awards may be renewed for up to 2 additional years; second-level awards may be renewed for up to 1 additional year.

Additional information From among the applicants to either level this program, 1 is selected to receive the Viva J. Erickson Scholarship for their academic leadership. The Patricia Leahy Scholarship is awarded to an applicant for a first-level award interested in doctoral study in neurology. The Marylou Barnes Scholarship is awarded to an applicant for a second-level award interested in doctoral study in neurology.

Number awarded Varies each year; recently, 7 first-level awards and 7 second-level awards were presented.

Deadline January of each year.

[220]
FRANK AND FLORENCE MARINO SCHOLARSHIPS

Hartford Foundation for Public Giving
85 Gillett Street
Hartford, CT 06105
(860) 548-1888   Fax: (860) 524-8346
E-mail: hfpg@hfpg.org
Web: www.hfpg.org

Summary To provide financial assistance for medical school to Connecticut residents.

Eligibility This program is open to students at medical schools anywhere in the United States who attended Connecticut schools for at least 8 years and graduated from a public or parochial high school in the state. Selection is based on academic record and financial need.

Financial data The stipend is at least $1,000 per year.

Duration 1 year; may be renewed.

Additional information Information is also available from Mrs. Rita Fry, P.O. Box 75, Brookfield, CT 06804.

Number awarded Varies each year.

Deadline April of each year.

[221]
FRED SCHEIGERT SCHOLARSHIPS

Council of Citizens with Low Vision International
c/o Pat Beattie, President
906 North Chambliss Street
Alexandria, VA 22312-3005
(703) 578-6513   Toll-free: (800) 733-2258
Fax: (703) 671-9053   E-mail: pbeattie@nib.org
Web: www.cclvi.org/scholarship.html

Summary To provide financial assistance to undergraduate and graduate students with low vision.

Eligibility Applicants must be certified by an ophthalmologist as having low vision (acuity of 20/70 or worse in the better seeing eye with best correction or side vision with a maximum diameter of no greater than 30 degrees). They may be part-time or full-time entering freshmen, undergraduates, or graduate students. A cumulative GPA of at least 3.0 is required.

Financial data The stipend is $1,000.

Duration 1 year.

Additional information Information is also available from Imogene Johnson, 5311 "B" Street, Little Rock, AR 72205-3509.

Number awarded 2 each year.

Deadline April of each year.

[222]
FULFILLING OUR DREAMS SCHOLARSHIP PROGRAM

Salvadoran American Leadership and Educational Fund
Attn: Education and Youth Programs Manager
1625 West Olympic Boulevard, Suite 718
Los Angeles, CA 90015
(213) 480-1052   Fax: (213) 487-2530
E-mail: info@salef.org
Web: www.salef.org/Scholarships.html

Summary To provide financial assistance for college and graduate school to Salvadoran Americans and other Americans of Hispanic descent.

Eligibility This program is open to high school seniors and graduates who have been accepted at a 4-year university, undergraduates in 2- and 4-year colleges and universities, and graduate students. Applicants do not need to provide proof of documented immigrant status, but they must be of Salvadoran, Central American, or other Latino background. Along with their application, they must submit a 800-word statement on their goals, aspirations, and ambitions, including short- and long-term goals; their background, family history, upbringing experiences, and obstacles confronted; leadership involvement, how they have contributed to their community, and their plans after graduation; and why they chose their field of study. They must be able to demonstrate financial need, have a GPA of at least 2.5, and have a history of community service and involvement. An interview may be required.

Financial data Stipends range from $500 to $2,500.

Duration 1 year; nonrenewable.

Additional information This program began in 1998. Recipients are paired with a professional in their field of study who serves as a mentor, providing moral support and direction. Funding for this program comes from the Bank of America Foundation and the Los Angeles Department of Water and Power.

Number awarded Approximately 50 each year.

Deadline June of each year.

[223]
GALA SCHOLARSHIPS

American Association of Nurse Anesthetists
Attn: AANA Foundation
222 South Prospect Avenue
Park Ridge, IL 60068-4001
(847) 692-7050, ext. 1171   Fax: (847) 692-7137
E-mail: foundation@aana.com
Web: www.aana.com/foundation/default.asp

Summary To provide financial assistance to members of the American Association of Nurse Anesthetists (AANA) who are interested in obtaining further education.

Eligibility This program is open to members of the association who are currently enrolled in an accredited nurse anesthesia education program. Gay and lesbian people are encouraged to apply. First-year students must have completed 6 months of nurse anesthesia classes; second-year students must have completed 12 months of nurse anesthesia classes. Along with their application, they must submit a 200-word essay describing why they have chosen nurse anesthesia as a profession and their professional goals for the future. Financial need is also considered in the selection process.

Financial data The stipend is $1,000 per year.

Duration 1 academic year.

Additional information The application processing fee is $25.

Number awarded 3 each year.

Deadline March of each year.

[224]
GALDERMA LABORATORIES CAREER MOBILITY SCHOLARSHIPS

Dermatology Nurses' Association
c/o A.J. Jannetti, Inc.
200 East Holly Avenue
P.O. Box 56
Pitman, NJ 08071-0056
(856) 256-2330   Toll-free: (800) 454-4DNA
Fax: (856) 589-7463   E-mail: dna@ajj.com
Web: www.dnanurse.org

Summary To provide financial assistance to members of the Dermatology Nurses' Association (DNA) who are working on an undergraduate or graduate degree.

Eligibility Applicants for these scholarships must 1) have been members of the association for at least 2 years, 2) be employed in the specialty of dermatology, and 3) be working on a degree or advanced degree in nursing. Selection is based on a letter in which applicants describe their professional goals, proposed course of study, time frame for completion of study, funds necessary to meet their educational goals, and financial need.

Financial data The stipend is $2,500.

Duration 1 year.

Additional information Funding for this program is provided by Galderma Laboratories.

Number awarded 1 each year.

Deadline September of each year.

[225]
GARDNER FOUNDATION INS EDUCATION SCHOLARSHIP

Infusion Nursing Society
Attn: Gardner Foundation
220 Norwood Park South
Norwood, MA 02062
(781) 440-9408, ext. 317   E-mail: chris.hunt@ins1.org
Web: www.ins1.org/gardner/scholarship_ins_edu.html

Summary To provide financial assistance to members of the Infusion Nursing Society (INS) who are interested in continuing education.

Eligibility This program is open to INS members interested in a program of continuing education, including working on a college or graduate degree or attending a professional meeting or seminar. Applicants must demonstrate how the continuing education activity will enhance their infusion career, describe their professional goals, and explain how the scholarship will be used.

Financial data The stipend is $1,000.

Duration This is a 1-time award.

Number awarded 2 each year.

Deadline February of each year.

[226]
GATES MILLENNIUM GRADUATE SCHOLARS PROGRAM

Bill and Melinda Gates Foundation
P.O. Box 10500
Fairfax, VA 22031-8044
Toll-free: (877) 690-GMSP   Fax: (703) 205-2079
Web: www.gmsp.org

Summary To provide financial assistance for graduate studies in selected subject areas to outstanding low-income minority students.

Eligibility This program is open to low-income African Americans, Native Alaskans, American Indians, Hispanic Americans, and Asian Pacific Islander Americans who are nominated by a professional educator. Nominees must be U.S. citizens who are enrolled or about to enroll in graduate school to work on a graduate degree in engineering, mathematics, science, education, public health, or library science. They must have a GPA of 3.3 or higher, be able to demonstrate significant financial need, and have demonstrated leadership commitment through participation in community service (i.e., mentoring/tutoring, volunteer work in social service organizations, and involvement in church initiatives), extracurricular activities (student government and athletics), or other activities that reflect leadership abilities.

Financial data The program covers the full cost of graduate study: tuition, fees, books, and living expenses not paid for by grants and scholarships already committed as part of the recipient's financial aid package.

Duration Up to 4 years (up to and including the doctorate), if the recipient maintains at least a 3.0 GPA.

Additional information This program, established in 1999, is funded by the Bill and Melinda Gates Foundation and administered by the United Negro College Fund with support from the American Indian Graduate Center, the Hispanic Scholarship Fund, and the Organization of Chinese Americans.

Number awarded Under the Gates Millennium Scholars Program, a total of 4,000 students receive support each year.

Deadline January of each year.

[227]
GE HEALTHCARE MANAGEMENT SCHOLARSHIP PROGRAM

American Society of Radiologic Technologists
Attn: ASRT Education and Research Foundation
15000 Central Avenue, S.E.
Albuquerque, NM 87123-3909
(505) 298-4500, ext. 2541
Toll-free: (800) 444-2778, ext. 2541   Fax: (505) 298-5063
E-mail: foundation@asrt.org
Web: www.asrt.org

Summary To provide financial assistance to members of the American Society of Radiologic Technologists (ASRT) who are interested in working on a masters' degree or higher in a field related to management.

Eligibility This program is open to licensed radiologic technologists who are current members of ASRT and have worked in the radiologic sciences profession for at least 1 year during the past 5 years in a clinical or didactic setting. Applicants must be interested in working on a master's degree or higher in a field related to management (e.g., business administration, health care administration). Along with their application, they must submit a written interview up to 1,000 words on their professional achievements, career goals, how their degree or certificate helps them achieve their career goals, their educational goals, and how this scholarship will help them to achieve their educational goals. Financial need is considered in the selection process.

Financial data The stipend is $5,000.

Duration 1 year; recipients may reapply but they may receive this scholarship only twice.

Additional information This program is supported by GE Healthcare.

Number awarded Varies each year; recently, 2 of these scholarships were awarded.

Deadline January of each year.

[228]
GEM PH.D. SCIENCE FELLOWSHIP PROGRAM

National Consortium for Graduate Degrees for Minorities in
   Engineering and Science (GEM)
P.O. Box 537
Notre Dame, IN 46556
(574) 631-7771   Fax: (574) 287-1486
E-mail: gem.1@nd.edu
Web: www.gemfellowship.org

Summary To provide financial assistance and summer work experience to underrepresented minority students interested in working on a Ph.D. degree in the life sciences, mathematics, or physical sciences.

Eligibility This program is open to U.S. citizens who are members of ethnic groups underrepresented in the natural sciences: Native Americans, African Americans, Latinos, Puerto Ricans, and other Hispanic Americans. Applicants must be juniors, seniors, or recent baccalaureate graduates in the life sciences, mathematics, or physical sciences (chemistry, computer science, earth sciences, and physics) with an academic record that indicates the ability to pursue doctoral studies (including a GPA of 3.0 or higher).

Financial data The stipend is $14,000 per year, plus tuition and fees. In addition, there is a summer internship program that provides a salary and reimbursement for travel expenses to and from the summer work site. The total value of the award is between $60,000 and $100,000, depending upon academic status at the time of application, summer employer, and graduate school attended.

Duration 3 to 5 years for the fellowship; 12 weeks during at least 1 summer for the internship. Fellows selected as juniors or seniors intern each summer until entrance to graduate school; fellows selected after college graduation intern at least 1 summer.

Additional information This program is valid only at 1 of 95 participating GEM member universities; write to GEM for a list. The fellowship award is designed to support the student in the first year of the doctoral program without working. Subsequent years are subsidized by the respective university and will usually include either a teaching or research assistantship. Recipients must participate in the GEM summer internship; failure to agree to accept the internship cancels the fellowship. Recipients must enroll in the same scientific discipline as their undergraduate major.

Number awarded Varies each year; recently, 40 of these fellowships were awarded.

Deadline October of each year.

[229]
GEORGE B. BOLAND ADVANCED DEGREE PROGRAM OF NURSING EDUCATION

National Forty and Eight
Attn: Voiture Nationale
777 North Meridian Street
Indianapolis, IN 46204-1170
(317) 634-1804   Fax: (317) 632-9365
E-mail: voiturenationale@msn.com
Web: fortyandeight.org/40_8programs.htm

Summary To provide financial assistance to students working on an advanced degree in nursing.

Eligibility This program is open to students working full time on an advanced degree in nursing. Applications must be submitted to the local Voiture of the Forty and Eight in the county of student's permanent residence; if the county organization has exhausted all of its nurses training funds, it will provide the student with an application for this scholarship. Students who are receiving assistance from the Eight and Forty Lung and Respiratory Disease Nursing Scholarship Program of the American Legion are not eligible. Financial need must be demonstrated.

Financial data Grants may be used to cover tuition, required fees, room and board or similar living expenses, and other school-related expenses.

Additional information National Forty and Eight is the Honor Society of the American Legion. Students may not apply directly to the National Forty and Eight for these scholarships.

Number awarded Varies each year.

[230]
GEORGE EAGLE MEMORIAL GRADUATE SCHOLARSHIP

Ohio Environmental Health Association
Attn: Scholarship Committee Chair
P.O. Box 234
Columbus, OH 43216-0234
Web: oeha.tripod.com/awards.htm

Summary To provide financial assistance to members of the Ohio Environmental Health Association (OEHA) who are interested in working on a graduate degree in the environmental health field.

Eligibility This program is open to OEHA members who are interested in expanding their career in environmental health in Ohio. They must have been a member of the association for 2 years before applying, be a registered sanitarian in Ohio, have at least 3 years of experience in the environmental health field, be enrolled in a graduate program, have a GPA of 3.0 or higher, be willing to be interviewed, and have been working on 1 of the following degrees: M.S.E.S., M.S.E.H., M.E.S.I., M.S.E.P.H., M.P.H., or a related graduate degree in environmental health.

Financial data The stipend is $2,000.

Duration 1 year.

Number awarded 1 each year.

Deadline February of each year.

[231]
GEORGE GUSTAFSON HSE MEMORIAL SCHOLARSHIP

American Society of Safety Engineers
Attn: ASSE Foundation
1800 East Oakton Street
Des Plaines, IL 60018
(847) 768-3435   Fax: (847) 768-3434
E-mail: agabanski@asse.org
Web: www.asse.org/foundation

Summary To provide financial assistance to upper-division and graduate student members of the American Society of Safety Engineers (ASSE), especially those from Texas, who are working on a degree in occupational health and related fields.

Eligibility This program is open to ASSE student members who are working on an undergraduate or graduate degree in occupational safety, health, and environment or a closely-related field (e.g., industrial or environmental engineering, environmental science, industrial hygiene, occupational health nursing). Priority is given to residents of Texas attending a university in the state. Undergraduates must be full-time students who have completed at least 60 semester hours with a GPA of 3.0 or higher. Graduate students must also be enrolled full time, have completed at least 9 semester hours with a GPA of 3.5 or higher, and have had a GPA of 3.0 or higher as an undergraduate. Along with their appli-

cation, they must submit 2 essays of 300 words or less: 1) why they are seeking a degree in occupational safety and health or a closely-related field, a brief description of their current activities, and how those relate to their career goals and objectives; and 2) why they should be awarded this scholarship (including career goals and financial need).

Financial data The stipend is $2,500.

Duration 1 year; nonrenewable.

Additional information This program, established in 2006, is supported by the Texas Safety Foundation.

Number awarded 1 each year.

Deadline November of each year.

[232]
GEORGE HI'ILANI MILLS PERPETUAL FELLOWSHIP AWARD

Ke Ali'i Pauahi Foundation
Attn: Financial Aid & Scholarship Services
567 South King Street, Suite 160
Honolulu, HI 96813
(808) 534-3966   Toll-free: (800) 842-4682, ext. 43966
Fax: (808) 534-3890   E-mail: giving@pauahi.org
Web: www.pauahi.org

Summary To provide financial assistance to Native Hawaiian students who are interested in working on a graduate degree in medicine or allied health.

Eligibility This program is open to Native Hawaiians (descendants of the aboriginal inhabitants of the Hawaiian islands prior to 1778) who are working on a graduate degree in medicine or the allied health-related fields. Applicants must be able to demonstrate financial need. Residency in Hawaii is not required.

Financial data The stipend is $1,500 per year.

Duration 1 year; may be renewed.

Number awarded Varies each year; recently, 2 of these fellowships were awarded.

Deadline May of each year.

[233]
GEORGE HUTCHENS GRADUATE STUDENT SCHOLARSHIP

International Union of Electronic, Electrical, Salaried, Machine, and Furniture Workers
Attn: IUE-CWA International Scholarship Program
501 Third Street, N.W., Suite 975
Washington, DC 20001
(202) 434-1417   Fax: (202) 434-1250
E-mail: bgray@iue-cwa.org
Web: www.iue-cwa.org/skills.html

Summary To provide financial assistance for graduate education to children and grandchildren of members of the International Union of Electronic, Electrical, Salaried, Machine, and Furniture Workers (IUE)-Communications Workers of America (CWA).

Eligibility This program is open to children and grandchildren of members of IUE-CWA (including retired or deceased members). Applicants must be accepted for admission or already enrolled as graduate students at an accredited college or university. Along with their application, they must submit an academic transcript (including rank in class and GPA); a short statement of interests and civic activities; an essay (300 to 500 words) describing their career goals and aspirations, highlighting their relationship with the union and the labor movement, and explaining why they are deserving of a union scholarship. They must also have demonstrated a commitment to equality of opportunity for all, a concern for improving the quality of life for all people, interest in service to the community, good character, leadership ability, and a desire to improve and move ahead.

Financial data The stipend is $1,500 per year.

Duration 1 year.

Additional information This scholarship was first awarded in 1999.

Number awarded 1 each year.

Deadline March of each year.

[234]
GEORGE W. NEIGHBOR, JR. MEMORIAL SCHOLARSHIP

Northeastern Association of Forensic Scientists
c/o Peter Diaczuk, Executive Secretary
John Jay College of Criminal Justice
445 West 59th Street
New York, NY 10019
(212) 237-8896   E-mail: pdiaczuk@jjay.cuny.edu
Web: www.neafs.org/scholarship.htm

Summary To provide financial assistance to upper-division and graduate students working on a degree in forensic science at colleges and universities in designated northeastern states.

Eligibility This program is open to full-time college juniors and seniors and full- or part-time graduate students enrolled in a forensic science or related science program. Applicants must be attending a college or university in Connecticut, Maine, Massachusetts, New Hampshire, New Jersey, New York, Pennsylvania, Rhode Island, or Vermont. Along with their application, they must submit a letter describing their personal goals, achievements, and reasons why they should be considered for this award.

Financial data A stipend is awarded (amount not specified).

Duration 1 year.

Additional information Information is also available from Margaret Lafond, NYSP FIC, State Campus Building 30, 1220 Washington Avenue, Albany, NY 12226-3000.

Number awarded 1 or more each year.

Deadline April of each year.

[235]
GERALD PEETE FELLOWSHIP

American Indian Graduate Center
Attn: Executive Director
4520 Montgomery Boulevard, N.E., Suite 1-B
Albuquerque, NM 87109-1291
(505) 881-4584   Toll-free: (800) 628-1920
Fax: (505) 884-0427   E-mail: aigc@aigc.com
Web: www.aigc.com

Summary To provide financial assistance to Native American students interested in working on a degree in medicine.

Eligibility This program is open to enrolled members of U.S. federally-recognized American Indian tribes and Alaska Native groups and other students who can document one-fourth degree federally-recognized Indian blood. Applicants must be enrolled as full-time students at a medical school in the United States. If insufficient medical school applicants appear, students from other health-related fields are considered. Selection is based on academic achievement, financial need, and an essay on the meaning of their graduate education to the Indian community.

Financial data A stipend is awarded (amount not specified).

Duration 1 year; may be renewed.

Additional information The application fee is $15. Since this a supplemental program, applicants must apply in a timely manner for federal financial aid and campus-based aid at the college they are attending to be considered for this program. Failure to apply will disqualify an applicant.

Number awarded 1 or more each year.

Deadline May of each year.

[236]
GIFT OF HOPE: 21ST CENTURY SCHOLARS PROGRAM

United Methodist Church
Attn: General Board of Higher Education and Ministry
Office of Loans and Scholarships
1001 19th Avenue South
P.O. Box 340007
Nashville, TN 37203-0007
(615) 340-7344   Fax: (615) 340-7367
E-mail: umscholar@gbhem.org
Web: www.gbhem.org/gbhem/loans2.html

Summary To provide financial assistance to undergraduate and graduate Methodist students who can demonstrate leadership in the church.

Eligibility This program is open to full-time undergraduate and graduate students at United Methodist institutions who have been active, full members of a United Methodist Church for at least 3 years prior to applying. Undergraduates must have a GPA of 3.0 or higher; graduate students must have a GPA of 3.5 or higher. Applicants must show evidence of leadership and participation in religious activities during college either through their campus ministry or through local United Methodist churches in the city where their college is located. They must also show how their education will provide leadership for the church and society and improve the quality of life for others. U.S. citizenship, permanent resident status, or membership in the Central Conferences of the United Methodist Church is required. Financial need is considered in the selection process.

Financial data The stipend is $1,000.

Duration 1 year; recipients may reapply.

Additional information This program was established in 1999.

Number awarded Varies each year; recently, 1,000 of these scholarships were awarded.

Deadline April of each year.

[237]
GILBERT RIOS MEMORIAL AWARD

Los Padres Foundation
P.O. Box 8421
McLean, VA 22106
Toll-free: (877) 843-7555   Fax: (866) 810-1361
E-mail: lpfadmin@lospadresfoundation.com
Web: www.lospadresfoundation.org

Summary To provide financial assistance to graduate students from low-income Hispanic families.

Eligibility This program is open to graduate students who are the first in their family to attend college and whose family meets the federal low-income guidelines. Applicants must be U.S. citizens or permanent residents of Hispanic origin planning to attend an accredited college or university. Along with their application, they must submit a 250-word personal essay that covers their future goals and objectives, the volunteer community service projects with which they have been involved as an undergraduate, the issue or problem that was the focus of each organization with which they were a volunteer, the influence or impact of this activity or program on their community, and what they consider to be the major issue affecting their community.

Financial data The stipend is $2,500 per year.

Duration 1 year.

Number awarded 1 or more each year.

Deadline January of each year.

[238]
GLAXOSMITHKLINE–HDA FOUNDATION SCHOLARSHIPS

Hispanic Dental Association
Attn: HDA Foundation
3085 Stevenson Drive, Suite 200
Springfield, IL 62703
(217) 529-6517   Toll-free: (800) 852-7921
Fax: (217) 529-9120   E-mail: HispanicDental@hdassoc.org
Web: www.hdassoc.org/site/epage/8351_351.htm

Summary To provide financial assistance to Hispanic students interested in preparing for a career in a dental profession.

Eligibility This program is open to Hispanics who have completed at least 1 year of an accredited dentistry or dental hygiene program. Applicants must have a GPA of 3.0 or higher. Along with their application, they must submit an essay on their career goals. Selection is based on scholastic achievement, community service, leadership skill, and commitment to improving health in the Hispanic community.

Financial data The stipend is $2,000.

Duration 1 year.

Additional information This program, which began in 2006, is sponsored by GlaxoSmithKline.

Number awarded 4 each year: 2 to dental students and 2 to dental hygiene students.

Deadline June of each year for dental students; July of each year for hygiene students.

[239]
GOLD COUNTRY SECTION AND REGION II SCHOLARSHIP

American Society of Safety Engineers
Attn: ASSE Foundation
1800 East Oakton Street
Des Plaines, IL 60018
(847) 768-3435   Fax: (847) 768-3434
E-mail: agabanski@asse.org
Web: www.asse.org/foundation

Summary To provide financial assistance to upper-division and graduate student members of the American Society of Safety Engineers (ASSE) from designated western states who are working on a degree in occupational health and related fields.

Eligibility This program is open to ASSE student members who are working on an undergraduate or graduate degree in occupational safety, health, and environment or a closely-related field (e.g., industrial or environmental engineering, environmental science, industrial hygiene, occupational health nursing). Priority is given to residents of ASSE Region II (Arizona, Colorado, Idaho, Montana, Nevada, New Mexico, Utah, and Wyoming). Undergraduates must be full-time students who have completed at least 60 semester hours with a GPA of 3.0 or higher. Graduate students must also be enrolled full time, have completed at least 9 semester hours with a GPA of 3.5 or higher, and have had a GPA of 3.0 or higher as an undergraduate. Along with their application,

they must submit 2 essays of 300 words or less: 1) why they are seeking a degree in occupational safety and health or a closely-related field, a brief description of their current activities, and how those relate to their career goals and objectives; and 2) why they should be awarded this scholarship (including career goals and financial need).

Financial data The stipend is $1,000.

Duration 1 year; nonrenewable.

Number awarded 1 each year.

Deadline November of each year.

[240]
GOLDEN KEY GRADUATE SCHOLAR AWARDS

Golden Key International Honour Society
621 North Avenue N.E., Suite C-100
Atlanta, GA 30308
(404) 377-2400   Toll-free: (800) 377-2401
Fax: (678) 420-6757   E-mail: scholarships@goldenkey.org
Web: www.goldenkey.org/GKweb/ScholarshipsandAwards

Summary To provide financial assistance for graduate school to members of the Golden Key International Honour Society.

Eligibility This program is open to members of the society who are either undergraduates or recent graduates (within the past 5 years). Applicants must be planning to enroll full time in a program of graduate or professional study in the year immediately following receipt of this award. They must include a 1,000-word essay that states why they are applying for the scholarship, explains why they are undertaking postbaccalaureate or professional study in a particular field, indicates how the society's commitment to academic excellence will be furthered by their studies, and describes their commitment to campus and community service. U.S. citizenship is not required and the graduate study does not have to be in the United States. Selection is based on academic achievement, involvement in their local chapter, and extra-curricular activities.

Financial data The stipend is $10,000.

Duration 1 year; nonrenewable.

Number awarded 12 each year.

Deadline January of each year.

[241]
GOLDIE BRANGMAN SCHOLARSHIP

American Association of Nurse Anesthetists
Attn: AANA Foundation
222 South Prospect Avenue
Park Ridge, IL 60068-4001
(847) 692-7050, ext. 1171   Fax: (847) 692-7137
E-mail: foundation@aana.com
Web: www.aana.com/foundation/default.asp

Summary To provide financial assistance to African American members of the American Association of Nurse Anesthetists (AANA) who are interested in obtaining further education.

Eligibility This program is open to African American members of the association who are currently enrolled in an accredited nurse anesthesia education program. Applicants must have a cumulative GPA of 3.0 or higher. First-year students must have completed 6 months of nurse anesthesia classes; second-year students must have completed 12 months of nurse anesthesia classes. Along with their application, they must submit a 200-word essay describing why they have chosen nurse anesthesia as a profession and their professional goals for the future. Financial need is also considered in the selection process.

Financial data The stipend is $1,000 per year.

Duration 1 academic year.

Additional information This program is supported by the Harlem Hospital School of Anesthesia Alumni. The application processing fee is $25.

Number awarded 1 each year.

Deadline March of each year.

[242]
GRACE LEGENDRE FELLOWSHIP FOR ADVANCED GRADUATE STUDY

Business and Professional Women's Clubs of New York State
Attn: Cynthia B. Gillmore, GLG Fellowship Chair
P.O. Box 200
Johnstown, NY 12095-0200
(518) 762-8483   Fax: (518) 762-2279
E-mail: CyndyG@aol.com
Web: www.gracelegendre.org

Summary To provide financial assistance to women in New York who wish to continue their education on the graduate level.

Eligibility This program is open to women who are permanent residents of New York state and citizens of the United States, have a bachelor's degree, and are currently registered full time or have completed 1 year in an advanced graduate degree program at a recognized college or university in New York. Applicants must show evidence of scholastic ability and need for financial assistance. They should be within 2 years of completing their degree.

Financial data The stipend is $1,000.

Duration 1 year; recipients may reapply.

Additional information This program was established in 1969. Requests for applications must be accompanied by a self-addressed stamped envelope.

Number awarded Varies each year; recently, 4 of these fellowships were awarded.

Deadline February of each year.

[243]
GRACE WALL BARREDA FELLOWSHIP

American Indian Graduate Center
Attn: Executive Director
4520 Montgomery Boulevard, N.E., Suite 1-B
Albuquerque, NM 87109-1291
(505) 881-4584   Toll-free: (800) 628-1920
Fax: (505) 884-0427   E-mail: aigc@aigc.com
Web: www.aigc.com

Summary To provide financial assistance to Native American students interested in working on a graduate degree in environmental studies or public health.

Eligibility This program is open to enrolled members of U.S. federally-recognized American Indian tribes and Alaska Native groups and other students who can document one-fourth degree federally-recognized Indian blood. Applicants must be enrolled full time in a master's, doctoral, or professional degree program at an accredited college or university in the United States. They must be studying public health or environmental sciences. Selection is based on academic achievement, financial need, and an essay on the meaning of their graduate education to the Indian community.

Financial data A stipend is awarded (amount not specified).

Duration 1 year; may be renewed.

Additional information The application fee is $15. Since this a supplemental program, applicants must apply in a timely manner for federal financial aid and campus-based aid at the college they are attending to be considered for this program. Failure to apply will disqualify an applicant.

Number awarded 1 or more each year.

Deadline May of each year.

[244]
GROTTO/JOB'S DAUGHTERS SCHOLARSHIP

International Order of Job's Daughters
Supreme Guardian Council Headquarters
Attn: Executive Manager
233 West Sixth Street
Papillion, NE 68046-2177
(402) 592-7987   Fax: (402) 592-2177
E-mail: sgc@iojd.org
Web: www.iojd.org

Summary To provide financial assistance to members of Job's Daughters who are working on an undergraduate or graduate degree in a dental field.

Eligibility This program is open to high school seniors and graduates; students in early graduation programs; junior college, technical, and vocational students; and college and graduate students. Applicants must be Job's Daughters in good standing in their Bethels; unmarried majority members under 30 years of age are also eligible. They must be working on a degree in a dental field, preferably with some training in the field of disabilities. Selection is based on scholastic standing, Job's Daughters activities, the applicant's self-help plan, recommendation by the Executive Bethel Guardian Council, faculty recommendations, achievements outside Job's Daughters, and financial need.

Financial data The stipend is $1,500.

Duration 1 year.

Additional information Information is also available from Barbara Hill, Education Scholarships Committee Chair, 337 Illinois Street, Pekin, IL 61554, (309) 346-5564.

Number awarded 1 or more each year.

Deadline April of each year.

[245]
GUAA GRADUATE FELLOWSHIP FUND

Gallaudet University Alumni Association
Attn: Graduate Fellowship Fund Committee
Peikoff Alumni House
Gallaudet University
800 Florida Avenue, N.E.
Washington, DC 20002-3695
(202) 651-5060   Fax: (202) 651-5062
TTY: (202) 651-5061
E-mail: alumni.relations@gallaudet.edu
Web: www.gallaudet.edu

Summary To provide financial assistance to deaf students who wish to work on a graduate degree at universities for people who hear normally.

Eligibility This program is open to deaf and hard of hearing graduates of Gallaudet University or other accredited academic institutions who have been accepted for graduate study at colleges or universities for people who hear normally. Applicants must be working on a doctoral or other terminal degree. Financial need is considered in the selection process.

Financial data The amount awarded varies, depending upon the number of qualified candidates applying for assistance, the availability of funds, and the needs of individual applicants.

Duration 1 year; may be renewed.

Additional information This program includes the following named fellowships: the Boyce R. Williams, '32, Fellowship, the David Peikoff, '29, Fellowship, the James N. Orman, '23, Fellowship, the John A. Trundle, 1885, Fellowship, the Old Dominion Foundation Fellowship, and the Waldo T., '49 and Jean Kelsch, '51, Cordano Fellowship. Recipients must carry a full-time semester load.

Number awarded Varies each year; recently, 9 of these fellowships were awarded.

Deadline April of each year.

[246]
GUARANTEED RESERVE FORCES DUTY (GRFD) SCHOLARSHIPS

U.S. Army
ROTC Cadet Command
Attn: ATCC-OP-I-S
55 Patch Road, Building 56
Fort Monroe, VA 23651-1052
(757) 727-4558   Toll-free: (800) USA-ROTC
E-mail: atccps@usaac.army.mil
Web: www.rotc.usaac.army.mil

Summary To provide financial assistance to college and graduate students who are willing to enroll in Army ROTC and serve in a Reserve component of the Army following graduation.

Eligibility This program is open to full-time students entering their junior year of college with a GPA of 2.5 or higher. Graduate students are also eligible if they have only 2 years remaining for completion of their graduate degree. Applicants must meet all other medical and moral character requirements for enrollment in Army ROTC. They must be willing to enroll in the Simultaneous Membership Program (SMP) of an ROTC unit on their campus; the SMP requires simultaneous membership in Army ROTC and the Army National Guard or Army Reserve.

Financial data Participants receive reimbursement of tuition (up to $28,000 per year), a grant of $600 per year for books, plus an ROTC stipend for 10 months of the year at $350 per month during their junior year and $400 per month during their senior year. As a member of the Army National Guard or Army Reserve, they also receive weekend drill pay at the pay grade of E-5 during their junior year or E-6 during their senior year.

Duration 2 years.

Additional information After graduation, participants serve 3 to 6 months on active duty in the Officer Basic Course (OBC). Following completion of OBC, they are released from active duty and are obligated to serve 8 years in the Army National Guard or Army Reserve.

Number awarded 54 each year (1 in each state or U.S. territory).

[247]
H. FLETCHER BROWN SCHOLARSHIP

H. Fletcher Brown Trust
PNC Bank Delaware
Attn: Donald W. Davis
222 Delaware Avenue, 16th Floor
Wilmington, DE 19899
(302) 429-2827   Fax: (302) 429-5658
E-mail: Robbie.testa@pncadvisors.com

Summary To provide financial assistance to residents of Delaware who are interested in studying engineering, chemistry, medicine, dentistry, or law.

Eligibility This program is open to Delaware residents who were born in Delaware, are either high school seniors entering the first year of college or college seniors entering the first year of graduate school, are of good moral character, and need financial assistance from sources outside their family. Applicants must have combined mathematics and verbal SAT scores of 1000 or higher, rank in the upper 20% of their class, and come from a family whose income is less than $75,000. Their proposed fields of study must be engineering, chemistry, medicine (for an M.D. or D.O. degree only), dentistry, or law. Finalists are interviewed.

Financial data The amount of the scholarship is determined by the scholarship committee and is awarded in installments over the length of study.

Duration 1 year; may be renewed if the recipient maintains a GPA of 2.5 or higher and continues to be worthy of and eligible for the award.

Deadline March of each year.

[248]
HANA SCHOLARSHIPS

United Methodist Church
Attn: General Board of Higher Education and Ministry
Office of Loans and Scholarships
1001 19th Avenue South
P.O. Box 340007
Nashville, TN 37203-0007
(615) 340-7344   Fax: (615) 340-7367
E-mail: umscholar@gbhem.org
Web: www.gbhem.org/gbhem/loans2.html

Summary To provide financial assistance to upper-division and graduate Methodist students who are of Hispanic, Asian, Native American, Alaska Native, or Pacific Islander ancestry.

Eligibility This program is open to full-time juniors, seniors, and graduate students at accredited colleges and universities in the United States who have been active, full members of a United Methodist Church for at least 1 year prior to applying. Applicants must have at least 1 parent who is Hispanic, Asian, Native American, Alaska Native, or Pacific Islander. They must be able to demonstrate involvement in their Hispanic, Asian, or Native American (HANA) community. Selection is based on that involvement, academic ability (GPA of at least 2.85 for undergraduates or 3.0 for graduate students) and financial need. U.S. citizenship or permanent resident status is required.

Financial data The maximum stipend is $3,000 for undergraduates or $5,000 for graduate students.

Duration 1 year; recipients may reapply.

Number awarded 50 each year.

Deadline March of each year.

[249]
HANK LEBONNE SCHOLARSHIP

National Federation of the Blind
c/o Peggy Elliott, Scholarship Committee Chair
805 Fifth Avenue
Grinnell, IA 50112
(641) 236-3366
Web: www.nfb.org/sch_intro.htm

Summary To provide financial assistance to legally blind students working on an undergraduate or graduate degree.

Eligibility This program is open to legally blind students who are working on or planning to work full time on an undergraduate or graduate degree. Selection is based on academic excellence, service to the community, and financial need.

Financial data The stipend is $5,000.

Duration 1 year; recipients may resubmit applications up to 2 additional years.

Additional information Scholarships are awarded at the federation convention in July. Recipients attend the convention at federation expense; that funding is in addition to the scholarship grant.

Number awarded 1 each year.

Deadline March of each year.

[250]
HAROLD B. & DOROTHY A. SNYDER SCHOLARSHIPS

Harold B. & Dorothy A. Snyder Scholarship Fund
P.O. Box 671
Moorestown, NJ 08057-0671
(856) 273-9745

Summary To provide financial assistance to undergraduate and graduate students preparing for a career in the areas of Presbyterian ministry, nursing, building construction, or engineering.

Eligibility This program is open to U.S. citizens who are attending or planning to attend institutions of higher learning. They must be preparing for a career in the areas of Presbyterian ministry (M.Div. degree), nursing (B.S.N.), building construction, or engineering. Applicants are evaluated on the basis of achievement, need, demonstrated commitment to community service, and character. Preference is given to applicants who are full-time students and who are New Jersey residents. In some instances, preference is also given to full-time enrollees of specific institutions and to members of certain denominations and congregations or residents of certain towns. There are no other preferences as to age, sex, religion (except when applicable), race, or country of origin. Personal interviews are required.

Financial data The amount awarded varies, depending upon the needs of the recipient. Funds are paid directly to the recipient's institution.

Duration 1 year; generally renewable until completion of the recipient's degree program.

Additional information Snyder Scholars are required, by contract, to submit periodic reports and attend meetings. The foundation will withdraw scholarship aid from any recipient who, in its opinion, has engaged in activities detrimental to the school or college being attended or to the country. In addition, the foundation will withdraw aid from any recipient (other than a divinity student) who seeks to avoid service in the U.S. armed forces as a conscientious objector.

Number awarded Varies each year.

Deadline March of each year.

[251]
HARRY J. HARWICK SCHOLARSHIPS

American College of Medical Practice Executives
Attn: ACMPE Scholarship Fund Inc.
104 Inverness Terrace East
Englewood, CO 80112-5306
(303) 799-1111, ext. 232   Toll-free: (877) ASK-MGMA
Fax: (303) 643-4439   E-mail: acmpe@mgma.com
Web: www.mgma.com/academics/scholar.cfm

Summary To provide financial assistance to undergraduate or graduate students who are interested in preparing for a career in medical group management.

Eligibility Eligible are 1) graduate students enrolled in a program accredited by the Accrediting Commission on Education for Health Services Administration and 2) undergraduate students enrolled in a program that is a member of the Association of University Programs in Health Administration. Applicants must be working on a degree in a program relevant to medical practice management, including public health, business administration, health care administration, or other related areas. Students working on a degree in medicine, physical therapy, nursing, or other clinically-related professions are not eligible. Along with their application, they must submit a letter describing their career goals and objectives relevant to medical practice management; a resume; 3 reference letters commenting on their performance, character, potential to succeed, and need for scholarship support; and either documentation indicating acceptance into an undergraduate or graduate school or academic transcripts indicating undergraduate or graduate work completed to date.

Financial data The stipend is $5,000. Funds are paid directly to the recipient's college or university.

Duration 1 year.

Additional information This program is managed by Scholarship Program Administrators, Inc. 1201 Eighth Avenue South, P.O. Box 23737, Nashville, TN 27202-3737, (615) 320-3149, (800) 310-4053, Fax: (615) 320-3151, E-mail: info@spaprog.com.

Number awarded 2 each year.

Deadline April of each year.

[252]
HARRY R. KENDALL LEADERSHIP DEVELOPMENT SCHOLARSHIPS

United Methodist Church
General Board of Global Ministries
Attn: Health and Welfare Program
475 Riverside Drive, Room 330
New York, NY 10115
(212) 870-3871   Toll-free: (800) UMC-GBGM
E-mail: jyoung@gbgm-umc.org
Web: hbs.gbgm-umc.org/umcor/work/health/scholarships

Summary To provide financial assistance to African Americans who are preparing for a career in a health-related field.

Eligibility This program is open to U.S. citizens who are of African American descent. Applicants must be planning to enter a health care field or already be a practitioner in such a field. They must be able to affirm their intention to serve needy persons upon completion of their study or experience. Financial need is considered in the selection process.

Financial data The stipend is $2,000.

Duration 1 year.

Additional information This program was established in 1980.

Number awarded Varies each year.

Deadline June of each year.

[253]
HARRY TABACK 9/11 MEMORIAL SCHOLARSHIP
American Society of Safety Engineers
Attn: ASSE Foundation
1800 East Oakton Street
Des Plaines, IL 60018
(847) 768-3435   Fax: (847) 768-3434
E-mail: agabanski@asse.org
Web: www.asse.org/foundation

Summary To provide financial assistance to upper-division and graduate student members of the American Society of Safety Engineers (ASSE) who are working on a degree in occupational health and related fields.

Eligibility This program is open to ASSE student members who are working on an undergraduate or graduate degree in occupational safety, health, and environment or a closely-related field (e.g., industrial or environmental engineering, environmental science, industrial hygiene, occupational health nursing). Undergraduates must be full-time students who have completed at least 60 semester hours with a GPA of 3.0 or higher. Graduate students must also be enrolled full time, have completed at least 9 semester hours with a GPA of 3.5 or higher, and have had a GPA of 3.0 or higher as an undergraduate. Along with their application, they must submit 2 essays of 300 words or less: 1) why they are seeking a degree in occupational safety and health or a closely-related field, a brief description of their current activities, and how those relate to their career goals and objectives; and 2) why they should be awarded this scholarship (including career goals and financial need). U.S. citizenship is required.

Financial data The stipend is $1,000.

Duration 1 year; nonrenewable.

Additional information This program was established to honor a victim of the attack on the World Trade Center on September 11, 2001.

Number awarded 1 each year.

Deadline November of each year.

[254]
HAWAI'I VETERANS MEMORIAL FUND SCHOLARSHIPS
Hawai'i Community Foundation
Attn: Scholarship Department
1164 Bishop Street, Suite 800
Honolulu, HI 96813
(808) 566-5570   Toll-free: (888) 731-3863
Fax: (808) 521-6286   E-mail: scholarships@hcf-hawaii.org
Web: www.hawaiicommunityfoundation.org

Summary To provide financial assistance to Hawaii residents who are interested in attending graduate school in Hawaii or on the mainland.

Eligibility This program is open to Hawaii residents who are planning to work on a graduate degree as full-time students at a college or university in Hawaii or the mainland. Applicants do not have to be veterans or children of veterans in order to apply for this scholarship. They must be able to demonstrate academic achievement (GPA of 3.5 or higher), good moral character, and financial need. Along with their application, they must submit a short statement indicating their reasons for attending college, their planned course of study, and their career goals. Preference is given to students with the greatest financial need. Each year, a special award is also presented in memory of Robert K. Murakami (founder and first president of the fund) to applicants who demonstrate the most outstanding academic record, charac-

ter, and potential for combining professional endeavors with community service.

Financial data The amounts of the awards depend on the availability of funds and the need of the recipient; recently, stipends averaged $1,000.

Duration 1 year.

Additional information The fund was established in 1945.

Number awarded Varies each year; recently, 35 of these scholarships were awarded.

Deadline February of each year.

[255]
HAWAIIAN CIVIC CLUB OF HONOLULU SCHOLARSHIP
Hawaiian Civic Club of Honolulu
Attn: Scholarship Committee
P.O. Box 1513
Honolulu, HI 96806
E-mail: newmail@hotbot.com
Web: www.hcchonolulu.org/scholarship

Summary To provide financial assistance for undergraduate or graduate studies to persons of Hawaiian descent.

Eligibility Applicants must be of Hawaiian descent (descendants of the aboriginal inhabitants of the Hawaiian Islands prior to 1778), residents of Hawaii, able to demonstrate academic achievement, and enrolled or planning to enroll full time in an accredited 2-year college, 4-year college, or graduate school. Graduating seniors and current undergraduate students must have a GPA of 2.5 or higher; graduate students must have at least a 3.0 GPA. As part of the selection process, applicants must submit a 2-page essay on a topic that changes annually but relates to issues of concern to the Hawaiian community; a recent topic related to the leadership, cultural and governmental, of the Hawaiian community. Selection is based on the quality of the essay, academic standing, financial need, and the completeness of the application package.

Financial data The amount of the stipend varies. Scholarship checks are made payable to the recipient and the institution and are mailed to the college or university financial aid office. Funds may be used for tuition, fees, books, and other educational expenses.

Duration 1 year.

Additional information Recipients may attend school in Hawaii or on the mainland. Information on this program is also available from Ke Ali'i Pauahi Foundation, Attn: Financial Aid and Scholarship Services, 567 King Street, Suite 160, Honolulu, HI 96813, (808) 534-3966.

Number awarded Varies each year; recently, 54 of these scholarships, worth $34,800, were awarded.

Deadline May of each year.

[256]
HAWAIIAN HOMES COMMISSION SCHOLARSHIPS
Hawai'i Community Foundation
Attn: Scholarship Department
1164 Bishop Street, Suite 800
Honolulu, HI 96813
(808) 566-5570   Toll-free: (888) 731-3863
Fax: (808) 521-6286   E-mail: scholarships@hcf-hawaii.org
Web: www.hawaiicommunityfoundation.org

Summary To provide financial assistance for undergraduate or graduate studies to persons of Hawaiian descent.

Eligibility Applicants must be 50% or more of Hawaiian descent (descendants of the aboriginal inhabitants of the Hawaiian Islands prior to 1778) or a homestead lessee (at least 25% Hawaiian ancestry). They must be U.S. citizens, enrolled in full-time study in an undergraduate or graduate degree program, and able to demonstrate financial need and academic excellence. Undergraduates must have a GPA of 2.0 or higher. Graduate students must have a GPA of 3.0 or higher. Current Hawaiian residency is not required. Special consideration is given to applicants with exceptional academic merit and proven commitment to serving the Native Hawaiian community. Along with their application, they must submit a short statement indicating their reasons for attending college, their planned course of study, and their career goals. Selection is based on academic achievement, good moral character, and financial need.

Financial data The amounts of the awards depend on the availability of funds and the need of the recipient; recently, stipends averaged $1,500.

Duration 1 year.

Additional information This program is sponsored by the state Department of Hawaiian Home Lands.

Number awarded Varies each year; recently, 105 of these scholarships were awarded.

Deadline February of each year.

[257]
HEALTH CAREERS FOUNDATION
SCHOLARSHIP/LOAN PROGRAM

Health Careers Foundation
3221 McKelvey Road, Suite 301
Bridgeton, MO 63044-2551
(314) 770-1626   Fax: (314) 770-1432
E-mail: info@hcfinfo.org
Web: www.hcfinfo.org

Summary To provide financial assistance (in the form of scholarships and loans) to individuals (particularly older students) who are interested in working on a degree in nursing, pharmacy, or the allied health professions.

Eligibility Applicants must be enrolled or planning to enroll in a course of study leading to a certificate, diploma, license, associate degree, or bachelor's degree in 1 of the following health care fields: dietetics, medical records/transcription, medical technology, nursing, occupational therapy, pharmacy, physical therapy, radiology, respiratory therapy, or speech pathology. They must be working on the degree required for an entry-level position in the appropriate field; advanced degrees are not eligible unless they are required in order to enter and practice in the profession (e.g., speech pathology, physical therapy). No correspondence programs at any level are acceptable. Selection is also based on academic record, statement of goals, work experience, and program completion date. Priority is given to nontraditional students (adults who either want to enter the workforce or change careers) and to individuals with financial need who have few financial aid options.

Financial data The amount awarded varies, up to $4,000 per year, depending upon the needs of the recipient. The award consists of half scholarship and half loan (the maximum lifetime loan indebtedness is $8,000). Funds may be used for educational purposes only (tuition, fees, and books) and are paid directly to the recipient in 2 equal installments. The first payment is mailed in August; the second payment is made in January, provided the recipient has maintained at least a 2.0 GPA. All recipients are required to sign a loan promissory note. Loans are interest free as long as the recipient remains a student or for a grace period

of 6 months after leaving school. After the grace period, the interest rate charged is 4% per year on the unpaid principal balance. Payment must begin 7 months after leaving school.

Duration 1 year; recipients may reapply.

Additional information The Health Careers Foundation was established in 1990 by the Health Services Corporation of America and the National Healthcare Coalition. Since then, the foundation has awarded more than $5 million in scholarships and loans to more than 4,500 recipients. Students may attend any appropriate 2-year college, 4-year college, university, vocational/technical school, nursing school, or institute accredited by an appropriate state licensing health career board.

Deadline March of each year.

[258]
HEALTH CAREERS SCHOLARSHIPS

International Order of the King's Daughters and Sons
Attn: Director, Health Careers Scholarship Department
34 Vincent Avenue
P.O. Box 1040
Chautauqua, NY 14722-1040
(716) 357-4951   Fax: (716) 357-3762
E-mail: iokds5@windstream.net
Web: www.iokds.org/scholarship.html

Summary To provide funding to students preparing for careers in medicine, dentistry, pharmacy, physical and occupational therapy, and selected medical technologies.

Eligibility This program is open to U.S. or Canadian citizens who are enrolled full time in an accredited college or university and studying medicine, dentistry, nursing, pharmacy, physical or occupational therapy, or medical technology. Applicants in undergraduate programs must be in at least the third year of college. Nursing students must have completed their first year of schooling. Students seeking M.D. or D.D.S. degrees must be in at least the second year of medical or dental school. Premed students are not eligible. Preference is given to students of Christian background. Selection is based on personal statistics, educational background, financial statement, and a statement from the applicant describing the reason for choosing the field of training and future plans.

Financial data The stipend is $1,000 per year.

Duration 1 year; may be renewed up to 2 additional years.

Additional information This program began in 1976. Requests for applications must be accompanied by a self-addressed stamped envelope. Requests for faxed materials and telephone calls will be not honored.

Number awarded Varies each year; recently, 43 of these scholarships were awarded.

Deadline March of each year.

[259]
HEALTH PHYSICS SOCIETY FELLOWSHIPS

Health Physics Society
Attn: Executive Secretary
1313 Dolley Madison Boulevard, Suite 402
McLean, VA 22101
(703) 790-1745   Fax: (703) 790-2672
Web: hps.org/students

Summary To provide funding to graduate students who are interested in working on a graduate degree that qualifies them to plan, direct, or conduct a program for the evaluation and control of radiation hazards.

Eligibility　This program is open to graduate students who are beginning or continuing full-time work toward a graduate degree offered by a U.S. graduate program in health physics or a closely-related field. Foreign nationals may apply. Preference is given to entering graduate students (less than 1 full-time academic year of graduate work in health physics). Financial need is considered in the selection process.

Financial data　The stipends are $7,500, $6,000, or $5,000.

Duration　1 year.

Additional information　These fellowships cannot be held by students who have accepted full-time grants (e.g., from the National Science Foundation or the Department of Energy).

Number awarded　7 each year, including the Burton J. Moyer Memorial Fellowship at $7,500, the Robert S. Landauer, Sr., Memorial Fellowship at $6,000, the Robert Gardner Memorial Fellowship at $5,000, the Richard J. Burk, Jr. Fellowship at $5,000, the J. Newell Stannard Fellowship at $5,000, and 2 unnamed fellowships at $5,000 each.

Deadline　February of each year.

[260]
HEALTH RESEARCH AND EDUCATIONAL TRUST SCHOLARSHIPS

New Jersey Hospital Association
Attn: Health Research and Educational Trust
760 Alexander Road
P.O. Box 1
Princeton, NJ 08543-0001
(609) 275-4224　　　　　　　　　　Fax: (609) 452-8097
Web: www.njha.com/hret/scholarship.aspx

Summary　To provide financial assistance to New Jersey residents working on an undergraduate or graduate degree in a health-related field.

Eligibility　This program is open to residents of New Jersey enrolled in an upper-division or graduate program in hospital or health care administration, public administration, nursing, or other allied health profession. Applicants must have a GPA of 3.0 or higher and be able to demonstrate financial need. Along with their application, they must submit a 2-page essay (on which 50% of the selection is based) describing their academic plans for the future. Minorities and women are especially encouraged to apply.

Financial data　The stipend is $2,000.

Duration　1 year.

Additional information　This program began in 1983.

Number awarded　Varies each year; recently, 2 of these scholarships were awarded.

Deadline　July of each year.

[261]
HEALTHCARE INFORMATION MANAGEMENT SYSTEMS SCHOLARSHIPS

Healthcare Information and Management Systems Society
Attn: HIMSS Foundation Scholarship Program Coordinator
230 East Ohio Street, Suite 500
Chicago, IL 60611-3270
(312) 664-HIMSS　　　　　　　　　Fax: (312) 664-6143
E-mail: foundation@himss.org
Web: www.himss.org/ASP/scholarship_hims.asp

Summary　To provide financial assistance to upper-division and graduate student members of the Healthcare Information and Management Systems Society (HIMSS) who are interested in the field of health care information and management systems.

Eligibility　This program is open to student members of the society, although an application for membership, including dues, may accompany the scholarship application. Applicants must be upper-division or graduate students enrolled in an accredited program designed to prepare them for a career in health care information or management systems, which may include industrial engineering, health care informatics, operations research, computer science and information systems, mathematics, and quantitative programs in business administration and hospital administration. Selection is based on academic achievement and demonstration of leadership potential, including communication skills and participation in society activity.

Financial data　The stipend is $5,000. The award also includes an all-expense paid trip to the annual HIMSS conference and exhibition.

Duration　1 year.

Additional information　This program was established in 1986 for undergraduate and master's degree students. The first Ph.D. scholarship was awarded in 2002.

Number awarded　3 each year: 1 to an undergraduate student, 1 to a master's degree student, and 1 to a Ph.D. candidate.

Deadline　October of each year.

[262]
HEALTHLINK INFORMATICS SCHOLARSHIP

Healthcare Information and Management Systems Society
Attn: HIMSS Foundation Scholarship Program Coordinator
230 East Ohio Street, Suite 500
Chicago, IL 60611-3270
(312) 664-HIMSS　　　　　　　　　Fax: (312) 664-6143
E-mail: foundation@himss.org
Web: www.himss.org/ASP/scholarship_his.asp

Summary　To provide financial assistance to student members of the Healthcare Information and Management Systems Society (HIMSS) who are working on a graduate degree in health care informatics.

Eligibility　This program is open to student members of the society, although an application for membership, including dues, may accompany the scholarship application. Applicants must be graduate students working on a degree in health care informatics. They must submit a personal statement that includes their career goals, past achievements, and future goals. Selection is based on that statement, academic achievement, and financial need.

Financial data　The stipend is $7,000. The award includes an all-expense paid trip to the annual HIMSS conference and exhibition.

Duration　1 year; nonrenewable.

Additional information　This program was established in 2004.

Number awarded　1 each year.

Deadline　October of each year.

[263]
HEART OF AMERICA CONTACT LENS SOCIETY GRANTS

Heart of America Contact Lens Society
c/o Kurt Finklang
84 Professional Parkway
Troy, MO 63379-2822
(636) 528-6104　　　　　　　E-mail: contact@hoacls.org
Web: www.hoacls.org

Summary　To provide financial assistance to optometry students from designated midwestern states.

Eligibility This program is open to residents of Arkansas, Illinois, Iowa, Kansas, Missouri, Nebraska, and Oklahoma who are enrolled in a school or college of optometry. Applicants must have completed at least 1 contact lens class. Along with their application, they must submit a publishable paper based on an aspect of contact lenses or primary care optometry. Selection is based on that paper (60%), overall GPA (20%), grades in contact lens courses (10%), and the selection committee's opinions and impressions (10%).

Financial data The stipend is $2,000.
Duration 1 year.
Number awarded 5 each year.
Deadline October of each year.

[264]
HELEN LAIDLAW FOUNDATION NURSING AND HEALTH CARE SCHOLARSHIPS

Helen Laidlaw Foundation
c/o Nancy E. Huck, President
314 Newman Street
East Tawas, MI 48730-1214
(989) 362-9117   Fax: (989) 362-7675

Summary To provide financial assistance to Michigan residents interested in preparing for a health care-related career.

Eligibility This program is open both to candidates seeking a degree (undergraduate or graduate) and candidates in nondegree programs. Applicants must be preparing for a health care career. Nursing candidates receive preference. In selecting recipients, consideration is given first to candidates from Iosco County, Michigan, then northeastern Michigan counties, and finally the entire state.

Financial data Stipends range from $500 to $1,500 per year. Funds are paid directly to the recipient's school.

Duration 1 year; may be renewed.

Additional information Recipients must attend school on a full-time basis.

Deadline February of each year.

[265]
HELLENIC TIMES SCHOLARSHIPS

Hellenic Times Scholarship Fund
Attn: Nick Katsoris
823 Eleventh Avenue, Fifth Floor
New York, NY 10019-3535
(212) 986-6881   Fax: (212) 977-3662
E-mail: HTSFund@aol.com
Web: www.HTSFund.org

Summary To provide financial assistance to undergraduate or graduate students of Greek descent.

Eligibility This program is open to undergraduate and graduate students of Greek descent who are between 17 and 25 years of age and enrolled in an accredited college or university. Students who are receiving other financial aid that exceeds 50% of their annual tuition are ineligible. Selection is based on need and merit.

Financial data The amount of the awards depends on the availability of funds and the number of recipients.

Additional information This program began in 1990.

Number awarded Varies; approximately $100,000 is available for this program each year.

Deadline January of each year.

[266]
HELPING HANDS BOOK SCHOLARSHIP PROGRAM

Helping Hands Foundation
Attn: Scholarship Director
4480-H South Cobb Drive
PMB 435
Smyrna, GA 30080
Fax: (770) 384-0376
E-mail: director@helpinghandsbookscholarship.com
Web: www.helpinghandsbookscholarship.com

Summary To provide high school seniors, undergraduates, and graduate students with funds to purchase textbooks and other study materials.

Eligibility This program is open to students who are 16 years of age or older and who are planning to attend or are currently attending a 2-year or 4-year college, university, or vocational/technical institute. Applicants must be enrolled as a high school, college, or graduate student in the United States, Canada, or Mexico. Along with their application, they must submit a 500-word essay describing their educational plans as they relate to their career objectives and why they feel this scholarship will help them achieve those goals. Selection is based on academic record and career potential.

Financial data Stipends range from $100 to $1,000. Funds are intended to be used to purchase textbooks and study materials. Checks are sent directly to the recipient.

Duration These are 1-time nonrenewable awards.

Additional information There is a $5 application fee.

Number awarded Up to 50 each year.

Deadline July of each year for fall semester; December of each year for spring semester.

[267]
HEMOPHILIA HEALTH SERVICES MEMORIAL SCHOLARSHIPS

Hemophilia Health Services
Attn: Scholarship Committee
6820 Charlotte Pike, Suite 100
Nashville, TN 37209-4234
(615) 850-5175   Toll-free: (800) 800-6606, ext. 5175
Fax: (615) 352-2588
E-mail: scholarship@HemophiliaHealth.com
Web: www.HemophiliaHealth.com

Summary To provide financial assistance for college or graduate school to people with hemophilia or other bleeding disorders.

Eligibility This program is open to individuals with hemophilia (factor VIII or IX), von Willebrand Disease (type 1, 2, 2A, 2B, 2M, 2N, or 3), or other bleeding disorders. Applicants must be 1) high school seniors; 2) college freshmen, sophomores, or juniors; or 3) college seniors planning to attend graduate school or students already enrolled in graduate school. They must be attending or planning to attend an accredited nonprofit college, university, or vocational/technical school in the United States or Puerto Rico as a full-time student. Along with their application, they must submit an essay, up to 250 words, on the following topic: "What has been your own personal challenge in living with a bleeding disorder?" U.S. citizenship is required. Selection is based on academic achievement in relation to tested ability, involvement in extracurricular and community activities, and financial need.

Financial data The stipend is $1,500. Funds are issued payable to the recipient's school.

Duration 1 year; recipients may reapply.

Additional information This program, which started in 1995, includes the following named scholarships: the Cindy Beck Scholarship, the Osborn DeWitt Scholarship, the Tim Haas Scholarship, the Ricky Hobson Scholarship, the Michael Moses Scholarship, and the Jim Stineback Scholarship. It is administered by Scholarship Program Administrators, Inc., 1201 Eighth Avenue South, P.O. Box 23737, Nashville, TN 27202-3737, (615) 320-3149, Fax: (615) 320-3151, E-mail: info@spaprog.com. Recipients must enroll full time.

Number awarded Several each year.

Deadline April of each year.

[268]
HENRY AND CHIYO KUWAHARA MEMORIAL SCHOLARSHIPS

Japanese American Citizens League
Attn: National Scholarship Awards
1765 Sutter Street
San Francisco, CA 94115
(415) 921-5225   Fax: (415) 931-4671
E-mail: jacl@jacl.org
Web: www.jacl.org/leadership_development_5.php

Summary To provide financial assistance for undergraduate or graduate study to members of the Japanese American Citizens League (JACL).

Eligibility This program is open to JACL members who are high school seniors, undergraduates, or graduate students. Applicants must be attending or planning to attend a college, university, trade school, or business college. They must submit a statement describing their current level of involvement in the Japanese American community or Asian Pacific community and how they will continue their involvement in future years. Selection is based on academic record, extracurricular activities, financial need, and community involvement.

Financial data The stipend depends on the availability of funds but usually ranges from $1,000 to $5,000.

Duration 1 year; nonrenewable.

Additional information Applications from high school seniors must be submitted to the local JACL chapter. All other applications must be submitted to the JACL National Scholarship Program, c/o San Diego JACL Chapter, 1031 25th Street, San Diego, CA 92102.

Number awarded 6 each year: 2 each to entering freshmen, continuing undergraduates, and entering or currently-enrolled graduate students.

Deadline February of each year for graduating high school seniors; March of each year for current undergraduate or graduate students.

[269]
HENRY H. STROUD, MD MEMORIAL SCHOLARSHIP

Delaware Community Foundation
Attn: Executive Vice President
100 West 10th Street, Suite 115
P.O. Box 1636
Wilmington, DE 19899
(302) 504-5222   Fax: (302) 571-1553
E-mail: rgentsch@delcf.org
Web: www.delcf.org

Summary To provide financial assistance to Delaware residents accepted at an accredited school of medicine.

Eligibility This program is open to residents of Delaware who have recently graduated from college and have been accepted at an accredited school of medicine. Applicants must submit a list of awards and extracurricular activities, letters of recommendation, and a 500-word essay on their current career plans. Selection is based on those submissions, demonstrated academic promise, and financial need. Special consideration is given to applicants demonstrating an entrepreneurial and innovative approach to medicine.

Financial data A stipend is awarded (amount not specified).

Duration 1 year; may be renewed up to 3 additional years.

Number awarded 1 or more each year.

Deadline March of each year.

[270]
HENRY HECAEN SCHOLARSHIP

American Psychological Foundation
750 First Street, N.E.
Washington, DC 20002-4242
(202) 336-5843   Fax: (202) 336-5812
E-mail: foundation@apa.org
Web: www.apa.org/apf/hecaen.html

Summary To provide financial assistance to neuropsychology graduate students with financial need.

Eligibility This program is open to students working on a graduate degree in the area of neuropsychology. Applicants must submit a letter documenting their scholarly or research accomplishments, their financial need for the award, and the purpose for which they plan to use it.

Financial data The stipend is $2,500 per year.

Duration 1 year.

Additional information This scholarship was first awarded in 1994.

Number awarded 1 each year.

Deadline May of each year.

[271]
HERBERT W. NICKENS MEDICAL STUDENT SCHOLARSHIPS

Association of American Medical Colleges
Attn: Division of Diversity Policy and Programs
2450 N Street, N.W.
Washington, DC 20037-1126
(202) 828-0570   Fax: (202) 828-1125
E-mail: nickensawards@aamc.org
Web: www.aamc.org

Summary To provide financial assistance to medical students who have demonstrated efforts to address the health-care needs of minorities.

Eligibility This program is open to U.S. citizens and permanent residents entering their third year of study at a U.S. allopathic medical school. Each medical school may nominate 1 student for these awards. The letter must describe the nominee's 1) academic achievement through the first and second year, including special awards and honors, clerkships or special research projects, and extracurricular activities in which the student has shown leadership abilities; 2) leadership efforts to eliminate inequities in medical education and health care; 3) demonstrated leadership efforts in addressing the educational, societal, and health-care needs of minorities; and 4) awards and honors, special research projects, and extracurricular activities in which the student has shown leadership abilities. Nominees must submit a curriculum vitae and a 250-word essay that discusses their motivation to pursue a medical career and how they anticipate working to improve the health and health care of minorities.

Financial data   The stipend is $5,000.

Duration   1 year.

Number awarded   5 each year.

Deadline   March of each year.

[272]
HERMIONE GRANT CALHOUN SCHOLARSHIPS

National Federation of the Blind
c/o Peggy Elliott, Scholarship Committee Chair
805 Fifth Avenue
Grinnell, IA 50112
(641) 236-3366
Web: www.nfb.org/sch_intro.htm

Summary   To provide financial assistance to female blind students interested in working on an undergraduate or graduate degree.

Eligibility   This program is open to legally blind women students who are working on or planning to work full time on an undergraduate or graduate degree. Selection is based on academic excellence, service to the community, and financial need.

Financial data   The stipend is $3,000.

Duration   1 year; recipients may resubmit applications up to 2 additional years.

Additional information   Scholarships are awarded at the federation convention in July. Recipients attend the convention at federation expense; that funding is in addition to the scholarship grant.

Number awarded   1 each year.

Deadline   March of each year.

[273]
HERSCHEL S. HOROWITZ SCHOLARSHIP

American Association of Public Health Dentistry
Attn: AAPHD Foundation
3085 Stevenson Drive, Suite 200
Springfield, IL 62703
(217) 529-6941   Fax: (217) 529-9120
E-mail: natoff@aaphd.org
Web: www.aaphd.org

Summary   To provide financial assistance to dentists interested in working on a master's degree in public health or a dental public health program.

Eligibility   This program is open to dentists enrolled in a full-time accredited M.P.H. program or the first year of a 2-year advanced education program in dental public health. Applicants must submit a curriculum vitae, a 500-word statement of their dental public health career plans, 2 letters of recommendation, and a 200- to 250-word statement of financial need.

Financial data   The stipend is $25,000.

Duration   1 year.

Additional information   Information is also available from Dr. Linda C. Niessen, AAPHD Foundation Chair, 3549 Haynie Avenue, Dallas, TX 75205-1219.

Number awarded   1 each year.

Deadline   October of each year.

[274]
HHMI-NIH RESEARCH SCHOLARS PROGRAM

Howard Hughes Medical Institute
One Cloister Court, Building 60, Room 253
Bethesda, MD 20814-1460
(301) 951-6770   Toll-free: (800) 424-9924
Fax: (301) 951-6776   E-mail: research_scholars@hhmi.org
Web: www.hhmi.org/cloister

Summary   To give outstanding students at U.S. medical or dental schools the opportunity to receive educational funding and research training at the National Institutes of Health (NIH), in Bethesda, Maryland.

Eligibility   This program is open to students who have completed their second or third year at a medical or dental school in the United States or Puerto Rico. Applicants must be interested in conducting a basic, translational, or applied biomedical research project while in residence at a facility on the NIH campus. There are no citizenship requirements, but applicants must be authorized to work in the United States. Those who are enrolled in an M.D./Ph.D. or D.D.S./Ph.D. program or who already have an M.D., D.D.S., or Ph.D. or Sc.D. in a laboratory-based biological science are not eligible.

Financial data   Scholars receive an annual salary of $25,000 for rent, food, and other living expenses. They are also eligible for medical, life, and accidental death and dismemberment insurance. Students are reimbursed for round-trip moving expenses for personal belongings (not furniture) for themselves and their dependents from and back to medical school. In addition, tuition is paid for Research Scholars who wish to take courses from the Foundation for Advanced Education in the Sciences (FAES). They also receive allowances for the purchase of textbooks and scientific journals related to their area of research and for travel to scientific meetings.

Duration   1 year, beginning in July or August.

Additional information   Research Scholars work as part of a research team in a laboratory at the NIH's main campus in Bethesda, conducting basic research under the mentorship of an NIH senior investigator or preceptor. They learn the latest laboratory techniques and experience the creative thinking involved in at least 1 of the following biomedical areas: biostatistics, cell biology, epidemiology, genetics, immunology, neuroscience, or structural biology. This program is unique in that it does not require students to propose a research project or select a laboratory at the NIH as part of the application process. Instead, Research Scholars are encouraged to take their first couple of weeks in the program to interview investigators and explore different laboratories at the NIH before making a selection. This program is jointly sponsored by the Howard Hughes Medical Institute and the National Institutes of Health—the largest private and public biomedical research institutions in the United States. It complements the HHMI Research Training Fellowships for Medical Students Program; students may not apply to both programs in the same year.

Number awarded   Approximately 42 each year.

Deadline   January of each year.

[275]
HISPANIC LEADERSHIP DEVELOPMENT FUND

United Methodist Church
General Board of Global Ministries
Attn: Health and Welfare Program
475 Riverside Drive, Room 330
New York, NY 10115
(212) 870-3871   Toll-free: (800) UMC-GBGM
E-mail: jyoung@gbgm-umc.org
Web: hbs.gbgm-umc.org/umcor/work/health/scholarships

Summary To provide financial assistance to Methodists and other Christians of Hispanic descent who are preparing for a career in a health-related field.

Eligibility This program is open to U.S. citizens who are of Hispanic descent. Applicants must be professed Christians, preferably United Methodists. They must be attending a college or university to enter or continue in a health-related field. Financial need is considered in the selection process.

Financial data The stipend is $2,000.

Duration 1 year.

Additional information This program was established in 1986.

Number awarded Varies each year.

Deadline June of each year.

[276]
HIV/AIDS RESEARCH FELLOWSHIPS

American Psychological Association
Attn: Minority Fellowship Program
750 First Street, N.E.
Washington, DC 20002-4242
(202) 336-6127   Fax: (202) 336-6012
TDD: (202) 336-6123   E-mail: mfp@apa.org
Web: www.apa.org/mfp/hprogram.html

Summary To provide financial assistance to psychology doctoral students (especially minorities) who are preparing for a career involving research on HIV/AIDS issues and ethnic minority populations.

Eligibility This program is open to full-time doctoral students who can demonstrate a strong commitment to a career in HIV/AIDS research related to ethnic minorities. Students from the complete range of psychology disciplines are encouraged to apply if their training and research interests are related to mental health and HIV/AIDS. Clinical, counseling, and school psychology students must demonstrate that they will receive substantial training in research and the delivery of services to people with HIV/AIDS. Members of minority groups (African Americans, Alaskan Natives, American Indians, Asian Americans, Hispanics/Latinos, Native Hawaiians, and Pacific Islanders) are especially encouraged to apply. U.S. citizenship or permanent resident status is required. Selection is based on commitment to a career in research that focuses on HIV/AIDS in ethnic minority communities, knowledge of ethnic minority psychology or HIV/AIDS issues, the fit between career goals and training environment selected, potential for a research career demonstrated through accomplishments and goals, scholarship and grades, and letters of recommendation.

Financial data The stipend is that established by the National Institutes of Health for predoctoral students, recently $20,772 per year.

Duration 1 year; may be renewed for up to 2 additional years.

Additional information Funding is provided by the U.S. National Institute of Mental Health. Students who receive a feder-

ally-funded grant from another source may not also accept funds from this program.

Number awarded Varies each year.

Deadline January of each year.

[277]
HO'OMAKA HOU SCHOLARSHIP

Hawai'i Community Foundation
Attn: Scholarship Department
1164 Bishop Street, Suite 800
Honolulu, HI 96813
(808) 566-5570   Toll-free: (888) 731-3863
Fax: (808) 521-6286   E-mail: scholarships@hcf-hawaii.org
Web: www.hawaiicommunityfoundation.org

Summary To provide financial assistance to Hawaii residents who are interested in attending college or graduate school and have turned their lives around after overcoming substance abuse.

Eligibility This program is open to Hawaii residents who have turned their lives around after overcoming substance abuse. Applicants must be or planning to become full-time students at the undergraduate or graduate school level. They must be able to demonstrate academic achievement (GPA of 2.7 or higher), good moral character, and financial need. Along with their application, they must submit a short statement indicating their reasons for attending college, their planned course of study, and their career goals.

Financial data The amounts of the awards depend on the availability of funds and the need of the recipient.

Duration 1 year.

Additional information Recipients may attend college in Hawaii or on the mainland.

Number awarded Varies each year.

Deadline February of each year.

[278]
HORIZON SCHOLARSHIPS

Maine Employers' Mutual Insurance Company
Attn: MEMIC Education Fund
261 Commercial Street
P.O. Box 11409
Portland, ME 04104
(207) 791-3300   Toll-free: (800) 660-1306
Fax: (207) 791-3335   E-mail: mbourque@memic.com
Web: www.memic.com

Summary To provide financial assistance for college or graduate school to Maine residents whose parent or spouse was killed or permanently disabled in a work-related accident.

Eligibility This program is open to Maine residents who are the child or spouse of a worker killed or permanently disabled as the result of a work-related injury. The worker must have been insured through the sponsor at the time of the workplace injury. Applicants must be attending or planning to attend an accredited college or university as an undergraduate or graduate student. They must submit a personal statement of 500 words or less on their aspirations and how their educational plans relate to them. Selection is based on financial need, academic performance, community involvement, and other life experiences.

Financial data Stipends range up to $5,000, depending on the need of the recipient. Funds are paid directly to the recipient's institution.

Duration 1 year; may be renewed.

Additional information The Maine Employers' Mutual Insurance Company (MEMIC) was established in 1993 as the result of reforms in Maine's workers' compensation laws. It is currently the largest workers' compensation insurance company in the state. It established this scholarship program in 2001.

Number awarded Varies each year; recently, 2 of these scholarships were awarded.

Deadline April of each year.

[279]
HOWARD BROWN RICKARD SCHOLARSHIPS

National Federation of the Blind
c/o Peggy Elliott, Scholarship Committee Chair
805 Fifth Avenue
Grinnell, IA 50112
(641) 236-3366
Web: www.nfb.org/sch_intro.htm

Summary To provide financial assistance for college or graduate school to blind students studying or planning to study law, medicine, engineering, architecture, or the natural sciences.

Eligibility This program is open to legally blind students who are enrolled in or planning to enroll in a full-time undergraduate or graduate course of study. Applicants must be studying or planning to study law, medicine, engineering, architecture, or the natural sciences. Selection is based on academic excellence, service to the community, and financial need.

Financial data The stipend is $3,000.

Duration 1 year; recipients may resubmit applications up to 2 additional years.

Additional information Scholarships are awarded at the federation convention in July. Recipients attend the convention at federation expense; that funding is in addition to the scholarship grant.

Number awarded 1 each year.

Deadline March of each year.

[280]
HOWARD HUGHES MEDICAL INSTITUTE RESEARCH TRAINING FELLOWSHIPS FOR MEDICAL STUDENTS

Howard Hughes Medical Institute
Attn: Office of Grants and Special Programs
4000 Jones Bridge Road
Chevy Chase, MD 20815-6789
(301) 215-8889   Toll-free: (800) 448-4882, ext. 8889
Fax: (301) 215-8888   E-mail: fellows@hhmi.org
Web: www.hhmi.org/grants/individuals/medfellows.html

Summary To provide financial assistance to medical students interested in pursuing research training.

Eligibility Applicants must be enrolled in a medical school in the United States, although they may be citizens of any country. They must describe a proposed research project to be conducted at an academic or nonprofit research institution in the United States, other than a facility of the National Institutes of Health in Bethesda, Maryland. Research proposals should reflect the interests of the Howard Hughes Medical Institute (HHMI), especially in biochemistry, bioinformatics, biomedical engineering, biophysics, biostatistics, cell biology, developmental biology, epidemiology, genetics, immunology, mathematical and computational biology, microbiology, molecular biology, neuroscience, pharmacology, physiology, structural biology, and virology. Applications from women and minorities underrepresented in the sciences (Blacks, Hispanics, American Indians, Native Alaskans, and Native Pacific Islanders) are especially encouraged. Students enrolled in M.D./Ph.D., Ph.D., or Sc.D. programs and those who have completed a Ph.D. or Sc.D. in a laboratory-based science are not eligible. Selection is based on the applicant's ability and promise for a research career as a physician-scientist and the quality of training that will be provided.

Financial data Fellows receive a stipend of $25,000 per year; their institution receives an institutional allowance of $5,500 and a research allowance of $5,500.

Duration 1 year.

Additional information This program complements the HHMI-NIH Research Scholars Program; students may not apply to both programs in the same year.

Number awarded Up to 60 each year.

Deadline January of each year.

[281]
HOWARD S. STERN SCHOLARSHIPS

American Society of Radiologic Technologists
Attn: ASRT Education and Research Foundation
15000 Central Avenue, S.E.
Albuquerque, NM 87123-3909
(505) 298-4500, ext. 2541
Toll-free: (800) 444-2778, ext. 2541   Fax: (505) 298-5063
E-mail: foundation@asrt.org
Web: www.asrt.org

Summary To provide financial assistance to members of the American Society of Radiologic Technologists (ASRT) who are interested in continuing their education.

Eligibility This program is open to licensed radiologic technologists who are current members of ASRT and have worked in the radiologic sciences profession for at least 1 year during the past 5 years in a clinical or didactic setting. Applicants must have applied to 1) an accredited certificate program related to the radiologic sciences, or 2) a course of study at the associate, bachelor's, master's, or doctoral level intended to further their career. Along with their application, they must submit a written interview up to 1,000 words on their professional achievements, their career goals, how their degree or certificate will help them to achieve their career goals, their educational goals, and how this scholarship will help them to achieve their educational goals. Financial need is considered in the selection process.

Financial data The stipend is $1,000.

Duration 1 year; may be renewed for 1 additional year.

Additional information This program, supported by E-Z-EM Inc., replaces the Jeanette C. and Isadore N. Stern Scholarship, established in 1993.

Number awarded Varies each year; recently, 9 of these scholarships were awarded.

Deadline January of each year.

[282]
HUGH J. ANDERSEN MEMORIAL SCHOLARSHIPS

National Medical Fellowships, Inc.
Attn: Scholarship Program
5 Hanover Square, 15th Floor
New York, NY 10004
(212) 483-8880   Fax: (212) 483-8897
E-mail: info@nmfonline.org
Web: www.nmf-online.org

Summary To provide financial assistance to underrepresented minority medical students who reside or attend school in Minnesota.

Eligibility This program is open to African Americans, Mexican Americans, Native Hawaiians, Alaska Natives, American Indians, and mainland Puerto Ricans who have completed at least 1 year of medical school. Applicants must be Minnesota residents enrolled in an accredited U.S. medical school. Selection is based on leadership, community service, and financial need. Direct applications are not accepted; candidates must be nominated by medical school deans.

Financial data The award is $2,500.

Duration 1 year.

Additional information This award was established in 1982.

Number awarded Up to 5 each year.

Deadline Nominations must be submitted by March of each year.

[283]
H.Y. BENEDICT FELLOWSHIPS

Alpha Chi
Attn: Executive Director
900 East Center Avenue
Harding University Box 12249
Searcy, AR 72149-0001
(501) 279-4443   Toll-free: (800) 477-4225
Fax: (501) 279-4589   E-mail: dorgan@harding.edu
Web: www.harding.edu/alphachi/benedict.htm

Summary To provide financial assistance for graduate school to members of Alpha Chi, a national honor society.

Eligibility Eligible to be nominated for these funds are graduating college seniors who have been initiated into Alpha Chi and are going on to a graduate or professional school. Members who are currently enrolled in graduate school may also be nominated. Only 2 nominations may be submitted by each chapter. Included in the nomination package must be an academic paper or other appropriate work in the student's major field (e.g., painting, music score, film, slides, video, cassette tape recording, or other medium). Students must also submit a letter of application outlining their plans for study and detailing their extracurricular activities. Financial need is not considered.

Financial data The stipend is $2,500.

Duration 1 year.

Additional information Recipients must enroll in graduate school on a full-time basis.

Number awarded 10 each year.

Deadline February of each year.

[284]
IADES FELLOWSHIP AWARD

International Alumnae of Delta Epsilon Sorority
Attn: Fellowship Award Committee
9406 Steeple Court
Laurel, MD 20723
(301) 490-5076   E-mail: Fellowship@iades.org
Web: www.iades.org

Summary To provide financial assistance to deaf women who are working on a graduate degree.

Eligibility Eligible to apply are deaf women who have completed 12 or more units in a doctoral-level program with a GPA of 3.0 or more. They need not be members of Delta Epsilon. Along with their application, they must submit official transcripts,

a recent copy of their audiogram, and 2 letters of recommendation.

Financial data The stipend is $1,200.

Duration 1 year.

Additional information This program, established in 1989, is also known as the Betty G. Miller Fellowship Award. Information is also available from Virginia Borgaard, 2453 Bear Den Road, Frederick, MD 21701-9321.

Number awarded 1 or more each year.

Deadline August of each year.

[285]
ILLINOIS HOSPITAL RESEARCH AND EDUCATION FOUNDATION SCHOLARSHIPS

Illinois Hospital Association
Attn: Illinois Hospital Research and Educational Foundation
1151 East Warrenville Road
P.O. Box 3015
Naperville, IL 60566
(630) 505-7777
Web: www.ihatoday.org

Summary To provide financial assistance to Illinois residents accepted into or enrolled in a hospital-related health care professional curriculum.

Eligibility This program is open to Illinois residents who have been accepted into or are currently enrolled in a hospital-related health care professional curriculum. Applicants enrolled in an associate degree or hospital-based program will be considered in their first year only. Students must have been accepted in a health care professional sequence; that is, when courses are open only to student candidates for the degree or certification; pre-nursing, pre-medicine, and pre-pharmacy applicants are not eligible until they are accepted into nursing clinics, medical school, etc. Applicants who have less than 1 academic year remaining until graduation are not eligible for consideration. Selection is based on academic record (GPA of 3.5 or higher) and financial need.

Financial data The stipend is $1,000. Funds must be used for tuition, fees, or books.

Duration 1 year.

Additional information The school attended need not be in Illinois, but it must be accredited or recognized as an approved program by the appropriate agencies.

Number awarded Varies each year; recently, 36 of these scholarships were awarded.

Deadline April of each year.

[286]
ILLINOIS VETERAN GRANT PROGRAM

Illinois Student Assistance Commission
Attn: Scholarship and Grant Services
1755 Lake Cook Road
Deerfield, IL 60015-5209
(847) 948-8550   Toll-free: (800) 899-ISAC
Fax: (847) 831-8549   TDD: (847) 831-8326, ext. 2822
E-mail: collegezone@isac.org
Web: www.collegezone.com

Summary To provide financial assistance for undergraduate and graduate education to Illinois veterans.

Eligibility This program is open to Illinois residents who served in the U.S. armed forces (including members of the Reserves and the Illinois National Guard) for at least 1 year on active duty and have been honorably discharged. The 1-year service requirement does not apply to veterans who 1) served in a foreign country in a time of hostilities in that country, 2) were medically discharged for service-related reasons, or 3) were discharged prior to August 11, 1967. Applicants must have been Illinois residents for at least 6 months before entering service and they must have returned to Illinois within 6 months after separation from service. Current members of the Reserve Officer Training Corps are not eligible.

Financial data This program pays all tuition and certain fees at all Illinois public colleges, universities, and community colleges.

Duration This scholarship may be used for the equivalent of up to 4 years of full-time enrollment, provided the recipient maintains the minimum GPA required by their college or university.

Additional information This is an entitlement program; once eligibility has been established, no further applications are necessary.

Number awarded Varies each year.

Deadline Applications may be submitted at any time.

[287]
INDIANA CHILD OF VETERAN AND PUBLIC SAFETY OFFICER SUPPLEMENTAL GRANT PROGRAM

State Student Assistance Commission of Indiana
Attn: Grant Division
150 West Market Street, Suite 500
Indianapolis, IN 46204-2811
(317) 232-2350 Toll-free: (888) 528-4719 (within IN)
Fax: (317) 232-3260 E-mail: grants@ssaci.state.in.us
Web: www.in.gov/ssaci/programs/cvo.html

Summary To provide financial assistance to undergraduate or graduate students in Indiana who are 1) the children of disabled or other veterans, and 2) the children and spouses of certain deceased or disabled public safety officers.

Eligibility The veterans portion of this program is open to Indiana residents who are the natural or adopted children of veterans who served in the active-duty U.S. armed forces during a period of wartime. Applicants may be of any age; parents must have lived in Indiana for at least 3 years during their lifetime. The veteran parent must also 1) have a service-connected disability as determined by the U.S. Department of Veterans Affairs or the Department of Defense; 2) have received a Purple Heart Medal; or 3) have been a resident of Indiana at the time of entry into the service and declared a POW or MIA after January 1, 1960. Students at the Indiana Soldiers' and Sailors' Children's Home are also eligible. The public safety officer portion of this program is open to 1) the children and spouses of regular law enforcement officers, regular fire fighters, volunteer fire fighters, county police reserve officers, city police reserve officers, paramedics, emergency medical technicians, and advanced emergency medical technicians killed in the line of duty, and 2) the children and spouses of Indiana state police troopers permanently and totally disabled in the line of duty. Children must be younger than 23 years of age and enrolled full time in an undergraduate or graduate degree program. Spouses must be enrolled in an undergraduate program and must have been married to the covered public safety officer at the time of death or disability.

Financial data Qualified applicants receive a 100% remission of tuition and all mandatory fees for undergraduate or graduate work at state-supported postsecondary schools and universities in Indiana. It does not cover such fees as room and board.

Duration Up to 124 semester hours of study.

Additional information The veterans portion of this program is administered by the Indiana Department of Veterans' Affairs, 302 West Washington Street, Room E-120, Indianapolis, IN

46204-2738, (317) 232-3910, (800) 400-4520, Fax: (317) 232-7721, E-mail: jkiser@dva.state.in.us.

Number awarded Varies each year.

Deadline Applications must be submitted at least 30 days before the start of the college term.

[288]
INDIVIDUAL PREDOCTORAL DENTAL SCIENTIST FELLOWSHIPS

National Institute of Dental and Craniofacial Research
Attn: Division of Extramural Research
45 Center Drive, Room 4AS-13B
Bethesda, MD 20892-6401
(301) 496-4263 Fax: (301) 402-7033
TTY: (301) 451-0088 E-mail: Albert.Avila/@nih.gov
Web: www.nidr.nih.gov

Summary To provide financial assistance to dental students who wish to participate in an integrated dental and graduate research training program that leads to both the D.D.S./D.M.D. and Ph.D. degrees.

Eligibility This program is open to U.S. citizens, nationals, and permanent residents who are enrolled in a formal program at an approved dental school that leads to a D.D.S. or D.M.D. degree; have been accepted in a Ph.D. program in dental, oral, and craniofacial health research from the basic, behavioral, and clinical perspectives; and have a confirmed mentor in that scientific field. Applicants may be in the third year of dental school, although preference is given to those in the first or second year. Individuals currently enrolled in a joint D.D.S./D.M.D.-Ph.D. program are eligible for consideration as trainees, but persons who obtained a Ph.D. prior to entering dental school and desire to pursue another research doctorate while in dental school are not eligible. Racial/ethnic minority individuals, women, and persons with disabilities are strongly encouraged to apply.

Financial data The fellowship provides an annual stipend of $20,772, a tuition and fee allowance (60% of costs up to $16,000 or 60% of costs up to $21,000 for dual degrees), and an institutional allowance of $4,200 for travel to scientific meetings and for laboratory and other training expenses.

Duration Up to 5 years of support for predoctoral study or up to 3 years of support at the postdoctoral level.

Number awarded Up to 4 each year.

Deadline April, August, or December of each year.

[289]
INEZ DEMONET SCHOLARSHIP

Vesalius Trust for Visual Communications in the Health Sciences
Attn: Wendy Hiller Gee, Student Grants and Scholarships
Krames-West Coast
1100 Grundy Lane
San Bruno, CA 94066
(650) 244-4320 E-mail: wendy.hillergee@krames.com
Web: www.vesaliustrust.org/scholarships.html

Summary To provide financial assistance to graduate students working on a degree in medical illustrating.

Eligibility This program is open to graduate students enrolled in the second year of a program in medical illustration accredited by the Association of Medical Illustrators. Applicants must submit a portfolio of 5 samples of their work and brief statements on why they decided to enter the field of medical illustration, the academic experiences that meant the most to them during their education (undergraduate or graduate school), what they plan to be doing in their professional life 10 years from now, and what else they would like the committee to know about them. Selection is based on academic breadth and depth, academic performance, quality of artwork, quality of references, and evidence of broad-based interests and accomplishments.

Financial data The stipend is $2,000. Travel support is provided for the recipient to attend the Vesalius Trust annual meeting.

Duration 1 year.

Additional information This scholarship was first awarded in 1989.

Number awarded 1 each year.

Deadline February of each year.

[290]
INTERNATIONAL DAIRY-DELI-BAKERY ASSOCIATION SCHOLARSHIP

International Dairy-Deli-Bakery Association
Attn: Scholarship Committee
636 Science Drive
P.O. Box 5528
Madison, WI 53705-0528
(608) 310-5000   Fax: (608) 238-6330
E-mail: iddba@iddba.org
Web: www.iddba.org/scholars.htm

Summary To provide financial assistance to undergraduate or graduate students employed in a supermarket dairy, deli, or bakery department who are interested in working on a degree in a food-related field.

Eligibility This program is open to high school seniors, college students, vocational/technical students, and graduate students. Applicants must be currently employed in a supermarket dairy, deli, or bakery department or be employed by a company that services those departments (e.g., food manufacturers, brokers, or wholesalers). They must be majoring in a food-related field, e.g., culinary arts, baking/pastry arts, food science, business, or marketing. Their employer must be a member of the International Dairy-Deli-Bakery Association (IDDBA). While a GPA of 2.5 or higher is required, this may be waived for first-time applicants. Selection is based on academic achievement, work experience, and a statement of career goals and/or how their degree will be beneficial to their job. Financial need is not considered.

Financial data Stipends range from $250 to $1,000. Funds are paid jointly to the recipient and the recipient's school. If the award exceeds tuition fees, the excess may be used for other educational expenses.

Duration 1 year; recipients may reapply.

Number awarded Varies each year; a total of $75,000 is available for this program annually.

Deadline Applications must be submitted prior to the end of March, June, September, or December of each year.

[291]
IOWA SPACE GRANT SCHOLARSHIP PROGRAM

Iowa Space Grant Consortium
Attn: Director
Iowa State University
2271 Howe Hall, Room 2365
Ames, IA 50011-2271
(515) 294-3106   Toll-free: (800) 854-1667
Fax: (515) 294-3361   E-mail: isgc@iastate.edu
Web: www.ia.spacegrant.org

Summary To provide financial assistance to undergraduate and graduate students majoring in science, technology, engineering, or mathematics (STEM) disciplines at member institutions of the Iowa Space Grant Consortium (ISGC).

Eligibility This program is open to U.S. citizens enrolled full time as undergraduate or graduate students at ISGC member institutions. Applicants must be majoring in a STEM discipline of interest to the National Aeronautics and Space Administration. They must be interested in working on the base research program at their institution. Students from underrepresented groups (women, minorities, and persons with disabilities) are especially encouraged to apply.

Financial data The stipend is $6,000.

Duration 1 year.

Additional information Member institutions of ISGC, and their base programs, include Drake University (molecular biology and space life sciences), Iowa State University (the Spacecraft Systems and Operations Laboratory), the University of Iowa (the Operator Performance Laboratory), and the University of Northern Iowa (student research program on Iowa's lakes and wetlands). Funding for this program is provided by NASA.

Number awarded Approximately 16 each year.

Deadline March of each year.

[292]
IRENE AND DAISY MACGREGOR MEMORIAL SCHOLARSHIP

National Society Daughters of the American Revolution
Attn: Committee Services Office, Scholarships
1776 D Street, N.W.
Washington, DC 20006-5303
(202) 628-1776
Web: www.dar.org/natsociety/edout_scholar.cfm

Summary To provide financial assistance for medical or psychiatric nursing study.

Eligibility This program is open to outstanding students who have been accepted into or are pursuing an approved program of graduate psychiatric nursing or medicine. Applicants must be U.S. citizens and attend an accredited medical school, college, or university in the United States. They must obtain a letter of sponsorship from a local Daughters of the American Revolution (DAR) chapter. Preference is given to women applicants if they are "equally qualified." Selection is based on academic excellence, commitment to the field of study, and financial need.

Financial data The stipend is $5,000.

Duration 1 year; may be renewed for up to 3 additional years.

Additional information Requests for applications must be accompanied by a self-addressed stamped envelope.

Number awarded 1 or more each year.

Deadline April of each year.

[293]
IRENE E. NEWMAN SCHOLARSHIP

American Dental Hygienists' Association
Attn: Institute for Oral Health
444 North Michigan Avenue, Suite 3400
Chicago, IL 60611
(312) 440-8918   Toll-free: (800) 735-4916
Fax: (312) 440-8929   E-mail: institute@adha.net
Web: www.adha.org/institute/Scholarship/index.htm

Summary To provide financial assistance to students in a baccalaureate or graduate degree program in dental hygiene who demonstrate strong potential in public health or community dental health.

Eligibility This program is open to students who have completed at least 1 year in a dental hygiene program at the baccalaureate, master's, or doctoral level with a GPA of at least 3.0. Applicants must demonstrate strong potential in public health or community dental health. They must be active members of the Student American Dental Hygienists' Association (SADHA) or the American Dental Hygienists' Association (ADHA) and be able to document financial need of at least $1,500. Along with their application, they must submit a statement that covers their long-term career goals, their intended contribution to the dental hygiene profession, their professional interests, a list of past and/or present involvement in professional and/or community activities, and the manner in which their degree will enhance their professional capacity. Selection is based on their potential in public health or community dental health.

Financial data Stipends range from $1,000 to $2,000.

Duration 1 year.

Number awarded 1 each year.

Deadline June of each year.

[294]
IRENE WOODALL GRADUATE SCHOLARSHIP

American Dental Hygienists' Association
Attn: Institute for Oral Health
444 North Michigan Avenue, Suite 3400
Chicago, IL 60611
(312) 440-8918   Toll-free: (800) 735-4916
Fax: (312) 440-8929   E-mail: institute@adha.net
Web: www.adha.org/institute/Scholarship/index.htm

Summary To provide financial assistance to licensed dental hygienists who are enrolled as full-time graduate students at a university.

Eligibility This program is open to licensed dental hygienists who have a baccalaureate degree and have completed at least 1 year of work as a full-time master's or doctoral degree student in a university graduate program. Applicants must be active members of the Student American Dental Hygienists' Association (SADHA) or the American Dental Hygienists' Association (ADHA), have a GPA of at least 3.0, and be able to document financial need of at least $1,500. Along with their application, they must submit a statement that covers their long-term career goals, their intended contribution to the dental hygiene profession, their professional interests, the manner in which their degree will enhance their professional capacity, a description of the research in which they are involved or would like to become involved, and a list of past and/or present involvement in professional and/or community activities.

Financial data Stipends range from $1,000 to $2,000.

Duration 1 year.

Number awarded 1 or more each year.

Deadline June of each year.

[295]
IRVING GRAEF MEMORIAL SCHOLARSHIP

National Medical Fellowships, Inc.
Attn: Scholarship Program
5 Hanover Square, 15th Floor
New York, NY 10004
(212) 483-8880   Fax: (212) 483-8897
E-mail: info@nmfonline.org
Web: www.nmf-online.org

Summary To provide financial assistance to third-year underrepresented minority medical school students.

Eligibility This competition is open only to rising third-year minority medical school students who received financial assistance from National Medical Fellowships during their second year. For the purposes of this program, "minority" is defined as African American, Native Hawaiian, Alaska Native, American Indian, Mexican American, and mainland Puerto Rican students. Candidates must be nominated by their medical schools. Selection is based on outstanding academic achievement, leadership, and community service.

Financial data This honor includes a certificate of merit and an annual stipend of $2,000.

Duration 1 year; renewable in the fourth year of medical school, if the recipient continues in good academic standing.

Additional information This program is named in honor of an active National Medical Fellowship board member who was also an associate professor of clinical medicine at New York University's School of Medicine. It was established in 1978.

Number awarded 1 each year.

Deadline Nominations must be submitted by November of each year.

[296]
JACK KENT COOKE GRADUATE SCHOLARSHIPS

Jack Kent Cooke Foundation
44115 Woodridge Parkway, Suite 200
Lansdowne, VA 20176-5199
(703) 723-8000   Toll-free: (800) 498-6478
Fax: (703) 723-8030
E-mail: jkc@jackkentcookefoundation.org
Web: www.jackkentcookefoundation.org

Summary To provide financial assistance to college seniors who are interested in working on a graduate degree in the United States or abroad.

Eligibility This program is open to seniors graduating from accredited U.S. colleges and universities and recent (within the past 5 years) graduates who are planning to enter graduate school in the United States or abroad as a full-time student. Applicants must be nominated by their undergraduate college or university and have a college GPA of 3.5 or higher. Along with their application, they must submit a narrative autobiography and documentation of financial need. Selection is based on academic ability and achievement, critical thinking ability, financial need, will to succeed, leadership and public service, and appreciation for and participation in the arts and humanities.

Financial data The maximum stipend is $50,000 per year.

Duration 1 year; may be renewed up to 5 additional years, as long as the fellow maintains high academic performance, good conduct, significant progress toward a degree, and compliance with the foundation's administrative requirements and requests.

Additional information This program was first offered in 2002. Accredited U.S. undergraduate institutions appoint a faculty representative to lead the nomination process and serve as liaison between the school and the foundation. Information is also available from the Jack Kent Cooke Foundation Graduate Scholarship Program, 301 ACT Drive, P.O. Box 4030, Iowa City, IA 52243, E-mail: jkc-g@act.org.
Number awarded 45 to 50 each year.
Deadline Campus faculty representatives must submit applications by April of each year.

[297]
JAMES P. DEARING SCHOLARSHIP
American Society of Extra-Corporeal Technology, Inc.
Attn: AmSECT Foundation
2209 Dickens Road
P.O. Box 11086
Richmond, VA 23230-1086
(804) 565-6363   Fax: (804) 282-0090
E-mail: AmSECT@amsect.org
Web: www.amsect.org
Summary To provide financial assistance to student members of the American Society of Extra-Corporeal Technology (AmSECT) who are enrolled in a perfusion training program.
Eligibility This program is open to student members of the society who are enrolled in (or accepted at) an accredited perfusion training program. Applicants must have completed at least half of the required course work and have at least a 2.75 GPA. They must submit 1) 250-word essays on how they would improve AmSECT and how they could improve the perfusion profession, and 2) a 500-word essay on a current topic affecting the conduct of perfusion. Financial need is not considered in the selection process.
Financial data The stipend is $2,000 per year.
Duration 1 year.
Number awarded 1 each year.
Deadline November of each year.

[298]
JAMES P. KOHN MEMORIAL SCHOLARSHIP
American Society of Safety Engineers
Attn: ASSE Foundation
1800 East Oakton Street
Des Plaines, IL 60018
(847) 768-3435   Fax: (847) 768-3434
E-mail: agabanski@asse.org
Web: www.asse.org/foundation
Summary To provide financial assistance to graduate student members of the American Society of Safety Engineers (ASSE) who are working on a degree in occupational health and related fields.
Eligibility This program is open to student members who are working on a graduate degree in occupational safety and health or a closely-related field (e.g., industrial or environmental engineering, environmental science, industrial hygiene, occupational health nursing). Applicants must be full-time students who have completed at least 9 semester hours with a GPA of 3.5 or higher. Their undergraduate GPA must have been 3.0 or higher. Along with their application, they must submit 2 essays of 300 words or less: 1) why they are seeking a degree in occupational safety and health or a closely-related field, a brief description of their current activities, and how those relate to their career goals and

objectives; and 2) why they should be awarded this scholarship (including career goals and financial need).
Financial data The stipend is $2,000.
Duration 1 year; nonrenewable.
Number awarded 1 each year.
Deadline November of each year.

[299]
JAMES Q. CANNON MEMORIAL SCHOLARSHIPS
James Q. Cannon Memorial Endowment
c/o Larry W. Pitman
Kansas Foundation for Medical Care, Inc.
2947 S.W. Wanamaker Drive
Topeka, KS 66614-4193
(785) 273-2552   Fax: (785) 273-5130
Summary To provide financial assistance to graduate students preparing for a career in the field of health care quality improvement.
Eligibility This program is open to students working on a graduate degree in a field related to the application of improvement methods in health care settings. Applicants must be able to demonstrate that their chosen program has a strong focus on the establishment of skills and knowledge about the measurement and improvement of health care quality. Selection is based on academic record, acceptance for graduate study in an appropriate academic program, and demonstrated commitment to the field of health care quality improvement.
Financial data The maximum stipend is $10,000.
Duration 1 year.
Additional information This program was established in 1999.
Number awarded Varies each year; recently, 6 of these scholarships were awarded.
Deadline May of each year.

[300]
JANEL PARKER CAREER MOBILITY SCHOLARSHIP
American Nephrology Nurses' Association
Attn: ANNA National Office
200 East Holly Avenue
P.O. Box 56
Pitman, NJ 08071-0056
(856) 256-2320   Toll-free: (888) 600-2662
Fax: (856) 589-7463   E-mail: annascholarships@ajj.com
Web: www.annanurse.org
Summary To provide financial assistance to members of the American Nephrology Nurses' Association (ANNA) who are interested in working on a baccalaureate or advanced degree in nursing.
Eligibility Applicants must be current association members, have been members for at least 2 years, be currently employed in nephrology nursing, and be accepted or enrolled in a baccalaureate or higher degree program in nursing. Along with their application, they must submit a 250-word essay on their career and education goals that includes how their degree will apply to nephrology nursing, provides a time frame for completing their program, and indicates how the funds will meet their educational needs.
Financial data The stipend is $2,500.
Duration 1 year.
Additional information These scholarships, first awarded in 1993, are sponsored by Anthony J. Jannetti, Inc. Information is

also available from Sharon Longton, Awards and Scholarships Chair, (313) 966-2674, E-mail: slongton@dmc.org.

Number awarded 1 each year.

Deadline October of each year.

[301]
JANICE MCGRAW MEMORIAL SCHOLARSHIP

American Occupational Therapy Foundation
Attn: Scholarship Coordinator
4720 Montgomery Lane
P.O. Box 31220
Bethesda, MD 20824-1220
(301) 652-2682   Fax: (301) 656-3620
TDD: (800) 377-8555   E-mail: aotf@aotf.org
Web: www.aotf.org

Summary To provide financial assistance to North Carolina residents who are members of the American Occupational Therapy Association (AOTA) and working on a master's degree in occupational therapy.

Eligibility This program is open to North Carolina residents who are full-time students working on a professional master's degree (entry level) in an accredited or developing occupational therapy educational program. Applicants must be members of the association, demonstrate a need for financial assistance, and have a sustained record of outstanding scholastic performance. As part of the application process, they must submit transcripts, 2 personal references, and a statement from their curriculum director.

Financial data The stipend is $1,000.

Duration 1 year; recipients may reapply.

Number awarded 1 each year.

Deadline January of each year.

[302]
JAPANESE MEDICAL SOCIETY OF AMERICA MEDICAL STUDENT SCHOLARSHIP

Japanese Medical Society of America, Inc.
c/o Yuzuru Anzai, M.D., Scholarship Committee Chair
285 Central Park West, Apartment 3W
New York, NY 10024
(212) 263-8682   Fax: (212) 883-5852
E-mail: yuzuru.anzai@med.nyu.edu
Web: www.jmsa.org

Summary To provide financial assistance to Japanese American medical school students.

Eligibility This program is open to Japanese Americans who are accepted at or currently enrolled in a medical school in the United States. Applicants must submit a 1-page essay about themselves and how they will be involved in the sponsoring organization's activities. Selection is based on academic excellence, honors and awards, community activities, financial need, and interest in the organization.

Financial data A stipend is awarded (amount not specified).

Duration 1 year.

Deadline February of each year.

[303]
JAPANESE WOMEN'S SOCIETY FOUNDATION ACADEMIC SCHOLARSHIP

Japanese Women's Society Foundation
Attn: Scholarship Committee
P.O. Box 3233
Honolulu, HI 96801
(808) 547-9192
Web: www.jwsonline.org/index.php?page=scholarships

Summary To provide financial assistance to graduate students from Hawaii working on a degree in a field related to gerontology or geriatrics.

Eligibility This program is open to residents of Hawaii who are enrolled or accepted in a graduate degree program at an accredited institution of higher learning. Applicants may be studying medicine, nursing, public health, social work, or the arts and sciences, but they must be able to demonstrate an interest and commitment in the field of gerontology or geriatrics based on course work, research, and/or volunteerism. Along with their application, they must submit a brief description of their plans for further academic training and how this will help them to achieve their career goals of working on behalf of Hawaii's elderly. Preference is given to citizens of the United States, although citizens of other countries may apply. Financial need is considered in the selection process.

Financial data The stipend is $5,000.

Duration 1 year.

Number awarded 1 each year.

Deadline March of each year.

[304]
J.C. AND RHEBA COBB MEMORIAL SCHOLARSHIP

National Community Pharmacists Association
Attn: NCPA Foundation
100 Daingerfield Road
Alexandria, VA 22314-2888
(703) 683-8200   Toll-free: (800) 544-7447
Fax: (703) 683-3619   E-mail: info@ncpanet.org
Web: www.ncpanet.org.org

Summary To provide financial assistance for full-time education in pharmacy to student members of the National Community Pharmacists Association (NCPA).

Eligibility All pharmacy students who are student members of the association and enrolled in an accredited U.S. school or college of pharmacy on a full-time basis are eligible. Applicants must submit a copy of their most recent college transcript, 2 letters of recommendation, a resume or curriculum vitae, and a statement outlining their scholastic achievement, leadership activities, objectives for the future, and interest in civic and government affairs. Selection is based on leadership qualities, demonstrated interest in civic and government affairs, and academic achievement.

Financial data The stipend is $2,000, paid directly to the recipient's school or college of pharmacy.

Duration 1 year; nonrenewable.

Additional information Until October 1996, the NCPA, the national association representing independent retail pharmacy, was known as NARD (the National Association of Retail Druggists).

Number awarded 1 each year.

Deadline February of each year.

[305]
JEAN STEFFAN SMITH MEMORIAL SCHOLARSHIP
Kentucky Occupational Therapy Foundation
Attn: Scholarship Chair
P.O. Box 21502
Louisville, KY 40221-0502
Toll-free: (888) 987-KOTA   Fax: (502) 451-4308
E-mail: kota@kotaweb.org
Web: www.kyotf.org

Summary To provide financial assistance to residents of Kentucky who are working on an professional master's degree in occupational therapy.

Eligibility This program is open to Kentucky residents who are enrolled full time in an accredited occupational therapy educational program in the state at the professional master's degree level. Applicants must have a GPA of 3.0 or higher and a record of leadership, service, and membership in professional occupational therapy organizations (e.g., Kentucky Occupational Therapy Association, American Occupational Therapy Association). Along with their application, they must submit 2 letters of reference, a personal essay, and an official transcript.

Financial data The stipend is $1,250.

Duration 1 year.

Number awarded 1 or more each year.

Deadline April of each year.

[306]
JENNICA FERGUSON MEMORIAL SCHOLARSHIP
National Federation of the Blind
c/o Peggy Elliott, Scholarship Committee Chair
805 Fifth Avenue
Grinnell, IA 50112
(641) 236-3366
Web: www.nfb.org/sch_intro.htm

Summary To provide financial assistance to undergraduate and graduate blind students.

Eligibility This program is open to legally blind students who are working on or planning to work full time on an undergraduate or graduate degree. Selection is based on academic excellence, service to the community, and financial need.

Financial data The stipend is $5,000.

Duration 1 year; recipients may resubmit applications up to 2 additional years.

Additional information Scholarships are awarded at the federation convention in July. Recipients attend the convention at federation expense; that funding is in addition to the scholarship grant.

Number awarded 1 each year.

Deadline March of each year.

[307]
JERRY RHEA/ATLANTA FALCONS GRADUATE SCHOLARSHIP AWARD
Southeast Athletic Trainers Association
c/o Janet Passman, Scholarship Committee Chair
Louisiana College
1140 College Drive
Pineville, LA 71359
(318) 487-7290   Fax: (318) 487-7174
E-mail: passman@lacollege.edu
Web: www.seata.org/Scholarshipdetails.htm

Summary To provide financial assistance to graduate student members of the Southeast Athletic Trainers Association (SEATA).

Eligibility This program is open to graduate students at colleges and universities in Alabama, Florida, Georgia, Kentucky, Louisiana, Mississippi, and Tennessee who are members of SEATA and the National Association of Athletic Trainers (NATA). Applicants must have worked as an athletic training student for a period of at least 2 years at the college level and have a GPA of 3.0 or higher. They must be sponsored by a certified athletic trainer who is a current member of SEATA and NATA. Along with their application, they must submit a brief biographical sketch that includes their reasons for wanting the scholarship, why they merit this award, high school and college awards and honors, athletic teams with which they have worked, and jobs they have held. Selection is based on academic achievement, character, and athletic training abilities and experiences.

Financial data The stipend is $1,000.

Duration 1 year; nonrenewable.

Additional information SEATA serves as District 9 of NATA.

Number awarded 1 each year.

Deadline December of each year.

[308]
JERRY W. RICHMOND MEMORIAL SCHOLARSHIP
American Society of Extra-Corporeal Technology, Inc.
Attn: AmSECT Foundation
2209 Dickens Road
P.O. Box 11086
Richmond, VA 23230-1086
(804) 565-6363   Fax: (804) 282-0090
E-mail: AmSECT@amsect.org
Web: www.amsect.org

Summary To provide financial assistance to student members of the American Society of Extra-Corporeal Technology (AmSECT) who are enrolled in a perfusion training program.

Eligibility This program is open to student members of the society who are enrolled in (or accepted at) an accredited perfusion training program. Applicants must have completed at least 1 quarter of the required course work and have at least a 2.75 GPA. They must submit 250-word essays on how they would improve AmSECT and how they could improve the perfusion profession. Financial need is not considered in the selection process.

Financial data The stipend is $1,000 per year.

Duration 1 year.

Number awarded 1 each year.

Deadline November of each year.

[309]
J.F. SCHIRMER SCHOLARSHIP

American Mensa Education and Research Foundation
1229 Corporate Drive West
Arlington, TX 76006-6103
(817) 607-0060   Toll-free: (800) 66-MENSA
Fax: (817) 649-5232   E-mail: info@mensafoundation.org
Web: www.mensafoundation.org

Summary To provide financial assistance for undergraduate or graduate study to qualified students.

Eligibility Any student who is enrolled or will enroll in a degree program at an accredited American institution of postsecondary education is eligible to apply. Membership in Mensa is not required, but applicants must be U.S. citizens or permanent residents. There are no restrictions as to age, race, gender, level of postsecondary education, GPA, or financial need. Selection is based on a 550-word essay that describes the applicant's career, vocational, or academic goals.

Financial data The stipend is $1,000.

Duration 1 year; may be renewed for up to 3 additional years if the recipient remains in school and achieves satisfactory grades.

Additional information Applications are available only through participating Mensa local groups.

Number awarded 3 each year.

Deadline January of each year.

[310]
JNMA AWARDS FOR MEDICAL JOURNALISM

National Medical Fellowships, Inc.
Attn: Scholarship Program
5 Hanover Square, 15th Floor
New York, NY 10004
(212) 483-8880   Fax: (212) 483-8897
E-mail: info@nmfonline.org
Web: www.nmf-online.org

Summary To provide financial assistance to African American medical students who are also interested in journalism.

Eligibility This program is open to African American medical students who are U.S. citizens attending accredited M.D. or D.O. degree-granting schools in the United States and in their third or fourth year. Only nominations are accepted. Nominees must have published articles and photographs in (or been writers, editors, or photographers on) the staffs of medical school newspapers, medical student journals (e.g., *Journal of the Student National Medical Association* or the *New Physician* magazine), recognized professional journals (e.g., the *Journal of the National Medical Association,* the *Journal of the American Medical Association,* or the *New England Journal of Medicine*), or other respected scientific journals. Students who have written, produced, or directed health-related films, commercials, or videos are also eligible. Selection is based on academic achievement, demonstrated journalistic skill, leadership and community involvement, and potential for outstanding contributions to medicine.

Financial data The awards are $2,500.

Duration 1 year.

Additional information This program is sponsored by the Journal of the National Medical Association (JNMA).

Number awarded 2 each year.

Deadline April of each year.

[311]
JOAN ALLEN EICHELBERGER SCHOLARSHIP

American Association of Nurse Anesthetists
Attn: AANA Foundation
222 South Prospect Avenue
Park Ridge, IL 60068-4001
(847) 692-7050, ext. 1171   Fax: (847) 692-7137
E-mail: foundation@aana.com
Web: www.aana.com/foundation/default.asp

Summary To provide financial assistance to African American members of the American Association of Nurse Anesthetists (AANA) who are interested in obtaining further education.

Eligibility This program is open to African American members of the association who are currently enrolled in an accredited nurse anesthesia education program. Applicants must have a cumulative GPA of 3.0 or higher. First-year students must have completed 6 months of nurse anesthesia classes; second-year students must have completed 12 months of nurse anesthesia classes. Along with their application, they must submit a 200-word essay describing why they have chosen nurse anesthesia as a profession and their professional goals for the future. Financial need is also considered in the selection process.

Financial data The stipend is $1,000 per year.

Duration 1 academic year.

Additional information This program is supported by the Harlem Hospital School of Anesthesia Alumni. The application processing fee is $25.

Number awarded 1 each year.

Deadline March of each year.

[312]
JOANNA F. REED MEDICAL SCHOLARSHIP

Joanna F. Reed Medical Scholarship Trust
c/o BancTrust Financial Group
227 Belleville Avenue
P.O. Box 469
Brewton, AL 36427-0469
(251) 867-3231   Fax: (251) 809-2274

Summary To provide financial assistance to students in Alabama and selected parts of Florida who are working on a pre-med (undergraduate) or medical (graduate) degree at a private university.

Eligibility This program is open to men and women who are working on a degree in medicine at a recognized private medical school and to men and women who are working on an undergraduate degree in pre-medicine at a private university. They must be residents of Alabama or northwest Florida (all counties in the state west of the Apalachicola River: Escambia, Santa Rosa, Okaloosa, Walton, Homes, Washington, Bay, Jackson, Calhoun, and Gulf). They may attend school anywhere in the United States. Selection is based on academic performance, recommendations, financial need, motivation, character, ability, and career potential. Special consideration is given to students who wish to become general practitioners or internists.

Financial data The stipend is $7,500.

Duration 1 year; may renewed.

Number awarded 1 or more each year.

Deadline May of each year.

[313]
JOANNE HOLBROOK PATTON MILITARY SPOUSE SCHOLARSHIP PROGRAM

National Military Family Association, Inc.
Attn: Spouse Scholarship Program
2500 North Van Dorn Street, Suite 102
Alexandria, VA 22302-1601
(703) 931-NMFA   Toll-free: (800) 260-0218
Fax: (703) 931-4600   E-mail: families@nmfa.org
Web: www.nmfa.org

Summary To provide financial assistance for college or graduate school to spouses of active and retired uniformed services personnel.

Eligibility This program is open to the spouses of uniformed services personnel (active, retired, Reserve, Guard, or survivor). Applicants must be attending or planning to attend an accredited postsecondary institution to work on a professional certificate or undergraduate or graduate degree. Selection is based on an essay question, community involvement, and academic achievement.

Financial data The stipend is $1,000. Funds are paid directly to the educational institution to be used for tuition, fees, books, and school room and board.

Duration 1 year; recipients may reapply.

Additional information This program began in 2004. It is currently sponsored by General Dynamics. Applications must be submitted online.

Number awarded Varies each year; recently, 25 of these scholarships were awarded.

Deadline March of each year.

[314]
JOHN AND BETTY POPE FELLOWSHIP PROGRAM

Rosalynn Carter Institute for Human Development
c/o Georgia Southwestern State University
800 Wheatley Street
Americus, GA 31709
(229) 928-1234   Fax: (229) 931-2663
E-mail: rci@canes.gsw.edu
Web: rci/gsw/edu/pope_program.htm

Summary To provide financial assistance to undergraduate and graduate students in Georgia interested in preparing for a career in a caregiving field.

Eligibility This program is open to undergraduate and graduate students enrolled at institutions that are components of the University System of Georgia. Applicants must have a GPA of 3.0 or higher. They must be committed to preparing for a career in a caregiving field as demonstrated by 1) completing an academic project on a caregiving topic; 2) practicing in caregiving organizations; 3) providing 10 hours of activity in 1 of the following areas: research/program evaluation, practice/service, education/training, policy, or field replications; 4) attending scheduled meetings with staff of the Rosalynn Carter Institute for Human Development; and 5) participating in an annual conference.

Financial data The stipend is $3,000 per year for undergraduates or $6,000 per year for graduate students.

Duration 1 year.

Additional information This program, established in 1995, defines caregiver as a person who assists individuals with physical diseases, mental illnesses, difficulties associated with aging, or development disabilities. Fields of study have included special education, nursing, pre-medicine, public administration, counsel-

ing psychology, social work, teaching mathematics, and teaching biology.

Number awarded Varies each year. Recently, 14 of these fellowships were awarded (8 to undergraduates and 6 to graduate students).

Deadline March each year.

[315]
JOHN DAWE DENTAL EDUCATION SCHOLARSHIP

Hawai'i Community Foundation
Attn: Scholarship Department
1164 Bishop Street, Suite 800
Honolulu, HI 96813
(808) 566-5570   Toll-free: (888) 731-3863
Fax: (808) 521-6286   E-mail: scholarships@hcf-hawaii.org
Web: www.hawaiicommunityfoundation.org

Summary To provide financial assistance to Hawaii residents who are interested in preparing for a career in the dental field.

Eligibility This program is open to Hawaii residents who are interested in full-time study in dentistry, dental hygiene, or dental assisting. Applicants must be able to demonstrate academic achievement (GPA of 2.7 or higher), good moral character, and financial need. Along with their application, they must submit a short statement indicating their reasons for attending college, their planned course of study, and their career goals.

Financial data The amounts of the awards depend on the availability of funds and the need of the recipient; recently, stipends averaged $2,150.

Duration 1 year.

Additional information Recipients may attend college in Hawaii or on the mainland.

Number awarded Varies each year; recently, 12 of these scholarships were awarded.

Deadline February of each year.

[316]
JOHN F. GARDE SCHOLARSHIP

American Association of Nurse Anesthetists
Attn: AANA Foundation
222 South Prospect Avenue
Park Ridge, IL 60068-4001
(847) 692-7050, ext. 1171   Fax: (847) 692-7137
E-mail: foundation@aana.com
Web: www.aana.com/foundation/default.asp

Summary To provide financial assistance to members of the American Association of Nurse Anesthetists (AANA) who are interested in obtaining further education.

Eligibility This program is open to members of the association who are currently enrolled in an accredited nurse anesthesia education program. First-year students must have completed 6 months of nurse anesthesia classes; second-year students must have completed 12 months of nurse anesthesia classes. Along with their application, they must submit a 200-word essay describing why they have chosen nurse anesthesia as a profession and their professional goals for the future. Financial need is also considered in the selection process.

Financial data The stipend is $1,000 per year.

Duration 1 academic year.

Additional information This program is sponsored by the Council on Accreditation of Nurse Anesthesia Educational Programs. The application processing fee is $25.

Number awarded 1 each year.

Deadline March of each year.

[317]
JOHN F. STEINMAN FELLOWSHIP

John F. Steinman Fellowship Fund
Attn: Secretary
8 West King Street
P.O. Box 1328
Lancaster, PA 17608-1328
Web: contests.lancasteronline.com/fellowshipfund

Summary To provide financial assistance to graduate and postdoctoral students in psychiatry, psychology, and social work.

Eligibility This program is open to applicants in the fields of psychiatry, psychology, and social case work. For awards in psychiatry, candidates must 1) have received an M.D. or D.O. degree and be interested in studying for 2 or 3 additional years to become trained as an adult psychiatrist or 2) have already been trained as an adult psychiatrist and be interested in advanced study to become trained as a child psychiatrist or other comparable psychiatric subspecialist. For awards in psychology, applicants must have completed at least a bachelor's degree and be interested in working on an advanced degree to become a clinical psychologist or public school psychologist. For awards in social work, applicants must have completed at least a bachelor's degree and be interested in working on an advanced degree to become trained as a social case worker. A personal interview may be required. Selection is based on scholastic record, personal qualifications, performance, and future promise. All applicants must agree to work in Lancaster County, Pennsylvania after they complete their advanced study if they receive this fellowship.

Financial data The stipend is $6,000.

Duration 1 year; may be renewed. Recipients must work in Lancaster County, after completion of their studies, for as many years as they received the fellowship.

Additional information Recipients must begin their advanced training within 12 month after receiving the award. They must pursue the course of study for which the fellowship was granted. They must not interrupt their course of study once they begin (except for military service or serious illness).

Number awarded 1 or more each year.

Deadline January of each year.

[318]
JOHN RAINER FELLOWSHIPS

American Indian Graduate Center
Attn: Executive Director
4520 Montgomery Boulevard, N.E., Suite 1-B
Albuquerque, NM 87109-1291
(505) 881-4584   Toll-free: (800) 628-1920
Fax: (505) 884-0427   E-mail: aigc@aigc.com
Web: www.aigc.com

Summary To provide financial assistance to Native American graduate students.

Eligibility This program is open to enrolled members of U.S. federally-recognized American Indian tribes and Alaska Native groups and other students who can document one-fourth degree federally-recognized Indian blood. Applicants must be enrolled full time in a master's, doctoral, or professional degree program at an accredited college or university in the United States. Selection is based on academic achievement, financial need, and an essay on the meaning of their graduate education to the Indian community. Males and females are considered in separate selection processes.

Financial data The stipend is $1,000.

Duration 1 year; may be renewed.

Additional information The application fee is $15. Since this a supplemental program, applicants must apply in a timely manner for federal financial aid and campus-based aid at the college they are attending to be considered for this program. Failure to apply will disqualify an applicant.

Number awarded 2 each year: 1 for a female and 1 for a male.

Deadline May of each year.

[319]
JOHNSON F. HAMMOND, MD, MEMORIAL SCHOLARSHIP

American Medical Association
Attn: AMA Foundation
515 North State Street
Chicago, IL 60610
(312) 464-4193   Fax: (312) 464-4142
E-mail: dina.lindenberg@ama-assn.org
Web: www.ama-assn.org/ama/pub/category/14772.html

Summary To provide financial assistance to medical students who are interested in a career in medical journalism.

Eligibility This program is open to U.S. citizens enrolled in accredited U.S. or Canadian medical schools that grant the M.D. degree. Only nominations are accepted. Nominees must be rising seniors and plan to specialize in medical journalism. The number of students who can be nominated per school depends upon the size of the third-year class: 1 nominee for a class size up to 150 students; 2 nominees for a class size between 151 and 250 students; 3 nominees for a class size of 251 students or more. Selection is based on demonstrated interest in medical journalism, academic record, and financial need.

Financial data The stipend is $10,000.

Duration 1 year.

Number awarded 1 each year.

Deadline May of each year.

[320]
JOSEPH E. PRYOR ALUMNI FELLOWSHIP

Alpha Chi
Attn: Executive Director
900 East Center Avenue
Harding University Box 12249
Searcy, AR 72149-0001
(501) 279-4443   Toll-free: (800) 477-4225
Fax: (501) 279-4589   E-mail: dorgan@harding.edu
Web: www.harding.edu/alphachi/pryor.htm

Summary To provide financial assistance for graduate school to members of Alpha Chi, a national honor society.

Eligibility Eligible to be nominated for these funds are active alumni members of Alpha Chi who are engaged in full-time graduate or professional study. Applicants must submit evidence of outstanding scholarship (a paper, painting, music score, film, slides, video, cassette tape recording, or other medium), an essay of 300 to 500 words introducing the applicant and his or her academic and professional goals (but not indicating financial need), 2 letters of recommendation, official transcripts, and results of standardized exams (GRE, LSAT, MCAT, or equivalent).

Financial data The stipend is $5,000.

Duration 1 year; nonrenewable.

Number awarded 1 each year.

Deadline January of each year.

[321]
JOSEPHINE DE KARMAN FELLOWSHIPS
Josephine de Kármán Fellowship Trust
Attn: Judy McClain, Secretary
P.O. Box 3389
San Dimas, CA 91773
(909) 592-0607   E-mail: info@dekarman.org
Web: www.dekarman.org
Summary To provide financial assistance to outstanding college seniors or students in their last year of a Ph.D. program.
Eligibility This program is open to students in any discipline who will be entering their senior undergraduate year or their terminal year of a Ph.D. program in the fall of the next academic year. Postdoctoral students are not eligible. Foreign students may apply if they are already enrolled in a university in the United States. Applicants must be able to demonstrate exceptional ability and seriousness of purpose. Special consideration is given to applicants in the humanities and to those who have completed their qualifying examinations for the doctoral degree.
Financial data The stipend is $16,000 per year for graduate students or $8,000 per year for undergraduates. Funds are paid in 2 installments to the recipient's school. No funds may be used for travel.
Duration 1 year; may not be renewed or postponed.
Additional information This fund was established in 1954 by Dr. Theodore von Kármán, renowned aeronautics expert and director of the Guggenheim Aeronautical Laboratory at the California Institute of Technology. Study must be carried out in the United States.
Number awarded At least 10 each year.
Deadline January of each year.

[322]
JOSH GOTTHEIL MEMORIAL BONE MARROW TRANSPLANT CAREER DEVELOPMENT AWARDS
Oncology Nursing Society
Attn: ONS Foundation
125 Enterprise Drive
Pittsburgh, PA 15275-1214
(412) 859-6100, ext. 8503   Toll-free: (866) 257-4ONS
Fax: (412) 859-6160   E-mail: foundation@ons.org
Web:
    www.ons.org/awards/foundawards/joshGottheil.sthml
Summary To provide funding for further education to professional registered nurses who can demonstrate meritorious practice in bone marrow transplant (BMT) nursing.
Eligibility This program is open to professional registered nurses who are interested in pursuing education at the bachelor's or master's degree level. Applicants must be currently employed as a registered nurse working in BMT (at least 75% of time must be devoted to patient care) or in the position of nurse manager, nurse practitioner, clinical nurse specialist, BMT coordinator, or equivalent position. They must have at least 2 years in BMT nursing practice. Candidates are evaluated on the following criteria: 1) clarity of professional goal statement; 2) demonstrated commitment to professional development in BMT nursing; 3) demonstrated commitment to continuing professional practice in BMT nursing; 4) recommendations; and 5) contributions and/or professional nursing practice. Applicants must not have previously received this career development award from the foundation.
Financial data The stipend is $2,000. Funds may be used to support a continuing education program or to supplement tuition in a bachelor's or master's program.

Duration 1 year.
Additional information These awards were first presented in 1995.
Number awarded 4 each year.
Deadline November of each year.

[323]
JOYCE W. KELLY SCHOLARSHIP
American Association of Nurse Anesthetists
Attn: AANA Foundation
222 South Prospect Avenue
Park Ridge, IL 60068-4001
(847) 692-7050, ext. 1171   Fax: (847) 692-7137
E-mail: foundation@aana.com
Web: www.aana.com/foundation/default.asp
Summary To provide financial assistance to members of the American Association of Nurse Anesthetists (AANA) who are interested in obtaining further education.
Eligibility This program is open to members of the association who are currently enrolled in an accredited nurse anesthesia education program. First-year students must have completed 6 months of nurse anesthesia classes; second-year students must have completed 12 months of nurse anesthesia classes. Along with their application, they must submit a 200-word essay describing why they have chosen nurse anesthesia as a profession and their professional goals for the future. Financial need is also considered in the selection process. Students attending Kaiser Permanente School of Anesthesia are not eligible.
Financial data The stipend is $2,000 per year.
Duration 1 academic year.
Additional information Funding for this program is provided by Kaiser Permanente School of Anesthesia. The application processing fee is $25.
Number awarded 1 each year.
Deadline March of each year.

[324]
JUANITA ROBLES-LOPEZ/PAMPERS PARENTING INSTITUTE AND PROCTER & GAMBLE SCHOLARSHIP
National Association of Hispanic Nurses
Attn: National Awards and Scholarship Committee Chair
1501 16th Street, N.W.
Washington, DC 20036
(202) 387-2477   Fax: (202) 483-7183
E-mail: info@thehispanicnurses.org
Web: www.thehispanicnurses.org
Summary To provide financial assistance to members of the National Association of Hispanic Nurses (NAHN) interested in working on a master's degree in maternal-child nursing.
Eligibility Eligible are members of the association enrolled in a master's degree program in a maternal-child nursing program. Applicants must submit a statement outlining the maternal child needs affecting Hispanic communities and their potential leadership in that area. U.S. citizenship or permanent resident status is required. Selection is based on academic excellence (preferably a GPA of 3.0 or higher), potential for leadership in nursing, and financial need.
Financial data The stipend is $2,000.
Duration 1 year.

Additional information Funding for this scholarship is provided by Procter & Gamble Company and Pampers Parenting Institute.
Number awarded 1 each year.
Deadline April of each year.

[325]
JUDGE WILLIAM M. BEARD SCHOLARSHIP
United Daughters of the Confederacy
Attn: Education Director
328 North Boulevard
Richmond, VA 23220-4057
(804) 355-1636　　　　　Fax: (804) 353-1396
E-mail: hqudc@rcn.com
Web: www.hqudc.org/scholarships/scholarships.html
Summary To provide financial assistance for graduate education in history or medicine to lineal descendants of Confederate veterans.
Eligibility Eligible to apply for these scholarships are lineal descendants of worthy Confederates or collateral descendants who are members of the Children of the Confederacy or the United Daughters of the Confederacy. Applicants must intend to work on a graduate degree in history or medicine and must submit certified proof of the Confederate record of 1 ancestor, with the company and regiment in which he served. They must have a GPA of 3.0 or higher.
Financial data The amount of the scholarship depends on the availability of funds.
Duration 1 year; may be renewed.
Additional information Information is also available from Mrs. Robert C. Kraus, Second Vice President General, 239 Deerfield Lane, Franklin, NC 28734-0112. Members of the same family may not hold scholarships simultaneously, and only 1 application per family will be accepted within any 1 year. Requests for applications must be accompanied by a self-addressed stamped envelope.
Number awarded 1 each year.
Deadline March of each year.

[326]
JULIA SMITH MEMORIAL NP STUDENT SCHOLARSHIP
American Academy of Nurse Practitioners
Attn: AANP Foundation
P.O. Box 10729
Glendale, AZ 85318-0729
(623) 376-9467　　　　　Fax: (623) 376-0369
E-mail: foundation@aanp.org
Web: www.aanpfoundation.org
Summary To provide financial assistance to members of the American Academy of Nurse Practitioners (AANP) who are working on a master's degree.
Eligibility This program is open to current student and full members of the academy who are enrolled in a M.S.N. degree program as a nurse practitioner (NP). Applicants must have a GPA of 3.5 or higher. They must have completed at least 25% but no more than 75% of their program requirements.
Financial data The stipend is $1,000. Funds may be used only for educational expenses (tuition, books, equipment, etc.), not for expenses related to master's thesis and/or general research projects.
Duration 1 year.

Additional information This program was established in 2003. There is a $10 application fee.
Number awarded 2 each year: 1 in each funding cycle.
Deadline April or October of each year.

[327]
KALA SINGH MEMORIAL SCHOLARSHIP
American Speech-Language-Hearing Foundation
Attn: Graduate Student Scholarship Competition
10801 Rockville Pike
Rockville, MD 20852-3279
(301) 897-5700　　　　　Toll-free: (800) 498-2071
Fax: (301) 571-0457　　　TTY: (800) 498-2071
E-mail: foundation@asha.org
Web: www.ashfoundation.org
Summary To provide financial assistance to international or minority students who are interested in working on a graduate degree in communication sciences and disorders.
Eligibility Applicants must be college graduates who are accepted for graduate study in the United States in a communication sciences and disorders program or enrolled as a full-time graduate student. The fund gives priority to foreign or minority (American Indian, Alaskan Native, Asian, Pacific Islander, Black, Hispanic) students. Students who previously received a scholarship from the American Speech-Language-Hearing Foundation are not eligible.
Financial data The stipend ranges from $2,000 to $4,000. Funds must be used for educational support (e.g., tuition, books, school living expenses), not for personal or conference travel.
Duration The award is granted annually.
Number awarded 1 each year.
Deadline June of each year.

[328]
KANSAS DISTINGUISHED SCHOLARSHIP PROGRAM
Kansas Board of Regents
Attn: Student Financial Aid
1000 S.W. Jackson Street, Suite 520
Topeka, KS 66612-1368
(785) 296-3518　　　　　Fax: (785) 296-0983
E-mail: dlindeman@ksbor.org
Web: www.kansasregents.com/financial_aid/awards.html
Summary To encourage award-winning undergraduate students from Kansas to attend graduate school in the state.
Eligibility This program is open to Kansas residents who have been Brasenose, Chevening, Fulbright, Madison, Marshall, Mellon, Rhodes, or Truman Scholars and are interested in working on a graduate degree at a public university in the state. Financial need must be demonstrated.
Financial data This program reimburses tuition and fees to recipients, subject to funding constraints.
Duration 1 year.
Number awarded Varies each year.

[329]
KAPPA DELTA PHI SCHOLARSHIPS

American Occupational Therapy Foundation
Attn: Scholarship Coordinator
4720 Montgomery Lane
P.O. Box 31220
Bethesda, MD 20824-1220
(301) 652-2682   Fax: (301) 656-3620
TDD: (800) 377-8555   E-mail: aotf@aotf.org
Web: www.aotf.org

Summary To provide financial assistance to full-time students who are members of the American Occupational Therapy Association (AOTA) and working on a master's degree in occupational therapy.

Eligibility Applicants must be full-time students who are working on a professional master's degree (entry level) in an accredited or developing occupational therapy educational program. In addition, applicants must be members of the association, demonstrate a need for financial assistance, and have a sustained record of outstanding scholastic performance. As part of the application process, they must submit transcripts, 2 personal references, and a statement from their curriculum director.

Financial data The stipend is $2,000.

Duration 1 year; recipients may reapply.

Number awarded 2 each year.

Deadline January of each year.

[330]
KAPPA EPSILON/AFPE/NELLIE WAKEMAN FIRST YEAR GRADUATE FELLOWSHIP

American Foundation for Pharmaceutical Education
Attn: Grants Manager
One Church Street, Suite 202
Rockville, MD 20850-4158
(301) 738-2160   Fax: (301) 738-2161
E-mail: info@afpenet.org
Web: www.afpenet.org/firstyr_kappa_eps.htm

Summary To provide financial assistance to members of Kappa Epsilon engaged in graduate study in pharmacy.

Eligibility Applicants must be members of Kappa Epsilon who have earned a B.S. in pharmacy or a Pharm.D. degree and are planning to pursue a master's or Ph.D. degree in a pharmacy discipline. Consideration is given to applicants who demonstrate financial need.

Financial data The grant is $4,000. Funds may be used for any purpose agreed upon by the recipient and faculty sponsor, including a student stipend, laboratory supplies or materials, travel, etc.

Duration 1 year.

Additional information This scholarship program is jointly administered by the American Foundation for Pharmaceutical Education (AFPE) and Kappa Epsilon. Applications and further information are available from the Kappa Epsilon Executive Office, 7700 Shawnee Mission Parkway, Overland Park, KS 66202, E-mail: KEFrat@aol.com. No funds may be used for indirect costs by the institution.

Number awarded 1 each year.

Deadline February of each year.

[331]
KAREN O'NEILL ENDOWED ADVANCED NURSING PRACTICE SCHOLARSHIP

Emergency Nurses Association
Attn: ENA Foundation
915 Lee Street
Des Plaines, IL 60016-6569
(847) 460-4100   Toll-free: (800) 900-9659, ext. 4100
Fax: (847) 460-4004   E-mail: foundation@ena.org
Web: www.ena.org/foundation/grants

Summary To provide financial assistance to members of the Emergency Nurses Association (ENA) who are working on an advanced clinical practice degree.

Eligibility This program is open to emergency nurses who are pursuing an advanced clinical degree to become a nurse practitioner or clinical nurse specialist. Applicants must have been members of the association for at least 12 months. They must submit a 1-page statement on their professional and educational goals and how this scholarship will help them attain those goals. Selection is based on content and clarity of the goal statement (45%), professional involvement (45%), and GPA (10%).

Financial data The stipend is $3,000.

Duration 1 year.

Number awarded 1 each year.

Deadline May of each year.

[332]
KATHERN F. GRUBER SCHOLARSHIPS

Blinded Veterans Association
477 H Street, N.W.
Washington, DC 20001-2694
(202) 371-8880   Toll-free: (800) 669-7079
Fax: (202) 371-8258   E-mail: bva@bva.org
Web: www.bva.org/services.html

Summary To provide financial assistance for undergraduate or graduate study to spouses and children of blinded veterans.

Eligibility This program is open to dependent children and spouses of blinded veterans of the U.S. armed forces. The veteran need not be a member of the Blinded Veterans Association. The veteran's blindness may be either service connected or non-service connected, but it must meet the following definition: central visual acuity of 20/200 or less in the better eye with corrective glasses, or central visual acuity of more than 20/200 if there is a field defect in which the peripheral field has contracted to such an extent that the widest diameter of visual field subtends an angular distance no greater than 20 degrees in the better eye. The applicant must have been accepted or be currently enrolled as a full-time student in an undergraduate or graduate program at an accredited institution of higher learning. Selection is based on high school and/or college transcripts, 3 letters of recommendation, and a 300-word essay on the applicant's career goals and aspirations.

Financial data The stipends are $2,000 or $1,000 and are intended to be used to cover the student's expenses, including tuition, other academic fees, books, dormitory fees, and cafeteria fees. Funds are paid directly to the recipient's school.

Duration 1 year; recipients may reapply.

Additional information Scholarships may be used for only 1 degree (vocational, bachelor's, or graduate) or nongraduate certificate (e.g., nursing, secretarial).

Number awarded 6 each year: 3 at $2,000 and 3 at $1,000.

Deadline April of each year.

[333]
KATIE GREATRIX ACADEMIC SCHOLARSHIP
National Association of Orthopaedic Nurses
Attn: NAON Foundation
2486 Paysphere Circle
Chicago, IL 60674
E-mail: info@naonfoundation.org
Web: www.naonfoundation.org

Summary To provide financial assistance to members of the National Association of Orthopaedic Nurses (NAON) who are interested in studying for a master's degree.

Eligibility This program is open to orthopedic nurses who are members of the association and working on a master's degree. Applicants must submit a detailed letter outlining the proposed course of study, professional goals and objectives, and relevance of the program to orthopedic nursing practice. Current members of the association's executive board, staff, and foundation trustees are not eligible for this scholarship.

Financial data The stipend is $20,000 per year. Funds may be used for tuition and other school-related fees.

Duration 2 years.

Additional information Recipients must complete a research project or provide a manuscript acceptable for publication in 1 of the association's publications by the completion of course study.

Number awarded 1 every other year.

Deadline October of even-numbered years.

[334]
KAY F. THOMPSON MEMORIAL FUND
Pittsburgh Foundation
Attn: Scholarship Coordinator
Five PPG Place, Suite 250
Pittsburgh, PA 15222-5414
(412) 391-5122   Fax: (412) 391-7259
E-mail: turnerd@pghfdn.org
Web: www.pittsburghfoundation.org

Summary To provide financial assistance to graduate students in health-related fields who have demonstrated an interest in hypnosis.

Eligibility This program is open to full-time students working on a graduate or professional degree in a health-related field (e.g., medicine, dentistry, psychology, social work, counseling). Applicants must be interested in pursuing formal training in hypnosis; the training must be acceptable for membership in and receiving credentials by the American Society of Clinical Hypnosis. Along with their application, they must submit a 1-page essay on their interest in hypnosis, its relationship to their chosen profession, and future plans for implementing the hypnosis training in that profession.

Financial data A stipend is awarded (amount not specified).

Duration 1 year.

Additional information This program also provides funding to dental students involved in training activities outside the formal classroom or attending extracurricular meetings, such as sessions of their national and state associations.

Number awarded Varies each year.

Deadline January, April, August, or September of each year.

[335]
KENNETH JERNIGAN SCHOLARSHIP
National Federation of the Blind
c/o Peggy Elliott, Scholarship Committee Chair
805 Fifth Avenue
Grinnell, IA 50112
(641) 236-3366
Web: www.nfb.org/sch_intro.htm

Summary To provide financial assistance to undergraduate and graduate blind students.

Eligibility This program is open to legally blind students who are working on or planning to work full time on an undergraduate or graduate degree. Selection is based on academic excellence, service to the community, and financial need.

Financial data The stipend is $12,000.

Duration 1 year; recipients may resubmit applications up to 2 additional years.

Additional information Scholarships are awarded at the federation convention in July. Recipients attend the convention at federation expense; that funding is in addition to the scholarship grant. This scholarship is given by the American Action Fund for Blind Children and Adults, a nonprofit organization that assists blind people.

Number awarded 1 each year.

Deadline March of each year.

[336]
KENTUCKY EXEMPTION FROM TUITION FEES FOR DEPENDENTS OF KENTUCKY VETERANS
Kentucky Department of Veterans Affairs
Attn: Division of Field Operations
545 South Third Street, Room 123
Louisville, KY 40202
(502) 595-4447   Toll-free: (800) 928-4012 (within KY)
Fax: (502) 595-4448
Web: www.kdva.net/tuitionwaiver.htm

Summary To provide financial assistance for undergraduate or graduate education to the children or unremarried widow(er)s of deceased Kentucky veterans.

Eligibility This program is open to the children, stepchildren, adopted children, and unremarried widow(er)s of veterans who were residents of Kentucky when they entered military service or joined the Kentucky National Guard. The qualifying veteran must have been killed in action during a wartime period or died as a result of a service-connected disability incurred during a wartime period. Applicants must be attending or planning to attend a state-supported college or university in Kentucky to work on an undergraduate or graduate degree.

Financial data Eligible dependents and survivors are exempt from tuition and matriculation fees at any state-supported institution of higher education in Kentucky.

Duration There are no age or time limits on the waiver.

Number awarded Varies each year.

[337]
KEPPRA FAMILY EPILEPSY SCHOLARSHIP PROGRAM

UCB Pharma, Inc.
Keppra Scholarship Program
c/o S&R Communications Group
2511 Old Cornwallis Road, Suite 200
Durham, NC 27713
Toll-free: (888) 275-7928
E-mail: kepprascholarship@srcomgroup.com
Web: www.keppra.com

Summary   To provide financial assistance for college or graduate school to epilepsy patients and their family members and caregivers.

Eligibility   This program is open to epilepsy patients and their family members and caregivers. Applicants must be working on or planning to work on an undergraduate or graduate degree at an institution of higher education in the United States. They must be able to demonstrate academic achievement, a record of participation in activities outside of school, and service as a role model. Along with their application, they must submit a 1-page essay explaining why they should be selected for the scholarship, how epilepsy has impacted their life either as a patient or as a family member or caregiver, and how they will benefit from the scholarship.

Financial data   The stipend is $50,000.

Duration   1 year; nonrenewable.

Number awarded   30 each year: 20 to epilepsy patients and 10 to family members or caregivers.

Deadline   May of each year.

[338]
KIDS' CHANCE OF INDIANA SCHOLARSHIP PROGRAM

Kids' Chance of Indiana, Inc.
Attn: Scholarship Committee
721 East Broadway
Fortville, IN 46040
(317) 485-0043, ext. 123   Fax: (317) 485-4299
E-mail: office@kidschancein.org
Web: www.kidschancein.org

Summary   To provide financial assistance for college or graduate school to Indiana residents whose parent was killed or permanently disabled in a work-related accident.

Eligibility   This program is open to Indiana residents between 16 and 25 years of age who are the children of workers fatally or catastrophically injured as a result of a work-related accident or occupational disease. The death or injury must be compensable by the Workers' Compensation Board of the state of Indiana and must have resulted in a substantial decline in the family's income that is likely to impede the student's pursuit of his or her educational objectives. Applicants must be attending or planning to attend a trade/vocational school, junior/community college, 4-year college or university, or graduate school. Financial need is considered in the selection process.

Financial data   Stipends range up to $6,000 per year. Funds may be used for tuition and fees, books, room and board, and utilities.

Duration   1 year; may be renewed.

Additional information   Recipients may attend a public or private educational institution in any state.

Number awarded   Varies each year.

[339]
KIDS' CHANCE OF SOUTH CAROLINA SCHOLARSHIPS

Kids' Chance of South Carolina
1135 Dixie Red Road
Leesville, SC 29070
(803) 532-0608   Fax: (803) 532-9892
Web: www.kidschancesc.org

Summary   To provide financial assistance for college or graduate school to South Carolina residents whose parent was killed or permanently disabled in a work-related accident.

Eligibility   This program is open to South Carolina residents between 16 and 25 years of age who are the children of workers fatally or catastrophically injured as a result of a work-related accident or occupational disease. Applicants must be attending or planning to attend a trade school, vocational school, community or junior college, 4-year college or university, or graduate school. The work-related injury or occupational disease from which their parent suffers or died must be compensable by the Workers' Compensation Board of the state of South Carolina and must have resulted in a substantial decline in the family's income that is likely to interfere with the student's pursuit of his or her educational objectives.

Financial data   Stipends range from $500 to $6,000 per year. Funds may be used for tuition and fees, books, room and board, and utilities.

Duration   1 year; may be renewed.

Additional information   Recipients may attend school in any state.

Number awarded   Varies each year.

[340]
KNIGHTS OF LITHUANIA SCHOLARSHIP PROGRAM

Knights of Lithuania
c/o John P. Baltrus, Scholarship Committee Chair
118 Vine Street
Jefferson Hills, PA 15025
(412) 233-2764   E-mail: jonaspb@verizon.net
Web: www.knightsoflithuania.com

Summary   To provide financial assistance to undergraduate or graduate students of Lithuanian ancestry.

Eligibility   Applicants must have been a member of the Knights of Lithuania for at least 2 years, be of Lithuanian ancestry, and be in financial need. There is no age limitation. Selection is based on recommendations, scholastic record, financial need, a personal interview, and organizational activity within the Knights of Lithuania.

Financial data   Stipends range up to $1,000 per year. Funds are generally paid in 2 equal installments.

Duration   1 year; nonrenewable.

Number awarded   Varies each year.

Deadline   June of each year.

[341]
KOSCIUSZKO FOUNDATION TUITION SCHOLARSHIPS FOR STUDY IN THE UNITED STATES

Kosciuszko Foundation
Attn: Educational Programs
15 East 65th Street
New York, NY 10021-6595
(212) 734-2130, ext. 210   Fax: (212) 628-4552
E-mail: addy@thekf.org
Web: www.thekf.org/EDScholarships_US_Tuition.html

Summary To provide financial assistance for graduate education to American students who are majoring in Polish studies or are of Polish descent.

Eligibility This program is open to students who are U.S. citizens or permanent residents of Polish descent. Americans of non-Polish descent who are majoring in Polish studies are also eligible. Applicants must be full-time graduate students at U.S. universities. Selection is based on academic excellence (minimum GPA of 3.0); academic achievements, interests, and motivation; interest in Polish subjects and/or involvement in the Polish American community; a personal statement on background and academic and career goals; and financial need.

Financial data Stipends range from $1,000 to $7,000.

Duration 1 year; may be renewed 1 additional year.

Additional information This program includes certain funds that are designated for specific groups of qualifying students. Those include students of law and engineering at DePaul University in Chicago; residents of Bayonne, New Jersey studying nursing, teaching, or business; and residents of Amsterdam, New York, Chicopee, Massachusetts, and the state of New Hampshire. There is a $25 nonrefundable application fee.

Number awarded Varies each year; recently, 148 of these scholarships were awarded.

Deadline January of each year.

[342]
KUCHLER-KILLIAN MEMORIAL SCHOLARSHIP

National Federation of the Blind
c/o Peggy Elliott, Scholarship Committee Chair
805 Fifth Avenue
Grinnell, IA 50112
(641) 236-3366
Web: www.nfb.org/sch_intro.htm

Summary To provide financial assistance to undergraduate and graduate blind students.

Eligibility This program is open to legally blind students who are working on or planning to work full time on an undergraduate or graduate degree. Selection is based on academic excellence, service to the community, and financial need.

Financial data The stipend is $3,000.

Duration 1 year; recipients may resubmit applications up to 2 additional years.

Additional information Scholarships are awarded at the federation convention in July. Recipients attend the convention at federation expense; that funding is in addition to the scholarship grant.

Number awarded 1 each year.

Deadline March of each year.

[343]
LADIES' AUXILIARY NATIONAL RURAL LETTER CARRIERS SCHOLARSHIP

Alexander Graham Bell Association for the Deaf
Attn: Financial Aid Coordinator
3417 Volta Place, N.W.
Washington, DC 20007-2778
(202) 337-5220   Fax: (202) 337-8314
TTY: (202) 337-5221   E-mail: financialaid@agbell.org
Web: www.agbell.org

Summary To provide financial assistance to undergraduate and graduate students with moderate to profound hearing loss.

Eligibility This program is open to undergraduate and graduate students who have been diagnosed with a moderate to profound hearing loss prior to acquiring spoken language (hearing loss averages 60dB or greater in the better ear in the speech frequencies of 500, 1000, and 2000 Hz). Applicants must be committed to using spoken language as their primary mode of communication. They must be accepted or enrolled at a mainstream college or university as a full-time student. Along with their application, they must submit a 1-page essay discussing their career goals and how spoken communication is helping them to reach those goals as a person with a hearing loss. Financial need is considered in the selection process. This scholarship is reserved for students who are deaf.

Financial data The stipend is $2,000 per year.

Duration 1 year; may be renewed 1 additional year.

Number awarded 1 each year.

Deadline April of each year.

[344]
LAKEVIEW SCHOLARSHIP

American Association of Nurse Anesthetists
Attn: AANA Foundation
222 South Prospect Avenue
Park Ridge, IL 60068-4001
(847) 692-7050, ext. 1171   Fax: (847) 692-7137
E-mail: foundation@aana.com
Web: www.aana.com/foundation/default.asp

Summary To provide financial assistance to members of the American Association of Nurse Anesthetists (AANA) who are interested in obtaining further education.

Eligibility This program is open to members of the association who are currently enrolled in an accredited nurse anesthesia education program. Applicants must be second-year students who have completed 12 months of nurse anesthesia classes. Along with their application, they must submit a 200-word essay describing why they have chosen nurse anesthesia as a profession and their professional goals for the future. Financial need is also considered in the selection process.

Financial data The stipend is $1,000 per year.

Duration 1 academic year.

Additional information The application processing fee is $25.

Number awarded 1 each year.

Deadline March of each year.

[345]
LARRY WILSON SCHOLARSHIP FOR ENVIRONMENTAL STUDIES

Arkansas Environmental Federation
Attn: Scholarship Program
1400 West Markham, Suite 250
Little Rock, AR 72201
(501) 374-0263   Fax: (501) 374-8752
E-mail: joliver@environmentark.org
Web: www.environmentark.org/randallmathis.htm

Summary To provide financial assistance to residents of Arkansas working on an undergraduate or graduate degree in environmental studies at a college or university in the state.

Eligibility This program is open to Arkansas residents who have completed at least 40 credit hours as a full-time undergraduate or graduate student at a college or university in the state. Applicants must be majoring in a field related to environmental studies, including agriculture with an environmental emphasis, chemical engineering with an environmental emphasis, civil engineering with an environmental emphasis, environmental engineering, environmental health science, fisheries and wildlife biology, forestry, geology, or wildlife management. They must have a GPA of 2.8 or higher. Along with their application, they must submit an essay of 1 to 3 pages explaining their professional career goals relating to the fields of environmental health and safety. U.S. citizenship is required. Financial need is not considered in the selection process.

Financial data The stipend is $2,500.
Duration 1 year.
Additional information This program is sponsored by Northstar Engineering Consultants, Inc.
Number awarded 1 each year.
Deadline January of each year.

[346]
LAURA N. DOWSETT FUND SCHOLARSHIPS

Hawai'i Community Foundation
Attn: Scholarship Department
1164 Bishop Street, Suite 800
Honolulu, HI 96813
(808) 566-5570   Toll-free: (888) 731-3863
Fax: (808) 521-6286   E-mail: scholarships@hcf-hawaii.org
Web: www.hawaiicommunityfoundation.org

Summary To provide financial assistance to Hawaii residents who are interested in preparing for a career in occupational therapy.

Eligibility This program is open to Hawaii residents who are studying occupational therapy as full-time juniors, seniors, or graduate students. They must be able to demonstrate academic achievement (GPA of 2.7 or higher), good moral character, and financial need. In addition to filling out the standard application form, applicants must write a short statement indicating their reasons for attending college, their planned course of study, and their career goals.

Financial data The amounts of the awards depend on the availability of funds and the need of the recipient; recently, stipends averaged $2,000.
Duration 1 year.
Additional information Recipients may attend college in Hawaii or on the mainland.
Number awarded Varies each year; recently, 2 of these scholarships were awarded.
Deadline February of each year.

[347]
LAWRENCE E. AND THELMA J. NORRIE MEMORIAL SCHOLARSHIP

Foundation for Amateur Radio, Inc.
Attn: Scholarship Committee
P.O. Box 831
Riverdale, MD 20738
E-mail: aa3of@arrl.net
Web: www.amateurradio-far.org/scholarships.php

Summary To provide funding to licensed radio amateurs who are interested in going to college or graduate school, particularly those majoring in engineering or the sciences.

Eligibility Applicants must be a resident of the United States and have an amateur radio license of any class with HF privileges. Special consideration is given to applicants who have demonstrated academic merit, financial need, and an interest in promoting the amateur radio service. Preference is given to juniors, seniors, and graduate students who have a GPA of 3.0 or higher and are working on a degree in science or engineering.

Financial data The stipend is $2,500.
Duration 1 year.
Additional information Recipients must attend an accredited school (university, college, or technical institute) on a full-time basis.
Number awarded 1 each year.
Deadline Requests for applications must be submitted by April of each year.

[348]
LAWRENCE R. FOSTER MEMORIAL SCHOLARSHIP

Oregon Student Assistance Commission
Attn: Grants and Scholarships Division
1500 Valley River Drive, Suite 100
Eugene, OR 97401-2146
(541) 687-7395   Toll-free: (800) 452-8807, ext. 7395
Fax: (541) 687-7419
E-mail: awardinfo@mercury.osac.state.or.us
Web: www.osac.state.or.us

Summary To provide financial assistance for college or graduate school to residents of Oregon who are interested in preparing for a public health career.

Eligibility This program is open to residents of Oregon who are attending a 4-year college or university in any state to prepare for a career in public health (not private practice). First preference is given to applicants who are either working in public health or enrolled as graduate students in that field. Second preference is given to undergraduates entering the junior or senior year of a health program, including nursing, medical technology, and physician assistant. A general preference is given to applicants from diverse cultures. Along with their application, they must submit a 1- to 2-page essay on their interest, experience, and future plans for a public health career.

Financial data Stipend amounts vary; recently, they were at least $4,167.
Duration 1 year.
Additional information This program is administered by the Oregon Student Assistance Commission (OSAC) with funds provided by the Oregon Community Foundation, 1221 S.W. Yamhill, Suite 100, Portland, OR 97205, (503) 227-6846, Fax: (503) 274-7771.
Number awarded Varies each year; recently, 6 of these scholarships were awarded.
Deadline February of each year.

[349]
LAZARIAN GRADUATE SCHOLARSHIP

Armenian Relief Society of Eastern U.S.A., Inc.
Attn: Scholarship Committee
80 Bigelow Avenue, Suite 200
Watertown, MA 02472
(617) 926-3801   Fax: (617) 924-7238
E-mail: arseastus@aol.com
Web: www.arseastus.com

Summary To provide financial assistance for degrees in selected fields to graduate students of Armenian ancestry.

Eligibility This program is open to students of Armenian ancestry who intend to pursue their studies at the graduate level (master's degree or doctorate) in 1 of the following fields: law, history, political science, international relations, journalism, government, economics, business administration, medicine, or public service. Selection is based on academic record, financial need, and Armenian community involvement.

Financial data A stipend is awarded (amount not specified).

Duration 1 year.

Additional information Students may not receive more than 2 scholarships from the Armenian Relief Society.

Deadline March of each year.

[350]
LEBANESE AMERICAN HERITAGE CLUB SCHOLARSHIPS

Lebanese American Heritage Club
Attn: Arab American Scholarship Foundation
4337 Maple Road
Dearborn, MI 48126
(313) 846-8480   Fax: (313) 846-2710
E-mail: lahc@lahc.org
Web: www.lahc.org/scholarship.htm

Summary To provide financial assistance for college or graduate school to Americans of Arab descent who reside in Michigan.

Eligibility This program is open to students who are already in college or graduate school. Only full-time students may apply. Applicants must be of Arab descent, be U.S. citizens or permanent residents, reside in the state of Michigan, and be able to demonstrate financial need. Undergraduate students must have at least a 3.0 GPA; graduate students must have at least a 3.5. Applicants must submit a completed application form, official copies of academic transcripts, 2 letters of recommendation, financial aid transcripts, copies of their current Student Aid Report, and a 500-word essay on their educational background, field of study, future goals, and contributions to their community.

Financial data The stipend is $1,000. Funds are paid directly to the recipient's institution.

Duration 1 year; recipients may reapply.

Additional information This program was established in 1989. Since then, more than half a million dollars has been awarded.

Number awarded 1 or more each year.

Deadline April of each year.

[351]
LEIGH CARTER SCHOLARSHIP

Community Foundation of Middle Tennessee
Attn: Scholarship Committee
3833 Cleghorn Avenue, Suite 400
Nashville, TN 37215-2519
(615) 321-4939   Toll-free: (888) 540-5200
Fax: (615) 327-2746   E-mail: mail@cfmt.org
Web: www.cfmt.org/scholarship_info.htm

Summary To provide financial assistance to residents of Tennessee preparing for a career in chiropractic.

Eligibility This program is open to full-time students at accredited chiropractic colleges and universities in the United States. Preference is given to residents of Tennessee. Applicants must demonstrate a strong interest in health care delivery. Along with their application, they must submit an essay explaining their career and educational goals, transcripts, 2 letters of recommendation, and documentation of financial need.

Financial data Stipends range from $500 to $2,500 per year. Funds are paid to the recipient's school and must be used for tuition, fees, books, supplies, room, board, or miscellaneous expenses.

Duration 1 year; recipients may reapply.

Additional information This program was established in 2001 by the Tennessee Chiropractic Association.

Number awarded 1 or more each year.

Deadline March of each year.

[352]
LEO DOERFLER MEMORIAL SCHOLARSHIP

Audiology Foundation of America
Attn: Scholarship Committee
8 North Third Street, Suite 406
Lafayette, IN 47901-1247
(765) 743-6AUD   Fax: (765) 743-9AUD
E-mail: info-afa@audfound.org
Web: www.audfound.org/index.cfm?pageID=49

Summary To provide financial assistance to audiologists interested in working on a Ph.D. degree.

Eligibility This program is open to audiologists who have an Au.D. degree. Applicants must be enrolled in a Ph.D. program in a scientific discipline where knowledge discovery will benefit the practice of audiology. They must be citizens or permanent residents of the United States and its territories or Canada. Along with their application, they must submit a 500-word essay on their research and how it will impact the practice of audiology.

Financial data The stipend is $5,000.

Duration 1 year; nonrenewable.

Number awarded 1 each year.

Deadline April of each year.

[353]
LEOPOLD SCHEPP FOUNDATION SCHOLARSHIPS

Leopold Schepp Foundation
551 Fifth Avenue, Suite 3000
New York, NY 10176-2597
(212) 692-0191

Summary To provide financial assistance to undergraduate and graduate students.

Eligibility This program is open to undergraduates under 30 years of age and graduate students under 40 years of age. Applicants must either be currently enrolled full time or have completed 1 year of undergraduate work at an accredited college or university. They must have a GPA of 3.0 or higher. High school seniors, graduate students completing a dissertation and not enrolled in class, and students working on a second degree at the same level are not eligible. U.S. citizenship or permanent resident status is required. Selection is based on character, ability, and financial need.

Financial data The maximum stipend is $8,000 per year.

Duration 1 year; may be renewed.

Additional information Finalists may be required to travel to New York at their own expense for an interview. Requests for applications must be accompanied by a self-addressed stamped envelope.

Number awarded Approximately 200 each year.

Deadline The foundation stops accepting applications when a sufficient number has been received, usually in January.

[354]
LESLIE ISENBERG FUND SCHOLARSHIP

American Speech-Language-Hearing Foundation
Attn: Graduate Student Scholarship Competition
10801 Rockville Pike
Rockville, MD 20852-3279
(301) 897-5700   Toll-free: (800) 498-2071
Fax: (301) 571-0457   TTY: (800) 498-2071
E-mail: foundation@asha.org
Web: www.ashfoundation.org

Summary To provide financial assistance to persons with disabilities and others who are interested in studying communication sciences or related programs in graduate school.

Eligibility Applicants must be accepted for full-time graduate study in an accredited communication sciences and disorders program. Priority is given to students with disabilities. Selection is based on academic and personal merit. Students who have received a prior scholarship from the American Speech-Language-Hearing Foundation are not eligible.

Financial data The stipend ranges from $2,000 to $4,000. Funds must be used for educational support (e.g., tuition, books, school-related living expenses), not for personal or conference travel.

Duration 1 year.

Number awarded 1 each year.

Deadline June of each year.

[355]
LEST WE FORGET POW/MIA/KIA SCHOLARSHIP FUND

Maine Community Foundation
Attn: Program Director
245 Main Street
Ellsworth, ME 04605
(207) 667-9735   Toll-free: (877) 700-6800
Fax: (207) 667-0447   E-mail: info@mainecf.org
Web: www.mainecf.org/html/scholarships/index.html

Summary To provide financial assistance for undergraduate or graduate study to Vietnam veterans or the dependents of Vietnam or other veterans in Maine.

Eligibility This program is open to residents of Maine who are Vietnam veterans or the descendants of veterans who served in the Vietnam Theater. As a second priority, children of veterans from other time periods are also considered. Graduating high school seniors, nontraditional students, undergraduates, and

graduate students are eligible to apply. Selection is based on financial need, extracurricular activities, work experience, academic achievement, and a personal statement of career goals and how the applicant's educational plans relate to them.

Financial data The stipend is $1,000 per year.

Duration 1 year.

Additional information This fund was transferred to the Maine Community Foundation in 1996. There is a $3 processing fee.

Number awarded 3 to 6 each year.

Deadline April of each year.

[356]
LIBERTY LEADERSHIP FUND ACADEMIC SCHOLARSHIP

American Association of Occupational Health Nurses, Inc.
Attn: AAOHN Foundation
2920 Brandywine Road, Suite 100
Atlanta, GA 30341-4146
(770) 455-7757   Fax: (770) 455-7271
E-mail: foundation@aaohn.org
Web: www.aaohn.org/foundation/scholarships/index.cfm

Summary To provide financial assistance to registered nurses who are working on a bachelor's or graduate degree to prepare for a career in occupational and environmental health.

Eligibility This program is open to registered nurses who are enrolled in a baccalaureate or graduate degree program. Applicants must demonstrate an interest in, and commitment to, occupational and environmental health. Along with their application, they must submit a 500-word narrative on their professional goals as they relate to the academic activity and the field of occupational and environmental health. Selection is based on that essay (50%), impact of education on applicant's career (20%), and 2 letters of recommendation (30%).

Financial data The stipend is $3,500.

Duration 1 year; may be renewed up to 2 additional years.

Additional information Funding for this program is provided by the Liberty Leadership Fund.

Number awarded 1 each year.

Deadline November of each year.

[357]
LILLY MOVING LIVES FORWARD REINTEGRATION SCHOLARSHIPS

The Center for Reintegration, Inc.
Attn: Lilly Secretariat
310 Busse Highway
PMB 327
Park Ridge, IL 60068-3251
Toll-free: (800) 809-8202
E-mail: lillyawards@reintegration.com
Web: www.reintegration.com

Summary To provide financial assistance to undergraduate and graduate students diagnosed with schizophrenia.

Eligibility This program is open to U.S. citizens diagnosed with bipolar disorder, schizophrenia, schizophreniform disorder, or schizoaffective disorder. Applicants must be receiving medical treatment for the disease and be actively involved in rehabilitative or reintegrative efforts. They must be interested in pursuing postsecondary education, including trade or vocational school programs, high school equivalency programs, associate degrees, bachelor's degrees, and graduate programs. Along with their application, they must submit an essay on their career goal and their rationale for choosing that goal, how this course of study will help them achieve their career goal, obstacles they have faced in life and how they have overcome them, steps they have taken to prepare for pursuit of this education, rationale for the specific school chosen, and their plans to continue treatment while pursuing an education. Selection is based on the quality of the essay, academic success, 3 references, thoughtfulness and appropriateness of academic and vocational/career goals, rehabilitation involvement, success in dealing with the disease, recent volunteer and/or vocational experience, and completion of application requirements.

Financial data The amount awarded varies, depending upon the specific needs of the recipient. Funds may be used to pay for tuition and related expenses, such as textbooks and laboratory fees.

Duration 1 year; may be renewed.

Additional information This program, established in 1998, is funded by Eli Lilly and Company.

Number awarded Varies each year; recently, 50 of these scholarships (including renewals) were awarded.

Deadline January of each year.

[358]
LINCOLN COMMUNITY FOUNDATION MEDICAL RESEARCH SCHOLARSHIP

Lincoln Community Foundation
215 Centennial Mall South, Suite 100
Lincoln, NE 68508
(402) 474-2345   Fax: (402) 476-8532
E-mail: lcf@lcf.org
Web: www.lcf.org

Summary To provide financial assistance to residents of Nebraska who are interested in working on an advanced degree in a medical field.

Eligibility This program is open to residents of Nebraska who are working on an advanced degree in a medical field (nursing students may apply as undergraduates). Applicants must submit an essay explaining their progress toward completing their education, why they have chosen to prepare for a career in a medical field, and their future career goals once they complete their degree. Preference is given to 1) female applicants; 2) students preparing for careers as physicians and nurses; and 3) applicants who demonstrate financial need.

Financial data Stipends provided by the foundation generally range from $500 to $2,000.

Duration 1 year; may be renewed.

Number awarded 1 or more each year.

Deadline May of each year.

[359]
LISTERINE PREVENTIVE DENTISTRY SCHOLARSHIPS

American Dental Education Association
Attn: Awards Program Coordinator
1400 K Street, N.W., Suite 1100
Washington, DC 20005
(202) 289-7201   Fax: (202) 289-7204
E-mail: morganm@adea.org
Web: www.adea.org/Awards/default.htm

Summary To provide financial assistance to predoctoral dental students who have demonstrated academic excellence in preventive dentistry.

Eligibility Dental school deans may nominate up to 3 students each. Candidates must be enrolled at a U.S. dental school on a full-time basis, possess a superior academic record, demonstrate (through activities and achievements) a strong interest in preventive dentistry, and belong to the American Dental Education Association. Financial need may be considered in the selection process.

Financial data The stipend is $2,500. Funds are applied to tuition and fees.

Duration 1 year; nonrenewable.

Additional information Funding for this program, which began in 2001, is provided by the Warner-Lambert Company.

Number awarded 12 each year.

Deadline November of each year.

[360]
LLOYD G. BALFOUR FELLOWSHIPS

North American Interfraternal Foundation.
Attn: Executive Director
10023 Cedar Point Drive
Carmel, IN 46032
(317) 848-7829   Fax: (317) 571-9686
E-mail: nancyfrick@nif-inc.net
Web: www.nif-inc.net/scholarships/lloyd_balfour

Summary To provide financial assistance for graduate studies to initiated fraternity or sorority members.

Eligibility This program is open to full-time students enrolled in an accredited graduate or professional school. Applicants must be initiated members of fraternities affiliated with the North-American Interfraternity Council (NIC), National Panhellenic Conference (NPC), National Pan-Hellenic Council (NPHC), or Professional Fraternity Association (PFA). Along with their application, they must submit an essay, up to 500 words, on their contributions to the enhancement of fraternal ideals and their application to their future career.

Financial data Stipends range from $1,000 to $5,000 per year.

Duration 1 year.

Additional information This fellowship was established in 1985.

Number awarded Varies each year; recently, 12 of these fellowships were awarded.

Deadline May of each year.

[361]
LOS ANGELES HILLEL COUNCIL

Los Angeles Hillel Council
6505 Wilshire Boulevard, Suite 450
Los Angeles, CA 90048-4906
(323) 761-8555   Fax: (323) 761-8566
E-mail: scholarship@lahillel.org
Web: www.lahillel.org/medicalscholarship.html

Summary To provide financial assistance for medical school to students from California or who have been active in Hillel.

Eligibility This program is open to 1) students attending California medical schools; 2) California residents attending medical school anywhere in the country; and 3) medical students nationwide who are or have been active in Hillel while in college. Applicants must submit a brief description of their religious philosophy, activities, and interests; information on hobbies and special interests and talents; a list of sports and extracurricular activities; and documentation of financial need.

Financial data The stipend is $2,500 per year.

Duration 1 year; may be renewed.
Number awarded 1 or more each year.
Deadline August of each year.

[362]
LOUIS DICARLO SCHOLARSHIP

Alexander Graham Bell Association for the Deaf
Attn: Financial Aid Coordinator
3417 Volta Place, N.W.
Washington, DC 20007-2778
(202) 337-5220   Fax: (202) 337-8314
TTY: (202) 337-5221   E-mail: financialaid@agbell.org
Web: www.agbell.org

Summary To provide financial assistance to graduate students with moderate to profound hearing loss.

Eligibility This program is open to graduate students who have been diagnosed with a moderate to profound hearing loss prior to acquiring spoken language (hearing loss averages 60dB or greater in the better ear in the speech frequencies of 500, 1000, and 2000 Hz). Applicants must be committed to using spoken language as their primary mode of communication. They must be accepted or enrolled at a mainstream college or university as a full-time student. Along with their application, they must submit a 1-page essay discussing their career goals and how spoken communication is helping them to reach those goals as a person with a hearing loss. Financial need is considered in the selection process.

Financial data The stipend is $2,000 per year.
Duration 1 year; may be renewed 1 additional year.
Number awarded 1 each year.
Deadline April of each year.

[363]
LUCILLE B. ABT SCHOLARSHIPS

Alexander Graham Bell Association for the Deaf
Attn: Financial Aid Coordinator
3417 Volta Place, N.W.
Washington, DC 20007-2778
(202) 337-5220   Fax: (202) 337-8314
TTY: (202) 337-5221   E-mail: financialaid@agbell.org
Web: www.agbell.org

Summary To provide financial assistance to undergraduate and graduate students with moderate to profound hearing loss.

Eligibility This program is open to undergraduate and graduate students who have been diagnosed with a moderate to profound hearing loss prior to acquiring spoken language (hearing loss averages 60dB or greater in the better ear in the speech frequencies of 500, 1000, and 2000 Hz). Applicants must be committed to using spoken language and lipreading as their preferred mode of communication. They must be accepted or enrolled at a mainstream college or university as a full-time student. Along with their application, they must submit a 1-page essay discussing their career goals and how spoken communication is helping them to reach those goals as a person with a hearing loss. Financial need is considered in the selection process.

Financial data The stipend is $5,000 per year.
Duration 1 year; may be renewed 1 additional year.
Number awarded 10 each year.
Deadline April of each year.

[364]
LULAC GENERAL AWARDS

League of United Latin American Citizens
Attn: LULAC National Education Service Centers
2000 L Street, N.W., Suite 610
Washington, DC 20036
(202) 835-9646   Fax: (202) 835-9685
E-mail: scholarships@lnesc.org
Web: www.lnesc.org

Summary To provide financial assistance to Hispanic American undergraduate and graduate students.

Eligibility This program is open to Hispanic Americans who are U.S. citizens or permanent residents currently enrolled or planning to enroll at an accredited college or university as a graduate or undergraduate student. Although grades are considered in the selection process, emphasis is placed on the applicant's motivation, sincerity, and integrity, as revealed through a personal interview and in an essay. Need, community involvement, and leadership activities are also considered. Candidates must live near a participating local council of the League of United Latin American Citizens (LULAC) and must apply directly to that council.

Financial data The stipend ranges from $250 to $1,000 per year, depending on the need of the recipient.
Duration 1 year.
Additional information This program represents an attempt to forge a partnership between the corporate world and the community. Under its fundsharing concept, LULAC's National Education Service Center gathers contributions nationally from corporations, while LULAC councils raise money locally. The total corporate donations are then apportioned back to the councils according to effort. Applications must be obtained directly from participating LULAC councils; for a list, send a self-addressed stamped envelope to the sponsor.
Number awarded Varies; approximately 500 each year.
Deadline March of each year.

[365]
LULAC HONORS AWARDS

League of United Latin American Citizens
Attn: LULAC National Education Service Centers
2000 L Street, N.W., Suite 610
Washington, DC 20036
(202) 835-9646   Fax: (202) 835-9685
E-mail: scholarships@lnesc.org
Web: www.lnesc.org

Summary To provide financial assistance to Hispanic American undergraduate and graduate students who are doing well in school.

Eligibility This program is open to Hispanic Americans who are U.S. citizens or permanent residents currently enrolled or planning to enroll at an accredited college or university as a graduate or undergraduate student. Applicants who are already in college must have a GPA of 3.25 or higher. Entering freshmen must have ACT scores of 20 or higher or SAT scores of 840 or higher. In addition, applicants must demonstrate motivation, sincerity, and integrity through a personal interview and in an essay. Need, community involvement, and leadership activities are also considered. Candidates must live near a participating local council of the League of United Latin American Citizens (LULAC) and must apply directly to that council.

Financial data The stipend ranges from $250 to $1,000 per year, depending on the need of the recipient.
Duration 1 year.

Additional information This program represents an attempt to forge a partnership between the corporate world and the community. Under its fundsharing concept, LULAC's National Education Service Center gathers contributions nationally from corporations, while LULAC councils raise money locally. The total corporate donations are then apportioned back to the councils according to effort. Applications must be obtained directly from participating LULAC councils; for a list, send a self-addressed stamped envelope to the sponsor.
Number awarded Varies each year.
Deadline March of each year.

[366]
LULAC NATIONAL SCHOLASTIC ACHIEVEMENT AWARDS

League of United Latin American Citizens
Attn: LULAC National Education Service Centers
2000 L Street, N.W., Suite 610
Washington, DC 20036
(202) 835-9646　　　　Fax: (202) 835-9685
E-mail: scholarships@lnesc.org
Web: www.lnesc.org
Summary To provide financial assistance to academically outstanding Hispanic American undergraduate and graduate students.
Eligibility This program is open to Hispanic Americans who are U.S. citizens or permanent residents currently enrolled or planning to enroll at an accredited college or university as a graduate or undergraduate student. Applicants who are already in college must have a GPA of 3.5 or higher. Entering freshmen must have ACT scores of 23 or higher or SAT scores of 970 or higher. In addition, applicants must demonstrate motivation, sincerity, and integrity through a personal interview and in an essay. Need, community involvement, and leadership activities are also considered. Candidates must live near a participating local council of the League of United Latin American Citizens (LULAC) and must apply directly to that council.
Financial data Stipends are at least $1,000 per year.
Duration 1 year.
Additional information This program represents an attempt to forge a partnership between the corporate world and the community. Under its fundsharing concept, LULAC's National Education Service Center gathers contributions nationally from corporations, while LULAC councils raise money locally. The total corporate donations are then apportioned back to the councils according to effort. Applications must be obtained directly from participating LULAC councils; for a list, send a self-addressed stamped envelope to the sponsor.
Number awarded Varies each year.
Deadline March of each year.

[367]
M. ELIZABETH CARNEGIE SCHOLARSHIP

Nurses Educational Funds, Inc.
Attn: Scholarship Coordinator
304 Park Avenue South, 11th Floor
New York, NY 10010
(212) 590-2443　　　　Fax: (212) 590-2446
E-mail: info@n-e-f.org
Web: www.n-e-f.org
Summary To provide financial assistance to African Americans who wish to work on a doctoral degree in nursing.

Eligibility This program is open to African American registered nurses who are members of a national professional nursing organization and are enrolled in or applying to a nursing or nursing-related program at the doctoral level. Applicants must submit a 2-page essay on their professional goals and potential for making a contribution to the nursing profession. They must be U.S. citizens or have declared their official intention of becoming a citizen. Selection is based on academic excellence and potential for contributing to the nursing profession.
Financial data Stipends range from $2,500 to $10,000, depending on the availability of funds.
Duration 1 year; nonrenewable.
Additional information There is a $20 application fee.
Number awarded 1 each year.
Deadline February of each year.

[368]
MAGOICHI AND SHIZUKO KATO MEMORIAL SCHOLARSHIP

Japanese American Citizens League
Attn: National Scholarship Awards
1765 Sutter Street
San Francisco, CA 94115
(415) 921-5225　　　　Fax: (415) 931-4671
E-mail: jacl@jacl.org
Web: www.jacl.org/leadership_development_5.php
Summary To provide financial assistance for graduate study to members of the Japanese American Citizens League (JACL).
Eligibility This program is open to JACL members who are attending or planning to attend an accredited college or university as a graduate student. Applicants must submit a statement describing their current level of involvement in the Japanese American community or Asian Pacific community and how they will continue their involvement in future years. Selection is based on academic record, extracurricular activities, financial need, and community involvement. Preference is given to applicants planning a career in medicine or the ministry.
Financial data The stipend depends on the availability of funds but usually ranges from $1,000 to $5,000.
Duration 1 year; nonrenewable.
Additional information Applications must be submitted to the JACL National Scholarship Program, c/o San Diego JACL Chapter, 1031 25th Street, San Diego, CA 92102.
Number awarded 1 each year.
Deadline March of each year.

[369]
MAIDS OF ATHENA SCHOLARSHIPS

Maids of Athena
1909 Q Street, N.W., Suite 500
Washington, DC 20009-1007
(202) 232-6300　　　　Fax: (202) 232-2140
Web: www.ahepa.org
Summary To provide financial assistance for undergraduate and graduate education to women of Greek descent.
Eligibility This program is open to women who are members of the Maids of Athena. Applicants may be a graduating high school senior, an undergraduate student, or a graduate student. Selection is based on academic merit, financial need, and participation in the organization.
Financial data The stipend is $1,000.
Duration 1 year.

Additional information   Membership in Maids of Athena is open to unmarried women between 14 and 24 years of age who are of Greek descent from either parent.
Number awarded   3 each year: 1 each to a graduating high school senior, undergraduate student, and graduate student.

[370]
MAINE LEGISLATURE MEMORIAL SCHOLARSHIP FUND

Maine Education Services
Attn: MES Foundation
One City Center, 11th Floor
Portland, ME 04101
(207) 791-3600   Toll-free: (800) 922-6352
Fax: (207) 791-3616   E-mail: info@mesfoundation.com
Web: www.mesfoundation.com

Summary   To provide financial assistance to residents of Maine planning to attend or currently attending a college or university in the state.
Eligibility   This program is open to residents of Maine who are either seniors graduating from high schools in the state or already in college. Applicants must be planning to enroll or be currently enrolled in an accredited 2- or 4-year degree-granting Maine college, university, or technical school as an undergraduate or graduate student. Selection is based on academic excellence as demonstrated by transcripts and GPA, contributions to community and employment, letters of recommendation, a 300-word essay on educational goals and intentions, and financial need.
Financial data   The stipend is $1,000.
Duration   1 year.
Additional information   This program was established in 1995 as a successor to the Gould-Michaud Scholarship Funds, which operated from 1981 to 1994 but were limited to students attending the universities in Orono and Fort Kent. Information is also available from the Legislative Information Office, 100 State House Station, Augusta ME 04333-0001, (207) 287-1692, (800) 301-3178, Fax: (207) 287-1580, TDD: (207) 287-6826, E-mail: Teen.Griffin@state.me.us.
Number awarded   16 each year: 1 from each county in Maine.
Deadline   April of each year.

[371]
MAINE MASONIC AID FOR CONTINUING EDUCATION

Maine Education Services
Attn: MES Foundation
One City Center, 11th Floor
Portland, ME 04101
(207) 791-3600   Toll-free: (800) 922-6352
Fax: (207) 791-3616   E-mail: info@mesfoundation.com
Web: www.mesfoundation.com

Summary   To provide financial assistance for college or graduate school to students in Maine who meet the federal definition of an independent student.
Eligibility   This program is open to residents of Maine who meet at least 1 of the following criteria: 1) are at least 24 years of age; 2) are married; 3) are enrolled in a graduate level or professional education program; 4) have legal dependents other than a spouse; 5) are an orphan or ward of the court (or were a ward of the court until age 18); or 6) are a veteran of the U.S. armed forces. Selection is based on work experience, educational history, school and community activities, an essay on career goals, a community reference, and financial need.

Financial data   The stipend is $1,000 per year.
Duration   1 year.
Number awarded   12 each year.
Deadline   April of each year.

[372]
MAINE OSTEOPATHIC ASSOCIATION MEMORIAL SCHOLARSHIP

Maine Osteopathic Association
Attn: Executive Director
693 Western Avenue, Suite 1
Manchester, ME 04351
(207) 623-1101   Fax: (207) 623-4228
E-mail: info@mainedo.org
Web: www.mainedo.org

Summary   To provide financial assistance to Maine residents who are attending osteopathic medical school.
Eligibility   This program is open to continuing students who have been Maine residents for at least 3 years and are able to present proof of enrollment at an approved college of osteopathic medicine in the second, third, or fourth year of study. Residency in Maine for the sole purpose of attending college is not considered evidence of Maine residence for the purpose of this scholarship. Applicants who are graduates of a public or private secondary school in Maine are considered eligible regardless of whether or not they have resided elsewhere in the interim between high school graduation and application.
Financial data   The stipend is $1,000.
Duration   1 year.
Number awarded   1 each year.
Deadline   April of each year.

[373]
MAINE OSTEOPATHIC ASSOCIATION SCHOLARSHIP

Maine Osteopathic Association
Attn: Executive Director
693 Western Avenue, Suite 1
Manchester, ME 04351
(207) 623-1101   Fax: (207) 623-4228
E-mail: info@mainedo.org
Web: www.mainedo.org

Summary   To provide financial assistance to Maine residents who are first-year osteopathic medical students.
Eligibility   This program is open to first-year medical students who have been Maine residents for at least 3 years and are able to present proof of enrollment at an approved college of osteopathic medicine. Residency in Maine for the sole purpose of attending college is not considered evidence of Maine residence for the purpose of this scholarship. Applicants who are graduates of a public or private secondary school in Maine are considered eligible regardless of whether or not they have resided elsewhere in the interim between high school graduation and application.
Financial data   The stipend is $1,000.
Duration   1 year.
Number awarded   1 each year.
Deadline   April of each year.

[374]
MAINE VETERANS DEPENDENTS EDUCATIONAL BENEFITS

Bureau of Veterans' Services
117 State House Station
Augusta, ME 04333-0117
(207) 626-4464   Toll-free: (800) 345-0116 (within ME)
Fax: (207) 626-4471   E-mail: mainebvs@maine.gov
Web: www.mainebvs.org/benefits.htm

Summary To provide financial assistance for undergraduate or graduate education to dependents of disabled and other Maine veterans.

Eligibility Applicants for these benefits must be children (high school seniors or graduates under 25 years of age), non-divorced spouses, or unremarried widow(er)s of veterans who meet 1 or more of the following requirements: 1) living and determined to have a total permanent disability resulting from a service-connected cause; 2) killed in action; 3) died from a service-connected disability; 4) died while totally and permanently disabled due to a service-connected disability but whose death was not related to the service-connected disability; or 5) a member of the armed forces on active duty who has been listed for more than 90 days as missing in action, captured, forcibly detained, or interned in the line of duty by a foreign government or power. The veteran parent must have been a resident of Maine at the time of entry into service or a resident of Maine for 5 years preceding application for these benefits. Children may be seeking no higher than a bachelor's degree. Spouses, widows, and widowers may work on an advanced degree if they already have a bachelor's degree at the time of enrollment into this program.

Financial data Recipients are entitled to free tuition at institutions of higher education supported by the state of Maine.

Duration Benefits extend for a maximum of 8 semesters. Recipients have 6 consecutive academic years to complete their education.

Additional information College preparatory schooling and correspondence courses do not qualify under this program.

Number awarded Varies each year.

[375]
MAINE VIETNAM VETERANS SCHOLARSHIP FUND

Maine Community Foundation
Attn: Program Director
245 Main Street
Ellsworth, ME 04605
(207) 667-9735   Toll-free: (877) 700-6800
Fax: (207) 667-0447   E-mail: info@mainecf.org
Web: www.mainecf.org/html/scholarships/index.html

Summary To provide financial assistance for college or graduate school to Vietnam veterans or the dependents of Vietnam or other veterans in Maine.

Eligibility This program is open to residents of Maine who are Vietnam veterans or the descendants of veterans who served in the Vietnam Theater. As a second priority, children of veterans from other time periods are also considered. Graduating high school seniors, nontraditional students, undergraduates, and graduate students are eligible to apply. Selection is based on financial need, extracurricular activities, work experience, academic achievement, and a personal statement of career goals and how the applicant's educational plans relate to them.

Financial data The stipend is $1,000 per year.

Duration 1 year.

Additional information This program was established in 1985. There is a $3 processing fee.

Number awarded 3 to 6 each year.

Deadline April of each year.

[376]
MALCOLM M. BERGLUND SCHOLARSHIP

United Daughters of the Confederacy
Attn: Education Director
328 North Boulevard
Richmond, VA 23220-4057
(804) 355-1636   Fax: (804) 353-1396
E-mail: hqudc@rcn.com
Web: www.hqudc.org/scholarships/scholarships.html

Summary To provide financial assistance for graduate education to lineal descendants of Confederate veterans.

Eligibility Eligible to apply for these scholarships are lineal descendants of worthy Confederates or collateral descendants who are members of the Children of the Confederacy or the United Daughters of the Confederacy. Applicants must intend to study at the graduate level and must submit certified proof of the Confederate record of 1 ancestor, with the company and regiment in which he served. They must have a GPA of 3.0 or higher.

Financial data The amount of this scholarship depends on the availability of funds.

Duration 1 year; may be renewed up to 2 additional years.

Additional information Information is also available from Mrs. Robert C. Kraus, Second Vice President General, 239 Deerfield Lane, Franklin, NC 28734-0112. Members of the same family may not hold scholarships simultaneously, and only 1 application per family will be accepted within any 1 year. All requests for applications must be accompanied by a self-addressed stamped envelope.

Number awarded 1 each year.

Deadline March of each year.

[377]
MANFRED MEIER SCHOLARSHIP

American Psychological Foundation
750 First Street, N.E.
Washington, DC 20002-4242
(202) 336-5843   Fax: (202) 336-5812
E-mail: foundation@apa.org
Web: www.apa.org/apf/hecaen.html

Summary To provide financial assistance to neuropsychology graduate students with financial need.

Eligibility This program is open to graduate students working in the area of neuropsychology. Applicants must submit a letter documenting their scholarly or research accomplishments, their financial need for the award, and the purpose for which they plan to use it.

Financial data The stipend is $2,500 per year.

Duration 1 year.

Additional information This scholarship was first awarded in 1997.

Number awarded 1 each year.

Deadline May of each year.

[378]
MARCH OF DIMES GRADUATE NURSING SCHOLARSHIPS

March of Dimes Birth Defects Foundation
Attn: Vice President for Research
1275 Mamaroneck Avenue
White Plains, NY 10605
(914) 997-4609   Fax: (914) 997-4560
E-mail: mlavan@marchofdimes.com
Web: www.marchofdimes.com

Summary   To provide financial assistance to registered nurses enrolled in graduate programs of maternal and child nursing.

Eligibility   This program is open to registered nurses who are enrolled in graduate programs in maternal and child nursing and have at least 1 academic term to complete. Applicants must be a member of the American College of Nurse-Midwives (ACNM), the National Association of Neonatal Nurses (NANN), or the Association of Women's Health, Obstetric and Neonatal Nurses (AWHONN). They must submit a 500-word essay on their educational plan; career goals and how they correlate with the mission of the March of Dimes to improve the health of babies by preventing birth defects and infant mortality; past, current, and planned involvement in nursing for mothers and infants; and why they should be awarded the scholarship. Financial need is not considered in the selection process.

Financial data   The stipend is $5,000.

Duration   1 year; nonrenewable.

Additional information   This program was established in 1997. Recently, it was supported by Pampers.

Number awarded   Varies each year; recently, 6 of these scholarships were awarded.

Deadline   January of each year.

[379]
MARIAN J. WETTRICK CHARITABLE FOUNDATION MEDICAL SCHOLARSHIPS

Marian J. Wettrick Charitable Foundation
c/o Citizens Trust Company
10 North Main Street
P.O. Box 229
Coudersport, PA 16915-0229
(814) 274-9150   Toll-free: (800) 921-9150
Fax: (814) 274-0401   E-mail: ctc.info@citztrust.com
Web: www.CitizensTrustCompany.com

Summary   To provide financial assistance to women who graduated from a college in Pennsylvania and are interested in attending a medical school in the state.

Eligibility   This program is open to women who graduated from a college or university in Pennsylvania with a recognized premedical major. They must be interested in attending a medical school in the state. Priority is given to applicants who are interested in practicing medicine at Charles Cole Medical Center in Coudersport (although this is not a binding requirement). A personal interview may be required. Financial need is considered in the selection process.

Financial data   Stipends range up to $10,000 per year.

Duration   1 year; may be renewed.

Number awarded   Up to 6 each year.

Deadline   May of each year.

[380]
MARION B. POLLOCK FELLOWSHIP

American Association for Health Education
Attn: Scholarship Committee
1900 Association Drive
Reston, VA 20191-1599
(703) 476-3437   Toll-free: (800) 213-7193, ext. 437
Fax: (703) 476-6638   E-mail: aahe@aahperd.org
Web: www.aahperd.org/aahe/heawards/Pollock.html

Summary   To provide financial assistance to health education teachers who are working on a master's degree.

Eligibility   This program is open to experienced teachers at the elementary, middle school, or high school level who are enrolled full time as a master's degree student in a health education program. Applicants must have completed at least 6 hours of graduate course work. They must submit a current resume or curriculum vitae, a transcript from the institution granting the most recent degree, 2 letters of recommendation, and a 5-page narrative describing the role of school health education in meeting the current health needs of children and youth, their personal and professional goals, and how the educational program is going to advance the health of children and youth. Selection is based on evidence of ability to link health needs of children to school health instruction, teaching experience, professional goals, potential to advance the practice of health education in schools, and caliber of documents.

Financial data   The stipend is $3,000.

Duration   1 year.

Number awarded   1 each year.

Deadline   November of each year.

[381]
MARTIN J. GREEN, SR. MEMORIAL SCHOLARSHIP

American Radio Relay League
Attn: ARRL Foundation
225 Main Street
Newington, CT 06111
(860) 594-0397   Fax: (860) 594-0259
E-mail: foundation@arrl.org
Web: www.arrl.org/arrlf/scholgen.html

Summary   To provide financial assistance to licensed radio amateurs who are interested in working on an undergraduate or graduate degree.

Eligibility   This program is open to undergraduate or graduate students in any field who are enrolled at accredited institutions and are licensed radio amateurs of general class. Applicants must submit an essay on the role amateur radio has played in their lives and provide documentation of financial need. Preference is given to students whose parents, grandparents, siblings, or other relatives are also ham radio operators.

Financial data   The stipend is $1,000.

Duration   1 year.

Number awarded   1 each year.

Deadline   January of each year.

[382]
MARY ANNE WILLIAMS SCHOLARSHIP

United Daughters of the Confederacy-Virginia Division
c/o Suzie Snyder, Education Committee Chair
8440 Bradshaw Road
Salem, VA 24153-2246
(540) 384-6884   E-mail: Suzienotes@aol.com
Web: users.erols.com/va-udc/scholarships.html

Summary To provide financial assistance for undergraduate or graduate study in medicine or engineering to Confederate descendants from Virginia.

Eligibility This program is open to residents of Virginia who are 1) lineal descendants of Confederates, or 2) collateral descendants and also members of the Children of the Confederacy or the United Daughters of the Confederacy. Applicants must be interested in working on an undergraduate or graduate degree in medicine or engineering. They must submit proof of the Confederate military record of at least 1 ancestor, with the company and regiment in which he served. They must also submit a personal letter pledging to make the best possible use of the scholarship; describing their health, social, family, religious, and fraternal connections within the community; and reflecting on what a Southern heritage means to them (using the term "War Between the States" in lieu of "Civil War"). They must have a GPA of 3.0 or higher and be able to demonstrate financial need.

Financial data The amount of the stipend depends on the availability of funds. Payment is made directly to the college or university the recipient attends.

Duration 1 year; may be renewed up to 3 additional years if the recipient maintains a GPA of 3.0 or higher.

Additional information Information is also available from Mrs. George W. Bryson, 10103 Rixeyville Road, Culpeper, VA 22701-4422, E-mail: brysdale@aol.com.

Number awarded This scholarship is offered whenever a prior recipient graduates or is no longer eligible.

Deadline May of years in which the scholarship is available.

[383]
MARY EILEEN DIXEY SCHOLARSHIP

American Occupational Therapy Foundation
Attn: Scholarship Coordinator
4720 Montgomery Lane
P.O. Box 31220
Bethesda, MD 20824-1220
(301) 652-2682   Fax: (301) 656-3620
TDD: (800) 377-8555   E-mail: aotf@aotf.org
Web: www.aotf.org

Summary To provide financial assistance to students in New Hampshire who are working on an associate or master's degree in occupational therapy.

Eligibility This program is open to New Hampshire residents who are enrolled in an accredited occupational therapy educational program in any state at the associate or master's degree level. Applicants must demonstrate a need for financial assistance and have a sustained record of outstanding scholastic performance. As part of the application process, they must submit transcripts, 2 personal references, and a statement from their curriculum director.

Financial data The stipend is $2,000.

Duration 1 year.

Number awarded 1 each year.

Deadline January of each year.

[384]
MARY GIBBON SCHOLARSHIP

American Society of Extra-Corporeal Technology, Inc.
Attn: AmSECT Foundation
2209 Dickens Road
P.O. Box 11086
Richmond, VA 23230-1086
(804) 565-6363   Fax: (804) 282-0090
E-mail: AmSECT@amsect.org
Web: www.amsect.org

Summary To provide financial assistance to student members of the American Society of Extra-Corporeal Technology (AmSECT) who are enrolled in a perfusion training program.

Eligibility This program is open to student members of the society who are enrolled in (or accepted at) an accredited perfusion training program. Applicants must have completed at least half of the required course work and have at least a 2.75 GPA. They must submit 1) 250-word essays on how they would improve AmSECT and how they could improve the perfusion profession, and 2) a 500-word essay on a current topic affecting the conduct of perfusion. Financial need is not considered in the selection process.

Financial data The stipend is $2,500 per year.

Duration 1 year.

Additional information The funding for this program comes from the Medtronic Cardiopulmonary, Inc.

Number awarded 1 each year.

Deadline November of each year.

[385]
MARY LEWIS WYCHE FELLOWSHIPS

North Carolina Nurses Association
Attn: North Carolina Foundation for Nursing
103 Enterprise Street
P.O. Box 12025
Raleigh, NC 27605-2025
(919) 828-1464   Toll-free: (800) 814-0126
Fax: (919) 829-5807   E-mail: rns@ncnurses.org
Web: www.ncnurses.org/ncfn.html

Summary To provide financial assistance to registered nurses in North Carolina who are interested in working on a graduate degree.

Eligibility This program is open to registered nurses in North Carolina who have been admitted to a master's or doctoral degree program in the state as a full-time student. Applicants must have been North Carolina residents for at least 12 months prior to application and have a cumulative GPA of 3.0 or higher. Selection is based on GPA, professional involvement, community involvement, potential for contribution to the profession, and honors and certifications. Preference is given to members of the North Carolina Nurses Association.

Financial data The stipend is $5,000 per year.

Duration 1 year.

Additional information This program was established in 2003.

Number awarded 1 or more each year.

Deadline June of each year.

[386]
MARY LOU BROWN SCHOLARSHIPS

American Radio Relay League
Attn: ARRL Foundation
225 Main Street
Newington, CT 06111
(860) 594-0397   Fax: (860) 594-0259
E-mail: foundation@arrl.org
Web: www.arrl.org/arrlf/scholgen.html

Summary To provide financial assistance to licensed radio amateurs, particularly from designated states, who are interested in working on an undergraduate or graduate degree.

Eligibility This program is open to undergraduate or graduate students at accredited institutions who are licensed radio amateurs of general class. Preference is given to students residing in Alaska, Idaho, Montana, Oregon, or Washington and attending school in those states. Applicants must have a GPA of 3.0 or better and a demonstrated interest in promoting the Amateur Radio Service. They must submit an essay on the role amateur radio has played in their lives and provide documentation of financial need.

Financial data The stipend is $2,500.

Duration 1 year.

Number awarded 1 or more each year.

Deadline January of each year.

[387]
MARY LOUISE ROLLER PANHELLENIC SCHOLARSHIPS

North American Interfraternal Foundation.
Attn: Executive Director
10023 Cedar Point Drive
Carmel, IN 46032
(317) 848-7829   Fax: (317) 571-9686
E-mail: nancyfrick@nif-inc.net
Web: www.nif-inc.net/scholarships/mary_louise_roller

Summary To provide financial assistance to women college seniors who have been members of a sorority and plan to attend graduate school.

Eligibility This program is open to undergraduate women who plan to attend graduate school the following fall. Each college Panhellenic council may nominate 1 member. Nominees must have displayed outstanding service to their local college Panhellenic during their undergraduate years. They must include an essay, up to 500 words, on how they have benefited from their Panhellenic experiences.

Financial data The stipend is $1,000 per year.

Duration 1 year.

Number awarded 2 each year.

Deadline May of each year.

[388]
MARY MCMILLAN DOCTORAL SCHOLARSHIPS

American Physical Therapy Association
Attn: Foundation for Physical Therapy
1111 North Fairfax Street
Alexandria, VA 22314-1488
(703) 706-8906   Toll-free: (800) 875-1378
Fax: (703) 706-8519   TDD: (703) 683-6748
E-mail: foundation@apta.org
Web: www.apta.org

Summary To provide financial assistance to physical therapists in their first year of postprofessional doctoral study.

Eligibility This program is open to licensed physical therapists who have been accepted as a student in an accredited post-professional doctoral program with a demonstrated relationship to physical therapy. Applicants may not have completed the equivalent of 1 academic year of doctoral-level course work prior to the start of the year for which the scholarship will be used. They must be U.S. citizens or permanent residents. Preference is given to applicants who 1) show promise of completing doctoral degree requirements in a timely fashion; 2) have a demonstrated potential for a career as an academic researcher and educator in an accredited physical therapy education program; and 3) plan to conduct research that is directly related to the sponsor's clinical research agenda. Selection is based on a statement of career goals, objectives of graduate study, plan for study and completion of degree, significance of research direction, and endorsement of faculty members.

Financial data Awards up to $5,000 are provided. Funds are paid directly to the recipient.

Duration 1 year; nonrenewable.

Number awarded Up to 6 each year.

Deadline August of each year.

[389]
MARY MCMILLAN SCHOLARSHIP AWARDS

American Physical Therapy Association
Attn: Honors and Awards Program
1111 North Fairfax Street
Alexandria, VA 22314-1488
(703) 684-APTA   Toll-free: (800) 999-APTA
Fax: (703) 684-7343   TDD: (703) 683-6748
E-mail: Governce@apta.org
Web: www.apta.org

Summary To provide financial assistance to students in physical therapist assistant, professional physical therapy education, and post-professional master's degree programs.

Eligibility This program is open to 1) physical therapist assistant education program students in the final year of study; 2) physical therapist professional education program students (including entry-level doctor of physical therapy degree students) who have completed at least 1 full year of entry-level education; and 3) post-professional master's degree students who have completed at least 1 term in the program and are enrolled at the time. Students must be nominated by the school they are attending. Selection is based on scholastic performance, past productivity, evidence of potential contribution to physical therapy, and service to the American Physical Therapy Association.

Financial data The stipend is $3,000 for physical therapist assistant students or $5,000 for physical therapist professional education students (including entry-level doctor of physical therapy degree students) and post-professional master's degree students.

Duration 1 year.

Number awarded Varies each year.

Deadline November of each year.

[390]
MARY MURPHY GRADUATE SCHOLARSHIP

Delta Sigma Theta Sorority, Inc.-Century City Alumnae
  Chapter
Attn: Scholarship Committee
P.O. Box 90956
Los Angeles, CA 90009
(213) 243-0594   E-mail: centurycitydst@yahoo.com
Web: www.centurycitydst.org/programs.html

Summary To provide financial assistance to African American women interested in working on a graduate degree.

Eligibility This program is designed to support women who have a bachelor's degree from an accredited institution and are pursuing (or interested in pursuing) graduate study in any field. Members of Delta Sigma Theta Sorority are not eligible to apply. Candidates must have a reputation as a person of good character, a commitment to serving others in the African American community, and an outstanding academic record (at least a 3.0 GPA). Each applicant is requested to submit a completed application form, 3 letters of recommendation, an official transcript, verification of application or admission to a graduate program, and a statement describing career goals and service to the African American community. Financial need is considered in the selection process.

Financial data A stipend is awarded (amount not specified).
Duration 1 year; may be renewed.
Number awarded 1 each year.
Deadline March of each year.

[391]
MARY OPAL WOLANIN GRADUATE SCHOLARSHIP

National Gerontological Nurses Association
7794 Grow Drive
Pensacola, FL 32514-7072
(850) 473-1174   Toll-free: (800) 723-0560
Fax: (850) 484-8762   E-mail: ngna@puetzamc.com
Web: www.ngna.org

Summary To provide financial assistance to graduate student members of the National Gerontological Nurses Association (NGNA).

Eligibility This program is open to members of the association who are majoring in gerontology/geriatric nursing and carrying at least 6 units at a school accredited by the NLN. Applicants must submit 3 letters of recommendation, a current school catalog describing courses with gerontological nursing content, all academic transcripts (at least a 3.0 GPA is required), a statement of purpose for requesting the scholarship, a statement of future professional and educational goals, and a statement of financial need. U.S. citizenship is required.

Financial data The stipend is $1,500.
Duration 1 year.
Additional information Recipients must be willing to serve on the honors and awards committee for a minimum of 1 year and must agree to attend the association's annual conference.
Number awarded 1 or more each year.
Deadline May of each year.

[392]
MARYLAND DELEGATE SCHOLARSHIP PROGRAM

Maryland Higher Education Commission
Attn: Office of Student Financial Assistance
839 Bestgate Road, Suite 400
Annapolis, MD 21401-3013
(410) 260-4565   Toll-free: (800) 974-1024
Fax: (410) 974-5376   TTY: (800) 735-2258
E-mail: osfamail@mhec.state.md.us
Web: www.mhec.state.md.us

Summary To provide financial assistance to vocational, undergraduate, and graduate students in Maryland.

Eligibility This program is open to students enrolled or planning to enroll either part time or full time in a vocational, undergraduate, or graduate program in Maryland. Applicants and their parents must be Maryland residents. Awards are made by state delegates to students in their district. Financial need must be demonstrated if the Office of Student Financial Assistance makes the award for the delegate.

Financial data The minimum annual award is $200. The total amount of all state awards may not exceed the cost of attendance as determined by the school's financial aid office or $17,800, whichever is less.

Duration 1 year; may be renewed for up to 3 additional years if the recipient maintains satisfactory academic progress.

Additional information Recipients may attend an out-of-state institution if their major is not available at a Maryland school and if their delegate agrees. Students should contact all 3 delegates in their state legislative district for application instructions.

Number awarded Varies each year.
Deadline February of each year.

[393]
MARYLAND FIRE FIGHTER, AMBULANCE, AND RESCUE SQUAD MEMBER TUITION REIMBURSEMENT PROGRAM

Maryland Higher Education Commission
Attn: Office of Student Financial Assistance
839 Bestgate Road, Suite 400
Annapolis, MD 21401-3013
(410) 260-4574   Toll-free: (800) 974-1024, ext. 4574
Fax: (410) 974-5376   TTY: (800) 735-2258
E-mail: osfamail@mhec.state.md.us
Web: www.mhec.state.md.us

Summary To provide financial assistance for college and graduate school to fire fighters, ambulance, and rescue squad members in Maryland.

Eligibility Eligible for this support are fire fighters, ambulance, and rescue squad members who are enrolled as full-time or part-time undergraduate or graduate students at an accredited institution of higher education in Maryland in a degree or certificate program for fire service technology or emergency medical technology. Applicants must have received at least a grade of "C" in any course required for completion of their program. They must be serving a Maryland community while they are taking college courses.

Financial data Awards provide full reimbursement of tuition charges the student has paid.

Duration 1 year; may be renewed if the recipient maintains satisfactory academic progress and remains enrolled in an eligible program.

Additional information Recipients must continue to serve a Maryland community for an additional year following completion of the courses.
Number awarded Varies each year.
Deadline June of each year.

[394]
MARYLAND GRADUATE AND PROFESSIONAL SCHOOL SCHOLARSHIPS

Maryland Higher Education Commission
Attn: Office of Student Financial Assistance
839 Bestgate Road, Suite 400
Annapolis, MD 21401-3013
(410) 260-4565   Toll-free: (800) 974-1024
Fax: (410) 974-5376   TTY: (800) 735-2258
E-mail: osfamail@mhec.state.md.us
Web: www.mhec.state.md.us

Summary To provide financial assistance to professional and graduate students in Maryland who are interested in preparing for a career in the legal or medical professions.
Eligibility This program is open to students enrolled at designated universities in graduate and professional programs in dentistry, law, medicine, nursing, pharmacy, social work, or veterinary medicine. Applicants must be Maryland residents and able to demonstrate financial need.
Financial data Stipends range from $1,000 to $5,000 per year.
Duration 1 year; may be renewed for up to 3 additional years if the recipient remains enrolled in an eligible program, maintains satisfactory academic progress, and continues to demonstrate financial need.
Additional information The selected institutions are the University of Maryland at Baltimore Schools of Medicine, Dentistry, Law, Pharmacy, and Social Work; the University of Baltimore School of Law, the Johns Hopkins University School of Medicine; the Virginia-Maryland Regional College of Veterinary Medicine; and certain Maryland institutions offering a master's degree in nursing or social work.
Number awarded Varies each year.
Deadline February of each year.

[395]
MARYLAND SENATORIAL SCHOLARSHIPS

Maryland Higher Education Commission
Attn: Office of Student Financial Assistance
839 Bestgate Road, Suite 400
Annapolis, MD 21401-3013
(410) 260-4565   Toll-free: (800) 974-1024
Fax: (410) 974-5376   TTY: (800) 735-2258
E-mail: osfamail@mhec.state.md.us
Web: www.mhec.state.md.us

Summary To provide financial assistance to vocational, undergraduate, and graduate students in Maryland.
Eligibility This program is open to students enrolled either part time or full time in a vocational, undergraduate, or graduate program in Maryland. Applicants and their parents must be Maryland residents and able to demonstrate financial need. Awards are made by state senators to students in their districts. Some senators ask the Office of Student Financial Assistance to make awards for them; those awards are made on the basis of financial need.
Financial data Stipends range from $200 to $2,000 per year, depending on the need of the recipient. The total amount of all

state awards may not exceed the cost of attendance as determined by the school's financial aid office or $17,800, whichever is less.
Duration 1 year; may be renewed for up to 3 additional years of full-time study or 7 additional years of part-time study, provided the recipient maintains satisfactory academic progress.
Additional information Recipients may attend an out-of-state institution if their major is not available at a Maryland school and if their senator agrees.
Number awarded Varies each year.
Deadline February of each year.

[396]
MASSACHUSETTS COLLABORATIVE TEACHERS TUITION WAIVER

Massachusetts Office of Student Financial Assistance
454 Broadway, Suite 200
Revere, MA 02151
(617) 727-9420   Fax: (617) 727-0667
E-mail: osfa@osfa.mass.edu
Web: www.osfa.mass.edu

Summary To provide financial assistance to teachers in Massachusetts who wish to take graduate classes in any field at a public college or university in the state and are willing to become a mentor to student teachers.
Eligibility This program is open to public school teachers who are Massachusetts residents and U.S. citizens or permanent residents. Applicants must agree to mentor a student teacher from a state college or university in their classroom. They must be interested in enrolling in graduate courses at 1 of the 9 Massachusetts state colleges or the 4 campuses of the University of Massachusetts. The courses may be in education or in the applicant's major field.
Financial data Participating teachers are eligible for a tuition waiver for up to 1 state-supported graduate course for each student teacher mentored.
Duration Teachers can request waivers for up to 2 years after the completion of the mentoring relationship.
Number awarded Varies each year.

[397]
MASTER'S AND POST-MASTER'S NURSE PRACTITIONER CERTIFICATE SCHOLARSHIPS

Oncology Nursing Society
Attn: ONS Foundation
125 Enterprise Drive
Pittsburgh, PA 15275-1214
(412) 859-6100, ext. 8503   Toll-free: (866) 257-4ONS
Fax: (412) 859-6160   E-mail: foundation@ons.org
Web: www.ons.org

Summary To provide financial assistance to registered nurses interested in pursuing a master's or post-master's degree in advanced practice oncology nursing.
Eligibility Candidates must 1) be registered nurses with a demonstrated interest in and commitment to oncology nursing; 2) have a previous bachelor's or master's degree in nursing; 3) be enrolled in or applying to an academic master's degree or post-master's nurse practitioner certificate program in an NLN- or CCNE-accredited school of nursing; and 4) never have received this award from this sponsor. Applicants must submit an essay of 250 words or less on their role in caring for persons with cancer and a statement of their professional goals and their relationship

to the advancement of oncology nursing. Financial need is not considered in the selection process.

Financial data The stipend is $3,000.

Duration 1 year.

Additional information This program is supported by Amgen, Inc., Novartis Oncology, Sanofi-Aventis, Oncology Education Services, Inc., and the Oncology Nursing Certification Corporation. At the end of each year of scholarship participation, recipients must submit a summary of the educational activities in which they participated. Applications must be accompanied by a $5 fee.

Number awarded Varies each year; recently, 9 of these scholarships were awarded.

Deadline January of each year.

[398]
MASTER'S DEGREE SCHOLARSHIPS IN CANCER NURSING

American Cancer Society
Attn: Extramural Grants Department
1599 Clifton Road, N.E.
Atlanta, GA 30329-4251
(404) 329-7558   Toll-free: (800) ACS-2345
Fax: (404) 321-4669   E-mail: grants@cancer.org
Web: www.cancer.org/research

Summary To provide financial assistance to graduate students working on a master's degree in cancer nursing.

Eligibility This program is open to registered nurses with a current license to practice who are enrolled in or applying to a master's degree program in cancer nursing at an academic institution within the United States. Applicants must be U.S. citizens or permanent residents, be committed to preparing for a career full time, have had experience in professional nursing (as well as cancer nursing), be involved in professional and academic organizations, be involved in the American Cancer Society and other volunteer organizations, have published or contributed to publications and creative works, have received professional and personal awards and honors, have a focus for scholarly activity in a specific area of cancer nursing, have explicit and realistic professional goals, and be committed to a career in cancer nursing. They must be preparing to work in the following fields of cancer nursing: research, education, administration, or clinical practice.

Financial data The stipend is $10,000 per year. Payments are made to the institution at the beginning of each semester.

Duration 1 to 2 years.

Number awarded Varies each year.

Deadline January of each year.

[399]
MATTIE J.T. STEPANEK INTERGENERATIONAL SCHOLARSHIP

Rosalynn Carter Institute for Human Development
c/o Georgia Southwestern State University
800 Wheatley Street
Americus, GA 31709
(229) 928-1234   Fax: (229) 931-2663
E-mail: rci@canes.gsw.edu
Web: www.rosalynncarter.org

Summary To provide financial assistance to caregivers interested in additional training and students preparing for a career in a caregiving field.

Eligibility This program is open to 1) students of any age and at any level who are preparing for a career in a caregiving field,

and 2) individuals already working as a paid caregiver and interested in receiving further training. Applicants must submit a resume that includes extracurricular activities, community involvement, and volunteer work; a 1-page description of their interests and aspirations in a career providing care to others; and 2 letters of recommendation. Current students must also submit official grade transcripts; current employees must also submit their most recent performance appraisal or letter from their direct supervisor.

Financial data The stipend is $2,000.

Duration 1 year.

Additional information This program, established in 2005, defines caregiver as a person who assists individuals with physical diseases, mental illnesses, difficulties associated with aging, or development disabilities.

Number awarded 4 each year.

Deadline April each year.

[400]
MCKNIGHT DOCTORAL FELLOWSHIP PROGRAM

Florida Education Fund
201 East Kennedy Boulevard, Suite 1525
Tampa, FL 33602
(813) 272-2772   Fax: (813) 272-2784
E-mail: mdf@fefonline.org
Web: www.fefonline.org/mdf.html

Summary To provide financial assistance to African American graduate students in Florida who are interested in teaching selected disciplines at colleges and universities in the state.

Eligibility This program is open to African Americans who are working on a Ph.D. degree at 1 of 9 universities in Florida. Fellowships may be in any discipline in the arts and sciences, business, engineering, health sciences, nursing, or the visual and performing arts; preference is given to the following fields of study: agriculture, biology, business administration, chemistry, computer science, engineering, marine biology, mathematics, physics, and psychology. Academic programs that lead to professional degrees (such as the M.D., D.B.A., D.D.S., J.D., or D.V.M.) are not covered by the fellowship. Graduate study in education, whether leading to an Ed.D. or a Ph.D., is generally not supported. U.S. citizenship is required. Because this program is intended to increase African American graduate enrollment at the 9 participating universities, currently-enrolled doctoral students at those universities are not eligible to apply.

Financial data Each award provides annual tuition up to $5,000 and an annual stipend of $12,000. Recipients are also eligible for the Fellows Travel Fund, which supports recipients who wish to attend and present papers at professional conferences.

Duration 3 years; an additional 2 years of support may be provided by the university if the recipient maintains satisfactory performance and normal progress toward the Ph.D. degree.

Additional information This program was established in 1984. The participating universities are Florida Agricultural and Mechanical University, Florida Atlantic University, Florida Institute of Technology, Florida International University, Florida State University, University of Central Florida, University of Florida, University of Miami, and University of South Florida.

Number awarded Up to 25 each year.

Deadline January of each year.

[401]
MCNEIL ANNUAL SCHOLARSHIPS

National Association of Pediatric Nurse Practitioners
Attn: Director
20 Brace Road, Suite 200
Cherry Hill, NJ 08034-2633
(856) 857-9700   Toll-free: (877) 662-7627
Fax: (856) 857-1600   E-mail: info@napnap.org
Web: www.napnap.org

Summary   To provide funding to students interested in working on a degree as a pediatric nurse practitioner.

Eligibility   This program is open to registered nurses who have at least 3 years' previous work experience in pediatrics. Applicants must have been accepted at a recognized pediatric nurse practitioner (PNP) program (the program must be associated with an academic institution authorized to award a master's degree in nursing); have no previous formal nurse practitioner education; and be able to demonstrate financial need. Along with their application, they must submit an essay of 500 to 1,000 words explaining why they want to become a PNP and describing their professional aspirations and plans.

Financial data   The stipend is $2,000.

Duration   1 year; may be renewed if the recipient maintains full-time status, a GPA of 3.0 or higher, and membership in the National Association of Pediatric Nurse Practitioners (NAPNAP).

Additional information   Funds for this program are provided by McNeil Consumer and Specialty Pharmaceuticals. Scholarships are awarded for both the fall and spring semesters/quarters. Recipients are formally recognized at the association's annual conference. Airfare and conference registration fees are paid by the association.

Number awarded   2 each year.

Deadline   May of each year for the fall semester; September of each year for the fall or spring semester. Students who begin a program in January may also apply the following May if clinical course work continues into the next academic year.

[402]
MEDICAL STUDENT TRAINING IN HUMAN IMMUNOLOGY

Charles A. Dana Foundation
Attn: Grants Office
745 Fifth Avenue, Suite 900
New York, NY 10151
(212) 223-4040   Fax: (212) 317-8721
E-mail: danainfo@dana.org
Web: www.dana.org

Summary   To provide funding to medical students interested in research training in immunology.

Eligibility   This program is open to medical students preparing for a research career in clinical immunology with a patient-oriented emphasis. Students must be recommended by an investigator who has received support for immunological research from the foundation and has agreed to serve as a mentor. The candidate can be either from the medical school at the investigator's institution or from another medical school.

Financial data   The stipend is $35,000 per year.

Duration   1 year; may be renewed for 1 additional year.

Number awarded   Varies each year.

[403]
MEDINA SCHOLARSHIP FOR HISPANICS IN SAFETY

American Society of Safety Engineers
Attn: ASSE Foundation
1800 East Oakton Street
Des Plaines, IL 60018
(847) 768-3435   Fax: (847) 768-3434
E-mail: agabanski@asse.org
Web: www.asse.org/foundation

Summary   To provide financial assistance to Hispanic upper-division and graduate student members of the American Society of Safety Engineers (ASSE) who are working on a degree in occupational health and related fields.

Eligibility   This program is open to ASSE student members who are working on an undergraduate or graduate degree in occupational safety, health, and environment or a closely-related field (e.g., industrial or environmental engineering, environmental science, industrial hygiene, occupational health nursing). Applicants must be bilingual (Spanish-English); Hispanic ethnicity is preferred. Students attending an ABET-accredited school also receive preference. Undergraduates must be full-time students who have completed at least 60 semester hours with a GPA of 3.0 or higher. Graduate students must also be enrolled full time, have completed at least 9 semester hours with a GPA of 3.5 or higher, and have had a GPA of 3.0 or higher as an undergraduate. Along with their application, they must submit 2 essays of 300 words or less: 1) why they are seeking a degree in occupational safety and health or a closely-related field, a brief description of their current activities, and how those relate to their career goals and objectives; and 2) why they should be awarded this scholarship (including career goals and financial need).

Financial data   The stipend is $1,500.

Duration   1 year; nonrenewable.

Additional information   This program was established in 2005.

Number awarded   1 each year.

Deadline   November of each year.

[404]
MEDTRONIC EMERGENCY RESPONSE SYSTEMS ACADEMIC SCHOLARSHIP

American Association of Occupational Health Nurses, Inc.
Attn: AAOHN Foundation
2920 Brandywine Road, Suite 100
Atlanta, GA 30341-4146
(770) 455-7757   Fax: (770) 455-7271
E-mail: foundation@aaohn.org
Web: www.aaohn.org/foundation/scholarships/index.cfm

Summary   To provide financial assistance to registered nurses who are working on a bachelor's or graduate degree to prepare for a career in occupational and environmental health.

Eligibility   This program is open to registered nurses who are enrolled in a baccalaureate or graduate degree program. Applicants must demonstrate an interest in, and commitment to, occupational and environmental health. Along with their application, they must submit a 500-word narrative on their professional goals as they relate to the academic activity and the field of occupational and environmental health. Selection is based on that essay (50%), impact of education on applicant's career (20%), and 2 letters of recommendation (30%).

Financial data   The stipend is $3,000.

Duration   1 year; may be renewed up to 2 additional years.

Additional information   Funding for this program is provided by Medtronic Physio-Control Corporation.

Number awarded 1 each year.

Deadline November of each year.

[405]
MEDTRONIC PHYSIO-CONTROL ADVANCED NURSING PRACTICE SCHOLARSHIP

Emergency Nurses Association
Attn: ENA Foundation
915 Lee Street
Des Plaines, IL 60016-6569
(847) 460-4100   Toll-free: (800) 900-9659, ext. 4100
Fax: (847) 460-4004   E-mail: foundation@ena.org
Web: www.ena.org/foundation/grants

Summary To provide financial assistance to members of the Emergency Nurses Association (ENA) who are pursuing an advanced clinical practice degree.

Eligibility This program is open to nurses pursuing an advanced clinical degree to become a nurse practitioner or clinical nurse specialist. Preference is given to nurses focusing on cardiac nursing, including cardiac resuscitation. Applicants must have been members of the association for at least 12 months. They must submit a 1-page statement on their professional and educational goals and how this scholarship will help them attain those goals. Selection is based on content and clarity of the goal statement (45%), professional involvement (45%), and GPA (10%).

Financial data The stipend is $3,000.

Duration 1 year.

Additional information This program is funded by the Medtronic Physio-Control Corporation.

Number awarded 1 each year.

Deadline May of each year.

[406]
MENSA MEMBER AWARDS

American Mensa Education and Research Foundation
1229 Corporate Drive West
Arlington, TX 76006-6103
(817) 607-0060   Toll-free: (800) 66-MENSA
Fax: (817) 649-5232   E-mail: info@mensafoundation.org
Web: www.mensafoundation.org

Summary To provide financial assistance for undergraduate or graduate study to members of American Mensa and their dependent children.

Eligibility This program is open to students who are enrolled or planning to enroll in a degree program at an accredited American institution of postsecondary education. Applicants must be current Mensa members or their dependent children. There are no restrictions as to age, race, gender, level of postsecondary education, GPA, or financial need. Selection is based on a 550-word essay that describes the applicant's career, vocational, or academic goals.

Financial data The stipend is $1,000.

Duration 1 year; nonrenewable.

Additional information Applications are only available through the advertising efforts of participating Mensa local groups. This program consists of the following named awards: the Tom and Elaine Ehrhorn Scholarship, the Verma Jeremiah Scholarship, the Pat Merk Scholarship, and the Scholarship in Memory of Jerry Salny.

Number awarded 4 each year.

Deadline January of each year.

[407]
MENTAL HEALTH AND SUBSTANCE ABUSE SERVICES FELLOWSHIP

American Psychological Association
Attn: Minority Fellowship Program
750 First Street, N.E.
Washington, DC 20002-4242
(202) 336-6127   Fax: (202) 336-6012
TDD: (202) 336-6123   E-mail: mfp@apa.org
Web: www.apa.org/mfp/cprogram.html

Summary To provide financial assistance to doctoral students committed to providing mental health and substance abuse services to ethnic minority populations.

Eligibility Applicants must be U.S. citizens or permanent residents, enrolled full time in an accredited doctoral program, and committed to a career in psychology related to ethnic minority mental health and substance abuse services. Members of ethnic minority groups (African Americans, Hispanics/Latinos, American Indians, Alaskan Natives, Asian Americans, Native Hawaiians, and other Pacific Islanders) are especially encouraged to apply. Preference is given to students specializing in clinical, school, and counseling psychology. Students of any other specialty will be considered if they plan careers in which their training will lead to delivery of mental health or substance abuse services to ethnic minority populations. Selection is based on commitment to ethnic minority health and substance abuse services, knowledge of ethnic minority psychology or mental health issues, the fit between career goals and training environment selected, potential to become a culturally competent mental health service provider demonstrated through accomplishments and goals, scholarship and grades, and letters of recommendation.

Financial data The stipend is the amount established by the National Institutes of Health for predoctoral students, recently $20,772 per year.

Duration 1 academic or calendar year; may be renewed for up to 2 additional years.

Additional information Funding is provided by the U.S. Substance Abuse and Mental Health Services Administration.

Number awarded Varies each year.

Deadline January of each year.

[408]
MENTAL HEALTH RESEARCH FELLOWSHIP

American Psychological Association
Attn: Minority Fellowship Program
750 First Street, N.E.
Washington, DC 20002-4242
(202) 336-6127   Fax: (202) 336-6012
TDD: (202) 336-6123   E-mail: mfp@apa.org
Web: www.apa.org/mfp/rprogram.html

Summary To provide financial assistance to doctoral students interested in preparing for a career in mental health or psychological research as it relates to ethnic minority populations.

Eligibility Applicants must be U.S. citizens or permanent residents, enrolled full time in an accredited doctoral program, and committed to a career as a researcher specializing in mental health issues of concern to ethnic minority populations. African American Hispanic/Latino, American Indian, Asian American, Alaskan Native, Native Hawaiian, and other Pacific Islander students are especially encouraged to apply. Students specializing in all disciplines of psychology are eligible as long as their training and research interests are related to mental health. Selection is based on commitment to a career in research that focuses on ethnic minority mental health, knowledge of ethnic minority psychology or mental health issues, fit between career goals and training environment selected, potential for a research career as demonstrated through accomplishments and productivity, scholarship and grades, and letters of recommendation.

Financial data The stipend is the amount established by the National Institutes of Health for predoctoral students, recently $20,772 per year.

Duration 1 academic or calendar year; may be renewed for up to 2 additional years.

Additional information Funding is provided by the U.S. National Institute of Mental Health, a component of the National Institutes of Health.

Number awarded Varies each year; recently, 22 of these fellowships were awarded.

Deadline January of each year.

[409]
MESBEC PROGRAM

Catching the Dream
8200 Mountain Road, N.E., Suite 203
Albuquerque, NM 87110-7835
(505) 262-2351   Fax: (505) 262-0534
E-mail: NScholarsh@aol.com
Web: www.catchingthedream.org/Scholarship.htm

Summary To provide financial assistance to American Indian students who are interested in working on an undergraduate or graduate degree in selected fields.

Eligibility This program is open to American Indians who can provide proof that they have at least one-quarter Indian blood and are a member of a U.S. tribe that is federally-recognized, state-recognized, or terminated. Applicants must be enrolled or planning to enroll full time and major in the 1 of the following fields: mathematics, engineering, science (including medicine), business administration, education, or computer science. They may be entering freshmen, undergraduate students, graduate students, or Ph.D. candidates. Along with their application, they must submit documentation of financial need, 3 letters of recommendation, copies of applications and responses for all other sources of funding for which they are eligible, official transcripts, standardized test scores (ACT, SAT, GRE, MCAT, LSAT, etc.), and an essay explaining their goals in life, college plans, and career plans (especially how those plans include working with and benefiting Indians). Selection is based on merit and potential for improving the lives of Indian people.

Financial data Stipends range from $500 to $5,000.

Duration 1 year; may be renewed.

Additional information MESBEC is an acronym that stands for the priority areas of this program: mathematics, engineering, science, business, education, and computers. The sponsor was formerly known as the Native American Scholarship Fund.

Number awarded Varies; generally, 30 to 35 each year.

Deadline April of each year for fall term; September of each year for spring and winter terms; March of each year for summer school.

[410]
METROPOLITAN LIFE FOUNDATION AWARDS PROGRAM FOR ACADEMIC EXCELLENCE IN MEDICINE

National Medical Fellowships, Inc.
Attn: Scholarship Program
5 Hanover Square, 15th Floor
New York, NY 10004
(212) 483-8880   Fax: (212) 483-8897
E-mail: info@nmfonline.org
Web: www.nmf-online.org

Summary To provide financial assistance to underrepresented minority medical students who reside or attend school in designated cities.

Eligibility This program is open to African American, mainland Puerto Rican, Mexican American, Native Hawaiian, Alaska Native, or American Indian medical students in their second through fourth year who are nominated by their dean. Nominees must be enrolled in medical schools located in (or residents of) the following cities: Phoenix, Arizona; San Francisco/Oakland/Bay area, California; Los Angeles, California; Denver, Colorado; Miami, Florida; Tampa/St. Petersburg, Florida; Atlanta, Georgia; Aurora/Chicago, Illinois; Boston, Massachusetts; St. Louis, Missouri; Albany, New York; metropolitan New York area (including New York City, southern New York, Long Island, central and northern New Jersey, and southern Connecticut); Rensselaer, New York; Utica, New York; Dayton, Ohio; Tulsa, Oklahoma; Philadelphia, Pennsylvania; Pittsburgh, Pennsylvania; Scranton, Pennsylvania; Warwick/Providence, Rhode Island; Greenville, South Carolina; Austin, Texas; Dallas/Fort Worth, Texas; or Houston, Texas. Selection is based on demonstrated financial need, outstanding academic achievement, leadership, and potential for distinguished contributions to medicine.

Financial data The stipend is $4,000.

Duration 1 year; nonrenewable.

Additional information Funding for this program, established in 1987, is provided by the Metropolitan Life Foundation of New York, New York.

Number awarded 17 each year.

Deadline February of each year.

[411]
MEXICAN AMERICAN ENGINEERS AND SCIENTISTS SCHOLARSHIP PROGRAM

Society of Mexican American Engineers and Scientists
Attn: Scholarship Committee
711 West Bay Area Boulevard, Suite 206
Webster, TX 77598-4051
(281) 557-3677   Fax: (281) 557-3757
E-mail: maesscholars@maes-natl.org
Web: www.maes-natl.org

Summary To provide financial assistance to undergraduate and graduate student members of the Society of Mexican American Engineers and Scientists (MAES).

Eligibility This program is open to MAES student members who are full-time undergraduate or graduate students at a college or university in the United States. Community college students must be enrolled in majors that can transfer to a 4-year institution offering a baccalaureate degree. All applicants must be majoring in a field of science or engineering. U.S. citizenship or permanent resident status is required. Selection is based on financial need; academic achievement; personal qualities, strengths, and leadership abilities; and timeliness and completeness of the application.

Financial data Stipends are $3,000, $2,000, or $1,000.

Duration 1 year.

Additional information Each year, this program awards the $4,000 Padrino/Madrina Scholarships, graduate student scholarships at $3,000, the Founder's Scholarship at $2,500, the President's Scholarship at $2,500, the Pipeline Scholarship at $2,000, and general scholarships at $2,000 and $1,000. Recipients must attend the MAES International Symposium's Medalla de Oro Banquet in December.

Number awarded Varies each year. Recently, 32 of these scholarships were awarded: 3 Padrino/Madrina Scholarships at $4,000, 1 graduate scholarship at $3,000, 2 (the Founder's Scholarship and the President's Scholarship) at $2,500, 1 (the Pipeline Scholarship) at $2,000, 12 general scholarships at $2,000 each, and 13 general scholarships at $1,000 each.

Deadline October of each year.

[412]
MICHIGAN TUITION GRANT PROGRAM

Michigan Department of Treasury
Michigan Higher Education Assistance Authority
Attn: Office of Scholarships and Grants
P.O. Box 30462
Lansing, MI 48909-7962
(517) 373-3394   Toll-free: (888) 4-GRANTS
Fax: (517) 335-5984   E-mail: osg@michigan.gov
Web: www.michigan.gov/mistudentaid

Summary To provide financial assistance for undergraduate or graduate education to residents of Michigan.

Eligibility This program is open to Michigan residents who are attending or planning to attend an independent, private, nonprofit degree-granting Michigan college or university at least half time as an undergraduate or graduate student. Applicants must demonstrate financial need and be a U.S. citizen, permanent resident, or approved refugee. Students working on a degree in theology, divinity, or religious education are ineligible.

Financial data Awards are limited to tuition and fees, recently to a maximum of $2,100 per academic year.

Duration 1 year; the award may be renewed for a total of 10 semesters or 15 quarters of undergraduate aid or 6 semesters or 9 quarters of graduate aid.

Number awarded Varies each year; recently, 28,441 of these grants were awarded.

Deadline Priority is given to students who apply by February of each year.

[413]
MIDWEST SECTION SCHOLARSHIPS

American College of Medical Practice Executives
Attn: ACMPE Scholarship Fund Inc.
104 Inverness Terrace East
Englewood, CO 80112-5306
(303) 799-1111, ext. 232   Toll-free: (877) ASK-MGMA
Fax: (303) 643-4439   E-mail: acmpe@mgma.com
Web: www.mgma.com/academics/scholar.cfm

Summary To provide financial assistance to members of the Medical Group Management Association (MGMA) Midwest Section who are interested in undergraduate or graduate education.

Eligibility Eligible to apply are individuals resident in the MGMA Midwest Section (Illinois, Indiana, Iowa, Michigan, Minnesota, Nebraska, North Dakota, Ohio, South Dakota, and Wisconsin) who wish to work on an undergraduate or graduate degree in medical practice management, including public health, business

administration, health care administration, or other related areas. Students working on a degree in medicine, physical therapy, nursing, or other clinically-related professions are not eligible. Applicants must submit a letter describing their career goals and objectives relevant to medical practice management; a resume; 3 reference letters commenting on their performance, character, potential to succeed, and need for scholarship support; and either documentation indicating acceptance into an undergraduate or graduate college or university or academic transcripts indicating undergraduate or graduate work completed to date.

Financial data The stipend is $2,000. Funds are paid directly to the recipient's college or university.

Duration 1 year.

Additional information This program is managed by Scholarship Program Administrators, Inc. 1201 Eighth Avenue South, P.O. Box 23737, Nashville, TN 27202-3737, (615) 320-3149, (800) 310-4053, Fax: (615) 320-3151, E-mail: info@spaprog.com.

Number awarded 1 each year.

Deadline April of each year.

[414]
MIDWEST STUDENT EXCHANGE PROGRAM

Midwestern Higher Education Commission
Attn: Midwest Student Exchange Program
1300 South Second Street, Suite 130
Minneapolis, MN 55454-1079
(612) 626-8288   Fax: (612) 626-8290
E-mail: mhec@mhec.org
Web: www.mhec.org/msep/index.htm

Summary To provide a tuition discount to undergraduate and graduate students from selected midwestern states who are attending schools affiliated with the Midwest Student Exchange Program.

Eligibility The Midwest Student Exchange Program is an interstate initiative established to increase interstate educational opportunities for students in the member states. The Tuition Discount Program includes the 6 participating states of Kansas, Michigan, Minnesota, Missouri, Nebraska and North Dakota. Residents of these states may enroll in programs in the other participating states, but only at the level at which their home state admits students. All of the enrollment and eligibility decisions for the program are made by the institution.

Financial data Participants in this program pay no more than 150% of the regular resident tuition, plus any required fees, at public colleges and universities in the state where they are enrolled. Students attending designated independent colleges and universities participating in the program receive at least a 10% reduction in their tuition. Savings typically range from $500 to $3,000 per year.

Duration Students receive these benefits as long as they are enrolled in the program to which they were originally admitted and are making satisfactory progress towards a degree.

Additional information Extension of the tuition privileges to students already enrolled is at the discretion of the institution.

Number awarded Varies each year.

[415]
MILDRED B. DAVIS NATIONAL FELLOWSHIP

American Association of Family and Consumer Sciences
Attn: Manager of Awards and Grants
400 North Columbus Street, Suite 202
Alexandria, VA 22314
(703) 706-4600   Toll-free: (800) 424-8080, ext. 119
Fax: (703) 706-4663   E-mail: staff@aafcs.org
Web: www.aafcs.org/programs/fellowships.html

Summary To provide financial assistance to student members of the American Association of Family and Consumer Sciences (AAFCS) who wish to work on a graduate degree in nutrition.

Eligibility Applicants must be student members of the association who have clearly defined plans to work on a degree in nutrition at the graduate level immediately after receiving their bachelor's degree. Selection is based on scholarship and special aptitudes for advanced study and research, educational and/or professional experiences, professional contributions to family and consumer sciences, and significance of the proposed research problem to the public well-being and the advancement of family and consumer sciences. Preference is given to applicants who have at least 1 year of work experience in family and consumer sciences, serving in such positions as a graduate/undergraduate assistant, trainee, or intern.

Financial data The stipend is $3,500.

Duration 1 year.

Additional information The application fee is $40. The association reserves the right to reconsider an award in the event the student receives a similar scholarship for the same academic year.

Number awarded Up to 2 each year.

Deadline January of each year.

[416]
MILDRED R. KNOLES OPPORTUNITY SCHOLARSHIPS

American Legion Auxiliary
Attn: Department of Illinois
2720 East Lincoln Street
P.O. Box 1426
Bloomington, IL 61702-1426
(309) 663-9366   Fax: (309) 663-5827
E-mail: ilala@ilala.org
Web: illegion.org/auxiliary/scholar.html

Summary To provide financial assistance for college or graduate school to Illinois veterans and their children.

Eligibility Eligible to apply for these scholarships are veterans or children and grandchildren of veterans of World War I, World War II, Korea, Vietnam, Grenada/Lebanon, Panama, or Desert Storm who have begun college but need financial assistance to complete their college or graduate education. Applicants must have resided in Illinois for at least 3 years prior to application. Selection is based on character, Americanism, leadership, financial need, and academic record.

Financial data Stipends are $1,200 or $800.

Duration 1 year.

Additional information Applications may be obtained only from a local unit of the American Legion Auxiliary.

Number awarded Varies; each year 1 scholarship at $1,200 and several at $800 are awarded.

Deadline March of each year.

[417]
MILITARY ORDER OF THE PURPLE HEART SCHOLARSHIP PROGRAM

Military Order of the Purple Heart
Attn: Scholarships
5413-B Backlick Road
Springfield, VA 22151-3960
(703) 642-5360   Fax: (703) 642-2054
E-mail: info@purpleheart.org
Web: www.purpleheart.org/scholar.html

Summary To provide financial assistance for college or graduate school to spouses and children of members of the Military Order of the Purple Heart.

Eligibility This program is open to children (natural, step-, and adopted), grandchildren, great-grandchildren and spouses of veterans who are members in good standing of the order or who received the Purple Heart. Applicants must be U.S. citizens, graduating seniors or graduates of an accredited high school, enrolled or accepted for enrollment in a full-time program of study in a college, trade school, or graduate school with a GPA of 3.5 or higher. Selection is based on merit; financial need is not considered in the selection process.

Financial data The stipend is $1,750 per year.

Duration 1 year; may be renewed up to 3 additional years.

Number awarded Varies each year; recently, 28 of these scholarships were awarded.

Deadline March of each year.

[418]
MINE AND GONSAKULTO SCHOLARSHIP

Far West Athletic Trainers' Association
c/o Jason Bennett, Scholarship Chair
Chapman University
1 University Drive
Orange, CA 92866
(714) 997-6567   E-mail: jbennett@chapman.edu
Web: www.fwata.org/com_scholarships.html

Summary To provide financial assistance to members of the National Athletic Trainers Association (NATA) who are of Asian descent and working on an undergraduate or graduate degree in its District 8.

Eligibility This program is open to students of Asian descent enrolled as undergraduate or graduate students at colleges and universities in California, Guam, Hawaii, or Nevada who are preparing for a career as an athletic trainer. Applicants must be student members of NATA and a District 8 member of NATA working on a bachelor's, master's, or doctoral degree in athletic training. They must have a GPA of 3.0 or higher and a record of distinction in their athletic training program, academic major, institution, intercollegiate athletics, and higher education. Along with their application, they must submit a statement on their athletic training background, experience, philosophy, and goals. Financial need is not considered in the selection process.

Financial data The stipend is $1,000.

Duration 1 year.

Additional information FWATA serves as District 8 of NATA.

Number awarded 1 each year.

Deadline February of each year.

[419]
MINNESOTA HIMSS SCHOLARSHIP

Healthcare Information and Management Systems Society-
  Minnesota Chapter
Attn: Scholarship Chair
P.O. Box 2331
Minneapolis, MN 55402-0031
(612) 325-9014   E-mail: scholarship@himss-mn.org
Web: www.himss-mn.org/scholarship/scholarship.html

Summary To provide financial assistance to members of the
Healthcare Information and Management Systems Society
(HIMSS) in Minnesota who are working on an undergraduate or
graduate degree.

Eligibility This program is open to HIMSS members who are
either residents of Minnesota or enrolled in a Minnesota institution
of higher education. Applicants must be working on an undergraduate, master's, or Ph.D. degree in a field related to health
care information or management systems, including industrial
engineering, operations research, health care informatics, computer science and information systems, mathematics, and quantitative programs in business administration and hospital administration. Selection is based on academic achievement, demonstration of leadership potential, communication skills, and participation in HIMSS activities.

Financial data The stipend is $1,000.

Duration 1 year; nonrenewable.

Number awarded 1 each year.

Deadline March of each year.

[420]
MINNIE L. MAFFETT FELLOWSHIPS

Texas Federation of Business and Professional Women's
  Foundation, Inc.
Attn: TFBPW Foundation
803 Forest Ridge Drive, Suite 207
Bedford, TX 76022
(817) 283-0862   Fax: (817) 283-0872
E-mail: bpwtx@swbell.net
Web: www.bpwtx.org/foundation.asp

Summary To provide financial assistance to women in Texas
interested in conducting research or continuing their education
in a medical field.

Eligibility This program is open to 1) women graduates of
Texas medical schools interested in postgraduate or research
work; 2) women who have been awarded a Ph.D. degree from a
Texas university and are doing research in a medical field; 3)
women who need financial aid for the first year in establishing a
family practice in a rural area of Texas with a population of less
than 5,000; and 4) fourth-year women medical students who are
completing an M.D. or O.D. degree in an accredited medical
school in Texas.

Financial data The stipend recently was $1,500.

Duration 1 year; nonrenewable.

Additional information This program was established in 1948.

Number awarded Varies each year; recently, 3 of these fellowships were awarded.

Deadline January of each year.

[421]
MINORITY DENTAL STUDENT SCHOLARSHIP

American Dental Association
Attn: ADA Foundation
211 East Chicago Avenue
Chicago, IL 60611
(312) 440-2547   Fax: (312) 440-3526
E-mail: adaf@ada.org
Web: www.ada.org

Summary To provide financial assistance to underrepresented
minorities who wish to enter the field of dentistry.

Eligibility This program is open to U.S. citizens from a minority
group that is currently underrepresented in the dental profession:
Native American, African American, or Hispanic. Applicants must
have a GPA of 3.0 or higher and be entering their second year
of study at a dental school in the United States accredited by the
Commission on Dental Accreditation. Selection is based upon
academic achievement, a written summary of personal and professional goals, letters of reference, and demonstrated financial
need.

Financial data The maximum stipend is $2,500. Funds are
sent directly to the student's financial aid office to be used to
cover tuition, fees, books, supplies, and living expenses.

Duration 1 year.

Additional information This program, established in 1991, is
supported by the Harry J. Bosworth Company, Colgate-
Palmolive, Sunstar Americas, and Procter & Gamble Company.
Students receiving a full scholarship from any other source are
ineligible to receive this scholarship.

Number awarded 25 each year.

Deadline October of each year.

[422]
MINORITY FACULTY DEVELOPMENT SCHOLARSHIP
AWARD IN PHYSICAL THERAPY

American Physical Therapy Association
Attn: Department of Minority/International Affairs
1111 North Fairfax Street
Alexandria, VA 22314-1488
(703) 706-3144   Toll-free: (800) 999-APTA, ext. 3144
Fax: (703) 706-8519   TDD: (703) 683-6748
E-mail: min-intl@apta.org
Web: www.apta.org

Summary To provide financial assistance to minority faculty
members in physical therapy who are interested in working on a
doctoral degree.

Eligibility This program is open to U.S. citizens and permanent
residents who are members of the following minority groups: African American or Black, Asian, Native Hawaiian or other Pacific
Islander, American Indian or Alaska Native, or Hispanic/Latino.
Applicants must be full-time faculty members teaching in an
accredited or developing professional physical therapist education program who will have completed the equivalent of 2 full
semesters of post-professional doctoral course work. They must
possess a license to practice physical therapy in a U.S. jurisdiction and be enrolled as a student in an accredited post-
professional doctoral program whose content has a demonstrated relationship to physical therapy. Along with their application, they must submit transcripts of all post-professional doctoral
course work, a curriculum vitae, and their plan of study for attaining the doctoral degree. Selection is based on 1) demonstrated
evidence of contributions in the area of minority affairs and services; 2) contributions to the professional of physical therapy; and
3) scholastic achievement.

Financial data The stipend is $7,000.
Duration 1 year.
Additional information This program was established in 1999.
Number awarded Varies each year; recently, 1 of these scholarships was awarded.
Deadline November of each year.

[423]
MONSTER HEALTHCARE-AACN NURSING FACULTY SCHOLARSHIP PROGRAM

American Association of Colleges of Nursing
One Dupont Circle, N.W., Suite 530
Washington, DC 20036
(202) 463-6930, ext. 231   Fax: (202) 785-8320
E-mail: rrosseter@aacn.nche.edu
Web: www.aacn.nche.edu/Education/financialaid.htm

Summary To provide financial assistance to students who are working on a doctoral degree in nursing to prepare for a career as a faculty member.
Eligibility This program is open to students enrolled full time at a school of nursing in 1) a baccalaureate to doctoral degree program, or 2) a doctor of nursing practice program. Members of minority groups (Alaska Native, American Indian, Asian, Black or African American, Hawaiian or Pacific Islander, or Hispanic) are especially encouraged to apply. Applicants must agree to 1) serve in a teaching capacity at a nursing school for a minimum of 1 year for each year of support they receive; 2) provide 6-month progress reports to the American Association of Colleges of Nursing (AACN) throughout the entire funding process and during the payback period; 3) work at least 10 hours per week while enrolled in the doctoral program so they can maintain clinical skills and obtain health care benefits; and 4) work with a mentor who will also submit progress reports. Selection is based on potential to contribute to the knowledge base in nursing education; leadership potential; nature and extent of goals reflecting education, research, and professional activities; and evidence of commitment to a career in nursing education.
Financial data The stipend is $25,000. The recipient's institution must agree to match at least 50% of tuition; preference is given to applicants whose institution agrees to provide a greater percentage match for tuition.
Duration 1 year; may be renewed up to 2 additional years provided the recipient continues to make appropriate progress toward their degree, as indicated by the required progress reports.
Additional information This program, established in 2005, is sponsored by Monster Healthcare, which attempts to provide students with the required part-time jobs.
Number awarded 5 each year.
Deadline September of each year.

[424]
MONSTER MEDICAL IMAGING EDUCATORS SCHOLARSHIP PROGRAM

American Society of Radiologic Technologists
Attn: ASRT Education and Research Foundation
15000 Central Avenue, S.E.
Albuquerque, NM 87123-3909
(505) 298-4500, ext. 2541
Toll-free: (800) 444-2778, ext. 2541   Fax: (505) 298-5063
E-mail: foundation@asrt.org
Web: www.asrt.org

Summary To provide financial assistance to members of the American Society of Radiologic Technologists (ASRT) who are interested in continuing their education to enhance their position in the field of medical imaging.
Eligibility This program is open to licensed radiologic technologists who are current members of ASRT and have worked in the radiologic sciences profession for at least 1 year during the past 5 years in a clinical or didactic setting. Applicants must be employed as a medical imaging program director, faculty member, clinical coordinator, or clinical instructor. They must have applied to a course of study at the bachelor's, master's, or doctoral level intended to further their career as a medical imaging educator Along with their application, they must submit a written interview up to 1,000 words on their professional achievements, their career goals, how their degree or certificate will help them to achieve their career goals, their educational goals, and how this scholarship will help them to achieve their educational goals. Financial need is considered in the selection process.
Financial data The stipend is $5,000.
Duration 1 year; may be renewed for 1 additional year.
Additional information This program is supported by Monster Healthcare.
Number awarded Varies each year; recently, 4 of these scholarships were awarded.
Deadline January of each year.

[425]
MONTGOMERY GI BILL (ACTIVE DUTY)

Department of Veterans Affairs
810 Vermont Avenue, N.W.
Washington, DC 20420
(202) 418-4343   Toll-free: (888) GI-BILL1
Web: www.gibill.va.gov

Summary To provide financial assistance for college, graduate school, and other types of postsecondary schools to new enlistees in any of the armed forces after they have completed their service obligation.
Eligibility This program is open to veterans who received an honorable discharge and have a high school diploma, a GED, or, in some cases, up to 12 hours of college credit. Applicants must also meet the requirements of 1 of the following categories: 1) entered active duty for the first time after June 30, 1985, had military pay reduced by $100 per month for the first 12 months, and continuously served for 3 years, or 2 years if that was their original enlistment, or 2 years if they entered Selected Reserve within a year of leaving active duty and served 4 years (the 2 by 4 program); 2) entered active duty before January 1, 1977, had remaining entitlement under the Vietnam Era GI Bill on December 31, 1989, served at least 1 day between October 19, 1984 and June 30, 1985, and stayed on active duty through June 30, 1988 (or June 30, 1987 if they entered Selected Reserve within 1 year of leaving active duty and served 4 years); 3) on active duty on September 30, 1990 and separated involuntarily after February 2,

1991, involuntarily separated on or after November 30, 1993, or voluntarily separated under either the Voluntary Separation Incentive (VSI) or Special Separation Benefit (SSB) program, and before separation had military pay reduced by $1,200; or 4) on active duty on October 9, 1996, had money remaining in an account from the Veterans Educational Assistance Program (VEAP), elected MGIB by October 9, 1997, and paid $1,200. Certain National Guard servicemembers may also qualify under category 4 if they served on full-time active duty between July 1, 1985 and November 28, elected MGIB between October 9, 1996 and July 8, 1997, and paid $1,200. Following completion of their service obligation, participants may enroll in colleges or universities for associate, bachelor, or graduate degrees; in courses leading to a certificate or diploma from business, technical, or vocational schools; for apprenticeships or on-job training programs; in correspondence courses; in flight training; for preparatory courses necessary for admission to a college or graduate school; for licensing and certification tests approved for veterans; or in state-approved teacher certification programs. Veterans who wish to enroll in certain high-cost technology programs (life science, physical science, engineering, mathematics, engineering and science technology, computer specialties, and engineering, science, and computer management) may be eligible for an accelerated payment.

Financial data For veterans in categories 1, 3, and 4 who served on active duty for 3 years or more, the current monthly stipend for college or university work is $1,034 for full-time study, $775.50 for three-quarter time study, or $517 for half-time study, or $258.50 for quarter-time study or less; for apprenticeship and on-the-job training, the monthly stipend is $878.90 for the first 6 months, $672.10 for the second 6 months, and $465.30 for the remainder of the program. For enlistees whose initial active-duty obligation was less than 3 years, the current monthly stipend for college or university work is $840 for full-time study, $630 for three-quarter time study, $420 for half-time study, or $210 for quarter-time study or less; for apprenticeship and on-the-job training, the monthly stipend is $714 for the first 6 months, $546 for the second 6 months, and $378 for the remainder of the program. For veterans in category 2 with remaining eligibility, the current monthly stipend for institutional study full time is $1,222 for no dependents, $1,258 with 1 dependent, $1,289 with 2 dependents, and $16 for each additional dependent; for three-quarter time study, the monthly stipend is $917 for no dependents, $943.50 with 1 dependent, $967 with 2 dependents, and $12 for each additional dependent; for half-time study, the monthly stipend is $611 for no dependents, $629 with 1 dependent, $644.50 with 2 dependents, and $8.50 for each additional dependent. For those veterans pursuing an apprenticeship or on-the-job training, the current monthly stipend for the first 6 months is $995.35 for no dependents, $1,009.38 with 1 dependent, $1,021.70 with 2 dependents, and $5.95 for each additional dependent; for the second 6 months, the current monthly stipend is $738.73 for no dependents, $749.78 with 1 dependent, $758.88 with 2 dependents, and $4.55 for each additional dependent; for the third 6 months, the current monthly stipend is $495.90 for no dependents, $503.78 with 1 dependent, $509.85 with 2 dependents, and $3.15 for each additional dependent; for the remainder of the training period, the current monthly stipend is $480.60 for no dependents, $488.03 with 1 dependent, $494.78 with 2 dependents, and $3.15 for each additional dependent. Other rates apply for less than half-time study, cooperative education, correspondence courses, and flight training. Veterans who qualify for the accelerated payment and whose entitlement does not cover 60% of tuition and fees receive an additional lump sum payment to make up the different between their entitlement and 60% of tuition and fees.

Duration 36 months; active-duty servicemembers must utilize the funds within 10 years of leaving the armed services; Reservists may draw on their funds while still serving.

Additional information Further information is available from local armed forces recruiters. This is the basic VA education program, referred to as Chapter 30.

Number awarded Varies each year.

[426]
MONTGOMERY GI BILL (SELECTED RESERVE)

Department of Veterans Affairs
810 Vermont Avenue, N.W.
Washington, DC 20420
(202) 418-4343   Toll-free: (888) GI-BILL1
Web: www.gibill.va.gov

Summary To provide financial assistance for college or graduate school to members of the Reserves or National Guard.

Eligibility Eligible to apply are members of the Reserve elements of the Army, Navy, Air Force, Marine Corps, and Coast Guard, as well as the Army National Guard and the Air National Guard. To be eligible, a Reservist must 1) have a 6-year obligation to serve in the Selected Reserves signed after June 30, 1985 (or, if an officer, to agree to serve 6 years in addition to the original obligation); 2) complete Initial Active Duty for Training (IADT); 3) meet the requirements for a high school diploma or equivalent certificate before completing IADT; and 4) remain in good standing in a drilling Selected Reserve unit. Reservists who enlisted after June 30, 1985 can receive benefits for undergraduate degrees, graduate training, or technical courses leading to certificates at colleges and universities. Reservists whose 6-year commitment began after September 30, 1990 may also use these benefits for a certificate or diploma from business, technical, or vocational schools; cooperative training; apprenticeship or on-the-job training; correspondence courses; independent study programs; tutorial assistance; remedial, deficiency, or refresher training; flight training; or state-approved alternative teacher certification programs.

Financial data The current monthly rate is $297 for full-time study, $222.75 for three-quarter time study, $148.50 for half-time study, or $74.25 for less than half-time study. For apprenticeship and on-the-job training, the monthly stipend is $252.45 for the first 6 months, $193.05 for the second 6 months, and $133.65 for the remainder of the program. Other rates apply for cooperative education, correspondence courses, and flight training.

Duration Up to 36 months for full-time study, 48 months for three-quarter study, 72 months for half-time study, or 144 months for less than half-time study.

Additional information This program is frequently referred to as Chapter 1606 (formerly Chapter 106). Reservists who are enrolled for three-quarter or full-time study are eligible to participate in the work-study program. The Department of Defense periodically offers "kickers" of additional benefits on behalf of individuals in critical military fields, as deemed necessary to encourage enlistment. Information on currently-available "kickers" is available from Reserve and National Guard recruiters. Benefits end 10 years from the date the Reservist became eligible for the program. The Department of Veterans Affairs (VA) may extend the 10-year period if the individual could not train because of a disability caused by Selected Reserve service. Certain individuals separated from the Selected Reserve due to downsizing of the military between October 1, 1991 and September 30, 1999 will also have the full 10 years to use their benefits.

Number awarded Varies each year.

Deadline Applications may be submitted at any time.

[427]
MONTGOMERY GI BILL TUITION ASSISTANCE TOP-UP

Department of Veterans Affairs
810 Vermont Avenue, N.W.
Washington, DC 20420
(202) 418-4343   Toll-free: (888) GI-BILL1
Web: www.gibill.va.gov

Summary To supplement the tuition assistance provided by the military services to their members.

Eligibility This program is open to military personnel who have served at least 2 full years on active duty and are approved for tuition assistance by their military service. Applicants must be participating in the Montgomery GI Bill (MGIB) Active Duty program and be eligible for MGIB benefits. This assistance is available to service members whose military service does not pay 100% of tuition and fees.

Financial data This program pays the difference between what the military services pay for tuition assistance and the full amount of tuition and fees.

Duration Up to 36 months of payments are available.

Additional information This program was established in 2000.

Number awarded Varies each year.

[428]
MUSIC THERAPY SCHOLARSHIP

Sigma Alpha Iota Philanthropies, Inc.
One Tunnel Road
Asheville, NC 28805
(828) 251-0606   Fax: (828) 251-0644
E-mail: philonline@sai-national.org
Web: www.sai-national.org/phil/philsch1.html

Summary To provide financial assistance to members of Sigma Alpha Iota (an organization of women musicians) who are interested in working on an undergraduate or graduate degree in music therapy.

Eligibility Members of the organization may apply for these scholarships if they wish to study music therapy at the undergraduate or graduate level. Applicants must submit an essay that includes their personal definition of music therapy, their career plans and professional goals as a music therapist, and why they feel they are deserving of this scholarship. Selection is based on music therapy skills, musicianship, fraternity service, community service, leadership, self-reliance, and dedication to the field of music therapy as a career.

Financial data The stipend is $1,000.

Duration 1 year.

Additional information There is a $25 nonrefundable application fee.

Number awarded 1 each year.

Deadline March of each year.

[429]
MYRA LEVICK SCHOLARSHIP FUND

American Art Therapy Association, Inc.
Attn: Scholarships and Grants Committee
5999 Stevenson Avenue
Alexandria, VA 22304
(703) 212-2238   Toll-free: (888) 290-0878
E-mail: info@arttherapy.org
Web: www.arttherapy.org/stscholarships.html

Summary To provide financial assistance to graduate student members of the American Art Therapy Association (AATA).

Eligibility This program is open to graduate student AATA members accepted or enrolled in an art therapy program approved by the association. Applicants must be able to demonstrate financial need and a GPA of 3.0 or higher. Along with their application, they must submit transcripts, 2 letters of reference, a student financial information form, and a 2-page essay that contains a brief biography and a statement of how they see their role in the future of art therapy.

Financial data A stipend is awarded (amount not specified).

Duration 1 year.

Number awarded 1 each year.

Deadline June of each year.

[430]
NAAMA SCHOLARSHIPS

National Arab American Medical Association
Attn: NAAMA Foundation
801 South Adams Road, Suite 208
Birmingham, MI 48009
(248) 646-3661   Fax: (248) 646-0617
E-mail: naama@naama.com
Web: www.naama.com/scholarship.htm

Summary To provide financial assistance to medical students of Arab descent.

Eligibility This program is open to Arab Americans who are enrolled in or accepted at an accredited U.S. or Canadian medical, osteopathic, or dental school. Selection is based on academic merit and financial need.

Financial data The stipend is $1,000.

Duration 1 year; may be renewed.

Additional information This program began in 1990.

Number awarded 2 each year.

Deadline June of each year.

[431]
NACDA FOOTBALL POSTGRADUATE SCHOLARSHIP PROGRAM

National Association of Collegiate Directors of Athletics
Attn: NACDA Foundation
24651 Detroit Road
P.O. Box 16428
Cleveland, OH 44116
(440) 892-4000   Fax: (440) 892-4007
E-mail: bhorning@nacda.com
Web: nacda.cstv.com

Summary To provide financial assistance for graduate school to college football players on teams that participate in the Kickoff Classic and the Pigskin Classic.

Eligibility This program provides scholarship grants for graduate school to 1 varsity letter winner on each of the teams that participate in the Kickoff Classic and Pigskin Classic, the preseason football games sponsored by the National Association of Collegiate Directors of Athletics (NACDA). The student-athlete chosen must be in his final year of athletics eligibility and carry a minimum GPA of 3.0. The recipients are chosen by the athletics department at each participating institution. Those selected to receive the scholarship need not be a star player or major contributor, but can be any player who meets the criteria that the athletics department chooses.

Financial data   The stipend is $5,000.

Duration   1 year.

Number awarded   4 each year.

[432]
NADONA/LTC ABOVE AND BEYOND SCHOLARSHIP

National Association Directors of Nursing Administration in
   Long Term Care
Attn: Education/Scholarship Committee
10101 Alliance Road, Suite 140
Cincinnati, OH 45242
(513) 791-3679   Toll-free: (800) 222-0539
Fax: (513) 791-3699   E-mail: info@nadona.org
Web: www.nadona.org

Summary   To provide financial assistance to students who are working on an advanced nursing degree and who are members of National Association of Directors of Nursing Administration in Long Term Care (NADONA/LTC).

Eligibility   This program is open to members of the association who are currently employed in long-term care (for at least 1 year) and plan to remain employed in long-term care for at least 2 years after graduation. Applicants must have graduated from a nursing program accredited by the National League for Nursing and be currently accepted or enrolled in a master's or higher degree program in nursing, gerontology, health administration, or a field related to long-term care nursing. Along with their application, they must submit an essay (up to 250 words) that describes why they are seeking this degree and how the education will be used in the future. Students who received funds/awards from a NADONA/LTC scholarship within the last 4 years are ineligible to apply for this award.

Financial data   A stipend is awarded (amount not specified); a total of $5,000 is currently available for this program each year.

Duration   1 year.

Additional information   Funds for this scholarship are provided by Johnson & Johnson Long Term Care Business Group.

Number awarded   At least 1 each year.

Deadline   February of each year.

[433]
NANCIE RIDEOUT-ROBERTSON INTERNSHIP SCHOLARSHIP

American Water Ski Educational Foundation
Attn: Director
1251 Holy Cow Road
Polk City, FL 33868-8200
(863) 324-2472   Fax: (863) 324-3996
E-mail: info@waterskihalloffame.com
Web: www.waterskihalloffame.com

Summary   To provide financial assistance and work experience to upper-division and graduate students who are interested in water skiing.

Eligibility   This program is open to upper-division and graduate students who are members of the United States Water Ski Asso-

ciation (USWSA) and the American Water Ski Educational Foundation (AWSEF). Applicants must have participated in the sport of water skiing as a skier, official, and/or volunteer worker and be able to demonstrate leadership potential. They must have a GPA of at least "B+" overall and an "A" average in their major field of study. Along with their application, they must submit 1) a 500-word personal statement on why they wish to be awarded this scholarship and serve as an intern at AWSEF; and 2) an internship proposal, covering their learning goals and how they want to apply the skills and knowledge related to their program of study in college or graduate school to their internship, the kinds of contributions they think they can make toward the goals of AWSEF, how they would allocate their time toward their internship activities, when they could complete their "onsite" requirement, and the kinds of skills and knowledge of people with whom they might like to work during their internship.

Financial data   The stipend is $2,500.

Duration   1 year, including at least 4 weeks (during semester breaks, spring break, summer) at AWSEF headquarters in Polk City, Florida.

Additional information   This program was established in 2004.

Number awarded   1 each year.

Deadline   January of each year.

[434]
NANCY REAGAN PATHFINDER SCHOLARSHIPS

National Federation of Republican Women
Attn: Scholarships and Internships
124 North Alfred Street
Alexandria, VA 22314-3011
(703) 548-9688   Fax: (703) 548-9836
E-mail: mail@nfrw.org
Web: www.nfrw.org/programs/scholarships.htm

Summary   To provide financial assistance for college or graduate school to Republican women.

Eligibility   This program is open to women currently enrolled as college sophomores, juniors, seniors, or master's degree students. Recent high school graduates and first-year college women are not eligible. Applicants must submit 3 letters of recommendation, an official transcript, a 1-page essay on why they should be considered for the scholarship, and a 1-page essay on career goals. Optionally, a photograph may be supplied. Applications must be submitted to the Republican federation president in the applicant's state. Each president chooses 1 application from her state to submit for scholarship consideration. Financial need is not a factor in the selection process. U.S. citizenship is required.

Financial data   The stipend is $2,500.

Duration   1 year; nonrenewable.

Additional information   This program, established in 1985, is also known as the National Pathfinder Scholarship.

Number awarded   3 each year.

Deadline   Applications must be submitted to the state federation president by May of each year.

[435]
NASN EDUCATIONAL ADVANCEMENT AWARDS

National Association of School Nurses
Attn: Scholarship Chair
163 U.S. Route 1
P.O. Box 1300
Scarborough, ME 04070-1300
(207) 883-2117   Toll-free: (877) NASN-4SN
Fax: (207) 883-2683   E-mail: nasn@nasn.org
Web: www.nasn.org

Summary To provide funding to members of the National Association of School Nurses (NASN) who are interested in advancing their education.

Eligibility This program is open to licensed registered nurses who are employed as a school nurse. Applicants must have been active members of NASN for at least the past 2 years. They must have a bachelor's degree (does not need to be in nursing) except for applicants who are pursuing a B.S.N./M.S.N. degree. Selection is based on brief essays by the applicant on the benefit of the advanced degree or course work to the applicant's school nursing practice (60%), impact on the community (25%), and educational goals (15%).

Financial data The stipend is $1,500.

Duration 1 year.

Additional information This program was established in 1994 as the Shirley Steel Awards. Information is also available from NASN's western office, 1416 Park Street, Suite A, Castle Rock, CO 80109, (303) 663-2329, (866) 627-6767, Fax: (303) 663-0403.

Number awarded 2 each year.

Deadline October of each year.

[436]
NATA DOCTORAL SCHOLARSHIPS

National Athletic Trainers' Association
Attn: Research and Education Foundation
2952 Stemmons Freeway, Suite 200
Dallas, TX 75247-6103
(214) 637-6282   Toll-free: (800) TRY-NATA, ext. 121
Fax: (214) 637-2206   E-mail: barbaran@nata.org
Web: www.natafoundation.org/scholarship.html

Summary To provide financial aid to members of the National Athletic Trainers' Association (NATA) who are working on a doctoral degree.

Eligibility Applicants must have been members of the association for at least 1 year, be recommended by a certified athletic trainer, have at least a 3.2 GPA, and intend to pursue athletic training as a profession. They must be enrolled or accepted for enrollment in a doctoral degree program. Along with their application, they must submit a statement on their athletic training background, experience, philosophy, and goals. Selection is based on that essay; participation in their school's athletic training program, academic major, institution, intercollegiate athletics, and American higher education; and participation in campus activities other than academic and athletic training. Financial need is not considered.

Financial data The stipend is $2,000 per year.

Duration 1 year.

Number awarded Varies each year; recently, 9 of these scholarships were awarded.

Deadline February of each year.

[437]
NATA MASTER'S SCHOLARSHIPS

National Athletic Trainers' Association
Attn: Research and Education Foundation
2952 Stemmons Freeway, Suite 200
Dallas, TX 75247-6103
(214) 637-6282   Toll-free: (800) TRY-NATA, ext. 121
Fax: (214) 637-2206   E-mail: barbaran@nata.org
Web: www.natafoundation.org/scholarship.html

Summary To provide financial aid to members of the National Athletic Trainers' Association (NATA) who are working on a master's degree.

Eligibility Applicants must have been members of the association for at least 1 year, be recommended by a certified athletic trainer, have at least a 3.2 GPA, and intend to pursue athletic training as a profession. They must be enrolled or accepted for enrollment in a master's degree program. Along with their application, they must submit a statement on their athletic training background, experience, philosophy, and goals. Selection is based on that essay; participation in their school's athletic training program, academic major, institution, intercollegiate athletics, and American higher education; and participation in campus activities other than academic and athletic training. Financial need is not considered.

Financial data The stipend is $2,000 per year.

Duration 1 year.

Number awarded Varies each year; recently, 25 of these scholarships were awarded.

Deadline February of each year.

[438]
NATIONAL ASSOCIATION OF HEALTH SERVICES EXECUTIVES SCHOLARSHIP PROGRAM

National Association of Health Services Executives
Attn: Educational Assistance Program
8630 Fenton Street, Suite 126
Silver Spring, MD 20910
(202) 628-3953   Fax: (301) 588-0011
E-mail: nahsehg@nahse.org
Web: www.nahse.org

Summary To provide financial assistance to African Americans who are members of the National Association of Health Services Executives (NAHSE) and interested in preparing for a career in health care administration.

Eligibility This program is open to African Americans who are either enrolled or accepted in an accredited college or university program, working on a bachelor's, master's, or doctoral degree in health care administration. Applicants must be members of NAHSE and able to demonstrate financial need. They must have a GPA of 2.5 or higher as undergraduates or 3.0 or higher as graduate students. Along with their application, they must submit 3 letters of recommendation, a recent resume, a 3-page essay on a topic related to health care management, a copy of their most recent federal income tax return, transcripts from all colleges attended, and 2 photographs.

Financial data The stipends are $2,500 per year. Funds are sent to the recipient's institution.

Duration 1 year.

Additional information This program consists of the following named awards: the Haynes Rice Scholarship, the Ellis J. Bonner Scholarship, and the Florence Small Gaynor Scholarship.

Number awarded 3 each year.

Deadline June of each year.

[439]
NATIONAL ASSOCIATION OF HISPANIC NURSES SCHOLARSHIPS

National Association of Hispanic Nurses
Attn: National Awards and Scholarship Committee Chair
1501 16th Street, N.W.
Washington, DC 20036
(202) 387-2477   Fax: (202) 483-7183
E-mail: info@thehispanicnurses.org
Web: www.thehispanicnurses.org

Summary   To provide financial assistance for nursing education to members of the National Association of Hispanic Nurses (NAHN).

Eligibility   Eligible are members of the association enrolled in associate, diploma, baccalaureate, graduate, or practical/vocational nursing programs at NLN-accredited schools of nursing. Applicants must submit a 1-page essay that reflects their qualifications and potential for leadership in nursing for the Hispanic community. U.S. citizenship or permanent resident status is required. Selection is based on academic excellence (preferably a GPA of 3.0 or higher), potential for leadership in nursing, and financial need.

Financial data   The stipend is $1,000.

Duration   1 year.

Number awarded   Varies each year, depending on the availability of funds.

Deadline   April of each year.

[440]
NATIONAL ASSOCIATION OF JUNIOR AUXILIARIES GRADUATE SCHOLARSHIP PROGRAM

National Association of Junior Auxiliaries, Inc.
Attn: Scholarship Committee
845 South Main Street
P.O. Box 1873
Greenville, MS 38702-1873
(662) 332-3000   Fax: (662) 332-3076
E-mail: najanet@bellsouth.net
Web: www.najanet.org/view/17

Summary   To provide financial assistance to students from selected states working on a graduate degree in fields that address the special needs of children and youth.

Eligibility   This program is open to U.S. citizens who are residents of states with a Junior Auxiliary chapter (Alabama, Arkansas, Florida, Louisiana, Missouri, Mississippi, Tennessee, and Texas). Applicants must have completed (or are about to complete) undergraduate studies, have applied to and been accepted by a graduate school, and have selected a field of study that focuses on working directly with children or youth with special needs (e.g., counseling, psychology, mental health, special education, speech pathology, exceptional children, remedial skills development, hearing impaired, gifted and talented). They may not be working on a degree in administration or general education. Finalists are interviewed. Selection is based on commitment to children with special needs, academic record, recommendations, motivation, and goals.

Financial data   The amount awarded varies, depending upon the amount of funds available each year.

Duration   1 year; recipients may reapply.

Additional information   Since this program was established in 1962, it has awarded more than 418 grants for more than $831,790. It includes the Betty W. Robbins Endowed Scholarship, established in 1995.

Number awarded   1 or more each year.

Deadline   January of each year.

[441]
NATIONAL ASSOCIATION OF UNIVERSITY WOMEN FELLOWSHIP

National Association of University Women
Attn: Fellowship Chair
1001 E Street, S.E.
Washington, DC 20003
(202) 547-3967   Fax: (202) 547-5226
E-mail: info@nauw1910.org
Web: www.nauw1910.org

Summary   To provide financial assistance to minority and other women who are working on a doctoral degree.

Eligibility   This program is open to women who already have a master's degree and are enrolled in a program leading to a doctoral degree. They should be close to completing their degree. Preference is given to applications from minority women.

Financial data   A stipend is awarded (amount not specified).

Duration   1 year.

Number awarded   1 or more each year.

Deadline   May of each year.

[442]
NATIONAL DENTAL ASSOCIATION FOUNDATION PRE-DOCTORAL SCHOLARSHIP PROGRAM

National Dental Association
Attn: National Dental Association Foundation, Inc.
3517 16th Street, N.W.
Washington, DC 20010
(202) 588-1697   Fax: (202) 588-1242
E-mail: admin@ndaonline.org
Web: www.nadonline.org/ndafoundation.asp

Summary   To provide financial assistance to underrepresented minority dental students.

Eligibility   This program is open to members of underrepresented minority groups who are entering their second, third, or fourth year of dental school. Applicants must be members of the Student National Dental Association (SNDA) and U.S. citizens or permanent residents. Along with their application, they must submit a letter explaining why they should be considered for this scholarship, 2 letters of recommendation, and documentation of financial need. Selection is based on academic performance and service to community and/or country.

Financial data   The stipend is $1,000 per year.

Duration   1 year. Recipients may reapply.

Additional information   This program, established in 1990, is supported by the Colgate-Palmolive Company.

Number awarded   Varies each year.

Deadline   May of each year.

[443]
NATIONAL FEDERATION OF THE BLIND SCHOLARSHIPS

National Federation of the Blind
c/o Peggy Elliott, Scholarship Committee Chair
805 Fifth Avenue
Grinnell, IA 50112
(641) 236-3366
Web: www.nfb.org/sch_intro.htm

Summary To provide financial assistance for college or graduate school to blind students.

Eligibility This program is open to legally blind students who are working on or planning to work on an undergraduate or graduate degree. In general, full-time enrollment is required, although 1 scholarship may be awarded to a part-time student who is working full time. Selection is based on academic excellence, service to the community, and financial need.

Financial data Stipends are $7,000 or $3,000.

Duration 1 year; recipients may resubmit applications up to 2 additional years.

Additional information Scholarships are awarded at the federation convention in July. Recipients attend the convention at federation expense; that funding is in addition to the scholarship grant.

Number awarded 17 each year: 2 at $7,000 and 15 at $3,000.

Deadline March of each year.

[444]
NATIONAL SCHOLAR-ATHLETE AWARDS

National Football Foundation
22 Maple Avenue
Morristown, NJ 07960
(973) 829-1933   Toll-free: (800) 486-1865
Fax: (973) 829-1737
E-mail: scholarship@footballfoundation.com
Web: www.footballfoundation.com/NSAaward.php

Summary To provide graduate fellowships to college football players who demonstrate both athletic and academic excellence.

Eligibility These awards are presented to college football players who combine outstanding athletic performance with academic distinction and civic leadership. Each 4-year college and university that plays football (I-A, I-AA, II, III, and NAIA) is encouraged to nominate 1 of its players who is a senior or graduate student in his final year of eligibility. Nominees must have a GPA of 3.0 or higher and have demonstrated football ability and performance as a first team player as well as outstanding school leadership and citizenship. Selection is based on academic accomplishment (up to 40 points), football ability (up to 40 points), and school, civic, and community activities (up to 20 points).

Financial data The awardees receive $18,000 graduate scholarships. Supplemental grants ranging from $1,000 to $5,000 are awarded for specialized areas of graduate study.

Duration The awards are presented annually.

Additional information These awards, first presented in 1959, are cosponsored by the National Football Foundation and College Hall of Fame, Inc.

Number awarded 15 each year.

Deadline Nominations must be submitted by September of each year.

[445]
NATIONAL STUDENT NURSES' ASSOCIATION CAREER MOBILITY SCHOLARSHIPS

National Student Nurses' Association
Attn: NSNA Foundation
45 Main Street, Suite 606
Brooklyn, NY 11201
(718) 210-0705   Fax: (718) 210-0710
E-mail: nsna@nsna.org
Web: www.nsna.org

Summary To provide financial assistance to nurses interested in pursuing additional education.

Eligibility This program is open to 1) registered nurses enrolled in programs leading to a baccalaureate or master's degree with a major in nursing or 2) licensed practical/vocational nurses enrolled in programs leading to licensure as a registered nurse. Graduating high school seniors are not eligible. Selection is based on academic achievement, financial need, and involvement in student nursing organizations and community activities related to health care.

Financial data Stipends range from $1,000 to $5,000. A total of more than $100,000 is awarded each year by the foundation for all its scholarship programs.

Duration 1 year.

Additional information Applications must be accompanied by a $10 processing fee.

Number awarded Varies each year. Recently, 3 of these scholarships were awarded: 1 sponsored by Advanstar Medical Economics Nursing Group and 2 sponsored by Anthony J. Jannetti, Inc.

Deadline January of each year.

[446]
NATIONAL STUDENT NURSES' ASSOCIATION GENERAL SCHOLARSHIPS

National Student Nurses' Association
Attn: NSNA Foundation
45 Main Street, Suite 606
Brooklyn, NY 11201
(718) 210-0705   Fax: (718) 210-0710
E-mail: nsna@nsna.org
Web: www.nsna.org

Summary To provide financial assistance to nursing or pre-nursing students.

Eligibility This program is open to students currently enrolled in state-approved schools of nursing or pre-nursing associate degree, baccalaureate, diploma, generic doctorate, or generic master's programs. Graduating high school seniors are not eligible. Support for graduate education is provided only for a first degree in nursing. Selection is based on academic achievement, financial need, and involvement in student nursing organizations and community health activities.

Financial data Stipends range from $1,000 to $5,000. A total of more than $100,000 is awarded each year by the foundation for all its scholarship programs.

Duration 1 year.

Additional information This program includes the following named scholarships: the Alice Robinson Memorial Scholarship, the Jeannette Collins Memorial Scholarship, the Cleo Doster Memorial Scholarship, and the Mary Ann Tuft Scholarships. Applications must be accompanied by a $10 processing fee.

Number awarded Varies each year. Approximately 30 of these scholarships were awarded recently.

Deadline January of each year.

[447]
NATIONAL STUDENT NURSES' ASSOCIATION SPECIALTY SCHOLARSHIPS

National Student Nurses' Association
Attn: NSNA Foundation
45 Main Street, Suite 606
Brooklyn, NY 11201
(718) 210-0705 Fax: (718) 210-0710
E-mail: nsna@nsna.org
Web: www.nsna.org

Summary To provide financial assistance to nursing students in designated specialties.

Eligibility This program is open to students currently enrolled in state-approved schools of nursing or pre-nursing associate degree, baccalaureate, diploma, generic doctorate, or generic master's programs. Graduating high school seniors are not eligible. Support for graduate education is provided only for a first degree in nursing. Applicants must designate their intended specialty, which may be anesthesia nursing, critical care, emergency, gerontology, informatics, nephrology, nurse educator, oncology, orthopedic, or perioperative. Selection is based on academic achievement, financial need, and involvement in student nursing organizations and community activities related to health care.

Financial data Stipends range from $1,000 to $5,000. A total of more than $100,000 is awarded each year by the foundation for all its scholarship programs.

Duration 1 year.

Additional information Funding for this program is provided by sponsors from industry who are interested in promoting specialties related to their products. Some scholarships are offered jointly with other nursing organizations, including the American Association of Nurse Anesthetists, the American Nephrology Nurses' Association, the American Organization of Nurse Executives, the Emergency Nurses Association, and the Oncology Nursing Society. Applications must be accompanied by a $10 processing fee.

Number awarded Varies each year; approximately 16 of these scholarships were awarded recently.

Deadline January of each year.

[448]
NATIONAL TEMPERANCE SCHOLARSHIP

United Methodist Higher Education Foundation
Attn: Scholarship Office
1001 19th Avenue South
P.O. Box 340005
Nashville, TN 37203-0005
(615) 340-7385 Toll-free: (800) 811-8110
Fax: (615) 340-7330
E-mail: umhefscholarships@gbhem.org
Web: www.umhef.org/othergroupa.html

Summary To provide financial assistance to undergraduate and graduate Methodist students at Methodist-related colleges and universities.

Eligibility This program is open to full-time undergraduate and graduate students at United Methodist-related colleges and universities. Applicants must have been active, full members of a United Methodist Church for at least 1 year prior to applying. They must be able to demonstrate financial need. U.S. citizenship or permanent resident status is required.

Financial data A stipend is awarded (amount not specified).

Duration 1 year; recipients may reapply.
Number awarded Varies each year.
Deadline May of each year.

[449]
NBRC/AMP GARETH B. GISH, MS, RRT MEMORIAL POSTGRADUATE EDUCATION RECOGNITION AWARD

American Association for Respiratory Care
Attn: American Respiratory Care Foundation
9425 North MacArthur Boulevard, Suite 100
Irving, TX 75063-4706
(972) 243-2272 Fax: (972) 484-2720
E-mail: info@arcfoundation.org
Web: www.arcfoundation.org

Summary To provide financial assistance to respiratory care therapists who are interested in working on an advanced degree.

Eligibility This program is open to respiratory care therapists who have at least a baccalaureate degree with a GPA of 3.0 or higher and have been accepted into an advanced degree program at a fully-accredited school. Applicants must submit 3 letters of reference and a 1,200-word essay on how this program will assist them in earning an advanced degree and working toward a role of leadership in health care.

Financial data The stipend is $1,500. The award also provides 1 night's lodging and registration for the international congress of the association.

Duration 1 year; recipients may reapply.

Additional information This program, first offered in 1999, is sponsored by the National Board for Respiratory Care (NBRC) and its wholly owned subsidiary, Applied Measurement Professionals, Inc. (AMP).

Number awarded 1 each year.
Deadline June of each year.

[450]
NCA SCHOLARSHIP PROGRAM

Healthcare Information and Management Systems Society-
National Capital Area Chapter
c/o Tony Smith
6024 Ascending Moon Path
Clarksville, MD 21029
E-mail: tony_smith@himss-nca.org
Web: www.himss-nca.org

Summary To provide financial assistance to students at colleges and universities in the Washington, D.C. metropolitan area who are working on an undergraduate or graduate degree in fields related to the health or management information systems industry.

Eligibility This program is open to students enrolled at a college or university in the Washington, D.C. metropolitan area and working on an associate, bachelor's, master's, or Ph.D. degree. Applicants must be studying health management, health information, informatics, or a management systems-related field. They must have a GPA of 3.0 or higher. Membership in the National Capital Area (NCA) chapter of the Healthcare Information and Management Systems Society (HIMSS) is required, but that requirement may be waived upon request. Along with their application, they must submit a 500-word essay on why they have chosen the field of information management/information technology (IM/IT), why IM/IT is important to health care today, and a major issue facing the community today and how IM/IT can address that issue. Selection is based on that essay, academic achievement, demonstration of leadership potential, communication skills, and participation in such professional activities as HIMSS-NCA.

Financial data The stipend is at least $3,000.

Duration 1 year; nonrenewable.

Number awarded 3 each year: 1 to an associate degree student, 1 to an undergraduate student, and 1 to a graduate student.

Deadline April of each year.

[451]
NCAA POSTGRADUATE SCHOLARSHIP PROGRAM

National Collegiate Athletic Association
Attn: Leadership Advisory Board
700 West Washington Avenue
P.O. Box 6222
Indianapolis, IN 46206-6222
(317) 917-6650   Fax: (317) 917-6888
E-mail: tksmith@ncaa.org
Web: www.ncaa.org

Summary To provide financial support for graduate education to student-athletes.

Eligibility Eligible are student-athletes who have excelled academically and athletically and who are in their final year of intercollegiate athletics competition at member schools of the National Collegiate Athletic Association (NCAA). Candidates must be nominated by the faculty athletic representative or director of athletics and must have a GPA of 3.2 or higher. Nominees must be planning full- or part-time graduate study. For the fall term, scholarships are presented to athletes who participated in men's and women's cross country, men's football, men's and women's soccer, men's water polo, women's volleyball, women's field hockey, women's equestrian, and women's badminton. For the winter term, scholarships are presented to athletes who participated in men's and women's basketball, men's and women's fencing, men's and women's gymnastics, men's and women's ice hockey, men's and women's rifle, men's and women's skiing, men's and women's swimming and diving, men's and women's indoor track and field, men's wrestling, women's archery, women's bowling, women's squash, and women's team handball. For the spring term, scholarships are presented to athletes who participated in men's baseball, men's and women's golf, men's and women's lacrosse, women's rowing, women's softball, men's and women's tennis, men's volleyball, men's and women's outdoor track and field, women's water polo, and women's synchronized swimming. Financial need is not considered in the selection process.

Financial data The stipend is $7,500.

Duration These are 1-time, nonrenewable awards.

Number awarded 174 each year: 87 for women and 87 for men. Each term, 29 scholarships are awarded to men and 29 to women.

Deadline December of each year for fall sports; February of each year for winter sports; May of each year for spring sports.

[452]
NCPA FOUNDATION PRESIDENTIAL SCHOLARSHIPS

National Community Pharmacists Association
Attn: NCPA Foundation
100 Daingerfield Road
Alexandria, VA 22314-2888
(703) 683-8200   Toll-free: (800) 544-7447
Fax: (703) 683-3619   E-mail: info@ncpanet.org
Web: www.ncpanet.org.org

Summary To provide financial assistance for full-time education in pharmacy to student members of the National Community Pharmacists Association (NCPA).

Eligibility All pharmacy students who are student members of the association and enrolled in an accredited U.S. school or college of pharmacy on a full-time basis are eligible. Applicants must submit a copy of the most recent transcript of their college grades, 2 letters of recommendation, a resume or curriculum vitae, and a statement outlining their school and citizenship accomplishments and future career objectives in independent community pharmacy. Selection is based on leadership qualities and academic achievement.

Financial data The stipend is $2,000, paid directly to the recipient's school or college of pharmacy.

Duration 1 year; nonrenewable.

Additional information Until October 1996, the NCPA, the national association representing independent retail pharmacy, was known as NARD (the National Association of Retail Druggists).

Number awarded 15 each year.

Deadline February of each year.

[453]
NDAF MEMORIAL AWARD

National Dental Association
Attn: National Dental Association Foundation, Inc.
3517 16th Street, N.W.
Washington, DC 20010
(202) 588-1697   Fax: (202) 588-1242
E-mail: admin@ndaonline.org
Web: www.nadonline.org/ndafoundation.asp

Summary To provide financial assistance to underrepresented minority dental postdoctoral students.

Eligibility This program is open to members of underrepresented minority groups who are dentists working on a degree in subspecialty areas of dentistry, public health, administration, research, or law. Students working on a master's degree beyond their residency may be considered. Applicants must be members of the National Dental Association (NDA) and U.S. citizens or permanent residents. Along with their application, they must submit a letter explaining why they should be considered for this scholarship, 2 letters of recommendation, a curriculum vitae, a description of the program, nomination by their program director, and documentation of financial need.

Financial data The stipend is $10,000.

Duration 1 year.

Additional information This program, established in 1990, is supported by the Colgate-Palmolive Company.

Number awarded 1 each year.

Deadline May of each year.

[454]
NEBRASKA SPACE GRANT STATEWIDE SCHOLARSHIP COMPETITION

Nebraska Space Grant Consortium
c/o University of Nebraska at Omaha
Allwine Hall 422
6001 Dodge Street
Omaha, NE 68182-0406
(402) 554-3772
Toll-free: (800) 858-8648, ext. 4-3772 (within NE)
Fax: (402) 554-3781   E-mail: nasa@unomaha.edu
Web: nasa.unomaha.edu/Funding/funding.php

Summary To provide financial assistance to undergraduate and graduate students at member institutions of the Nebraska Space Grant Consortium.

Eligibility This program is open to undergraduate and graduate students at schools that are members of the Nebraska Space Grant Consortium. Students in all academic disciplines are eligible. This program is sponsored by the U.S. National Aeronautics and Space Administration (NASA), which strongly encourages women, minorities, and students with disabilities to apply. U.S. citizenship is required. Financial need is not considered in the selection process.

Financial data A stipend is awarded (amount not specified).

Duration 1 year.

Additional information The following schools are members of the Nebraska Space Grant Consortium: University of Nebraska at Omaha, University of Nebraska at Lincoln, University of Nebraska at Kearney, University of Nebraska Medical Center, Creighton University, Western Nebraska Community College, Chadron State College, College of St. Mary, Metropolitan Community College, Grace University, Hastings College, Little Priest Tribal College, and Nebraska Indian Community College.

Number awarded At least 2 students from each institution are supported each year.

Deadline April of each year.

[455]
NEF DOCTORAL SCHOLARSHIPS

Nurses Educational Funds, Inc.
Attn: Scholarship Coordinator
304 Park Avenue South, 11th Floor
New York, NY 10010
(212) 590-2443   Fax: (212) 590-2446
E-mail: info@n-e-f.org
Web: www.n-e-f.org

Summary To provide financial assistance to African American nurses who are interested in working on a doctoral degree.

Eligibility This program is open to African American registered nurses who are members of a national professional nursing organization and enrolled in or applying to a nursing or nursing-related program at the doctoral level. Applicants must submit a 2-page essay on their professional goals and potential for making a contribution to the nursing profession. They must be U.S. citizens or have declared their official intention of becoming a citizen. Selection is based on academic excellence and potential for contributing to the nursing profession.

Financial data Awards range from $2,500 to $10,000, depending on the availability of funds.

Duration 1 year.

Additional information The highest-ranked applicant is awarded the Isabel Hampton Robb Scholarship. There is a $20 application fee.

Number awarded Varies each year; recently, 9 of these scholarships were awarded.

Deadline February of each year.

[456]
NEF MASTER'S SCHOLARSHIPS

Nurses Educational Funds, Inc.
Attn: Scholarship Coordinator
304 Park Avenue South, 11th Floor
New York, NY 10010
(212) 590-2443   Fax: (212) 590-2446
E-mail: info@n-e-f.org
Web: www.n-e-f.org

Summary To provide financial assistance to nurses who are interested in working on a master's degree.

Eligibility This program is open to registered nurses who are members of a national professional nursing organization and enrolled in or applying to an accredited master's degree program in nursing. Applicants must submit a 2-page essay on their professional goals and potential for making a contribution to the nursing profession. They must be U.S. citizens or have declared their official intention of becoming a citizen. Selection is based on academic excellence and potential for contributing to the nursing profession.

Financial data Awards range from $2,500 to $10,000, depending on the availability of funds.

Duration 1 year.

Additional information The highest-ranked applicant is awarded the Isabel McIsaac Scholarship. Recipients must study on a full-time basis. There is a $20 application fee.

Number awarded Varies each year; recently, 7 of these scholarships were awarded.

Deadline February of each year.

[457]
NEHA/AAS SCHOLARSHIPS

National Environmental Health Association
Attn: Scholarship Coordinator
720 South Colorado Boulevard, Suite 1000-N
Denver, CO 80246-1926
(303) 756-9090, ext. 343   Fax: (303) 691-9490
E-mail: cdimmitt@neha.org
Web: www.neha.org/scholarship/scholarship.html

Summary To provide financial assistance to upper-division and graduate students interested in preparing for a career in environmental health.

Eligibility This program is open to undergraduate and graduate students preparing for a career in environmental health. Undergraduates must be entering their junior or senior year in an approved environmental health curriculum at a 4-year college or university accredited by the Environmental Health Accreditation Council (EHAC). Graduate applicants may be enrolled in a college or university with a program of studies in environmental health sciences and/or public health. Selection for both levels is based on academic record and letters of recommendation; at least 1 letter of recommendation must be from an active member of the National Environmental Health Association (NEHA).

Financial data Stipends range from $400 to $1,000.

Duration 1 year; may be renewed.

Additional information The NEHA began this scholarship program in 1984; the American Academy of Sanitarians (AAS) joined it in 1989. Information is also available from the AAS, Executive

Secretary/Treasurer, 3815 Stone Briar Court, Duluth, GA 30097-2240, (770) 623-5691.

Number awarded Up to 3 each year.

Deadline January of each year.

[458]
NESBITT MEDICAL STUDENT FOUNDATION SCHOLARSHIP

Nesbitt Medical Student Foundation
c/o National Bank & Trust Company of Sycamore
230 West State Street
Sycamore, IL 60178
(815) 895-2125, ext. 228

Summary To provide financial assistance to needy medical students residing in Illinois and to encourage their entry into general practice in the state.

Eligibility The applicant must be a U.S. citizen, a resident of Illinois, and either accepted for enrollment or a regular full-time student in good standing at an approved college of medicine. Applicants must be interested in entry into general practice either in DeKalb County or in any county in Illinois having a population of less than 50,000 residents. Preference is given to women, persons who are or have been residents of DeKalb County, and students already attending an approved medical school in Illinois. Financial need must be demonstrated.

Financial data The maximum stipend is $2,000 per year, depending upon the needs of the recipient.

Duration 1 academic year; renewable.

Deadline April of each year.

[459]
NEUROSCIENCE NURSING FOUNDATION REGULAR SCHOLARSHIPS

American Association of Neuroscience Nurses
Attn: Neuroscience Nursing Foundation
4700 West Lake Avenue
Glenview, IL 60025-1485
(847) 375-4733   Toll-free: (888) 557-2266
Fax: (877) 734-8677   E-mail: info@aann.org
Web: www.aann.org/nnf/index.htm

Summary To provide financial assistance to nurses interested in further study in neuroscience nursing.

Eligibility This program is open to nurses who have a diploma or associate degree and are working on an advanced degree in neuroscience nursing. Applicants must submit their resume and a personal statement on their anticipated contribution to neuroscience nursing practice, research, and/or education.

Financial data The stipend is $1,500.

Duration 1 year.

Additional information This program was established in 1994.

Number awarded The award is presented when a suitable candidate applies.

Deadline January of each year.

[460]
NEVADA SPACE GRANT CONSORTIUM GRADUATE FELLOWSHIP PROGRAM

Nevada Space Grant Consortium
c/o University of Nevada at Reno
Mackay School of Mines Building, Room 308
MS 168
Reno, NV 89557
(775) 784-6261   Fax: (775) 327-2235
E-mail: nvsg@mines.unr.edu
Web: www.unr.edu/spacegrant

Summary To provide financial assistance for space-related study or research to graduate students at institutions that are members of the University and Community College System of Nevada (UCCSN) and participate in the Nevada Space Grant Consortium (NSGC).

Eligibility This program is open to graduate students at UCCSN member institutions. Applicants must be working on a degree in an aerospace-related field (including engineering, mathematics, physical and life sciences, and technology) that will prepare them for a career in aerospace science, technology, and related fields. They must be U.S. citizens, be enrolled full time (or accepted for full-time study), present a proposed study or research plan related to aerospace, include in the research or activity plan an extramural experience at a field center of the U.S. National Aeronautics and Space Administration (NASA), plan to be involved in NSGC outreach activities, not receive other federal funds, and intend to prepare for a career in a field of interest to NASA. Members of underrepresented groups (African Americans, Hispanics, American Indians, Pacific Islanders, people with physical disabilities, and women of all races) who have an interest in aerospace fields are encouraged to apply. Selection is based on the academic qualifications of the applicant, the quality of the proposed research program or plan of study and its relevant to NASA's aerospace science and technology program, the quality of the approach to achieving the objectives of the proposed utilization of a NASA center in carrying out the objectives of the program, the prospects for completion of the project within the allotted time, and the applicant's motivation for an aerospace career.

Financial data The grant is $22,500, including $16,000 as a stipend for the student and $6,500 for tuition and a student research and travel allowance.

Duration 12 months; may be renewed up to 24 additional months.

Additional information Funding for this program is provided by NASA.

Number awarded Varies each year; recently, 3 of these awards were granted.

Deadline March of each year.

[461]
NEVADA STATE MEDICAL ASSOCIATION SCHOLARSHIPS

Nevada State Medical Association
3660 Baker Lane, Suite 101
Reno, NV 89509
(775) 825-6788   Fax: (775) 798-6711
E-mail: nsma@nsmadocs.org
Web: www.nsmadocs.org

Summary To provide financial assistance to Nevada residents who are attending medical school in other states.

Eligibility Nevada residents who are attending an accredited medical school outside the state are eligible to apply. Selection is based on financial need, career plans, and awards received.
Financial data Stipends are based on need and usually range from $500 to $3,000.
Duration 1 year.
Number awarded 1 or more each year.
Deadline July of each year.

[462]
NEW CENTURY SCHOLARS PROGRAM
American Speech-Language-Hearing Foundation
Attn: Graduate Student Scholarship Competition
10801 Rockville Pike
Rockville, MD 20852-3279
(301) 897-5700 Toll-free: (800) 498-2071
Fax: (301) 571-0457 TTY: (800) 498-2071
E-mail: foundation@asha.org
Web: www.ashfoundation.org
Summary To provide financial assistance to doctoral students in communication sciences and disorders programs.
Eligibility This program is open to doctoral students who are enrolled in or accepted by a research program in communication sciences and disorders. Applicants must be committed to a teacher-investigator career in the field. They must be a member of the National Student Speech Language Hearing Association or the American Speech-Language-Hearing Association. Preference is given to full-time students.
Financial data The stipend is $10,000.
Duration 1 year.
Number awarded 4 each year.
Deadline March of each year.

[463]
NEW ENGLAND FEMARA SCHOLARSHIPS
American Radio Relay League
Attn: ARRL Foundation
225 Main Street
Newington, CT 06111
(860) 594-0397 Fax: (860) 594-0259
E-mail: foundation@arrl.org
Web: www.arrl.org/arrlf/scholgen.html
Summary To provide financial assistance to licensed radio amateurs who are interested in working on an undergraduate or graduate degree.
Eligibility This program is open to undergraduate or graduate students at accredited institutions who are licensed radio amateurs of technician class. Applicants must submit an essay on the role amateur radio has played in their lives and provide documentation of financial need. Preference is given to applicants from the 6 New England states.
Financial data The stipend is $1,000.
Duration 1 year.
Number awarded Varies, depending upon the availability of funds; recently, 5 of these scholarships were awarded per year.
Deadline January of each year.

[464]
NEW ENGLAND REGIONAL STUDENT PROGRAM
New England Board of Higher Education
45 Temple Place
Boston, MA 02111
(617) 357-9620 Fax: (617) 338-1577
E-mail: tuitionbreak@nebhe.org
Web: www.nebhe.org
Summary To enable students in New England to attend a college or graduate school within the region at reduced tuition when their area of study is not offered at their own state's public institutions.
Eligibility This program is open to residents of the 6 New England states: Connecticut, Maine, Massachusetts, New Hampshire, Rhode Island, and Vermont. Students may apply for this support when their chosen field of study is not offered at any of the public institutions within their own state. Contact the New England Board of Higher Education for a catalog of degree programs and states that qualify for this program. Undergraduate program eligibility is based on entire degree programs only, not on concentrations or options within degree programs. Some highly specialized graduate programs might be available even if they are not listed in the catalog. Eligibility is not based on financial need.
Financial data With this program, students accepted at a public college or university in New England (but outside their own state) generally pay 150% of the in-state tuition for residents of the state. The average tuition savings is approximately $5,000.
Duration Up to 4 years.
Additional information In addition to reduced tuition, participants in this program also receive admission preference among out-of-state applicants. Because this is a tuition-reduction program, not a financial assistance program, participants are still eligible to apply for financial aid from other sources. Students must apply for this program when they apply to their chosen out-of-state public college or university.
Number awarded Varies each year; recently, more than 8,050 New England students took advantage of this program.

[465]
NEW HAMPSHIRE CHARITABLE FOUNDATION STATEWIDE STUDENT AID PROGRAM
New Hampshire Charitable Foundation
37 Pleasant Street
Concord, NH 03301-4005
(603) 225-6641 Toll-free: (800) 464-6641
Fax: (603) 225-1700 E-mail: info@nhcf.org
Web: www.nhcf.org/page16960.cfm
Summary To provide scholarships or loans for undergraduate or graduate study to New Hampshire residents.
Eligibility This program is open to New Hampshire residents who are graduating high school seniors planning to enter a 4-year college or university, undergraduate students between 17 and 23 years of age working on a 4-year degree, or graduate students of any age. Applicants must be enrolled on at least a half-time basis at a school in New Hampshire or another state. Selection is based on financial need, academic merit, community service, school activities, and work experience. Priority is given to students with the fewest financial resources.
Financial data Awards range from $500 to $2,500 and average $1,800. Most are made in the form of grants (recently, 82% of all awards) or no-interest or low-interest loans (recently, 18% of all awards).

Duration 1 year; approximately one third of the awards are renewable.

Additional information Through this program, students submit a single application for more than 270 different scholarship and loan funds. Many of the funds have additional requirements, including field of study; residency in region, county, city, or town; graduation from designated high schools; and special attributes (e.g., of Belgian descent, employee of designated firms, customer of Granite State Telephone Company, disabled, suffering from a life-threatening or serious chronic illness, of Lithuanian descent, dependent of a New Hampshire police officer, dependent of a New Hampshire Episcopal minister, of Polish descent, former Sea Cadet or Naval Junior ROTC, or employed in the tourism industry). The Citizens' Scholarship Foundation of America reviews all applications; recipients are selected by the New Hampshire Charitable Foundation. A $20 application fee is required.

Number awarded Varies each year; recently, a total of $3 million was awarded.

Deadline April of each year.

[466]
NEW JERSEY EDUCATIONAL OPPORTUNITY FUND GRANTS

New Jersey Commission on Higher Education
Attn: Educational Opportunity Fund
20 West State Street, Seventh Floor
P.O. Box 542
Trenton, NJ 08625-0542
(609) 984-2709   Fax: (609) 292-7225
E-mail: nj_che@che.state.nj.us
Web: www.nj.gov/highereducation/eligible.htm

Summary To provide financial assistance for undergraduate or graduate study in New Jersey to students from disadvantaged backgrounds.

Eligibility This program is open to students from economically and educationally disadvantaged backgrounds who have been legal residents of New Jersey for at least 12 consecutive months. Applicants must be from families with annual incomes below specified limits, ranging from $18,620 for a household size of 1 to $63,140 for a household size of 8. They must be attending or accepted for attendance as full-time undergraduate or graduate students at institutions of higher education in New Jersey. To apply, students must fill out the Free Application for Federal Student Aid. Some colleges may also require students to complete the College Scholarship Service's (CSS) Financial Aid Form to apply for institutional aid.

Financial data Undergraduate grants range from $200 to $2,400 and graduate grants from $200 to $4,250, depending on college costs and financial need.

Duration 1 year; renewable annually (based on satisfactory academic progress and continued eligibility).

Additional information This is a campus-based program; each college or university has its own specific criteria for admission and program participation; students should contact the Educational Opportunity Fund (EOF) director at their institution for specific admissions information and requirements for participating in the program. Participants are also eligible for supportive services, such as counseling, tutoring, and developmental course work.

Deadline September of each year.

[467]
NEW MEXICO GRADUATE SCHOLARSHIP PROGRAM

New Mexico Higher Education Department
Attn: Financial Aid Director
1068 Cerrillos Road
P.O. Box 15910
Santa Fe, NM 87506-5910
(505) 476-6506   Toll-free: (800) 279-9777
Fax: (505) 476-6511   E-mail: ofelia.morales@state.nm.us
Web: hed.state.nm.us/collegefinance/gradshol.asp

Summary To provide financial assistance for graduate education to underrepresented groups in New Mexico.

Eligibility Applicants for this program must be New Mexico residents who are members of underrepresented groups, particularly minorities and women. Preference is given to 1) students enrolled in business, engineering, computer science, mathematics, or agriculture and 2) American Indian students enrolled in any graduate program. All applicants must be U.S. citizens or permanent residents enrolled in graduate programs at public institutions of higher education in New Mexico.

Financial data The maximum stipend is $7,500 per year.

Duration 1 year; may be renewed.

Additional information Information is available from the dean of graduate studies at the participating New Mexico public institution. Recipients must serve 10 hours per week in an unpaid internship or assistantship.

Number awarded Varies each year, depending on the availability of funds.

Deadline Deadlines are established by the participating institutions.

[468]
NEW MEXICO VIETNAM VETERANS SCHOLARSHIPS

New Mexico Department of Veterans' Services
P.O. Box 2324
Santa Fe, NM 87504-2324
(505) 827-6300   Toll-free: (866) 433-VETS
Fax: (505) 827-6372   E-mail: nmdvs@state.nm.us
Web: www.state.nm.us/veterans/scholarship.html

Summary To provide financial assistance for undergraduate and graduate education to Vietnam veterans in New Mexico.

Eligibility This program is open to Vietnam veterans who have been residents of New Mexico for at least 10 years. Applicants must have been honorably discharged and have been awarded the Vietnam Service Medal or the Vietnam Campaign Medal. They must be planning to attend a state-supported college, university, or community college in New Mexico to work on an undergraduate or graduate degree.

Financial data The scholarships pay tuition, fees, and books at any postsecondary institution in New Mexico, up to $1,520 for tuition and fees and $500 for books.

Duration 1 year.

[469]
NEW MEXICO 3 PERCENT SCHOLARSHIP PROGRAM

New Mexico Higher Education Department
Attn: Financial Aid Director
1068 Cerrillos Road
P.O. Box 15910
Santa Fe, NM 87506-5910
(505) 476-6506   Toll-free: (800) 279-9777
Fax: (505) 476-6511   E-mail: ofelia.morales@state.nm.us
Web: hed.state.nm.us/collegefinance/three.asp

Summary To provide financial assistance for college or graduate school to residents of New Mexico.
Eligibility This assistance is available to residents of New Mexico enrolled or planning to enroll at a public institution of higher education in the state as an undergraduate or graduate student. Selection is based on moral character, satisfactory initiative, scholastic standing, personality, and additional criteria established by each participating college or university. At least a third of the scholarships are based on financial need.
Financial data The amount of assistance varies but covers at least tuition and some fees.
Duration 1 year; may be renewed.
Additional information Information is available at the financial aid office of any New Mexico public postsecondary institution.
Number awarded Varies each year.
Deadline Deadlines are established by the participating institutions.

[470]
NEW YORK STATE OCCUPATIONAL THERAPY ASSOCIATION SCHOLARSHIP

American Occupational Therapy Foundation
Attn: Scholarship Coordinator
4720 Montgomery Lane
P.O. Box 31220
Bethesda, MD 20824-1220
(301) 652-2682   Fax: (301) 656-3620
TDD: (800) 377-8555   E-mail: aotf@aotf.org
Web: www.aotf.org

Summary To provide financial assistance to students who are members of the New York State Occupational Therapy Association and working on a professional master's degree in occupational therapy.
Eligibility This program is open to New York residents who are enrolled in an accredited professional occupational therapy educational program in the state. Applicants must demonstrate a need for financial assistance, have a sustained record of outstanding scholastic performance, and be members of the New York State Occupational Therapy Association. As part of the application process, they must submit transcripts, 2 personal references, and a statement from their curriculum director.
Financial data The stipend is $1,000.
Duration 1 year.
Number awarded 1 or more each year.
Deadline January of each year.

[471]
NEW YORK VIETNAM TUITION AWARD (VTA) PROGRAM

New York State Higher Education Services Corporation
Attn: Student Information
99 Washington Avenue
Albany, NY 12255
(518) 473-1574   Toll-free: (888) NYS-HESC
Fax: (518) 473-3749   TDD: (800) 445-5234
E-mail: webmail@hesc.com
Web: www.hesc.com

Summary To provide tuition assistance to eligible veterans enrolled in an undergraduate or graduate program in New York.
Eligibility This program is open to veterans who served in the U.S. armed forces in 1) Indochina between December 22, 1961 and May 7, 1975; 2) in the Persian Gulf on or after August 2, 1990; or 3) in Afghanistan on or after September 11, 2001. Applicants must have been discharged from the service under other than dishonorable conditions, must be a New York resident, must be enrolled full or part time at an undergraduate or graduate degree-granting institution in New York State or in an approved vocational training program in the state, and must apply for a New York Tuition Assistance Program (TAP) award if a full-time student (12 or more credits) or a Pell Grant if a part-time student (at least 3 but less than 12 credits).
Financial data Awards are $1,000 per semester for full-time study or $500 for part-time study, but in no case can the award exceed the amount charged for tuition. Total lifetime awards for undergraduate and graduate study under this program cannot exceed $10,000.
Duration For full-time undergraduate study, up to 8 semesters, or up to 10 semesters for a program requiring 5 years for completion; for full-time graduate study, up to 6 semesters; for full-time vocational programs, up to 4 semesters; for part-time undergraduate study, up to 16 semesters, or up to 20 semesters for a 5-year program; for part-time graduate study, up to 12 semesters; for part-time vocational programs, up to 8 semesters.
Additional information If a TAP award is also received, the combined academic year award cannot exceed tuition costs. If it does, the TAP award will be reduced accordingly.
Number awarded Varies each year.
Deadline April of each year.

[472]
NICHOLAS AND MARY TRIVILLIAN MEMORIAL SCHOLARSHIPS

Greater Kanawha Valley Foundation
Attn: Scholarship Coordinator
1600 Huntington Square
900 Lee Street, East
P.O. Box 3041
Charleston, WV 25331-3041
(304) 346-3620   Fax: (304) 346-3640
E-mail: tgkvf@tgkvf.com
Web: www.tgkvf.com/scholar.html

Summary To provide financial assistance to residents of West Virginia who are working on a degree in medicine or pharmacy.
Eligibility This program is open to residents of West Virginia who are working full time on a degree in the field of medicine or pharmacy at a college or university in the state. Applicants must have an ACT score of 20 or higher, be able to demonstrate good moral character and financial need, and have a GPA of 2.5 or higher.

Financial data   The stipend is $1,000 per year.
Duration   1 year; may be renewed.
Number awarded   Varies each year; recently, 24 of these scholarships were awarded.
Deadline   February of each year.

[473]
NICK COST SCHOLARSHIPS

American Hellenic Educational Progressive Association
Attn: AHEPA Educational Foundation
1909 Q Street, N.W., Suite 500
Washington, DC 20009
(202) 232-6300   Fax: (202) 232-2140
E-mail: ahepa@ahepa.org
Web: www.ahepa.org

Summary   To provide financial assistance to undergraduate and graduate students with a connection to the American Hellenic Educational Progressive Association (AHEPA).

Eligibility   This program is open to 1) members in good standing of the Order of Ahepa, Daughters of Penelope, Sons of Pericles, or Maids of Athena, and 2) the children of Order of Ahepa or Daughters of Penelope members in good standing. Applicants must be currently enrolled or planning to enroll as undergraduate or graduate students. High school seniors must submit their most recent official transcript as well as SAT or ACT scores; college freshmen and sophomores must submit high school transcripts, SAT or ACT scores, and their most recent college transcript; college juniors and seniors must submit their most recent college transcript; graduate students must submit college transcripts, GRE or MCAT scores (if available), and their most recent graduate school transcript. Along with their application, they must also submit a 500-word biographical essay. Selection is based on academic achievement; extracurricular, personal, and volunteer activities; athletic achievements; and work experience. Financial need is not considered.

Financial data   Stipends range from $500 to $2,000 per year.
Duration   1 year.
Additional information   A processing fee of $20 must accompany each application.
Number awarded   Varies each year; recently, 2 of these scholarships were awarded.
Deadline   March of each year.

[474]
NISABURO AIBARA MEMORIAL SCHOLARSHIP

Japanese American Citizens League
Attn: National Scholarship Awards
1765 Sutter Street
San Francisco, CA 94115
(415) 921-5225   Fax: (415) 931-4671
E-mail: jacl@jacl.org
Web: www.jacl.org/leadership_development_5.php

Summary   To provide financial assistance for graduate study to members of the Japanese American Citizens League (JACL).

Eligibility   This program is open to JACL members who are attending or planning to attend an accredited college or university as a graduate student. Applicants must submit a statement describing their current level of involvement in the Japanese American community or Asian Pacific community and how they will continue their involvement in future years. Selection is based on academic record, extracurricular activities, financial need, and community involvement.

Financial data   The stipend depends on the availability of funds but usually ranges from $1,000 to $5,000.
Duration   1 year; nonrenewable.
Additional information   The funds for this program are provided by the Turlock Social Club of California, in honor of the late Issei pioneer. Applications must be submitted to the JACL National Scholarship Program, c/o San Diego JACL Chapter, 1031 25th Street, San Diego, CA 92102.
Number awarded   At least 1 each year.
Deadline   March of each year.

[475]
NMA EMERGING SCHOLARS AWARDS

National Medical Fellowships, Inc.
Attn: Scholarship Program
5 Hanover Square, 15th Floor
New York, NY 10004
(212) 483-8880   Fax: (212) 483-8897
E-mail: info@nmfonline.org
Web: www.nmf-online.org

Summary   To provide financial assistance to African American medical students.

Eligibility   This program is open to African American medical students who are U.S. citizens in their first, second, or third year at an accredited M.D. or D.O. degree-granting school in the United States. Only nominations are accepted. All nominees must submit a personal essay on their motivation for a career in medicine and career plans over the next 10 years. Selection is based on financial need, community involvement, academic achievement, and potential for a responsible role in medicine.

Financial data   The stipend is $2,250.
Duration   1 year.
Additional information   This program is sponsored by the National Medical Association (NMA).
Number awarded   6 each year.
Deadline   April of each year.

[476]
NMF NEED-BASED SCHOLARSHIP PROGRAM

National Medical Fellowships, Inc.
Attn: Scholarship Program
5 Hanover Square, 15th Floor
New York, NY 10004
(212) 483-8880   Fax: (212) 483-8897
E-mail: info@nmfonline.org
Web: www.nmf-online.org

Summary   To provide financial assistance to underrepresented minority medical students.

Eligibility   This program is open to U.S. citizens enrolled in the first or second year of an accredited M.D. or D.O. degree-granting program in the United States. Applicants must be African American, Mexican American, Native Hawaiian, Alaska Native, American Indian, or mainland Puerto Rican. They must submit an essay of 500 to 1,000 words on their motivation for a career in medicine and their personal and professional goals over the next 10 years. Selection is based primarily on financial need.

Financial data   The amount of the award depends on the student's total resources (including parental and spousal support), cost of education, and receipt of additional scholarships; recently, individual awards ranged from $500 to $10,000 per year.
Duration   1 year for first-year students; may be renewed for the second year only.

Number awarded Varies each year; recently, more than 300 students received support from this program.
Deadline June of each year.

[477]
NNCC CAREER MOBILITY SCHOLARSHIPS

American Nephrology Nurses' Association
Attn: ANNA National Office
200 East Holly Avenue
P.O. Box 56
Pitman, NJ 08071-0056
(609) 256-2320   Toll-free: (888) 600-2662
Fax: (856) 589-7463   E-mail: annascholarships@ajj.com
Web: www.annanurse.org

Summary To provide financial assistance to members of the American Nephrology Nurses' Association (ANNA) who are Certified Nephrology Nurses and are interested in working on a baccalaureate or graduate degree in nursing to enhance their nephrology nursing practice.

Eligibility Applicants must have a current credential as a Certified Nephrology Nurse (CNN) by the Nephrology Nursing Certification Commission (NNCC), be a current full member of the association, have been a member for at least 2 years, be currently employed in nephrology nursing, and be accepted or enrolled in a baccalaureate or higher degree program in nursing. Along with their application, they must submit a 250-word essay on their career and education goals that includes how their degree will apply to nephrology nursing, provides a time frame for completing their program, and indicates how the funds will meet their educational needs.

Financial data The stipend is $2,000.
Duration 1 year.
Additional information Funds for this program, established in 1993, are supplied by the NNCC. Information is also available from Sharon Longton, Awards and Scholarships Chair, (313) 966-2674, E-mail: slongton@dmc.org.
Number awarded 3 each year.
Deadline October of each year.

[478]
NORTHWEST OSTEOPATHIC MEDICAL FOUNDATION SCHOLARSHIPS

Northwest Osteopathic Medical Foundation
Tiffany Center
1410 S.W. Morrison Street, Suite 700
Portland, OR 97205
(503) 222-7161   Toll-free: (888) NW-OSTEO
Fax: (503) 222-2841   E-mail: lavery@nwosteo.org
Web: www.nwosteo.org

Summary To provide financial assistance to residents of the Pacific Northwest who are attending osteopathic medical schools.

Eligibility This program is open to 1) residents of Alaska, Idaho, Montana, Oregon, and Washington and 2) people who have lived, worked, or attended institutions of higher education in those states. Applicants must be in their second, third, or fourth year of a medical school approved by the American Osteopathic Association. Selection is based on prior and current academic work, professional activity, aptitude for medical school work, and recommendations.

Financial data Stipends range from $1,000 to $6,000 per year.
Duration 1 year.

Number awarded Varies each year; recently, 25 of these fellowships, for a total of $70,000, were awarded.
Deadline January of each year.

[479]
NSCA MINORITY SCHOLARSHIPS

National Strength and Conditioning Association
Attn: Grants and Scholarships
1885 Bob Johnson Drive
Colorado Springs, CO 80906
(719) 632-6722, ext. 105   Toll-free: (800) 815-6826
Fax: (719) 632-6367   E-mail: nsca@nsca-lift.org
Web: www.nsca-lift.org/Foundation

Summary To provide financial assistance to minorities who are members of the National Strength and Conditioning Association (NSCA) and interested in preparing for a career in strength training and conditioning.

Eligibility This program is open to members who are minorities 17 years of age and older. Applicants must have been accepted into an accredited postsecondary institution to work on a graduate degree in the strength and conditioning field. They must submit a 500-word essay describing their course of study, career goals, and financial need.

Financial data The stipend is $1,000.
Duration 1 year.
Additional information The NSCA is a nonprofit organization of strength and conditioning professionals, including coaches, athletic trainers, physical therapists, educators, researchers, and physicians. This program was first offered in 2003.
Number awarded 2 each year.
Deadline March of each year.

[480]
NSCA WOMEN'S SCHOLARSHIPS

National Strength and Conditioning Association
Attn: Grants and Scholarships
1885 Bob Johnson Drive
Colorado Springs, CO 80906
(719) 632-6722, ext. 105   Toll-free: (800) 815-6826
Fax: (719) 632-6367   E-mail: nsca@nsca-lift.org
Web: www.nsca-lift.org/Foundation

Summary To provide financial assistance to women who are members of the National Strength and Conditioning Association (NSCA) and interested in working on a graduate degree.

Eligibility This program is open to members who are women 17 years of age and older. Applicants must have been accepted into an accredited postsecondary institution to work on a graduate degree in the strength and conditioning field. They must submit a 500-word essay describing their course of study, career goals, and financial need.

Financial data The stipend is $1,000.
Duration 1 year.
Additional information The NSCA is a nonprofit organization of strength and conditioning professionals, including coaches, athletic trainers, physical therapists, educators, researchers, and physicians. This program was first offered in 2003.
Number awarded 2 each year.
Deadline March of each year.

[481]
NSF GRADUATE RESEARCH FELLOWSHIPS

National Science Foundation
Directorate for Education and Human Resources
Attn: Division of Graduate Education
4201 Wilson Boulevard, Room 907N
Arlington, VA 22230
(703) 331-3424   Toll-free: (866) NSF-GRFP
Fax: (703) 292-9048   E-mail: grfp@nsf.gov
Web: www.nsf.gov/funding/pgm_summ.jsp?pims_id=6201

Summary To provide financial assistance to graduate students, especially those who will increase diversity, interested in working on a master's or doctoral degree in fields supported by the National Science Foundation (NSF).

Eligibility This program is open to U.S. citizens, nationals, and permanent residents who wish to work on research-based master's or doctoral degrees in a field of science (including social science), technology, engineering, or mathematics (STEM) supported by NSF. Research in bioengineering is eligible if it involves 1) diagnosis or treatment-related goals that apply engineering principles to problems in biology and medicine while advancing engineering knowledge, or 2) aiding persons with disabilities. Other work in medical, dental, law, public health, or practice-oriented professional degree programs, or in joint science-professional degree programs, such as M.D./Ph.D. and J.D./Ph.D. programs, is not eligible. Other categories of ineligible support include 1) clinical, counseling, business, or management fields; 2) education (except science education); 3) history (except in history of science); 4) social work; 5) medical sciences or research with disease-related goals, including work on the etiology, diagnosis, or treatment of physical or mental disease, abnormality, or malfunction in human beings or animals; 6) research involving animal models of research with disease-related goals; and 7) testing of drugs or other procedures for disease-related goals. Applications normally should be submitted during the senior year in college or in the first year of graduate study; eligibility is limited to those who have completed no more than 12 months of graduate study since completion of a baccalaureate degree. Applicants who have already earned an advanced degree in science, engineering, or medicine (including an M.D., D.D.S., or D.V.M.) are ineligible. Selection is based on intellectual merit and broader impacts. Intellectual merit includes intellectual ability and other accepted requisites for scholarly scientific study, such as the ability to work as a member of a team as well as independently, to interpret and communicate research findings, and to plan and conduct research. The broader impacts criterion includes contributions that 1) effectively integrate research and education at all levels, infuse learning with the excitement of discovery, and assure that the findings and methods of research are communicated in a broad context and to a large audience; 2) encourage diversity, broaden opportunities, and enable the participation of all citizens (including women and men, underrepresented minorities, and persons with disabilities) in science and engineering; 3) enhance scientific and technical understanding; and 4) benefit society.

Financial data The stipend is $30,000 per year, plus a $10,500 cost-of-education allowance given to the recipient's institution. If a fellow affiliates with a foreign institution, tuition and fees are reimbursed to the fellow up to a maximum of $10,500 per tenure year and an additional international research travel allowance of $1,000 is provided.

Duration Up to 3 years, usable over a 5-year period.

Additional information Fellows may choose as their fellowship institution any appropriate nonprofit U.S. or foreign institution of higher education.

Number awarded Approximately 1,000 each year.

Deadline November of each year. Deadlines are staggered for life sciences; psychology and mathematical sciences; social sciences; chemistry, physics, and astronomy; engineering; and computer and information science and engineering (CISE) and geosciences.

[482]
NURSE PRACTITIONER HEALTHCARE FOUNDATION/PROCTER & GAMBLE ENDOWED SCHOLARSHIPS

Nurse Practitioner Healthcare Foundation
Attn: Scholarship Selection Committee
2647 134th Avenue N.E.
Bellevue, WA 98005-1813
(425) 861-0911   Fax: (425) 861-0907
Web: www.nphealthcarefoundation.org/projects.html

Summary To provide financial assistance to students preparing for a career as a nurse practitioner.

Eligibility This program is open to students currently enrolled in a nationally-accredited nurse practitioner program at the master's, postmaster's, or doctoral level. Applicants in the leadership category must have made a significant, positive leadership contribution on campus, in the community, or in patient care while working on an advanced degree. Applicants in the gastroenterology category must have clinical and/or research interests in the field of gastroenterology. For the leadership category, they must describe how they will use this scholarship to advance their skills as a nurse practitioner leader, including past and current leadership experience and potential opportunities to enact the leadership role to influence the profession and their care of patients as a nurse practitioner. For the gastroenterology category, they must describe what they plan to do in their chosen area to enhance their ability to make an innovative or unique contribution to the overall care of patients with potential or ongoing gastroenterological problems.

Financial data The stipend is $1,000.

Duration 1 year; nonrenewable.

Additional information This program is sponsored by the Procter & Gamble Company.

Number awarded 2 each year: 1 in the leadership category and 1 in the gastroenterology category.

Deadline May of each year.

[483]
NURSE QUEST SCHOLARSHIP

National Association Directors of Nursing Administration in Long Term Care
Attn: Education/Scholarship Committee
10101 Alliance Road, Suite 140
Cincinnati, OH 45242
(513) 791-3679   Toll-free: (800) 222-0539
Fax: (513) 791-3699   E-mail: info@nadona.org
Web: www.nadona.org

Summary To provide financial assistance to certified nursing assistants who are currently employed in long-term care and are interested in pursuing higher education, with a career focus on gerontology.

Eligibility This program is open to certified nursing assistants (C.N.A.s) (evidence of certification must accompany the application) who are currently accepted or enrolled in 1 of the following programs: 1) an L.P.N. or R.N. program; 2) an accredited R.N. program or undergraduate health care management program; 3) a baccalaureate or master's degree program in nursing or gerontology; 4) an undergraduate or graduate program in health care management. Candidates must be currently employed in long-term care (for at least 1 year) and have a career focus in gerontology. They must be members of the National Association of Directors of Nursing Administration in Long Term Care or sponsored by a member.

Financial data A stipend is awarded (amount not specified); a total of $1,000 is currently available for this program each year.

Duration 1 year.

Number awarded At least 1 each year.

Deadline February of each year.

[484]
NURSING ECONOMIC$ FOUNDATION SCHOLARSHIP

Nursing Economic$ Foundation
c/o Anthony J. Jannetti, Inc.
200 East Holly Avenue
P.O. Box 56
Pitman, NJ 08071-0056
(856) 256-2318   Fax: (856) 589-7463
E-mail: nefoun@ajj.com
Web: www.nursingeconomics.net

Summary To provide financial assistance to students working on a master's or doctoral nursing degree with an emphasis on administration or management.

Eligibility This program is open to R.N.s who have been accepted at or are currently enrolled in an accredited, degree-granting master's or doctoral nursing program with an emphasis on administration or management. Applicants must plan to continue in the field of nursing in a leadership, administration, or management position upon completion of the degree. Along with their application, they must submit tuition information for their degree program, a curriculum vitae, transcripts, and official GRE or Miller Analogies test scores (even if their school does not require them).

Financial data The stipend is $5,000. Checks are made out jointly to the recipient and the school. Funds must be used for tuition and other school-related fees (excluding room, board, insurance, and athletic fees).

Duration 1 year; nonrenewable.

Number awarded Varies each year; recently, 3 of these scholarships were awarded.

Deadline April of each year.

[485]
NURSING FOUNDATION OF RHODE ISLAND STUDENT SCHOLARSHIPS

Nursing Foundation of Rhode Island
Attn: Scholarship Committee
Corliss Landing
550 South Water Street
Providence, RI 02903
(401) 421-9703   Fax: (401) 421-6793
E-mail: risna@prodigy.net
Web: www.rinursingfoundation.org/StudentNurse.htm

Summary To provide financial assistance to students currently enrolled in nursing schools in Rhode Island.

Eligibility This program is open to students enrolled in a nursing program in Rhode Island who demonstrate financial need, have maintained at least a 3.0 GPA, and have demonstrated clinical proficiency, enthusiasm, and motivation in their studies. Preference is given to students who are in the latter half of their nursing program.

Financial data The stipend of the Elsie L. Drew Memorial Scholarship is $1,000. All other stipends are $500. Checks are written jointly to the recipient and the recipient's school.

Duration 1 year.

Additional information In addition to the Elsie L. Drew Memorial Scholarship, this program includes these other named scholarships: the Francis H. Sherman Memorial Scholarship, the Gerald and Trudy Mulvey Scholarship, and the Helen Capocci Enright Scholarship.

Number awarded Varies each year; recently, more than 70 of these scholarships were awarded.

Deadline May of each year.

[486]
OCCUPATIONAL THERAPY ASSOCIATION OF OREGON SCHOLARSHIPS

Occupational Therapy Association of Oregon
Attn: Office Manager
P.O. Box 7133
Aloha, OR 97007
(503) 658-6384   Fax: (503) 690-1819
E-mail: otao@otao.com
Web: www.otao.com

Summary To provide financial assistance to members of the Occupational Therapy Association of Oregon (OTAO) who are working on a degree as an occupational therapist or occupational therapy assistant.

Eligibility This program is open to OTAO members who are accepted by or enrolled in an occupational therapy professional master's degree program or an occupational therapy assistant program.

Financial data The stipend is $1,000.

Duration 1 year.

Number awarded 4 each year.

[487]
O'CONNOR MEMORIAL SCHOLARSHIP

American Association of Nurse Anesthetists
Attn: AANA Foundation
222 South Prospect Avenue
Park Ridge, IL 60068-4001
(847) 692-7050, ext. 1171   Fax: (847) 692-7137
E-mail: foundation@aana.com
Web: www.aana.com/foundation/default.asp

Summary To provide financial assistance to members of the American Association of Nurse Anesthetists (AANA) who are interested in obtaining further education.

Eligibility This program is open to members of the association who are currently enrolled in an accredited nurse anesthesia education program. Applicants must be second-year students who have completed 12 months of nurse anesthesia classes. Along with their application, they must submit a 200-word essay describing why they have chosen nurse anesthesia as a profession and their professional goals for the future. Financial need is also considered in the selection process.

Financial data The stipend is $1,000 per year.

Duration 1 academic year.

Additional information Funds for this program are provided by the David L. Jelinek Agency, LLC. The application processing fee is $25.

Number awarded 1 each year.

Deadline March of each year.

[488]
OHIO OCCUPATIONAL THERAPY ASSOCIATION SCHOLARSHIPS

American Occupational Therapy Foundation
Attn: Scholarship Coordinator
4720 Montgomery Lane
P.O. Box 31220
Bethesda, MD 20824-1220
(301) 652-2682   Fax: (301) 656-3620
TDD: (800) 377-8555   E-mail: aotf@aotf.org
Web: www.aotf.org

Summary To provide financial assistance to students in Ohio who are working on an an associate or professional master's degree in occupational therapy.

Eligibility This program is open to Ohio residents who are enrolled in an accredited occupational therapy educational program in the state at the associate or professional master's degree level. Applicants must demonstrate a need for financial assistance and have a sustained record of outstanding scholastic performance. As part of the application process, they must submit transcripts, 2 personal references, and a statement from their curriculum director.

Financial data The stipend is $1,000.

Duration 1 year.

Number awarded Normally 2 each year: 1 to an associate degree student and 1 to a professional master's degree student.

Deadline January of each year.

[489]
OHIO REGENTS GRADUATE/PROFESSIONAL FELLOWSHIP PROGRAM

Ohio Board of Regents
Attn: State Grants and Scholarships
57 East Main Street, Fourth Floor
P.O. Box 182452
Columbus, OH 43218-2452
(614) 466-7420   Toll-free: (888) 833-1133
Fax: (614) 752-5903
E-mail: bmetheney@regents.state.oh.us
Web: www.regents.state.oh.us/sgs/regentsfellowship.htm

Summary To provide financial assistance to college graduates in Ohio who agree to go directly to graduate school in the state.

Eligibility To be nominated for this award, a student must 1) have earned a baccalaureate degree at a public or private college or university in Ohio; 2) be a U.S. citizen; and 3) be enrolled or intend to enroll as a full-time graduate or professional program student at an eligible Ohio institution of higher learning within the same year as receiving the bachelor's degree. Selection is based on undergraduate GPA, graduate or professional examination scores and percentile rankings, a written essay, letters of recommendation, and an interview. Financial need is not considered.

Financial data The stipend is $3,500 each year.

Duration 2 years.

Additional information Residents of other states who receive this award are granted Ohio residency status. This program was established in 1986. Recipients must attend graduate school on a full-time basis.

Number awarded Varies each year. Generally, at least 1 of these fellowships is awarded to a student from each nominating undergraduate institution. Recently, 113 students received these fellowships.

Deadline February of each year.

[490]
ONCOLOGY PRACTICE ALLIANCE SCHOLARSHIP

American College of Medical Practice Executives
Attn: ACMPE Scholarship Fund Inc.
104 Inverness Terrace East
Englewood, CO 80112-5306
(303) 799-1111, ext. 232   Toll-free: (877) ASK-MGMA
Fax: (303) 643-4439   E-mail: acmpe@mgma.com
Web: www.mgma.com/academics/scholar.cfm

Summary To provide financial assistance to residents of Ohio and West Virginia who are working on an undergraduate or graduate degree in health care management related to hematology or oncology.

Eligibility This program is open to full-time students working on an undergraduate or graduate degree in a program relevant to medical practice management (e.g., public health, business administration, health care administration) with a specialty in oncology or hematology. Students working on a degree in medicine, physical therapy, nursing, or other clinically-related professions are not eligible. Applicants must have been residents of Ohio or West Virginia for at least 12 months prior to applying. They must submit a letter describing their career goals and objectives related to medical practice management; a resume; 3 reference letters commenting on their performance, character, potential to succeed, and need for scholarship support; and either documentation indicating acceptance into an undergraduate or graduate program or academic transcripts indicating undergraduate or graduate work completed to date.

Financial data The stipend is at least $1,000. Funds are paid directly to the recipient's college or university.

Duration 1 year.

Additional information This program is managed by Scholarship Program Administrators, Inc. 1201 Eighth Avenue South, P.O. Box 23737, Nashville, TN 27202-3737, (615) 320-3149, (800) 310-4053, Fax: (615) 320-3151, E-mail: info@spaprog.com.

Number awarded 1 each year.

Deadline April of each year.

[491]
ONS FOUNDATION DOCTORAL SCHOLARSHIPS

Oncology Nursing Society
Attn: ONS Foundation
125 Enterprise Drive
Pittsburgh, PA 15275-1214
(412) 859-6100, ext. 8503   Toll-free: (866) 257-4ONS
Fax: (412) 859-6160   E-mail: foundation@ons.org
Web: www.ons.org/awards/foundawards/doctoral.shtml

Summary To provide financial assistance to registered nurses interested in pursuing doctoral studies in oncology nursing.

Eligibility Candidates must be registered nurses with a demonstrated interest in and commitment to oncology nursing; be enrolled in or applying to a doctoral nursing degree program or related program; and never have received a doctoral scholarship from this sponsor. Along with their application, they must submit brief essays on why they chose their doctoral program; the courses and clinical experience of the program that are related to cancer nursing; their research area of interest and plans for a dissertation; their professional goals and their relationship to the advancement of oncology nursing; and how the doctoral program will assist them in achieving their goals.

Financial data The stipend is $3,000.

Duration 1 year; nonrenewable.

Additional information This program began in 1991. At the end of each year of scholarship participation, recipients must submit a summary of their educational activities. Applications must be accompanied by a $5 fee.

Number awarded 1 or more each year.

Deadline January of each year.

[492]
OREGON DECEASED OR DISABLED PUBLIC SAFETY OFFICER GRANT PROGRAM

Oregon Student Assistance Commission
Attn: Grants and Scholarships Division
1500 Valley River Drive, Suite 100
Eugene, OR 97401-2130
(541) 687-7466   Toll-free: (800) 452-8807, ext. 7466
Fax: (541) 687-7419
E-mail: awardinfo@mercury.osac.state.or.us
Web: www.ossc.state.or.us/grants.html

Summary To provide financial assistance for college or graduate school to the children of disabled or deceased Oregon peace officers.

Eligibility This program is open to the natural, adopted, or stepchildren of Oregon public safety officers (fire fighters, state fire marshals, chief deputy fire marshals, deputy state fire marshals, police chiefs, police officers, sheriffs, deputy sheriffs, county adult parole and probation officers, correction officers, and investigators of the Criminal Justice Division of the Department of Justice) who, in the line of duty, were killed or disabled. Applicants must be enrolled or planning to enroll as a full-time undergraduate student at a public or private college or university in Oregon. Children of deceased officers are also eligible for graduate study. Financial need must be demonstrated.

Financial data At a public 2- or 4-year college or university, the amount of the award is equal to the cost of tuition and fees. At an eligible private college, the award amount is equal to the cost of tuition and fees at the University of Oregon.

Duration 1 year; may be renewed for up to 3 additional years of undergraduate study, if the student maintains satisfactory academic progress and demonstrates continued financial need. Children of deceased public safety officers may receive support for 12 quarters of graduate study.

Number awarded Varies each year.

[493]
OREGON OCCUPATIONAL SAFETY AND HEALTH DIVISION WORKERS MEMORIAL SCHOLARSHIPS

Oregon Student Assistance Commission
Attn: Grants and Scholarships Division
1500 Valley River Drive, Suite 100
Eugene, OR 97401-2146
(541) 687-7395   Toll-free: (800) 452-8807, ext. 7395
Fax: (541) 687-7419
E-mail: awardinfo@mercury.osac.state.or.us
Web: www.osac.state.or.us

Summary To provide financial assistance for undergraduate or graduate education to the children and spouses of disabled or deceased workers in Oregon.

Eligibility This program is open to residents of Oregon who are U.S. citizens or permanent residents. Applicants must be high school seniors or graduates who 1) are dependents or spouses of an Oregon worker who has suffered permanent total disability on the job; or 2) are receiving, or have received, fatality benefits as dependents or spouses of a worker fatally injured in Oregon. Selection is based on financial need and an essay of up to 500 words on "How has the injury or death of your parent or spouse affected or influenced your decision to further your education?"

Financial data Stipend amounts vary; recently, they were at least $4,786.

Duration 1 year.

Number awarded 1 or more each year.

Deadline February of each year.

[494]
OSCAR AND MILDRED LARSON AWARD

Vasa Order of America
Attn: Vice Grand Master
3236 Berkeley Avenue
Cleveland Heights, OH 44118-2055
(216) 371-5141   E-mail: rolf.bergman@sbcglobal.net
Web: www.vasaorder.com

Summary To provide financial assistance for college or graduate school to students of Swedish heritage.

Eligibility Applicants must be Swedish born or of Swedish ancestry; residents of the United States, Canada, or Sweden; and enrolled or accepted as full-time undergraduate or graduate students in an accredited 4-year college or university in the United States. Membership in Vasa Order of America is not required. Selection is based on a grade transcript, letters of recommendation from school and local Vasa lodge officials, and an essay of up to 1,000 words on a topic related to Vasa.

Financial data The stipend is $3,000 per year.

Duration 1 year; may be renewed up to 3 additional years.

Additional information Vasa Order of America is a Swedish American fraternal organization incorporated in 1899.

Number awarded 1 each year.

Deadline February of each year.

[495]
P.A. MARGARONIS SCHOLARSHIPS

American Hellenic Educational Progressive Association
Attn: AHEPA Educational Foundation
1909 Q Street, N.W., Suite 500
Washington, DC 20009
(202) 232-6300   Fax: (202) 232-2140
E-mail: ahepa@ahepa.org
Web: www.ahepa.org

Summary To provide financial assistance to undergraduate and graduate students of Hellenic heritage.

Eligibility Applicants must be of Hellenic heritage (although their ancestry does not need to be 100% Greek) and currently enrolled or planning to enroll as undergraduate or graduate students. High school seniors must submit their most recent official transcript as well as SAT or ACT scores; college freshmen and sophomores must submit high school transcripts, SAT or ACT scores, and their most recent college transcript; college juniors and seniors must submit their most recent college transcript; graduate students must submit college transcripts, GRE or MCAT scores (if available), and their most recent graduate school transcript. Along with their application, they must also submit a 500-word biographical essay. Selection is based on academic achievement; extracurricular, personal, and volunteer activities; athletic achievements; work experience; and financial need.

Financial data   Stipends range from $500 to $2,000 per year.

Duration   1 year.

Additional information   A processing fee of $20 must accompany each application.

Number awarded   Varies each year. Recently, 14 of these scholarships were awarded: 6 to graduate students and 8 to undergraduates.

Deadline   March of each year.

[496]
PALMER CARRIER DOCTORAL SCHOLARSHIP
American Association of Nurse Anesthetists
Attn: AANA Foundation
222 South Prospect Avenue
Park Ridge, IL 60068-4001
(847) 692-7050, ext. 1171   Fax: (847) 692-7137
E-mail: foundation@aana.com
Web: www.aana.com/foundation/default.asp

Summary   To provide financial assistance to members of the American Association of Nurse Anesthetists (AANA) who are working on a doctoral degree.

Eligibility   This program is open to members of the association who are certified or recertified CRNAs working on a doctoral degree. Applicants must have a long-term goal to remain in a leadership capacity in education and/or research, be actively involved at the state or national level in the profession of nurse anesthesia, and demonstrate a commitment to furthering the profession of nurse anesthesia. Preference is given to applicants who have been advanced to candidacy in their program. Along with their application, they must submit a curriculum vitae; a 250-word essay on their current involvement in nurse anesthesia education, practice, or research and how funding will enhance their education and professional goals; 2 letters of reference; and documentation of the course work they have completed in their doctoral program.

Financial data   The stipend is $1,000 per year.

Duration   1 academic year.

Additional information   This program was established in 2001.

Number awarded   1 each year.

Deadline   May of each year.

[497]
PALMER CARRIER STUDENT SCHOLARSHIP
American Association of Nurse Anesthetists
Attn: AANA Foundation
222 South Prospect Avenue
Park Ridge, IL 60068-4001
(847) 692-7050, ext. 1171   Fax: (847) 692-7137
E-mail: foundation@aana.com
Web: www.aana.com/foundation/default.asp

Summary   To provide financial assistance to members of the American Association of Nurse Anesthetists (AANA) who are interested in obtaining further education.

Eligibility   This program is open to members of the association who are currently enrolled in an accredited nurse anesthesia education program. First-year students must have completed 6 months of nurse anesthesia classes; second-year students must

have completed 12 months of nurse anesthesia classes. Along with their application, they must submit a 200-word essay describing why they have chosen nurse anesthesia as a profession and their professional goals for the future. Financial need is also considered in the selection process. Preference is given to second-year students in Illinois.

Financial data   The stipend is $1,000 per year.

Duration   1 academic year.

Additional information   The application processing fee is $25.

Number awarded   1 each year.

Deadline   March of each year.

[498]
PAMELA STINSON KIDD MEMORIAL DOCTORAL SCHOLARSHIP
Emergency Nurses Association
Attn: ENA Foundation
915 Lee Street
Des Plaines, IL 60016-6569
(847) 460-4100   Toll-free: (800) 900-9659, ext. 4100
Fax: (847) 460-4004   E-mail: foundation@ena.org
Web: www.ena.org/foundation/grants

Summary   To provide financial assistance for doctoral study to nurses who are members of the Emergency Nurses Association (ENA).

Eligibility   This program is open to nurses (R.N.) who are working on a doctoral degree in emergency nursing. Applicants must have been members of the association for at least 12 months. They must submit a 1-page statement on their professional and educational goals and how this scholarship will help them attain those goals. Selection is based on content and clarity of the goal statement (45%), professional association involvement (45%), and GPA (10%).

Financial data   The stipend is $10,000.

Duration   1 year; nonrenewable.

Number awarded   1 each year.

Deadline   May of each year.

[499]
PATIENT ADVOCATE FOUNDATION SCHOLARSHIPS FOR SURVIVORS
Patient Advocate Foundation
Attn: Vice President of Special Programs
700 Thimble Shoals Boulevard, Suite 200
Newport News, VA 23606
Toll-free: (800) 532-5274   Fax: (757) 873-8999
E-mail: help@patientadvocate.org
Web: www.patientadvocate.org

Summary   To provide financial assistance for college or graduate school to students seeking to initiate or complete a course of study that has been interrupted or delayed by a diagnosis of cancer or other life threatening disease.

Eligibility   This program is open to students working full time on a 2-year, 4-year, or advanced degree with a GPA of 3.0 or higher. The college or graduate education of applicants must have been interrupted or delayed by a diagnosis of cancer or other life threatening, chronic, or debilitating disease. They must be able to demonstrate that their course of study will make them immediately employable after graduation. Along with their application, they must submit a 1,000-word essay on why they have chosen to further their education, how the illness has affected their family and their decision to continue their education, and how they feel they can help others by earning their degree. Financial need is also considered in the selection process.

Financial data The stipend is $2,000. Funds are paid directly to the college or university to help cover tuition and other fee costs. The cost of books is not included.

Duration 1 year; recipients may reapply.

Additional information This program includes the Cheryl Grimmel Award and the Monica Bailes Award. Support has come from a variety of sources, including Pfizer, Inc., AstraZeneca Pharmaceuticals, Aventis Pharmaceuticals, GlaxoSmithKline, and Novartis Oncology. Students must complete 20 hours of community service during each year they receive support.

Number awarded Varies each year; recently, 10 of these scholarships were awarded.

Deadline April of each year.

[500]
PATTI LABELLE MEDICAL STUDENT SCHOLARSHIP

National Medical Fellowships, Inc.
Attn: Scholarship Program
5 Hanover Square, 15th Floor
New York, NY 10004
(212) 483-8880   Fax: (212) 483-8897
E-mail: info@nmfonline.org
Web: www.nmf-online.org

Summary To provide financial assistance to African American medical students.

Eligibility This program is open to African American medical students who are U.S. citizens in their first, second, or third year at an accredited M.D. or D.O. degree-granting school in the United States. Only nominations are accepted. All nominees must submit a personal essay on their motivation for a career in medicine and career plans over the next 10 years. Selection is based on financial need, community involvement, academic achievement, and potential for responsible role in medicine.

Financial data The stipend is $5,000.

Duration 1 year.

Additional information This program is sponsored by the National Medical Association (NMA).

Number awarded 1 each year.

Deadline April of each year.

[501]
PAUL AND DAISY SOROS FELLOWSHIP PROGRAM FOR NEW AMERICANS

Paul and Daisy Soros Fellowships for New Americans
Attn: Program Officer
400 West 59th Street
New York, NY 10019
(212) 547-6926   Fax: (212) 548-4623
E-mail: pdsoros_fellows@sorosny.org
Web: www.pdsoros.org

Summary To provide funding for graduate study in the United States to new Americans.

Eligibility This program defines new Americans as individuals who 1) have a Green Card, 2) have been naturalized as a U.S. citizen, or 3) are the children of parents who are both naturalized citizens. Applicants must be younger than 30 years of age. Preference is given to graduating college students who will be entering graduate school, although students who are completing the first or second year of graduate study are also eligible; graduate students in their third or fourth year of work are not eligible. Appli-

cants may be studying any academic discipline in the arts (including the fine and performing arts), humanities, social sciences, or sciences. Candidates must demonstrate evidence of at least 2 of the following attributes: 1) creativity, originality, and initiative; 2) accomplishment, demonstrated by activity that has required drive and sustained effort; and 3) a commitment to the values expressed in the U.S. Constitution and the Bill of Rights.

Financial data Fellows receive an annual stipend of $20,000 (paid directly to the fellow in 3 installments) and a grant equal to half the tuition at the institution the fellow attends (to a maximum of $16,000) paid directly to the institution.

Duration Up to 2 years; may be renewed for a third year if necessary and appropriate.

Additional information This program was established in 1997.

Number awarded 30 each year.

Deadline October of each year.

[502]
PAUL AND ELLEN RUCKES SCHOLARSHIP

American Foundation for the Blind
Attn: Scholarship Committee
11 Penn Plaza, Suite 300
New York, NY 10001
(212) 502-7661   Toll-free: (800) AFB-LINE
Fax: (212) 502-7771   TDD: (212) 502-7662
E-mail: afbinfo@afb.net
Web: www.afb.org/scholarships.asp

Summary To provide financial assistance to visually impaired students who wish to work on a graduate or undergraduate degree in engineering or computer, physical, or life sciences.

Eligibility This program is open to visually impaired undergraduate or graduate students who are U.S. citizens working on a degree in engineering or the computer, physical, or life sciences. Legal blindness is not required. Along with their application, they must submit an essay that includes the field of study they are pursuing and why they have chosen it; their educational and personal goals; their work experience; any extracurricular activities with which they have been involved, including those in school, religious organizations, and the community; and how they intend to use scholarship monies that may be awarded.

Financial data The stipend is $1,000.

Duration 1 year.

Number awarded 1 each year.

Deadline April of each year.

[503]
PAUL PRIVITERA SCHOLARSHIP

American Association of Nurse Anesthetists
Attn: AANA Foundation
222 South Prospect Avenue
Park Ridge, IL 60068-4001
(847) 692-7050, ext. 1171   Fax: (847) 692-7137
E-mail: foundation@aana.com
Web: www.aana.com/foundation/default.asp

Summary To provide financial assistance to members of the American Association of Nurse Anesthetists who are interested in obtaining further education.

Eligibility This program is open to members of the association who are currently enrolled in an accredited nurse anesthesia education program. Applicants must be second-year students who have completed 12 months of nurse anesthesia classes. Along with their application, they must submit a 200-word essay describing why they have chosen nurse anesthesia as a profession and their professional goals for the future. Financial need is also considered in the selection process.

Financial data The stipend is $1,000 per year.

Duration 1 academic year.

Additional information The application processing fee is $25.

Number awarded 1 each year.

Deadline March of each year.

[504]
PAULINA L. SORG SCHOLARSHIPS

Hawai'i Community Foundation
Attn: Scholarship Department
1164 Bishop Street, Suite 800
Honolulu, HI 96813
(808) 566-5570   Toll-free: (888) 731-3863
Fax: (808) 521-6286   E-mail: scholarships@hcf-hawaii.org
Web: www.hawaiicommunityfoundation.org

Summary To provide financial assistance to Hawaii residents who are interested in preparing for a career in physical therapy.

Eligibility This program is open to Hawaii residents who are studying physical therapy as full-time juniors, seniors, or graduate students. They must be able to demonstrate academic achievement (GPA of 2.7 or higher), good moral character, and financial need. In addition to filling out the standard application form, applicants must write a short statement indicating their reasons for attending college, their planned course of study, and their career goals.

Financial data The amounts of the awards depend on the availability of funds and the need of the recipient; recently, stipends averaged $1,000.

Duration 1 year.

Additional information Recipients may attend college in Hawaii or on the mainland.

Number awarded Varies each year; recently, 5 of these scholarships were awarded.

Deadline February of each year.

[505]
PDEF PROFESSIONAL DEVELOPMENT SCHOLARSHIP

Society of Nuclear Medicine
Attn: Committee on Awards
1850 Samuel Morse Drive
Reston, VA 20190-5316
(703) 708-9000, ext. 1255   Fax: (703) 708-9020
E-mail: grantinfo@snm.org
Web: www.snm.org

Summary To provide financial support to students working on a graduate degree in nuclear medicine.

Eligibility This program is open to students working on a master's or doctoral degree in a field related to nuclear medicine. Applicants must have worked in the nuclear medicine profession for at least 1 year during the past 5 years in a clinical or didactic setting. They must be able to demonstrate financial need and U.S. citizenship or permanent resident status. Along with their application, they must submit a 2-page essay on their professional achievements, their career and educational goals, and how their degree will advance their career goals in the field of nuclear medicine.

Financial data The stipend is $5,000.

Duration 1 year; may be renewed 1 additional year.

Additional information This program is supported by corporate sponsors of the Professional Development and Education Fund (PDEF) of the Society of Nuclear Medicine Technologist Section.

Number awarded 1 each year.

Deadline October of each year.

[506]
PENNSYLVANIA KNIGHTS TEMPLAR EDUCATIONAL FOUNDATION SCHOLARSHIPS

Pennsylvania Masonic Youth Foundation
Attn: Educational Endowment Fund
1244 Bainbridge Road
Elizabethtown, PA 17022-9423
(717) 367-1536   Toll-free: (800) 266-8424 (within PA)
Fax: (717) 367-0616   E-mail: pyf@pagrandlodge.org
Web: www.pagrandlodge.org/pyf/scholar/index.html

Summary To provide financial assistance for college or graduate school to residents of Pennsylvania.

Eligibility This program is open to residents of Pennsylvania who are working on a 2-year college, trade school, 4-year college, or graduate degree. Applicants are considered without regard to age, race, religion, national origin, sex, or Masonic ties or affiliations.

Financial data The stipend varies.

Duration 1 year.

Additional information Further information is also available from Knights Templar Educational Foundation, Office of Walter G. DePrefontaine, Eminent Grand Recorder, Masonic Temple, One North Broad Street, Philadelphia, PA 19107-2598, (215) 567-5836.

Number awarded 1 or more each year.

Deadline March of each year.

[507]
PENS ACADEMIC EDUCATION SCHOLARSHIPS

Pediatric Endocrinology Nursing Society
Attn: President-Elect
7794 Grow Drive
Pensacola, FL 32514
(850) 484-5223   Toll-free: (877) 936-7367
Fax: (850) 484-8762   E-mail: pens@peutzamc.com
Web: www.pens.org

Summary To provide financial assistance for further education to members of the Pediatric Endocrinology Nursing Society (PENS).

Eligibility This program is open to R.N.s currently employed in pediatric endocrine nursing who have been members of PENS for at least 3 years. Applicants must be working on a degree in nursing; preference is given to those working on a B.S.N. degree and to first-time applicants. Along with their application, they must submit a copy of their R.N. license card, curriculum vitae or resume, statement of fees from the college or university, transcript of grades or (if beginning course work) a letter of acceptance, a list of professional organizations to which they belong, information on PENS activities in which they have participated, a list of volunteer or community service, and documentation of financial need.

Financial data The stipend is $1,000 per year.

Duration 1 year. Members are eligible for 2 scholarships in a 5-year period.

Number awarded Varies each year.

Deadline March or August of each year.

[508]
P.E.O. SCHOLAR AWARDS

P.E.O. Sisterhood
Attn: Executive Office
3700 Grand Avenue
Des Moines, IA 50312-2899
(515) 255-3153   Fax: (515) 255-3820
Web: www.peointernational.org

Summary To provide financial assistance for graduate education to women in the United States or Canada.

Eligibility This program is open to women who are working on a graduate degree or research as full-time students at universities in the United States or Canada. Applicants must be within 2 years of achieving their educational goal with at least 1 full academic year remaining. They must be sponsored by a local P.E.O. chapter. Selection is based on academic excellence and achievement, career goals, recommendations, and potential of applicant to make a significant contribution to her field; financial need is not considered.

Financial data The stipend is $10,000.

Duration 1 year; nonrenewable.

Additional information This program was established in 1991 by the Women's Philanthropic Educational Organization (P.E.O.).

Number awarded 75 each year.

Deadline November of each year.

[509]
PERFUSION STUDENT SCHOLARSHIP

American Society of Extra-Corporeal Technology, Inc.
Attn: AmSECT Foundation
2209 Dickens Road
P.O. Box 11086
Richmond, VA 23230-1086
(804) 565-6363   Fax: (804) 282-0090
E-mail: AmSECT@amsect.org
Web: www.amsect.org

Summary To provide financial assistance to student members of the American Society of Extra-Corporeal Technology (AmSECT) who are enrolled in a perfusion training program.

Eligibility This program is open to student members of the society who are enrolled in (or accepted at) an accredited perfusion training program. Applicants must have completed at least 1 quarter of the required course work and have at least a 2.75 GPA. They must submit 250-word essays on how they would improve AmSECT and how they could improve the perfusion profession. Financial need is not considered in the selection process.

Financial data The stipend is $1,000 per year.

Duration 1 year.

Number awarded 1 each year.

Deadline November of each year.

[510]
PETER CONNACHER MEMORIAL TRUST FUND

Oregon Student Assistance Commission
Attn: Grants and Scholarships Division
1500 Valley River Drive, Suite 100
Eugene, OR 97401-2146
(541) 687-7395   Toll-free: (800) 452-8807, ext. 7395
Fax: (541) 687-7419
E-mail: awardinfo@mercury.osac.state.or.us
Web: www.osac.state.or.us

Summary To provide financial assistance for college or graduate school to ex-prisoners of war and their descendants.

Eligibility Applicants must be American citizens who 1) were military or civilian prisoners of war or 2) are the descendants of ex-prisoners of war. They may be undergraduate or graduate students. A copy of the ex-prisoner of war's discharge papers from the U.S. armed forces must accompany the application. In addition, written proof of POW status must be submitted, along with a statement of the relationship between the applicant and the ex-prisoner of war (father, grandfather, etc.). Selection is based on academic record and financial need. Preference is given to Oregon residents or their dependents.

Financial data The stipend amount varies; recently, it was at least $1,150.

Duration 1 year; may be renewed for up to 3 additional years for undergraduate students or 2 additional years for graduate students. Renewal is dependent on evidence of continued financial need and satisfactory academic progress.

Additional information This program is administered by the Oregon Student Assistance Commission (OSAC) with funds provided by the Oregon Community Foundation, 1221 S.W. Yamhill, Suite 100, Portland, OR 97205, (503) 227-6846, Fax: (503) 274-7771. Funds are also provided by the Columbia River Chapter of the American Ex-prisoners of War, Inc. Recipients must attend college on a full-time basis.

Number awarded Varies each year; recently, 4 of these scholarships were awarded.

Deadline February of each year.

[511]
PFIZER EPILEPSY SCHOLARSHIP AWARD

Pfizer Inc.
c/o Eden Communications Group
515 Valley Street, Suite 200
Maplewood, NJ 07040
(973) 275-6518   Toll-free: (800) AWARD-PF
Fax: (973) 275-9792
E-mail: info@epilepsy-scholarship.com
Web: www.epilepsy-scholarship.com

Summary To provide financial assistance for undergraduate or graduate study to individuals with epilepsy.

Eligibility Applicants must be under a physician's care for epilepsy (taking prescribed medication) and must submit an application with 2 letters of recommendation (1 from the physician) and verification of academic status. They must be high school seniors entering college in the fall; college freshmen, sophomores, or juniors continuing in the fall; or college seniors planning to enter graduate school in the fall. Along with their application, they must submit a 250-word essay on something of direct personal importance to them as a person with epilepsy. Selection is based on demonstrated achievement in academic and extracurricular activities; financial need is not considered.

Financial data The stipend is $3,000.

Duration 1 year; nonrenewable.
Number awarded 25 each year.
Deadline February of each year.

[512]
PHARMACY STUDENT SCHOLARSHIP PROGRAM

National Association of Chain Drug Stores
Attn: NACDS Foundation
413 North Lee Street
Alexandria, VA 22314
(703) 837-4276   Fax: (703) 683-3587
E-mail: foundation@nacds.org
Web: www.nacdsfoundation.org

Summary To provide financial assistance to pharmacy students.

Eligibility This program is open to students working full time on a Pharm.D. degree at an accredited U.S. college or school of pharmacy. Applicants must have completed at least 1 year of professional study with a GPA of "C" or better. They must have experience in chain community pharmacy and a desire to prepare for a career in chain community pharmacy; experience may be current or recent employment. Along with their application, they must submit a letter explaining their interest and career goals in chain community pharmacy practice. Selection is based on that letter, a recommendation from a chain pharmacy employer, their credentials (including leadership activities and professional and community involvement), and chain community pharmacy experience.

Financial data Stipends are $2,500 (for the named scholarships) or $2,000.

Duration 1 year.

Additional information This program currently includes 2 named scholarship programs (each of which awards 2 scholarships): the Robert J. Bolger Scholarship (established in 2002) and the Taro Research Foundation Scholarship (established in 2003).

Number awarded Varies each year. Recently, 37 of these scholarships were awarded: 4 at $2,500 and 33 at $2,000.

Deadline October of each year.

[513]
PHI KAPPA PHI GRADUATE FELLOWSHIPS

Phi Kappa Phi
7576 Goodwood Boulevard
P.O. Box 16000
Baton Rouge, LA 70893-6000
(225) 388-4917   Toll-free: (800) 804-9880
Fax: (225) 706-1062   E-mail: fellows@phikappaphi.org
Web: www.phikappaphi.org

Summary To support first-year graduate or professional study for members of Phi Kappa Phi honor society.

Eligibility Applicants must be active members of the society; individuals selected for membership but not yet initiated are also eligible. Applicants must have applied or been accepted for an advanced degree in a graduate or professional school (preferably in the United States). Preference is given to students working on a doctorate or other advanced professional degree. Applications must be filed with the student's local chapter. Each chapter selects their most worthy applicant and forwards that application to the national office. Selection is based on undergraduate academic achievement; service and leadership experience, on and off campus; letters of recommendation; and a personal statement regarding career goals.

Financial data Stipends are either $5,000 or $2,000.

Duration Support is offered for the first year of graduate/professional study only (normally to be undertaken within a year following receipt of the baccalaureate degree).

Additional information This program includes the following named awards: the Slater Fellow (preference to applicants whose undergraduate major is in the biological sciences), the Yoerger Presidential Fellow (reserved for a student in the basic science disciplines, such as agriculture or engineering), the Kathleen Greey Fellow (reserved for a student whose undergraduate field is other than the basic sciences), the Marjorie Schoch Fellow (for a top-ranking applicant), the Alfred M. Wolfe Fellow (for a student majoring in agriculture, classical Latin, ancient Greek, or English), and the Walter and Adelheid Hohenstein Fellows (for a top-ranking applicant from each of the 5 regions). Recipients are expected to attend graduate school on a full-time basis.

Number awarded 100 each year: 60 at $5,000 and 40 at $2,000.

Deadline Applications must be submitted to chapters by the end of January of each year; chapter nominations must reach the national office before the end of February of each year.

[514]
PHI LAMBDA SIGMA–GLAXOSMITHKLINE–AFPE FIRST YEAR GRADUATE SCHOLARSHIP

American Foundation for Pharmaceutical Education
Attn: Grants Manager
One Church Street, Suite 202
Rockville, MD 20850-4158
(301) 738-2160   Fax: (301) 738-2161
E-mail: info@afpenet.org
Web: www.afpenet.org/firstyr_phi_lambda.htm

Summary To provide financial assistance to members of Phi Lambda Sigma who are interested in pursuing a Ph.D. in a college of pharmacy graduate program.

Eligibility This program is open to Phi Lambda Sigma members who are in the final year of a pharmacy B.S. or Pharm.D. program or who hold a B.S. or Pharm.D. degree. Applicants must submit 2 letters of recommendation, the name of the graduate school they plan to attend, a 1- or 2-page statement on their reasons for attending graduate school, a list of special honors and awards in high school and college, and official transcripts and achievement test scores. U.S. citizenship or permanent resident status is required.

Financial data The award is $7,500. Funds may be used for any purpose agreed upon by the recipient and faculty sponsor, including a student stipend, laboratory supplies or materials, travel, etc.

Duration 1 year.

Additional information This scholarship program is administered by the American Foundation for Pharmaceutical Education (AFPE) and Phi Lambda Sigma, with additional funding provided by GlaxoSmithKline. Additional information is available from Mary Euler, Phi Lambda Sigma Executive Director, University of Missouri at Kansas City, 5005 Rockhill Road, Kansas City, MO 64110. No funds may be used for indirect costs by the institution.

Number awarded 1 each year.

Deadline January of each year.

[515]
PHILLIP R. LEE SCHOLARSHIP

California Rural Indian Health Board, Inc.
Attn: Administrative Services Department
4400 Auburn Boulevard, Second Floor
Sacramento, CA 95841
(916) 929-9761   Toll-free: (800) 274-4288
Fax: (916) 929-7246   E-mail: shelley.whitebear@ihs.gov
Web: www.crihb.org/scholarship.htm

Summary To provide financial assistance to California Indians working on an undergraduate or graduate degree in a health-related field.

Eligibility This program is open to California Indians who have completed at least 1 semester of undergraduate or graduate study at an accredited college or vocational program. Applicants must be enrolled in a health or related field of study and have a GPA of 3.0 or higher. They must submit tribal certification from their tribe or the U.S. Bureau of Indian Affairs. Financial need is considered in the selection process.

Financial data Stipends range from $300 to $2,500.

Duration 1 year; may be renewed as long as the recipient maintains a GPA of 3.0 or higher.

Number awarded Varies; a total of $25,000 is available to this program each year.

Deadline February or June of each year.

[516]
PHONAK/AFA SCHOOL-BASED PRACTITIONER SCHOLARSHIPS

Audiology Foundation of America
Attn: Scholarship Committee
8 North Third Street, Suite 406
Lafayette, IN 47901-1247
(765) 743-6AUD   Fax: (765) 743-9AUD
E-mail: info-afa@audfound.org
Web: www.audfound.org/index.cfm?pageID=49

Summary To provide financial assistance to school-based audiologists interested in working on a doctoral degree.

Eligibility This program is open to licensed audiology practitioners with at least 4 years of post-master's or doctoral experience. Applicants must be employed (full or part time) as a birth through 12+ school-based practitioner. They must be applying to, but not yet enrolled in, a distance-learning doctor of audiology (Au.D.) program. Citizenship or permanent resident status of the United States and its territories or Canada is required.

Financial data The stipend is $1,000. Funds are disbursed to the Au.D. program after verification of enrollment by the recipient.

Duration 1 year.

Additional information This program, established in 2005, is sponsored by Phonak AG of Switzerland.

Number awarded 11 each year.

Deadline March of each year.

[517]
PHYLLIS V. ROBERTS SCHOLARSHIPS

General Federation of Women's Clubs of Virginia
Attn: Scholarships/Fellowships/Loan Committee
513 Forest Avenue
P.O. Box 8750
Richmond, VA 23226
(804) 288-3724   Toll-free: (800) 699-8392
Fax: (804) 288-0341   E-mail: h.vfwcofgfwc@verizon.net
Web: www.gfwcvirginia.org

Summary To provide financial assistance to residents of Virginia who are working on a graduate degree at a college or university in the state.

Eligibility This program is open to residents of Virginia who are enrolled in graduate school at a college or university in the state. The field of study changes annually. Applicants must have an undergraduate GPA of 3.0 or higher. Selection is based on 3 letters of recommendation (1 of a general nature, 2 from recent professors); a short statement of reasons for choosing a graduate degree in the designated field; and a resume of educational and employment history, community service, and awards received.

Financial data The stipend is $1,000. Funds are paid to the college or university the recipient attends.

Duration 1 year.

Additional information Each year, the new administration of the sponsoring organization selects the field of study for that year.

Number awarded 6 each year.

Deadline March of each year.

[518]
PHYSICIAN ASSISTANT FOUNDATION SCHOLARSHIPS

American Academy of Physician Assistants
Attn: Physician Assistant Foundation
950 North Washington Street
Alexandria, VA 22314-1552
(703) 519-5686   Fax: (703) 684-1924
E-mail: aapa@aapa.org
Web: www.aapa.org/paf/pafprog.html

Summary To provide financial assistance to student members of the American Academy of Physician Assistants (AAPA).

Eligibility This program is open to AAPA student members attending a physician assistant program accredited by the Commission on Accreditation of Allied Health Education Programs. Applicants must have entered the professional phase of the program. Selection is based on financial need, academic achievement, extracurricular activities, and future goals.

Financial data Stipends are $5,000, $3,000, or $2,000.

Duration 1 year; nonrenewable.

Additional information This program, established in 1989, is sponsored by the following firms: AstraZeneca Pharmaceuticals, Eli Lilly and Company, GlaxoSmithKline, McNeil Consumer and Specialty Pharmaceuticals, Pfizer Inc., Procter and Gamble Pharmaceuticals, Purdue Pharma, Roche Pharmaceuticals, and Wyeth Pharmaceuticals.

Number awarded Varies each year; recently, 35 of these scholarships were awarded.

Deadline January of each year.

[519]
PIONEER IN PERFUSION SCHOLARSHIP

American Society of Extra-Corporeal Technology, Inc.
Attn: AmSECT Foundation
2209 Dickens Road
P.O. Box 11086
Richmond, VA 23230-1086
(804) 565-6363   Fax: (804) 282-0090
E-mail: AmSECT@amsect.org
Web: www.amsect.org

Summary To provide financial assistance to student members of the American Society of Extra-Corporeal Technology (AmSECT) who are enrolled in a perfusion training program.

Eligibility This program is open to student members of the society who are enrolled in (or accepted at) an accredited perfusion training program. Applicants must have completed at least half of the required course work and have at least a 2.75 GPA. They must submit 1) 250-word essays on how they would improve AmSECT and how they could improve the perfusion profession, and 2) a 1,000-word essay on myocardial perfusion. Financial need is not considered in the selection process.

Financial data The stipend is $1,500 per year.

Duration 1 year.

Additional information The funds for this program are provided by Quest Medical, Inc.

Number awarded 1 each year.

Deadline November of each year.

[520]
PISACANO SCHOLARS LEADERSHIP PROGRAM

Pisacano Leadership Foundation
Attn: Executive Director
2228 Young Drive
Lexington, KY 40505-4294
(859) 269-5626   Toll-free: (888) 995-5700
Fax: (859) 335-7501
Web: www.fpleaders.org

Summary To offer career development opportunities and scholarship funding to medical students and physicians interested in becoming leaders in the field of family practice.

Eligibility This program is open to medical students entering their fourth year. Applicants must be able to demonstrate a strong commitment to the specialty of family practice, leadership qualities, academic achievement, interpersonal skills, communication skills, and involvement in serving others. Along with their application, they must submit a 700-word topical essay on a current issue relevant to the specialty of family practice, including their professional goals and special strengths that will allow them to address that issue. Financial need is not considered in the selection process.

Financial data The maximum scholarship award is $28,000 (up to $7,000 per year for 4 years). Funds are intended to reimburse the scholars a portion of medical school debt incurred until completion of residency.

Duration A portion of the funds are distributed to students during medical school and the remainder of the funds are distributed over the required 3-year residency.

Additional information This program was established in 1991. There is no limitation on the number of applications that may be submitted from a particular medical school. Pisacano Scholars participate in semiannual Leadership Skills Development Symposia and are offered numerous educational programs and mentoring relations with current leaders in the field of family practice.

Examples of these programs are: negotiation skills, problem-based learning, journal writing and peer-review process, evidence based medicine, professional presentation and media skills, and health policy and primary care research. The Pisacano Leadership Foundation is the philanthropic foundation of the American Board of Family Practice, Inc.

Number awarded Up to 15 each year.

Deadline February of each year.

[521]
POINT FOUNDATION SCHOLARSHIPS

Point Foundation
P.O. Box 11210
Chicago, IL 60611
Toll-free: (866) 33-POINT   Fax: (866) 39-POINT
E-mail: info@thepointfoundation.org
Web: www.thepointfoundation.org

Summary To provide financial assistance for college or graduate school to students who have been involved in the lesbian, gay, bisexual, or transgender (LGBT) community.

Eligibility This program is open to citizens of any country who are attending or planning to attend a college or university in the United States to work on an undergraduate or graduate degree. Applicants are not required to be LGBT, but they should have a history of leadership in the LGBT community and plan to be a LGBT leader in the future. Selection is based on academic accomplishment; financial, emotional, and social need; extracurricular activities; personal circumstances; and goals.

Financial data Stipends range from $5,000 to $28,000 per year.

Duration 1 year; may be renewed if the recipient maintains a GPA of 3.5 or higher.

Additional information This program began in 2001. It includes the following named scholarships: the Merle Aronson Scholarship, the Carlos Enrique Cisneros Scholarship (for students at American University in Washington, D.C.), the Walter M. Decker Scholarship, the Bryan L. Knapp Scholarship (for students from the New York City area at Cornell University in Ithaca, New York), the Elsie De Wolfe Scholarship, and the mtvU Scholarship (for students at universities participating in the mtvU program).

Number awarded Varies each year; recently, 20 of these scholarships were awarded.

Deadline February of each year.

[522]
POLONIA FOUNDATION OF OHIO SCHOLARSHIPS

Polonia Foundation of Ohio
Attn: Scholarship Committee
6966 Broadway Avenue
Cleveland, OH 44105
(440) 843-8041

Summary To provide financial assistance for college, medical school, or law school to Ohio residents who are of Polish descent.

Eligibility Eligible to apply for this support are students attending or planning to attend college, law school, or medical school. Applicants must be Ohio residents and of Polish descent. Financial need, academic achievement, and involvement in Polish groups are considered in the selection process.

Financial data The stipend ranges from $750 to $1,500.

Duration 1 year; may be renewed.

Number awarded Approximately 10 to 15 each year; of these, at least 1 is presented to students working on a degree in the following fields: music, law, and family medicine.
Deadline June of each year.

[523]
PORTUGUESE FOUNDATION SCHOLARSHIPS

Portuguese Foundation of Connecticut
Attn: Gabriel R. Serrano, President
86 New Park Avenue
P.O. Box 331441
West Hartford, CT 06133-1441
(860) 236-5514   Fax: (860) 236-5514
E-mail: info@pfict.org
Web: www.pfict.org/scholar.html

Summary To provide financial assistance for college or graduate school to students of Portuguese ancestry in Connecticut.
Eligibility This program is open to residents of Connecticut who are U.S. citizens or permanent residents of Portuguese ancestry. Applicants must be attending, or planning to attend, a 4-year college or university as a full-time undergraduate or full- or part-time graduate student. Along with their application, they must submit an essay describing financial need, an essay detailing proof of Portuguese ancestry and interest in the Portuguese language and culture, 2 letters of recommendation, their high school or college transcripts, a copy of the FAFSA form or their most recent federal income tax return, and their SAT report. Selection is based on financial need and academic record.
Financial data Stipends are at least $1,000 each.
Duration 1 year; recipients may reapply.
Additional information This program started in 1992. Undergraduate recipients must attend school on a full-time basis; graduate students may attend school on a part-time basis. No recipient may receive more than 4 scholarships from the foundation.
Number awarded Varies each year; recently, 4 of these scholarships were awarded.
Deadline March of each year.

[524]
POSSIBLE WOMAN FOUNDATION INTERNATIONAL SCHOLARSHIP

Possible Woman Enterprises
Attn: Possible Woman Foundation International
3475 Oak Valley Road, Suite 3040
P.O. Box 78851
Atlanta, GA 30357
Fax: (404) 869-7202
E-mail: linda@possiblewomanfoundation.org
Web: www.possiblewomanfoundation.org/Home.htm

Summary To provide financial assistance for college or graduate school to women who are at least 25 years old.
Eligibility This program is open to women who are returning to school after a hiatus, changing careers, seeking advancement in their career or work life, or stay-at-home mothers entering the work place and in need of additional education or training. Applicants must be at least 25 years of age and may be at any level of education (high school graduate, some college, 4-year college graduate, graduate school, doctoral). Along with their application, they must submit a 2-page essay on the topic, "How Having the Opportunity for Beginning or Continuing My Academic Education Will Positively Impact My Life." Selection is based on the essay, career and life goals, leadership and participation in community activities, honors and awards received, and financial need.

Financial data The stipend ranges from $3,000 to $5,000.
Duration 1 year; nonrenewable.
Additional information Information is also available from Stacie Shelby, P.O. Box 117740, Carrollton, TX 75011-7740, Fax: (817) 497-2497, E-mail: stacie@possiblewomanfoundation.org.
Number awarded Varies each year; recently, 6 of these scholarships were awarded.
Deadline February of each year.

[525]
POWER SYSTEMS PROFESSIONAL SCHOLARSHIP

National Strength and Conditioning Association
Attn: Grants and Scholarships
1885 Bob Johnson Drive
Colorado Springs, CO 80906
(719) 632-6722, ext. 105   Toll-free: (800) 815-6826
Fax: (719) 632-6367   E-mail: nsca@nsca-lift.org
Web: www.nsca-lift.org/Foundation

Summary To provide financial assistance for undergraduate or graduate study in strength training and conditioning to members of the National Strength and Conditioning Association (NSCA).
Eligibility This program is open to undergraduate and graduate students working as a strength and conditioning coach (student assistant, volunteer, or graduate assistant) in their school's athletic department. Applicants must have been members of the association for at least 1 year. They must be nominated by the head strength coach at their school. Along with their application, they must submit an essay of no more than 500 words explaining their career goals and objectives. Selection is based on scholarship (25 points), strength and conditioning experience (15 points), the essay (15 points), recommendations (5 points), honors and awards (10 points), community involvement (10 points), and NSCA involvement (20 points).
Financial data The stipend is $1,000, to be applied toward tuition.
Additional information The NSCA is a nonprofit organization of strength and conditioning professionals, including coaches, athletic trainers, physical therapists, educators, researchers, and physicians. This program is funded in part by Power Systems, Inc.
Number awarded 1 each year.
Deadline March of each year.

[526]
PREDOCTORAL FELLOWSHIPS IN HEALTH OUTCOMES

Pharmaceutical Research and Manufacturers of America
Attn: PhRMA Foundation
950 F Street, N.W., Suite 300
Washington, DC 20004
(202) 572-7756   Fax: (202) 572-7799
E-mail: foundation@phrma.org
Web: www.phrmafoundation.org

Summary To provide financial assistance to doctoral candidates interested in pursuing research training in health outcomes.
Eligibility Applicants must be enrolled as full-time, in-residence Ph.D. candidates in health outcomes in U.S. schools of medicine, pharmacy, dentistry, or veterinary medicine and starting their thesis research after 2 years of pre-thesis study. Students just starting in graduate school are not eligible. U.S. citizenship or permanent resident status is required. Candidates enrolled in an

M.D./Ph.D. program should not be taking required clinical course work or clerkships during the tenure of the fellowship.

Financial data The grant is $20,000 per year, payable directly to the university on behalf of the fellow. Of the grant award, $500 a year is provided for incidentals directly associated with thesis research preparation.

Duration 1 to 2 years.

Additional information This program is to assist in the predoctoral training of the applicant, not to fund a research project.

Number awarded 1 or 2 each year.

Deadline September of each year.

[527]
PREDOCTORAL FELLOWSHIPS IN PHARMACEUTICS

Pharmaceutical Research and Manufacturers of America
Attn: PhRMA Foundation
950 F Street, N.W., Suite 300
Washington, DC 20004
(202) 572-7756   Fax: (202) 572-7799
E-mail: foundation@phrma.org
Web: www.phrmafoundation.org

Summary To provide financial assistance to doctoral candidates interested in pursuing research training in pharmaceutics.

Eligibility Applicants must have a B.S., M.S., or Pharm.D. degree in pharmacy or a related area, such as chemistry or biology, from an accredited school in the United States. They must be enrolled as full-time, in-residence Ph.D. candidates in pharmaceutics with 2 years or less to complete their degree in a school of pharmacy accredited by the American Council on Pharmaceutical Education. In addition, they must be U.S. citizens or permanent residents and have a firm commitment from a university in the United States for a program of research and training in an area related to pharmaceutics. Students just starting in graduate school are not eligible. For the purposes of this program, pharmaceutics includes basic pharmaceutics, biopharmaceutics, and pharmaceutical technology, but not pharmacokinetics.

Financial data The grant is $20,000 per year, payable directly to the university on behalf of the fellow. Of the grant award, $500 a year is provided for incidentals directly associated with thesis research preparation.

Duration 1 to 2 years.

Additional information This program began in 1987. This program is to assist in the predoctoral training of the applicant, not to fund a research project.

Number awarded Varies each year; recently, 4 of these fellowships were awarded.

Deadline September of each year.

[528]
PREDOCTORAL FELLOWSHIPS IN PHARMACOLOGY AND TOXICOLOGY

Pharmaceutical Research and Manufacturers of America
Attn: PhRMA Foundation
950 F Street, N.W., Suite 300
Washington, DC 20004
(202) 572-7756   Fax: (202) 572-7799
E-mail: foundation@phrma.org
Web: www.phrmafoundation.org

Summary To provide financial assistance to doctoral candidates interested in pursuing research training in pharmacology or toxicology.

Eligibility Applicants must be enrolled as full-time, in-residence Ph.D. candidates in pharmacology or toxicology in U.S. schools of medicine, pharmacy, dentistry, or veterinary medicine and starting their thesis research after 2 years of pre-thesis study. Students just starting in graduate school are not eligible. U.S. citizenship or permanent resident status is required. Candidates enrolled in an M.D./Ph.D. program should not be taking required clinical course work or clerkships during the tenure of the fellowship.

Financial data The grant is $20,000 per year, payable directly to the university on behalf of the fellow. Of the grant award, $500 a year is provided for incidentals directly associated with thesis research preparation.

Duration 1 to 2 years.

Additional information This program began in 1978. This program is to assist in the predoctoral training of the applicant, not to fund a research project.

Number awarded Varies each year; recently, 6 of these fellowships were awarded.

Deadline August of each year.

[529]
PREDOCTORAL FELLOWSHIPS IN THE NEUROSCIENCES

American Psychological Association
Attn: Minority Fellowship Program
750 First Street, N.E.
Washington, DC 20002-4242
(202) 336-6127   Fax: (202) 336-6012
TDD: (202) 336-6123   E-mail: mfp@apa.org
Web: www.apa.org/mfp/prprogram.html

Summary To provide financial assistance to minority and other students who are interested in completing a doctorate in neuroscience.

Eligibility This program is open to all U.S. citizens and permanent residents who are enrolled full time in a Ph.D. program. Applicants must have career goals that are consistent with those of the program: 1) to increase ethnic and racial diversity among neuroscience researchers with a special emphasis on increasing the numbers of underrepresented ethnic minorities; and 2) to increase numbers of neuroscientists whose work is related to the federal initiative to eliminate health disparities. They must be interested in engaging in predoctoral research training in behavioral neuroscience, cellular neurobiology, cognitive neuroscience, computational neuroscience, developmental neurobiology, membrane biophysics, molecular neurobiology, neuroanatomy, neurobiology of aging, neurobiology of disease, neurochemistry, neurogenetics, neuroimmunology, neuropathology, neuropharmacology, neurophysiology, neurotoxicology, or systems neuroscience. Students identified as underrepresented ethnic minorities in the neurosciences (African Americans, Native Americans, Hispanic Americans, and Pacific Islanders) are especially encouraged to apply. Students working on a doctoral degree with a primarily clinical focus (e.g., M.D. or Psy.D) are not eligible. Selection is based on commitment to a research career in neuroscience, potential demonstrated through accomplishments and goals, fit between career goals and training environment selected, scholarship and grades, and letters of recommendation.

Financial data The stipend is the amount established by the National Institutes of Health for predoctoral students, recently $20,772 per year. The fellowship also provides travel funds to visit universities being considered for graduate training, travel funds to attend the annual meeting of the Society for Neuroscience, and a program of summer training at the Marine Biological Laboratory in Woods Hole, Massachusetts.

Duration 1 year; may be renewed for up to 2 additional years.

Additional information The program was established in 1987. It is funded by the U.S. National Institute of Mental Health of the National Institutes of Health and administered by the American Psychological Association.

Number awarded Varies each year.

Deadline January of each year.

[530]
PREDOCTORAL RESEARCH FELLOWSHIPS IN AUTISM

National Alliance for Autism Research
Attn: Grants Administrator
99 Wall Street, Research Park
Princeton, NJ 08540
(609) 430-9160, ext. 23   Toll-free: (888) 777-NAAR
Fax: (609) 430-9163   E-mail: grantadmin@naar.org
Web: www.naar.org/research/research.asp

Summary To provide funding to doctoral candidates interested in a program of research training related to autism.

Eligibility This program is open to predoctoral students enrolled in a program leading to a research doctorate (e.g., Ph.D., Sc.D., M.D./Ph.D.) in a relevant academic department of a university or health/medical institution. Students must be interested in working on a dissertation related to autism. Relevant scientific disciplines include (but are not limited to) biochemistry, cellular physiology, clinically based studies, cognitive development, development biology and teratology, epidemiology, genetics, immunology, language, molecular biology, neuroanatomy, neuroimaging, pharmacology, structural biology, toxicology, and virology, The research training must be conducted with a mentor who submits the application and chooses the fellow. Selection of grantees is based on the quality and activity of the mentor's autism research programs, his or her experience with training graduate fellows, evidence of sufficient research support and adequate facilities to provide an appropriate training environment for a predoctoral fellow, quality and nature of the research plan, and presence of institutional research programs and/or clinical assets that enhance the richness of fellow training in the multidisciplinary complexity of autism spectrum disorder investigation.

Financial data Stipends range from $21,000 to $24,000 per year, depending upon the years of prior training. A research allowance of $4,000 is provided to partially cover fringe benefits, supplies, and travel. No indirect costs are covered.

Duration 2 years.

Additional information Fellows must devote at least 80% of their time to working on the project outlined in the research plan of the application. They may not simultaneously hold another named fellowship award.

Number awarded 1 or more each year.

Deadline Letters of intent must be submitted by March; the completed application is due in the following June.

[531]
PREDOCTORAL RESEARCH FELLOWSHIPS ON LANGUAGE AND COMMUNICATIONS IN INDIVIDUALS WITH AUTISM SPECTRUM DISORDERS

National Alliance for Autism Research
Attn: Grants Administrator
99 Wall Street, Research Park
Princeton, NJ 08540
(609) 430-9160, ext. 23   Toll-free: (888) 777-NAAR
Fax: (609) 430-9163   E-mail: grantadmin@naar.org
Web: www.naar.org/research/research.asp

Summary To provide funding to doctoral candidates interested in a program of research training in language and autism.

Eligibility This program is open to predoctoral students enrolled in a program leading to a research doctorate (e.g., Ph.D., Sc.D., M.D./Ph.D.) in a relevant academic department of a university or health/medical institution. Students must be interested in working on a dissertation related to autism and language. Relevant scientific disciplines include (but are not limited to) cognitive development, language, linguistics and augmentative communication strategies, child language development, speech-language pathology, pharmacology, psychology, and neuropsychology. The research training must be conducted with co-mentors, 1 with research expertise in communication and language and the other from the field of autism. Applications must be submitted by the co-mentors, who choose the fellow. Selection of grantees is based on the quality and activity of the mentors' autism research programs, their experience with training graduate fellows, evidence of sufficient research support and adequate facilities to provide an appropriate training environment for a predoctoral fellow, quality and nature of the research plan, and presence of institutional research programs and/or clinical assets that enhance the richness of fellow training in the multidisciplinary complexity of autism spectrum disorder investigation.

Financial data Stipends range from $21,000 to $24,000 per year, depending upon the years of prior training. A research allowance of $4,000 is provided to partially cover fringe benefits, supplies, and travel. No indirect costs are covered.

Duration 2 years.

Additional information Fellows must devote at least 80% of their time to working on the project outlined in the research plan of the application. They may not simultaneously hold another named fellowship award.

Number awarded 1 or more each year.

Deadline Letters of intent must be submitted by March; the completed application is due in the following June.

[532]
PROCTER & GAMBLE ORAL CARE–HDA FOUNDATION SCHOLARSHIPS

Hispanic Dental Association
Attn: HDA Foundation
3085 Stevenson Drive, Suite 200
Springfield, IL 62703
(217) 529-6517   Toll-free: (800) 852-7921
Fax: (217) 529-9120 E-mail: HispanicDental@hdassoc.org
Web: www.hdassoc.org/site/epage/8351_351.htm

Summary To provide financial assistance to Hispanic students interested in preparing for a career in a dental profession.

Eligibility This program is open to Hispanics who are entering as first-year students into an accredited dental, dental hygiene, dental assisting, or dental technician program. Applicants must have a GPA of 3.0 or higher. Along with their application, they must submit an essay on their career goals. Selection is based on scholastic achievement, community service, leadership skill, and commitment to improving health in the Hispanic community.

Financial data Stipends are $1,000 or $500.

Duration 1 year.

Additional information This program, which began in 1994, is sponsored by Procter & Gamble Company.

Number awarded Varies each year; recently, scholarships were awarded to 8 dental students, 8 dental hygiene students, 2 dental assisting students, and 2 dental technician students.

Deadline June of each year for dental students; July of each year for hygiene, assisting, and laboratory technician students.

[533]
PROFESSIONAL MASTER'S DEGREE SCHOLARSHIPS IN OCCUPATIONAL THERAPY

American Occupational Therapy Foundation
Attn: Scholarship Coordinator
4720 Montgomery Lane
P.O. Box 31220
Bethesda, MD 20824-1220
(301) 652-2682   Fax: (301) 656-3620
TDD: (800) 377-8555   E-mail: aotf@aotf.org
Web: www.aotf.org

Summary To provide financial assistance to practitioners who are members of the American Occupational Therapy Association (AOTA) and interested in working on a professional master's degree in occupational therapy.

Eligibility This program is open to AOTA members who are currently enrolled in a professional master's degree program. Applicants must demonstrate a need for financial assistance and have a sustained record of outstanding scholastic performance. As part of the application process, they must submit transcripts, 2 personal references, and a statement from their curriculum director.

Financial data Stipends range from $1,000 to $5,000 per year.

Duration 1 year; recipients may reapply.

Additional information This program includes a number of named scholarships that are offered from year to year. Among them are the North Coast Medical Scholarship, the Naida Ackley Memorial Scholarship, the Ethel Beard Burstein Scholarship, the Renee Achter Memorial Scholarship, the Diane Blicksilver Aja Memorial Scholarship, the Mary K. Minglin Memorial Scholarship, the Ethel Weingarten Memorial Scholarship, the Willard and Spackman Memorial Scholarship, the Alice Jantzen Memorial Scholarship, and the Oppenheimer Scholarship.

Number awarded 1 each year.

Deadline January of each year.

[534]
PROFESSIONAL STUDENT EXCHANGE PROGRAM

Western Interstate Commission for Higher Education
Attn: Student Exchange Programs
3035 Center Green Drive
P.O. Box 9752
Boulder, CO 80301-9752
(303) 541-0210   Fax: (303) 541-0291
E-mail: info-sep@wiche.edu
Web: www.wiche.edu/sep/psep

Summary To underwrite some of the cost of out-of-state professional schooling for students in selected Western states.

Eligibility This program is open to residents of 13 western states who are interested in pursuing professional study at selected out-of-state institutions, usually because those fields of study are not available in their home states. The eligible programs, and the states whose residents are eligible, presently include: 1) architecture (master's degree), for residents of Wyoming, to study at designated institutions in Arizona, California, Colorado, Idaho, Montana, New Mexico, Oregon, Utah, or Washington); 2) dentistry, for residents of Alaska, Arizona, Hawaii, Montana, New Mexico, North Dakota, and Wyoming, to study at designated institutions in Arizona, California, Colorado, Nevada, Oregon, or Washington; 3) library studies (master's degree), for residents of New Mexico and Wyoming, to study at designated institutions in Arizona, California, Hawaii, or Washington; 4) medicine, for residents of Montana and Wyoming, to study at designated institutions in Arizona, California, Colorado, Hawaii, Nevada, New Mexico, North Dakota, Oregon, or Utah; 5) nursing (graduate degree), for residents of Wyoming, to study at designated institutions in California, Hawaii, North Dakota, or Oregon; 6) occupational therapy (bachelors' or master's degree), for residents of Alaska, Arizona, Hawaii, Montana, and Wyoming, to study at designated institutions in Arizona, California, Idaho, New Mexico, North Dakota, Oregon, Utah, or Washington; 7) optometry, for residents of Alaska, Arizona, Colorado, Hawaii, Idaho, Montana, Nevada, New Mexico, North Dakota, Utah, Washington, and Wyoming, to study at designated institutions in California or Oregon; 8) osteopathic medicine, for residents of Arizona, Montana, New Mexico, Washington, and Wyoming, to study at designated institutions in Arizona or California; 9) pharmacy, for residents of Alaska, Hawaii, and Nevada, to study at designated institutions in Arizona, California, Colorado, Idaho, Montana, New Mexico, North Dakota, Oregon, Utah, Washington, or Wyoming; 10) physical therapy (master's or doctoral degree), for residents of Alaska, Hawaii, and Wyoming, to study at designated institutions in Arizona, California, Colorado, Idaho, Montana, New Mexico, North Dakota, Oregon, Utah, or Washington; 11) physician assistant, for residents of Alaska, Arizona, Nevada, and Wyoming, to study at designated institutions in Arizona, California, Colorado, Idaho, Oregon, Utah, or Washington; 12) podiatry, for residents of Alaska, Montana, New Mexico, Utah, and Wyoming, to study at a designated institution in California; 13) public health, for residents of Montana and New Mexico, to study at designated institutions in California, Colorado, or Washington; and 14) veterinary medicine, for residents of Arizona, Hawaii, Montana, Nevada, New Mexico, North Dakota, Utah, and Wyoming, to study at designated institutions in California, Colorado, Oregon, or Washington. The financial status of the applicants is not considered. Interested students must apply for admission and for PSEP assistance directly from the institution of their choice. They must be certified by their state of residence to become an exchange student and be seeking enrollment at the first professional degree level.

Financial data The assistance consists of reduced levels of tuition, usually resident tuition in public institutions or reduced standard tuition at private schools. The home state pays a support fee to the admitting school to help cover the cost of the recipient's education.

Duration 1 year; may be renewed.

Number awarded Varies each year.

Deadline In most states, the deadline for receiving completed applications for certification is in October. After obtaining certification, students must still apply to the school of their choice, which also sets its own deadline.

[535]
PROJECT RED FLAG ACADEMIC SCHOLARSHIP FOR WOMEN WITH BLEEDING DISORDERS

National Hemophilia Foundation
Attn: Department of Finance, Administration & MIS
116 West 32nd Street, 11th Floor
New York, NY 10001-3212
(212) 328-3700   Toll-free: (800) 42-HANDI, ext. 3700
Fax: (212) 328-3777   E-mail: info@hemophilia.org
Web: www.hemophilia.org

Summary To provide financial assistance for college or graduate school to women who have a bleeding disorder.

Eligibility This program is open to women who are entering or already enrolled in an undergraduate or graduate program at a university, college, or accredited vocational school. Applicants must have von Willebrand disease, hemophilia or other clotting factor deficiency, or carrier status. Along with their application, they must submit a 250-word essay that describes their educational and future career plans, including how they intend to use their education to enhance the bleeding disorders community. Financial need is not considered in the selection process.

Financial data The stipend is $2,500.

Duration 1 year.

Additional information The program was established in 2005.

Number awarded 2 each year.

Deadline May of each year.

[536]
RADIOLOGY CENTENNIAL SCHOLARSHIP AWARD

American Academy of Oral and Maxillofacial Radiology
Attn: Executive Director
P.O. Box 1010
Evans, GA 30809-1010
(706) 721-2607   E-mail: mshrout@mail.mcq.edu
Web: www.aaomr.org/Rad_Centennial.htm

Summary To provide financial assistance to graduate students in oral and maxillofacial radiology programs in the United States and Canada.

Eligibility Applicants must be currently enrolled as an entering or fully matriculated graduate student in oral and maxillofacial radiology in the United States and Canada. As part of the selection process, they must submit a list of honors and awards received while in dental school or postgraduate programs, 3 letters of reference, and a description of their personal and professional goals as they relate to oral and maxillofacial radiology.

Financial data The stipend is $5,000 per year.

Duration 1 year. May be renewed for 1 additional year.

Additional information This program was established in 1995 to celebrate the centennial of the discovery of x-rays.

Number awarded 1 or more each year.

Deadline March of each year.

[537]
RAILROAD AND MINE WORKERS MEMORIAL SCHOLARSHIP

Japanese American Citizens League
Attn: National Scholarship Awards
1765 Sutter Street
San Francisco, CA 94115
(415) 921-5225   Fax: (415) 931-4671
E-mail: jacl@jacl.org
Web: www.jacl.org/leadership_development_5.php

Summary To provide financial assistance for graduate study to members of the Japanese American Citizens League (JACL).

Eligibility This program is open to JACL members who are attending or planning to attend an accredited college or university as a graduate student. Applicants must submit a statement describing their current level of involvement in the Japanese American community or Asian Pacific community and how they will continue their involvement in future years. Selection is based on academic record, extracurricular activities, financial need, and community involvement.

Financial data The stipend depends on the availability of funds but usually ranges from $1,000 to $5,000.

Duration 1 year; nonrenewable.

Additional information Applications must be submitted to the JACL National Scholarship Program, c/o San Diego JACL Chapter, 1031 25th Street, San Diego, CA 92102.

Number awarded At least 1 each year.

Deadline March of each year.

[538]
RANDALL MATHIS SCHOLARSHIP FOR ENVIRONMENTAL STUDIES

Arkansas Environmental Federation
Attn: Scholarship Program
1400 West Markham, Suite 250
Little Rock, AR 72201
(501) 374-0263   Fax: (501) 374-8752
E-mail: joliver@environmentark.org
Web: www.environmentark.org/randallmathis.htm

Summary To provide financial assistance to residents of Arkansas working on an undergraduate or graduate degree in environmental studies at a college or university in the state.

Eligibility This program is open to Arkansas residents who have completed at least 40 credit hours as a full-time undergraduate or graduate student at a college or university in the state. Applicants must be majoring in a field related to environmental studies, including agriculture with an environmental emphasis, chemical engineering with an environmental emphasis, civil engineering with an environmental emphasis, environmental engineering, environmental health science, fisheries and wildlife biology, forestry, geology, or wildlife management. They must have a GPA of 2.8 or higher. Along with their application, they must submit an essay of 1 to 3 pages explaining their professional career goals relating to the fields of environmental health and safety. U.S. citizenship is required. Financial need is not considered in the selection process.

Financial data The stipend is $2,500.

Duration 1 year.

Number awarded 1 each year.

Deadline January of each year.

[539]
RAWLEY SILVER SCHOLARSHIP FUND

American Art Therapy Association, Inc.
Attn: Scholarships and Grants Committee
5999 Stevenson Avenue
Alexandria, VA 22304
(703) 212-2238   Toll-free: (888) 290-0878
E-mail: info@arttherapy.org
Web: www.arttherapy.org/stscholarships.html

Summary To provide financial assistance to graduate student members of the American Art Therapy Association (AATA).

Eligibility This program is open to AATA student members accepted or enrolled in a graduate level art therapy program approved by the association. Applicants must be able to demonstrate financial need. Along with their application, they must submit transcripts, 2 letters of reference, a student financial information form, and a 2-page essay that contains a brief biography and a statement of how they see their role in the future of art therapy.

Financial data The amount of the award varies, depending on the need of the recipient; however, applicants who have no financial need receive only a $100 honorarium.

Duration 1 year.

Number awarded 1 each year.

Deadline June of each year.

[540]
REDI-TAG CORPORATION SCHOLARSHIP

American Health Information Management Association
Attn: Foundation of Research and Education
233 North Michigan Avenue, Suite 2150
Chicago, IL 60601-5806
(312) 233-1131   Fax: (312) 233-1431
E-mail: fore@ahima.org
Web: www.ahima.org/fore/student/programs.asp

Summary To provide financial assistance to members of the American Health Information Management Association (AHIMA) who are single parents interested in working on an undergraduate or graduate degree in health information administration or technology.

Eligibility This program is open to AHIMA members who are single parents enrolled in a health information administration or health information technology program accredited by the Commission on Accreditation of Allied Health Education Programs. Applicants must be working on an undergraduate or graduate degree on at least a half-time basis and have a GPA of 3.0 or higher. U.S. citizenship is required. Selection is based (in order of importance) on GPA and academic achievement, volunteer and work experience, commitment to the health information management profession, suitability to the health information management profession, quality and suitability of references provided, and clarity of application.

Financial data The stipend ranges from $1,000 to $5,000.

Duration 1 year; nonrenewable.

Additional information Funding for this program is provided by the Redi-Tag Corporation.

Number awarded 1 each year.

Deadline April of each year.

[541]
RESOUND SCHOLARSHIPS

Audiology Foundation of America
Attn: Scholarship Committee
8 North Third Street, Suite 406
Lafayette, IN 47901-1247
(765) 743-6AUD   Fax: (765) 743-9AUD
E-mail: info-afa@audfound.org
Web: www.audfound.org/index.cfm?pageID=49

Summary To provide financial assistance to audiologists interested in working on a doctoral degree.

Eligibility This program is open to licensed audiology practitioners with at least 4 years of experience. Applicants must be interested in working on a doctor of audiology (Au.D.) degree. They must be citizens or permanent residents of the United States and its territories or Canada. Along with their application, they must submit an essay of 250 to 500 words on issues related to open fittings for patients.

Financial data The stipend is $1,000.

Duration 1 year.

Additional information This program is sponsored by GN ReSound North America.

Number awarded 5 each year.

Deadline July of each year.

[542]
REVEREND H. JOHN YAMASHITA MEMORIAL SCHOLARSHIP

Japanese American Citizens League
Attn: National Scholarship Awards
1765 Sutter Street
San Francisco, CA 94115
(415) 921-5225   Fax: (415) 931-4671
E-mail: jacl@jacl.org
Web: www.jacl.org/leadership_development_5.php

Summary To provide financial assistance for graduate study to members of the Japanese American Citizens League (JACL).

Eligibility This program is open to JACL members who are attending or planning to attend an accredited college or university as a graduate student. Applicants must submit a statement describing their current level of involvement in the Japanese American community or Asian Pacific community and how they will continue their involvement in future years. Selection is based on academic record, extracurricular activities, financial need, and community involvement.

Financial data The stipend depends on the availability of funds but usually ranges from $1,000 to $5,000.

Duration 1 year; nonrenewable.

Additional information Applications must be submitted to the JACL National Scholarship Program, c/o San Diego JACL Chapter, 1031 25th Street, San Diego, CA 92102.

Number awarded At least 1 each year.

Deadline March of each year.

[543]
RHO CHI–SCHERING-PLOUGH–AFPE FIRST YEAR GRADUATE SCHOLARSHIP

American Foundation for Pharmaceutical Education
Attn: Grants Manager
One Church Street, Suite 202
Rockville, MD 20850-4158
(301) 738-2160   Fax: (301) 738-2161
E-mail: info@afpenet.org
Web: www.afpenet.org/firstyr_rho_chi.htm

Summary To provide financial assistance to members of Rho Chi who are interested in pursuing a Ph.D. in a college of pharmacy.

Eligibility This program is open to Rho Chi members who are either currently enrolled in a dual-degree pathway leading to a professional degree in pharmacy and the Ph.D. or first-year graduate students entering a Ph.D. program in an accredited school of pharmacy as full-time students. Applicants must be in the final year of professional studies or have completed professional studies. Along with their application, they must submit a 1-page description of their present academic status, including all previous scholarships and fellowships and memberships in professional, scientific, scholastic, and honor societies; a 1-page account of involvement in professional and extracurricular activities; a statement of their financial status; GRE scores; a 1- to 2-page statement describing their career goals; official transcripts; and 3 letters of recommendation. U.S. citizenship or permanent resident status is required.

Financial data The award is $7,500. Funds may be used for any purpose agreed upon by the recipient and faculty sponsor, including a student stipend, laboratory supplies or materials, travel, etc. No funds may be used for indirect costs by the institution.

Duration 1 year; nonrenewable.

Additional information This scholarship program is administered by the American Foundation for Pharmaceutical Education (AFPE) and Rho Chi. Funding is provided by Schering-Plough Corporation. Information is also available from Rho Chi, University of North Carolina School of Pharmacy, CB #7360, Kerr Hall, Chapel Hill, NC 27599-7360.

Number awarded 1 each year.

Deadline January of each year.

[544]
RICHARD CECIL TODD AND CLAUDA PENNOCK TODD TRIPOD SCHOLARSHIP

Phi Sigma Pi
2119 Ambassador Circle
Lancaster, PA 17603
(717) 299-4710   Fax: (717) 390-3054
E-mail: pspoffice@phisigmapi.org
Web: www.phisigmapi.org/contribute/todd.html

Summary To provide financial assistance for college or graduate school to members of Phi Sigma Pi Honor Society.

Eligibility This program is open to members of the society who are undergraduates working on a bachelor's degree or graduating seniors entering graduate school. Applicants must have a GPA of 3.0 or higher. Along with their application, they must submit a 1- to 3-page statement on how they have promoted scholarship, leadership, and fellowship within the fraternity, campus, and community since becoming a member of Phi Sigma Pi. Financial need is not considered in the selection process.

Financial data The stipend is $1,500.

Duration 1 year; nonrenewable.

Additional information This program was established in 1991.

Number awarded 1 or more each year.

Deadline April of each year.

[545]
RICHARD L. DAVIS MANAGERS SCHOLARSHIP

American College of Medical Practice Executives
Attn: ACMPE Scholarship Fund Inc.
104 Inverness Terrace East
Englewood, CO 80112-5306
(303) 799-1111, ext. 232   Toll-free: (877) ASK-MGMA
Fax: (303) 643-4439   E-mail: acmpe@mgma.com
Web: www.mgma.com/academics/scholar.cfm

Summary To provide financial assistance to individuals currently employed in medical group management who wish to pursue professional development on the undergraduate or graduate level.

Eligibility This program is open to medical group management professionals who want to pursue professional development through undergraduate or graduate education in a program relevant to medical practice management, including public health, business administration, health care administration, or other related areas. Professionals interested in studying medicine, physical therapy, nursing, or other clinically-related professions are not eligible. Applicants must submit a letter describing their career goals and objectives related to medical practice management; a resume; 3 reference letters commenting on their performance, character, potential to succeed, and need for scholarship support; and either documentation indicating acceptance into an undergraduate or graduate college or university or academic transcripts indicating undergraduate or graduate work completed to date.

Financial data The stipend is $1,500. Funds are paid directly to the recipient's college or university.

Duration 1 year.

Additional information This program is managed by Scholarship Program Administrators, Inc. 1201 Eighth Avenue South, P.O. Box 23737, Nashville, TN 27202-3737, (615) 320-3149, (800) 310-4053, Fax: (615) 320-3151, E-mail: info@spaprog.com.

Number awarded 1 each year.

Deadline April of each year.

[546]
RICHARD L. DAVIS/BARBARA B. WATSON NATIONAL SCHOLARSHIP

American College of Medical Practice Executives
Attn: ACMPE Scholarship Fund Inc.
104 Inverness Terrace East
Englewood, CO 80112-5306
(303) 799-1111, ext. 232   Toll-free: (877) ASK-MGMA
Fax: (303) 643-4439   E-mail: acmpe@mgma.com
Web: www.mgma.com/academics/scholar.cfm

Summary To provide financial assistance to undergraduate and graduate students who are interested in preparing for a career in medical group management.

Eligibility This program is open to full-time students working on an undergraduate or graduate degree in a program relevant to medical practice management, including public health, business administration, health care administration, or other related areas. Students working on a degree in medicine, physical therapy, nursing, or other clinically-related professions are not eligible. Applicants must submit a letter describing their career goals and objectives related to medical practice management; a resume; 3 reference letters commenting on their performance, character, potential to succeed, and need for scholarship support; and either documentation indicating acceptance into an undergraduate or graduate college or university or academic transcripts indicating undergraduate or graduate work completed to date.

Financial data The stipend is $1,500. Funds are paid directly to the recipient's college or university.

Duration 1 year.

Additional information This program is managed by Scholarship Program Administrators, Inc. 1201 Eighth Avenue South, P.O. Box 23737, Nashville, TN 27202-3737, (615) 320-3149, (800) 310-4053, Fax: (615) 320-3151, E-mail: info@spaprog.com.

Number awarded 1 each year.

Deadline April of each year.

[547]
ROBERT H. WEITBRECHT SCHOLARSHIP

Alexander Graham Bell Association for the Deaf
Attn: Financial Aid Coordinator
3417 Volta Place, N.W.
Washington, DC 20007-2778
(202) 337-5220   Fax: (202) 337-8314
TTY: (202) 337-5221   E-mail: financialaid@agbell.org
Web: www.agbell.org

Summary To provide financial assistance to undergraduate and graduate students with moderate to profound hearing loss.

Eligibility This program is open to undergraduate and graduate students who have been diagnosed with a moderate to profound hearing loss prior to acquiring spoken language (hearing loss averages 60dB or greater in the better ear in the speech frequencies of 500, 1000, and 2000 Hz). Applicants must be able to demonstrate leadership potential and be committed to using spoken language as their primary mode of communication. They must be accepted or enrolled at a mainstream college or university as a full-time student. Along with their application, they must submit a 1-page essay discussing their career goals and how spoken communication is helping them to reach those goals as a person with a hearing loss. Financial need is considered in the selection process. Priority for this scholarship is given to applicants studying engineering or science.

Financial data The stipend is $2,500 per year.

Duration 1 year; may be renewed 1 additional year.

Number awarded 1 each year.

Deadline April of each year.

[548]
ROBERT W. SLEDGE FELLOWSHIPS

Alpha Chi
Attn: Executive Director
900 East Center Avenue
Harding University Box 12249
Searcy, AR 72149-0001
(501) 279-4443   Toll-free: (800) 477-4225
Fax: (501) 279-4589   E-mail: dorgan@harding.edu
Web: www.harding.edu/alphachi/benedict.htm

Summary To provide financial assistance for graduate school to members of Alpha Chi, a national honor society.

Eligibility Eligible to be nominated for these funds are graduating college seniors who have been initiated into Alpha Chi and

are going on to a graduate or professional school. Members who are currently enrolled in graduate school may also be nominated. Only 2 nominations may be submitted by each chapter. Included in the nomination package must be an academic paper or other appropriate work in the student's major field (e.g., painting, music score, film, slides, video, cassette tape recording, or other medium). Students must also submit a letter of application outlining their plans for study and detailing their extracurricular activities. Financial need is not considered.

Financial data The stipend is $3,500.

Duration 1 year.

Additional information Recipients must enroll in graduate school on a full-time basis.

Number awarded 2 each year.

Deadline February of each year.

[549]
ROBERTA PIERCE SCOFIELD DOCTORAL SCHOLARSHIP

Oncology Nursing Society
Attn: ONS Foundation
125 Enterprise Drive
Pittsburgh, PA 15275-1214
(412) 859-6100, ext. 8503   Toll-free: (866) 257-4ONS
Fax: (412) 859-6160   E-mail: foundation@ons.org
Web: www.ons.org/awards/foundawards/doctoral.shtml

Summary To provide financial assistance to registered nurses interested in pursuing doctoral studies in oncology nursing.

Eligibility Candidates must be registered nurses with a demonstrated interest in and commitment to oncology nursing; be enrolled in or applying to a doctoral nursing degree program or related program; and never have received a doctoral scholarship from this sponsor. Along with their application, they must submit brief essays on why they chose their doctoral program; the courses and clinical experience of the program that are related to cancer nursing; their research area of interest and plans for a dissertation; their professional goals and their relationship to the advancement of oncology nursing; and how the doctoral program will assist them in achieving their goals.

Financial data The stipend is $5,000.

Duration 1 year; nonrenewable.

Additional information At the end of each year of scholarship participation, recipients must submit a summary of their educational activities. Applications must be accompanied by a $5 fee.

Number awarded 1 each year.

Deadline January of each year.

[550]
ROCK SLEYSTER, MD, MEMORIAL SCHOLARSHIP

American Medical Association
Attn: AMA Foundation
515 North State Street
Chicago, IL 60610
(312) 464-4193   Fax: (312) 464-4142
E-mail: dina.lindenberg@ama-assn.org
Web: www.ama-assn.org/ama/pub/category/14772.html

Summary To provide financial assistance to medical students who plan to specialize in psychiatry.

Eligibility This program is open to U.S. citizens enrolled in accredited U.S. or Canadian medical schools that grant the M.D. degree. Only nominations are accepted. Nominees must be rising seniors and plan to specialize in psychiatry. The number of students who can be nominated per school depends upon the size of the third-year class: 1 nominee for a class size up to 150 students; 2 nominees for a class size between 151 and 250 students; 3 nominees for a class size of 251 students or more. Selection is based on demonstrated interest in psychiatry, academic record, and financial need.

Financial data The stipend is $10,000.

Duration 1 year.

Number awarded 1 each year.

Deadline May of each year.

[551]
ROLLA F. WOOD GRADUATE SCHOLARSHIP

Phi Sigma Pi
2119 Ambassador Circle
Lancaster, PA 17603
(717) 299-4710   Fax: (717) 390-3054
E-mail: pspoffice@phisigmapi.org
Web: www.phisigmapi.org/contribute/scholarship.html

Summary To provide financial assistance for graduate school to members of Phi Sigma Pi Honor Society.

Eligibility This program is open to members of the society who graduated with a GPA of 3.0 or higher. Applicants must be members of the national alumni association who have been accepted to a graduate or professional school. Along with their application, they must submit a 1,500-word essay describing how they have lived the ideals of the fraternity since their graduation.

Financial data The stipend is $1,000.

Duration 1 year; nonrenewable.

Additional information This program was established in 2004.

Number awarded 1 or more each year.

Deadline April of each year.

[552]
ROSA HARTSOOK SCHOLARSHIP

American Occupational Therapy Foundation
Attn: Scholarship Coordinator
4720 Montgomery Lane
P.O. Box 31220
Bethesda, MD 20824-1220
(301) 652-2682   Fax: (301) 656-3620
TDD: (800) 377-8555   E-mail: aotf@aotf.org
Web: www.aotf.org

Summary To provide financial assistance to occupational therapists in Ohio who are working on a graduate degree.

Eligibility This program is open to occupational therapists in Ohio who are enrolled in an accredited graduate degree program in the state in a field related to occupational therapy. Applicants must demonstrate a need for financial assistance and have a sustained record of outstanding scholastic performance. As part of the application process, they must submit transcripts, 2 personal references, and a statement from their curriculum director.

Financial data The stipend is $1,000.

Duration 1 year.

Number awarded 1 each year.

Deadline January of each year.

[553]
ROSE FEATHERSTONE MEMORIAL SCHOLARSHIP

American Association of Nurse Anesthetists
Attn: AANA Foundation
222 South Prospect Avenue
Park Ridge, IL 60068-4001
(847) 692-7050, ext. 1171   Fax: (847) 692-7137
E-mail: foundation@aana.com
Web: www.aana.com/foundation/default.asp

Summary To provide financial assistance to members of the American Association of Nurse Anesthetists (AANA) who are interested in obtaining further education.

Eligibility This program is open to members of the association who are currently enrolled in an accredited nurse anesthesia education program. Preference is given to students from Idaho. First-year students must have completed 6 months of nurse anesthesia classes; second-year students must have completed 12 months of nurse anesthesia classes. Along with their application, they must submit a 200-word essay describing why they have chosen nurse anesthesia as a profession and their professional goals for the future. Financial need is also considered in the selection process.

Financial data The stipend is $1,500 per year.

Duration 1 academic year.

Additional information This program is supported by the Idaho Association of Nurse Anesthetists. The application processing fee is $25.

Number awarded 1 each year.

Deadline March of each year.

[554]
ROSS N. AND PATRICIA PANGERE FOUNDATION SCHOLARSHIPS

American Council of the Blind
Attn: Coordinator, Scholarship Program
1155 15th Street, N.W., Suite 1004
Washington, DC 20005
(202) 467-5081   Toll-free: (800) 424-8666
Fax: (202) 467-5085   E-mail: info@acb.org
Web: www.acb.org

Summary To provide financial assistance for undergraduate or graduate study to outstanding blind students.

Eligibility Eligible to apply for this scholarship are legally blind U.S. citizens or resident aliens who are undergraduate or graduate students. In addition to letters of recommendation and copies of academic transcripts, applications must include an autobiographical sketch. A cumulative GPA of 3.3 or higher is generally required. Selection is based on demonstrated academic record, involvement in extracurricular and civic activities, and academic objectives. The severity of the applicant's visual impairment and his/her study methods are also taken into account.

Financial data A stipend is awarded (amount not specified). In addition, the winner receives a Kurzweil-1000 Reading System.

Duration 1 year.

Additional information The scholarship winner is expected to be present at the council's annual national convention; the council will cover all reasonable costs connected with convention attendance.

Number awarded 1 each year.

Deadline February of each year.

[555]
ROSS-FAHEY SCHOLARSHIPS

National Association for Campus Activities
Attn: NACA Foundation
13 Harbison Way
Columbia, SC 29212-3401
(803) 732-6222   Fax: (803) 749-1047
E-mail: scholarships@naca.org
Web: www.naca.org

Summary To provide financial assistance to graduate students and new professionals at colleges and universities within the former New England region of the National Association for Campus Activities (NACA).

Eligibility This program is open to graduate students and new professional employees at colleges and universities in Connecticut, Maine, Massachusetts, New Hampshire, Rhode Island, and Vermont. Applicants must be seeking funding for tuition, fees, books, or professional development (such as conference fees). Selection is based on demonstrated significant leadership skills and abilities plus a record of volunteer activities (either on or off campus). Financial need is not considered in the selection process.

Financial data A stipend is awarded (amount not specified).
Duration 1 year.
Number awarded 1 or 2 each year.
Deadline September of each year.

[556]
RUDOLPH DILLMAN MEMORIAL SCHOLARSHIP

American Foundation for the Blind
Attn: Scholarship Committee
11 Penn Plaza, Suite 300
New York, NY 10001
(212) 502-7661   Toll-free: (800) AFB-LINE
Fax: (212) 502-7771   TDD: (212) 502-7662
E-mail: afbinfo@afb.net
Web: www.afb.org/scholarships.asp

Summary To provide financial assistance to legally blind undergraduate or graduate students studying in the field of rehabilitation and/or education of visually impaired and blind persons.

Eligibility Applicants must be able to submit evidence of legal blindness, U.S. citizenship, and acceptance in an accredited undergraduate or graduate training program within the broad field of rehabilitation and/or education of blind and visually impaired persons. Along with their application, they must submit an essay that includes the field of study they are pursuing and why they have chosen it; their educational and personal goals; their work experience; any extracurricular activities with which they have been involved, including those in school, religious organizations, and the community; and how they intend to use scholarship monies that may be awarded. They may also include documentation of financial need.

Financial data The stipend is $2,500 per year.
Duration 1 academic year; previous recipients may not reapply.
Number awarded 4 each year: 3 without consideration of financial need and 1 based on financial need.
Deadline April of each year.

[557]
RURAL FAMILY MEDICINE SCHOLARSHIPS

Iowa Farm Bureau Federation
Attn: Community Resources Department
5400 University Avenue
West Des Moines, IA 50266
(515) 225-5461   Fax: (515) 225-5419
E-mail: blykins@ifbf.org
Web: www.iowafarmbureau.com

Summary To provide financial assistance to medical students and residents who are interested in practicing in rural areas of Iowa.

Eligibility This program is open to 1) medical residents who are completing an Iowa family practice residency, locating their practice in a rural Iowa setting with a population less than 10,000, members of the American Academy of Family Physicians (AAFP), and able to demonstrate scholarship and achievement in medical school; and 2) students who are graduating from medical school in Iowa, entering an Iowa family practice residency program, members of the AAFP, and able to demonstrate scholarship and achievement in medical school. Applicants must submit a 1,000-word essay explaining their personal philosophy about medical care, especially family practice, and outlining their intended career plans. They should have a demonstrated interest in rural practice as shown by completing a preceptorship or elective experience in a rural Iowa community with a population less than 10,000. Selection is based on the quality of the essay (40%), demonstrated interest in rural practice or likelihood of preparing for a career as a family physician in rural Iowa (30%) demonstrated scholarship and achievement in medical school (15%), and quality of letters of recommendation (15%).

Financial data The stipend is $2,500.
Duration 1 year.
Additional information This program, established in 1993, is operated by the Farm Bureau Agricultural Foundation in cooperation with the Iowa Academy of Family Physicians Foundation, 100 East Grand Avenue, Suite 170, Des Moines, IA 50309-1800, (515) 283-9370, (800) 283-9370.
Number awarded 4 each year: 2 medical students and 2 residents.
Deadline June of each year.

[558]
RUTH ABERNATHY GRADUATE PRESIDENTIAL SCHOLARSHIP

American Alliance for Health, Physical Education, Recreation and Dance
Attn: Presidential Scholarships
1900 Association Drive
Reston, VA 20191-1598
(703) 476-3400   Toll-free: (800) 213-7193
E-mail: dcallis@aahperd.org
Web: www.aahperd.org

Summary To provide financial assistance to graduate student members of the American Alliance for Health, Physical Education, Recreation and Dance (AAHPERD).

Eligibility This program is open to AAHPERD members who are full-time graduate students. Applicants must be majoring in health, physical education, recreation, or dance and have a GPA of 3.5 or higher. They must submit a statement of their professional goals. Selection is based on academic proficiency; evidence of leadership; school, community, and professional activity and service; and character attributes.

Financial data The stipend is $1,500.

Duration 1 year; nonrenewable.

Additional information This program, established in 1995, was formerly designated the National Presidential Graduate Scholarship of AAHPERD.

Number awarded 2 each year.

Deadline October of each year.

[559]
RUTH H. BUFTON SCHOLARSHIP

American Business Women's Association
Attn: Stephen Bufton Memorial Educational Fund
9100 Ward Parkway
P.O. Box 8728
Kansas City, MO 64114-0728
(816) 361-6621   Toll-free: (800) 228-0007
Fax: (816) 361-4991   E-mail: abwa@abwahq.org
Web: www.abwahq.org/ProfDev.asp

Summary To provide financial assistance to women graduate students who are working on a degree in a specified field.

Eligibility This program is open to women who are working on a graduate degree and have a cumulative GPA of 2.5 or higher. Applicants are not required to be members of the American Business Women's Association, but they must be sponsored by an ABWA chapter that has contributed to the fund in the previous chapter year. Each year, the trustees designate an academic discipline for which the scholarship will be presented that year. U.S. citizenship is required.

Financial data The stipend is $10,000. Funds are paid directly to the recipient's institution to be used only for tuition, books, and fees.

Duration 1 year.

Additional information This program was created in 1986 as part of ABWA's Stephen Bufton Memorial Education Fund. The ABWA does not provide the names and addresses of local chapters; it recommends that applicants check with their local Chamber of Commerce, library, or university to see if any chapter has registered a contact's name and number.

Number awarded 1 each odd-numbered year.

Deadline May of each odd-numbered year.

[560]
RUTH L. KIRSCHSTEIN NATIONAL RESEARCH SERVICE AWARD FOR INDIVIDUAL PREDOCTORAL FELLOWS IN NURSING RESEARCH

National Institute of Nursing Research
Attn: Division of Extramural Research
6701 Democracy Boulevard, Room 710
Bethesda, MD 20892-4870
(301) 594-5970   Fax: (301) 480-8260
E-mail: hussk@nih.gov
Web: ninr.nih.gov/ninr/research/dea/PARFApage.html

Summary To provide financial aid to registered nurses who are pursuing doctoral study in a field relevant to the work of the National Institute of Nursing Research (NINR).

Eligibility This program is open to registered nurses who are enrolled or accepted for enrollment full time in a doctoral degree program (but not a health professional degree such as M.D., D.O., D.D.S., or D.V.M.). Applicants must be U.S. citizens, nationals, or permanent residents. Members of underrepresented racial and ethnic groups and individuals with disabilities are especially encouraged to apply.

Financial data The award provides an annual stipend of $20,772; a tuition, fee, and health insurance allowance of 100% of all costs up to $3,000 plus 60% of costs above $3,000; and an annual institutional allowance of $2,500.

Duration Up to 5 years.

Number awarded Varies each year, depending on the availability of funds.

Deadline April, August, or December of each year.

[561]
RUTH L. KIRSCHSTEIN NATIONAL RESEARCH SERVICE AWARDS FOR INDIVIDUAL PREDOCTORAL FELLOWSHIPS TO PROMOTE DIVERSITY IN HEALTH-RELATED RESEARCH

National Institutes of Health
Division of Extramural Outreach and Information Resources
Attn: Grants Information
6701 Rockledge Drive, Suite 6095
Bethesda, MD 20892-7910
(301) 435-0714   Fax: (301) 480-0525
TTY: (301) 451-0088   E-mail: NIHTrain@mail.nih.gov
Web: www.nih.gov

Summary To provide financial assistance to students from underrepresented groups interested in working on a graduate degree and preparing for a career in biomedical and behavioral research.

Eligibility This program is open to students enrolled or accepted for enrollment in a Ph.D. or equivalent research degree program; a formally combined M.D./Ph.D. program; or other combined professional doctoral/research Ph.D. graduate program in the biomedical, behavioral, health, or clinical sciences. Students in health professional degree programs (e.g., M.D., D.O., D.D.S., D.V.M.) are not eligible. Applicants must be 1) members of an ethnic or racial group underrepresented in biomedical or behavioral research; 2) individuals with disabilities; or 3) individuals from socially, culturally, economically, or educationally disadvantaged backgrounds that have inhibited their ability to prepare for a career in health-related research. They must be U.S. citizens, nationals, or permanent residents.

Financial data The fellowship provides an annual stipend of $20,772, a tuition and fee allowance (60% of costs up to $16,000 or 60% of costs up to $21,000 for dual degrees), and an institutional allowance of $4,200 for travel to scientific meetings and for laboratory and other training expenses.

Duration Up to 5 years.

Additional information These fellowships are offered by most components of the National Institutes of Health (NIH). Write for a list of names and telephone numbers of responsible officers at each component.

Number awarded Varies each year.

Deadline April, August, or December of each year.

[562]
RUTH L. KIRSCHSTEIN NRSA PROGRAM FOR NIGMS MARC PREDOCTORAL FELLOWSHIPS
National Institute of General Medical Sciences
Attn: Minority Access to Research Careers Branch
45 Center Drive, Room 2AS.37
Bethesda, MD 20892-6200
(301) 594-3900   Fax: (301) 480-2753
TTY: (301) 451-0088   E-mail: at21z@nih.gov
Web: www.nigms.nih.gov

Summary To provide financial assistance to minority doctoral students who are interested in preparing for a research career in the biomedical sciences.

Eligibility This program is open to students from minority groups underrepresented in the behavioral and biomedical sciences who are currently enrolled in a Ph.D. or equivalent research degree program, a combined M.D./Ph.D. program, or other combined professional and Ph.D. degree program in the behavioral or biomedical sciences, including mathematics. Support is not available to individuals enrolled in medical or other professional schools unless they are working on a degree combined with a Ph.D. Applicants must have graduated from an undergraduate program supported by the Minority Access to Research Careers (MARC) Branch of the National Institute of General Medical Sciences (NIGMS). Only U.S. citizens, nationals, and permanent residents are eligible.

Financial data The fellowship provides an annual stipend of $20,772, a tuition and fee allowance (60% of costs up to $16,000 or 60% of costs up to $21,000 for dual degrees), and an institutional allowance of $4,200 for travel to scientific meetings and for laboratory and other training expenses.

Duration Up to 5 years.

Additional information This program is part of the National Research Service Award program of the National Institutes of Health (NIH), named in honor of Ruth L. Kirschstein in 2002.

Deadline April, August, or December of each year.

[563]
RUTH M. FRENCH GRADUATE OR UNDERGRADUATE SCHOLARSHIP
Alpha Mu Tau Fraternity
c/o American Society for Clinical Laboratory Science
6701 Democracy Boulevard, Suite 300
Bethesda, MD 20817
(301) 657-2768   Fax: (301) 657-2909
E-mail: ascls@ascls.org
Web: www.ascls.org/leadership/awards/amt.asp

Summary To provide financial assistance for undergraduate or graduate studies to members of Alpha Mu Tau, a national fraternity for professionals in the clinical laboratory sciences.

Eligibility Applicants must be U.S. citizens or permanent residents, members of Alpha Mu Tau, and accepted into or currently enrolled in a program in clinical laboratory science, including clinical laboratory education or management programs for graduate students and clinical laboratory science/medical technology and clinical laboratory technician/medical laboratory technician for undergraduates. Undergraduate applicants must be entering their last year of study. Along with their application, they must submit a 500-word statement describing their interest and reasons for preparing for a career in clinical laboratory science. Financial need is also considered in the selection process.

Financial data The stipend is $3,000.

Duration 1 year.

Additional information Information is also available from Joe Briden, Alpha Mu Tau Fraternity Scholarship Coordinator, 7809 South 21st Drive, Phoenix, AZ 85041-7736, E-mail: alphamutau-joe@yahoo.com.

Number awarded 1 each year.

Deadline March of each year.

[564]
RUTH MUSKRAT BRONSON FELLOWSHIP
American Indian Graduate Center
Attn: Executive Director
4520 Montgomery Boulevard, N.E., Suite 1-B
Albuquerque, NM 87109-1291
(505) 881-4584   Toll-free: (800) 628-1920
Fax: (505) 884-0427   E-mail: aigc@aigc.com
Web: www.aigc.com

Summary To provide financial assistance to Native American students interested in working on a graduate degree in nursing.

Eligibility This program is open to enrolled members of U.S. federally-recognized American Indian tribes and Alaska Native groups and other students who can document one-fourth degree federally-recognized Indian blood. Applicants must be working full time on a graduate degree in nursing at a college, university, or professional school in the United States. If insufficient nursing applicants appear, students from other health-related fields are considered. Selection is based on academic achievement, financial need, and an essay on the meaning of their graduate education to the Indian community.

Financial data A stipend is awarded (amount not specified).

Duration 1 year; may be renewed.

Additional information The application fee is $15. Since this a supplemental program, applicants must apply in a timely manner for federal financial aid and campus-based aid at the college they are attending to be considered for this program. Failure to apply will disqualify an applicant.

Number awarded 1 or more each year.

Deadline May of each year.

[565]
S. EVELYN LEWIS MEMORIAL SCHOLARSHIP IN MEDICAL HEALTH SCIENCES
Zeta Phi Beta Sorority, Inc.
Attn: National Education Foundation
1734 New Hampshire Avenue, N.W.
Washington, DC 20009
(202) 387-3103   Fax: (202) 232-4593
E-mail: scholarship@ZPhiBNEF.org
Web: www.zphib1920.org/nef

Summary To provide financial assistance to women interested in studying medicine or health sciences on the undergraduate or graduate school level.

Eligibility This program is open to women enrolled in a program on the undergraduate or graduate school level leading to a degree in medicine or health sciences. Proof of enrollment is required. Applicants need not be members of Zeta Phi Beta Sorority. They must submit 3 letters of recommendation, high school or university transcripts, a 150-word essay on their educational and professional goals, and information on financial need.

Financial data The stipend ranges from $500 to $1,000. Funds are paid directly to the college or university.

Duration 1 academic year.

Additional information Information is also available from Cheryl Williams, National Second Vice President, 6322 Bocage Drive, Shreveport, LA 71119. Recipients must attend school on a full-time basis. No awards are made just for summer study.

Number awarded 1 or more each year.

Deadline January of each year.

[566]
SCHOLARSHIP AWARDS FOR NURSE DIRECTORS/MANAGERS

American Organization of Nurse Executives
Attn: Institute for Patient Care Research and Education
Liberty Place
325 Seventh Street, N.W., Suite 700
Washington, DC 20004
(202) 626-2274   Fax: (202) 638-5499
E-mail: voven@aha.org
Web: www.hospitalconnect.com/aone/institute/about.html

Summary To provide financial assistance to members of the American Organization of Nurse Executives (AONE) who are interested in working on an advanced degree in nursing administration.

Eligibility This program is open to members of the organization who have been accepted into an advanced course of study in nursing administration.

Financial data The stipend is $2,500.

Duration 1 year.

Additional information This program is sponsored by *Nursing Spectrum/NurseWeek.*

Number awarded 1 or more each year.

[567]
SCHOLARSHIP AWARDS FOR NURSE EXECUTIVES

American Organization of Nurse Executives
Attn: Institute for Patient Care Research and Education
Liberty Place
325 Seventh Street, N.W., Suite 700
Washington, DC 20004
(202) 626-2274   Fax: (202) 638-5499
E-mail: voven@aha.org
Web: www.aone.org/aone/institute/award.html

Summary To provide financial assistance to members of the American Organization of Nurse Executives (AONE) who are interested in working on a doctoral degree in nursing administration.

Eligibility This program is open to members of the organization who have been accepted into an advanced course of study in nursing administration.

Financial data The stipend is $2,500.

Duration 1 year.

Additional information Recent sponsors of this program included Thomson Micromedex and Siemens.

Number awarded Varies each year; recently, 2 of these scholarships were awarded.

[568]
SCIENCE GRADUATE STUDENT GRANT FUND

Foundation for Science and Disability, Inc.
c/o Dr. E.C. Keller, Jr., Treasurer
West Virginia University-Department of Biology
P.O. Box 6057
Morgantown, WV 26506-6057
(304) 293-5201, ext. 2513   Fax: (304) 293-6363
E-mail: ekeller@wvu.edu
Web: www.as.wvu.edu

Summary To provide supplemental grants to students with disabilities who are interested in working on a graduate degree in a science-related field.

Eligibility This program is open to 1) college seniors who have a disability and have been accepted to a graduate or professional school in the sciences, and 2) graduate science students who have a disability. Applicants must be U.S. citizens interested in working on a degree in an area of engineering, mathematics, medicine, science, or technology. Along with their application, they must submit an essay (about 250 words) describing professional goals and objectives, as well as the specific purpose for which the grant would be used. Selection is based on financial need, sincerity of purpose, and scholarship and/or research ability.

Financial data The grant is $1,000. Funds may be used for an assistive device or instrument, as financial support to work with a professor on an individual research project, or for some other special need.

Duration The award is granted annually.

Additional information The Foundation for Science and Disability, Inc. is an affiliate society of the American Association for the Advancement of Science. Information is also available from Richard Mankin, Science Student Grant Committee Chair, 503 N.W. 89th Street, Gainesville, FL 32607-1400, (352) 374-5774, Fax: (352) 374-5781, E-mail: rmankin@gainesville.usda.ufl.edu.

Number awarded Varies each year.

Deadline November of each year.

[569]
SCOTT DOMINGUEZ-CRATERS OF THE MOON CHAPTER SCHOLARSHIP

American Society of Safety Engineers
Attn: ASSE Foundation
1800 East Oakton Street
Des Plaines, IL 60018
(847) 768-3435   Fax: (847) 768-3434
E-mail: agabanski@asse.org
Web: www.asse.org/foundation

Summary To provide financial assistance to undergraduate and graduate student members of the American Society of Safety Engineers (ASSE) from designated western states who are working on a degree in occupational health and related fields.

Eligibility This program is open to undergraduate and graduate students who are working on a degree in occupational safety, health, and environment or a closely-related field (e.g., industrial or environmental engineering, environmental science, industrial hygiene, occupational health nursing). First priority is given to residents within the service area of Craters of the Moon Chapter in Idaho; second priority is given to residents of other states in ASSE Region II (Arizona, Colorado, Montana, Nevada, New Mexico, Utah, and Wyoming). Special consideration is also given to 1) employees of a sponsoring organization or their dependents; 2) students who are serving their country through active duty in the armed forces or are honorably discharged; 3) former members of the Boy Scouts, Girl Scouts, FFA, or 4-H; 4) recipients of awards from service organizations; and 5) students who have provided volunteer service to an ASSE chapter in a leadership role. Undergraduates must have completed at least 60 semester hours with a GPA of 3.0 or higher. Graduate students must have completed at least 9 semester hours with a GPA of 3.5 or higher and have had a GPA of 3.0 or higher as an undergraduate. Full-time students must be ASSE student members; part-time students must be ASSE general or professional members. Along with their application, they must submit 2 essays of 300 words or less: 1) why they are seeking a degree in occupational safety and health or a closely-related field, a brief description of their current activities, and how those relate to their career goals and objectives; and 2) why they should be awarded this scholarship (including career goals and financial need).

Financial data   The stipend is $1,000.
Duration   1 year; nonrenewable.
Number awarded   1 each year.
Deadline   November of each year.

[570]
SCUDDER ASSOCIATION EDUCATIONAL GRANTS

Scudder Association, Inc.
Attn: Educational Grants Chair
33 Christian Avenue, Suite 119
Concord, NH 03301-6128
E-mail: info@scudder.org
Web: www.scudder.org/philanthropy.html

Summary   To assist undergraduate and graduate students preparing for "careers as servants of God in various forms of ministry to men and women around the world."
Eligibility   This program is open to undergraduate and graduate students who are preparing for careers in the ministry, medicine, nursing, teaching, or social service. Applicants must be a Scudder family member or recommended by a member of the Scudder Association. They are requested to submit an official transcript, 2 letters of recommendation from faculty members, a statement (up to 500 words) on their goals and objectives, and a verification of financial need from their school (financial need is considered in the selection process).
Financial data   Stipends range from $1,000 to $2,500. A total of $25,000 is distributed each year.
Duration   Up to 4 years of undergraduate studies, graduate studies, or a combination of the two.
Number awarded   Up to 25 each year.

[571]
SEATA MEMORIAL GRADUATE SCHOLARSHIP

Southeast Athletic Trainers Association
c/o Janet Passman, Scholarship Committee Chair
Louisiana College
1140 College Drive
Pineville, LA 71359
(318) 487-7290   Fax: (318) 487-7174
E-mail: passman@lacollege.edu
Web: www.seata.org/Scholarshipdetails.htm

Summary   To provide financial assistance to graduate student members of the Southeast Athletic Trainers Association (SEATA).
Eligibility   This program is open to graduate students at colleges and universities in Alabama, Florida, Georgia, Kentucky, Louisiana, Mississippi, and Tennessee who are members of SEATA and the National Association of Athletic Trainers (NATA). Applicants must have worked as an athletic training student for

a period of at least 2 years at the college level and have a GPA of 3.0 or higher. They must be sponsored by a certified athletic trainer who is a current member of SEATA and NATA. Along with their application, they must submit a brief biographical sketch that includes their reasons for wanting the scholarship, why they merit this award, high school and college awards and honors, athletic teams with which they have worked, and jobs they have held. Selection is based on academic achievement, character, and athletic training abilities and experiences.
Financial data   The stipend is $1,000.
Duration   1 year; nonrenewable.
Additional information   SEATA serves as District 9 of NATA. This program was established in 1981.
Number awarded   1 each year.
Deadline   December of each year.

[572]
SECOND YEAR OUTSTANDING AU.D. STUDENT AWARD

Audiology Foundation of America
Attn: Scholarship Committee
8 North Third Street, Suite 406
Lafayette, IN 47901-1247
(765) 743-6AUD   Fax: (765) 743-9AUD
E-mail: info-afa@audfound.org
Web: www.audfound.org/index.cfm?pageID=49

Summary   To provide financial assistance to students entering the second year of a doctoral program in audiology.
Eligibility   This program is open to students enrolled full time in the first year of a 4-year doctor of audiology (Au.D.) program. Applicants may not be a licensed or registered practicing audiologist. They must be nominated by their program director. Citizenship or permanent resident status of the United States and its territories or Canada is required.
Financial data   The stipend is $4,500.
Duration   1 year; nonrenewable.
Additional information   This program is sponsored by the Oticon Foundation.
Number awarded   2 each year.
Deadline   July of each year.

[573]
SENTILLION SCHOLARSHIP

Healthcare Information and Management Systems Society
Attn: HIMSS Foundation Scholarship Program Coordinator
230 East Ohio Street, Suite 500
Chicago, IL 60611-3270
(312) 664-HIMSS   Fax: (312) 664-6143
E-mail: foundation@himss.org
Web: www.himss.org/ASP/scholarship_sentil.asp

Summary   To provide financial assistance to students who are working on a graduate degree in health care information technology.
Eligibility   This program is open to graduate students working on a degree in health care information technology. Applicants must be residents of North America who can demonstrate knowledge of health care information technology through work as a vendor, care provider, researcher, or administrator. They must submit a personal statement that includes their career goals, past achievements, and future goals. Selection is based on that statement, academic achievement, and financial need.

Financial data The stipend is $7,000. The award includes an all-expense paid trip to the annual conference and exhibition of the Healthcare Information and Management Systems Society.

Duration 1 year; nonrenewable.

Number awarded 1 each year.

Deadline October of each year.

[574]
SEQUOYAH GRADUATE FELLOWSHIPS

Association on American Indian Affairs, Inc.
Attn: Director of Scholarship Programs
966 Hungerford Drive, Suite 12-B
Rockville, MD 20850
(240) 314-7155   Fax: (240) 314-7159
E-mail: lw.aaia@verizon.net
Web: www.indian-affairs.org/scholarships.htm

Summary To provide financial assistance to Native Americans interested in working on a graduate degree.

Eligibility This program is open to American Indians and Alaskan Natives working full time on a graduate degree. Applicants must submit documentation of financial need, a Certificate of Indian Blood showing at least one-quarter Indian blood, proof of tribal enrollment, an essay on their educational goals, 2 letters of recommendation, and their most recent transcript.

Financial data The stipend is $1,500 per year.

Duration 1 year; may be renewed.

Number awarded Varies each year.

Deadline July of each year.

[575]
SEYMOUR L. KAPLAN SCHOLARSHIP

Seymour L. Kaplan Scholarship Foundation Fund
315 Glendale Road
Scarsdale, NY 10583-1509

Summary To provide financial assistance to students enrolled in medical school.

Eligibility This program is open to students enrolled or planning to enroll in medical school. Applicants must submit a brief summary of their academic goals, extracurricular activities, and other interests unrelated to their professional career. Selection is based on previous academic achievement, excellence in general citizenship, academic goals, and financial need.

Financial data The stipend is $5,000.

Duration 1 year.

Number awarded 2 each year.

Deadline November of each year.

[576]
SGNA RN ADVANCING EDUCATION SCHOLARSHIP

Society of Gastroenterology Nurses and Associates, Inc.
Attn: Awards Committee
401 North Michigan Avenue
Chicago, IL 60611-4267
(312) 321-5165   Toll-free: (800) 245-SGNA
Fax: (312) 527-6658   E-mail: sgna@smithbucklin.com
Web: www.sgna.org/Education/scholarships.cfm

Summary To provide financial assistance to registered nurses (R.N.s) working in gastroenterology who are interested in enrolling in an advanced degree program.

Eligibility This program is open to R.N.s working in gastroenterology who are members of the Society of Gastroenterology

Nurses and Associates (SGNA). Applicants must be enrolled in an accredited advanced degree program working on a B.S.N., M.S.N., or Ph.D. degree with a GPA of 3.0 or higher. Along with their application, they must submit a 500-word essay on a challenging situation they see in the health care environment today and how they, as an R.N., would best address and meet that challenge. Financial need is not considered in the selection process.

Financial data The stipend is $2,500 for full-time students or $1,000 for part-time students. Funds are issued as reimbursement after the recipient has completed the proposed course work with a GPA of 3.0 or higher.

Duration 1 year.

Number awarded 1 or more each year.

Deadline July of each year.

[577]
SHEPHERD SCHOLARSHIP

Ancient and Accepted Scottish Rite of Freemasonry,
   Southern Jurisdiction
Supreme Council, 33°
Attn: Director of Education
1733 16th Street, N.W.
Washington, DC 20009-2103
(202) 232-3579   Fax: (202) 464-0487
E-mail: grndexec@srmason-sj.org
Web: www.srmason-sj.org

Summary To provide financial assistance to undergraduate and graduate students who are working on degrees in areas associated with public service.

Eligibility This program is open to undergraduate and graduate students who have taken part in social, civic, religious, or fraternal activities in their communities. Applicants must be working on a baccalaureate or graduate degree in a field "associated with service to country and generally perceived as benefiting the human race." U.S. citizenship is required. Selection is based on dedication, ambition, academic record, financial need, and promise of outstanding performance at the advanced level.

Financial data The stipend is $1,500 per year.

Duration 4 years.

Number awarded 1 or more each year.

Deadline March of each year.

[578]
SHERRY R. ARNSTEIN MINORITY STUDENT SCHOLARSHIP

American Association of Colleges of Osteopathic Medicine
Attn: Office of Government Relations
5550 Friendship Boulevard, Suite 310
Chevy Chase, MD 20815-7231
(301) 968-4151   Fax: (301) 968-4101
Web: www.aacom.org

Summary To provide financial assistance to underrepresented minority students enrolled in osteopathic medical school.

Eligibility This program is open to Black, Hispanic, and Native American students currently enrolled in good standing in their first, second, or third year of osteopathic medical school. Applicants must submit a 750-word essay on what osteopathic medical schools can do to recruit and retain more underrepresented minority students, what they personally plan to do as a student and as a future D.O. to help increase minority student enrollment at a college of osteopathic medicine, and how and why they were drawn to osteopathic medicine.

Financial data Stipends are generally $1,000.

Duration 1 year; nonrenewable.

Deadline March of each year.

[579]
SHERRY R. ARNSTEIN NEW STUDENT MINORITY STUDENT SCHOLARSHIP

American Association of Colleges of Osteopathic Medicine
Attn: Office of Government Relations
5550 Friendship Boulevard, Suite 310
Chevy Chase, MD 20815-7231
(301) 968-4151   Fax: (301) 968-4101
Web: www.aacom.org

Summary To provide financial assistance to underrepresented minority students planning to enroll at an osteopathic medical school.

Eligibility This program is open to Black, Hispanic, and Native American students who have been accepted and are planning to enroll as a first-time student at any of the 20 colleges of osteopathic medicine that are members of the American Association of Colleges of Osteopathic Medicine (AACOM). Applicants must submit a 750-word essay on what osteopathic medical schools can do to recruit and retain more underrepresented minority students, what they personally plan to do as a student and as a future D.O. to help increase minority student enrollment at a college of osteopathic medicine, and how and why they were drawn to osteopathic medicine.

Financial data Stipends are generally $1,000.

Duration 1 year; nonrenewable.

Deadline March of each year.

[580]
SHIP ISLAND–MRS. J.O. JONES MEMORIAL SCHOLARSHIP

United Daughters of the Confederacy
Attn: Education Director
328 North Boulevard
Richmond, VA 23220-4057
(804) 355-1636   Fax: (804) 353-1396
E-mail: hqudc@rcn.com
Web: www.hqudc.org/scholarships/scholarships.html

Summary To provide financial assistance for graduate nursing education to lineal descendants of Confederate veterans.

Eligibility Eligible to apply for these scholarships are lineal descendants of worthy Confederates or collateral descendants who are members of the Children of the Confederacy or the United Daughters of the Confederacy. Applicants must intend to study nursing at the graduate level and must submit certified proof of the Confederate record of 1 ancestor, with the company and regiment in which he served. They must have a GPA of 3.0 or higher.

Financial data The amount of this scholarship depends on the availability of funds.

Duration 1 year; may be renewed up to 2 additional years.

Additional information Information is also available from Mrs. Robert C. Kraus, Second Vice President General, 239 Deerfield Lane, Franklin, NC 28734-0112. Members of the same family may not hold scholarships simultaneously, and only 1 application per family will be accepted within any 1 year. All requests for applica-

tions must be accompanied by a self-addressed stamped envelope.

Number awarded 1 each year.

Deadline March of each year.

[581]
SHUI KUEN AND ALLEN CHIN SCHOLARSHIP

Shui Kuen and Allen Chin Foundation
c/o Curtis Chin
215 South Santa Fe, Suite 3
Los Angeles, CA 90012
E-mail: info@skacfoundation.org
Web: blog.skacfoundation.org

Summary To provide financial assistance for college or graduate school to students who have worked or whose parent has worked in an Asian restaurant.

Eligibility This program is open to students currently working on an undergraduate or graduate degree at an accredited college or university. Applicants or their parents must have worked in the Asian/Pacific Islander food service industry in the United States.

Financial data The stipend is $1,000.

Duration 1 year.

Additional information This scholarship was first awarded in 2007.

Number awarded 1 each year.

Deadline December of each year.

[582]
SIEMENS CLINICAL ADVANCEMENT SCHOLARSHIP PROGRAM

American Society of Radiologic Technologists
Attn: ASRT Education and Research Foundation
15000 Central Avenue, S.E.
Albuquerque, NM 87123-3909
(505) 298-4500, ext. 2541
Toll-free: (800) 444-2778, ext. 2541   Fax: (505) 298-5063
E-mail: foundation@asrt.org
Web: www.asrt.org

Summary To provide financial assistance to members of the American Society of Radiologic Technologists (ASRT) who are interested in continuing their education.

Eligibility This program is open to licensed radiologic technologists who are current members of ASRT and have worked in the radiologic sciences profession for at least 1 year during the past 5 years in a clinical or didactic setting. Applicants must have applied to 1) an accredited certificate program related to the radiologic sciences, or 2) a course of study at the associate, bachelor's, master's, or doctoral level intended to further their career. Along with their application, they must submit a written interview up to 1,000 words on their professional achievements, their career goals, how their degree or certificate will help them to achieve their career goals, their educational goals, and how this scholarship will help them to achieve their educational goals. Financial need is considered in the selection process.

Financial data The stipend is $3,000.

Duration 1 year; may be renewed for 1 additional year.

Additional information This program is supported by the Oncology Care Group of Siemens Medical Solutions USA, Inc.

Number awarded Varies each year; recently, 6 of these scholarships were awarded.

Deadline January of each year.

[583]
SIGMA PHI ALPHA GRADUATE SCHOLARSHIP PROGRAM

American Dental Hygienists' Association
Attn: Institute for Oral Health
444 North Michigan Avenue, Suite 3400
Chicago, IL 60611
(312) 440-8918   Toll-free: (800) 735-4916
Fax: (312) 440-8929   E-mail: institute@adha.net
Web: www.adha.org/institute/Scholarship/index.htm

Summary To provide financial assistance to full-time students enrolled in graduate programs in dental hygiene who are members of Sigma Phi Alpha.

Eligibility This program is open to licensed dental hygienists who have a baccalaureate degree and have completed at least 1 year of work as a full-time master's or doctoral degree student in a university graduate program. Applicants must be active members of Sigma Phi Alpha, have a GPA of at least 3.5, and be able to document financial need of at least $1,500. Along with their application, they must submit a statement that covers their long-term career goals, their intended contribution to the dental hygiene profession, their professional interests, the manner in which their degree will enhance their professional capacity, a description of the research in which they are involved or would like to become involved, and a list of past and/or present involvement in professional and/or community activities.

Financial data Stipends range from $1,000 to $2,000.

Duration 1 year.

Additional information Recipients are required to submit a manuscript to the American Dental Hygienists' Association for publication.

Number awarded 1 each year.

Deadline June of each year.

[584]
SIGMA PHI ALPHA LINDA DEVORE SCHOLARSHIP

American Dental Education Association
Attn: Awards Program Coordinator
1400 K Street, N.W., Suite 1100
Washington, DC 20005
(202) 289-7201   Fax: (202) 289-7204
E-mail: morganm@adea.org
Web: www.adea.org/Awards/default.htm

Summary To provide financial assistance to undergraduate and graduate students working on a degree in an allied dental field.

Eligibility This program is open to students working on a baccalaureate, master's, or doctoral degree in dental hygiene, education, or public health. Applicants must be in good academic standing, able to demonstrate a commitment to leadership in education or health care (as by serving as an exemplary class officer or organizing a major class or schoolwide community service activity), and be an individual member of the American Dental Education Association (ADEA). Along with their application, they must submit a personal statement providing details of their personal qualities and leadership experiences. Financial need is not considered in the selection process.

Financial data The stipend is $1,000.

Duration Up to 1 year.

Additional information This program was established in 2006 to honor Linda DeVore, who served as president of the predecessor of the ADEA in 1994 and of Sigma Phi Alpha, the national honorary society of the dental hygiene profession, in 1997-98.

Number awarded 1 each year.

Deadline November of each year.

[585]
THE SISTERS' ECONOMIC AND SOCIAL JUSTICE SCHOLARSHIP FUND

The Sisters of Perpetual Indulgence, Inc.
Attn: Scholarship Fund Committee Chair
584 Castro Street
PMB 392
San Francisco, CA 94114
Web: www.SisterFund.com

Summary To provide financial assistance for college or graduate school to students who are committed to working for social and economic justice.

Eligibility This program is open to students enrolled in an accredited college or university and working on a bachelor's, master's, M.D., J.D., or Ph.D. degree. Applicants must be able to demonstrate a history of working for social and economic justice in their local or national community and be able to describe their plans to use their education to further economic and social justice. Ineligible students include those who are attending 1) military schools, law enforcement academies, or related preparatory programs; 2) institutions associated with religious groups known for discrimination or intolerance; or 3) institutions that, either through intentional or unintentional action or inaction, promote, encourage, or foster social or economic injustice. Selection is based on financial need, prior community involvement, future community involvement, and commitment to economic and social justice issues. Age, ethnicity, race or national origin, gender, and sexual orientation are not considered.

Financial data Stipends are either $1,000 or $500.

Duration 1 year.

Additional information The Sisters of Perpetual Indulgence is an organization of gay men established in San Francisco in 1979. It began offering scholarships in 2001. Applications must be submitted online.

Number awarded Varies each year; recently, 23 of these scholarships were awarded.

Deadline November of each year.

[586]
SOHN GRADUATE SCHOLARSHIPS

Society of Otorhinolaryngology and Head-Neck Nurses, Inc.
Attn: Ear, Nose and Throat Nursing Foundation
116 Canal Street, Suite A
New Smyrna Beach, FL 32168
(386) 428-1695   Fax: (386) 423-7566
E-mail: info@sohnnurse.com
Web: www.sohnnurse.com/awards.html

Summary To provide financial assistance to members of the Society of Otorhinolaryngology and Head-Neck Nurses (SOHN) who are working on a graduate degree in nursing.

Eligibility This program is open to members of the society who are able to demonstrate progress toward a master's degree in nursing.

Financial data Stipends range from $1,000 to $1,500.

Duration 1 year.

Number awarded 1 each year.

Deadline June of each year.

[587]
SONJA STEFANADIS GRADUATE STUDENT FELLOWSHIP

Daughters of Penelope
Attn: Daughters of Penelope Foundation, Inc.
1909 Q Street, N.W., Suite 500
Washington, DC 20009-1007
(202) 234-9741   Fax: (202) 483-6983
E-mail: daughters@ahepa.org
Web: www.ahepa.org

Summary To provide financial assistance for graduate study to women of Greek descent.

Eligibility This program is open to women who have been members of the Daughters of Penelope or the Maids of Athena for at least 2 years, or whose parents or grandparents have been members of the Daughters of Penelope or the Order of Ahepa for at least 2 years. Applicants must be accepted or currently enrolled in at least 9 units per academic year in an M.A., M.S., M.B.A., Ph.D., D.D.S., M.D., or other university graduate degree program. They must have taken the GRE or other entrance examination (or Canadian, Greek, or Cypriot equivalent) and must write an essay (in English) about their educational and vocational goals. Selection is based on academic merit.

Financial data The stipend is $1,000.

Duration 1 year; nonrenewable.

Additional information Information is also available from Helen Santire, National Scholarship Chair, P.O. Box 19709, Houston, TX 77242-9709, (713) 468-6531.

Number awarded 1 each year.

Deadline May of each year.

[588]
SOOZIE COURTER SHARING A BRIGHTER TOMORROW HEMOPHILIA SCHOLARSHIP

Wyeth Pharmaceuticals
Attn: Wyeth Hemophilia Hotline
5 Giralda Farms
Madison, NJ 07940
Toll-free: (888) 999-2349
Web: www.hemophiliavillage.com/programs_scholar.asp

Summary To provide financial assistance for college or graduate school to persons with hemophilia.

Eligibility This program is open to persons with hemophilia (A or B) who are high school seniors, have a GED, or are currently attending an accredited college, university, junior college, vocational school, or graduate school. They must need financial assistance to work on an undergraduate or graduate degree.

Financial data The stipends are $5,000 for undergraduate students, $7,500 for graduate students, or $2,500 for recipients at a vocational school.

Duration 1 year.

Additional information This program was established in 1998 and given its current name in 2000.

Number awarded 19 each year: 16 to undergraduates, 2 to graduate students, and 1 to a vocational student.

Deadline April of each year.

[589]
SOUTHERN MEDICAL ASSOCIATION MEDICAL STUDENT SCHOLARSHIP PROGRAM

Southern Medical Association
Attn: Research and Education Endowment Fund
35 Lakeshore Drive
P.O. Box 190088
Birmingham, AL 35219-0088
(205) 945-1840   Toll-free: (800) 423-4992, ext. 147
Fax: (205) 942-4454   E-mail: jfowler@sma.org
Web: www.sma.org

Summary To provide financial assistance to medical students at schools within the territorial boundaries of the Southern Medical Association.

Eligibility This program is open to third-year medical students at schools within the association's territory. Applicants must be able to demonstrate financial need.

Financial data The maximum stipend is $1,000. Funds are paid directly to the student's medical school.

Duration 1 year.

Additional information The association covers the states of Alabama, Arkansas, Florida, Georgia, Kentucky, Louisiana, Maryland, Mississippi, Missouri, North Carolina, Oklahoma, South Carolina, Tennessee, Texas, Virginia, West Virginia, and the District of Columbia.

Number awarded Varies each year; recently, 22 of these scholarships were awarded:

Deadline October of each year.

[590]
SREB DOCTORAL SCHOLARS PROGRAM

Southern Regional Education Board
592 10th Street N.W.
Atlanta, GA 30318-5790
(404) 875-9211, ext. 273   Fax: (404) 872-1477
E-mail: doctoral.scholars@sreb.org
Web: www.sreb.org/programs/dsp/dspindex.asp

Summary To provide financial assistance to minority students who wish to work on a doctoral degree in the sciences at designated universities in the southern states.

Eligibility This program is open to U.S. citizens who are members of racial/ethnic minority groups (Native Americans, Hispanic Americans, Asian Americans, and African Americans) and have or will receive a bachelor's degree from an accredited college or university. Applicants must intend to work on a Ph.D. in science, mathematics, engineering, or science or mathematics education at a participating institution. They must indicate an interest in becoming a college professor at an institution in the South. Students who are already enrolled in a doctoral program are not eligible. Study for professional degrees, such as the M.D., D.D.S., J.D., or D.V.M., as well as graduate study in education leading to an Ed.D., does not qualify.

Financial data Scholars receive a waiver of tuition and fees (in or out of state) for up to 5 years, an annual stipend of $15,000 for 3 years, an annual allowance for professional development activities, and reimbursement of travel expenses to attend the Doctoral Scholars annual meeting.

Duration Up to 5 years.

Number awarded Varies each year; recently, the program was supporting 208 scholars at 54 institutions in 22 states.

Deadline March of each year.

[591]
SREB REGIONAL CONTRACT PROGRAM

Southern Regional Education Board
592 10th Street N.W.
Atlanta, GA 30318-5790
(404) 875-9211, ext. 261   Fax: (404) 872-1477
E-mail: acm-rcp@sreb.org
Web: www.sreb.org/programs/acm/rcp/aboutrcp.asp

Summary To enable students from specified southern states to study designated health-related professions in other states at reduced tuition.

Eligibility Eligible are residents of 11 southern states who wish to enroll in a program not available at any public institution of higher education in their home state. If their state has made arrangements to send students to another institution, they may participate in this program. Contract programs currently operating include the following: for Alabama, dentistry and medicine at Meharry Medical College in Tennessee, and osteopathic medicine at Nova Southeastern College of Osteopathic Medicine in Florida; for Arkansas, dentistry at Baylor College of Dentistry in Texas, Louisiana State University, Meharry Medical College, University of Alabama at Birmingham, University of Louisville in Kentucky, University of Oklahoma, and University of Tennessee, optometry at Northeastern State University in Oklahoma and Southern College of Optometry in Tennessee, osteopathic medicine at Oklahoma State University, podiatry at Barry University in Florida, Ohio College of Podiatric Medicine, and the William M. Scholl College of Podiatric Medicine, and veterinary medicine at Louisiana State University and Mississippi State University; for Delaware, veterinary medicine at Oklahoma State University and University of Georgia; for Georgia, optometry at Southern College of Optometry and University of Alabama at Birmingham, and osteopathic medicine at Nova Southeastern College of Osteopathic Medicine; for Kentucky, optometry at Southern College of Optometry and University of Alabama at Birmingham, and veterinary medicine at Auburn University and Tuskegee University in Alabama; for Louisiana, optometry at Southern College of Optometry, University of Alabama at Birmingham, and University of Houston, osteopathic medicine at Nova Southeastern College of Osteopathic Medicine, and podiatry at William M. Scholl College of Podiatric Medicine; for Mississippi, optometry at Southern College of Optometry, University of Alabama at Birmingham, and University of Houston, and osteopathic medicine at Nova Southeastern College of Osteopathic Medicine; for North Carolina, dentistry and medicine at Meharry Medical College, and optometry at Southern College of Optometry, University of Alabama at Birmingham, and University of Houston; for South Carolina, arts at North Carolina School of the Arts, optometry at Southern College of Optometry and University of Alabama at Birmingham, and veterinary medicine at Tuskegee University and University of Georgia; for Tennessee, dentistry and medicine at Meharry Medical College, and optometry at Southern College of Optometry; for Virginia, optometry at Southern College of Optometry and University of Alabama at Birmingham.

Financial data Participants attending a public institution outside their home state pay only the in-state tuition. Students in programs at private institutions pay a reduced tuition rate.

Duration 1 year; may be renewed.

Number awarded Varies each year; during the past decade, more than 13,000 students have participated in this program.

[592]
ST. FRANCIS SCHOOL OF NURSING ALUMNI OF PITTSBURGH, PA SCHOLARSHIP FUND

Pittsburgh Foundation
Attn: Scholarship Coordinator
Five PPG Place, Suite 250
Pittsburgh, PA 15222-5414
(412) 391-5122   Fax: (412) 391-7259
E-mail: turnerd@pghfdn.org
Web: www.pittsburghfoundation.org

Summary To provide financial assistance to students working on an undergraduate or graduate degree in nursing.

Eligibility This program is open to 1) students working on their first academic degree or diploma that leads to professional licensure as a registered nurse, and 2) licensed registered nurses working on an advanced degree in nursing. Applicants must have a GPA of 3.0 or higher and be able to demonstrate financial need. Along with their application, they must submit brief essays on their prior work experience, prior education, financial obligations, extracurricular activities and volunteer work, past achievements related to nursing, and career goals. U.S. citizenship is required.

Financial data A stipend is awarded (amount not specified).

Duration 1 year.

Additional information This scholarship was first awarded in 2007.

Number awarded 1 or more each year.

Deadline December of each year.

[593]
STATE VOCATIONAL REHABILITATION SERVICES PROGRAM

Department of Education
Office of Special Education and Rehabilitative Services
Attn: Rehabilitation Services Administration
400 Maryland Avenue, S.W.,
Washington, DC 20202-2800
(202) 245-7488
Web: www.ed.gov/about/offices/list/osers/rsa/index.html

Summary To provide financial assistance to individuals with disabilities for undergraduate or graduate study pursued as part of their program of vocational rehabilitation.

Eligibility To be eligible for vocational rehabilitation services, an individual must 1) have a physical or mental impairment that is a substantial impediment to employment; 2) be able to benefit in terms of employment from vocational rehabilitation services; and 3) require vocational rehabilitation services to prepare for, enter, engage in, or retain gainful employment. Priority is given to applicants with the most significant disabilities. Persons accepted for vocational rehabilitation develop an Individualized Written Rehabilitation Program (IWRP) in consultation with a counselor for the vocational rehabilitation agency in the state in which they live. The IWRP may include a program of postsecondary education, if the disabled person and counselor agree that such a program will fulfill the goals of vocational rehabilitation. In most cases, the IWRP will provide for postsecondary education only to a level at which the disabled person will become employable, but that may include graduate education if the approved occupation requires an advanced degree as a minimum condition of entry. Students accepted to a program of postsecondary education as part of their IWRP must apply for all available federal, state, and private financial aid.

Financial data Funding for this program is provided by the federal government through grants to state vocational rehabilitation agencies. Grants under the basic support program currently total nearly $2.7 billion per year. States must supplement federal funding with matching funds of 21.3%. Persons who are accepted for vocational rehabilitation by the appropriate state agency receive financial assistance based on the cost of their education and other funds available to them, including their own or family contribution and other sources of financial aid. Allowable costs in most states include tuition, fees, books, supplies, room, board, transportation, personal expenses, child care, and expenses related to disability (special equipment, readers, attendants, interpreters, or notetakers).

Duration Assistance is provided until the disabled person achieves an educational level necessary for employment as provided in the IWRP.

Additional information You will need to contact your state vocational rehabilitation agency to apply for this program.

Number awarded Varies each year. Recently, more than 1.2 million people (of whom more than 80% have significant disabilities) were participating in this program.

[594]
STEPHANIE CARROLL MEMORIAL SCHOLARSHIP

National Association Directors of Nursing Administration in
  Long Term Care
Attn: Education/Scholarship Committee
10101 Alliance Road, Suite 140
Cincinnati, OH 45242
(513) 791-3679   Toll-free: (800) 222-0539
Fax: (513) 791-3699   E-mail: info@nadona.org
Web: www.nadona.org

Summary To provide financial assistance to undergraduate and graduate nursing students interested in specializing in geriatrics or long-term care.

Eligibility This program is open to students enrolled in a nursing program accredited by the National League for Nursing (NLN) or the Commission on Collegiate Nursing Education (CCNE). Applicants must be working on an undergraduate or graduate degree with long-term care or geriatrics as their practice area after graduation. They must be a member of the National Association of Directors of Nursing Administration in Long Term Care or sponsored by a member.

Financial data A stipend is awarded (amount not specified); a total of $5,000 is currently available for this program each year.

Duration 1 year.

Number awarded At least 1 each year.

Deadline February of each year.

[595]
STEPHEN BUFTON MEMORIAL EDUCATION FUND GRANTS

American Business Women's Association
Attn: Stephen Bufton Memorial Educational Fund
9100 Ward Parkway
P.O. Box 8728
Kansas City, MO 64114-0728
(816) 361-6621   Toll-free: (800) 228-0007
Fax: (816) 361-4991   E-mail: abwa@abwahq.org
Web: www.abwahq.org/ProfDev.asp

Summary To provide financial assistance to women undergraduate and graduate students in any field who are sponsored by a chapter of the American Business Women's Association (ABWA).

Eligibility This program is open to women who are at least sophomores at an accredited college or university. Applicants must be working on an undergraduate or graduate degree and have a GPA of 2.5 or higher. They are not required to be ABWA members, but they must be sponsored by an ABWA chapter that has contributed to the fund in the previous chapter year. U.S. citizenship is required.

Financial data The maximum grant is $1,200. Funds are paid directly to the recipient's institution to be used only for tuition, books, and fees.

Duration 1 year. Grants are not automatically renewed, but recipients may reapply.

Additional information This program was established in 1953. The ABWA does not provide the names and addresses of local chapters; it recommends that applicants check with their local Chamber of Commerce, library, or university to see if any chapter has registered a contact's name and number.

Number awarded Varies each year; since the inception of this program, it has awarded more than $14 million to more than 14,000 students.

Deadline May of each year.

[596]
STEVE DEARDUFF SCHOLARSHIP

Community Foundation for Greater Atlanta, Inc.
50 Hurt Plaza, Suite 449
Atlanta, GA 30303
(404) 688-5525   Fax: (404) 688-3060
E-mail: scholarships@atlcf.org
Web: www.atlcf.org

Summary To provide financial assistance to Georgia residents who are working on an undergraduate or graduate degree in medicine or social work.

Eligibility This program is open to legal residents of Georgia who are enrolled in or accepted at an accredited institution of higher learning to work on an undergraduate or graduate degree in medicine or social work. Applicants must be able to demonstrate a history of outstanding community service and potential for success in their chosen field. They must have a GPA of 2.0 or higher.

Financial data Stipends range up to $2,500 per year.

Duration 1 year; recipients may reapply.

Number awarded 3 each year.

Deadline March of each year.

[597]
STEVE FASTEAU PAST PRESIDENTS' SCHOLARSHIP

California Association for Postsecondary Education and
  Disability
Attn: Executive Assistant
71423 Biskra Road
Rancho Mirage, CA 92270
(760) 346-8206   Fax: (760) 340-5275
TTY: (760) 341-4084   E-mail: caped2000@aol.com
Web: www.caped.net/scholarship.html

Summary To provide financial assistance to undergraduate and graduate students in California who have a disability.

Eligibility This program is open to students at public and private colleges and universities in California who have a disability. Undergraduates must have completed at least 6 semester credits and have a GPA of 2.5 or higher. Graduate students must have completed at least 3 semester units and have a GPA of 3.0 or higher. Applicants must submit a 1-page personal letter that demonstrates writing skills; progress toward meeting educational and vocational goals; how they accommodate their disability; involvement in community activities; and any other personal factor that might strengthen their application. They must also submit a letter of recommendation from a faculty person, verification of disability, official transcripts, proof of current enrollment, and documentation of financial need.

Financial data The stipend is $1,000.

Duration 1 year.

Additional information Information is also available from Janet Shapiro, Disabled Student Programs and Services, Santa Barbara City College, 721 Cliff Drive, Santa Barbara, CA 93109, (805) 965-0581, ext. 2365, E-mail: shapiro@sbcc.net.

Number awarded 1 each year.

Deadline August of each year.

[598]
STUDENT PHARMACISTS SCHOLARSHIP PROGRAM

American Pharmacists Association
Attn: Foundation
1100 15th Street, N.W., Suite 400
Washington, DC 20005
(202) 429-7565   Fax: (202) 429-6300
E-mail: info@aphafoundation.org
Web: www.aphafoundation.org

Summary To provide financial assistance to members of the Academy of Student Pharmacists of the American Pharmacists Association (APhA-ASP).

Eligibility This program is open to full-time pharmacy students who have been actively involved in their school's APhA-ASP chapter. Applicants must have completed at least 1 year in the professional sequence of courses with a GPA of 2.75 or higher. Along with their application, they must submit a 500-word essay on a designated topic, 2 letters of recommendation, a current resume or CV, and a list of pharmacy and non-pharmacy related activities. Selection is based on the essay (50 points), voluntary service activities (30 points), GPA (10 points), and letters of recommendation (10 points).

Financial data The stipend is $1,000.

Duration 1 year; recipients may reapply.

Additional information This program was established in 2000 when the APhA Auxiliary decided to cease operations and transfer its assets to the APhA Foundation.

Number awarded Varies each year; recently, 9 of these scholarships were awarded.

Deadline November of each year.

[599]
SUBSTANCE ABUSE RESEARCH FELLOWSHIPS

American Psychological Association
Attn: Minority Fellowship Program
750 First Street, N.E.
Washington, DC 20002-4242
(202) 336-6127   Fax: (202) 336-6012
TDD: (202) 336-6123   E-mail: mfp@apa.org
Web: www.apa.org/mfp/sarprogram.html

Summary To provide financial assistance to psychology doctoral students (especially minorities) who are preparing for a career involving research on substance abuse issues and ethnic minority populations.

Eligibility This program is open to full-time doctoral students who can demonstrate a strong commitment to a career in substance abuse research and the mental health or psychological well-being of ethnic minorities. Students from all psychology disciplines are encouraged to apply if their training and research interests are related to mental health and substance abuse. Clinical, counseling, and school psychology students may be eligible if they intend to specialize in substance abuse treatment and research. Members of minority groups (African Americans, Alaskan Natives, American Indians, Asian Americans, Hispanics/Latinos, Native Hawaiians, and Pacific Islanders) are especially encouraged to apply. U.S. citizenship or permanent resident status is required. Selection is based on commitment to a career in research that focuses on substance abuse in ethnic minority communities, knowledge of ethnic minority psychology or mental health issues, the fit between career goals and training environment selected, potential for a research career demonstrated through accomplishments and goals, scholarship and grades, and letters of recommendation.

Financial data The stipend is the amount established by the National Institutes of Health for predoctoral students, recently $20,772 per year.

Duration 1 year; may be renewed for up to 2 additional years.

Additional information Funding is provided by the U.S. National Institute of Mental Health. Students who receive a federally-funded grant from another source may not also accept funds from this program.

Number awarded Varies each year.

Deadline January of each year.

[600]
SUPERCOLLEGE.COM STUDENT SCHOLARSHIPS

SuperCollege.com
Attn: Scholarship Application Request
4546 B10 El Camino Real, Number 281
Los Altos, CA 94022
(650) 618-2221   E-mail: supercollege@supercollege.com
Web: www.supercollege.com

Summary To provide financial assistance for undergraduate or graduate study to U.S. citizens and permanent residents.

Eligibility This program is open to U.S. citizens and permanent residents who are high school students (grades 9-12), college undergraduates, or graduate students. Applicants must submit an essay, up to 1,000 words, on 1 of the following topics: 1) describe a person, place, or issue that is important to you; 2) tell us why you deserve to win this scholarship; or 3) if you could have 1 superpower, what would it be and why? They must also submit 5 20-word statements on their 5 most important academic or non-academic achievements (e.g., projects, honors, awards, leadership positions, athletics, talents). Selection is based on the essays and academic and extracurricular achievement.

Financial data Stipends range from $500 to $2,500 per year. Funds must be used for tuition or tuition-related fees, textbooks, or room and board for study at an accredited college or university in the United States.

Duration 1 year.

Number awarded 1 each year.

Deadline July of each year.

[601]
SURVIVORS' AND DEPENDENTS' EDUCATIONAL ASSISTANCE PROGRAM

Department of Veterans Affairs
810 Vermont Avenue, N.W.
Washington, DC 20420
(202) 418-4343   Toll-free: (888) GI-BILL1
Web: www.gibill.va.gov

Summary To provide financial assistance for undergraduate or graduate study to children and spouses of deceased and disabled veterans, MIAs, and POWs.

Eligibility Eligible for this assistance are spouses and children of 1) veterans who died or are permanently and totally disabled as the result of active service in the armed forces; 2) veterans who died from any cause while rated permanently and totally disabled from a service-connected disability; 3) servicemembers listed for more than 90 days as currently missing in action or captured in the line of duty by a hostile force; and 4) servicemembers listed for more than 90 days as presently detained or interned by a foreign government or power. Children must be between 18 and 26 years of age, although extensions may be granted. Spouses and children over 14 years of age with physical or mental disabilities are also eligible.

Financial data Monthly stipends from this program for study at an academic institution are $827 for full time, $621 for three-quarter time, or $413 for half-time. For farm cooperative work, the monthly stipends are $667 for full-time, $500 for three-quarter time, or $334 for half-time. For an apprenticeship or on-the-job training, the monthly stipend is $650 for the first 6 months, $507 for the second 6 months, $366 for the third 6 months, and $151 for the remainder of the program.

Duration Up to 45 months (or the equivalent in part-time training). Spouses must complete their training within 10 years of the date they are first found eligible.

Additional information Benefits may be used to work on associate, bachelor, or graduate degrees at colleges and universities, including independent study, cooperative training, and study abroad programs. Courses leading to a certificate or diploma from business, technical, or vocational schools may also be taken. Other eligible programs include apprenticeships, on-job training programs, farm cooperative courses, correspondence courses (for spouses only), secondary school programs (for recipients who are not high school graduates), tutorial assistance, remedial deficiency and refresher training, or work-study (for recipients who are enrolled at least three-quarter time). Eligible children who are handicapped by a physical or mental disability that prevents pursuit of an educational program may receive special restorative training that includes language retraining, lip reading, auditory training, Braille reading and writing, and similar programs. Eligible spouses and children over 14 years of age who are handicapped by a physical or mental disability that prevents pursuit of an educational program may receive specialized vocational training that includes specialized courses, alone or in combination with other courses, leading to a vocational objective that is suitable for the person and required by reason of physical or mental handicap. Ineligible courses include bartending or personality development courses; correspondence courses by dependent or surviving children; non-accredited independent study courses; any course given by radio; self-improvement courses, such as reading, speaking, woodworking, basic seamanship, and English as a second language; audited courses; any course that is avocational or recreational in character; courses not leading to an educational, professional, or vocational objective; courses taken and successfully completed previously; courses taken by a federal government employee and paid for under the Government Employees' Training Act; and courses taken while in receipt of benefits for the same program from the Office of Workers' Compensation Programs.

Number awarded Varies each year.

Deadline Applications may be submitted at any time.

[602]
TAYLOR J. ERTEL SCHOLARSHIPS

Taylor J. Ertel Foster Children Foundation
2245 Heim Hill Road
Montoursville, PA 17754-9699
(570) 433-3494   Fax: (570) 326-1050
E-mail: aertel@regscan.com
Web: www.tjefoundation.org

Summary To provide financial assistance for college or graduate school to residents of Pennsylvania who have been in foster care.

Eligibility This program is open to Pennsylvania residents who have been placed in foster care by a child welfare agency. Applicants must be attending or planning to attend a vocational school, college, university, or graduate school in the state. Along with their application, they must submit information on their school activities, educational record, school awards and honors, community activities, employment record, and a budget.

Financial data The stipend is $2,000 per year.

Duration 1 year.

Additional information This program was established in 1993.

Number awarded 1 or more each year.

[603]
TEXAS AMATEUR ATHLETIC FEDERATION ATHLETE SCHOLARSHIPS

Texas Amateur Athletic Federation
P.O. Box 1789
Georgetown, TX 78627-1789
(512) 863-9400   Fax: (512) 869-2393
E-mail: marklord@cox-internet.com
Web: www.taaf.com/pages/schlorship.asp

Summary To provide financial assistance to undergraduate and graduate students who have participated in activities of the Texas Amateur Athletic Federation (TAAF).

Eligibility This program is open to past and present Texas Amateur Athletic Federation (TAAF) athletes who have competed in 1 or more state level competitions or tournaments. Applicants must be enrolled or planning to enroll at a college or university, preferably in Texas, in an accredited bachelor's, master's, or doctoral degree program. They must have a GPA of 2.5 or higher. Selection is based on honors and awards from, and participation in, activities, endeavors, volunteerism, and work related to athletics and/or the field of parks and recreation. Financial need is not considered.

Financial data A stipend is awarded (amount not specified).

Duration 1 year.

Number awarded 1 or more each year.

Deadline April of each year.

[604]
TEXAS LEVERAGING EDUCATIONAL ASSISTANCE PARTNERSHIP PROGRAM

Texas Higher Education Coordinating Board
Attn: Grants and Special Programs
1200 East Anderson Lane
P.O. Box 12788, Capitol Station
Austin, TX 78711-2788
(512) 427-6101   Toll-free: (800) 242-3062
Fax: (512) 427-6127   E-mail: grantinfo@thecb.state.tx.us
Web: www.collegefortexans.com

Summary To provide financial assistance to undergraduate and graduate students at colleges and universities in Texas who are also receiving other state funds.

Eligibility This program is open to Texas residents who are enrolled or accepted for enrollment at least half time at a college or university in Texas on the undergraduate or graduate school level. Financial need must be demonstrated. Applicants must also be receiving funding from another state program (either the Texas Student Incentive Grant Program for students at public colleges and universities or the Texas Tuition Equalization Grant Program for students at private colleges and universities).

Financial data The stipend depends on the need of the recipient, to a maximum of $1,250.

Duration 1 year; may be renewed.

Number awarded Varies each year.

[605]
TEXAS OCCUPATIONAL THERAPY ASSOCIATION SCHOLARSHIPS

American Occupational Therapy Foundation
Attn: Scholarship Coordinator
4720 Montgomery Lane
P.O. Box 31220
Bethesda, MD 20824-1220
(301) 652-2682   Fax: (301) 656-3620
TDD: (800) 377-8555   E-mail: aotf@aotf.org
Web: www.aotf.org

Summary To provide financial assistance to students who are members of the Texas Occupational Therapy Association and working on a degree in occupational therapy.

Eligibility This program is open to Texas residents who are enrolled in an accredited occupational therapy educational program (associate or professional master's) in the state. Applicants must demonstrate a need for financial assistance, have a sustained record of outstanding scholastic performance, and be members of the Texas Occupational Therapy Association. As part of the application process, they must submit transcripts, 2 personal references, and a statement from their curriculum director.

Financial data The stipend is $2,000.

Duration 1 year.

Number awarded 2 each year: 1 at the professional master's degree level and 1 at the associate degree level.

Deadline January of each year.

[606]
TEXAS PUBLIC EDUCATIONAL GRANT PROGRAM

Texas Higher Education Coordinating Board
Attn: Grants and Special Programs
1200 East Anderson Lane
P.O. Box 12788, Capitol Station
Austin, TX 78711-2788
(512) 427-6101   Toll-free: (800) 242-3062
Fax: (512) 427-6127   E-mail: grantinfo@thecb.state.tx.us
Web: www.collegefortexans.com

Summary To provide financial assistance to undergraduate and graduate students in Texas.

Eligibility This program is open to residents of Texas, nonresidents, and foreign students. Applicants may be undergraduate or graduate students. They must be attending a public college or university in Texas. Financial need is considered as part of the selection process.

Financial data The amount awarded varies, depending upon the financial need of the recipient. No award may exceed the student's unmet financial need. Each institution sets its own maximum award amounts.

Duration 1 year; may be renewed.

Additional information Information and application forms may be obtained from the director of financial aid at the public college or university in Texas the applicant attends. Study must be conducted in Texas; funds cannot be used to support attendance at an out-of-state institution.

Number awarded Varies each year; recently, 102,696 of these grants were awarded.

[607]
TEXAS TUITION EQUALIZATION GRANT PROGRAM

Texas Higher Education Coordinating Board
Attn: Grants and Special Programs
1200 East Anderson Lane
P.O. Box 12788, Capitol Station
Austin, TX 78711-2788
(512) 427-6101   Toll-free: (800) 242-3062
Fax: (512) 427-6127   E-mail: grantinfo@thecb.state.tx.us
Web: www.collegefortexans.com

Summary To provide financial assistance to undergraduate and graduate students attending private postsecondary schools in Texas.

Eligibility This program is open to 1) residents of Texas, and 2) residents of other states who are National Merit Scholarship finalists. Applicants must be enrolled at least half time as an undergraduate or graduate student at an eligible nonprofit independent college in the state. They may not be receiving an athletic scholarship. Financial need is considered in the selection process.

Financial data The maximum awarded is the lesser of the student's unmet need or the amount they would pay at a public institution (currently, $3,653).

Duration 1 year; may be renewed.

Additional information Information and application forms may be obtained from the director of financial aid at any participating nonprofit independent college or university in Texas.

Number awarded Varies each year; recently, 27,994 of these grants were awarded.

[608]
TEXAS WAIVER FOR STUDENTS FROM MEXICO ENROLLED IN GRADUATE DEGREE PROGRAMS IN PUBLIC HEALTH

Texas Higher Education Coordinating Board
Attn: Grants and Special Programs
1200 East Anderson Lane
P.O. Box 12788, Capitol Station
Austin, TX 78711-2788
(512) 427-6323   Toll-free: (800) 242-3062, ext. 6323
Fax: (512) 427-6127   E-mail: grantinfo@thecb.state.tx.us
Web: www.collegefortexans.com

Summary To enable Mexican residents to work on a graduate degree in public health at Texas public institutions at reduced rates.

Eligibility This program is open to residents of Mexico who are non-immigrant aliens in Texas. Applicants must enroll in a graduate degree program in public health conducted by a public university or health-related institution in a Texas county immediately adjacent to Mexico. They must be able to demonstrate financial need.

Financial data Eligible students are able to attend Texas public institutions and pay the resident tuition rate.

Duration 1 year; may be renewed.

Additional information Applications must be submitted through the financial aid office or international student office at the college or university attended.

Number awarded Varies each year.

[609]
THIRD YEAR OUTSTANDING AU.D. STUDENT AWARD

Audiology Foundation of America
Attn: Scholarship Committee
8 North Third Street, Suite 406
Lafayette, IN 47901-1247
(765) 743-6AUD   Fax: (765) 743-9AUD
E-mail: info-afa@audfound.org
Web: www.audfound.org/index.cfm?pageID=49

Summary To provide financial assistance to students entering the second year of a doctoral program in audiology.

Eligibility This program is open to students enrolled full time in the second year of a 4-year doctor of audiology (Au.D.) program. Applicants may not be a licensed or registered practicing audiologist. They must be nominated by their program director. Citizenship or permanent resident status of the United States and its territories or Canada is required.

Financial data The stipend is $4,500.

Duration 1 year; nonrenewable.

Additional information This program is sponsored by the Oticon Foundation.

Number awarded 2 each year.

Deadline July of each year.

[610]
THOMAS JORDAN DOCTORAL SCHOLARSHIP

Oncology Nursing Society
Attn: ONS Foundation
125 Enterprise Drive
Pittsburgh, PA 15275-1214
(412) 859-6100, ext. 8503   Toll-free: (866) 257-4ONS
Fax: (412) 859-6160   E-mail: foundation@ons.org
Web: www.ons.org/awards/foundawards/doctoral.shtml

Summary To provide financial assistance to registered nurses interested in pursuing doctoral studies in oncology nursing.

Eligibility Candidates must be registered nurses with a demonstrated interest in and commitment to oncology nursing; be enrolled in or applying to a doctoral nursing degree program or related program; and never have received a doctoral scholarship from this sponsor. Along with their application, they must submit brief essays on why they chose their doctoral program; the courses and clinical experience of the program that are related to cancer nursing; their research area of interest and plans for a dissertation; their professional goals and their relationship to the advancement of oncology nursing; and how the doctoral program will assist them in achieving their goals.

Financial data The stipend is $3,000.

Duration 1 year.

Additional information Funding for this program, which began in 1993, is provided by Bristol-Myers Squibb Oncology Division. At the end of each year of scholarship participation, recipients must submit a summary of their educational activities. Applications must be accompanied by a $5 fee.

Number awarded 1 each year.

Deadline January of each year.

[611]
THOMPSON SCHOLARSHIP FOR WOMEN IN SAFETY

American Society of Safety Engineers
Attn: ASSE Foundation
1800 East Oakton Street
Des Plaines, IL 60018
(847) 768-3435   Fax: (847) 768-3434
E-mail: agabanski@asse.org
Web: www.asse.org/foundation

Summary To provide financial assistance to women working on a graduate degree in safety-related fields (including occupational health and medicine).

Eligibility This program is open to women who are working on a graduate degree in safety engineering, safety management, occupational health nursing, occupational medicine, risk management, ergonomics, industrial hygiene, fire safety, environmental safety, environmental health, or another safety-related field. Applicants must be full-time students who have completed at least 9 semester hours with a GPA of 3.5 or higher. Their undergraduate GPA must have been 3.0 or higher. Along with their application, they must submit 2 essays of 300 words or less: 1) why they are seeking a degree in occupational safety and health or a closely-related field, a brief description of their current activities, and how those relate to their career goals and objectives; and 2) why they should be awarded this scholarship (including career goals and financial need).

Financial data The stipend is $1,000.

Duration 1 year; nonrenewable.

Number awarded 1 each year.

Deadline November of each year.

[612]
T.L. MCCLELLAN MEMORIAL SCHOLARSHIP

North Carolina Rehabilitation Association
c/o Ardell Allen, Commissioner of Professional Concerns
Division of Services for the Deaf and the Hard of Hearing
31 College Place, Building C-100
Asheville, NC 28801
(828) 251-6190   Fax: (828) 251-6860
E-mail: Ardell.allen@ncmail.net
Web: www.ncrehab.org

Summary To provide financial assistance to undergraduate and graduate students in North Carolina who are preparing for a career in rehabilitation.

Eligibility This program is open to undergraduate and graduate students enrolled full time at accredited colleges and universities in North Carolina. Applicants must be studying rehabilitation or human services to prepare for a career in rehabilitation in North Carolina. Along with their application, they must submit official transcripts; any certificates for academic excellence; a resume of work experiences, publications, and vocational objectives; and 3 letters of reference. Applicants who have a physical or mental impairment and would like that to be considered must also describe how they have dealt with or overcome societal barriers to their impairment.

Financial data The stipend is $1,000.

Duration 1 year.

Additional information This scholarship was first awarded in 1969. Recipients are required to attend the sponsor's awards breakfast.

Number awarded 1 or more each year.

Deadline May of each year.

[613]
TRIAD HOSPITALS CORRIS BOYD SCHOLARSHIP

Association of University Programs in Health Administration
Attn: Prizes, Fellowships and Scholarships
2000 14th Street North, Suite 780
Arlington, VA 22201
(703) 894-0940, ext. 131   Fax: (703) 894-0941
E-mail: aupha@aupha.org
Web: www.aupha.org

Summary To provide financial assistance to minority students entering graduate schools affiliated with the Association of University Programs in Health Administration (AUPHA).

Eligibility This program is open to members of racial and ethnic minority groups (African Americans, American Indians, Alaska Natives, Asian Americans, Hispanic Americans, Native Hawaiians, and other Pacific Islanders) who have applied to but not yet enrolled in a master's degree program in health care management at an AUPHA member institution. Applicants must be U.S. citizens and have a GPA of 3.0 or higher. Selection is based on leadership qualities, academic achievement, community involvement, and commitment to health care; financial need may be considered if all other factors are equal.

Financial data Fellows receive full payment of tuition at the AUPHA member institution of their choice. The school receives a grant of $13,000 to provide the student with an assistantship.

Duration 1 year.

Additional information These fellowships are funded by Triad Hospitals, Inc. The program is jointly administered by AUPHA and the Institute for Diversity in Healthcare Management. Recipients are offered, and required to accept, a residency placement with Triad Hospitals upon graduation.

Number awarded 2 each year.

Deadline May of each year.

[614]
TYCO KENDALL HEALTHCARE PRODUCTS SCHOLARSHIP FOR CONTINUING EDUCATION

American Nephrology Nurses' Association
Attn: ANNA National Office
200 East Holly Avenue
P.O. Box 56
Pitman, NJ 08071-0056
(856) 256-2320   Toll-free: (888) 600-2662
Fax: (856) 589-7463   E-mail: annascholarships@ajj.com
Web: www.annanurse.org

Summary To provide financial assistance to members of the American Nephrology Nurses' Association (ANNA) who are interested in working on an advanced degree that will enhance their ability to contribute to the renal community.

Eligibility Applicants must be full members of the association, have been members for at least 2 years, be currently employed in nephrology nursing, be actively working in a clinical setting, and provide evidence of active participation in the local association chapter. Along with their application, they must submit a 250-word essay on their career and education goals that includes how their degree will apply to nephrology nursing, provides a time frame for completing their program, and indicates how the funds will meet their educational needs.

Financial data The stipend is $1,000.

Duration 1 year.

Additional information Funds for this program, established in 2000, are supplied by Tyco Kendall Healthcare Products. Information is also available from Sharon Longton, Awards and Scholarships Chair, (313) 966-2674, E-mail: slongton@dmc.org.

Number awarded 1 each year.

Deadline October of each year.

[615]
TYLENOL SCHOLARSHIPS

McNeil Consumer Healthcare
c/o Scholarship America
Attn: Scholarship Management Services
One Scholarship Way
P.O. Box 297
St. Peter, MN 56082
(507) 931-0479   Toll-free: (800) 537-4180
Fax: (507) 931-9168   E-mail: margjohnson@csfa.org
Web: www.tylenolscholarship.com

Summary To provide financial assistance for college or graduate school to students intending to prepare for a career in a health-related field.

Eligibility This program is open to students who will be enrolled in an undergraduate or graduate course of study at an accredited 2-year or 4-year college, university, or vocational/technical school and have 1 or more years of school remaining. Applicants must intend to major in an area that will lead to a career in a health-related field. Selection is based on the number, length of commitment, and quality of leadership responsibilities in community activities and school activities, awards, and honors (40%), a clear statement of education and career goals (10%), and academic record (50%).

Financial data Stipends are $5,000 or $1,000.

Duration 1 year.

Additional information This program is sponsored by McNeil Consumer Healthcare, maker of Tylenol products, and administered by Scholarship America.

Number awarded 170 each year: 20 at $5,000 and 150 at $1,000.

Deadline April of each year.

[616]
UNITED METHODIST GENERAL SCHOLARSHIP PROGRAM

United Methodist Church
Attn: General Board of Higher Education and Ministry
Office of Loans and Scholarships
1001 19th Avenue South
P.O. Box 340007
Nashville, TN 37203-0007
(615) 340-7344   Fax: (615) 340-7367
E-mail: umscholar@gbhem.org
Web: www.gbhem.org/gbhem/loans2.html

Summary To provide financial assistance to undergraduate and graduate students who are members of United Methodist Church congregations.

Eligibility This program includes a number of individual scholarships that were established by private donors through wills and annuities. The basic criteria for eligibility include 1) U.S. citizenship or permanent resident status; 2) active, full membership in a United Methodist Church for at least 1 year prior to applying (some scholarships require 3-years' membership); 3) GPA of 2.5 or higher (some scholarships require 3.0 or higher); 4) demonstrated financial need; and 5) full-time enrollment in an undergraduate or graduate degree program at an accredited educational institution in the United States. Students from the Central Conferences must be enrolled at a United Methodist-related institution. Most graduate scholarships are designated for persons working on a degree in theological studies (M.Div., D.Min., Ph.D.) or higher education administration. Some scholarships stipulate that the applicant meet more than the basic eligibility criteria (e.g., resident of specific conference, majoring in specified field).

Financial data The funding is intended to supplement the students' own resources.

Duration 1 year; renewal policies are set by participating universities.

Number awarded Varies each year.

Deadline May of each year.

[617]
UPWARD BOUND! SCHOLARSHIP

National Association Directors of Nursing Administration in
    Long Term Care
Attn: Education/Scholarship Committee
10101 Alliance Road, Suite 140
Cincinnati, OH 45242
(513) 791-3679   Toll-free: (800) 222-0539
Fax: (513) 791-3699   E-mail: info@nadona.org
Web: www.nadona.org

Summary To provide financial assistance to nurses who are currently employed in long-term care and are interested in pursuing higher education, with a career focus on long-term care.

Eligibility This program is open to registered nurses, licensed practical nurses, and certified nursing assistants (evidence of licensure or certification must accompany the application) who are currently accepted or enrolled in 1 of the following programs: 1) an L.P.N. or R.N. program; 2) an accredited R.N. program or

undergraduate health care management program; 3) a baccalaureate or master's degree program in nursing or gerontology; 4) an undergraduate or graduate program in health care management. Applicants must be currently employed in long-term care (for at least 1 year) and plan to remain employed in that field for at least 2 years after graduation. They must be members of the National Association of Directors of Nursing Administration in Long Term Care or sponsored by a member.

Financial data A stipend is awarded (amount not specified); a total of $5,000 is currently available for this program each year.

Duration 1 year.

Additional information Funds for this scholarship are provided by Pfizer.

Number awarded At least 1 each year.

Deadline February of each year.

[618]
USA FUNDS ACCESS TO EDUCATION SCHOLARSHIPS

Scholarship America
Attn: Scholarship Management Services
One Scholarship Way
P.O. Box 297
St. Peter, MN 56082
(507) 931-1682   Toll-free: (800) 537-4180
Fax: (507) 931-9168   E-mail: scholarship@usafunds.org
Web: www.usafunds.org

Summary To provide financial assistance to undergraduate and graduate students, especially those who are members of ethnic minority groups or have physical disabilities.

Eligibility This program is open to high school seniors and graduates who plan to enroll or are already enrolled in full-time undergraduate or graduate course work at an accredited 2- or 4-year college, university, or vocational/technical school. Half-time undergraduate students are also eligible. Up to 50% of the awards are targeted at students who have a documented physical disability or are a member of an ethnic minority group, including but not limited to Native Hawaiian, Alaskan Native, Black/African American, Asian, Pacific Islander, American Indian, or Hispanic/Latino. Residents of all 50 states, the District of Columbia, Puerto Rico, Guam, the U.S. Virgin Islands, and all U.S. territories and commonwealths are eligible. Applicants must also be U.S. citizens or eligible noncitizens and come from a family with an annual adjusted gross income of $35,000 or less. In addition to financial need, selection is based on past academic performance and future potential, leadership and participation in school and community activities, work experience, career and educational aspirations, and goals.

Financial data The stipend is $1,500 per year for full-time undergraduate or graduate students or $750 per year for half-time undergraduate students. Funds are paid jointly to the student and the school.

Duration 1 year; may be renewed until the student receives a final degree or certificate or until the total award to a student reaches $6,000, whichever comes first. Renewal requires the recipient to maintain a GPA of 2.5 or higher.

Additional information This program, established in 2000, is sponsored by USA Funds, which serves as the education loan guarantor and administrator in selected states.

Number awarded Varies each year; recently, a total of $3 million was available for this program.

Deadline February of each year.

[619]
UTAH GOLF ASSOCIATION SCHOLARSHIPS

Utah Golf Association
Attn: Scholarship Committee
9121 South 150 West, Suite D
P.O. Box 5601
Sandy, UT 84091-5601
(801) 563-0400   Fax: (801) 563-0632
Web: www.uga.org/awards/scholarship/index.html

Summary To provide financial assistance for college or graduate school to students in Utah who have been active in golf.

Eligibility This program is open to students enrolled or planning to enroll at a postsecondary institution in Utah. Preference is given to applicants already in college or working on an advanced degree. At least 1 scholarship is reserved for a student interested in preparing for a career in agronomy, turfgrass management, or as a golf course superintendent. Applicants have been involved in golf, but skill is not considered. They must describe their long-range educational and occupational goals and objectives, what they like about golf, and their background, interests, and future plans in golf. Selection is based on educational experience, achievements, GPA, test scores, goals, and objectives (25%); leadership, extracurricular activities, work experience, volunteerism, and character (25%); golf affiliation and interest (25%); and financial need (25%).

Financial data The stipend is $1,200.

Duration 1 year.

Number awarded At least 3 each year.

Deadline April of each year.

[620]
VICTOR E. SCHIMMEL MEMORIAL NURSING SCHOLARSHIPS

The Camden Group
Attn: Barbara Patton
100 North Sepulveda, Suite 600
El Segundo, CA 90245
(310) 320-3990, ext. 4044   Fax: (310) 606-5811
E-mail: Bpatton@thecamdengroup.com
Web: www.thecamdengroup.com

Summary To provide financial assistance to California residents interested in working on an advanced degree in nursing.

Eligibility This program is open to residents of California who are currently enrolled or have been accepted into a college or university to work on an advanced degree in nursing. Nurse managers, directors, educators, and nursing program faculty are invited to apply. Both full- and part-time graduate students are eligible. As part of the application process, they must submit 2 essays of 400 words or less: 1) the professional goals they want to achieve in the next 5 years; and 2) their ability to guide, inspire, direct, or set examples for others and how they have accomplished this in their professional life.

Financial data The stipend is $2,500.

Duration 1 year.

Additional information These scholarships were first awarded in 2001.

Number awarded 2 each year.

Deadline March of each year.

[621]
VICTORIA S. AND BRADLEY L. GEIST FOUNDATION SCHOLARSHIP

Hawai'i Community Foundation
Attn: Scholarship Department
1164 Bishop Street, Suite 800
Honolulu, HI 96813
(808) 566-5570   Toll-free: (888) 731-3863
Fax: (808) 521-6286   E-mail: scholarships@hcf-hawaii.org
Web: www.hawaiicommunityfoundation.org

Summary To provide financial assistance to Hawaii residents who are interested in attending college or graduate school and have been in the foster care (or similar) system.

Eligibility This program is open to Hawaii residents who are permanently separated from their parents and currently in (or formerly in) the foster care system. Applicants must be or planning to become full-time students at the undergraduate or graduate school level. They must be able to demonstrate academic achievement, good moral character, and financial need. In addition to filling out the standard application form, applicants must 1) write a short statement indicating their reasons for attending college, their planned course of study, and their career goals, and 2) supply a confirmation letter from their social worker, foster parent, hanai parent, or other appropriate individual.

Financial data The amounts of the awards depend on the availability of funds and the need of the recipient; recently, stipends averaged $2,400.

Duration 1 year.

Additional information Recipients may attend college in Hawaii or on the mainland.

Number awarded Varies each year; recently, 54 of these scholarships were awarded.

Deadline February of each year.

[622]
VINCENT DEPAUL DRADDY AWARD

National Football Foundation
22 Maple Avenue
Morristown, NJ 07960
(973) 829-1933   Toll-free: (800) 486-1865
Fax: (973) 829-1737
E-mail: scholarship@footballfoundation.com
Web: www.footballfoundation.com/draddy.php

Summary To provide financial assistance for graduate school to college football players who demonstrate both athletic and academic excellence.

Eligibility This award is presented to college football players who combine outstanding athletic performance with academic distinction and civic leadership. Each 4-year college and university that plays football (I-A, I-AA, II, III, and NAIA) is encouraged to nominate 1 of its players who is a senior or graduate student in his final year of eligibility. Nominees must have a GPA of 3.0 or higher and have demonstrated football ability and performance as a first team player as well as outstanding school leadership and citizenship. Selection is based on academic accomplishment (up to 40 points), football ability (up to 40 points), and school, civic, and community activities (up to 20 points).

Financial data The awardee receives a trophy and a $25,000 graduate scholarship.

Duration The award is presented annually.

Additional information This award, first presented in 1990, is cosponsored by the National Football Foundation and College Hall of Fame, Inc. with funding from HealthSouth.

Number awarded 1 each year.
Deadline Nominations must be submitted by September of each year.

[623]
VIRGINIA ASSOCIATION FOR HEALTH, PHYSICAL EDUCATION, RECREATION, AND DANCE GRADUATE AWARD

Virginia Association for Health, Physical Education,
  Recreation, and Dance
c/o Jack Schiltz, Executive Director
817 West Franklin Street
P.O. Box 842020
Richmond, VA 23284-2020
(804) 828-1948   Toll-free: (800) 918-9899
Fax: (804) 828-1946   E-mail: info@vahperd.org
Web: www.vahperd.org

Summary To provide financial assistance to graduate students working on a degree in health, physical education, recreation, or dance in Virginia.
Eligibility This program is open to students working on a master's or doctoral degree in health, physical education, recreation, or dance at a college or university in Virginia. Applicants must be members of the Virginia Association of Health, Physical Education, Recreation, and Dance (VAHPERD) and the American Alliance for Health, Physical Education, Recreation and Dance (AAHPERD). Selection is based on honors and awards received, services to school and community, and achievements in the field of health, physical education, recreation, or dance.
Financial data A stipend is awarded (amount not specified).
Duration 1 year.
Number awarded 1 each year.
Deadline September of each year.

[624]
VIRGINIA C. PHILLIPS GRADUATE SCHOLARSHIP AWARD

South Carolina Nurses Foundation, Inc.
Attn: Virginia C. Phillips Scholarship Fund
1821 Gadsden Street
Columbia, SC 29201
(803) 788-9054   Fax: (803) 779-3870
E-mail: info@scnursesfoundation.org
Web: www.scnursesfoundation.org

Summary To provide financial assistance to residents of South Carolina who are enrolled in a graduate program in public health or nursing.
Eligibility This program is open to South Carolina residents who are have successfully completed at least 12 hours of graduate course work in a program in nursing or public health. Applicants must be a current member of a professional organization and have already made some contribution to the field of public/community health nursing. Along with their application, they must submit a 1- to 2-page statement that describes their future career goals in public/community health nursing. Financial need is not considered in the selection process.
Financial data The stipend is $1,000.
Duration 1 year.
Additional information This program, which began in 1980, is operated in partnership with the South Carolina Department of Health and Environmental Control (SCDHEC). Information is also available from the VCP/HHS Planning Committee, SCDHEC,

Office of Public Health Nursing, Mills/Jarrett Complex, Box 101106, Columbia, SC 29211.
Number awarded 1 each year.
Deadline July of each year.

[625]
VIRGINIA TUITION ASSISTANCE GRANT PROGRAM

State Council of Higher Education for Virginia
Attn: Financial Aid Office
James Monroe Building
101 North 14th Street, Ninth Floor
Richmond, VA 23219-3659
(804) 225-2600   Toll-free: (877) 515-0138
Fax: (804) 225-2604   TDD: (804) 371-8017
E-mail: fainfo@schev.edu
Web: www.schev.edu

Summary To provide financial assistance to undergraduate and graduate students attending private colleges or universities in Virginia.
Eligibility Undergraduate and graduate or professional students who are Virginia residents attending private colleges or universities in the state on a full-time basis in a degree program are eligible for this program. There is no financial need requirement. Students pursuing religious training or theological education are not eligible.
Financial data The amount awarded varies, depending on annual appropriations and number of applicants; recently, the maximum award was $2,700 for undergraduates or $1,900 for graduate students.
Duration 1 year; may be renewed.
Additional information This program was established in 1972.
Number awarded Varies each year.
Deadline The deadline for priority consideration for fall semester is July of each year. Applicants submitted through the end of November are considered only if funds are available.

[626]
VIRGINIA WAR ORPHANS EDUCATION PROGRAM

Virginia Department of Veterans' Affairs
270 Franklin Road, S.W., Room 503
Roanoke, VA 24011-2215
(540) 857-7104   Fax: (540) 857-7573
Web: www.dvs.virginia.gov/education_benefits.htm

Summary To provide educational assistance to the children of disabled and other Virginia veterans or service personnel.
Eligibility This program is open to residents of Virginia who have at least 1 parent who served in the U.S. armed forces and is permanently and totally disabled due to an injury or disease incurred in a time of war or other period of armed conflict, has died as a result of war or other armed conflict, or is listed as a prisoner of war or missing in action. Applicants must be between 16 and 25 years of age and be accepted at a public secondary or postsecondary educational institution in Virginia. The veteran parent must have been a resident of Virginia at the time of entry into active military service or for at least 5 consecutive years immediately prior to the date of application or death. The surviving parent must have been a resident of Virginia for at least 5 years prior to marrying the deceased parent or for at least 5 years immediately prior to the date on which the application was submitted.
Financial data Eligible individuals receive free tuition and are exempted from any fees charged by state-supported schools in Virginia.

Duration Entitlement extends to a maximum of 48 months.

Additional information Individuals entitled to this benefit may use it to pursue any vocational, technical, undergraduate, or graduate program of instruction. Generally, programs listed in the academic catalogs of state-supported institutions are acceptable, provided they have a clearly defined educational objective (such as a certificate, diploma, or degree).

Number awarded Varies; generally more than 150 each year.

[627]
VOCATIONAL REHABILITATION FOR DISABLED VETERANS

Department of Veterans Affairs
810 Vermont Avenue, N.W.
Washington, DC 20420
(202) 418-4343   Toll-free: (800) 827-1000
Web: www.va.gov

Summary To provide vocational rehabilitation to certain categories of veterans with disabilities.

Eligibility This program is open to veterans who have a service-connected disability of at least 10% and a serious employment handicap or 20% and an employment handicap. They must have been discharged or released from military service under other than dishonorable conditions. The Department of Veterans Affairs (VA) must determine that they would benefit from a training program that would help them prepare for, find, and keep suitable employment. The program may be 1) institutional training at a certificate, 2-year college, 4-year college or university, or technical program; 2) unpaid on-the-job training in a federal, state, or local agency or a federally-recognized Indian tribal agency, training in a home, vocational course in a rehabilitation facility or sheltered workshop, independent instruction, or institutional non-farm cooperative; or 3) paid training through a farm cooperative, apprenticeship, on-the-job training, or on-the-job non-farm cooperative.

Financial data While in training and for 2 months after, eligible disabled veterans may receive subsistence allowances in addition to their disability compensation or retirement pay. For training at an institution of higher education or in an unpaid work experience program, the full-time monthly rate is $474.27 with no dependents, $588.30 with 1 dependent, $693.25 with 2 dependents, and $50.54 for each additional dependent; the three-quarter time monthly rate is $356.36 with no dependents, $441.86 with 1 dependent, $518.31 with 2 dependents, and $38.86 for each additional dependent; the half-time monthly rate is $238.45 with no dependents, $295.44 with 1 dependent, $347.27 with 2 dependents, and $25.93 for each additional dependent. For unpaid on-the-job training, the monthly rate is $474.27 with no dependents, $588.30 with 1 dependent, $693.25 with 2 dependents, and $50.54 for each additional dependent. For paid training, the monthly rate is based on the wage received, to a maximum of $414.67 with no dependents, $501.46 with 1 dependent, $577.92 with 2 dependents, and $37.59 for each additional dependent. The VA also pays the costs of tuition, books, fees, supplies, and equipment; it may also pay for special supportive services, such as tutorial assistance, prosthetic devices, lipreading training, and signing for the deaf. If during training or employment services the veteran's disabilities cause transportation expenses that would not be incurred by nondisabled persons, the VA will pay for at least a portion of those expenses. If the veteran encounters financial difficulty during training, the VA may provide an advance against future benefit payments.

Duration Up to 48 months of full-time training or its equivalent in part-time training. If a veteran with a serious disability receives services under an extended evaluation to improve training potential, the total of the extended evaluation and the training phases of the rehabilitation program may exceed 48 months. Usually, the veteran must complete a rehabilitation program within 12 years from the date of notification of entitlement to compensation by the VA. Following completion of the training portion of a rehabilitation program, a veteran may receive counseling and job search and adjustment services for 18 months.

Additional information The program may also provide employment assistance, self-employment assistance, training in a rehabilitation facility, or college and other training. Veterans who are seriously disabled may receive services and assistance to improve their ability to live more independently in their community. After completion of the training phase, the VA will assist the veteran to find and have a suitable job.

Number awarded Varies each year.

Deadline Applications are accepted at any time.

[628]
VOLTA SCHOLARSHIP FUND

Alexander Graham Bell Association for the Deaf
Attn: Financial Aid Coordinator
3417 Volta Place, N.W.
Washington, DC 20007-2778
(202) 337-5220   Fax: (202) 337-8314
TTY: (202) 337-5221   E-mail: financialaid@agbell.org
Web: www.agbell.org

Summary To provide financial assistance to undergraduate and graduate students with moderate to profound hearing loss.

Eligibility This program is open to undergraduate and graduate students who have been diagnosed with a moderate to profound hearing loss prior to acquiring spoken language (hearing loss averages 60dB or greater in the better ear in the speech frequencies of 500, 1000, and 2000 Hz). Applicants must be committed to using spoken language as their primary mode of communication. They must be accepted or enrolled at a mainstream college or university as a full-time student. Along with their application, they must submit a 1-page essay discussing their career goals and how spoken communication is helping them to reach those goals as a person with a hearing loss. Financial need is considered in the selection process. This scholarship is reserved for students who are oral deaf.

Financial data The stipend is $2,000 per year.

Duration 1 year; may be renewed 1 additional year.

Number awarded 1 each year.

Deadline April of each year.

[629]
WALMAN OPTICAL COMPANY SCHOLARSHIP

Walman Optical Company
c/o Scholarship America
Attn: Scholarship Management Services
One Scholarship Way
P.O. Box 297
St. Peter, MN 56082
(507) 931-1682   Toll-free: (800) 537-4180
Fax: (507) 931-9168   E-mail: smsinfo@csfa.org
Web: www.walman.com/scholarship.html

Summary To provide financial assistance to students enrolled at designated schools and colleges of optometry.

Eligibility This program is open to students currently enrolled in the second or third year of a full-time 4-year program leading to a Doctor of Optometry degree at a school selected by Walman

Optical Company. Selection is based on academic record, demonstrated leadership and participation in school and community activities, honors, work experience, a statement of goals and aspirations, unusual personal or family circumstances, and an outside appraisal.

Financial data The stipend ranges from $500 to $3,000 per year, depending on the need of the recipient.

Duration 1 year; nonrenewable, although recipients may reapply.

Additional information The designated schools are University of Alabama at Birmingham, School of Optometry (Birmingham, Alabama); University of California at Berkeley, School of Optometry (Berkeley, California); Southern California College of Optometry (Fullerton, California); Nova Southeastern University, Health Professions Division, College of Optometry (Ft. Lauderdale, Florida); Illinois College of Optometry (Chicago, Illinois); Indiana University, School of Optometry (Bloomington, Indiana); New England College of Optometry (Boston, Massachusetts); Michigan College of Optometry, Ferris State University (Big Rapids, Michigan); University of Missouri at St. Louis, School of Optometry (St. Louis, Missouri); State University of New York, State College of Optometry (New York, New York); Ohio State University, College of Optometry (Columbus, Ohio); Northeastern State University, College of Optometry (Tahlequah, Oklahoma); Pacific University, College of Optometry (Forest Grove, Oregon); Pennsylvania College of Optometry (Elkins Park, Pennsylvania); Inter American University of Puerto Rico, School of Optometry (San Juan, Puerto Rico); Southern College of Optometry (Memphis, Tennessee); and University of Houston, College of Optometry (Houston, Texas).

Number awarded Varies each year.

Deadline April of each year.

[630]
WALTER BYERS POSTGRADUATE SCHOLARSHIP PROGRAM

National Collegiate Athletic Association
Attn: Walter Byers Scholarship Committee Staff Liaison
700 West Washington Avenue
P.O. Box 6222
Indianapolis, IN 46206-6222
(317) 917-6477   Fax: (317) 917-6888
Web: www1.ncaa.org

Summary To provide financial assistance for graduate education in any field to student-athletes with outstanding academic records.

Eligibility This program is open to student-athletes who are seniors or already enrolled in graduate school while completing their final year of athletics eligibility at a member institution of the National Collegiate Athletic Association (NCAA). Men and women compete for scholarships separately. Applicants must be planning to work full time on a graduate degree or postbaccalaureate professional degree. They must have a GPA of 3.5 or higher, have evidenced superior character and leadership, and have demonstrated that participation in athletics has been a positive influence on their personal and intellectual development. Candidates must be nominated by their institution's faculty athletic representative or chief academics officer. Financial need is not considered in the selection process.

Financial data The stipend is $21,500 per year.

Duration 2 years.

Additional information This program was established in 1988 in honor of the former executive director of the NCAA.

Number awarded 2 each year: 1 is set aside for a female and 1 for a male.

Deadline January of each year.

[631]
WALTER W. AND THELMA C. HISSEY COLLEGE SCHOLARSHIPS

Alexander Graham Bell Association for the Deaf
Attn: Financial Aid Coordinator
3417 Volta Place, N.W.
Washington, DC 20007-2778
(202) 337-5220   Fax: (202) 337-8314
TTY: (202) 337-5221   E-mail: financialaid@agbell.org
Web: www.agbell.org

Summary To provide financial assistance to undergraduate and graduate students with moderate to profound hearing loss.

Eligibility This program is open to undergraduate and graduate students who have been diagnosed with a moderate to profound hearing loss prior to acquiring spoken language (hearing loss averages 60dB or greater in the better ear in the speech frequencies of 500, 1000, and 2000 Hz). Applicants must be committed to using spoken language as their primary mode of communication. They must be accepted or enrolled at a mainstream college or university as a full-time student. Along with their application, they must submit a 1-page essay discussing their career goals and how spoken communication is helping them to reach those goals as a person with a hearing loss. Financial need is considered in the selection process.

Financial data The stipend is $5,000 per year.

Duration 1 year; may be renewed 1 additional year.

Number awarded 2 each year.

Deadline April of each year.

[632]
WASHINGTON OCCUPATIONAL THERAPY ASSOCIATION SCHOLARSHIP

Washington Occupational Therapy Association
Attn: Scholarship Program
P.O. Box 731356
Puyallup, WA 98373
(206) 242-9862   Fax: (253) 864-7992
E-mail: intouch@wota.org
Web: www.wota.org

Summary To provide financial assistance to members of the Washington Occupational Therapy Association who are working on a degree in occupational therapy.

Eligibility This program is open to Washington residents who are enrolled in an accredited occupational therapy educational program (associate or professional master's level) in the state. Applicants must demonstrate a need for financial assistance, have a sustained record of outstanding scholastic performance, and be members of the Washington Occupational Therapy Association. As part of the application process, they must submit transcripts, 2 personal references, and a statement from their curriculum director.

Financial data The stipend is $500 for students at the associate degree level or $1,000 for students at the professional master's degree level.

Duration 1 year.

Number awarded 2 each year: 1 for students at the professional degree level and 1 for students at the associate degree level.

Deadline January of each year.

[633]
WATSON MIDWIVES OF COLOR SCHOLARSHIP

American College of Nurse-Midwives
Attn: ACNM Foundation, Inc.
8403 Coleville Road, Suite 1550
Silver Spring, MD 20915
(240) 485-1850   Fax: (240) 485-1818
Web: www.midwife.org

Summary To provide financial assistance for midwifery education to student members of color of the American College of Nurse-Midwives (ACNM).

Eligibility This program is open to ACNM members of color who are currently enrolled in an accredited basic midwife education program and have successfully completed 1 academic or clinical semester/quarter or clinical module. Applicants must submit a 150-word essay on their midwifery career plans and a 100-word essay on their intended future participation in the local, regional, and/or national activities of the ACNM. Selection is based on leadership potential, financial need, academic history, and potential for future professional contribution to the organization.

Financial data The stipend is $3,000.

Duration 1 year.

Number awarded Varies each year; recently, 2 of these scholarships were awarded.

Deadline March of each year.

[634]
WATSON PHARMA CAREER MOBILITY SCHOLARSHIP

American Nephrology Nurses' Association
Attn: ANNA National Office
200 East Holly Avenue
P.O. Box 56
Pitman, NJ 08071-0056
(856) 256-2320   Toll-free: (888) 600-2662
Fax: (856) 589-7463   E-mail: annascholarships@ajj.com
Web: www.annanurse.org

Summary To provide financial assistance to members of the American Nephrology Nurses' Association (ANNA) who are interested in working on a baccalaureate or advanced degree in nursing.

Eligibility Applicants must be current association members, have been members for at least 2 years, be currently employed in nephrology nursing, and be accepted or enrolled in a baccalaureate or higher degree program in nursing. Along with their application, they must submit a 250-word essay on their career and education goals that includes how their degree will apply to nephrology nursing, provides a time frame for completing their program, and indicates how the funds will meet their educational needs.

Financial data The stipend is $2,500.

Duration 1 year.

Additional information This scholarship, first awarded in 2003, is sponsored by Watson Pharma, Inc. Information is also available from Sharon Longton, Awards and Scholarships Chair, (313) 966-2674, E-mail: slongton@dmc.org.

Number awarded 1 each year.

Deadline October of each year.

[635]
WEISBERG POST GRADUATE SCHOLARSHIP

American Society for Clinical Laboratory Science-Wisconsin
c/o Sue Jahnke, P.A.C.E. Program
Marshfield Laboratories
1000 North Oak
Marshfield, WI 54449
(715) 387-5835   Toll-free: (800) 222-5835
Fax: (715) 387-7877
E-mail: jahnke.susan@marshfieldclinic.org
Web: www.wiscls.org/scholarship.htm

Summary To provide financial assistance to laboratory technician students in Wisconsin who are enrolled in a postgraduate program.

Eligibility This program is open to graduate students accepted into an accredited graduate or professional studies program directly related to professional development in clinical laboratory science. Applicants must have been members of the Wisconsin affiliate of the American Society for Clinical Laboratory Science (ASCLS) for the past 3 years.

Financial data A stipend is awarded (amount not specified).

Duration 1 year.

Number awarded 1 each year.

Deadline November of each year.

[636]
WELCH SCHOLARS GRANTS

American Osteopathic Foundation
Attn: Program Manager
142 East Ontario Street
Chicago, IL 60611-2864
(312) 202-8232   Toll-free: (800) 621-1773
Fax: (312) 202-8216   E-mail: vheck@aof-foundation.org
Web: www.aof-foundation.org/stu.asp

Summary To provide financial assistance to students enrolled in colleges of osteopathic medicine.

Eligibility Eligible to apply for this support are students entering their second, third, or fourth year at accredited colleges of osteopathic medicine. Selection is based on financial need; academic achievement; participation in school, community, and professional activities; and demonstrated commitment to the osteopathic profession.

Financial data The stipend is $2,000.

Duration 1 year.

Additional information This program was established in 2001 as the Foundation Scholars Grant and given its current name in 2002.

Number awarded 1 or more at each accredited college of osteopathic medicine in the United States.

Deadline April of each year.

[637]
WESTERN REGIONAL GRADUATE PROGRAM

Western Interstate Commission for Higher Education
Attn: Student Exchange Programs
3035 Center Green Drive
P.O. Box 9752
Boulder, CO 80301-9752
(303) 541-0210   Fax: (303) 541-0291
E-mail: info-sep@wiche.edu
Web: www.wiche.edu/sep/wrgp

Summary To underwrite some of the cost of out-of-state graduate school for students in selected western states.

Eligibility This program is open to residents of 14 states that participate in the Western Regional Graduate Program (WRGP): Alaska, Arizona, Colorado, Hawaii, Idaho, Montana, Nevada, New Mexico, North Dakota, Oregon, South Dakota, Utah, Washington, and Wyoming. To be eligible, students should be resident in 1 of these states for at least 1 year before applying and be interested in enrolling in graduate school in 1 of the other participating states in specified subject fields. The financial status of the applicants is not considered. Interested students apply for admission and for WRGP assistance directly from the institution of their choice.

Financial data Participants in this program attend out-of-state graduate schools but pay only resident rates.

Duration 1 year; may be renewed.

Additional information Part-time students are eligible to participate in WRGP if they have been admitted to a WRGP program. For a list of participating institutions and the programs they offer to students from other states, contact the commission.

Number awarded Varies each year.

Deadline Deadline dates vary; check with the institution you wish to attend.

[638]
WESTERN SECTION SCHOLARSHIPS

American College of Medical Practice Executives
Attn: ACMPE Scholarship Fund Inc.
104 Inverness Terrace East
Englewood, CO 80112-5306
(303) 799-1111, ext. 232   Toll-free: (877) ASK-MGMA
Fax: (303) 643-4439   E-mail: acmpe@mgma.com
Web: www.mgma.com/academics/scholar.cfm

Summary To provide financial assistance to members of the Medical Group Management Association (MGMA) Western Section who are interested in undergraduate or graduate education.

Eligibility Eligible to apply are individuals who reside in and have been members of the MGMA Western Section (Alaska, Arizona, California, Colorado, Hawaii, Idaho, Montana, Nevada, New Mexico, Oregon, Utah, Washington, and Wyoming) for at least 2 years. Applicants must wish to work on an undergraduate or graduate degree in medical practice management, including public health, business administration, health care administration, or other related areas. Students working on a degree in medicine, physical therapy, nursing, or other clinically-related professions are not eligible. Applicants must submit a letter describing their career goals and objectives relevant to medical practice management; a resume; 3 reference letters commenting on their performance, character, potential to succeed, and need for scholarship support; and either documentation indicating acceptance into an undergraduate or graduate college or university or academic transcripts indicating undergraduate or graduate work completed to date.

Financial data The stipend is $2,000. Funds are paid directly to the recipient's college or university.

Duration 1 year.

Additional information This program is managed by Scholarship Program Administrators, Inc. 1201 Eighth Avenue South, P.O. Box 23737, Nashville, TN 27202-3737, (615) 320-3149, (800) 310-4053, Fax: (615) 320-3151, E-mail: info@spaprog.com.

Number awarded 1 each year.

Deadline April of each year.

[639]
WILHELM-FRANKOWSKI SCHOLARSHIP

American Medical Women's Association Foundation
Attn: AMWA Foundation
211 North Union Street, Suite 100
Alexandria, VA 22314
(703) 838-0500   Fax: (703) 549-3864
E-mail: foundation@amwa-doc.org
Web: www.amwa-doc.org

Summary To provide financial assistance for medical education to members of the American Medical Women's Association (AMWA).

Eligibility Eligible for this scholarship are student members of the association attending an accredited U.S. medical or osteopathic medical school in their first, second, or third year. Selection is based on community service; work, research, and participation in women's health issues; participation in association activities; and participation in women-in-medicine or medical student groups other than this association.

Financial data The stipend is $4,000.

Duration 1 year.

Additional information This scholarship was first awarded in 1996.

Number awarded 1 each year.

Deadline April of each year.

[640]
WILL ROGERS INSTITUTE FELLOWSHIP

American Association for Health Education
Attn: Scholarship Committee
1900 Association Drive
Reston, VA 20191-1599
(703) 476-3437   Toll-free: (800) 213-7193, ext. 437
Fax: (703) 476-6638   E-mail: aahe@aahperd.org
Web: www.aahperd.org/aahe/heawards/rogers.html

Summary To provide financial assistance to doctoral students working on a degree in health education with an emphasis on lung health.

Eligibility This program is open to graduate students who have completed at least 1 year (preferably 2 years) in a health education program at an accredited college or university in the United States or a U.S. territory. Applicants must have a cumulative graduate GPA of 3.5 or higher. They must submit a resume or curriculum vitae, a transcript from the institution granting the most recent degree, a letter of recommendation, and a 3-page statement that describes either their history of work related to research in lung health or their commitment to conduct lung health research during their doctoral studies.

Financial data The stipend is $10,000.

Duration 1 year.

Number awarded 1 each year.

Deadline November of each year.

[641]
WILLARD B. SIMMONS SCHOLARSHIP

National Community Pharmacists Association
Attn: NCPA Foundation
100 Daingerfield Road
Alexandria, VA 22314-2888
(703) 683-8200   Toll-free: (800) 544-7447
Fax: (703) 683-3619   E-mail: info@ncpanet.org
Web: www.ncpanet.org.org

Summary   To provide financial assistance for full-time education in pharmacy to student members of the National Community Pharmacists Association (NCPA).

Eligibility   All pharmacy students who are student members of the association and enrolled in an accredited U.S. school or college of pharmacy on a full-time basis are eligible. Applicants must submit a copy of the most recent transcript of their college grades, 2 letters of recommendation, a resume or curriculum vitae, and a statement outlining their school and citizenship accomplishments and future career objectives in independent community pharmacy. Selection is based on leadership qualities and academic achievement.

Financial data   The stipend is $2,000, paid directly to the recipient's school or college of pharmacy.

Duration   1 year; nonrenewable.

Additional information   Until October 1996, the NCPA, the national association representing independent retail pharmacy, was known as NARD (the National Association of Retail Druggists).

Number awarded   1 each year.

Deadline   February of each year.

[642]
WILLARD BERNBAUM SCHOLARSHIP

Cystic Fibrosis Foundation
Attn: President
6931 Arlington Road, Suite 200
Bethesda, MD 20814
(301) 951-4422   Toll-free: (800) FIGHT CF
Fax: (301) 951-6378
Web: www.cysticfibrosis.com

Summary   To provide financial assistance to graduate students who have cystic fibrosis (CF).

Eligibility   This program is open to graduate students who have CF. Applicants must submit a 1-page letter describing their educational program and financial need.

Financial data   The stipend is $1,000.

Duration   1 year.

Number awarded   1 or more each year.

[643]
WILLIAM C. EZELL FELLOWSHIPS

American Academy of Optometry
Attn: American Optometric Foundation
6110 Executive Boulevard, Suite 506
Rockville, MD 20852
(301) 984-4734, ext. 3007   Fax: (301) 984-4737
E-mail: laraf@aaoptom.org
Web: www.aaopt.org/aof/scholarship/ezell/index.asp

Summary   To provide financial assistance to students working on a graduate degree or conducting graduate research in optometric education.

Eligibility   Students entering or continuing a full-time program of study and training in research that leads to a master's or doctoral degree relating to optometric education are eligible to apply.

Financial data   The stipend is $8,000 per year. Funds are paid quarterly.

Duration   1 year; may be renewed for up to 2 additional years.

Additional information   This program was established in 1949 in honor of the first president of the American Optometric Foundation. Sponsors of the program include Bausch & Lomb, CIBA Vision, Essilor, and Vistakon. Recipients are expected to attend school on a full-time basis (although other arrangements can be made).

Number awarded   Varies; recently, 9 of these fellowships were awarded.

Deadline   March of each year.

[644]
WILLIAM E. DOCTER SCHOLARSHIPS

William E. Docter Educational Fund
c/o St. Mary Armenian Church
P.O. Box 39224
Washington, DC 20016
(202) 363-1923   Fax: (202) 527-0229
E-mail: WEDFund@aol.com
Web: www.WEDFund.org

Summary   To provide financial assistance to undergraduate or graduate students of Armenian ancestry.

Eligibility   This program is open to U.S. citizens of Armenian ancestry; preference is given to those with 2 parents of Armenian ancestry. Applicants must be working on undergraduate, graduate, or vocational study or training in the United States or Canada. Along with their application, they must submit a 1-page statement of their goals and what they plan to do after completing their education, 2 letters of recommendation, and evidence of financial need.

Financial data   The stipend is $5,000.

Duration   1 year; may be renewed.

Additional information   This fund was established in 1998.

Number awarded   Varies each year; recently, 39 students received support from this fund.

Deadline   June of each year.

[645]
WILLIAM F. AUSTIN SCHOLARSHIPS

Starkey Laboratories, Inc.
Attn: Scholarship
6600 Washington Avenue South
Eden Prairie, MN 55344
Toll-free: (800) 328-8602
Web: www.starkeyfirst.com/pages/wfas.html

Summary   To provide financial assistance to students working on a graduate degree in audiology.

Eligibility   This program is open to students accepted to or currently enrolled in an accredited graduate (M.S., M.A., Au.D., or Ph.D.) program in audiology. Applicants must be committed to a clinical, teaching, and/or research career in audiology. Part-time students are eligible, but priority is given to those with full-time status. Along with their application, they must submit a 750-word letter that focuses on why they are pursuing graduate study in audiology, a description of their study plans, their intended goals after completing the program, and an overview of their academic interests and activities.

Financial data The stipend is $10,000. Funds may be used for tuition only.

Duration Recipients have up to 4 years to use this nonrenewable award.

Number awarded Up to 5 each year.

Deadline June of each year.

[646]
WILLIAM F. MILLER, MD POSTGRADUATE EDUCATION RECOGNITION AWARD

American Association for Respiratory Care
Attn: American Respiratory Care Foundation
9425 North MacArthur Boulevard, Suite 100
Irving, TX 75063-4706
(972) 243-2272   Fax: (972) 484-2720
E-mail: info@arcfoundation.org
Web: www.arcfoundation.org

Summary To provide financial assistance to respiratory care therapists who are interested in working on an advanced degree.

Eligibility This program is open to respiratory care therapists who have at least a baccalaureate degree with a GPA of 3.0 or higher and have been accepted into an advanced degree program at a fully-accredited school. Applicants must submit 3 letters of reference and a 1,200-word essay on how this program will assist them in earning an advanced degree and working toward a role of leadership in health care.

Financial data The stipend is $1,500. The award also provides 1 night's lodging and registration for the international congress of the association.

Duration 1 year; recipients may reapply.

Additional information This support was first offered in 1992.

Number awarded 1 each year.

Deadline June of each year.

[647]
WILLIAM G. ANDERSON, D.O. SCHOLARSHIP FOR MINORITY STUDENTS

American Osteopathic Foundation
Attn: Program Manager
142 East Ontario Street
Chicago, IL 60611-2864
(312) 202-8232   Toll-free: (800) 621-1773
Fax: (312) 202-8216   E-mail: vheck@aof-foundation.org
Web: www.aof-foundation.org/stu.asp

Summary To provide financial assistance to minority students enrolled in colleges of osteopathic medicine.

Eligibility This program is open to minority (African American, Native American, Asian American, Pacific Islander, or Hispanic) students entering their second, third, or fourth year at an accredited college of osteopathic medicine. Applicants must demonstrate 1) interest in osteopathic medicine, its philosophy, and its principles; 2) academic achievement; 3) leadership efforts in addressing the educational, societal, and health needs of minorities; 4) leadership efforts to eliminate inequities in medical education and health care; 5) accomplishments, awards and honors, clerkships or special projects; and 6) extracurricular activities in which the student has shown leadership abilities; and 6) financial need.

Financial data The stipend is $5,000.

Duration 1 year.

Additional information This program was established in 1998.

Number awarded 1 each year.

Deadline April of each year.

[648]
WILLIAM J. FEINGOLD SCHOLARSHIP

American Society for Quality
Attn: Biomedical Division
600 North Plankinton Avenue
P.O. Box 3005
Milwaukee, WI 53201-3005
(414) 272-8575   Toll-free: (800) 248-1946
Fax: (414) 272-1734   E-mail: cs@asqu.org
Web: www.asq.org/biomed/scholarship/index.html

Summary To provide financial assistance to undergraduate and graduate students working on a degree in a field related to quality in the biomedical community.

Eligibility This program is open to students who have completed at least 2 years of study in a program that involves the use of quality principles, concepts, and technologies in the biomedical community. Applicants must have a GPA of 3.0 or higher. Along with their application, they must submit essays on 1) their career objectives and how they relate to quality issues within the biomedical community; and 2) why quality systems are important in the biomedical community. Graduate students are eligible, but preference is given to undergraduates. Priority is given to students who 1) are enrolled in a technical or scientific course of study; 2) have contributed to or participated in activities related to quality in the biomedical community; and 3) have a higher GPA or more compelling essay.

Financial data The stipend is $5,000 per year.

Duration 1 year; may be renewed 1 additional year.

Additional information This program was approved in 2004. Information is also available from Hal Greenberg, 6 Coe Road, Framingham, MA 01701.

Number awarded 1 each year.

Deadline April of each year.

[649]
WILLIAM MAY MEMORIAL SCHOLARSHIP

California Association for Postsecondary Education and
    Disability
Attn: Executive Assistant
71423 Biskra Road
Rancho Mirage, CA 92270
(760) 346-8206   Fax: (760) 340-5275
TTY: (760) 341-4084   E-mail: caped2000@aol.com
Web: www.caped.net/scholarship.html

Summary To provide financial assistance to undergraduate and graduate students in California who have a disability.

Eligibility This program is open to students at public and private colleges and universities in California who have a disability. Undergraduates must have completed at least 6 semester credits and have a GPA of 2.5 or higher. Graduate students must have completed at least 3 semester units and have a GPA of 3.0 or higher. Applicants must submit a 1-page personal letter that demonstrates writing skills; progress toward meeting educational and vocational goals; how they accommodate their disability; involvement in community activities; and any other personal factor that might strengthen their application. They must also submit a letter of recommendation from a faculty person, verification of disability, official transcripts, proof of current enrollment, and documentation of financial need.

Financial data The stipend is $1,000.

Duration 1 year.

Additional information Information is also available from Janet Shapiro, Disabled Student Programs and Services, Santa Barbara City College, 721 Cliff Drive, Santa Barbara, CA 93109, (805) 965-0581, ext. 2365, E-mail: shapiro@sbcc.net.
Number awarded 1 each year.
Deadline August of each year.

[650]
WILLIAM T. PORTER PHYSIOLOGY FELLOWSHIP AWARDS

American Physiological Society
Attn: Education Office
9650 Rockville Pike, Room 3111
Bethesda, MD 20814-3991
(301) 634-7132   Fax: (301) 634-7098
E-mail: education@the-aps.org
Web: www.the-aps.org

Summary To provide financial assistance to minorities interested in working on a doctoral degree in physiology.
Eligibility This program is open to U.S. citizens and permanent residents who are members of racial or ethnic minority groups (Hispanic or Latino, American Indian or Alaska Native, Asian, Black or African American, and Native Hawaiian or other Pacific Islander). Applicants must be currently enrolled in or accepted to a doctoral program in physiology at a university as full-time students. They must be planning a program of research training under the supervision of a qualified preceptor. Selection is based on the applicant's potential for success (academic record, statement of interest, previous awards and experiences, letters of recommendation); applicant's proposed training environment (including quality of preceptor); and applicant's research and training plan (clarity and quality).
Financial data The stipend is $20,772. No provision is made for a dependency allowance or tuition and fees.
Duration 1 year; may be renewed for 1 additional year and, in exceptional cases, for a third year.
Additional information This program is supported by the William Townsend Porter Foundation (formerly the Harvard Apparatus Foundation). The first Porter Fellowship was awarded in 1920. In 1966 and 1967, the American Physiological Society established the Porter Physiology Development Committee to award fellowships to minority students engaged in graduate study in physiology.
Number awarded Varies each year; recently, 8 of these fellowships were awarded.
Deadline January of each year.

[651]
WILSON MEMORIAL EDUCATIONAL GRANTS

Arkansas Business and Professional Women
c/o Cari Griffith White
Jonesboro Regional Chamber of Commerce
P.O. Box 789
Jonesboro, AR 72403
(870) 932-6691   Fax: (870) 933-5758
Web: www.arkansasbpw.org/scholarships.htm

Summary To provide financial assistance to female residents of Arkansas who are working on a graduate degree.
Eligibility This program is open to women who are Arkansas residents attending an accredited college or university. Applicants must be working on a master's or doctoral degree and have a GPA as set forth by their institution. Along with their application,

they must submit a statement covering their goals, choice of major, and reasons why the grant is needed.
Financial data The stipend is $1,000.
Duration 1 year.
Number awarded 1 or more each year.
Deadline March of each year.

[652]
WISCONSIN G.I. BILL

Wisconsin Department of Veterans Affairs
30 West Mifflin Street
P.O. Box 7843
Madison, WI 53707-7843
(608) 266-1311   Toll-free: (800) WIS-VETS
Fax: (608) 267-0403   E-mail: wdvaweb@dva.state.wi.us
Web: dva.state.wi.us/Ben_education.asp

Summary To provide financial assistance for college or graduate school to Wisconsin veterans and their dependents.
Eligibility This program is open to current residents of Wisconsin who 1) were residents of the state when they entered or reentered active duty in the U.S. armed forces, or 2) have moved to the state and have been residents for any consecutive 12-month period after entry or reentry into service. Applicants must have served on active duty for at least 2 continuous years or for at least 90 days during specified wartime periods. Also eligible are 1) qualifying children and unremarried surviving spouses of Wisconsin veterans who died in the line of duty; and 2) children and spouses of Wisconsin veterans who have a service-connected disability rated by the U.S. Department of Veterans Affairs as 30% or greater. Children must be between 18 and 26 years of age (regardless of the date of the veteran's death or initial disability rating), be a Wisconsin resident for tuition purposes, and register as a full-time student. Spouses remain eligible for 10 years following the date of the veteran's death or initial disability rating; they must be Wisconsin residents for tuition purposes but they may enroll full or part time. Students may attend any institution, center, or school within the University of Wisconsin (UW) System or the Wisconsin Technical College System (WCTS). There are no income limits, delimiting periods following military service during which the benefit must be used, or limits on the level of study (e.g., vocational, undergraduate, professional, or graduate).
Financial data Veterans who qualify as a Wisconsin resident for tuition purposes are eligible for a remission of 50% of tuition and fees at a UW or WCTS institution. Veterans who qualify as a Wisconsin veteran for purposes of this program but for other reasons fail to meet the definition of a Wisconsin resident for tuition purposes at the UW system are eligible for a remission of 100% of non-resident fees. Spouses and children of deceased or disabled veterans are entitled to a remission of 100% of tuition and fees at a UW or WCTS institution.
Duration Up to 8 semesters or 128 credits, whichever is greater.
Additional information This program was established in 2005 as a replacement for Wisconsin Tuition and Fee Reimbursement Grants.
Number awarded Varies each year.
Deadline Applications may be submitted at any time, but they should be received as early as possible prior to the intended date of enrollment.

[653]
WISCONSIN MEDICAL SOCIETY GENERAL MEDICAL EDUCATION SCHOLARSHIPS

Wisconsin Medical Society
Attn: Executive Director, Wisconsin Medical Society
   Foundation
330 East Lakeside Street
P.O. Box 1109
Madison, WI 53701-1109
(608) 442-3722   Toll-free: (866) 442-3800, ext. 3722
Fax: (608) 442-3802   E-mail: eileenw@wismed.org
Web: www.wisconsinmedicalsociety.org

Summary   To provide financial assistance to Wisconsin residents working on a degree in medicine, nursing, or a related field.

Eligibility   This program is open to Wisconsin residents who are enrolled in medical school or in a nursing, physician assistant, or other allied health career program. Preference is given to students at educational institutions in Wisconsin, those close to completing their degree, and those who show a strong interest in practicing in Wisconsin. U.S. citizenship is required. Selection is based on financial need, academic achievement, personal qualities and strengths, and letters of recommendation.

Financial data   The stipend is $1,500 for medical students or $750 for registered nurses, physician assistants, and other allied health care careers.

Duration   1 year.

Number awarded   1 or more each year.

Deadline   March of each year.

[654]
WISCONSIN MEDICAL SOCIETY PRESIDENTIAL SCHOLAR AWARD

Wisconsin Medical Society
Attn: Executive Director, Wisconsin Medical Society
   Foundation
330 East Lakeside Street
P.O. Box 1109
Madison, WI 53701-1109
(608) 442-3722   Toll-free: (866) 442-3800, ext. 3722
Fax: (608) 442-3802   E-mail: eileenw@wismed.org
Web: www.wisconsinmedicalsociety.org

Summary   To provide financial assistance to residents of Wisconsin working on a degree in medicine at a school in the state.

Eligibility   This program is open to Wisconsin residents entering their fourth year as a full-time student at a medical school in the state. Applicants must be able to demonstrate active involvement with the Wisconsin Medical Society or a county medical society and must include a letter of recommendation from a Wisconsin Medical Society member. Preference is given to students who show strong interest in practicing in Wisconsin, especially in areas of need. U.S. citizenship is required. Selection is based on financial need, academic achievement, personal qualities and strengths, and letters of recommendation.

Financial data   The stipend is $3,000.

Duration   1 year.

Number awarded   1 or more each year.

Deadline   January of each year.

[655]
WISCONSIN SCHOLARSHIPS OF THE AMERICAN OCCUPATIONAL THERAPY FOUNDATION

American Occupational Therapy Foundation
Attn: Scholarship Coordinator
4720 Montgomery Lane
P.O. Box 31220
Bethesda, MD 20824-1220
(301) 652-2682   Fax: (301) 656-3620
TDD: (800) 377-8555   E-mail: aotf@aotf.org
Web: www.aotf.org

Summary   To provide financial assistance to students in Wisconsin who are working on an associate or professional degree in occupational therapy.

Eligibility   This program is open to Wisconsin residents who are enrolled in an accredited occupational therapy professional master's degree program in the state. Applicants must demonstrate a need for financial assistance and have a sustained record of outstanding scholastic performance. As part of the application process, they must submit transcripts, 2 personal references, and a statement from their curriculum director.

Financial data   The stipend is $1,000.

Duration   1 year.

Number awarded   2 each year.

Deadline   January of each year.

[656]
W.K. KELLOGG FOUNDATION DOCTORAL FELLOWSHIP IN HEALTH POLICY

National Medical Fellowships, Inc.
Attn: Scholarship Program
5 Hanover Square, 15th Floor
New York, NY 10004
(212) 483-8880   Fax: (212) 483-8897
E-mail: info@nmfonline.org
Web: www.nmf-online.org

Summary   To provide financial assistance to minorities enrolled in a doctoral program in health policy research who are committed to working with underserved populations.

Eligibility   This program is open to members of minority groups (African Americans, Native Americans, Asians, and Hispanics) enrolled in doctoral programs in public health, social policy, or health policy (Ph.D., Dr.P.H., or Sc.D.). Applicants must demonstrate a willingness to complete relevant dissertation research and a commitment to work with underserved populations upon completion of the doctorate. They must include an essay of 500 to 1,000 words discussing their reasons for applying for a fellowship, their qualifications, how it will support their career plans, and which of 4 areas of focus (health policy, men's health, mental health, substance abuse) most interests them and why.

Financial data   Fellowships cover tuition, fees, and a partial living stipend.

Duration   Up to 5 years: 2 years to do the necessary course work and 3 years to complete the dissertation.

Additional information   The program was created in 1998 with grant support from the W.K. Kellogg Foundation. Recently, it operated at 8 institutions: the RAND Graduate School, the Heller Graduate School at Brandeis University, the Joseph L. Mailman School of Public Health at Columbia University, the Harvard School of Public Health, the Johns Hopkins School of Hygiene and Public Health, the UCLA School of Public Health, the University of Michigan School of Public Health, and the University of Pennsylvania. Information is also available from the sponsor's

Washington office at 1627 K Street, N.W., Suite 1200, Washington, DC 20006-1702, (202) 296-4431, Fax: (202) 293-1990.
Number awarded 5 each year.
Deadline June of each year.

[657]
WOCN SOCIETY ADVANCED EDUCATION SCHOLARSHIP PROGRAM

Wound, Ostomy and Continence Nurses Society
Attn: Scholarship Committee
15000 Commerce Parkway, Suite C
Mt. Laurel, NJ 08054
Toll-free: (888) 224-WOCN   E-mail: info@wocn.org
Web: www.wocn.org/education/scholarship

Summary To provide financial assistance to members of the Would, Ostomy and Continence Nurses (WOCN) Society interested in working on an undergraduate or graduate degree.
Eligibility This program is open to active members of the society who have a current, unrestricted R.N. license and are working on a baccalaureate, master's, or doctoral degree or N.P. certificate. Applicants must provide evidence of current or previous employment as a wound, ostomy, and/or continence nurse during the last 3 years, proof of WOCNCB certification, and proof of current enrollment or acceptance into an accredited nursing program or other accredited college or university program for non-nursing degrees. Selection is based on merit, compliance with the eligibility requirements, and financial need.
Financial data Stipends range from $1,000 to $2,000 per year.
Duration 1 year.
Additional information This program is supported, in part, by the ConvaTec Fund.
Number awarded Varies each year. Recently, 3 of these scholarships were awarded: 1 at $2,000, 1 at $1,500, and 1 at $1,000.
Deadline April or October of each year.

[658]
WOMEN IN SCIENCE AND TECHNOLOGY SCHOLARSHIP

Business and Professional Women of Virginia
Attn: Virginia BPW Foundation
P.O. Box 4842
McLean, VA 22103-4842
Web: www.bpwva.org/scholarships.shtml

Summary To provide financial assistance to women in Virginia who are interested in working on a bachelor's or advanced degree in science or technology.
Eligibility This program is open to women who are at least 18 years of age, U.S. citizens, Virginia residents, accepted at or currently studying at a Virginia college or university, and working on a bachelor's, master's, or doctoral degree in 1 of the following fields: actuarial science, biology, bioengineering, chemistry, computer science, dentistry, engineering, mathematics, medicine, physics, or a similar scientific or technical field. Applicants must have a definite plan to use their education in a scientific or technical profession. They must be able to demonstrate financial need.
Financial data Stipends range from $500 to $1,000 per year, depending on the need of the recipient; funds may be used for tuition, fees, books, transportation, living expenses, and dependent care.
Duration 1 year; recipients may reapply (but prior recipients are not given priority).

Additional information Recipients must complete their studies within 2 years.
Number awarded At least 1 each year.
Deadline March of each year.

[659]
WOMEN'S BASKETBALL COACHES ASSOCIATION SCHOLARSHIP AWARDS

Women's Basketball Coaches Association
Attn: Manager of Awards
4646 Lawrenceville Highway
Lilburn, GA 30047-3620
(770) 279-8027, ext. 102   Fax: (770) 279-6290
E-mail: alowe@wbca.org
Web: www.wbca.org/WBCAScholarAward.asp

Summary To provide financial assistance for undergraduate or graduate study to women's basketball players.
Eligibility This program is open to women's basketball players who are competing in any of the 4 intercollegiate divisions (NCAA Divisions I, II, and III, and NAIA). Applicants must be interested in completing an undergraduate degree or beginning work on an advanced degree. They must be nominated by a member of the Women's Basketball Coaches Association (WBCA). Selection is based on sportsmanship, commitment to excellence as a student-athlete, honesty, ethical behavior, courage, and dedication to purpose.
Financial data The stipend is $1,000 per year.
Duration 1 year.
Number awarded 2 each year.

[660]
YOUNG LADIES' RADIO LEAGUE SCHOLARSHIP

Foundation for Amateur Radio, Inc.
Attn: Scholarship Committee
P.O. Box 831
Riverdale, MD 20738
E-mail: aa3of@arrl.net
Web: www.amateurradio-far.org/scholarships.php

Summary To provide funding to licensed radio amateurs (especially women) who are interested in earning a bachelor's or graduate degree in the United States.
Eligibility Applicants must have at least an FCC Technician Class or equivalent foreign authorization and intend to work on a bachelor's or graduate degree in the United States. There are no restrictions on the course of study or residency location. Preference is given to female applicants.
Financial data The stipend is $1,500.
Duration 1 year.
Additional information This program is sponsored by the Young Ladies' Radio League. It includes the following named scholarships: the Ethel Smith-K4LMB Memorial Scholarship and the Mary Lou Brown-NM7N Memorial Scholarship. Recipients must attend an accredited school (university, college, or technical institute) on a full-time basis.
Number awarded 2 each year.
Deadline Requests for applications must be submitted by April of each year.

[661]
ZELDA WALLING VICHA MEMORIAL TRUST FUND

American Society of Podiatric Medical Assistants
Attn: Executive Office
2124 South Austin Boulevard
Cicero, IL 60804
(708) 863-6303   Toll-free: (888) 88-ASPMA
E-mail: aspmaex@aol.com
Web: www.aspma.org

Summary To provide financial assistance to podiatry college students.

Eligibility Applicants must be fourth-year podiatry students who have at least a 3.2 GPA, are in good academic standing, have demonstrated leadership ability, and can demonstrate financial need.

Financial data The stipend is $1,500.

Duration 1 year.

Additional information Information is also available from the Scholarship Chair, Janet B. Grace, E-mail: Janetgpmac@aol.com.

Number awarded 2 each year.

Deadline May of each year.

[662]
ZETA PHI BETA GENERAL GRADUATE FELLOWSHIPS

Zeta Phi Beta Sorority, Inc.
Attn: National Education Foundation
1734 New Hampshire Avenue, N.W.
Washington, DC 20009
(202) 387-3103   Fax: (202) 232-4593
E-mail: scholarship@ZPhiBNEF.org
Web: www.zphib1920.org/nef

Summary To provide financial assistance to women who are working on professional degrees, master's degrees, doctorates, or postdoctoral studies.

Eligibility Women graduate or postdoctoral students are eligible to apply if they have achieved distinction or shown promise of distinction in their chosen fields. Applicants need not be members of Zeta Phi Beta. They must submit 3 letters of recommendation, university transcripts, a 150-word essay on their educational and professional goals, and information on financial need.

Financial data The stipend ranges up to $2,500, paid directly to the recipient.

Duration 1 academic year; may be renewed.

Additional information Information is also available from Cheryl Williams, National Second Vice President, 6322 Bocage Drive, Shreveport, LA 71119.

Deadline January of each year.

[663]
10-10 INTERNATIONAL NET SCHOLARSHIPS

Foundation for Amateur Radio, Inc.
Attn: Scholarship Committee
P.O. Box 831
Riverdale, MD 20738
E-mail: aa3of@arrl.net
Web: www.amateurradio-far.org/scholarships.php

Summary To provide funding to licensed radio amateurs who are interested in working on an undergraduate or graduate degree.

Eligibility Applicants must be radio amateurs who have HF privileges and are working on an associate, bachelor's, or graduate degree. There is no restriction on the course of study. Non-U.S. amateurs are also eligible. Applicants must provide a recommendation from a member of the 10-10 International Net or be a member of that organization.

Financial data The stipend is $1,000.

Duration 1 year.

Additional information This program is sponsored by 10-10 International Net, Inc. Information is also available from Larry Berger, Scholarship Manager, 9 Nancy Boulevard, Merrick, NY 11566, E-mail: wa2suh@aol.com. Recipients must attend an accredited school (university, college, or technical institute) on a full-time basis.

Number awarded 5 each year.

Deadline Requests for applications must be submitted by April of each year.

Research and Creative Activities

Listed alphabetically by program title are 271 grants, traineeships, and awards that support research and creative activities in the health sciences on the graduate level in the United States. Check here if you need funding for research, lectureships, research traineeships, or creative activities in any health-related field, including dentistry, genetics, medicine, nursing, nutrition, pharmacology, rehabilitation, etc.

[664]
AABB-FENWAL SBB SCHOLARSHIP AWARDS

AABB
Attn: Scholarship Coordinator
8101 Glenbrook Road
Bethesda, MD 20814-2749
(301) 215-6482   Fax: (301) 907-6895
E-mail: education@aabb.org
Web: www.aabb.org

Summary To recognize and reward essays by students enrolled in programs accredited by AABB (formerly the American Association of Blood Banks).

Eligibility This program is open to students enrolled in an accredited program for the education of Specialists in Blood Banking (SBB). Applicants must submit 1 of the following types of entries: 1) a scientific paper reporting experimental work (the work may be an original concept, extension of a major concept, or application of a procedure in blood substitutes, IV immune globulin, hemophilia, or other transfusion medical topics); 2) an analytical or interpretational review suitable for publication in a professional journal; or 3) an innovative educational syllabus using traditional or advanced technology modalities. The essays or scientific papers must be less than 3,000 words on a subject pertaining to blood banking or a related field. Scientific papers should describe materials and methods used, including experimental design, in sufficient detail to enable other scientists to evaluate or duplicate the work. Reviews should analyze or interpret the subject and not just restate the literature. Educational entries should include a brief summary covering the need for the program, how the program is innovative, and a list of references. A student may submit more than 1 entry; however, no student may receive more than 1 award.

Financial data The award is $1,500.

Duration The competition is held annually.

Additional information This program began in 1968. Funding is provided by Fenwal Inc. Winning entries may not be published or printed elsewhere without the prior approval of AABB.

Number awarded Up to 5 each year.

Deadline June of each year.

[665]
AADR STUDENT RESEARCH FELLOWSHIPS

American Association for Dental Research
Attn: Awards, Grants and Fellowships Administrator
1619 Duke Street
Alexandria, VA 22314-3406
(703) 299-8094   Fax: (703) 548-1883
E-mail: sherren@iadr.com
Web: www.iadr.com/awards/studentresearch.html

Summary To provide funding to students interested in conducting research on oral health.

Eligibility This program is open to students currently enrolled at an accredited D.D.S./D.M.D. or hygiene program in a dental (health-associated) institution in the United States. Applicants must be sponsored by a faculty member at their school and should not have received their degree or be scheduled to receive their degree in the year of the award. They may have an advanced degree in a basic science subject. Students who have already received a fellowship from the American Association for Dental Research (AADR) are not eligible for a second award. Along with their application, they must submit a proposal (to 8 pages) that includes the following: objectives and significance, rational and hypotheses, materials and methods, statistical management of the data, preliminary studies (if any), facilities and equipment, and

appropriate clearance, if the study involves human subjects, vertebrate animals, or recombinant DNA. Selection is based on the presence of a testable hypothesis, suitability of methods and facilities, significance of problem, likelihood of success, clarity and style, student potential, and experience of mentor.

Financial data The grant is $2,100. In addition, $300 is provided to the faculty preceptor for supplies.

Duration The research must be completed within 2 years.

Additional information When the research is completed, recipients are awarded funds for transportation and accommodations to present their findings at an annual AADR meeting. This fellowship is supported by several major companies, including Johnson & Johnson, GlaxoSmithKline, Sunstar Butler, Pfizer Consumer Healthcare Procter & Gamble, 3M Dental Products, and Dentsply International.

Number awarded Varies each year; recently, 19 of these grants were awarded.

Deadline January of each year.

[666]
AANA FOUNDATION DOCTORAL FELLOWSHIP

American Association of Nurse Anesthetists
Attn: AANA Foundation
222 South Prospect Avenue
Park Ridge, IL 60068-4001
(847) 692-7050, ext. 1171   Fax: (847) 692-7137
E-mail: foundation@aana.com
Web: www.aana.com/foundation/default.asp

Summary To provide financial assistance to members of the American Association of Nurse Anesthetists (AANA) who are working on a doctoral degree.

Eligibility This program is open to members of the association who are certified or recertified CRNAs working on a doctoral degree. Applicants must be able to provide evidence of past commitment and a high likelihood of future commitment to nurse anesthesia. Preference is given to applicants who are involved in the dissertation phase of their research within their doctoral program. Along with their application, they must submit a curriculum vitae; a 250-word essay on their current involvement in nurse anesthesia education, practice, or research and how funding will support their research; 2 letters of reference; and a copy of a brochure describing their doctoral program.

Financial data The maximum stipend is $60,000 per year.

Duration 1 academic year.

Number awarded 1 each year.

Deadline May of each year.

[667]
AAPD FOUNDATION INVESTIGATOR INITIATED RESEARCH PROJECTS

American Academy of Pediatric Dentistry
Attn: AAPD Foundation
211 East Chicago Avenue, Suite 700
Chicago, IL 60611-2663
(312) 337-2169, ext. 22   Fax: (312) 337-6329
E-mail: foundation@aapd.org
Web: www.aapd.org/foundation/grants

Summary To provide funding for research to investigators, including graduate students, in pediatric dentistry.

Eligibility This program is open to researchers interested in conducting projects that contribute to the knowledge base in pediatric dentistry and lead to improved oral health for children.

Graduate students overseen by a senior investigator are eligible. Membership in the American Academy of Pediatric Dentistry (AAPD) is not required. Grants are available for projects on topics that are selected when funding is available. Recently, research on non-pharmacological behavior management was supported.

Financial data The grant is $15,000 per year.

Duration 2 years.

Additional information This program was established in 2001. Grants are issued in response to specific requests for proposals (RFPs).

Number awarded 1 whenever a specific RFP is issued.

Deadline June of years when funding is available.

[668]
AAPS-AFPE GATEWAY RESEARCH SCHOLARSHIPS

American Foundation for Pharmaceutical Education
Attn: Grants Manager
One Church Street, Suite 202
Rockville, MD 20850-4158
(301) 738-2160   Fax: (301) 738-2161
E-mail: info@afpenet.org
Web: www.afpenet.org/under_research_scholar.htm

Summary To provide funding to pharmacy students interested in conducting a research project.

Eligibility This program is open to students who are enrolled in either 1) a Pharm.D. program, have completed at least 2 years of college, and are enrolled in at least the first year of the professional pharmacy curriculum; or 2) a baccalaureate degree program and have completed at least 1 year of the degree program. All applicants must be enrolled for at least 1 full year after initiation of the award. Students enrolled in joint Pharm.D./Ph.D. programs are not eligible. Candidates must be nominated by a faculty member at a school of pharmacy accredited by the American Council on Pharmaceutical Education or a faculty member in a college awarding baccalaureate degrees who is actively undertaking research in the pharmaceutical sciences. Each faculty member may nominate up to 2 students. U.S. citizenship or permanent resident status is not required for the student. Preference is given to students who need relevant research experience in order to have a basis to decide whether to pursue a Ph.D. degree in the basic, clinical, or administrative pharmaceutical sciences.

Financial data The total grant is $5,000, including $4,000 as a student stipend, $500 for the student to attend the annual meeting of the American Association of Pharmaceutical Scientists (AAPS), and $500 to be used by the supporting faculty member in direct support of the research effort.

Duration Up to 1 calendar year.

Additional information This program is jointly administered by the AAPS and the American Foundation for Pharmaceutical Education (AFPE). Funding is provided by a number of corporate sponsors, including Abbott Laboratories, AstraZeneca Pharmaceuticals, Bristol-Myers Squibb, GlaxoSmithKline, Novartis, Pfizer Inc., Schering Laboratories, and Wyeth Pharmaceuticals.

Number awarded 3 each year.

Deadline January of each year.

[669]
AAUW DISSERTATION FELLOWSHIPS

American Association of University Women
Attn: AAUW Educational Foundation
301 ACT Drive, Department 60
P.O. Box 4030
Iowa City, IA 52243-4030
(319) 337-1716   Fax: (319) 337-1204
E-mail: aauw@act.org
Web: www.aauw.org/fga/fellowships_grants/American.cfm

Summary To provide funding to women in the final year of writing their dissertation.

Eligibility This program is open to U.S. citizens and permanent residents who are women and intend to pursue professional careers in the United States. They should have successfully completed all required course work for their doctorate, passed all preliminary examinations, and received written acceptance of their prospectus. Applicants may propose research in any field except engineering (the association offers Engineering Dissertation Fellowships as a separate program). Selection is based on scholarly excellence, quality of project design, originality of project, scholarly significance of project to discipline, feasibility of project and proposed schedule, qualifications of applicant, potential of applicant to make a significant contribution to field, applicant's commitment to women's issues in profession and community, and applicant's mentoring of other women.

Financial data The stipend is $20,000.

Duration 1 year, beginning in July.

Additional information The filing fee is $40. It is expected that the fellowship will be used for the final year of doctoral work and that the degree will be received at the end of the fellowship year. The fellowship is not intended to fund extended field research. The recipient should be prepared to devote full time to the dissertation during the fellowship year.

Number awarded Varies each year; recently, 48 of these fellowships were awarded.

Deadline November of each year.

[670]
ABBOTT HEALTH PROFESSIONAL GRADUATE STUDENT RESEARCH PRECEPTORSHIPS

American College of Rheumatology
Attn: Research and Education Foundation
1800 Century Place, Suite 250
Atlanta, GA 30345
(404) 633-3777   Fax: (404) 633-1870
E-mail: ref@rheumatology.org
Web: www.rheumatology.org

Summary To provide funding to graduate students who are interested in participating in a rheumatology research program.

Eligibility This program is open to students currently enrolled in a rheumatology-related health care graduate program. Applicants must be interested in participating in a research program under the supervision of a preceptor who is a member of the American College of Rheumatology (ACR) or the Association of Rheumatology Health Professionals (ARHP). They must be U.S. citizens, nationals, or permanent residents. Selection is based on scientific merit and relevance to rheumatic disease research (either clinical or basic science), preceptor's credentials as related to the project and previous experience as a mentor, appropriateness and feasibility of the students' role in the project, and the institutional research environment (including any course work or seminars specifically for summer students).

Financial data Awardees receive $3,500 as a stipend and up to $1,000 in travel funds to attend the ACR annual scientific meeting. The mentor receives a $1,500 stipend and a grant of $1,000 to cover related laboratory expenses.
Duration 8 weeks anytime during the year.
Additional information This program is supported by the Abbott Endowment for Rheumatology Development.
Number awarded Approximately 4 each year.
Deadline January of each year.

[671]
ABBOTT MEDICAL STUDENT CLINICAL PRECEPTORSHIPS

American College of Rheumatology
Attn: Research and Education Foundation
1800 Century Place, Suite 250
Atlanta, GA 30345
(404) 633-3777   Fax: (404) 633-1870
E-mail: ref@rheumatology.org
Web: www.rheumatology.org
Summary To provide funding to medical students who are interested in participating in a clinical rheumatology program during the summer.
Eligibility This program is open to students between the first and second year of medical school; M.D./Ph.D. students are not eligible. Applicants must be interested in participating in a clinical experience related to rheumatology under the supervision of a preceptor who is a member of the American College of Rheumatology (ACR). They must be U.S. citizens, nationals, or permanent residents.
Financial data Awardees receive $1,500 per 4-week period as a stipend and up to $1,000 in travel funds to attend the ACR annual scientific meeting. The mentor receives a stipend of $500 per 4-week period to cover related laboratory expenses.
Duration 4 or 8 weeks during the summer.
Additional information This program is supported by the Abbott Endowment for Rheumatology Development.
Number awarded Varies each year; recently, 8 of these awards were granted.
Deadline January of each year.

[672]
ABBOTT MEDICAL STUDENT RESEARCH PRECEPTORSHIPS

American College of Rheumatology
Attn: Research and Education Foundation
1800 Century Place, Suite 250
Atlanta, GA 30345
(404) 633-3777   Fax: (404) 633-1870
E-mail: ref@rheumatology.org
Web: www.rheumatology.org
Summary To provide funding to medical students who are interested in participating in a rheumatology research program during the summer.
Eligibility This program is open to students currently enrolled in medical school; M.D./Ph.D. students are not eligible. Applicants must be interested in participating in a research program under the supervision of a preceptor who is a member of the American College of Rheumatology (ACR). They must be U.S. citizens, nationals, or permanent residents. Selection is based on scientific merit and relevance to rheumatic disease research (either clinical or basic science), the preceptor's credentials as

related to the project and previous experience as a mentor, appropriateness and feasibility of the students' role in the project, and the institutional research environment (including any course work or seminars specifically for summer students).
Financial data Awardees receive $3,000 as a stipend and up to $1,000 in travel funds to attend the ACR annual scientific meeting. The mentor receives a $1,000 stipend to cover related laboratory expenses.
Duration 8 weeks during the summer.
Additional information This program is supported by the Abbott Endowment for Rheumatology Development.
Number awarded Approximately 10 each year.
Deadline January of each year.

[673]
ABRAHAM LILIENFELD PRIZE

Society for Epidemiologic Research
P.O. Box 900
Clearfield, UT 84098
(801) 525-0231   Fax: (801) 774-9211
E-mail: membership@epiresearch.org
Web: www.epiresearch.org
Summary To recognize and reward outstanding graduate student research papers in epidemiology.
Eligibility This program is open to graduate students in epidemiology who have completed a research project, have written up the results, and wish to submit it for consideration. The work must be recent (not more than 2 years since completion) and unpublished.
Financial data The prize is $1,000 plus travel expenses to the society's annual meeting.
Duration The prize is awarded annually.
Additional information The winning paper may be published in the *American Journal of Epidemiology*. This award was first presented in 1979. Information is also available from Joseph L. Lyon, University of Utah School of Medicine, 375 Chipeta Way, Suite A, Salt Lake City, UT 84119, (801) 587-3350, E-mail: jlyon@dfpm.utah.edu.
Number awarded 1 each year.
Deadline January of each year.

[674]
ABTA MEDICAL STUDENT SUMMER FELLOWSHIPS

American Brain Tumor Association
Attn: Executive Director
2720 River Road, Suite 146
Des Plaines, IL 60018-4110
(847) 827-9910   Toll-free: (800) 886-2282
Fax: (847) 827-9918   E-mail: info@abta.org
Web: www.abta.org/research.htm
Summary To provide funding to medical students who are interested in conducting neuro-oncology research during the summer.
Eligibility This program is open to students at medical schools in the United States or Canada. Applicants must be interested in preparing for a career in brain tumor research. The fellow who submits the most outstanding research paper at the end of the summer receives the Lucien J. Rubinstein Memorial Award.
Financial data The grant is $2,500. The winner of the Lucien J. Rubinstein Memorial Award receives an additional award of $1,000.
Duration Summer months.

Number awarded Varies each year; recently, 9 of these fellowships were awarded.

Deadline January of each year.

[675]
ACADEMIA RESOURCE MANAGEMENT GRADUATE STUDENT INTERNSHIPS AND FELLOWSHIPS

Academia Resource Management
535 East 4500 South, Suite D120
Salt Lake City, UT 84107-2988
(801) 273-8911   Toll-free: (866) 863-3570
Fax: (801) 277-5632   E-mail: info@armanagement.org
Web: www.armanagement.org

Summary To enable science, mathematics, engineering, and technology graduate students to participate in and contribute to research at various national laboratories, other federal agencies, and private industries.

Eligibility This program is open to master's and doctoral candidates who are working on a degree in science, mathematics, engineering, or technology. Applicants may be interested in 1) conducting thesis or dissertation research; or 2) exploring research and technology career options or gaining practical training at a sponsoring facility. U.S. citizenship is required at some facilities. Selection is based on academic performance, research potential, career goals, recommendations, and compatibility of scientific interests and proposed research with the resources of the host facility.

Financial data A stipend is awarded (amount not specified); tuition assistance and a travel allowance are also available.

Duration Assignments normally range from 1 to 12 months; non-thesis research fellows or interns are generally placed for 8 to 16 weeks in the summer or for a semester.

Additional information Current sponsoring facilities include Fluor Fernald (Cincinnati, Ohio), Hewlett-Packard Company (Palo Alto, California), Office of Naval Research (Washington, D.C.), CH2M Hill Hanford Group (Richland, Washington), MSE, Inc. (Butte, Montana), National Petroleum Technology Office (Tulsa, Oklahoma), Naval Air Warfare Center (China Lake, California), Rocky Mountain Oilfield Testing Center (Casper, Wyoming), Department of Energy Seattle Support Office (Seattle, Washington), Strategic Petroleum Reserve Project Office (New Orleans, Louisiana), Sun Microsystems (San Francisco, California), and XL Sci-Tech, Inc. (Richland, Washington).

Number awarded Varies each year.

Deadline Applications may be submitted at any time, but complete applications received by January of each year are given priority consideration for summer fellowships.

[676]
ADHA INSTITUTE RESEARCH GRANT COMPETITION

American Dental Hygienists' Association
Attn: Institute for Oral Health
444 North Michigan Avenue, Suite 3400
Chicago, IL 60611
(312) 440-8918   Toll-free: (800) 243-2342, ext. 244
Fax: (312) 440-8929   E-mail: institute@adha.net
Web: www.adha.org

Summary To provide funding to dental hygienists and dental hygiene students who are interested in conducting research.

Eligibility This program is open to licensed dental hygienists and to dental hygiene students, undergraduate or graduate, full-time or part-time. Applicants must be proposing to conduct research related to dental hygiene. They must be active members of the Student American Dental Hygienists' Association (SADHA) or the American Dental Hygienists' Association (ADHA). Priority is given to proposals addressing these topics: access to care/underserved populations, health promotion and disease prevention, alternative practice settings, and oral health public policy.

Financial data Grants range from $1,000 to $10,000 for licensed hygienists or from $1,000 to $5,000 for dental hygiene students.

Duration 1 year.

Number awarded 1 or more each year.

Deadline January of each year.

[677]
ADSA DENTAL STUDENT ESSAY CONTEST

American Dental Society of Anesthesiology, Inc.
211 East Chicago Avenue, Suite 780
Chicago, IL 60611
(312) 664-8270   Toll-free: (877) 255-3742
Fax: (312) 224-8624   E-mail: adsahome@mac.com
Web: www.adsahome.org/essay.html

Summary To recognize and reward outstanding essays written by dental students in the United States or Canada.

Eligibility Eligible to compete in this contest are students in U.S. and Canadian dental schools. They are invited to write an essay, up to 5,000 words in length, on anesthesiology in dentistry. Selection is based on clear and concise expression, logical thought, and originality.

Financial data The prize is $1,000 and payment of travel and lodging expenses to attend the sponsor's annual meeting.

Duration The prize is given annually.

Additional information This award was established in 1963. The winning essay is published in the society's journal.

Number awarded 1 each year.

Deadline December of each year.

[678]
AFPE GATEWAY RESEARCH SCHOLARSHIPS

American Foundation for Pharmaceutical Education
Attn: Grants Manager
One Church Street, Suite 202
Rockville, MD 20850-4158
(301) 738-2160   Fax: (301) 738-2161
E-mail: info@afpenet.org
Web: www.afpenet.org/under_research_scholar.htm

Summary To provide funding to pharmacy students interested in conducting a research project.

Eligibility This program is open to students who are enrolled in either 1) a Pharm.D. program, have completed at least 2 years of college, and are enrolled in at least the first year of the professional pharmacy curriculum; or 2) a baccalaureate degree program and have completed at least 1 year of the degree program. All applicants must be enrolled for at least 1 full year after initiation of the award. Students enrolled in joint Pharm.D./Ph.D. programs are not eligible. Candidates must be nominated by a faculty member at a school of pharmacy accredited by the American Council on Pharmaceutical Education or a faculty member in a college awarding baccalaureate degrees who is actively undertaking research in the pharmaceutical sciences. Each faculty member may nominate up to 2 students. U.S. citizenship or permanent resident status is required for the student. Preference is given to students who need relevant research experience in order to have a basis to decide whether to pursue a Ph.D. degree in the basic, clinical, or administrative pharmaceutical sciences.

Financial data The total grant is $5,000, including $4,000 as a student stipend and $1,000 to be used by the supporting faculty member in direct support of the research effort.

Duration Up to 1 calendar year.

Additional information Funding for this program is provided by a number of corporate sponsors, including Abbott Laboratories, AstraZeneca Pharmaceuticals, Bristol-Myers Squibb, GlaxoSmithKline, Novartis, Pfizer Inc., Schering Laboratories, and Wyeth Pharmaceuticals.

Number awarded 12 each year.

Deadline January of each year.

[679]
AGA GRADUATE STUDENT RESEARCH FELLOWSHIP AWARDS

Foundation for Digestive Health and Nutrition
Attn: Research Awards Program
4930 Del Ray Avenue
Bethesda, MD 20814-2512
(301) 222-4012   Fax: (301) 652-3890
E-mail: info@fdhn.org
Web: www.fdhn.org/html/awards/elect_app.html

Summary To provide funding to graduate students conducting doctoral research related to the gastrointestinal tract, liver, or pancreas.

Eligibility This program is open to Ph.D. candidates conducting research in the biology and epidemiology or diseases of the gastrointestinal tract, liver, or pancreas. Applicants should have completed between 1 and 3 years of training towards the doctoral degree and have selected the laboratory or department in which they will conduct their doctoral research. Their research advisor must be a member of the American Gastroenterological Association (AGA). U.S. citizenship, permanent resident status, or visa status to pursue education in North America is required. Selection is based on scientific merit, credentials, and long-term potential for a research career. Priority is given to students aiming for long-term careers in research in the biology and disease of the gastrointestinal tract, liver, or pancreas.

Financial data The grant includes $18,000 per year as a stipend and $2,000 per year to be used for such fringe benefits as medical insurance and travel to a national meeting. Tuition costs are expected to be covered by the institution or host department and laboratory. Indirect costs are not allowed.

Duration 2 years.

Additional information This award is administered by the Foundation for Digestive Health and Nutrition (FDHN) and sponsored by the AGA.

Number awarded 2 each year.

Deadline March of each year.

[680]
AGA STUDENT ABSTRACT PRIZES

Foundation for Digestive Health and Nutrition
Attn: Research Awards Program
4930 Del Ray Avenue
Bethesda, MD 20814-2512
(301) 222-4012   Fax: (301) 652-3890
E-mail: info@fdhn.org
Web: www.fdhn.org/html/awards/elect_app.html

Summary To recognize and reward students at any level who submit outstanding abstracts for presentation during Digestive Disease Week (DDW).

Eligibility This program is open to high school, undergraduate, premedical, predoctoral, and medical students and medical residents (up to and including postgraduate year 3) who have performed original research related to gastroenterology and hepatology. Postdoctoral fellows, technicians, visiting scientists, and M.D. research fellows are not eligible. Applicants must submit an abstract on their research and must be the designated presenter or first author of the abstract. They must be sponsored by a member of the American Gastroenterological Association (AGA). Travel awards are presented to authors of outstanding abstracts to enable them to attend DDW, the most outstanding abstracts receive prizes. Selection is based on novelty, significance of the proposal, clarity of the abstract, and contribution of the student. Women and minority students are strongly encouraged to apply.

Financial data The prizes are $1,000; the travel awards are $500.

Duration Awards and prizes are presented annually.

Additional information This award is administered by the Foundation for Digestive Health and Nutrition (FDHN) and sponsored by the AGA.

Number awarded 10 travel awards are presented each year. Of the 10 awardees, 3 receive additional prizes of $1,000.

Deadline March of each year.

[681]
AGA STUDENT RESEARCH FELLOWSHIP AWARDS

Foundation for Digestive Health and Nutrition
Attn: Research Awards Program
4930 Del Ray Avenue
Bethesda, MD 20814-2512
(301) 222-4012   Fax: (301) 652-3890
E-mail: info@fdhn.org
Web: www.fdhn.org/html/awards/elect_app.html

Summary To provide funding for research on digestive diseases or nutrition to students at any level.

Eligibility This program is open to high school, college, graduate, and medical students at accredited institutions in North America who are not yet engaged in thesis research. They must be interested in conducting research on digestive diseases or nutrition. Candidates must not hold similar salary support awards from other agencies (e.g., American Liver Foundation, Crohn's and Colitis Foundation). Women and underrepresented minority students are strongly encouraged to apply. Research must be conducted under the supervision of a preceptor who is a full-time faculty member at a North American institution, directing a research project in a gastroenterology-related area, and a member of the American Gastroenterological Association (AGA). Selection is based on novelty, feasibility, and significance of the proposal; attributes of the candidate; record of the preceptor; evidence of institutional commitment; and the laboratory environment. Applicants are grouped and evaluated according to educational level.

Financial data Grants range from $2,000 to $3,000. No indirect costs are allowed. The award is paid directly to the student and is to be used as a stipend or for thesis research.

Duration At least 10 weeks. The work may take place at any time during the year.

Additional information In an effort to attract and encourage minorities, several of the awards are set aside specifically for underrepresented minority students, defined as African Americans, Mexican Americans, Mainland Puerto Ricans, and Native Americans (Alaskan Natives, American Indians, and Native Hawaiians). This award is administered by the Foundation for Digestive Health and Nutrition (FDHN) and sponsored by the AGA. Funds may not be used to support thesis research.

Number awarded Varies each year. Recently, 21 of these awards were granted, including several set aside specifically for underrepresented minorities (African Americans, American Indians, Alaska and Hawaiian Natives, Mexican Americans, and Mainland Puerto Ricans).

Deadline March of each year.

[682]
AGING RESEARCH DISSERTATION AWARDS TO INCREASE DIVERSITY

National Institute on Aging
Attn: Office of Extramural Affairs
7201 Wisconsin Avenue, Room 2C-218
Bethesda, MD 20892-9205
(301) 496-9322   Fax: (301) 402-2945
E-mail: rb42h@nih.gov
Web: www.nia.nih.gov

Summary To provide financial assistance to doctoral candidates from underrepresented groups who wish to conduct research on aging.

Eligibility This program is open to doctoral candidates conducting research on a dissertation with an aging-related focus, including the 4 extramural programs within the National Institute on Aging (NIA): the biology of aging program, the behavioral and social research program, the neuroscience and neuropsychology of aging program, and the geriatrics and clinical gerontology program. Applicants must be 1) members of an ethnic or racial group underrepresented in biomedical or behavioral research; 2) individuals with disabilities; or 3) individuals from socially, culturally, economically, or educationally disadvantaged backgrounds that have inhibited their ability to prepare for a career in health-related research. They must be U.S. citizens, nationals, or permanent residents.

Financial data Grants provide $20,772 per year for stipend and up to $15,000 for additional expenses. No funds may be used to pay tuition or fees associated with completion of doctoral studies. The institution may receive up to 8% of direct costs as facilities and administrative costs per year.

Duration Up to 2 years.

Number awarded 6 to 8 each year.

Deadline Letters of intent must be submitted by February or October of each year.

[683]
ALBERT G. RICHARDS GRADUATE STUDENT RESEARCH GRANT

American Academy of Oral and Maxillofacial Radiology
Attn: Executive Director
P.O. Box 1010
Evans, GA 30809-1010
(706) 721-2607   E-mail: mshrout@mail.mcq.edu
Web: www.aaomr.org/a_richards.htm

Summary To provide funding to members of the American Academy of Oral and Maxillofacial Radiology doing applied research in oral and maxillofacial radiology.

Eligibility This award is open to students enrolled in graduate programs with an oral and maxillofacial radiology track. Applicants should be active or associate members of the academy or should have applied for membership. Funded projects should involve research in some area of oral and maxillofacial radiology and should result in the eventual publication of a master's thesis or an article suitable for publication. Selection is based on originality, soundness of methodology, and significance of contribution of the research to the science of oral and maxillofacial radiology.

Financial data The grant is $1,000. Funds may be used for supplies, equipment, and other research-related costs (e.g., computer time or shop work).

Duration 1 year.

Number awarded 1 each year.

Deadline April of each year.

[684]
ALICE FISHER SOCIETY HISTORICAL SCHOLARSHIP

University of Pennsylvania
School of Nursing
Attn: Barbara Bates Center for the Study of the History of Nursing
307 Nursing Education Building
Philadelphia, PA 19104-6906
(215) 898-4502   Fax: (215) 573-2168
E-mail: nhistory@nursing.upenn.edu
Web: www.nursing.upenn.edu/history/research/fisher.htm

Summary To provide funding to graduate students interested in conducting research at the Barbara Bates Center for the Study of the History of Nursing in Philadelphia, Pennsylvania.

Eligibility This program is open to nurses working on a master's or doctoral degree on the history of nursing. Proposals should cover aims, background significance, previous work, methods, facilities needed, other research support needed, budget, and professional accomplishments. Selection is based on evidence of interest in and aptitude for historical research related to nursing.

Financial data The grant is $2,500.

Duration 4 to 6 weeks.

Additional information Scholars work under the general direction of nurse historians associated with the center. They may be asked to present their work before a meeting of the Philadelphia General Hospital School of Nursing Alumni—the founders of this scholarship. Scholars must be in residence at the Barbara Bates Center for the Study of the History of Nursing for the duration of the program.

Number awarded 1 each year.

Deadline December of each year.

[685]
ALLEGIANCE HEALTHCARE GRADUATE RESEARCH AWARD

American Society for Clinical Laboratory Science
Attn: ASCLS Education & Research Fund
6701 Democracy Boulevard, Suite 300
Bethesda, MD 20817
(301) 657-2768   Fax: (301) 657-2909
E-mail: ascls@ascls.org
Web: www.ascls.org/leadership/awards/e_and_r.asp

Summary To provide funding to graduate students who are interested in conducting research in clinical laboratory science.

Eligibility This program is open to clinical laboratory scientists or clinical laboratory technicians conducting graduate research in the field. Applicants must be U.S. citizens or permanent residents, be enrolled or accepted for enrollment in an approved master's or doctoral program in an area related to clinical laboratory science, and not be completing their education before the grant is awarded.

Financial data The grant is $3,000. Funds must be used for direct support of the research; they may not be used for education programs or curriculum development, stipends for applicants or assistants, manuscript preparation or publication, purchase of standard equipment and supplies, travel to scientific meetings, or tuition.

Duration 1 year.

Number awarded 1 each year.

Deadline May of each year.

[686]
AMERICAN ACADEMY OF AMBULATORY CARE NURSING RESEARCH AWARD

American Academy of Ambulatory Care Nursing
Attn: Scholarships
200 East Holly Avenue
P.O. Box 56
Pitman, NJ 08071-0056
(856) 256-2350   Toll-free: (800) AMN-NURS
Fax: (856) 589-7463   E-mail: aaacn@ajj.com
Web: www.aaacn.org

Summary To provide funding to members of the American Academy of Ambulatory Care Nursing (AAACN) who are interested in conducting a research project.

Eligibility This program is open to nurses who have been AAACN members for at least 2 years. Applicants must be interested in conducting a research project that has been accepted by their academic institution or the investigational review board of their employing or sponsoring institution. Along with their application, they must submit a brief paragraph describing why they are applying for this research award.

Financial data Grants range from $100 to $1,000.

Duration 1 year.

Additional information Recipients must 1) write an article for *Viewpoint* describing the research study and its outcomes, and 2) submit an abstract for presentation of the research study and its outcomes at the next annual meeting of AAACN.

Number awarded 1 or more each year.

Deadline January of each year.

[687]
AMERICAN ASSOCIATION FOR THE HISTORY OF NURSING COMPETITIVE STUDENT RESEARCH AWARD

American Association for the History of Nursing
Attn: Executive Secretary
P.O. Box 175
Lanoka Harbor, NJ 08734
(609) 693-7250   Fax: (609) 693-1037
E-mail: aahn@aahn.org
Web: www.aahn.org/awards.html

Summary To provide funding for graduate student research to members of the American Association for the History of Nursing (AAHN).

Eligibility This program is open to members of the association enrolled in either an NLN-accredited master's program or a doctoral program at a regionally-accredited university. Proposals must focus on a significant question in the history of nursing. The applicant's research advisor must be a scholar who is actively involved in the field of nursing history and who has prior experience in guiding student research. Selection is based on the scholarly merit of the proposal, the student's preparation for the study, the advisor's qualifications for guiding the study, and the project's potential for contributing to scholarship in the field of nursing history.

Financial data The grant is $1,000.

Duration 1 year.

Number awarded 1 each year.

Deadline May of each year.

[688]
AMERICAN ASSOCIATION OF CRITICAL-CARE NURSES MENTORSHIP GRANT

American Association of Critical-Care Nurses
Attn: Research Department
101 Columbia
Aliso Viejo, CA 92656-4109
(949) 362-2050, ext. 321
Toll-free: (800) 394-5995, ext. 321   Fax: (949) 362-2020
E-mail: research@aacn.org
Web: www.aacn.org

Summary To provide funding to members of the American Association of Critical-Care Nurses (AACN) who are interested in conducting research under the direction of a mentor.

Eligibility Registered nurses who are current members of the association and have limited or no research experience may apply for these grants. They must propose to conduct research under the direction of a mentor with expertise in the area of proposed investigation. The role of the mentor must be clearly defined. The recipient may use the proposed research to meet the requirements for an academic degree, but the mentor may not. The mentor may not be a mentor on another AACN Mentorship Grant in 2 consecutive years.

Financial data The grant is $10,000. Funds may be used to support direct project expenses, such as research assistants, secretarial support, equipment, supplies, and consultative assistance. They may not be used for salaries of the principle or co-investigators, travel to presentations, preparation of slides, presentation or publication of findings, or such educational expenses as tuition or books. Indirect costs are limited to 10% of direct costs.

Number awarded 1 each year.

Deadline December of each year.

[689]
AMERICAN COLLEGE OF SPORTS MEDICINE DOCTORAL RESEARCH SCHOLARSHIPS FOR MINORITY STUDENTS

American College of Sports Medicine
Attn: Director of Membership and Chapter Services
401 West Michigan Street
P.O. Box 1440
Indianapolis, IN 46206-1440
(317) 637-9200, ext. 104   Fax: (317) 637-7817
E-mail: csawyer@acsm.org
Web: www.acsm.org

Summary To provide funding for research to minority doctoral students who are interested in preparing for a career in sports medicine or exercise science.

Eligibility This program is open to minorities who have been accepted in a full-time doctoral program in sports medicine, exercise science, kinesiology, or other related field. Minorities are defined as American Indians, Alaskan Natives, Asians, Native Hawaiians and other Pacific Islanders, Blacks or African Americans, and Latinos or Hispanics. Applicants must submit 2 letters of professional recommendation (including at least 1 from a current member of the American College of Sports Medicine),a summary of participation in scholarly activities associated with sports medicine, exercise science, kinesiology, or a related field (including documentation of research and scholarly activities), transcripts, GRE or MCAT scores, and a 300-word description of short- and long-term academic and career goals in sports medicine, exercise science, kinesiology, or a related field. U.S. or Canadian citizenship is required.

Financial data The stipend is $8,000 per year.

Duration 1 year.

Additional information Recipients are given a 1 year's free membership in the American College of Sports Medicine.

Number awarded 1 or more each year.

Deadline January of each year.

[690]
AMERICAN COLLEGE OF SPORTS MEDICINE DOCTORAL STUDENT RESEARCH GRANTS

American College of Sports Medicine
Attn: Research Administration and Programs Office
401 West Michigan Street
P.O. Box 1440
Indianapolis, IN 46206-1440
(317) 637-9200, ext. 143   Fax: (317) 634-7817
Web: www.acsm.org

Summary To provide funding for research to doctoral students who are members of the American College of Sports Medicine (ACSM).

Eligibility This program is open to doctoral students enrolled full time in programs in sports medicine or exercise science. Applicants must be current members of ACSM interested in conducting basic, applied, or clinical research.

Financial data The grant is $5,000 per year. Funds are to be used for experimental subjects, supplies, and small equipment needs.

Duration 1 year.

Deadline January of each year.

[691]
AMERICAN DIABETES ASSOCIATION PHYSICIAN-SCIENTIST TRAINING AWARDS

American Diabetes Association
Attn: Research Program Specialist
1701 North Beauregard Street
Alexandria, VA 22311
(703) 549-1500, ext. 2250   Toll-free: (800) DIABETES
Fax: (703) 549-1715   E-mail: mrowan@diabetes.org
Web: www.diabetes.org

Summary To provide funding to students working on joint degrees and interested in diabetes-related clinical investigation or basic research.

Eligibility This program is open to students working on a joint degree in medicine with a research-oriented Ph.D., master's in clinical research, or master's in public health degree. Application must be initiated by a student who has a qualified sponsor. The student's sponsor must hold a faculty position at an accredited medical school in the United States and be a U.S. citizen or have permanent resident status. The sponsor must also be a member of the Professional Section of the American Diabetes Association and should have a demonstrated record of success in conducting research and in working with research trainees. Students should develop a proposal with their sponsors. The entire research protocol may not exceed 2 pages and must include the following: purpose, background, experimental design and methodology, expected results and data analysis, and significance. Selection is based on the proposed research, qualifications of the student and sponsor, and the training environment.

Financial data The grant is $30,000; that includes $20,000 as a stipend for the student and up to $10,000 for tuition, materials, supplies, and travel to the association's scientific sessions. No indirect costs are funded.

Duration 3 years.

Additional information A progress report must be submitted within 12 months. Funds not spent in any award year must be returned to the association. Recipients must conduct their research in the United States or U.S. possessions. Acknowledgement of support from the association must be made in all research publications arising from funds provided by this award.

Number awarded 1 or more each year.

Deadline January of each year.

[692]
AMERICAN INSTITUTE OF THE HISTORY OF PHARMACY GRANTS-IN-AID

American Institute of the History of Pharmacy
Attn: Director
Rennebohm Hall
777 Highland Avenue
Madison, WI 53706-2222
(608) 262-5378   E-mail: grants@aihp.org
Web: www.pharmacy.wisc.edu/aihp/grant.htm

Summary To provide funding to graduate students interested in conducting historical research on an aspect of pharmacy.

Eligibility This program is open to graduate students (in any department) working on a master's thesis or Ph.D. dissertation that is clearly and significantly related to pharmaceutical history or some other branch of humanistic study utilizing a pharmaco-historical approach. Applicants must be attending school in the United States, but they need not be a U.S. citizen and the research topic does not need to be in the field of U.S. history. A member of the graduate faculty must co-sign the application, to indicate willingness to supervise the thesis research and to share responsibility for proper expenditure of any funds awarded. Selection is based on originality and significance of the proposed master's or doctoral thesis; relevance to the history of pharmacy; and demonstrated need for outside funds to enhance or complete the research project.

Financial data Grants up to $5,000 are available. Funds must be used to defray the direct costs of thesis research (supplies and other expenses) that cannot normally be reimbursed by the degree-granting institution. Examples of eligible expenses are: computer time and assistance in programming; travel and maintenance at a site removed from the home university for research in sources necessary to the project; obtaining a photocopy or microform of essential sources; application of investigative methods unusual in the history of pharmacy. Examples of ineligible expenses include: living expenses of the applicant at the home university; routine typing to produce research notes or the thesis manuscript; routine illustrations for the manuscript; and publication of the research results.

Duration 1 year.

Number awarded 1 or more each year.

Deadline January of each year.

[693]
AMERICAN MEDICAL ASSOCIATION FOUNDATION SEED GRANT RESEARCH PROGRAM

American Medical Association
Attn: AMA Foundation
515 North State Street
Chicago, IL 60610
(312) 464-4200   Fax: (312) 464-4142
E-mail: seedgrants@ama-assn.org
Web: www.ama-assn.org/ama/pub/category/7785.html

Summary To provide funding to medical students and residents interested in conducting small research projects.

Eligibility This program is open to medical students, residents, and physician fellows interested in conducting small research projects in the following areas: arthritis and rheumatism, cardiovascular and pulmonary diseases, HIV/AIDS, leukemia, neoplastic diseases, and psychiatric diseases. Proposals should be to round out new project budgets, not to sustain current initiatives. Projects must have a worthy research objective; scientifically sound design; no association with product research and development activities; demonstrated need for start-up, interim, or supplemental funding on a time-limited basis; and no effective funding from other sources available. Research must be conducted in the United States.

Financial data Grants range from $1,500 to $2,500.

Number awarded Varies each year; recently, 40 of these grants were awarded.

Deadline November of each year.

[694]
AMERICAN METEOROLOGICAL SOCIETY GRADUATE FELLOWSHIP IN THE HISTORY OF SCIENCE

American Meteorological Society
Attn: Fellowship/Scholarship Program
45 Beacon Street
Boston, MA 02108-3693
(617) 227-2426, ext. 246   Fax: (617) 742-8718
E-mail: scholar@ametsoc.org
Web: www.ametsoc.org

Summary To provide funding to graduate students interested in conducting dissertation research on the history of meteorology.

Eligibility This program is open to graduate students who are planning to complete a dissertation on the history of the atmospheric or related oceanic or hydrologic sciences. Applicants must be U.S. citizens or permanent residents and working on a degree at a U.S. institution. Fellowships may be used to support research at a location away from the student's institution, provided the plan is approved by the student's thesis advisor. In such an instance, an effort is made to place the student into a mentoring relationship with a member of the society at an appropriate institution. The sponsor specifically encourages applications from women, minorities, and students with disabilities who are traditionally underrepresented in the atmospheric and related oceanic sciences.

Financial data The stipend is $15,000 per year.

Duration 1 year.

Number awarded 1 each year.

Deadline February of each year.

[695]
AMERICAN NURSES ASSOCIATION PRESIDENTIAL SCHOLAR AWARD

American Nurses Foundation
Attn: Nursing Research Grants Program
8515 Georgia Avenue, Suite 400
Silver Spring, MD 20910-3492
(301) 628-5298   Fax: (301) 628-5354
E-mail: anf@ana.org
Web: www.anfonline.org

Summary To provide funding to nurses interested in conducting research.

Eligibility This program is open to registered nurses who have earned a baccalaureate or higher degree. Applicants must be beginning researchers who have had no more than 3 research-based publications in refereed journals and have received, as a principal investigator, no more than $15,000 in extramural funding in any 1 research area. The topic of the research changes periodically; recently, it was health disparities. Proposed research may be for a master's thesis or doctoral dissertation if the project has been approved by the principal investigator's thesis or dissertation committee.

Financial data The grant is $3,500. Funds may not be used as a salary for the principal investigator.

Duration 1 year.

Additional information This program was established in 1993. There is a $75 application fee.

Number awarded 1 each year.

Deadline April of each year.

[696]
AMERICAN OCCUPATIONAL THERAPY FOUNDATION DISSERTATION RESEARCH AWARDS

American Occupational Therapy Foundation
Attn: Office of Research Resources
4720 Montgomery Lane
P.O. Box 31220
Bethesda, MD 20824-1220
(301) 652-6611, ext. 2556   Fax: (301) 656-3620
TDD: (800) 377-8555   E-mail: hross@aotf.org
Web: www.aotf.org/html/student.shtml

Summary To provide funding to members of the American Occupational Therapy Association (AOTA) interested in conducting doctoral research in occupational therapy.

Eligibility This program is open to members of the association who are registered occupational therapists. Applicants must be enrolled in a doctoral program and have an approved dissertation proposal. They must have a GPA of 3.5 or higher. Along with their application, they must submit an abstract of their dissertation proposal, a statement of their career goals and their plans to continue contributing to occupational therapy, resources currently available to complete their dissertation research, a statement describing their relationship with a mentor, and a budget request and justification.

Financial data Grants range up to $5,000.

Duration 1 year.

Additional information This program operated from 1981 to 1999 and was reestablished in 2006. Recipients must agree to complete their doctoral program within 3 years of the initial award or repay the entire amount of the grant.

Number awarded Up to 5 each year.

Deadline February, May, August, or November of each year.

[697]
AMERICAN OTOLOGICAL SOCIETY RESEARCH TRAINING FELLOWSHIPS

American Otological Society Research Fund
c/o Lloyd B. Minor, Executive Secretary
Johns Hopkins University, School of Medicine
Division of Otolaryngology-Head and Neck Surgery
601 North Caroline Street, JHOC 6210
Baltimore, MD 21287-0910
(410) 955-1080   Fax: (410) 955-6526
E-mail: lminor2@jhmi.edu
Web: www.americanotologicalsociety.org/funding.html

Summary To provide funding to students and resident physicians conducting research on otosclerosis or Meniere's Disease.

Eligibility Applicants must be medical students, residents, or fellows (not nonmedical postgraduate researchers). Appropriate areas of research include diagnosis, management, and pathogenesis of otosclerosis or Meniere's Disease, as well as underlying processes. These can involve anatomical, physiological, biochemical, pharmacological, physical, genetic, environmental, psychological, pathological, or audiological investigations. The applicant should describe correlations between proposed research and these clinical pathological entities.

Financial data The maximum award is $35,000 for a stipend and $5,000 for supplies (plus up to 10% indirect costs). Awards are made to an institution on behalf of the grantee.

Duration The fellowships support full-time research for 1 or 2 years conducted outside of residency training.

Additional information Recipients are relieved of all clinical duties during the fellowship period. All research must be performed in U.S. or Canadian institutions.

Number awarded Varies each year.

Deadline January of each year.

[698]
AMERICAN PEDIATRIC SOCIETY/SOCIETY FOR PEDIATRIC RESEARCH STUDENT RESEARCH PROGRAM

American Pediatric Society/Society for Pediatric Research
3400 Research Forest Drive, Suite B-7
The Woodlands, TX 77381
(281) 419-0052   Fax: (281) 419-0082
E-mail: student-research@aps-spr.org
Web: www.aps-spr.org/Student_Research

Summary To provide financial assistance to gifted medical students who are considering careers in research related to pediatrics.

Eligibility This program is open to students seeking a pediatric research opportunity at an institution (in the United States or Canada) other than their own medical school. Applicants must be enrolled in a medical school in good standing at the time of their application. If they already have a medical degree, they are ineligible. Letters of recommendation are required.

Financial data The stipend is $57.70 per day, to a maximum of $4,270.

Duration 8 to 10 weeks.

Additional information Participants choose or are assigned to leading research laboratories in the United States or Canada to work under the direct supervision of experienced scientists in the field of pediatrics.

Deadline January of each year.

[699]
AMERICAN PHILOSOPHICAL SOCIETY LIBRARY RESIDENT RESEARCH FELLOWSHIPS

American Philosophical Society
Attn: Library
105 South Fifth Street
Philadelphia, PA 19106-3386
(215) 440-3443   Fax: (215) 440-3436
E-mail: jjahern@amphilsoc.org
Web: www.amphilsoc.org/grants/resident.htm

Summary To provide funding for scholars, including doctoral candidates, who wish to conduct research at the American Philosophical Society Library.

Eligibility Eligible to apply are holders of the Ph.D. or its equivalent, Ph.D. candidates who have passed their preliminary exams, and independent scholars in any field of study relevant to the holdings of the American Philosophical Society Library. They may be foreign nationals or U.S. citizens who reside beyond a 75-mile radius of Philadelphia.

Financial data The stipend is $2,000 per month.

Duration 1 to 3 months.

Additional information The library's holdings focus on the history of American science and technology and its European roots, as well as early American history and culture. Collections and subject areas include the papers of Benjamin Franklin; the American Revolution; 18th- and 19th-century natural history; western scientific expeditions and travel, including the journals of Lewis and Clark; polar exploration; American Indian languages;

anthropology including the papers of Franz Boas; the papers of Charles Darwin and his forerunners, colleagues, critics, and successors; 20th-century medical research; and the history of physics, biophysics, biochemistry, physiology, genetics, eugenics, and evolution. These fellowships are funded by the Andrew W. Mellon Foundation, the Grundy Foundation, the Isaac Comly Martindale Fund, and the Phillips Fund. Fellows are expected to be in residence in Philadelphia for at least 4 consecutive weeks during the period of their award.

Number awarded Varies each year; recently, 23 of these grants were awarded.

Deadline February of each year.

[700]
AMERICAN SKIN ASSOCIATION MEDICAL STUDENT STIPENDS

American Skin Association
346 Park Avenue South, Fourth Floor
New York, NY 10010
(212) 889-4858   Toll-free: (800) 499-SKIN
Fax: (212) 889-4959   E-mail: info@americanskin.org
Web: www.americanskin.org/research.htm

Summary To provide funding to medical students interested in conducting research related to dermatology or skin cancer.

Eligibility This program is open to medical students working actively in areas related to dermatology. Applicants must be seeking support of a new or ongoing research/clinical investigation project related to melanoma or skin cancer. Along with their application, they must submit a cover letter describing their career goals and the relevance of the grant at this time, a curriculum vitae, a letter of endorsement from their dermatology department chair or mentor, and a research proposal.

Financial data The grant is $7,000.

Duration 1 year.

Number awarded 3 each year.

Deadline September of each year.

[701]
AMERICAN SOCIETY FOR CLINICAL LABORATORY SCIENCE RESTRICTED GRANTS-IN-AID OF RESEARCH

American Society for Clinical Laboratory Science
Attn: ASCLS Education & Research Fund
6701 Democracy Boulevard, Suite 300
Bethesda, MD 20817
(301) 657-2768   Fax: (301) 657-2909
E-mail: ascls@ascls.org
Web: www.ascls.org/leadership/awards/e_and_r.asp

Summary To provide funding to members of the American Society for Clinical Laboratory Science (ASCLS) who are interested in conducting research on designated topics in the field.

Eligibility This program is open to clinical laboratory science scientists and technicians who are ASCLS members (including graduate students) conducting scientific investigations in the field. The proposed research must relate to 1 of the areas targeted for funding by the program's sponsor: 1) investigation of the extent and nature of problems caused by inaccurate test results in the diagnosis and treatment of patients; 2) investigation of the link between proficiency testing, personnel standards, internal quality control, and quality assurance on the reliability and accuracy of test results; 3) investigation of the clinical laboratory scientist's or clinical laboratory technician's role in test utilization decisions; 4) development and testing of a model for the study

of clinical laboratory test utilization in clinical decision-making; 5) assessment of patient centered outcomes for point of care testing; 6) development and testing of strategies to improve the public image of clinical laboratory science; 7) investigation of the need for curriculum restructuring to meet market demands for laboratory professionals in the 21st century; 8) examination of the extent to which each step in the laboratory testing process influences the overall test accuracy in patient results; or 9) design and test strategies that lead to recognition of the contributions of laboratory professionals.

Financial data The amount of the grant depends on the nature of the proposal. Funds must be used for direct support of the research; they are not available for stipends for applicants or assistants, manuscript preparation and publication costs, purchase of standard equipment that should normally be available in an institutional research laboratory, travel to scientific meetings, or indirect costs.

Duration Grants may be expended over 3 years.

Number awarded Up to 2 each year.

Deadline May of each year.

[702]
AMERICAN SOCIETY FOR CLINICAL LABORATORY SCIENCE UNRESTRICTED GRANT-IN-AID OF RESEARCH

American Society for Clinical Laboratory Science
Attn: ASCLS Education & Research Fund
6701 Democracy Boulevard, Suite 300
Bethesda, MD 20817
(301) 657-2768   Fax: (301) 657-2909
E-mail: ascls@ascls.org
Web: www.ascls.org/leadership/awards/e_and_r.asp

Summary To provide funding to members of the American Society for Clinical Laboratory Science (ASCLS) who are interested in conducting research on designated topics in the field.

Eligibility This program is open to clinical laboratory science scientists and technicians who are ASCLS members (including graduate students) conducting scientific investigations in the field. The proposed research must relate to 1 of the areas targeted for funding by the program's sponsor: 1) investigation of the extent and nature of problems caused by inaccurate test results in the diagnosis and treatment of patients; 2) investigation of the link between proficiency testing, personnel standards, internal quality control, and quality assurance on the reliability and accuracy of test results; 3) investigation of the clinical laboratory scientist's or clinical laboratory technician's role in test utilization decisions; 4) development and testing of a model for the study of clinical laboratory test utilization in clinical decision-making; 5) assessment of patient centered outcomes for point of care testing; 6) development and testing of strategies to improve the public image of clinical laboratory science; 7) investigation of the need for curriculum restructuring to meet market demands for laboratory professionals in the 21st century; 8) examination of the extent to which each step in the laboratory testing process influences the overall test accuracy in patient results; or 9) design and test strategies that lead to recognition of the contributions of laboratory professionals.

Financial data The grant is $5,000. Funds must be used for direct support of the research, but their use is not restricted except for excluding payment of indirect costs.

Duration Grants may be expended over 3 years.

Number awarded 1 each year.

Deadline May of each year.

[703]
AMERICAN SOCIETY OF HEMATOLOGY TRAINEE RESEARCH AWARDS

American Society of Hematology
Attn: Award Program Coordinator
1900 M Street, N.W., Suite 200
Washington, DC 20036
(202) 776-0544, ext. 1168   Fax: (202) 776-0545
E-mail: ASH@hematology.org
Web: www.hematology.org/education/awards/trainee.cfm

Summary To provide an opportunity for medical students, residents, and selected undergraduates to work on a research training project in hematology.

Eligibility This program is open to medical students and residents who are interested in working on a research project in hematology under the supervision of a mentor or training director who is a member of the American Society of Hematology (ASH). Undergraduates may participate at the discretion of the mentor or training director. Applications must be submitted by the institution, which must have an accredited training program with a director in hematology or a hematology-related area. The institution must be in the United States, Canada, or Mexico. The mentor and the student should work collaboratively to complete the application. It should include a 500-word research outline, covering the scientific question, background, proposed method, proposed results, and impact. Both laboratory research and clinical investigation are eligible.

Financial data The grant includes $4,000 for research support and an additional $1,000 to support travel to the annual meeting of the ASH. Research stipends are paid directly to the institution, not the student.

Duration 3 months any time during the year.

Additional information Trainees are required to submit a final summary of their work at the end of their research.

Number awarded Varies each year; each training program may support only 1 student unless there are unclaimed funds available.

Deadline March of each year.

[704]
AMERICAN SOCIETY OF PERIANESTHESIA NURSES ADVANCED BEGINNER RESEARCHER GRANTS

American Society of PeriAnesthesia Nurses
Attn: Foundation
10 Melrose Avenue, Suite 110
Cherry Hill, NJ 08003-3696
(856) 616-9600   Toll-free: (877) 737-9696, ext. 13
Fax: (856) 616-9601   E-mail: aspan@aspan.org
Web: www.aspan.org/ResearchPack.htm

Summary To provide funding to members of the American Society of PeriAnesthesia Nurses (ASPAN) who have limited previous research experience and are interested in conducting a research project.

Eligibility This program is open to members of the society who have limited previous exposure to or experience with research. Applicants must be registered nurses conducting 1) self-initiated graduate research projects as part of their requirements for a master's degree, or 2) small, individual projects for the purpose of individual and clinical advancement. All projects must be related to and contribute to the growth of evidence-based perianesthesia nursing practice. Applicants must provide evidence of expert consultation, mentorship, and support with a co-

investigator who can be a student's faculty advisor, head of research at an institution, or director of nursing.

Financial data Grants range from $500 to $5,000. Funds may be used to support direct project expenses only (e.g., equipment, supplies, secretarial support). Indirect costs are not funded.

Duration 1 year.

Number awarded Varies each year.

Deadline January or June of each year.

[705]
AMERICAN SOCIETY OF PERIANESTHESIA NURSES COMPETENT RESEARCHER GRANTS

American Society of PeriAnesthesia Nurses
Attn: Foundation
10 Melrose Avenue, Suite 110
Cherry Hill, NJ 08003-3696
(856) 616-9600   Toll-free: (877) 737-9696, ext. 13
Fax: (856) 616-9601   E-mail: aspan@aspan.org
Web: www.aspan.org/ResearchPack.htm

Summary To provide funding to members of the American Society of PeriAnesthesia Nurses (ASPAN) who have documented competency in the research process and are interested in conducting a research project.

Eligibility This program is open to members of the society who have documented competency in the research process. Applicants must be registered nurses conducting 1) self-initiated graduate research projects as part of their requirements for a doctoral degree, or 2) individual projects for the purpose of individual and clinical advancement. All projects must be related to and contribute to the growth of evidence-based perianesthesia nursing practice. Applicants must provide evidence of research expertise and/or expert consultation, mentorship, and support.

Financial data Grants range from $500 to $5,000. Funds may be used to support direct project expenses only (e.g., equipment, supplies, secretarial support). Indirect costs are not funded.

Duration 1 year.

Number awarded Varies each year.

Deadline January or June of each year.

[706]
AMERICAN SOCIETY OF RADIOLOGIC TECHNOLOGISTS PROFESSIONAL RESEARCH GRANT AWARD PROGRAM

American Society of Radiologic Technologists
Attn: ASRT Education and Research Foundation
15000 Central Avenue, S.E.
Albuquerque, NM 87123-3909
(505) 298-4500, ext. 2541
Toll-free: (800) 444-2778, ext. 2541   Fax: (505) 298-5063
E-mail: foundation@asrt.org
Web: www.asrt.org

Summary To provide funding to members of the American Society of Radiologic Technologists (ASRT) who are interested in conducting research, including dissertation research, in the radiological sciences.

Eligibility This program is open to licensed radiologic technologists who are current members of ASRT. Applicants must be interested in conducting research related to radiation therapy, dosimetry, or medical imaging, including nuclear medicine and sonography. Proposals related to education and administration in those fields are also eligible. Research may be for completion of a doctoral dissertation or in affiliation with an academic or clinical institution.

Financial data The grant is $10,000.

Duration Up to 2 years.

Number awarded 1 or 2 each year.

Deadline February or August of each year.

[707]
AMERICAN SOCIETY OF RADIOLOGIC TECHNOLOGISTS RESEARCH GRANT AWARD PROGRAM FOR GRADUATE STUDENTS

American Society of Radiologic Technologists
Attn: ASRT Education and Research Foundation
15000 Central Avenue, S.E.
Albuquerque, NM 87123-3909
(505) 298-4500, ext. 2541
Toll-free: (800) 444-2778, ext. 2541   Fax: (505) 298-5063
E-mail: foundation@asrt.org
Web: www.asrt.org

Summary To provide funding to student members of the American Society of Radiologic Technologists (ASRT) who are interested in conducting a research project in the radiological sciences.

Eligibility This program is open to licensed radiologic technologists who are current members of ASRT. Applicants must be enrolled in a planned course of study at the associate, baccalaureate, master's, or doctoral degree level to further their career in the radiologic sciences. They must be interested in conducting a research project related to their degree that they will complete prior to graduation. Projects must be related to radiation therapy, dosimetry, or medical imaging, including nuclear medicine and sonography. Proposals related to education and administration in those fields are also eligible. Selection is based on appropriateness of methodology and experimental design, thoroughness of literature review, and soundness of budget.

Financial data The grant is $1,500 per year.

Duration 1 year; may be renewed.

Number awarded 4 each year.

Deadline March or September of each year.

[708]
AMTA FELLOWSHIP FOR MEMBRANE TECHNOLOGY

National Water Research Institute
Attn: Fellowship Program
10500 Ellis Avenue
P.O. Box 20865
Fountain Valley, CA 92728-0865
(714) 378-3278   Fax: (714) 378-3375
E-mail: fellow@nwri-usa.org
Web: www.nwri-usa.org

Summary To provide funding to graduate students interested in conducting research on the use of membranes in water science and technology (including health sciences).

Eligibility This program is open to full-time graduate students interested in conducting research in areas of interest to the American Membrane Technology Association (AMTA): to promote, advocate, and advance the understanding and application of membrane technology to create safe, affordable, and reliable water supplies, and to treat municipal, industrial, agricultural, and waste waters for beneficial use. Possible topics include innovative membrane treatment technologies, use of advanced materials,

membrane bioreactors, membrane fouling/scaling control, membrane removal efficiency, membrane pretreatment, or improved feedwater recovery. Research areas include, but are not limited to, engineering, physical and chemical sciences, biological sciences, health sciences, political sciences, economics, and planning and public policy that are related to water and/or water resources. Preference is given to doctoral candidates, but outstanding students in master's programs may be considered. Applicants must submit a letter of inquiry describing the importance of the research to them and the water community, how their research will contribute to water science in general, what they expect to accomplish, and how their research relates to the mission of the National Water Research Institute (NWRI) to create new sources of water through research and technology and to protect the freshwater and marine environments.

Financial data The grant is $10,000 per year.

Duration 2 years.

Additional information This fellowship is jointly sponsored by AMTA and the NWRI.

Number awarded 2 each year.

Deadline February of each year.

[709]
ANESTHESIOLOGY DENTAL STUDENT RESEARCH AWARDS

American Dental Society of Anesthesiology, Inc.
211 East Chicago Avenue, Suite 780
Chicago, IL 60611
(312) 664-8270   Toll-free: (877) 255-3742
Fax: (312) 224-8624   E-mail: adsahome@mac.com
Web: www.adsahome.org/researchaward.html

Summary To recognize and reward outstanding research completed by dental students in the United States or Canada.

Eligibility This program is open to students in U.S. and Canadian dental schools. Applicants must submit a manuscript describing research they have completed.

Financial data First prize is $1,000 and payment of travel and lodging expenses to attend the sponsor's annual meeting. Second prize is $500.

Duration The prizes are given annually.

Number awarded 2 each year.

Deadline October of each year.

[710]
ANNE S. CHATHAM FELLOWSHIP IN MEDICINAL BOTANY

Missouri Botanical Garden
Attn: William L. Brown Center for Plant Genetic Resources
P.O. Box 299
St. Louis, MO 63166-0299
(314) 577-9503   Fax: (314) 577-9465
E-mail: james.miller@mobot.org
Web: www.wlbcenter.org/chatham.htm

Summary To provide funding to Ph.D. candidates and Ph.D.s interested in conducting research in medicinal botany in the United States or abroad.

Eligibility This program is open to students currently enrolled in Ph.D. programs at recognized universities and postdoctorates who received their Ph.D. within the last 5 years. Applicants must be interested in conducting research on the medicinal use of plants. They must submit a description of their proposed research, budget, current curriculum vitae, and documentation that appropriate permits, research clearances, and permissions from governmental agencies have been obtained for foreign research.

Financial data   The stipend is $4,000. Funds may be used to cover direct costs associated with travel, field studies, or laboratory research but cannot be used for indirect costs or institutional overhead.

Duration   1 year.

Additional information   The Missouri Botanical Garden administers this program, established in 1997 as part of the scholarship program of the Garden Club of America. Information is also available from its Scholarship Committee, 14 East 60th Street, New York, NY 10022-1006, (212) 753-8287, Fax: (212) 753-0134, E-mail: scholarship@gcamerica.org.

Number awarded   1 each year.

Deadline   January of each year.

[711]
ANNE ZIMMERMAN SCHOLAR AWARD
American Nurses Foundation
Attn: Nursing Research Grants Program
8515 Georgia Avenue, Suite 400
Silver Spring, MD 20910-3492
(301) 628-5298   Fax: (301) 628-5354
E-mail: anf@ana.org
Web: www.anfonline.org

Summary   To provide funding to nurses interested in conducting research related to nursing practice or social policy issues that will advance the profession.

Eligibility   This program is open to registered nurses who have earned a baccalaureate or higher degree. Applicants may be either beginning or experienced researchers. They must be planning to conduct research that is intended to advance the profession of nursing by strengthening clinical nursing practice, supporting pertinent social policies, and underpinning the economic and general welfare of both nurses and nursing. Proposed research may be for a master's thesis or doctoral dissertation if the project has been approved by the principal investigator's thesis or dissertation committee.

Financial data   The grant is $5,000. Funds may not be used as a salary for the principal investigator.

Duration   1 year.

Additional information   This program was established in 1995. There is a $75 application fee. A publication, preferably a monograph, is expected at the conclusion of the award term.

Number awarded   1 each year.

Deadline   April of each year.

[712]
AOA PRESIDENTIAL MEMORIAL LEADERSHIP AWARD
American Osteopathic Foundation
Attn: Program Manager
142 East Ontario Street
Chicago, IL 60611-2864
(312) 202-8232   Toll-free: (800) 621-1773
Fax: (312) 202-8216   E-mail: vheck@aof-foundation.org
Web: www.aof-foundation.org/stu.asp

Summary   To recognize and reward outstanding students enrolled in colleges of osteopathic medicine.

Eligibility   This program is open to students entering their second, third, or fourth year at accredited colleges of osteopathic

medicine. Applicants must be members of the Student Osteopathic Medical Association. Selection is based on demonstrated commitment to the osteopathic profession; strong leadership skills and demonstrated use of those skills; noteworthy accomplishments demonstrating role as a leader; and outstanding character, academic achievements, and the drive to be a leader.

Financial data   The award is $3,000.

Duration   1 year.

Additional information   This program was established in 2002.

Number awarded   1 each year.

Deadline   March of each year.

[713]
AORN DEGREE COMPLETION RESEARCH GRANT PROGRAM
Association of periOperative Registered Nurses
Attn: Research Grant Program
2170 South Parker Road, Suite 300
Denver, CO 80231-5711
(303) 755-6300, ext. 230
Toll-free: (800) 755-2676, ext. 230   Fax: (303) 755-4219
E-mail: research@aorn.org
Web: www.aorn.org/research/grantprgm.htm

Summary   To provide funding for research to student members of the Association of periOperative Registered Nurses (AORN).

Eligibility   This program is open to student members of the association who are enrolled in an accredited baccalaureate, master's, or doctoral program. Applicants must be interested in conducting a research project that is related to perioperative nursing practice and consistent with AORN's research priorities: health and safety issues affecting perioperative nurses and patients; preoperative nursing leadership and management; evidence based practice; validation, testing, and refinement of the Perioperative Nursing Data Set; and perioperative nursing care that contributes to quality, cost-effective patient outcomes related to safety, physiological integrity, and behavioral responses. Except for generic baccalaureate nursing students, they must be a registered nurse with a current and valid license.

Financial data   The maximum grant is $15,000.

Duration   These are 1-time grants.

Number awarded   Varies each year.

Deadline   March or October of each year.

[714]
APA MINORITY MEDICAL STUDENT SUMMER MENTORING PROGRAM
American Psychiatric Association
Attn: Department of Minority and National Affairs
1000 Wilson Boulevard, Suite 1825
Arlington, VA 22209-3901
(703) 907-8653   Toll-free: (888) 35-PSYCH
Fax: (703) 907-7852   E-mail: mking@psych.org
Web: www.psych.org

Summary   To provide funding to minority medical students who are interested in working on a summer project with a psychiatrist mentor.

Eligibility   This program is open to minority medical students who are interested in psychiatric issues. Minorities include American Indians, Alaska Natives, Native Hawaiians, Asian Americans, Hispanic/Latinos, and African Americans. Applicants must be interested in working with a psychiatrist mentor, primarily on clinical work with underserved minority populations and mental health care disparities. Work settings may be in a research, academic, or clinical environment. Most of them are inner-city or rural, preferably those dealing with psychiatric subspecialties, particularly substance abuse and geriatrics. Selection is based on interest of the medical student and specialty of the mentor, practice setting, and geographic proximity of the mentor to the student.

Financial data Fellowships provide $1,500 for living expenses and up to another $1,500 for out-of-pocket expenses directly related to the conduct of the fellowship.

Duration Summer months.

Number awarded Varies each year.

Deadline February of each year.

[715]
ASHA STUDENT RESEARCH GRANTS

American School Health Association
Attn: ASHA Research Council
7263 State Route 43
P.O. Box 708
Kent, OH 44240-0708
(330) 678-1601   Fax: (330) 678-4526
E-mail: asha@ashaweb.org
Web: www.ashaweb.org/studentmembership.html

Summary To provide funding to undergraduate and graduate student members of the American School Health Association (ASHA) interested in conducting a research project.

Eligibility This program is open to ASHA members who are undergraduate or graduate students specializing in 1 of the following areas: 1) school health education, 2) school nursing, or 3) pediatric or adolescent medicine or dentistry. Applicants must be interested in conducting a research project that will protect and promote the health of children and youth.

Financial data Grants are $500 for undergraduates, $750 for master's degree students, or $1,000 for doctoral students.

Duration 1 year.

Number awarded Varies each year.

Deadline April of each year.

[716]
ASHP FOUNDATION STUDENT RESEARCH AWARD

American Society of Health-System Pharmacists
Attn: Research and Education Foundation
7272 Wisconsin Avenue
Bethesda, MD 20814-1439
(301) 664-8612   Fax: (301) 634-5712
E-mail: foundation@ashp.org
Web: www.ashpfoundation.org

Summary To recognize and reward outstanding papers or reports on pharmacy practice written by pharmacy students.

Eligibility This award is given to the student author of the best unpublished paper or report on a completed research project, prepared during the past year, that relates to pharmacy practice in hospitals or health systems. When a nomination is submitted (students may nominate themselves), it should be accompanied by a letter from a faculty member certifying that the nominated paper is the student's own work. At the time the nominated paper or report was written, the student author should have been a full-time student in an entry-level program at an accredited college of pharmacy. The nominated paper should be in publishable format. Selection is based on originality (20 points), significance (15 points), research methodology (25 points), data analysis (25 points), and validity of conclusions (15 points).

Financial data The award consists of a plaque, a $1,500 honorarium, and a $1,000 travel allowance (to cover the costs of attending the society's mid-year meeting, where the award is presented).

Duration The award is presented annually.

Number awarded 1 each year.

Deadline May of each year.

[717]
ASHP STUDENT LEADERSHIP AWARDS

American Society of Health-System Pharmacists
Attn: Pharmacy Student Forum
7272 Wisconsin Avenue
Bethesda, MD 20814-1439
(301) 664-8607   Fax: (301) 657-8278
E-mail: students@ashp.org
Web: www.ashp.org/s_ashp/cat1c.asp?CID=667&DID=709

Summary To recognize and reward outstanding pharmacy students who are members of the American Society of Health-System Pharmacists (ASHP).

Eligibility This program is open to ASHP members who have completed at least the first year of full-time study in a professional Pharm.D. program at an accredited college of pharmacy with a GPA of 2.5 or higher. Applicants must submit a resume or curriculum vitae, 3 letters of recommendation, and a 750-word essay on a contemporary issue impacting the health-system pharmacy (professional, societal, or therapeutic issue) and the role they might play as a practicing pharmacist in helping to address that issue. Selection is based on health-system pharmacy practice achievement, professional organization leadership, and personal leadership attributes.

Financial data The award includes $2,500 in cash, a plaque, and a drug information reference library from AHSP.

Duration The awards are presented annually.

Number awarded 12 each year: 4 for students in each professional year of pharmacy school.

Deadline January of each year.

[718]
ASIP MERIT AWARDS

American Society for Investigative Pathology
Attn: Executive Officer
9650 Rockville Pike
Bethesda, MD 20814-3993
(301) 634-7130   Fax: (301) 634-7990
E-mail: asip@asip.org
Web: www.asip.org/awds/epit.htm

Summary To recognize and reward graduate student and postdoctoral fellow members of the American Society for Investigative Pathology (ASIP) who submit outstanding research reports.

Eligibility These awards are presented to trainee members of the society who are currently graduate students or postdoctoral fellows/residents. Applicants must have excelled in their investigative efforts in studying mechanisms of disease, as evidenced by their abstract submission to the ASIP annual meeting, an extended research report, and a letter of recommendation attesting to their role in the work and potential as a biomedical research investigator.

Financial data The award is $1,250.

Duration The awards are presented annually.

Additional information This award was first presented in 1998.

Number awarded Varies each year. Recently, 4 of these awards were presented: 3 to predoctoral graduate students and 1 to a postdoctoral fellow.
Deadline November of each year.

[719]
ASSOCIATION FOR WOMEN IN SCIENCE PREDOCTORAL AWARDS

Association for Women in Science
Attn: AWIS Educational Foundation
1200 New York Avenue, N.W., Suite 650
Washington, DC 20005
(202) 326-8940   Toll-free: (866) 657-AWIS
Fax: (202) 326-8960   E-mail: awisedfd@awis.org
Web: www.awis.org/careers/edfoundation.html

Summary To provide research funding to predoctoral women students interested in preparing for careers in the natural and social sciences.
Eligibility This program is open to women enrolled in a Ph.D. program who have passed their department's qualifying exam and expect to complete their degree within 2 years. Applicants must be enrolled in a program in a natural or social science, including anthropology, archaeology, astronomy, biology, chemistry, computer and information science, demography, economics, engineering, geography, geoscience, history of science, linguistics, mathematics, philosophy of science, physics, political science, psychology, or sociology. Foreign students are eligible if they are enrolled in a U.S. institution of higher education. Selection is based on academic achievement, the importance of the research question addressed, the quality of the research, and the applicant's potential for future contributions to science or engineering.
Financial data The stipends are $1,000. Citations of merit are $300. Funds may be used for any aspect of education, including tuition, books, housing, research, travel and meeting registration, or publication costs.
Duration 1 year.
Additional information This program includes the Amy Lutz Rechel Award for a student in the field of plant biology, the Luise Meyer-Schutzmeister Award for a student in physics, the Diane H. Russell Award for a student in the fields of biochemistry or pharmacology, the Gail Naughton Graduate Award for an outstanding graduate student, and the Ruth Satter Memorial Awards for women who interrupted their education for 3 years or more to raise a family. Information is also available from Barbara Filner, President, AWIS Educational Foundation, 7008 Richard Drive, Bethesda, MD 20817-4838.
Number awarded 5 to 10 each year.
Deadline January of each year.

[720]
AUGUST KROGH YOUNG INVESTIGATOR AWARD

Microcirculatory Society
c/o Leslie Ritter, Awards Committee Chair
University of Arizona
College of Nursing
1305 North Martin, Room 6211A
Tucson, AZ 85721-0203
(520) 626-7434   E-mail: lritter@nursing.arizona.edu
Web: microcirc.org

Summary To recognize and reward outstanding research in the field of microcirculation by graduate students and recent doctorates.

Eligibility Eligible to be nominated for this award are 1) graduate students and 2) recent graduates who received a Ph.D. or completed their first residency following receipt of an M.D. within the past 3 years. Nominees must demonstrate excellence in microcirculatory research.
Financial data The award is $1,000.
Duration The award is presented annually.
Number awarded 1 each year.
Deadline October of each year.

[721]
AWARDS FOR STUDENT RESEARCH TRAINING IN ALTERNATIVE METHODS

Society of Toxicology
Attn: Education Committee
1821 Michael Faraday Drive, Suite 300
Reston, VA 20190-5348
(703) 438-3115   Fax: (703) 438-3113
E-mail: sothq@toxicology.org
Web: www.toxicology.org/ai/af/awards.aspx

Summary To provide funding to graduate student members of the Society of Toxicology (SOT) interested in research training in alternative methods for the use of animals in toxicological research.
Eligibility This program is open to society members who are enrolled in Ph.D. or master's degree study in toxicology. Applicants must be interested in developing expertise in the use of alternative methods that involve the use of the "3 R's": replacement (methods that do not employ animals), reduction (methods that result in the use of fewer animals than existing methods), or refinement (methods or techniques that reduce pain, distress, or discomfort to the animal). The proposed research training may take place at 1) a laboratory away from their home institution, 2) a laboratory at their home institution that would not be available to them otherwise, or 3) approved workshops, symposia, or continuing education programs where hands-on training is provided. The training should help them enhance their thesis or dissertation research and gain appreciation of the use of alternatives in toxicology. work planned for the future, relevance of graduate work to toxicology, and description of the techniques the applicant proposes to learn and how those would enhance the research program. Letters of support from the applicant's research advisor and director of the hosting laboratory are also required. The research director must also be an SOT member.
Financial data The grant is $3,500. Funds may be used for travel, per diem, and training expenses (including research costs at the home and host institutions).
Additional information This program, first offered in 2000, is funded by Colgate-Palmolive Company.
Number awarded 2 each year.
Deadline February, June, or October of each year.

[722]
BAMFORD-LAHEY SCHOLARSHIPS

Bamford-Lahey Children's Foundation
2995 Woodside Road, Suite 400
Woodside, CA 94062
E-mail: info@bamford-lahey.org
Web: bamford-lahey.org/scholarships.html

Summary To provide financial assistance to doctoral students interested in a program of study and research in children's language disorders.

Eligibility This program is open to doctoral students who have been accepted at an accredited university that provides sufficient course work and faculty advisement for study and research in children's language disorders and that has an emphasis on research skills. Applicants must be able to demonstrate an ability to complete a doctoral program and a commitment to become a teacher-investigator with an emphasis on children's language disorders at a college or university. Selection is based on motivation to complete the doctoral program, academic skills necessary to complete the program successfully, promise as a teacher who will educate future clinicians about children's language disorders, promise as a researcher who will contribute to the body of knowledge about children's language disorders, commitment to the field of children's language disorders, and responsibility for appropriate use of the funds. The ability of the institution to provide the applicant with mentors and course work in children's language disorders and related fields is also considered.

Financial data The stipend is $10,000.

Duration 1 year.

Additional information This foundation was established in 2000.

Number awarded Varies each year; recently, 3 of these fellowships were awarded.

Deadline March of each year.

[723]
BEHAVIORAL SCIENCES STUDENT FELLOWSHIPS IN EPILEPSY

Epilepsy Foundation
Attn: Research Department
8301 Professional Place
Landover, MD 20785-2237
(301) 459-3700   Toll-free: (800) EFA-1000
Fax: (301) 577-2684   TDD: (800) 332-2070
E-mail: grants@efa.org
Web: www.epilepsyfoundation.org/research/grants.cfm

Summary To provide funding to undergraduate and graduate students interested in working on a summer research training project in a field relevant to epilepsy.

Eligibility This program is open to undergraduate and graduate students in a behavioral science program relevant to epilepsy research or clinical care, including, but not limited to, sociology, social work, psychology, anthropology, nursing, economics, vocational rehabilitation, counseling, and political science. Applicants must be interested in working on an epilepsy research project under the supervision of a qualified mentor. Because the program is designed as a training opportunity, the quality of the training plans and environment are considered in the selection process. Other selection criteria include the quality of the proposed project, the relevance of the proposed work to epilepsy, the applicant's interest in the field of epilepsy, the applicant's qualifications, and the mentor's qualifications, including his or her commitment to the student and the project. U.S. citizenship is not required, but the project must be conducted in the United States. Applications from women, members of minority groups, and people with disabilities are especially encouraged. The program is not intended for students working on a dissertation research project.

Financial data The grant is $3,000.

Duration 3 months during the summer.

Additional information This program is supported by the American Epilepsy Society, Abbott Laboratories, Ortho-McNeil Pharmaceutical Corporation, and Pfizer Inc.

Number awarded Varies each year; recently, 2 of these fellowships were awarded.

Deadline February of each year.

[724]
BERNARD F. THORN EFFICACY RESEARCH GRANTS

American Therapeutic Recreation Association
Attn: American Therapeutic Recreation Foundation
1414 Prince Street, Suite 204
Alexandria, VA 22314
(703) 683-9420   Fax: (703) 683-9431
E-mail: conferences@atra-tr.org
Web: www.atra-tr.org

Summary To provide funding to members of the American Therapeutic Recreation Association (ATRA) interested in conducting a research project.

Eligibility This program is open to professional and student members of the association. Applicants must be interested in conducting an efficacy research project in the field of recreational therapy. They should submit evidence of the need for the study, relationship of the proposed study to ATRA research priorities, researcher capacity and qualifications to conduct the study, management plan for the research study, and projected plan for project dissemination. Priority consideration is given to 1) collaborative efficacy research between practitioners and educators based on practice issues; 2) projects that demonstrate a direct connection to the ATRA research agency by examining outcomes and cost effectiveness of recreational therapy protocols; 3) projects that provide evidence of the effectiveness of recreational therapy interventions; and 4) graduate students completing a thesis or dissertation in recreational therapy.

Financial data The amount of the grant depends on the availability of funds.

Duration 1 year.

Number awarded 1 or more each year.

Deadline June or December of each year.

[725]
BEST PRACTICES AWARDS

American Health Information Management Association
Attn: Foundation of Research and Education
233 North Michigan Avenue, Suite 2150
Chicago, IL 60601-5806
(312) 233-1131   Fax: (312) 233-1431
E-mail: fore@ahima.org
Web: www.ahima.org/fore/practice.asp

Summary To recognize and reward members of the American Health Information Management Association (AHIMA) who have implemented programs that meet or set new standards or introduce innovations in the management of health information.

Eligibility This program is open to active, associate, and student members of AHIMA who have fully implemented a project that applies to the health information management (HIM) field. The project must have demonstrated sustainable benefits; be innovative; include innovative elements or implement known information in new ways; have demonstrable positive impact on cost and resource efficiency (expenses are appropriate to the degree of benefit achieved); and have broad impact, applicability, and benefits to HIM practice that are adaptable beyond the setting or practice category in which it was implemented. Project outcomes must have been rigorously measured, evaluated, and documented. Benchmarking is required.

Financial data Awards are $2,500 for first place, $1,000 for second, and $500 for third.

Duration The awards are presented annually.
Number awarded 3 each year.
Deadline October of each year.

[726]
BRACCO DIAGNOSTICS IMAGING AWARD

Society of Diagnostic Medical Sonography
Attn: SDMS Educational Foundation
2745 North Dallas Parkway, Suite 350
Plano, TX 75093-8730
(214) 473-8057   Toll-free: (800) 229-9506
Fax: (214) 473-8563   E-mail: foundation@sdms.org
Web: www.sdms.org/foundation/bracco.asp

Summary To provide funding to members of the Society of Diagnostic Medical Sonography (SDMS) interested in conducting research in sonography.
Eligibility This program is open to active SDMS members, including undergraduate and graduate student members, who are interested in conducting research of interest to the ultrasound profession and Bracco Diagnostics. Applicants must submit information on their goals and proposed plan of study and research, relevant experience, origin of their interest in ultrasound research, vision for the future of sonography, and how their research relates to that vision.
Financial data The grant is $1,000.
Duration 1 year.
Additional information This program is sponsored by Bracco Diagnostics, Inc.
Number awarded 1 or more each year.
Deadline May of each year.

[727]
BUDWEISER CONSERVATION SCHOLARSHIP

National Fish and Wildlife Foundation
1120 Connecticut Avenue, N.W., Suite 900
Washington, DC 20036
(202) 857-0166   Fax: (202) 857-0162
E-mail: Alison.Bolz@nfwf.org
Web: www.nfwf.org/programs/budscholarship

Summary To provide financial assistance to undergraduate and graduate students who are interested in studying or conducting research related to the field of conservation.
Eligibility This program is open to U.S. citizens at least 21 years of age and enrolled in an accredited institution of higher education in the United States. Applicants must be working on a graduate or undergraduate degree (sophomores and juniors in the current academic year only) in environmental science, natural resource management, biology, public policy, geography, political science, or a related discipline. They must submit transcripts, 3 letters of recommendation, and an essay (up to 1,500 words) describing their academic objectives and focusing on a specific issue affecting the conservation of fish, wildlife, or plant species in the United States and the research or study they propose to address the issue. Selection is based on the merits of the proposed research or study, its significance to the field of conservation, its feasibility and overall quality, the innovativeness of the proposed research or study, the student's academic achievements, and their commitment to leadership in the conservation field.
Financial data Stipends range up to $10,000. Funds must be used to cover expenses related to the recipients' studies, including tuition, fees, books, room, and board. Payments may supplement but not duplicate benefits from their educational institution

or from other foundations, institutions, or organizations. The combined benefits from all sources may not exceed the recipient's educational expenses.
Duration 1 year.
Additional information This program, established in 2001, is jointly sponsored by Anheuser-Busch and the National Fish and Wildlife Foundation.
Number awarded At least 10 each year.
Deadline April of each year.

[728]
CALIFORNIA BREAST CANCER DISSERTATION FELLOWSHIPS

California Breast Cancer Research Program
c/o University of California, Office of the President
300 Lakeside Drive, Sixth Floor
Oakland, CA 94612-3550
(510) 987-9884   Toll-free: (888) 313-BCRD
Fax: (510) 987-6325   E-mail: CBCRP2ucop.edu
Web: www.cbcrp.org

Summary To provide funding for research training related to breast cancer to graduate students at universities in California.
Eligibility This program is open to students who have advanced to candidacy for a master's or doctoral degree at a California university. The proposed research training should relate to 1 of the current priorities of the sponsor: 1) the community impact of breast cancer, especially studies of the factors that contribute to the unequal burden of the disease among diverse communities; 2) etiology and prevention; 3) the basic science of the disease; or 4) detection, prognosis, and treatment. The student must act as the principal investigator and must prepare the application. A full-time faculty member at the institution must serve as mentor; the mentor should either be experienced and have published in breast cancer or collaborate with a breast cancer researcher. Applications must include a training plan focused on breast cancer.
Financial data The grant is $38,000 per year. Funds may be used for stipend, fringe benefits, tuition and fee remission, supplies, and travel; no indirect costs are allowed.
Duration 1 year for master's students or 2 years for doctoral students.
Number awarded Varies each year; recently, 17 of these fellowships were awarded.
Deadline January of each year.

[729]
CARL V. GISOLFI MEMORIAL FUND

American College of Sports Medicine
Attn: Research Administration and Programs Office
401 West Michigan Street
P.O. Box 1440
Indianapolis, IN 46206-1440
(317) 637-9200, ext. 143   Fax: (317) 634-7817
E-mail: jsenior@acsm.org
Web: www.acsm.org

Summary To provide funding for research to graduate students who are members of the American College of Sports Medicine (ACSM).
Eligibility This program is open to graduate students enrolled full time in programs in sports medicine or exercise science. Applicants must be current members of ACSM interested in conducting research in thermoregulation, exercise, and hydration.

Financial data Grants up to $5,000 per year are provided.

Duration 1 year.

Additional information Funding for this program is provided by Stokely-Van Camp, the maker of Gatorade.

Number awarded 1 each year.

Deadline January of each year.

[730]
CAROLYN L. KUCKEIN STUDENT RESEARCH FELLOWSHIPS

Alpha Omega Alpha Honor Medical Society
Attn: Research Fellowship Selection Committee
525 Middlefield Road, Suite 130
Menlo Park, CA 94025
(650) 329-0291   Fax: (650) 329-1618
E-mail: c wong@alphaomegaalpha.org
Web: www.alphaomegaalpha.org

Summary To provide funding to medical students interested in conducting summer research projects.

Eligibility Medical students may apply for this funding if they are interested in conducting research, including clinical investigations, basic research, epidemiology, and social science/health service research. Applicants may be in the first, second, or third year of their medical degree program (fourth-year students are not eligible). Because the program is designed to attract students who have not had extensive research experience, those with Ph.D. degrees and those enrolled in Ph.D. or M.D./Ph.D. programs are not eligible. Qualified students from any school with an active Alpha Omega Alpha chapter may apply, but each school may nominate only 1 candidate. The application must include a 1-page outline of the research project, the student's curriculum vitae and bibliography, a letter of support from the faculty supervisor, and letters of endorsement from the Alpha Omega Alpha councilor and the dean. All supporting letters must accompany the original submission; incomplete applications will not be accepted.

Financial data The student grant is $4,000; one half is paid upon announcement of the award and one half upon completion of the project. The faculty supervisor is also awarded $500, to meet expenses incurred in support of the student project.

Duration 8 to 10 weeks during the summer.

Additional information This program began in 1982. Within 6 months of receipt of the award, the recipient must submit either a progress report or a final report. Credit to Alpha Omega Alpha must be given in any publication that results from the supported research.

Number awarded Up to 50 each year.

Deadline Applications must be submitted to the chapter councilor by December of each year.

[731]
CARROLL L. BIRCH STUDENT RESEARCH AWARD

American Medical Women's Association Foundation
Attn: AMWA Foundation
211 North Union Street, Suite 100
Alexandria, VA 22314
(703) 838-0500   Fax: (703) 549-3864
E-mail: foundation@amwa-doc.org
Web: www.amwa-doc.org

Summary To recognize and reward the most outstanding paper written by a student member of the American Medical Women's Association (AMWA).

Eligibility This competition is open to national AMWA medical student members who attend an accredited U.S. allopathic or osteopathic medical school. Applicants must submit an original research paper (and a 250-word abstract) that has not been previously published.

Financial data The prize is $1,000 and publication in the *Journal of the American Medical Women's Association.*

Duration The award is presented annually.

Additional information This award is sponsored by the association's Chicago Branch. It has been presented since 1965.

Number awarded 1 each year.

Deadline June of each year.

[732]
CDC/PRC MINORITY FELLOWSHIPS

Association of Schools of Public Health
Attn: Senior Manager, Graduate Training Programs
1101 15th Street, N.W., Suite 910
Washington, DC 20005
(202) 296-1099, ext. 143   Fax: (202) 296-1252
E-mail: mstadtler@asph.org
Web: www.asph.org

Summary To provide an opportunity for minority doctoral students to conduct research at Prevention Research Centers (PRCs) funded by the U.S. Centers for Disease Control and Prevention (CDC).

Eligibility This program is open to minority (African American/Black American, Hispanic/Latino, American Indian/Alaska Native, and Asian/Pacific Islander) students working on a doctoral degree at a school of public health with a CDC-funded PRC. Applicants must be proposing to conduct a research project that is related to the PRC activities and is endorsed by the PRC director. Along with their application, they must submit a personal statement (2 pages or less) on why they are interested in this fellowship, including specifics regarding their interest in the opportunity, benefits they expect to receive from the fellowship experience, how the experience will shape their future career plans, and how the proposed project will advance the field of public health prevention research. Selection is based on the personal statement (30 points), curriculum vitae and transcripts (20 points), and the project proposal (50 points). U.S. citizenship or permanent resident status is required.

Financial data The stipend is $22,500 per year. Fellows are also reimbursed up to $3,000 per year for health-related expenses, project-related travel, tuition, journal subscriptions, and association dues.

Duration 2 years.

Additional information Currently, PRCs are funded at 33 universities: University of Alabama at Birmingham, University of Albany, University of Arizona, Boston University, University of California at Berkeley, University of California at Los Angeles, University of Colorado, Columbia University, Emory University, Harvard University, Oregon Health and Science University, San Diego State University and University of California at San Diego, Texas A&M University System Health Science Center, University of Illinois at Chicago, University of Iowa, Johns Hopkins University, University of Kentucky, University of Michigan, University of Minnesota, Morehouse School of Medicine, University of New Mexico, University of North Carolina at Chapel Hill, University of Oklahoma, University of Pittsburgh, University of Rochester, St. Louis University, University of South Carolina, University of South Florida, University of Texas Health Science Center at Houston, Tulane University, University of Washington, West Virginia University, and Yale University.

Number awarded Varies each year; recently, 11 of these fellowships were awarded.
Deadline February of each year.

[733]
CENTER FOR AMERICAN NURSES RESEARCH GRANT

American Nurses Foundation
Attn: Nursing Research Grants Program
8515 Georgia Avenue, Suite 400
Silver Spring, MD 20910-3492
(301) 628-5298   Fax: (301) 628-5354
E-mail: anf@ana.org
Web: www.anfonline.org

Summary To provide funding to nurses interested in conducting research on the use of technology.
Eligibility This program is open to registered nurses who have earned a baccalaureate or higher degree. Applicants may be either beginning or experienced researchers. They must be interested in conducting research on the use of technology in workplace design and by the mature nurse workforce. Research may deal with any aspect of technology use, implementation, and/or barriers to implementation. Proposed research may be for a master's thesis or doctoral dissertation if the project has been approved by the principal investigator's thesis or dissertation committee.
Financial data The grant is $5,000. Funds may not be used as a salary for the principal investigator.
Duration 1 year.
Additional information Funding for this program is provided by the Center for American Nurses. There is a $75 application fee.
Number awarded 1 each year.
Deadline April of each year.

[734]
CENTRAL ASSOCIATION OF OBSTETRICIANS AND GYNECOLOGISTS PRESIDENT'S CERTIFICATE OF MERIT AWARD

Central Association of Obstetricians and Gynecologists
c/o Executive Director
P.O. Box 3010
Minot, ND 58702-3010
(701) 838-8323   Fax: (701) 852-8733
E-mail: rhickel@caog.org
Web: www.caog.org

Summary To recognize and reward outstanding investigative or clinical work submitted by members of the Central Association of Obstetricians and Gynecologists (CAOG).
Eligibility This program is open to accredited physicians, teachers, research workers, and medical students whose work was done within the geographic areas of the association: Alabama, Arizona, Arkansas, Colorado, Idaho, Illinois, Indiana, Iowa, Kansas, Kentucky, Louisiana, Michigan, Minnesota, Mississippi, Missouri, Montana, Nebraska, Nevada, New Mexico, North Dakota, Ohio, Oklahoma, South Dakota, Tennessee, Texas, Utah, West Virginia, Wisconsin, and Wyoming. Applicants must submit an abstract of their work for presentation at the annual meeting of the CAOG. Abstracts must be original and not have been previously presented, submitted, accepted, or published. At least 1 of the authors must be a member of the association.
Financial data The award is $1,500.
Duration The award is presented annually.

Additional information The winning paper is offered for publication to the *American Journal of Obstetrics and Gynecology.*
Number awarded 1 each year.
Deadline April of each year.

[735]
CENTRAL PRIZE AWARD

Central Association of Obstetricians and Gynecologists
c/o Executive Director
P.O. Box 3010
Minot, ND 58702-3010
(701) 838-8323   Fax: (701) 852-8733
E-mail: rhickel@caog.org
Web: www.caog.org

Summary To recognize and reward outstanding investigative or clinical work submitted by members of the Central Association of Obstetricians and Gynecologists (CAOG).
Eligibility This program is open to accredited physicians, teachers, research workers, and medical students whose work was done within the geographic areas of the association: Alabama, Arizona, Arkansas, Colorado, Idaho, Illinois, Indiana, Iowa, Kansas, Kentucky, Louisiana, Michigan, Minnesota, Mississippi, Missouri, Montana, Nebraska, Nevada, New Mexico, North Dakota, Ohio, Oklahoma, South Dakota, Tennessee, Texas, Utah, West Virginia, Wisconsin, and Wyoming. Applicants must submit an abstract of their work for presentation at the annual meeting of the CAOG. Abstracts must be original and not have been previously presented, submitted, accepted, or published. At least 1 of the authors must be a member of the association.
Financial data The award is $2,000.
Duration The award is presented annually.
Additional information The winning paper is offered for publication to the *American Journal of Obstetrics and Gynecology.*
Number awarded 1 each year.
Deadline April of each year.

[736]
CHARLES R. MORRIS STUDENT RESEARCH AWARD

American Academy of Oral and Maxillofacial Radiology
Attn: Executive Director
P.O. Box 1010
Evans, GA 30809-1010
(706) 721-2607   E-mail: mshrout@mail.mcq.edu
Web: www.aaomr.org/crm_info1.htm

Summary To recognize and reward outstanding student papers on oral and maxillofacial radiology.
Eligibility This award is open to candidates from accredited dental and dental hygiene programs who, at the time the research was conducted, were full-time predoctoral or undergraduate students. The manuscript must be accompanied by a nomination from the institution in which the research was conducted. Applicants are judged on the following: clarity of conceptual definition, adequacy of literature review, originality, soundness of methodology, significance of contribution to the science of oral and maxillofacial radiology, and manuscript format and style. Students are encouraged to secure faculty guidance in designing the research project, in determining the extent of the literature review, and in composing the manuscript. All manuscripts must represent original research not submitted for publication elsewhere.
Financial data The awardee receives a certificate, a check for $1,000, free conference registration, an invitation to present the

research paper at the annual meeting, and free membership in the academy.

Duration The prize is awarded annually.

Additional information Information is also available from Dr. J. Sean Hubar, Louisiana State University, School of Dentistry, 1100 Florida Avenue, New Orleans, LA 70119, (504) 619-8623.

Number awarded At least 1 each year.

Deadline June of each year.

[737]
CHARLES S. HOUSTON RESEARCH AWARD

Wilderness Medical Society
810 East Tenth Street
P.O. Box 1897
Lawrence, KS 66044
Toll-free: (800) 627-0629   Fax: (785) 843-1853
E-mail: wms@wms.org
Web: www.wms.org

Summary To provide funding to medical students interested in conducting research in the fields of wilderness and environmental medicine.

Eligibility This program is open to medical students at accredited American or Canadian medical schools who are interested in conducting research in the fields of wilderness and environmental medicine. A wide variety of research projects are acceptable for submission, including clinical investigation, laboratory ("basic") science, epidemiological surveys, development of new techniques or novel application of existing techniques, improvements in equipment design or use, public information, and injury prevention. Projects may be part of existing research programs, but they should be easily distinguishable as a separate component. Letters of support from faculty, sponsors, collaborators, and co-sponsoring funding agencies, if appropriate, must be included with the application.

Financial data Grants up to $5,000 are available.

Duration 1 year.

Additional information The successful applicant is expected to conduct the project during the ensuing year and present an abstract of the findings at the society's next annual meeting. It is expected that the project will result in at least 1 article for publication in the peer-reviewed medical literature.

Number awarded 1 or more each year.

Deadline December of each year.

[738]
CLINICAL PRACTICE GRANT

American Association of Critical-Care Nurses
Attn: Research Department
101 Columbia
Aliso Viejo, CA 92656-4109
(949) 362-2050, ext. 321
Toll-free: (800) 394-5995, ext. 321   Fax: (949) 362-2020
E-mail: research@aacn.org
Web: www.aacn.org

Summary To provide funding to members of the American Association of Critical-Care Nurses (AACN) who wish to conduct research directly related to the association's clinical practice research priorities.

Eligibility Registered nurses who are current members of the association may apply for these grants. They must propose to conduct research on a topic that the association has identified as a priority for critical care nursing: effective and appropriate use of technology to achieve optimal patient assessment, management, and/or outcomes; creating a healing, humane environment; processes and systems that foster the optimal contribution of critical care nurses; effective approaches to symptom management; and prevention and management of complications. Funds may be sought for research required for an academic degree.

Financial data The grant is $6,000. Funds may be used to support direct project expenses, such as research assistants, secretarial support, equipment, supplies, and consultative assistance. They may not be used for salaries of the principle or co-investigators, travel to presentations, preparation of slides, presentation or publication of findings, or such educational expenses as tuition or books. Indirect costs are limited to 10% of direct costs.

Number awarded 1 each year.

Deadline September of each year.

[739]
CLINICAL RESEARCH PRE-DOCTORAL FELLOWSHIP PROGRAM

American Nurses Association
Attn: SAMHSA Minority Fellowship Programs
8515 Georgia Avenue, Suite 400
Silver Spring, MD 20910-3492
(301) 628-5247   Fax: (301) 628-5339
E-mail: jjackson@ana.org
Web: www.nursingworld.org/emfp/fellowships/pre.htm

Summary To provide financial assistance to minority nurses who are doctoral candidates interested in psychiatric, mental health, and substance abuse issues that impact the lives of ethnic minority people.

Eligibility This program is open to nurses who have a master's degree and are members of an ethnic or racial minority group, including but not limited to Blacks or African Americans, Hispanics or Latinos, American Indians and Alaska Natives, Asian Americans, and Native Hawaiians and other Pacific Islanders. Applicants must be able to demonstrate a commitment to a research career in nursing and psychiatric/mental health issues affecting ethnic minority populations. They must be interested in a program of full-time doctoral study, with a research focus on such issues of concern to minority populations as child abuse, violence in intimate relationships, mental health disorders, substance abuse, mental health service utilization, and stigma as a barrier to mental health care and personal resilience. U.S. citizenship or permanent resident status and membership in the American Nurses Association are required. Selection is based on research potential, scholarship, writing ability, knowledge of broad issues in mental health nursing, and professional commitment to ethnic minority concerns.

Financial data The program provides an annual stipend (amount not specified) and tuition assistance.

Duration 3 to 5 years.

Additional information Funds for this program are provided by the Substance Abuse and Mental Health Services Administration (SAMHSA).

Number awarded 1 or more each year.

Deadline February of each year.

[740]
COLIN HIGGINS FOUNDATION YOUTH COURAGE AWARDS

Colin Higgins Foundation
Attn: Youth Courage Awards
P.O. Box 29903
San Francisco, CA 94129-0903
(415) 561-6350   Fax: (415) 561-6401
E-mail: info@colinhiggins.org
Web: www.colinhiggins.org/courageawards/index.cfm

Summary To recognize and reward young people who have shown courage in the face of adversity related to discrimination against members of the lesbian, gay, bisexual, transgender, and questioning (LGBTQ) communities.

Eligibility Eligible to be nominated for these awards are young people under 24 years of age who are 1) LGBTQ youth who have "bravely stood up to hostility and intolerance based on their sexual orientation and triumphed over bigotry"; or 2) allies who are working to end homophobia and discrimination against LGBTQ communities. Letters of nomination must include 350-word essays describing why the nominee represents the ideals of this award. Self-nominations are not accepted.

Financial data The award is a $10,000 grant.

Duration The awards are presented annually.

Additional information This award program was established in 2000.

Number awarded 2 or 3 each year.

Deadline March of each year.

[741]
COLLEGIATE INVENTORS COMPETITION

National Inventors Hall of Fame
Attn: Collegiate Inventors Competition
221 South Broadway Street
Akron, OH 44308-1595
(330) 849-6887   E-mail: collegiate@invent.org
Web: www.invent.org/collegiate

Summary To recognize and reward outstanding inventions by college or university students in the fields of science, engineering, and technology.

Eligibility This competition is open to undergraduate and graduate students who are (or have been) enrolled full time at least part of the 12-month period prior to entry in a college or university in the United States. Entries may also be submitted by teams, up to 4 members, of whom at least 1 must meet the full-time requirement and all others must have been enrolled at least half time sometime during the preceding 24-month period. Applicants must submit a description of their invention, including a patent search and summary of current literature that describes the state of the art and identifies the originality of the invention; test data demonstrating that the idea, invention, or design is workable; the societal, economic, and environmental benefits of the invention; and supplemental material that may include photos, slides, disks, videotapes, and even samples. Entries must be original ideas and the work of a student or team and a university advisor; the invention should be reproducible and may not have been 1) made available to the public as a commercial product or process, or 2) patented or published more than 1 year prior to the date of submission for this competition. Entries are first reviewed by a committee of judges that selects the finalists. The committee is comprised of mathematicians, engineers, biologists, chemists, environmentalists, physicists, computer specialists, members of the medical and veterinary profession, and specialists in invention and development of technology. Entries are judged on the basis

of originality, inventiveness, potential value to society (socially, environmentally, and economically), and range or scope of use.

Financial data Finalists receive an all-expense paid trip to Washington, D.C. to participate in a final round of judging and in the awards dinner and presentation. The Grand Prize winner or team receives $25,000. Other prizes are $10,000 for an undergraduate winner or team and $15,000 for a graduate winner or team. Academic advisors of the winning entries each receive a $3,000 cash prize. Awards are unrestricted cash gifts, not scholarships or grants.

Duration The competition is held annually.

Additional information This program is co-sponsored by Abbott Laboratories and the United States Patent and Trademark Office. It was established in 1990 as the BFGoodrich Collegiate Inventors Program.

Number awarded 15 semifinalists are selected each year; of those, 3 individuals or teams win prizes.

Deadline May of each year.

[742]
COLLINS SCHOLARSHIP

Autism Society of America
Attn: Awards and Scholarships
7910 Woodmont Avenue, Suite 300
Bethesda, MD 20814-3015
(301) 657-0881   Toll-free: (800) 3-AUTISM
Fax: (301) 657-0869   E-mail: info@autism-society.org
Web: www.autism-society.org

Summary To provide funding to graduate students or postdoctorates who are interested in conducting research on autism.

Eligibility This program is open to graduate students, postgraduates, and postdoctorates who are interested in conducting basic or applied research related to autism prevention, cure, or amelioration. Each candidate must submit 3 copies of the following: brief overview of the research project and biographies of all university staff researchers or professionals overseeing the project.

Financial data The grant is $1,000.

Duration 1 year.

Number awarded 1 each year.

Deadline February of each year.

[743]
COMMISSION ON GRADUATES OF FOREIGN NURSING SCHOOLS/AMERICAN NURSES FOUNDATION SCHOLAR AWARD PROGRAM

American Nurses Foundation
Attn: Nursing Research Grants Program
8515 Georgia Avenue, Suite 400
Silver Spring, MD 20910-3492
(301) 628-5298   Fax: (301) 628-5354
E-mail: anf@ana.org
Web: www.anfonline.org

Summary To provide funding to nurses interested in conducting research on international aspects.

Eligibility This program is open to registered nurses who have earned a baccalaureate or higher degree. Applicants may be either beginning or experienced researchers. They must be interested in conducting research on international nursing issues or issues related to internationally educated nurses in the U.S. workforce. Proposed research may be for a master's thesis or doctoral dissertation if the project has been approved by the principal investigator's thesis or dissertation committee.

Financial data The grant is $5,000. Funds may not be used as a salary for the principal investigator.

Duration 1 year.

Additional information Funding for this program is provided by the Commission on Graduates of Foreign Nursing Schools. There is a $75 application fee.

Number awarded 1 each year.

Deadline April of each year.

[744]
COSMOS CLUB FOUNDATION PROGRAM OF GRANTS-IN-AID TO JUNIOR SCHOLARS

Consortium of Universities of the Washington Metropolitan Area
Attn: Director of Programs
One DuPont Circle, N.W., Suite 200
Washington, DC 20036-1166
(202) 331-8080, ext. 3008   Fax: (202) 331-7925
TDD: (202) 331-7955   E-mail: faulkner@consortium.org
Web: www.consortium.org/cosmos_club_grants.asp

Summary To provide grants-in-aid for research to full-time graduate students at selected universities in the Washington, D.C. area.

Eligibility This program is open to graduate students at schools belonging to the Consortium of Universities of the Washington Metropolitan Area. Applicants must need research funding for equipment, special supplies, travel to research facilities or relevant meetings, etc. There is no restriction as to academic field, but the proposed project should be focused on scholarly research rather than commercial or political activity, social activism, or other nonacademic goals. Along with their application, they must submit a 1-page description of their research project, a statement that alternative support for the specific research need is not available, and verification of their status from their academic advisor.

Financial data The amount awarded varies, depending upon the research needs of the recipient, up to a maximum of $3,000. The average is approximately $1,500. Funds are paid directly to individual recipients. No part of the award may be used to pay indirect costs to the recipient's institution.

Duration 1 year.

Additional information Funding for this award is provided by the Cosmos Club Foundation. The Consortium includes American University, Catholic University of America, Gallaudet University, George Mason University, George Washington University, Georgetown University, Howard University, Joint Military Intelligence College, Marymount University, National Defense University, Southeastern University, Trinity College, University of the District of Columbia, and University of Maryland at College Park. Recipients must agree to devote substantial time to the research project. They may also be required to make an oral presentation of the research results. Progress reports during the academic year may be requested.

Number awarded At least 15 each year.

Deadline November of each year.

[745]
CYSTIC FIBROSIS FOUNDATION STUDENT TRAINEESHIP

Cystic Fibrosis Foundation
Attn: Office of Grants Management
6931 Arlington Road, Suite 200
Bethesda, MD 20814
(301) 951-4422   Toll-free: (800) FIGHT CF
Fax: (301) 951-6378   E-mail: grants@cff.org
Web: www.cff.org

Summary To introduce undergraduate and graduate students to research related to cystic fibrosis.

Eligibility Applicants must be students in or about to enter a doctoral program (Ph.D., M.D., or M.D./Ph.D.). Senior level undergraduate students planning to pursue graduate training also may apply. Previous research experience is not a requirement.

Financial data The amount of the grant is $1,500, of which up to $300 may be used for laboratory expenses. The remainder must be used as a stipend for the trainee. Payments are made directly to the trainee in 2 equal installments.

Duration 10 weeks or more; recipients may apply for support in the subsequent year.

Additional information Recipients work with a faculty sponsor on a research project related to cystic fibrosis. A final progress report must be submitted before the second payment installment will be issued.

Deadline Applications are accepted throughout the year but should be submitted at least 2 months prior to the scheduled start date of the project.

[746]
DAN DAVID PRIZE SCHOLARSHIPS

Dan David Prize
c/o Ms. Smadar Fisher, Director
Tel-Aviv University
Eitan Berglas Building 119
P.O. Box 39040
Tel Aviv 69978
Israel
972 3 640 6614   Fax: 972 3 640 6613
E-mail: ddprize@post.tau.ac.il
Web: www.dandavidprize.org/scholarships.html

Summary To provide funding to doctoral and postdoctoral students at universities in fields related to the Dan David Prizes.

Eligibility This program is open to doctoral and postdoctoral students at universities throughout the world and at Tel Aviv university. Applicants must be conducting research in a field selected annually for the Dan David Prizes. Along with their application, they must submit a full curriculum vitae, a description of their research project, and list of publications. Selection is based on merit, without consideration for gender, race, religion, nationality, or political affiliation.

Financial data The stipend is $15,000.

Duration 1 year.

Additional information Each year, Dan David Prizes of $1 million each are presented to 3 internationally distinguished individuals or organizations for their work in fields selected annually by the prize committee. The prizes are awarded in 3 categories based on time dimensions: past, present, and future. Recently, the category for the past dimension was authors of major works of history, for the present it was contemporary music, and for the future it was quest for energy. The laureates then donate funds for these scholarships.

Number awarded 20 each year: 10 for students and scholars at Tel Aviv University and 10 for students and scholars at universities anywhere else in the world.
Deadline March of each year.

[747]
DEMPSTER NP DOCTORAL DISSERTATION RESEARCH GRANT

American Academy of Nurse Practitioners
Attn: AANP Foundation
P.O. Box 10729
Glendale, AZ 85318-0729
(623) 376-9467   Fax: (623) 376-0369
E-mail: foundation@aanp.org
Web: www.aanpfoundation.org

Summary To provide funding to members of the American Academy of Nurse Practitioners (AANP) who wish to conduct research for a doctoral degree project.
Eligibility This program is open to current student and full members of the academy who are working on a doctoral degree and their dissertation research. Applicants must be a currently licensed, practicing nurse practitioner (NP) in the United States and the principal investigator on a research project that is to be used for their degree program. Their GPA in their doctoral program must be 3.75 or higher. The research must have an outcomes-based primary care focus relevant to health care provided by NPs within the United States.
Financial data The grant is $2,000. Funds must be used for the proposed research, not tuition expenses.
Duration 1 year.
Additional information This grant was first awarded in 2000. There is a $10 application fee.
Number awarded 1 each year.
Deadline April of each year.

[748]
DEPARTMENT OF HOMELAND SECURITY GRADUATE FELLOWSHIPS

Oak Ridge Institute for Science and Education
Attn: Science and Engineering Education
P.O. Box 117
Oak Ridge, TN 37831-0117
(865) 576-8239   Fax: (865) 241-5219
E-mail: igrid.gregory@orau.gov
Web: www.orau.gov/orise.htm

Summary To provide financial assistance and summer research experience to graduate students who are working on a degree in a field of interest to the Department of Homeland Security (DHS).
Eligibility This program is open to students working on a master's or doctoral degree in a program that includes a thesis requirement. Applicants must have a GPA of 3.3 or higher. Their field of study must be in the agricultural sciences, biological and life sciences, computer and information sciences, engineering, mathematics, physical sciences, psychology, social sciences, selected humanities (religious studies, cultural studies, public policy, advocacy, communications, or science writing), or selected fields limited to D.V.M. or Ph.D. programs (basic biomedical sciences, infectious diseases and zoonoses, animal health and food safety, comparative medicine and laboratory animal medicine, population medicine, public health, and epidemiology). Along with their application, they must submit 2 statements on 1) their educational and professional goals, the kinds of research they are interested in conducting, specific questions that interest them, and how they became interested in them; and 2) how they think their interests, talents, and initiative would contribute to make the homeland safer and secure. Selection is based on those statements, academic record, references, and GRE scores, As part of their program, they must be interested in participating in summer research activities at a DHS-designated facility. U.S. citizenship is required.
Financial data This program provides a stipend of $2,300 per month for 12 months plus full payment of tuition and mandatory fees.
Duration 3 academic years plus 10 weeks during the summer after the first year.
Additional information This program, established in 2003, is funded by DHS and administered by Oak Ridge Institute for Science and Education (ORISE). Recipients must enroll full time.
Number awarded Approximately 50 each year.
Deadline January of each year.

[749]
DIBNER LIBRARY RESIDENT SCHOLAR PROGRAM

Smithsonian Institution Libraries
Attn: Resident Scholar Program
National Museum of American History, Room 1041, MRC 672
P.O. Box 37012
Washington, DC 20013-7012
(202) 633-3872   Fax: (202) 786-2866
E-mail: SILResidentScholars@si.edu
Web: www.sil.si.edu

Summary To offer short-term research grants to graduate students, postdoctorates, and professionals interested in conducting research on the history of science and technology at the Smithsonian Institution's Dibner Library.
Eligibility This program is open to historians, librarians, doctoral students, and postdoctoral scholars interested in using the Dibner Library's special collections on the history of science and technology. Applicants whose native language is not English must be able to demonstrate the ability to write and converse fluently in English. Selection is based on the quality of the research proposal (importance of the topic, originality, and sophistication of the approach, feasibility of research objectives, relevance to the collections) and evidence of the applicant's ability to carry out the proposed research.
Financial data The stipend is $2,500 per month; the funds may be used for any purpose, including travel to Washington.
Duration Up to 6 months.
Additional information The library provides study space and necessary equipment. Recipients must be in residence at the Dibner full time during the award period, devote full time to the proposed research, submit a final report no later than 30 days following the award period, and give credit to the program in any publication based on research performed during the award tenure.
Number awarded Varies each year; recently, 5 of these fellows were appointed.
Deadline February of each year.

[750]
DIVISION OF MEDICINAL CHEMISTRY PREDOCTORAL FELLOWSHIPS

American Chemical Society
Division of Medicinal Chemistry
1155 16th Street, N.W.
Washington, DC 20036
Toll-free: (800) 227-5558   E-mail: divisions@acs.org
Web: www.acsmedchem.org

Summary   To provide funding to students in graduate programs engaged in medicinal chemistry research.

Eligibility   This program is open to predoctoral students engaged in medicinal chemistry research in a medicinal chemistry, pharmaceutical chemistry, biochemistry, or chemistry department listed in the current American Chemical Society *Directory of Graduate Research*. Nominees must be U.S. citizens or permanent residents enrolled in their third or fourth year of graduate study. Nominations should contain a complete student curriculum vitae, including education and work experience; a student bibliography, including reprints of articles; a complete project description, including rationale (5-page limit) prepared by the candidate; transcripts of all post-high school work, including GRE scores if available; 3 letters, including a nomination letter from the student's research advisor; and a letter from a university official with a commitment to cover tuition and all fees granted to other regular graduate students.

Financial data   The grant is $24,000 per year.

Duration   1 year.

Additional information   This program is supported by pharmaceutical companies Bristol-Myers Squibb, Wyeth, Eli Lilly, Pfizer, Novartis, Sanofi-Aventis, and Amgen.

Number awarded   7 each year.

Deadline   January of each year.

[751]
DOCTORAL DISSERTATION AWARD FOR ARTHRITIS HEALTH PROFESSIONALS

Arthritis Foundation
Attn: Research Department
1330 West Peachtree Street, Suite 100
Atlanta, GA 30309-2904
(404) 965-7637   Fax: (404) 872-9559
E-mail: Grantsupport@arthritis.org
Web: www.arthritis.org/research/ProposalCentral.asp

Summary   To provide funding to advance the research training of doctoral candidates interested in rheumatic diseases.

Eligibility   This program is open to doctoral candidates entering the research phase of their program. Their doctoral chair must approve the proposed project. The project must relate to arthritis management, comprehensive patient care in rheumatology practice, or arthritis research. Suitable studies include, but are not limited to, functional, behavioral, educational, nutritional, occupational, or epidemiological aspects of patient care and management. Drug studies and laboratory in vitro studies are not appropriate. Applicants must be U.S. citizens or permanent residents, members of their professional organization or eligible for membership, and able to pursue their research under the direction of a supervisor who is a recognized expert in their specific field of study. Awards may be given to candidates for study abroad if it seems in the best interest of their future career. Preference is given to applicants who propose work on projects with demonstrable relationship to arthritis or who, with their mentor, have established a real working relationship with a clinical academic

rheumatology or musculoskeletal unit. Selection is based on the proposed research environment, background and potential of the research, and potential significance and relevance of the project to rheumatic diseases.

Financial data   The grant is $30,000 per year. Funds may be used for salary or research expenses. Indirect costs are not allowed.

Duration   1 or 2 years.

Deadline   August of each year.

[752]
DOLORES ZOHRAB LIEBMANN FELLOWSHIPS

Dolores Zohrab Liebmann Fund
c/o JPMorgan Private Bank
Philanthropic Services
345 Park Avenue, Fourth Floor
New York, NY 10154
(212) 464-2443   E-mail: sara.j.rosen@jpmchase.com

Summary   To provide financial assistance for graduate study or research in any field.

Eligibility   Candidates for this fellowship must have received a baccalaureate degree and have an outstanding academic record. They must be U.S. citizens, be currently enrolled in an academic institution in the United States, be able to show promise for achievement and distinction in their chosen field of study, and be able to document financial need. They may request funds for degree work or for independent research or study projects. All applications must be submitted through the dean of their university (each university is permitted to submit only 3 candidates for review each year). Candidates may be working on a degree in any field in the humanities, social sciences, or natural sciences, including law, medicine, engineering, architecture, or other formal professional training. They may be of any national descent or background.

Financial data   Fellowships provide a stipend of $18,000 plus full payment of tuition.

Duration   1 year; may be renewed for 2 additional years.

Additional information   Recipients must submit periodic progress reports. They must study or conduct their independent research projects in the United States. For a list of the 81 universities at which the fellowship is current tenable, contact the sponsor.

Number awarded   Varies each year; recently, this program awarded $909,377 for fellowships and $43,075 for independent research projects.

Deadline   January of each year.

[753]
DONALD D. HAMMILL FOUNDATION RESEARCH SCHOLARSHIPS

Donald D. Hammill Foundation
Attn: Executive Secretary
8700 Shoal Creek Boulevard
Austin, TX 78757-6897
(512) 451-0784   Fax: (512) 451-8542
E-mail: DDHFound@aol.com

Summary   To provide funding to doctoral students who need to complete a dissertation that pertains to characteristics, services, or issues related to disability areas.

Eligibility   Applicants requesting financial aid to complete their dissertation must be 1) admitted to candidacy; 2) conducting a study pertaining to characteristics, services, or issues related to a disability area; and 3) planning to complete their study by the end of the award period. Selection is based on the perceived importance of the study, the academic background of the applicant, and the need for financial assistance. Preference is given to applicants who have a disability or who are experiencing serious financial distress.

Financial data Grants up to $5,000 are awarded. Funds must be used for living expenses, materials, child care, data collections, clerical services, and other related activities.

Duration Up to 1 year.

Additional information Recipients must provide a brief progress report midway through the study and submit a copy of their dissertation upon completion. Publications that result from the funded research must acknowledge support of the foundation.

Number awarded 1 or more each year.

Deadline May of each year.

[754]
DORIS BLOCH RESEARCH AWARD

Sigma Theta Tau International
Attn: Research Department
550 West North Street
Indianapolis, IN 46202-3191
(317) 634-8171   Toll-free: (888) 634-7575
Fax: (317) 634-8188   E-mail: research@stti.iupui.edu
Web: www.nursingsociety.org/research/grant_vh.html

Summary To provide funding to nurses, especially members of Sigma Theta Tau International, interested in conducting research.

Eligibility This program is open to registered nurses who have a current license. Applicants must have a master's or doctoral degree in nursing or be enrolled in a doctoral program. Novice researchers who have received no other national research funds are especially encouraged to apply. Preference is given to members of Sigma Theta Tau International. Selection is based on the quality of the proposed research, future potential of the applicant, and appropriateness of the research budget.

Financial data The maximum grant is $5,000.

Duration 1 year.

Number awarded 1 each year.

Deadline November of each year.

[755]
DORIS DUKE CLINICAL RESEARCH FELLOWSHIPS FOR MEDICAL STUDENTS

Doris Duke Charitable Foundation
Attn: Grantmaking Programs
650 Fifth Avenue, 19th Floor
New York, NY 10019
(212) 974-7000   Fax: (212) 974-7590
E-mail: ddcfcrf@aibs.org
Web: www.ddcf.org/page.asp?pageId=292

Summary To provide funding to medical students interested in conducting clinical research.

Eligibility This program is open to students who have completed 2 or more years of full-time study at a medical school in the United States. Applicants must be interested in conducting clinical research at 1 of 10 participating medical schools under the supervision of an experienced mentor.

Financial data Fellows receive a stipend of $27,000, health insurance, financial support to attend research meetings, and supplementary research and training funds.

Duration 1 year.

Additional information This program was established in 2000. The participating medical schools are the Columbia University College of Physicians and Surgeons, Harvard Medical School, Mount Sinai School of Medicine, University of California at San Francisco School of Medicine, University of Iowa Roy J. and Lucille A. Carver College of Medicine, University of North Carolina at Chapel Hill School of Medicine, University of Pennsylvania School of Medicine, University of Texas Southwestern Medical Center at Dallas, Washington University School of Medicine in St. Louis, and Yale University School of Medicine.

Number awarded At least 50 each year (at least 5 at each participating medical school).

[756]
DOROTHY CORNELIUS, RN SCHOLAR AWARD

American Nurses Foundation
Attn: Nursing Research Grants Program
8515 Georgia Avenue, Suite 400
Silver Spring, MD 20910-3492
(301) 628-5298   Fax: (301) 628-5354
E-mail: anf@ana.org
Web: www.anfonline.org

Summary To provide funding to nurses interested in conducting research.

Eligibility This program is open to registered nurses who have earned a baccalaureate or higher degree. Applicants must be beginning researchers who have had no more than 3 research-based publications in refereed journals and have received, as a principal investigator, no more than $15,000 in extramural funding in any 1 research area. Proposed research may be for a master's thesis or doctoral dissertation if the project has been approved by the principal investigator's thesis or dissertation committee. There are no restrictions on the research topic.

Financial data The grant is $5,000. Funds may not be used as a salary for the principal investigator.

Duration 1 year.

Additional information There is a $75 application fee.

Number awarded 1 each year.

Deadline April of each year.

[757]
DOROTHY REILLY, RN RESEARCH GRANTS

American Nurses Foundation
Attn: Nursing Research Grants Program
8515 Georgia Avenue, Suite 400
Silver Spring, MD 20910-3492
(301) 628-5298   Fax: (301) 628-5354
E-mail: anf@ana.org
Web: www.anfonline.org

Summary To provide funding to nurses interested in conducting research on pediatric or life-span immunization issues.

Eligibility This program is open to registered nurses who have earned a baccalaureate or higher degree. Applicants may be either beginning or experienced researchers. They must be interested in conducting research on nursing education or curriculum development. Proposed research may be for a master's thesis or doctoral dissertation if the project has been approved by the principal investigator's thesis or dissertation committee.

Financial data The grant is $5,000. Funds may not be used as a salary for the principal investigator.

Duration 1 year.

Additional information This program was established in 2005. There is a $75 application fee. Recipients are expected to make the results of their research available to nurses either through publication (monograph, abstract, or journal article) or conference presentation.

Number awarded 1 each year.

Deadline April of each year.

[758]
DOW CHEMICAL COMPANY GRADUATE FELLOWSHIP AWARD

National Organization for the Professional Advancement of Black Chemists and Chemical Engineers
c/o Howard University
P.O. Box 77040
Washington, DC 20013
(202) 667-1699   Toll-free: (800) 776-1419
Fax: (267) 200-0156
Web: www.nobcche.org

Summary To provide funding to African American doctoral students for research in chemistry, chemical engineering, or life sciences.

Eligibility This program is open to African American candidates in a Ph.D. program for chemistry, chemical engineering, or life sciences. Applicants must submit 3 letters of recommendation, a resume, official transcripts for undergraduate and graduate study, a description of their proposed research, and a statement of their career objective. Preference is given to those who have completed at least 1 year of graduate study. U.S. citizenship is required.

Financial data The grant is $10,000.

Duration 1 year.

Additional information This program is sponsored by the Dow Chemical Company. Information is also available from Dr. Marlon L. Walker, Awards and Scholarships Committee Chair, National Institute of Standards and Technology, 100 Bureau Drive, Gaithersburg, MD 20899-8372, (301) 975-5593, E-mail: marlon.walker@nist.gov.

Number awarded 1 each year.

Deadline January of each year.

[759]
DR. ALEXANDRA KIRKLEY TRAVELING FELLOWSHIPS

Ruth Jackson Orthopaedic Society
6300 North River Road, Suite 727
Rosemont, IL 60018-4226
(847) 698-1637   Fax: (847) 823-0536
E-mail: rjos@aaos.org
Web: www.rjos.org/awards/index.htm

Summary To provide funding to women orthopedic medical students who are interested in traveling to enrich their academic career.

Eligibility This program is open to women medical students who are members of the Ruth Jackson Orthopaedic Society (RJOS). Applicants must be Board Eligible orthopedic surgeons and citizens of the United States or Canada. They must be interested in a program of travel to 1) enrich their academic career or 2) learn new techniques or expand their sub-specialty interests.

Financial data Grants up to $6,000 are available.

Number awarded 2 each year: 1 academic grant and 1 practice enrichment grant.

Deadline November of each year.

[760]
DR. FREDERICK E.G. VALERGAKIS RESEARCH GRANTS

Hellenic University Club of New York
Attn: Scholarship Committee
P.O. Box 1169, Grand Central Station
New York, NY 10150-6882
(914) 381-5192   Fax: (914) 318-2752
E-mail: info@hucny.org
Web: www.hucny.org

Summary To support graduate or postdoctoral research in the sciences or behavioral sciences by students of Hellenic ancestry.

Eligibility Candidates must meet all the following criteria: be of Hellenic ancestry, be either a graduate student or postdoctoral scholar engaged in research, be affiliated with an accredited university in the United States, and be conducting research in the biological, medical, or behavioral sciences.

Financial data Grants average $1,000. Funds may be used for research only, not for tuition or living expenses.

Duration Up to 1 year.

Number awarded 4 to 6 each year.

Deadline June of each year.

[761]
DR. RAYMOND K.J. LUOMANEN FUND

Finlandia Foundation-New York Metropolitan Chapter
Attn: Scholarships
P.O. Box 165, Bowling Green Station
New York, NY 10274-0165
E-mail: scholarships@finlandiafoundationny.org
Web: www.finlandiafoundationny.org/scholarships.html

Summary To provide financial assistance to students interested in studying or conducting research on medicine and health care in Finland or the United States.

Eligibility This program is open to students at colleges and universities in the United States who are interested in studying or conducting research on medicine or health care in Finland or the United States. Applicants must submit information on their language proficiency, work experience, memberships (academic, professional, and social), fellowships and scholarships, awards, publications, exhibitions, performances, and future goals and ambitions. Financial need is not considered in the selection process.

Financial data Stipends range from $500 to $5,000 per year.

Duration 1 year.

Additional information Information is also available from Leena Toivonen, (718) 680-1716, E-mail: leenat@hotmail.com.

Number awarded 1 or more each year.

Deadline February of each year.

[762]
DR. SHERI SMITH MEMORIAL GRANT

Wound, Ostomy and Continence Nurses Society
Attn: Scholarship Committee
15000 Commerce Parkway, Suite C
Mt. Laurel, NJ 08054
Toll-free: (888) 224-WOCN   E-mail: info@wocn.org
Web: www.wocn.org/education/scholarship

Summary To provide financial assistance to members of the Would, Ostomy and Continence Nurses (WOCN) Society interested in working on an advanced degree, conducting research, or developing educational materials.

Eligibility This program is open to active members of the society who have a current, unrestricted R.N. license and proof of WOCNCB certification. Applicants must be able to provide evidence of current or previous employment as a wound, ostomy, and/or continence nurse during the last 3 years. They must 1) provide proof of current enrollment or acceptance into an accredited nursing program or other accredited college or university program for non-nursing degrees to work on a master's or doctoral degree or N.P. certificate; 2) be conducting or planning to conduct innovative and theory-driven empirical research in the wound, ostomy, and/or continence specialty; or 3) be interested in developing professional or patient programs and/or materials. Self-nominations and nominations by another WOCN member are accepted.

Financial data The grant is $2,500.

Duration 1 year.

Additional information This program is sponsored by Carrington Laboratories.

Number awarded 2 each year: 1 in the fall and 1 in the spring.

Deadline April or October of each year.

[763]
DRUG ABUSE DISSERTATION RESEARCH: EPIDEMIOLOGY, PREVENTION, TREATMENT, SERVICES, AND WOMEN AND SEX/GENDER DIFFERENCES

National Institute on Drug Abuse
Attn: Division of Clinical Neuroscience, Development, and
    Behavioral Treatment
6101 Executive Boulevard, Room 4230
Bethesda, MD 20892-9593
(301) 443-2261   Fax: (301) 443-6814
E-mail: mraciopp@nida.nih.gov
Web: www.nida.nih.gov

Summary To provide financial assistance to doctoral candidates interested in conducting dissertation research on drug abuse treatment and health services.

Eligibility This program is open to doctoral candidates who are conducting dissertation research in a field of the behavioral, biomedical, or social sciences related to drug abuse treatment, including research in epidemiology, prevention, treatment, services, and women and sex/gender differences. Students working on an M.D., D.O., D.D.S., or similar professional degree are not eligible. Applicants must be U.S. citizens nationals, or permanent residents and must have completed all requirements for the doctoral degree except the dissertation. Special attention is paid to recruiting members of racial and ethnic groups underrepresented in the biomedical and behavioral sciences (African Americans, Hispanic Americans, Native Americans, Alaskan Natives, and Pacific Islanders).

Financial data The maximum grant is $50,000 per year, including support for the recipient's salary (up to $20,772 per year), research assistant's salary and direct research project expenses. Funding may not be used for tuition, alterations or renovations, faculty salary, contracting costs, or space rental. The recipient's institution may receive facilities and administrative costs of up to 8% of total direct costs.

Duration Up to 2 years; may be extended for 1 additional year.

Number awarded Varies each year, depending on the availability of funds.

Deadline April, August, or December of each year.

[764]
EASTMAN KODAK-DR. THEOPHILUS SORRELL GRADUATE FELLOWSHIP AWARD

National Organization for the Professional Advancement of
    Black Chemists and Chemical Engineers
c/o Howard University
P.O. Box 77040
Washington, DC 20013
(202) 667-1699   Toll-free: (800) 776-1419
Fax: (267) 200-0156
Web: www.nobcche.org

Summary To provide research funding to African American doctoral candidates in chemistry, chemical engineering, or life sciences.

Eligibility This program is open to African American candidates in a Ph.D. program related to chemistry, chemical engineering, or life sciences. Applicants must submit 3 letters of recommendation, a resume, official transcripts for undergraduate and graduate study, a description of their proposed research, and a statement of their career objective. Preference is given to those who have completed at least 1 year of graduate study. U.S. citizenship is required.

Financial data The grant is $13,500.

Duration 1 year.

Additional information This program is sponsored by the Eastman Kodak Company. Information is also available from Dr. Marlon L. Walker, Awards and Scholarships Committee Chair, National Institute of Standards and Technology, 100 Bureau Drive, Gaithersburg, MD 20899-8372, (301) 975-5593, E-mail: marlon.walker@nist.gov.

Number awarded 1 each year.

Deadline January of each year.

[765]
E.I. DUPONT GRADUATE FELLOWSHIP AWARD

National Organization for the Professional Advancement of
    Black Chemists and Chemical Engineers
c/o Howard University
P.O. Box 77040
Washington, DC 20013
(202) 667-1699   Toll-free: (800) 776-1419
Fax: (267) 200-0156
Web: www.nobcche.org

Summary To provide research funding to African American doctoral candidates in chemistry, chemical engineering, or life sciences.

Eligibility This program is open to African American candidates working on a Ph.D. in chemistry, chemical engineering, or life sciences. Applicants must submit 3 letters of recommendation, a resume, official transcripts for undergraduate and graduate study, a description of their proposed research, and a statement of their career objective. Preference is given to those who have completed at least 1 year of graduate study. U.S. citizenship is required.

Financial data The grant is $10,000.

Duration 1 year.

Additional information This program is sponsored by the E.I. duPont de Nemours and Company, Inc. Information is also available from Dr. Marlon L. Walker, Awards and Scholarships Committee Chair, National Institute of Standards and Technology, 100 Bureau Drive, Gaithersburg, MD 20899-8372, (301) 975-5593 E-mail: marlon.walker@nist.gov.

Number awarded 1 each year.

Deadline January of each year.

[766]
ELEANOR LAMBERTSON, RN SCHOLAR AWARD

American Nurses Foundation
Attn: Nursing Research Grants Program
8515 Georgia Avenue, Suite 400
Silver Spring, MD 20910-3492
(301) 628-5298   Fax: (301) 628-5354
E-mail: anf@ana.org
Web: www.anfonline.org

Summary To provide funding to nurses interested in conducting research.

Eligibility This program is open to registered nurses who have earned a baccalaureate or higher degree. Applicants must be beginning researchers who have had no more than 3 research-based publications in refereed journals and have received, as a principal investigator, no more than $15,000 in extramural funding in any 1 research area. Proposed research may be for a master's thesis or doctoral dissertation if the project has been approved by the principal investigator's thesis or dissertation committee. There are no restrictions on the research topic.

Financial data The grant is $3,500. Funds may not be used as a salary for the principal investigator.

Duration 1 year.

Additional information There is a $75 application fee.

Number awarded 1 each year.

Deadline April of each year.

[767]
ELIZABETH MUNSTERBERG KOPPITZ FELLOWSHIP

American Psychological Foundation
750 First Street, N.E.
Washington, DC 20002-4242
(202) 336-5843   Fax: (202) 336-5812
E-mail: foundation@apa.org
Web: www.apa.org/apf/hecaen.html

Summary To provide funding to doctoral students interested in conducting research in child psychology.

Eligibility This program is open to graduate students who have progressed academically through the qualifying examinations, usually after the third or fourth year of doctoral study. Applicants must be interested in conducting psychological research that breaks new ground or creates significant new understandings that facilitate the development and/or functioning of children and youth.

Financial data The stipend is $20,000. Fellows also receive travel funds to attend the American Psychological Association convention and other relevant conferences.

Duration 1 year.

Additional information This fellowship was first awarded in 2003.

Number awarded Up to 3 each year.

Deadline November of each year.

[768]
EMERGENCY MEDICINE FOUNDATION/SOCIETY FOR ACADEMIC EMERGENCY MEDICINE MEDICAL STUDENT RESEARCH GRANT

American College of Emergency Physicians
Attn: Emergency Medicine Foundation
P.O. Box 619911
Dallas, TX 75261-9911
(972) 550-0911, ext. 3216   Toll-free: (800) 798-1822
Fax: (972) 580-2816   E-mail: emf@acep.org
Web: www.acep.org

Summary To provide funding to medical students and residents interested in conducting research in emergency medicine.

Eligibility This program is open to medical students and residents proposing to conduct investigations focused on basic science research, clinical research, preventive medicine, epidemiology, cost containment, and research in emergency medicine teaching and education. Applications must be submitted by a medical student or by an emergency medicine residency program wishing to sponsor a medical student research project. All proposals must designate a preceptor who has a primary appointment in the department or division of emergency medicine. Selection is based on the project's relevance to the goals of the program; the quality and scientific value of the project; the preceptor's ability to mentor; institutional support personnel, facilities, and commitment to research; the research background and experience of the preceptor; and the educational experience for the applicant.

Financial data The grant is $2,400, of which at least $1,200 must be used as a student stipend.

Duration 3 months.

Number awarded Varies each year; recently, 5 of these grants were awarded.

Deadline February of each year.

[769]
ENDODONTIC RESEARCH GRANTS

American Association of Endodontists
Attn: AAE Foundation
211 East Chicago Avenue, Suite 1100
Chicago, IL 60611-2691
(312) 266-7255, ext. 3008   Toll-free: (800) 872-3636
Fax: (312) 266-9867   E-mail: info@aae.org
Web: www.aae.org

Summary To provide funding to dental students, postgraduate students, dental faculty, and practicing dentists who are interested in conducting research in endodontics.

Eligibility This program is open to 1) students in an advanced specialty education program in endodontics at an accredited dental school; 2) postgraduate students who are members of the American Association of Endodontists (AAE), with preference given to students in the first year of a 2-year endodontic program or the first or second year of a 3-year program; 3) faculty or researchers in endodontology or a related field (microbiology, pathology, physiology) at an accredited dental school; and 4) practicing dentists who are AAE members. Applicants must be interested in conducting research on topics relevant to current

AAE research priorities. Selection is based on the significance of the research and its relation to AAE research priorities, scientific merit and potential for discovering new information, excellence of research design and statistical methods, probability of successful completion, extent to which the project has been previously funded, extent to which alternative funding sources were sought, extent to which the research can lead to future innovations in clinical endodontics or future research that is funded by national or federal funding agencies.

Financial data The amounts of the grants vary, but rarely exceed $20,000 per project. No funds may be used for payment of indirect costs to a recipient's institution.

Additional information A progress report must be submitted within 30 days of the project's completion and an abstract must be submitted within 6 months after completion. The failure of grantees to submit a final project report will make their school ineligible for funding for 1 year.

Number awarded Varies each year. Recently, 12 grants, worth $156,623, were granted for the spring and summer cycle and 9 grants, worth $96,300, were granted for the fall and winter cycle.

Deadline February of each year for spring and summer grants; August of each year for fall and winter grants.

[770]
EVIDENCE-BASED CLINICAL PRACTICE GRANTS

American Association of Critical-Care Nurses
Attn: Research Department
101 Columbia
Aliso Viejo, CA 92656-4109
(949) 362-2050, ext. 321
Toll-free: (800) 394-5995, ext. 321   Fax: (949) 362-2020
E-mail: research@aacn.org
Web: www.aacn.org

Summary To provide funding to members of the American Association of Critical-Care Nurses (AACN) who wish to conduct research directly related to the association's clinical practice research priorities.

Eligibility Registered nurses who are current members of the association may apply for these grants. They must propose to conduct research on a topic that the association has identified as a priority for critical care nursing: effective and appropriate use of technology to achieve optimal patient assessment, management, and/or outcomes; creating a healing, humane environment; processes and systems that foster the optimal contribution of critical care nurses; effective approaches to symptom management; and prevention and management of complications. Funds may be sought for new projects, projects in progress, or projects required for an academic degree. Eligible projects may include research utilization studies, CQI projects, or outcomes evaluation projects. Interdisciplinary and collaborative projects are encouraged and may involve interdisciplinary teams, multiple nursing units, home health, subacute and transitional care, and other institutions or community agencies.

Financial data The maximum grant is $1,000. Funds may be used to cover direct project expenses, such as printed materials, small equipment, and supplies (including computer software). They may not be used for salaries or institutional overhead.

Number awarded Up to 6 each year.

Deadline September or December of each year.

[771]
EXCELLENCE IN SONOGRAPHY AWARD

Society of Diagnostic Medical Sonography
Attn: SDMS Educational Foundation
2745 North Dallas Parkway, Suite 350
Plano, TX 75093-8730
(214) 473-8057   Toll-free: (800) 229-9506
Fax: (214) 473-8563   E-mail: foundation@sdms.org
Web: www.sdms.org/foundation/gems.asp

Summary To recognize and reward members of the Society of Diagnostic Medical Sonography (SDMS) who make outstanding contributions to research in sonography.

Eligibility This award is available to SDMS members, including undergraduate and graduate student members, who have conducted research that advances the goals of promoting the art and science of diagnostic ultrasound to the sonography and medical communities. Selection is based on the significance and quality of the achievement, innovation, impact on diagnostic medical sonography, and impact on enhancing patient care.

Financial data The award is $1,000.

Duration The award is presented annually.

Additional information This award is sponsored by GE Healthcare.

Number awarded 1 each year.

Deadline May of each year.

[772]
EXTENDED NEUROSCIENCE AWARD

American Academy of Neurology
Attn: Customer Service
1080 Montreal Avenue
St. Paul, MN 55116-2325
(651) 695-2704   Toll-free: (800) 879-1960
Fax: (651) 695-2791   E-mail: memberservices@aan.com
Web: www.aan.com

Summary To recognize and reward outstanding research papers written by medical students on neurology.

Eligibility Applicants must be currently enrolled and in good standing at an accredited medical school in North America. They are invited to submit an original essay (not previously published) written about neurology for the general neurologist. Essays must be typewritten, double spaced, and up to 30 pages using a standard font. Applicants must have spent more than 1 year on the project leading to the essay.

Financial data The prize is $1,000. In addition, winners receive an award certificate, 1-year complimentary subscription to the journal *Neurology,* round-trip transportation plus a travel allowance to attend the academy's annual meeting, and complimentary registration at the meeting.

Duration The prize is awarded annually.

Additional information The award is presented at the academy's annual meeting. Only deceased persons may be the subject of a biographical paper. Recipients are expected to make a poster presentation based on the selected manuscript at the academy's annual program.

Number awarded 1 each year.

Deadline October of each year.

[773]
FELLOWSHIPS IN SCIENCE AND INTERNATIONAL AFFAIRS

Harvard University
John F. Kennedy School of Government
Belfer Center for Science and International Affairs
Attn: Fellowship Coordinator
79 John F. Kennedy Street
Cambridge, MA 02138
(617) 495-8806   Fax: (617) 495-8963
E-mail: bcsia_fellowships@ksg.harvard.edu
Web: bcsia.ksg.harvard.edu

Summary To provide funding to professionals, postdoctorates, and graduate students interested in conducting research in areas of concern to the Belfer Center for Science and International Affairs at Harvard University in Cambridge, Massachusetts.

Eligibility The postdoctoral fellowship is open to recent recipients of the Ph.D. or equivalent degree, university faculty members, and employees of government, military, international, humanitarian, and private research institutions who have appropriate professional experience. Applicants for predoctoral fellowships must have passed their general examinations. Lawyers, economists, physical scientists, and others of diverse disciplinary backgrounds are also welcome to apply. The program especially encourages applications from women, minorities, and citizens of all countries. All applicants must be interested in conducting research in 1 of the 4 major program areas of the center: the International Security Program (ISP); the Science, Technology, and Public Policy Program (STPP); the Program on Intrastate Conflict and Conflict Resolution (ICP); and the Dubai initiative. Fellowships may also be available in other specialized programs, such as science, technology, and globalization; managing the atom; and energy technology and innovation.

Financial data The stipend is $34,000 for postdoctoral research fellows or $20,000 for predoctoral research fellows. Health insurance is also provided.

Duration 10 months.

Number awarded A limited number each year.

Deadline December of each year.

[774]
FORE DISSERTATION ASSISTANCE AWARDS

American Health Information Management Association
Attn: Foundation of Research and Education
233 North Michigan Avenue, Suite 2150
Chicago, IL 60601-5806
(312) 233-1167   Fax: (312) 233-1431
E-mail: fore@ahima.org
Web: www.ahima.org/fore/research/dissertation.asp

Summary To provide funding to doctoral student members of the American Health Information Management Association (AHIMA) who are completing a dissertation in health information management.

Eligibility This program is open to doctoral candidates who are active, associate, or student members of AHIMA. Applicants must have completed all requirements for a doctoral degree (except the dissertation) in a program related to health information management (e.g., computer science, business management, education, public health). Priority is given to applicants proposing dissertation topics that relate to 1 or more of the AHIMA research priorities: transition to e-HIM and the role of technology in health care, quality of coded data, or clinical outcomes (data quality, impact and use of data). Selection is based on the proposed dissertation's impact, methodology, feasibility, and evaluation.

Financial data There are no limits on the amounts of the grants, but most have ranged from $5,000 to $10,000.

Duration Work should be completed within 18 months.

Number awarded Varies each year.

Deadline March or September of each year.

[775]
FORE GRANT-IN-AID RESEARCH AWARDS

American Health Information Management Association
Attn: Foundation of Research and Education
233 North Michigan Avenue, Suite 2150
Chicago, IL 60601-5806
(312) 233-1131   Fax: (312) 233-1431
E-mail: fore@ahima.org
Web: www.ahima.org/fore/research/grantinaid.asp

Summary To provide funding to members of the American Health Information Management Association (AHIMA) who are interested in conducting a research project in health information management.

Eligibility This program is open to active, associate, and student members of AHIMA. Applicants must be interested in conducting a research project related to health information management (computer science, business management, education, public health, etc.). Preference is given to applicants proposing dissertation topics that relate to 1 or more of the AHIMA research priorities: transition to e-HIM and the role of technology in health care, quality of coded data, or clinical outcomes (data quality, impact and use of data). Proposed research should be directed toward achieving 1 or more of the following outcomes: policy development, documentation of current status, standards development and establishment, validation of a theory, obtaining benchmark data, validating best practice, or improving current practice. The following categories of projects are given priority: research that clearly advances knowledge in the health information management field, proposals demonstrating potential for future funding, seed grants, and proposals with an interdisciplinary focus.

Financial data There are no limits on the amounts of the grants, but most have ranged from $15,000 to $40,000.

Duration Work should be completed within 18 months.

Number awarded Varies each year.

Deadline March or September of each year.

[776]
FOUNDATION FOR PHYSICAL THERAPY PROMOTION OF DOCTORAL STUDIES PROGRAM

American Physical Therapy Association
Attn: Foundation for Physical Therapy
1111 North Fairfax Street
Alexandria, VA 22314-1488
(703) 706-8906   Toll-free: (800) 875-1378
Fax: (703) 706-8519   TDD: (703) 683-6748
E-mail: foundation@apta.org
Web: www.apta.org

Summary To provide financial assistance for doctoral training to members of the American Physical Therapy Association.

Eligibility This program is open to members of the association who are 1) licensed physical therapists or eligible for licensure; 2) U.S. citizens, noncitizen nationals, or permanent residents; 3) enrolled in an accredited postprofessional doctoral program with a demonstrated relationship to physical therapy; and 4) able to demonstrate a commitment to further the physical therapy profession through teaching and research in the United States and its territories. Applicants for first-level awards must have completed at least 1 year of graduate study and be seeking funding to continue course work; applicants for second-level awards must have been admitted to candidacy for the Ph.D. and be seeking funding to work on their dissertation. Selection is based on 1) the objectives in the applicant's plan for development of an academically-based research career; 2) the significance of the total experience and its potential impact on teaching and research; and 3) the mentor, facilities, and resources available to the applicant to support the career development plan.

Financial data First-level awards are up to $7,500 per year for support of the course work phase of postprofessional doctoral studies; second-level awards are up to $15,000 per year for support of the postcandidacy phase of postprofessional doctoral studies. Funds are paid directly to the scholarship recipient.

Duration 1 year; first-level awards may be renewed for up to 2 additional years; second-level awards may be renewed for up to 1 additional year.

Additional information From among the applicants to either level this program, 1 is selected to receive the Viva J. Erickson Scholarship for their academic leadership. The Patricia Leahy Scholarship is awarded to an applicant for a first-level award interested in doctoral study in neurology. The Marylou Barnes Scholarship is awarded to an applicant for a second-level award interested in doctoral study in neurology.

Number awarded Varies each year; recently, 7 first-level awards and 7 second-level awards were presented.

Deadline January of each year.

[777]
FOUNDATION FOR THE HISTORY OF WOMEN IN MEDICINE FELLOWSHIPS

College of Physicians of Philadelphia
Attn: Francis C. Wood Institute for the History of Medicine
19 South 22nd Street
Philadelphia, PA 19103-3097
(215) 563-3737, ext. 305   Fax: (215) 561-6477
E-mail: mpatton@collphyphil.org
Web: www.collphyphil.org/woodfell.htm

Summary To provide funding to students and scholars interested in short-term use of resources in the Philadelphia area to conduct research on the history of women and medicine.

Eligibility This program is open to doctoral candidates and other advanced scholars interested in using the historical collections of the Historical Medical Library of the College of Physicians of Philadelphia, the Mütter Museum, or the archives and special collections on women in medicine at the Drexel University College of Medicine. The proposed research must related to the history of women and medicine. Preference is given to projects that deal specifically with women as physicians or other health workers, but proposals dealing with the history of women's health issues are also considered.

Financial data Grants up to $1,000 are available.

Duration Grants are available for spring, summer, or fall visits of at least 1 week.

Number awarded Up to 2 each year.

Deadline February of each year.

[778]
FRANCIS CLARK WOOD INSTITUTE FOR THE HISTORY OF MEDICINE RESIDENT RESEARCH FELLOWSHIPS

College of Physicians of Philadelphia
Attn: Francis C. Wood Institute for the History of Medicine
19 South 22nd Street
Philadelphia, PA 19103-3097
(215) 563-3737, ext. 305   Fax: (215) 561-6477
E-mail: mpatton@collphyphil.org
Web: www.collphyphil.org/woodfell.htm

Summary To provide funding to students and scholars interested in short-term use of the College of Physicians of Philadelphia's library or Mütter Museum.

Eligibility This program is open to doctoral candidates and other advanced scholars interested in using the historical collections of the library or the museum. The project proposal should demonstrate that the College of Physicians has print, manuscript, and artifactual collections central to the applicant's research project.

Financial data Grants up to $1,000 are available.

Duration Grants are available for spring, summer, or fall visits of at least 1 week.

Additional information The library of the College is among the largest medical history collections in the world. The Historical Collections of the library contain more than 225,000 books and journals published before 1966, including 430 incunabula and more than 12,000 pre-1801 imprints. The rare book collection is augmented by extensive archival, manuscript, and print/photograph collections. The Mütter Museum houses an exceptional collection of medical artifacts, instruments, pathological specimens, and anatomical models that complement the holdings of the library. Fellows must present a seminar at the institute and submit a report on their research.

Number awarded Varies each year; recently, 22 of these grants were awarded.

Deadline February of each year.

[779]
FRANKLIN C. MCLEAN AWARD

National Medical Fellowships, Inc.
Attn: Scholarship Program
5 Hanover Square, 15th Floor
New York, NY 10004
(212) 483-8880   Fax: (212) 483-8897
E-mail: info@nmfonline.org
Web: www.nmf-online.org

Summary To recognize and reward the outstanding academic achievement, leadership, and community service of senior medical school minority students.

Eligibility This competition is open to African American, Native Hawaiian, Alaska Native, American Indian, Mexican American, and mainland Puerto Rican students enrolled in accredited U.S. medical schools or osteopathic colleges. Candidates must be nominated by their schools during the summer preceding their senior year. Selection is based on academic achievement, leadership, and community service. U.S. citizenship is required.

Financial data This honor includes a certificate of merit and a $3,000 award.

Duration 1 year; nonrenewable.

Additional information This award, the first award offered by the National Medical Fellowship, was established in 1968 in memory of the Chicago bone physiologist who founded the organization.

Number awarded 1 each year.

Deadline Nominations must be submitted by July of each year.

[780]
FUTURE OF PERFUSION SCHOLARSHIP

Perfusion.com, Inc.
17080 Safety Street, Suite 108
Fort Myers, FL 33908
(239) 243-9171   Toll-free: (866) 892-0265
Fax: (425) 795-0565   E-mail: info@perfusion.com
Web: www.perfusion.com

Summary To recognize and reward graduate students in perfusion who submit outstanding research papers.

Eligibility This competition is open to graduate students in perfusion who submit research papers that relate to new technology and how it may apply to the future of the profession. Entries should demonstrate ingenuity, creativity, and forward thinking.

Financial data The award is $2,500.

Duration The award is presented annually.

Number awarded 1 each year.

Deadline January of each year.

[781]
GEORGE C. PAFFENBARGER STUDENT RESEARCH AWARD

Academy of Operative Dentistry
c/o Nairn H.F. Wilson, Research Committee Chair
King's College, Guy's Tower, Floor 18
London SE1 1UL
England
44 20 7955 4343   Fax: 44 20 7955 8873
E-mail: nairn.wilson@kd.ac.uk
Web: www.operativedentistry.com/awards.html

Summary To provide funding to dental students interested in conducting research on operative dentistry.

Eligibility This program is open to dental students at all levels and in all countries. Applicants must be proposing to undertake novel research related to contemporary operative dentistry. They must submit a protocol outlining the background, aims, and hypothesis of the proposed research, the methodology to be employed, and the anticipated effect on the clinical practice of operative dentistry. The protocol must be approved by a research mentor who is a member of the Academy of Operative Dentistry.

Financial data Grants up to $6,000 are available. Additional funding, up to $1,000, is available to help pay the costs of attending the annual meeting of the Academy of Operative Dentistry.

Additional information This program, sponsored by the American Dental Association Foundation, began in 2007. Recipients are required to present the findings of their research at the annual meeting of the Academy of Operative Dentistry. If the research leads to a report intended for publication, the sponsor expects that the report will first be submitted to *Operative Dentistry*.

Number awarded 1 or more each year.

Deadline December of each year.

[782]
GERBER ENDOWMENT IN PEDIATRIC NUTRITION GRADUATE FELLOWSHIP

Institute of Food Technologists
Attn: Scholarship Department
525 West Van Buren, Suite 1000
Chicago, IL 60607
(312) 782-8424   Fax: (312) 782-8348
E-mail: info@ift.org
Web: www.ift.org

Summary To provide funding to graduate students interested in conducting research on pediatric nutrition.

Eligibility Applicants must be currently enrolled in graduate studies leading to a master's or doctoral degree in an approved program in food science or food technology at an educational institution in the United States or Canada. They must have an above average interest in research, a demonstrated scientific aptitude, and an interest in conducting research in nutrition with an emphasis on pediatrics. Research in such disciplines as genetics, horticulture, nutrition, microbiology, biochemistry, engineering, and chemistry is eligible unless if it is directly related to pediatric nutrition.

Financial data The grant is $3,000.

Duration 1 year; recipients may reapply if they are members of the Institute of Food Technologists.

Additional information Correspondence and completed applications must be submitted to the department head of the educational institution the applicant is attending.

Number awarded 1 each year.

Deadline January of each year.

[783]
GERBER FELLOWSHIP IN PEDIATRIC NUTRITION

National Medical Fellowships, Inc.
Attn: Scholarship Program
5 Hanover Square, 15th Floor
New York, NY 10004
(212) 483-8880   Fax: (212) 483-8897
E-mail: info@nmfonline.org
Web: www.nmf-online.org

Summary To provide funding to underrepresented minority medical students and residents who are interested in conducting research on pediatric nutrition.

Eligibility This program is open to African Americans, Native Hawaiians, Alaska Natives, American Indians, Mexican Americans, and mainland Puerto Ricans who are 1) students enrolled in accredited U.S. medical schools, 2) students enrolled in U.S. colleges of osteopathic medicine, or 3) medical residents in U.S. programs. Candidates must be nominated by their deans or graduate education directors. They must be participating in ongoing research in the area of pediatric nutrition. U.S. citizenship is required. Selection is based on academic achievement and motivation to prepare for a career in pediatric nutrition research.

Financial data The grant is $3,000.

Duration 1 year; nonrenewable.

Additional information This award was established in 1997 with grant support from the Gerber Companies Foundation.

Number awarded 1 each year.

Deadline October of each year.

[784]
GINA FINZI MEMORIAL STUDENT SUMMER FELLOWSHIPS

Lupus Foundation of America
Attn: Student Fellowship Program
2000 L Street, N.W., Suite 710
Washington, DC 20036
(202) 349-1155   Toll-free: (800) 558-0121
Fax: (202) 349-1156   E-mail: Finzifellowship@lupus.org
Web: www.lupus.org/research/student.html

Summary To provide funding to conduct basic, clinical, or psychosocial research on lupus during the summer under the supervision of an established investigator.

Eligibility This program is open to undergraduate, graduate, and medical students, although preference is given to applicants with a college degree. Applicants must be interested in conducting basic, clinical, or psychosocial research related to systemic lupus erythematosus (SLE) during the summer in the United States. Selection is based on the applicant's past performance and competence to undertake the project, the institution where the project will be conducted, originality and timeliness of the project, and the project plan (design, methods, feasibility, relevance to lupus, and appropriateness of budget).

Financial data Fellowships are $2,000.

Duration Summer months; nonrenewable.

Number awarded Between 15 and 30 each year.

Deadline March of each year.

[785]
GLASGOW-RUBIN ESSAY AWARD

American Medical Women's Association Foundation
Attn: AMWA Foundation
211 North Union Street, Suite 100
Alexandria, VA 22314
(703) 838-0500   Fax: (703) 549-3864
E-mail: foundation@amwa-doc.org
Web: www.amwa-doc.org

Summary To recognize and reward outstanding papers written by women medical students.

Eligibility This award is presented for the best essay (approximately 1,000 words) identifying a woman physician who has been a significant mentor and role model. Applicants must be student members of the American Medical Women's Association (AMWA) attending an accredited U.S. allopathic or osteopathic medical school.

Financial data The award consists of $1,000 and a plaque.

Duration The award is presented annually.

Additional information The winning paper may be published in AMWA's journal. This award was formerly known as the Janet M. Glasgow Essay Award.

Number awarded 1 monetary award each year.

Deadline May of each year.

[786]
GLAXOSMITHKLINE-DR. LENDON N. PRIDGEN GRADUATE FELLOWSHIP AWARD

National Organization for the Professional Advancement of
   Black Chemists and Chemical Engineers
c/o Howard University
P.O. Box 77040
Washington, DC 20013
(202) 667-1699   Toll-free: (800) 776-1419
Fax: (267) 200-0156
Web: www.nobcche.org

Summary To provide funding to African American doctoral students for research in chemistry, chemical engineering, or life sciences.

Eligibility This program is open to African American candidates in a Ph.D. program for chemistry, chemical engineering, or life sciences. Applicants must submit 3 letters of recommendation, a resume, official transcripts for undergraduate and graduate study, a description of their proposed research, and a statement of their career objective. Preference is given to those who have completed at least 1 year of graduate study. U.S. citizenship is required.

Financial data The grant is $25,000.

Duration 1 year.

Additional information Information is also available from Dr. Marlon L. Walker, Awards and Scholarships Committee Chair, National Institute of Standards and Technology, 100 Bureau Drive, Gaithersburg, MD 20899-8372, (301) 975-5593. This program is sponsored by GlaxoSmithKline.

Number awarded 1 each year.

Deadline January of each year.

[787]
GLORIA SMITH, RN SCHOLAR AWARD

American Nurses Foundation
Attn: Nursing Research Grants Program
8515 Georgia Avenue, Suite 400
Silver Spring, MD 20910-3492
(301) 628-5298   Fax: (301) 628-5354
E-mail: anf@ana.org
Web: www.anfonline.org

Summary To provide funding to nurses interested in conducting research on health care delivery to socioeconomic and ethnic minority populations.

Eligibility This program is open to registered nurses who have earned a baccalaureate or higher degree. Applicants may be either beginning or experienced researchers. They must be interested in conducting research on accessibility or quality of health care delivery to socioeconomic and ethnic minority populations. Proposed research may be for a master's thesis or doctoral dissertation if the project has been approved by the principal investigator's thesis or dissertation committee.

Financial data The grant is either $15,000 or $5,000. Funds may not be used as a salary for the principal investigator.

Duration 1 year.

Additional information There is a $75 application fee.

Number awarded 2 each year: 1 at $15,000 and 1 at $5,000.

Deadline April of each year.

[788]
GNC NUTRITION RESEARCH GRANT

National Strength and Conditioning Association
Attn: Grants and Scholarships
1885 Bob Johnson Drive
Colorado Springs, CO 80906
(719) 632-6722, ext. 105　　Toll-free: (800) 815-6826
Fax: (719) 632-6367　　E-mail: nsca@nsca-lift.org
Web: www.nsca-lift.org/Foundation

Summary To provide funding for research related to strength and conditioning to graduate student members of the National Strength and Conditioning Association (NSCA).

Eligibility This program is open to graduate students who are members of the association studying in the field of strength and conditioning. Applicants must be proposing to conduct research related to nutrition that falls within the mission of NSCA.

Financial data The grant is $2,500; funds may not be used for overhead costs.

Additional information The National Strength and Conditioning Association (NSCA) is a nonprofit organization of strength and conditioning professionals, including coaches, athletic trainers, physical therapists, educators, researchers, and physicians. This program, established in 2003, is sponsored by General Nutrition Centers, Inc.

Number awarded 1 each year.

Deadline March of each year for letters of intent; May of each year for final applications.

[789]
GOOD GOVERNMENT STUDENT PHARMACIST-OF-THE-YEAR AWARD

American Pharmacists Association
Attn: Academy of Student Pharmacists
1100 15th Street, N.W., Suite 400
Washington, DC 20005
Toll-free: (800) 237-2742, ext. 7586　　Fax: (202) 628-0443
E-mail: jathay@aphanet.org
Web: www.aphanet.org

Summary To recognize and reward pharmacy students who demonstrate outstanding grassroots activity and advocacy for the profession.

Eligibility This award is available to pharmacy students who are active members of the Academy of Student Pharmacists of the American Pharmacists Association (APhA-ASP) and a state pharmacy association. Nominees must have raised student pharmacists' awareness of current state and federal issues and made a positive impact on the pharmacy profession. Priority is given to students who utilize a political information "network" that includes, but is not limited to, students, practitioners, and state association members.

Financial data The award consists of a $1,000 honorarium, a plaque, a U.S. flag previously flown over the U.S. Capitol, and complimentary registration to an APhA meeting.

Duration The award is presented annually.

Additional information This award was first presented in 2005.

Number awarded 1 each year.

Deadline Nominations must be submitted by October of each year.

[790]
GRADUATE FELLOWSHIPS IN ALTERNATIVES IN SCIENTIFIC RESEARCH

International Foundation for Ethical Research
Attn: Executive Director
53 West Jackson Boulevard, Suite 1552
Chicago, IL 60604
(312) 427-6025　　Fax: (312) 427-6524
E-mail: IFER@navs.org
Web: www.ifer.org/fellowships.html

Summary To provide funding to graduate students whose proposed research involves animal welfare.

Eligibility This program is open to students enrolled in master's and doctoral programs in the sciences, humanities, psychology, and journalism. Applicants must be interested in conducting research on scientifically valid alternatives to the use of animals in research, product testing, and education. Research may deal with tissue, cell, and organ cultures; clinical studies using animals or humans; epidemiological studies; enhanced use of existing tissue repositories and patient databases; public education; or computer modeling. Applications must be submitted by the student's faculty advisor; at least 1 member of the student's graduate advisory committee must have interest or expertise in the area of alternatives to the use of animals in scientific research.

Financial data Grants provide an annual stipend of $12,500 and $2,500 for supplies.

Duration 1 year; may be renewed up to 2 additional years.

Number awarded Varies each year; recently, 2 of these fellowships were awarded.

Deadline March of each year.

[791]
GRADUATE PARTNERSHIPS PROGRAM

National Institutes of Health
Attn: Office of Intramural Training and Education
2 Center Drive
Building 2, Room 2E06
Bethesda, MD 20892-0234
(301) 594-9605　　Fax: (301) 594-9606
E-mail: gpp@nih.gov
Web: gpp.nih.gov

Summary To provide funding to doctoral candidates who are interested at conducting dissertation research at laboratories in the United States or abroad partnering with the National Institutes of Health (NIH).

Eligibility This program is open to U.S. citizens and permanent residents who have or are completing an undergraduate degree. Applicants must either 1) be planning to enter a university in the United States or abroad that has a partnership agreement with the NIH; or 2) be able to develop an individual agreement with an NIH investigator to do all or part of their dissertation research at NIH. They must be interested in working on a Ph.D. degree in a biomedical field that involves study at the home institution and research at an NIH laboratory.

Financial data First-year stipends are currently $24,000 per year at U.S. universities or $23,100 per year at foreign universities. Small increases are provided in subsequent years.

Duration Until completion of a doctoral degree.

Additional information Currently, NIH has formal partnership agreements with the following institutions: Boston University (bioinformatics); Georgetown University (biomedical sciences); University of Maryland at College Park (biophysics and hearing and speech science); Johns Hopkins University (cell, molecular, and developmental biology and biophysics); University of North Carolina at Chapel Hill (cell motility and cytoskeleton); George Washington University (genetics); University of Pennsylvania (immunology); University of Montana, in collaboration with the National Institute of Allergy and Infectious Diseases and the Rocky Mountain Laboratory (molecular basis for infectious diseases); Brown University (neuroscience); New York University (structural biology); University of Oxford (biochemistry, bioinformatics, cell biology, developmental biology, genetics, immunology, microbiology, molecular biology, neuroscience, pharmacology, structural biology, any other areas of biomedical research); University of Cambridge (same areas as at Oxford); and Karolinska Institute, Sweden (neuroscience). In addition, a program offering a laboratory animal medicine residency and master's degree in comparative medicine is available from the Uniformed Services University of the Health Sciences; a program in nursing and biobehavioral research is offered through the National Institute of Nursing Research at a consortium of schools of nursing at Johns Hopkins University, Oregon Health and Sciences University, University of California at San Francisco, University of Iowa, University of Pittsburgh, and University of Utah; and a program in molecular pathology in offered by the National Cancer Institute, the National Institute of Allergy and Infectious Diseases, the National Institute of Diabetes and Digestive and Kidney Diseases, and the National Heart, Lung, and Blood Institute at North Carolina State University, Michigan State University, University of Illinois at Urbana-Champaign, and University of Maryland at College Park.

Number awarded 50 to 75 new graduate students are admitted to this program each year. That includes up to 6 each at the 2 English universities.

Deadline January of each year.

[792]
GRANTS FOR HEALTH SERVICES RESEARCH DISSERTATION

Agency for Healthcare Research and Quality
Attn: Office of Extramural Research, Education and Priority
    Populations
540 Gaither Road
Rockville, MD 20850
(301) 427-1527   Fax: (301) 427-1562
TTY: (301) 451-0088   E-mail: bharding@ahrq.gov
Web: www.ahrq.gov

Summary To provide funding to doctoral candidates engaged in research for a dissertation that examines some aspect of the health care system.

Eligibility This program is open to student enrolled in an accredited research doctoral degree (e.g., Ph.D., Sc.D., Dr.P.H., Ed.D.) program. Applicants must have completed all requirements for the doctoral degree other than the dissertation. The dissertation topic must relate to the strategic goals of the Agency for Healthcare Research and Quality (AHRQ) to enhance patient safety and quality of care. Priority is given to research on health issues related to designated populations, including individuals living in inner city and rural areas, low-income and minority groups, women, children, the elderly, and individuals with special health care needs (such as individuals with disabilities and individuals who need chronic care or end-of-life health care). U.S. citizenship or permanent resident status is required. Underrepresented racial and ethnic groups as well as individuals with disabilities are encouraged to apply.

Financial data Total direct costs may not exceed $35,000. Funds may be used for the investigator's salary, direct project

expenses (travel, data purchasing, data processing, and supplies), and matriculation fees. The institution will receive facilities and administrative costs of 8% of total allowable direct costs exclusive of tuition and related fees, health insurance, and expenditures for equipment.

Duration 9 to 17 months.

Number awarded Up to 30 each year.

Deadline April, August, or December of each year.

[793]
GRASS FELLOWSHIPS IN NEUROSCIENCE

Grass Foundation
Attn: President
400 Franklin Street, Suite 302
Braintree, MA 02184
(781) 843-0219   Fax: (781) 843-0474
E-mail: info@grassfoundation.org
Web: www.grassfoundation.org

Summary To encourage independent research in neurophysiology by pre- or postdoctoral investigators at the Marine Biological Laboratory in Woods Hole, Massachusetts during the summer.

Eligibility Individuals in the late predoctoral or early postdoctoral category who are academically prepared for independent neurophysiological research are eligible to apply for this grant. For the purposes of this program, neurobiological approaches used to study nervous system functions may include neurophysiology, membrane biophysics, integrative neurobiology and neuroethology, neuroanatomy, neuropharmacology, systems neuroscience, cellular and developmental neurobiology, and computational approaches to neural systems. Applications to conduct research in any of these categories will be considered. The application process involves the presentation of a research proposal, a budget, and a letter of recommendation from a senior investigator familiar with the candidate's work. Selection is based on the ability of the applicant to organize and present pertinent information and to work independently. Preference is given to applicants who have no prior research experience at the Marine Biological Laboratory (MBL) in Woods Hole, Massachusetts, who have no more than 5 years of postdoctoral research, and who have demonstrated a commitment to a research career.

Financial data Fellowships provide funds to support an investigator, spouse, and dependent children for 1 summer at the Marine Biological Laboratory in Woods Hole, Massachusetts. Laboratory research space, equipment, housing, and board are provided. Travel expenses to and from the laboratory are covered. However, fellows coming from outside continental North America receive travel funds for the fellow only (not for their spouse or children).

Duration 14 weeks during the summer.

Additional information Information is also available from the Grass Fellowship Program, 7 MBL Street, Candle House, Woods Hole, MA 02543, (508) 289-7173, Fax: (508) 289-7934, E-mail: gfp@fassfoundation.org. Fellows should not attempt to combine a summer fellowship at MBL with writing a dissertation.

Number awarded Varies each year; recently, 10 of these fellowships were awarded.

Deadline December of each year.

[794]
GREEN TEXTBOOKS FELLOWSHIP
National Wildlife Federation
Attn: Campus Ecology Coordinator
11100 Wildlife Center Drive
Reston, VA 20190-5362
(703) 438-6000   Toll-free: (800) 822-9919
E-mail: campus@nwf.org
Web: www.nwf.org/campusecology/dspfellowships.cfm

Summary To provide funding to undergraduate and graduate students interested in conducting a project to encourage publishers to print textbooks on environmentally preferably paper.

Eligibility This program is open to undergraduate, graduate, and law students at colleges and universities. Preference is given to students in New England, New York, Florida, and California, but applicants from other locations in the United States are also eligible. Applicants must be interested in developing and conducting a project to encourage educational textbook publishers to print K-12 and college textbooks on environmentally preferable paper in order to reduce paper consumption, conserve natural resources, and help protect endangered forests. Students must work with an advisor (a member of the staff, faculty, or administration on their campus who is willing to serve in an advisory capacity for the duration of the grant period) and a verifier (a staff member in charge of the department that is most closely related to their project and who can validate that the proposed project is supported by the department and/or campus that will implement and most closely benefit from the project). Selection is based on whether or not the proposal demonstrates increased awareness on campuses and surrounding communities about forestry impacts and solutions related to educational textbooks; states an awareness of issues surrounding traditional forestry and paper-making practices; incorporates hands-on action-oriented efforts to advance solutions to virgin paper use; engages and tracks students, faculty, and other stakeholder activities; demonstrates a keen interest in and experience working within or with diverse constituencies; conducts outreach to local and campus newspapers through press releases; secures matching funds or other financial support; arranges academic credit for successful completion of the project; and serves as a model for the national environmental movement. Attributes of a strong applicant include commitment to advancing environmental initiatives on academic, personal, and professional levels; creative thinking to engage stakeholders, including campus bookstore managers, faculty members, state procurement officers, key associations, and organizations; commitment to working with multicultural communities; strong communication skills; initiative to overcome barriers and seek alternative avenues of project advancement when necessary; proactive research and outreach to ensure project will successfully achieve its goals; interest in learning about, serving as a representative of, and pursuing engagement with the National Wildlife Federation (NWF) and its affiliate organizations; and desire to remain an active member of NWF after the conclusion of the fellowship.

Financial data The maximum grant is $2,000. Funds may be used for direct project expenses and/or living expenses. Grants are intended to serve as seed money, not to cover the full cost of the project.

Duration 1 academic year.

Number awarded 1 each year.

Deadline September of each year.

[795]
HAND-CARRIED ULTRASOUND RESEARCH AWARD
Society of Diagnostic Medical Sonography
Attn: SDMS Educational Foundation
2745 North Dallas Parkway, Suite 350
Plano, TX 75093-8730
(214) 473-8057   Toll-free: (800) 229-9506
Fax: (214) 473-8563   E-mail: foundation@sdms.org
Web: www.sdms.org/foundation/medison.asp

Summary To recognize and reward members of the Society of Diagnostic Medical Sonography (SDMS) who make outstanding contributions to research on hand-carried ultrasound.

Eligibility This award is available to SDMS members, including undergraduate and graduate student members, who have conducted research related to hand-carried ultrasound (HCU), defined as systems that weigh less than 10 pounds, have the capability to run on battery, and have at least 2-dimensional capability. The research must relate to the benefits of using HCU systems, including novel methods of incorporating HCU into clinical practice, innovative clinical applications for HCU technology, innovative technical applications for HCU technology, positive economic benefits of the use of HCU technology, or positive ergonometric benefits of the use of HCU technology.

Financial data The award is $1,500.

Duration The award is presented annually.

Additional information This award is sponsored by SonoSite Inc.

Number awarded 1 each year.

Deadline May of each year.

[796]
HEALTH SCIENCES STUDENT FELLOWSHIPS IN EPILEPSY
Epilepsy Foundation
Attn: Research Department
8301 Professional Place
Landover, MD 20785-2237
(301) 459-3700   Toll-free: (800) EFA-1000
Fax: (301) 577-2684   TDD: (800) 332-2070
E-mail: grants@efa.org
Web: www.epilepsyfoundation.org/research/grants.cfm

Summary To provide financial assistance to medical and health science graduate students interested in working on an epilepsy project during the summer.

Eligibility This program is open to students enrolled, or accepted for enrollment, in a medical school, a doctoral program, or other graduate program. Applicants must have a defined epilepsy-related study or research plan to be carried out under the supervision of a qualified mentor. Because the program is designed as a training opportunity, the quality of the training plans and environment are considered in the selection process. Other selection criteria include the quality of the proposed project, the relevance of the proposed work to epilepsy, the applicant's interest in the field of epilepsy, the applicant's qualifications, and the mentor's qualifications, including his or her commitment to the student and the project. U.S. citizenship is not required, but the project must be conducted in the United States. Applications from women, members of minority groups, and people with disabilities are especially encouraged. The program is not intended for students working on a dissertation research project.

Financial data Stipends are $3,000.

Duration 3 months during the summer.

Additional information Support for this program is provided by many individuals, families, and corporations, especially the American Epilepsy Society, Abbott Laboratories, Ortho-McNeil Pharmaceutical, and Pfizer Inc.

Number awarded Varies each year; recently, 3 of these fellowships were awarded.

Deadline February of each year.

[797]
HELEN H. GLASER STUDENT ESSAY AWARD

Alpha Omega Alpha Honor Medical Society
Attn: Managing Editor
525 Middlefield Road, Suite 130
Menlo Park, CA 94025
(650) 329-0291   Fax: (650) 329-1618
E-mail: d.lancaster@alphaomegaalpha.org
Web: www.alphaomegaalpha.org

Summary To recognize and reward outstanding essays written by medical students on nontechnical aspects of medicine.

Eligibility This competition is open to medical students who submit essays on nontechnical aspects of medicine, including education, ethics, history, philosophy, and policy; well-referenced scholarly fiction is also eligible. Manuscripts must be original and unpublished, should not exceed 15 double-spaced pages, and may not include more than 20 bibliographic references.

Financial data First prize is $2,000, second $750, third $500, and honorable mentions $250.

Duration The competition is held annually.

Additional information The winning manuscript may be published in *The Pharos*, the official publication of Alpha Omega Alpha.

Number awarded Up to 6 each year: 1 first, 1 second, 1 third, and up to 3 honorable mentions.

Deadline January of each year.

[798]
HENRY R. VIETS FELLOWSHIP

Myasthenia Gravis Foundation of America, Inc.
Attn: Chief Executive Officer
1821 University Avenue West, Suite S256
St. Paul, MN 55104
(651) 917-6256   Toll-free: (800) 541-5454
Fax: (651) 917-1835   E-mail: mgfa@myasthenia.org
Web: www.myasthenia.org/research

Summary To provide funding to medical and graduate students interested in conducting research on the cause or treatment of Myasthenia Gravis.

Eligibility This program is open to graduate and medical students who are interested in conducting either basic or clinical research on the cause or treatment of Myasthenia Gravis or related neuromuscular conditions. Applicants must submit a cover letter, a summary of their research proposal and its relationship to Myasthenia Gravis or related neuromuscular conditions, a curriculum vitae, and a letter of recommendation from the proposed sponsor who will be supervising the research.

Financial data The grant is $3,000.

Duration Up to 1 year.

Number awarded Varies each year; recently, 3 of these fellowships were awarded.

Deadline March of each year.

[799]
HHMI-NIH RESEARCH SCHOLARS PROGRAM

Howard Hughes Medical Institute
One Cloister Court, Building 60, Room 253
Bethesda, MD 20814-1460
(301) 951-6770   Toll-free: (800) 424-9924
Fax: (301) 951-6776   E-mail: research_scholars@hhmi.org
Web: www.hhmi.org/cloister

Summary To give outstanding students at U.S. medical or dental schools the opportunity to receive educational funding and research training at the National Institutes of Health (NIH), in Bethesda, Maryland.

Eligibility This program is open to students who have completed their second or third year at a medical or dental school in the United States or Puerto Rico. Applicants must be interested in conducting a basic, translational, or applied biomedical research project while in residence at a facility on the NIH campus. There are no citizenship requirements, but applicants must be authorized to work in the United States. Those who are enrolled in an M.D./Ph.D. or D.D.S./Ph.D. program or who already have an M.D., D.D.S., or Ph.D. or Sc.D. in a laboratory-based biological science are not eligible.

Financial data Scholars receive an annual salary of $25,000 for rent, food, and other living expenses. They are also eligible for medical, life, and accidental death and dismemberment insurance. Students are reimbursed for round-trip moving expenses for personal belongings (not furniture) for themselves and their dependents from and back to medical school. In addition, tuition is paid for Research Scholars who wish to take courses from the Foundation for Advanced Education in the Sciences (FAES). They also receive allowances for the purchase of textbooks and scientific journals related to their area of research and for travel to scientific meetings.

Duration 1 year, beginning in July or August.

Additional information Research Scholars work as part of a research team in a laboratory at the NIH's main campus in Bethesda, conducting basic research under the mentorship of an NIH senior investigator or preceptor. They learn the latest laboratory techniques and experience the creative thinking involved in at least 1 of the following biomedical areas: biostatistics, cell biology, epidemiology, genetics, immunology, neuroscience, or structural biology. This program is unique in that it does not require students to propose a research project or select a laboratory at the NIH as part of the application process. Instead, Research Scholars are encouraged to take their first couple of weeks in the program to interview investigators and explore different laboratories at the NIH before making a selection. This program is jointly sponsored by the Howard Hughes Medical Institute and the National Institutes of Health—the largest private and public biomedical research institutions in the United States. It complements the HHMI Research Training Fellowships for Medical Students Program; students may not apply to both programs in the same year.

Number awarded Approximately 42 each year.

Deadline January of each year.

[800]
HIGHER EDUCATION RESEARCH EXPERIENCES AT ORNL FOR THESIS RESEARCH

Oak Ridge Institute for Science and Education
Attn: Science and Engineering Education
P.O. Box 117
Oak Ridge, TN 37831-0117
(865) 576-3427   Fax: (865) 241-5219
E-mail: terryc@orau.gov
Web: www.orau.gov/orise.htm

Summary To provide funding to graduate students interested in conducting their thesis research at Oak Ridge National Laboratory (ORNL).

Eligibility This program is open to graduate students who have completed course work and are ready to conduct research for a master's thesis or Ph.D. dissertation. Applicants must be preparing for a career in science, mathematics, engineering, technology, or a related field and have a GPA of 3.0 or higher. They must be interested in conducting research at ORNL, especially in computer science; earth, environmental, and marine sciences; engineering; life, health, and medical sciences; mathematics; or physical sciences. U.S. citizenship or permanent resident status is required.

Financial data Stipends are $525 per week for master's degree students or $550 per week for Ph.D. candidates. Students whose permanent residence is outside a radius of 60 miles from ORNL also receive a $75 per week housing allowance. They may also receive payment of tuition and fees for advanced academic course work and for ORNL research academic credit at the discretion of their research mentor.

Duration 1 year; may be renewed for 1 additional year for master's thesis research or for 2 additional years for Ph.D. dissertation research.

Additional information This program is funded by ORNL and administered by Oak Ridge Institute for Science and Education (ORISE).

Number awarded Varies each year.

Deadline Applications may be submitted at any time.

[801]
HILDEGARD E. PEPLAU, RN SCHOLAR AWARD

American Nurses Foundation
Attn: Nursing Research Grants Program
8515 Georgia Avenue, Suite 400
Silver Spring, MD 20910-3492
(301) 628-5298   Fax: (301) 628-5354
E-mail: anf@ana.org
Web: www.anfonline.org

Summary To provide funding to nurses interested in conducting research on psychiatric-mental health nursing.

Eligibility This program is open to registered nurses who have earned a baccalaureate or higher degree. Applicants may be either beginning or experienced researchers. They must be interested in conducting research on psychiatric-mental health nursing with an interpersonal relations focus. The research outcomes should advance the clinical practice of nursing and contribute to knowledge about psycho-social phenomena in nursing. Proposed research may be for a master's thesis or doctoral dissertation only if the project has been approved by the principal investigator's thesis or dissertation committee.

Financial data The grant is $3,500. Funds may not be used as a salary for the principal investigator.

Duration 1 year.

Additional information This program was established in 1995. There is a $75 application fee.

Number awarded 1 each year.

Deadline April of each year.

[802]
HIRSH AWARD

American College of Legal Medicine
Attn: Student Writing Competition
1111 North Plaza Drive, Suite 550
Schaumburg, IL 60173-4946
(847) 969-0283   Toll-free: (800) 433-9137
Fax: (847) 517-7229   E-mail: info@aclm.org
Web: www.aclm.org/resources/swc.asp

Summary To recognize and reward outstanding original papers on legal medicine written by graduate students in dentistry, podiatry, nursing, pharmacy, health science, health care administration, or public health.

Eligibility This competition is open to currently-enrolled graduate students in health-related areas in the United States or Canada. They are invited to submit an original essay on legal medicine. The topic should stress the interface of law and medicine or law and health care, including delivery. Appropriate topics could address the ethical/moral issues of refusal of treatment, futile treatment, right to die, patient rights, alternative care, or transfer trauma. No paper that has been previously published in any form will be considered. Papers must contain only uncollaborated original work.

Financial data The prize is $1,000.

Duration The prize is given annually.

Additional information All papers submitted are considered for publication in the *Journal of Legal Medicine* or other medical legal publications.

Number awarded 1 each year.

Deadline January of each year.

[803]
HOSPICE AND PALLIATIVE NURSES FOUNDATION END OF LIFE NURSING CARE RESEARCH GRANT

Sigma Theta Tau International
Attn: Research Department
550 West North Street
Indianapolis, IN 46202-3191
(317) 634-8171   Toll-free: (888) 634-7575
Fax: (317) 634-8188   E-mail: research@stti.iupui.edu
Web: www.nursingsociety.org/research/grant_hpnf.html

Summary To provide funding to nurses interested in conducting research on end of life nursing care.

Eligibility This program is open to registered nurses who have a master's or doctoral degree or are enrolled in a doctoral program. Applicants must be interested in conducting a research project, including pilot and/or developmental research, on end of life nursing care. Preference is given to members of Sigma Theta Tau International and/or the Hospice and Palliative Nurses Association.

Financial data The maximum grant is $10,000.

Duration 1 year.

Additional information This program is sponsored jointly by Sigma Theta Tau International and the Hospice and Palliative Nurses Foundation, Penn Center West One, Suite 229, Pittsburgh, PA 15276, (412) 787-9301, Fax: (412) 787-9305, E-mail: hpna@hpna.org.

Number awarded 1 each year.
Deadline March of each year.

[804]
HOWARD HUGHES MEDICAL INSTITUTE RESEARCH TRAINING FELLOWSHIPS FOR MEDICAL STUDENTS

Howard Hughes Medical Institute
Attn: Office of Grants and Special Programs
4000 Jones Bridge Road
Chevy Chase, MD 20815-6789
(301) 215-8889   Toll-free: (800) 448-4882, ext. 8889
Fax: (301) 215-8888   E-mail: fellows@hhmi.org
Web: www.hhmi.org/grants/individuals/medfellows.html

Summary To provide financial assistance to medical students interested in pursuing research training.

Eligibility Applicants must be enrolled in a medical school in the United States, although they may be citizens of any country. They must describe a proposed research project to be conducted at an academic or nonprofit research institution in the United States, other than a facility of the National Institutes of Health in Bethesda, Maryland. Research proposals should reflect the interests of the Howard Hughes Medical Institute (HHMI), especially in biochemistry, bioinformatics, biomedical engineering, biophysics, biostatistics, cell biology, developmental biology, epidemiology, genetics, immunology, mathematical and computational biology, microbiology, molecular biology, neuroscience, pharmacology, physiology, structural biology, and virology. Applications from women and minorities underrepresented in the sciences (Blacks, Hispanics, American Indians, Native Alaskans, and Native Pacific Islanders) are especially encouraged. Students enrolled in M.D./Ph.D., Ph.D., or Sc.D. programs and those who have completed a Ph.D. or Sc.D. in a laboratory-based science are not eligible. Selection is based on the applicant's ability and promise for a research career as a physician-scientist and the quality of training that will be provided.

Financial data Fellows receive a stipend of $25,000 per year; their institution receives an institutional allowance of $5,500 and a research allowance of $5,500.

Duration 1 year.

Additional information This program complements the HHMI-NIH Research Scholars Program; students may not apply to both programs in the same year.

Number awarded Up to 60 each year.
Deadline January of each year.

[805]
HUBERT HUMPHREY RESEARCH GRANT

School Nutrition Association
Attn: Child Nutrition Foundation
700 South Washington Street, Suite 300
Alexandria, VA 22314-4287
(703) 739-3900   Toll-free: (800) 877-8822
Fax: (703) 739-3915   E-mail: cnf@schoolnutrition.org
Web: www.schoolnutrition.org/CNF.aspx?ID=1126

Summary To provide funding to graduate students who wish to conduct research that will advance the knowledge base of school food service and nutrition programs.

Eligibility This program is open to graduate students who are members of the School Nutrition Association (SNA) or supervised on the grant by an active member of SNA, and studying foods and nutrition, food service management, nutrition education, or a related field at an accredited university with a minimum GPA

of 3.0. Applicants must demonstrate competency to conduct a proposed research project applicable to school food service and child nutrition. Selection is based on significance and importance of the research to advance knowledge in the school food service and nutrition profession, understanding of the research problem, appropriateness of the research design and methodology, appropriateness of the budget request, practicality and realism of the timeline to conduct the research, and completeness of the application.

Financial data Awards are at least $2,500.

Duration 1 year.

Additional information Funding for this grant is provided by Lincoln Foodservice Products Company, Inc. The SNA was formerly the American School Food Service.

Number awarded 1 each year.
Deadline April of each year.

[806]
IMPLANT RESEARCH GRANTS

Academy of Osseointegration
Attn: Osseointegration Foundation
85 West Algonquin Road, Suite 550
Arlington Heights, IL 60005-4425
(847) 439-1919   Toll-free: (800) 65-OSSEO
Fax: (847) 439-1569   E-mail: academy.osseo.org
Web: www.osseo.org/resources/grants.htm

Summary To provide funding to dental faculty and students interested in conducting research in the field of dental implants.

Eligibility This program is open to faculty and students at academic dental institutions accredited by the American Dental Association. There are no age or citizenship requirements. Applicants must be interested in conducting research on the basic, clinical, or behavioral aspects of dental implants. Selection is based on the originality and innovativeness of the proposal, appropriateness of the materials and methods of investigation, evidence of sufficient level of support and commitment by the sponsoring institution, duration of the investigation, appropriateness of the budget, and overall scientific merit of the proposal.

Financial data The grant is $10,000. Funds may be used only for direct support of the proposed research. No indirect cost allocation is allowed. The grant may not be used for costs related to degree completion or salary.

Duration 1 year.

Additional information The awardee is required to present the results of the investigation at the annual meeting of the Academy of Osseointegration. Travel funds are provided by the Osseointegration Foundation.

Number awarded 1 each year.
Deadline October of each year.

[807]
INDIANA SPACE GRANT CONSORTIUM GRADUATE FELLOWSHIPS

Indiana Space Grant Consortium
c/o Purdue University
550 Stadium Mall Drive
West Lafayette, IN 47907
(765) 494-5873   Fax: (765) 494-1299
E-mail: bauermm@purdue.edu
Web: www.insgc.org

Summary To provide funding to graduate students at member institutions of the Indiana Space Grant Consortium (INSGC) interested in conducting research related to space.

Eligibility This program is open to graduate students enrolled full time at institutions that are members of the INSGC. Applicants must be working on a master's degree in space-related science or engineering, a doctoral degree in space-related science or engineering, or a doctoral degree in science education. They must be involved in a research project related to the interests of the U.S. National Aeronautics and Space Administration (NASA) in science, technology, engineering, and mathematics (STEM). U.S. citizenship is required. The program encourages representation of women, underrepresented minorities, and persons with disabilities.

Financial data The maximum grant is $5,000 per year for master's degree students or $10,000 for doctoral students.

Duration 1 year; students may not receive an award in consecutive years.

Additional information This program is funded by NASA. The academic member institutions of the INSGC are Purdue University, Ball State University, Indiana University, Indiana University-Purdue University at Indianapolis, Indiana State University, Purdue University at Calumet, Taylor University, University of Evansville, and Valparaiso University.

Number awarded Varies each year.

Deadline December of each year.

[808]
INDIVIDUAL PREDOCTORAL DENTAL SCIENTIST FELLOWSHIPS

National Institute of Dental and Craniofacial Research
Attn: Division of Extramural Research
45 Center Drive, Room 4AS-13B
Bethesda, MD 20892-6401
(301) 496-4263   Fax: (301) 402-7033
TTY: (301) 451-0088   E-mail: Albert.Avila/@nih.gov
Web: www.nidr.nih.gov

Summary To provide financial assistance to dental students who wish to participate in an integrated dental and graduate research training program that leads to both the D.D.S./D.M.D. and Ph.D. degrees.

Eligibility This program is open to U.S. citizens, nationals, and permanent residents who are enrolled in a formal program at an approved dental school that leads to a D.D.S. or D.M.D. degree; have been accepted in a Ph.D. program in dental, oral, and craniofacial health research from the basic, behavioral, and clinical perspectives; and have a confirmed mentor in that scientific field. Applicants may be in the third year of dental school, although preference is given to those in the first or second year. Individuals currently enrolled in a joint D.D.S./D.M.D.-Ph.D. program are eligible for consideration as trainees, but persons who obtained a Ph.D. prior to entering dental school and desire to pursue another research doctorate while in dental school are not eligible. Racial/ethnic minority individuals, women, and persons with disabilities are strongly encouraged to apply.

Financial data The fellowship provides an annual stipend of $20,772, a tuition and fee allowance (60% of costs up to $16,000 or 60% of costs up to $21,000 for dual degrees), and an institutional allowance of $4,200 for travel to scientific meetings and for laboratory and other training expenses.

Duration Up to 5 years of support for predoctoral study or up to 3 years of support at the postdoctoral level.

Number awarded Up to 4 each year.

Deadline April, August, or December of each year.

[809]
INTERNATIONAL STUDENT LEADER AWARDS

Golden Key International Honour Society
621 North Avenue N.E., Suite C-100
Atlanta, GA 30308
(404) 377-2400   Toll-free: (800) 377-2401
Fax: (678) 420-6757   E-mail: scholarships@goldenkey.org
Web: www.goldenkey.org/GKweb/ScholarshipsandAwards

Summary To recognize and reward members of the Golden Key International Honour Society who perform outstanding service to the society, campus, and community.

Eligibility This competition is open to active members of the society worldwide who are currently enrolled in an accredited undergraduate or graduate program. Applicants may apply for the international award, a regional award (for 10 regions within the United States, Canada, South Africa, or the Asia-Pacific region that covers Australia, New Zealand, and Malaysia), or both. Along with their application, they must submit a personal statement of up to 1,000 words explaining why they feel they should receive the award; a detailed list of Golden Key involvement and accomplishments; a list of extracurricular involvement in other organizations, honors and awards received, community service activities, and work experience; and a letter of recommendation from the Golden Key chapter advisor. Selection is based on leadership and involvement in Golden Key (50%), other extracurricular involvement (25%), and academic performance (25%).

Financial data The international award is $1,000; regional awards are $500.

Duration The awards are presented annually.

Number awarded 1 international and 13 regional awards are presented each year.

Deadline May of each year.

[810]
JEAN E. JOHNSON, RN SCHOLAR AWARD

American Nurses Foundation
Attn: Nursing Research Grants Program
8515 Georgia Avenue, Suite 400
Silver Spring, MD 20910-3492
(301) 628-5298   Fax: (301) 628-5354
E-mail: anf@ana.org
Web: www.anfonline.org

Summary To provide funding to nurses interested in conducting research on reducing the impact of physical illness.

Eligibility This program is open to registered nurses who have earned a baccalaureate or higher degree. Applicants may be either beginning or experienced researchers. They must be interested in conducting research on reducing the negative impact of physical illness, especially cancer. Proposed research may be for a master's thesis or doctoral dissertation if the project has been approved by the principal investigator's thesis or dissertation committee.

Financial data The grant is $3,500. Funds may not be used as a salary for the principal investigator.

Duration 1 year.

Additional information This program was established in 1999. There is a $75 application fee.

Number awarded 1 each year.

Deadline April of each year.

[811]
JERALD A. BREITMAN AND STEPHEN J. DORN ENDOWED RESEARCH FELLOWSHIP

American Academy of Physician Assistants
Attn: Physician Assistant Foundation
950 North Washington Street
Alexandria, VA 22314-1552
(703) 519-5686   Fax: (703) 684-1924
E-mail: aapa@aapa.org
Web: www.aapa.org/paf/pafprog.html

Summary To provide funding to doctoral students interested in conducting research on the contributions of physician assistants to medical care.

Eligibility This program is open to doctoral students who intend to devote their career to conducting research on the contributions of physician assistants to medical care. Applicants are not required to be physician assistants and the research does not need to focus exclusively on the physician assistant profession; it must address physician assistant issues and benefit physician assistants and/or the physician assistant profession.

Financial data The grant is $3,000. Funds may be used to 1) offset the cost of fees and tuition, 2) purchase materials for research, or 3) support other direct dissertation-related costs.

Duration Grants must be used within 3 years of the date of the award.

Additional information This program was established in 1998. Recipients must provide an annual summary of progress and expenditures of the grant to date; a final statement of the expenditure of funds and a copy of the completed work; at the conclusion of the research, a statement of how the fellowship has contributed to the candidate's capacity to conduct physician assistant research; and a copy of the dissertation after its completion.

Number awarded 1 each year.

Deadline April of each year.

[812]
JESSUP AWARD

Academy of Natural Sciences of Philadelphia
Attn: Chair, Jessup/McHenry Fund Committee
1900 Benjamin Franklin Parkway
Philadelphia, PA 19103-1195
(215) 299-1000   Fax: (215) 299-1028
Web: www.acnatsci.org/research/jessupinfo.html

Summary To provide funding to pre- and postdoctoral students who are interested in conducting research under the supervision or sponsorship of a member of the curatorial staff of the Academy of Natural Sciences of Philadelphia.

Eligibility These awards are intended to assist predoctoral and recent postdoctoral students. Students commuting within the Philadelphia area are ineligible. Proposed research may be in any specialty in which the Academy's curators have expertise.

Financial data The stipend for subsistence is $300 per week; round-trip travel is reimbursed up to $500 (or $1,000 for travel from outside North America).

Duration From 2 to 16 weeks.

Additional information Recipients are expected to give a seminar after their arrival and are encouraged to publish at least some of the work accomplished at the academy.

Number awarded Varies each year.

Deadline February or September of each year.

[813]
JOHN C. THIEL FACULTY RESEARCH FELLOWSHIP

American Dental Hygienists' Association
Attn: Institute for Oral Health
444 North Michigan Avenue, Suite 3400
Chicago, IL 60611
(312) 440-8918   Toll-free: (800) 243-2342, ext. 244
Fax: (312) 440-8929   E-mail: institute@adha.net
Web: www.adha.org

Summary To provide funding for research to dental hygiene faculty members who are working on a master's degree.

Eligibility This program is open to faculty members (including part-time and adjunct faculty) who have a valid license to practice dental hygiene and are working on a master's degree in dental hygiene or a related field. Applicants must be interested in conducting research on 1 of the following topics: access to care/underserved populations, health promotion and disease prevention, alternative practice settings, and oral health public policy. They must be active members of the American Dental Hygienists' Association (ADHA). Selection is based on demonstrated commitment to dental hygiene education and research and the advancement of the dental hygiene practice.

Financial data The maximum stipend is $5,000.

Duration 1 year; recipients may reapply.

Number awarded 2 each year.

Deadline June of each year.

[814]
JOHN F. GARDE RESEARCH AWARD

American Association of Nurse Anesthetists
Attn: AANA Foundation
222 South Prospect Avenue
Park Ridge, IL 60068-4001
(847) 692-7050, ext. 1171   Fax: (847) 692-7137
E-mail: foundation@aana.com
Web: www.aana.com/foundation/default.asp

Summary To provide funding to student members of the American Association of Nurse Anesthetists who are interested in conducting research.

Eligibility This program is open to nurse anesthesia students in good academic standing who are members of the association. Applicants must be proposing a research project related to their field. Along with their application, they must submit a letter of support from their research advisor and a 100-word statement on how their research impacts nurse anesthesia practice and/or education. Preference is given to CRNAs.

Financial data Grants are currently limited to $1,000.

Duration 1 academic year.

Number awarded 1 each year.

Deadline April of each year.

[815]
JOHN HOPE FRANKLIN DISSERTATION FELLOWSHIP
American Philosophical Society
Attn: Committee on Research
104 South Fifth Street
Philadelphia, PA 19106-3387
(215) 440-3429   Fax: (215) 440-3436
E-mail: lmusumeci@amphilsoc.org
Web: www.amphilsoc.org/grants/johnhopefranklin.htm
Summary To provide funding to African American graduate students conducting research for a doctoral dissertation.
Eligibility This program is open to African American graduate students working on a degree at a Ph.D. granting institution in the United States. Applicants must have completed all course work and examinations preliminary to the doctoral dissertation and be able to devote full-time effort, with no teaching obligations, to researching or writing their dissertation. All fields of study are eligible.
Financial data The grant is $25,000.
Duration 12 months, to begin at the discretion of the grantee.
Additional information This program was established in 2005.
Number awarded 1 each year.
Deadline April of each year.

[816]
JULIA HARDY, RN SCHOLAR AWARDS
American Nurses Foundation
Attn: Nursing Research Grants Program
8515 Georgia Avenue, Suite 400
Silver Spring, MD 20910-3492
(301) 628-5298   Fax: (301) 628-5354
E-mail: anf@ana.org
Web: www.anfonline.org
Summary To provide funding to nurses interested in conducting research on health care systems.
Eligibility This program is open to registered nurses who have earned a baccalaureate or higher degree. Applicants must be experienced researchers who have had more than 3 research-based publications in refereed journals and have received, as a principal investigator, more than $15,000 in extramural funding in any 1 research area. They must be interested in conducting research related to health care systems. Proposed research may be for a master's thesis or doctoral dissertation if the project has been approved by the principal investigator's thesis or dissertation committee.
Financial data The grant is $7,500. Funds may not be used as a salary for the principal investigator.
Duration 1 year.
Additional information There is a $75 application fee.
Number awarded 2 each year.
Deadline April of each year.

[817]
LEININGER TRANSCULTURAL NURSING GRANT AWARD
American Nurses Foundation
Attn: Nursing Research Grants Program
8515 Georgia Avenue, Suite 400
Silver Spring, MD 20910-3492
(301) 628-5298   Fax: (301) 628-5354
E-mail: anf@ana.org
Web: www.anfonline.org
Summary To provide funding to nurses interested in conducting research on immunization.
Eligibility This program is open to registered nurses who have been admitted to a doctoral or master's degree program in nursing and will have a research mentor to guide their research in transcultural nursing. Applicants may be either beginning or experienced researchers. They must be interested in conducting research on transcultural nursing that will use Leininger's Theory of Culture Care or a similar theory.
Financial data The grant is $5,000. Funds may not be used as a salary for the principal investigator.
Duration 1 year.
Additional information There is a $75 application fee.
Number awarded 1 each year.
Deadline April of each year.

[818]
LESBIAN HEALTH FUND GRANTS
Gay and Lesbian Medical Association
Attn: Lesbian Health Fund
459 Fulton Street, Suite 107
San Francisco, CA 94102
(415) 255-4547   Fax: (415) 255-4784
E-mail: lhf@glma.org
Web: www.glma.org
Summary To provide funding to pre- and postdoctoral investigators interested in conducting research related to the health of lesbians.
Eligibility This program is open to investigators interested in conducting research in the following areas: determination of rates and risk factors for cancers and other diseases among lesbians; access to medical care for lesbians; methodological exploration of diversity in the lesbian population; mental health concerns of lesbians and their families; and definition and investigation of lesbian family issues. If the principal investigator is a student, a faculty supervisor must submit a letter of support. Selection is based on research design (40 points), feasibility of accomplishing the project (20 points), investigator's qualifications (15 points), budget justification (10 points), and significance of the project to the lesbian community (15 points).
Financial data Grants range from $500 to $10,000.
Duration 1 year.
Additional information The Lesbian Health Fund (LHF) was established in 1992 to define, study, and educate lesbians and their health care providers about lesbian health issues. Interim 6-month and 12-month reports must be submitted by the principal investigator. Upon completion of the project, the investigator is expected to present the results at a conference selected by LHF. Within 6 months of project completion, the investigator is expected to submit a manuscript to a peer-reviewed journal for publication.

Number awarded Varies each year; recently, 2 of these grants were awarded. Since the program began, it has provided more than $335,000 to support research.
Deadline April or September of each year.

[819]
LILLIAN SHOLTIS BRUNNER SUMMER FELLOWSHIP FOR HISTORICAL RESEARCH IN NURSING

University of Pennsylvania
School of Nursing
Attn: Barbara Bates Center for the Study of the History of Nursing
307 Nursing Education Building
Philadelphia, PA 19104-6096
(215) 898-4502   Fax: (215) 573-2168
E-mail: nhistory@nursing.upenn.edu
Web: www.nursing.upenn.edu

Summary To support pre- and postdoctoral research to be conducted at the Barbara Bates Center for the Study of the History of Nursing in Philadelphia, Pennsylvania during the summer.
Eligibility This program is open to scholars interested in conducting research on the history of nursing at the center. Although postdoctoral candidates are preferred, the fellowship is also available to those at the predoctoral level. Proposals should cover aims, background significance, previous work, methods, facilities needed, other research support needed, budget, and professional accomplishments. Selection is based on evidence of preparation and/or productivity in historical research related to nursing.
Financial data The grant is $2,500.
Duration 6 to 8 weeks during the summer.
Additional information Brunner scholars work under the general direction of nurse historians associated with the center. Scholars must be in residence at the Barbara Bates Center for the Study of the History of Nursing for the duration of the program.
Number awarded 1 each year.
Deadline December of each year.

[820]
LIZETTE PETERSON HOMER MEMORIAL INJURY RESEARCH GRANT

American Psychological Foundation
750 First Street, N.E.
Washington, DC 20002-4242
(202) 336-5843   Fax: (202) 336-5812
E-mail: foundation@apa.org
Web: www.apa.org/apf/homer.html

Summary To provide funding to graduate students interested in conducting research related to the prevention of injuries in children.
Eligibility This program is open to graduate students and faculty interested in conducting research that focuses on the prevention of physical injury in children and young adults through accidents, violence, abuse, or suicide. Applicants must submit a 100-word abstract, description of the project, detailed budget, curriculum vitae, and letter from the supporting faculty supervisor.
Financial data Grants up to $1,000 are available.
Additional information This program, established in 1999, was formerly the Rebecca Routh Coon Injury Research Award. It is supported by Division 54 (the Society of Pediatric Research) of the American Psychological Association and the American Psychological Foundation. Information is also available from

Sharon Berry, Children's Hospital and Clinic, 17-301, 2525 Chicago Avenue South, Minneapolis, MN 55404, (612) 813-6727, Fax: (612) 813-8263, E-mail: sharon.berry@childrenshc.org.
Number awarded 1 or 2 each year.
Deadline March of each year.

[821]
L'OREAL USA FOR WOMEN IN SCIENCE FELLOWSHIP PROGRAM

L'Oréal USA
Attn: Women in Science Fellowship Program
575 Fifth Avenue
New York, NY 10017
(212) 818-1500   E-mail: infoofice@us.loreal.com
Web: www.lorealusa.com/?uid=forwomeninscience

Summary To provide research funding to pre- and postdoctoral women scientists.
Eligibility This program is open to women who are 1) enrolled in the third or fourth year of a Ph.D. program, or 2) postdoctoral researchers. Applicants must have completed or be working on a degree in the natural sciences (biological and physical), engineering, computer science, or mathematics. They must be U.S. citizens, plan to become citizens by the time the awards are announced, or permanent residents.
Financial data The grant is $20,000.
Duration 1 year.
Additional information This program, established in 2003, is sponsored by L'Oréal USA.
Number awarded 5 each year.
Deadline October of each year.

[822]
LOUIS R. OSTERNIG MASTER'S GRANT PROGRAM

National Athletic Trainers' Association
Attn: Research and Education Foundation
2952 Stemmons Freeway, Suite 200
Dallas, TX 75247-6103
(214) 637-6282   Toll-free: (800) TRY-NATA, ext. 147
Fax: (214) 637-2206   E-mail: patsyb@nata.org
Web: www.natafoundation.org/research-progs.html

Summary To provide funding for research to master's degree candidates who are members of the National Athletic Trainers' Association (NATA).
Eligibility Applicants must be current certified members of the association and master's degree students at the institution where they are proposing to conduct research. The proposed research may involve basic science, clinical studies, sports injury epidemiology, or observational studies.
Financial data The grant is $1,000 per year.
Duration 1 year.
Additional information Information is also available from Mark Hoffman, NATA Foundation Research Committee Chair, Oregon State University, Women's Building, Room 107B, Corvallis, OR 97331-3303, (541) 737-6787, Fax: (541) 737-2788, E-mail: mark.hoffman@oregonstate.edu.
Number awarded Varies each year; recently, 11 of these grants were awarded.
Deadline April or October of each year.

[823]
LUCILE V. LUKENS, RN SCHOLAR AWARD

American Nurses Foundation
Attn: Nursing Research Grants Program
8515 Georgia Avenue, Suite 400
Silver Spring, MD 20910-3492
(301) 628-5298   Fax: (301) 628-5354
E-mail: anf@ana.org
Web: www.anfonline.org

Summary To provide funding to nurses interested in conducting research on diabetes and chronic pulmonary disease.

Eligibility This program is open to registered nurses who have earned a baccalaureate or higher degree. Applicants may be either beginning or experienced researchers. Proposed research may be for a master's thesis or doctoral dissertation if the project has been approved by the principal investigator's thesis or dissertation committee. There are no restrictions on the research topic.

Financial data The grant is $10,000. Funds may not be used as a salary for the principal investigator.

Duration 1 year.

Additional information This program was established in 2006. There is a $75 application fee.

Number awarded 1 each year.

Deadline April of each year.

[824]
LUNG HEALTH RESEARCH DISSERTATION GRANTS

American Lung Association
Attn: Grants and Awards
61 Broadway, Sixth Floor
New York, NY 10006
(212) 315-8793   Toll-free: (800) LUNG-USA
Fax: (212) 265-5642   E-mail: emendoza@lungusa.org
Web: www.lungusa.org

Summary To provide funding to doctoral candidates interested in conducting dissertation research on issues relevant to people with lung disease.

Eligibility This program is open to full-time doctoral students in nursing and the social sciences who have an academic career focus. Areas of interest include psychosocial lung health research, behavioral lung health research, health services and health policy research, epidemiological and biostatistical lung health research, and public health education research. Nurses in any field who are interested in lung disease may also apply. Individuals with an M.D. degree who wish to acquire a Ph.D. are not eligible. Generally, individuals conducting laboratory research that does not involve patients or patient data are not eligible. Applicants must be U.S. citizens, permanent residents, or foreign residents authorized to work in the United States and enrolled in a U.S. institution. Selection is based on the applicant's education and experience; the scientific merit, innovation, and feasibility of the research plan and its relevance to the mission of the American Lung Association; and the research environment.

Financial data The grant is $21,000 per year (including up to $16,000 for stipend and $5,000 for research support).

Duration Up to 2 years.

Number awarded 1 or more each year.

Deadline August of each year.

[825]
M. LOUISE CARPENTER GLOECKNER, M.D. SUMMER RESEARCH FELLOWSHIP

Drexel University College of Medicine
Attn: Director, Archives and Special Collections on Women in Medicine
Hagerty Library
33rd and Market Streets
Philadelphia, PA 19104
(215) 895-6661   Fax: (215) 895-6660
E-mail: archives@drexelmed.edu
Web: archives.drexelmed.edu/fellowship.php

Summary To provide funding to scholars and students interested in conducting research during the summer on the history of medicine at the Archives and Special Collections on Women in Medicine at Drexel University in Philadelphia.

Eligibility This program is open to students at all levels, scholars, and general researchers. Applicants must be interested in conducting research utilizing the archives, which emphasize the history of women in medicine, nursing, medical missionaries, the American Medical Women's Association, American Women's Hospital Service, and other women in medicine organizations. Selection is based on research background of the applicant, relevance of the proposed research project to the goals of the applicant, overall quality and clarity of the proposal, appropriateness of the proposal to the holdings of the collection, and commitment of the applicant to the project.

Financial data The grant is $4,000.

Duration 4 to 6 weeks during the summer.

Number awarded 1 each year.

Deadline January of each year.

[826]
MARGRETTA MADDEN STYLES CREDENTIALING SCHOLARS GRANTS

American Nurses Credentialing Center
Attn: Institute for Credentialing Innovation
8515 Georgia Avenue, Suite 400
Silver Spring, MD 20910-3492
Toll-free: (800) 284-2378
Web: www.nursingworld.org/ancc/inside/grants.html

Summary To provide funding to registered nurses interested in conducting research related to credentialing for nurses.

Eligibility This program is open to registered nurses who have earned a baccalaureate or higher degree. Applicants may be either beginning or experienced researchers. They must be interested in conducting research on the relationship of credentialing in nursing to quality outcomes in patient care. Proposed research may be for a master's thesis or doctoral dissertation if the project has been approved by the principal investigator's thesis or dissertation committee.

Financial data The grant is $10,000.

Duration 1 year.

Additional information Applications must be accompanied by a $35 fee.

Number awarded 1 or more each year.

Deadline September of each year.

[827]
MARTHA E. BRILL, RN SCHOLAR AWARD

American Nurses Foundation
Attn: Nursing Research Grants Program
8515 Georgia Avenue, Suite 400
Silver Spring, MD 20910-3492
(301) 628-5298   Fax: (301) 628-5354
E-mail: anf@ana.org
Web: www.anfonline.org

Summary To provide funding to nurses interested in conducting research.

Eligibility This program is open to registered nurses who have earned a baccalaureate or higher degree. Applicants must be beginning researchers who have had no more than 3 research-based publications in refereed journals and have received, as a principal investigator, no more than $15,000 in extramural funding in any 1 research area. Proposed research may be for a master's thesis or doctoral dissertation if the project has been approved by the principal investigator's thesis or dissertation committee. There are no restrictions on the research topic.

Financial data The grant is $10,000. Funds may not be used as a salary for the principal investigator.

Duration 1 year.

Additional information This program was established in 2006. There is a $75 application fee.

Number awarded 1 each year.

Deadline April of each year.

[828]
MEDICAL SCHOLARS PROGRAM

American Diabetes Association
Attn: Research Program Specialist
1701 North Beauregard Street
Alexandria, VA 22311
(703) 549-1500, ext. 2250   Toll-free: (800) DIABETES
Fax: (703) 549-1715   E-mail: mrowan@diabetes.org
Web: www.diabetes.org

Summary To provide funding to medical students interested in diabetes-related clinical investigation or basic research.

Eligibility This program is open to students who have completed at least 2 years of medical school. M.D./Ph.D. students are not eligible. Application must be initiated by a student who has a qualified sponsor. The student's sponsor must hold a faculty position at an accredited medical school in the United States and be a U.S. citizen or have permanent resident status. The sponsor must also be a member of the Professional Section of the American Diabetes Association and should have a demonstrated record of success in conducting research and in working with research trainees. Students should develop a proposal with their sponsors. The entire research protocol may not exceed 2 pages and must include the following: purpose, background, experimental design and methodology, expected results and data analysis, and significance. Selection is based on the proposed research, qualifications of the student and sponsor, and training environment.

Financial data The grant is $30,000; that includes $20,000 as a stipend for the student and up to $10,000 for tuition, laboratory expenses, and grant-related travel. No indirect costs are funded.

Duration 12 months.

Additional information A progress report must be submitted within 12 months. Funds not spent in any award year must be returned to the association. Recipients must conduct their research in the United States or U.S. possessions. Acknowledge-

ment of support from the association must be made in all research publications arising from funds provided by this award.

Number awarded Up to 12 each year.

Deadline January of each year.

[829]
MEDICAL STUDENT EYE RESEARCH FELLOWSHIPS

Research to Prevent Blindness
Attn: Grants Administrator
645 Madison Avenue, 21st Floor
New York, NY 10022-1010
(212) 752-4333   Toll-free: (800) 621-0026
Fax: (212) 688-6231   E-mail: info@rpbusa.org
Web: www.rpbusa.org/grants.htm

Summary To provide funding to medical students interested on conducting eye research.

Eligibility This program is open to students entering their third or fourth year of medical school. Only 1 nomination may be submitted from any department of ophthalmology. Nominations should include 25 copies of a cover letter from the ophthalmology department chair, a brief letter from the principal preceptor, letters of recommendation from faculty members, the nominee's official transcript, and a completed application summary form.

Financial data The stipend is $25,000.

Duration 1 year.

Additional information Under this program, established in 1993, recipients are allowed to take a year off from their medical school studies and devote that time to the conduct of a research project within a department of ophthalmology. While it is hoped that department heads will be able to attract talented students, it is not intended that the program become a vehicle to assure the candidate a future ophthalmologic residency or that the fellowship be utilized simply to provide the services of a technician within the department.

Number awarded Varies each year; recently, 3 of these fellowships were awarded.

Deadline June or December of each year.

[830]
MEDICAL STUDENT SUMMER ORTHOPAEDIC RESEARCH FELLOWSHIPS

Orthopaedic Research and Education Foundation
Attn: Vice President, Grants
6300 North River Road, Suite 700
Rosemont, IL 60018-4261
(847) 384-4348   Fax: (847) 698-7806
E-mail: mcquire@oref.org
Web: www.oref.org

Summary To provide funding to medical students interested in conducting a summer research project.

Eligibility This program is open to medical students who have an interest in orthopedics. Applicants must identify an investigator with an ongoing orthopedic research project who is willing to accept the student as a research assistant and serve as a mentor. Along with their application, they must submit a 1- to 2-paragraph statement on why they are interested in orthopedic research at this time in their career.

Financial data The stipend is $2,500. The institution receives $200 as reimbursement for FICA taxes and up to $200 for supplies, but no other fringe benefits are authorized.

Duration 8 weeks during the summer.

Number awarded Varies each year; recently, 6 of these fellowships were awarded.
Deadline February of each year.

[831]
MEDICAL STUDENT TRAINING IN HUMAN IMMUNOLOGY

Charles A. Dana Foundation
Attn: Grants Office
745 Fifth Avenue, Suite 900
New York, NY 10151
(212) 223-4040   Fax: (212) 317-8721
E-mail: danainfo@dana.org
Web: www.dana.org

Summary To provide funding to medical students interested in research training in immunology.
Eligibility This program is open to medical students preparing for a research career in clinical immunology with a patient-oriented emphasis. Students must be recommended by an investigator who has received support for immunological research from the foundation and has agreed to serve as a mentor. The candidate can be either from the medical school at the investigator's institution or from another medical school.
Financial data The stipend is $35,000 per year.
Duration 1 year; may be renewed for 1 additional year.
Number awarded Varies each year.

[832]
MEDICAL STUDENTS SUMMER FELLOWSHIPS

American Parkinson Disease Association Inc.
135 Parkinson Avenue
Staten Island, NY 10305
(718) 981-8001   Toll-free: (800) 223-2732
Fax: (718) 981-4399   E-mail: apda@apdaparkinson.org
Web: www.apdaparkinson.org

Summary To provide funding to medical students interested in conducting research on Parkinson's disease during the summer.
Eligibility This program is open to full-time medical students who are interested in conducting supervised laboratory or clinical research related to Parkinson's disease (its nature, manifestations, etiology, or treatment). The proposed research must be conducted at an academic medical center or recognized research institute in the United States and be sponsored by a full-time faculty member or established institute scientist. Both laboratory and clinical research are eligible.
Financial data The stipend is $4,000; one half is paid at the outset of the project and the balance upon submission of a final report.
Duration Summer months.
Number awarded 2 each year.
Deadline December of each year.

[833]
MEDTRONICS PHYSIO-CONTROL AACN SMALL PROJECTS GRANTS

American Association of Critical-Care Nurses
Attn: Research Department
101 Columbia
Aliso Viejo, CA 92656-4109
(949) 362-2050, ext. 321
Toll-free: (800) 394-5995, ext. 321   Fax: (949) 362-2020
E-mail: research@aacn.org
Web: www.aacn.org

Summary To provide funding to members of the American Association of Critical-Care Nurses (AACN) who wish to conduct research on acute myocardial infarction or resuscitation.
Eligibility Registered nurses who are regular or affiliated members of the association may apply for these grants. They must be proposing to conduct research related to patient education, competency-based education, staff development, CQI projects, outcomes evaluation, or small clinical research studies. Topics should focus on aspects of acute myocardial infarction, cardiac resuscitation, use of defibrillation, synchronized cardioversion, non-invasive pacing, or interpretive 12-lead electrocardiogram. Funds may be awarded for new projects, projects in progress, or projects required for an academic degree. Collaborative projects are encouraged and may involve interdisciplinary teams, multiple nursing units, home health, subacute and transitional care, other institutions, or community agencies.
Financial data The maximum grant is $1,500. Funds may be used to cover direct project expenses, such as printed materials, small equipment, supplies (including computer software), and assistive personnel. They may not be used for salaries or institutional overhead.
Additional information Funds for these grants are provided by the Medtronic Physio-Control Corporation.
Number awarded 1 each year.
Deadline June of each year.

[834]
MENTAL HEALTH DISSERTATION RESEARCH GRANTS TO INCREASE DIVERSITY IN THE MENTAL HEALTH RESEARCH ARENA

National Institute of Mental Health
Attn: Division of Extramural Activities
6001 Executive Boulevard, Room 6138
Bethesda, MD 20892-9609
(301) 443-3534   Fax: (301) 443-4720
TTY: (301) 451-0088   E-mail: armstrda@mail.nih.gov
Web: www.nimh.nih.gov

Summary To provide financial support to doctoral candidates from underrepresented groups planning to prepare for a research career in any area relevant to mental health and/or mental disorders.
Eligibility This program is open to doctoral candidates conducting dissertation research in a field related to mental health and/or mental disorders at a university, college, or professional school with an accredited doctoral degree granting program. Applicants must be 1) members of an ethnic or racial group that has been determined by their institution to be underrepresented in biomedical or behavioral research; 2) individuals with disabilities; or 3) individuals from socially, culturally, economically, or educationally disadvantaged backgrounds that have inhibited their ability to prepare for a career in health-related research. They must be U.S. citizens, nationals, or permanent residents.

Financial data Grants provide up to $35,000 per year in direct costs. Facilities and administrative costs are limited to 8% of direct costs.

Duration Up to 2 years.

Number awarded Varies each year.

Deadline April, August, or December of each year.

[835]
MENTOR REHABILITATION NURSING RESEARCH GRANTS

Association of Rehabilitation Nurses
Attn: Rehabilitation Nursing Foundation
4700 West Lake Avenue
Glenview, IL 60025-1485
(847) 375-4710   Toll-free: (800) 229-7530
Fax: (877) 734-9384   E-mail: info@rehabnurse.org
Web: www.rehabnurse.org/research/researchgrants.hmtl

Summary To provide funding to nursing graduate students and professionals interested in conducting research into bladder management, urinary dysfunction, and bladder cancer.

Eligibility The principal investigator for the research project must be a registered nurse who is active in rehabilitation or who has demonstrated interest in and significant contributions to rehabilitation nursing. Membership in the Association of Rehabilitation Nurses is not required. Graduate students may apply. Research proposals that address the clinical, educational, or administrative dimensions of bladder management, urinary dysfunction, and bladder cancer are requested.

Financial data Up to $13,500 per year is available and may be awarded in the form of multiple grants.

Duration The project must be completed within 2 years.

Additional information Funding for this program is provided by Mentor HealthCare, Inc.

Number awarded 1 or more each year.

Deadline January of each year.

[836]
MICHAEL PESSIN STROKE LEADERSHIP PRIZE

American Academy of Neurology
Attn: Customer Service
1080 Montreal Avenue
St. Paul, MN 55116-2325
(651) 695-2724   Toll-free: (800) 879-1960
Fax: (651) 695-2791   E-mail: memberservices@aan.com
Web: www.aan.com

Summary To recognize and reward future or emerging stroke neurologists who have demonstrated an active involvement in providing patients with the highest quality of compassionate care.

Eligibility This program is open to medical students, residents, fellows, and junior faculty members involved in or considering a career in neurology, emphasizing the care of stroke patients. Applicants must be no more than 5 years from completion of their most recent training program and hold an academic rank no higher than assistant professor. Special consideration is given to those involved in clinical research, aimed at enhancing the understanding of stroke or improving acute treatment protocols.

Financial data The award consists of $1,500 and a certificate of recognition.

Duration The prize is awarded annually.

Additional information This award was established in 1998.

Number awarded 1 each year.

Deadline October of each year.

[837]
MIDWEST NURSING RESEARCH SOCIETY/AMERICAN NURSES FOUNDATION SCHOLAR AWARD PROGRAM

American Nurses Foundation
Attn: Nursing Research Grants Program
8515 Georgia Avenue, Suite 400
Silver Spring, MD 20910-3492
(301) 628-5298   Fax: (301) 628-5354
E-mail: anf@ana.org
Web: www.anfonline.org

Summary To provide funding to members of the Midwest Nursing Research Society (MNRS) who are interested in conducting research.

Eligibility This program is open to registered nurses who have earned a baccalaureate or higher degree. Applicants may be either beginning or experienced researchers. Proposed research may be for a master's thesis or doctoral dissertation if the project has been approved by the principal investigator's thesis or dissertation committee. There are no restrictions on the research topic, but applicants must be current MNRS members.

Financial data The grant is $5,000. Funds may not be used as a salary for the principal investigator.

Duration 1 year.

Additional information Funding for this program is provided by the MNRS. There is a $75 application fee.

Number awarded 1 each year.

Deadline April of each year.

[838]
MINNIE L. MAFFETT FELLOWSHIPS

Texas Federation of Business and Professional Women's Foundation, Inc.
Attn: TFBPW Foundation
803 Forest Ridge Drive, Suite 207
Bedford, TX 76022
(817) 283-0862   Fax: (817) 283-0872
E-mail: bpwtx@swbell.net
Web: www.bpwtx.org/foundation.asp

Summary To provide financial assistance to women in Texas interested in conducting research or continuing their education in a medical field.

Eligibility This program is open to 1) women graduates of Texas medical schools interested in postgraduate or research work; 2) women who have been awarded a Ph.D. degree from a Texas university and are doing research in a medical field; 3) women who need financial aid for the first year in establishing a family practice in a rural area of Texas with a population of less than 5,000; and 4) fourth-year women medical students who are completing an M.D. or O.D. degree in an accredited medical school in Texas.

Financial data The stipend recently was $1,500.

Duration 1 year; nonrenewable.

Additional information This program was established in 1948.

Number awarded Varies each year; recently, 3 of these fellowships were awarded.

Deadline January of each year.

[839]
MINORITY MEDICAL STUDENT AWARD PROGRAM OF THE AMERICAN SOCIETY OF HEMATOLOGY

American Society of Hematology
Attn: Award Program Coordinator
1900 M Street, N.W., Suite 200
Washington, DC 20036
(202) 776-0544, ext. 1168   Fax: (202) 776-0545
E-mail: ASH@hematology.org
Web: www.hematology.org/education/awards/mmsap.cfm

Summary To provide an opportunity for underrepresented minority medical students to conduct a research project in hematology.

Eligibility This program is open to medical students enrolled in D.O., M.D., or M.D./Ph.D. programs in the United States or Canada who are members of minority groups. For purposes of this program, minority is defined as those groups that the sponsor has identified as underrepresented in the field of hematology related to biomedical, behavioral, clinical, or social science research, including racial/ethnic minorities and persons from disadvantaged socioeconomic groups. Applicants must be interested in conducting a research project in hematology with a mentor who focuses on the research experience and another mentor who serves as an adviser. Mentors must be members of the American Society of Hematology (ASH) and the advisory mentor must be from a minority group. Students self-identify themselves as minorities. Along with their application, they must submit a brief essay on their interest in learning more about hematology and hematology research. U.S. or Canadian citizenship or permanent resident status is required.

Financial data The grant includes $5,000 for research support and an additional $2,000 to support travel to the annual meeting of the ASH. During subsequent years of medical school and residency, travel support of $1,000 for the annual meeting is also provided. Research mentors receive an allowance for supplies of $2,000 and a travel allowance of $1,000 if they accompany the student to the ASH annual meeting. Advisory mentors receive a $1,000 travel allowance every time they accompany the student to an ASH annual meeting.

Duration 8 to 12 weeks.

Additional information This program is supported by Genentech BioOncology.

Number awarded Up to 10 each year.

Deadline March of each year.

[840]
MINORITY MEDICAL STUDENT SUMMER EXTERNSHIP IN ADDICTION PSYCHIATRY

American Psychiatric Association
Attn: Department of Minority and National Affairs
1000 Wilson Boulevard, Suite 1825
Arlington, VA 22209-3901
(703) 907-8653   Toll-free: (888) 35-PSYCH
Fax: (703) 907-7852   E-mail: mking@psych.org
Web: www.psych.org

Summary To provide funding to minority medical students who are interested in working on a summer project with a mentor who specializes in addiction psychiatry.

Eligibility This program is open to minority medical students who have a specific interest in services related to substance abuse treatment and prevention. Minorities include American Indians, Alaska Natives, Native Hawaiians, Asian Americans, Hispanic/Latinos, and African Americans. Applicants must be interested in working with a mentor who specializes in addiction psychiatry. Work settings provide an emphasis on working clinically with or studying underserved minority populations and issues of co-occurring disorders, substance abuse treatment, and mental health disparity. Most of them are in inner-city or rural settings.

Financial data Externships provide $1,500 for travel expenses to go to the work setting of the mentor and up to another $1,500 for out-of-pocket expenses directly related to the conduct of the externship.

Duration 1 month during the summer.

Additional information Funding for this program is provided by the Substance Abuse and Mental Health Services Administration (SAMHSA).

Number awarded 10 each year.

Deadline February of each year.

[841]
MINORITY VISITING STUDENT AWARDS PROGRAM

Smithsonian Institution
Attn: Office of Research Training and Services
470 L'Enfant Plaza, Suite 7102, MRC 902
P.O. Box 37012
Washington, DC 20013-7012
(202) 633-7070   Fax: (202) 275-0489
E-mail: siofg@si.edu
Web: www.si.edu/ofg/fell.htm

Summary To provide funding to minority graduate students interested in conducting research at the Smithsonian Institution.

Eligibility This program is open to members of U.S. minority groups underrepresented in Smithsonian scholarly programs. Applicants must be advanced graduate students interested in conducting research in the Institution's disciplines and in the museum field.

Financial data Students receive a grant of $400 per week.

Duration Up to 10 weeks.

Additional information Recipients carry out independent research projects in association with the Smithsonian's research staff. Fellows are required to be in residence at the Smithsonian for the duration of the fellowship.

Number awarded Varies each year.

Deadline January of each year for summer and fall residency; September of each year for spring residency.

[842]
MORTAR AND PESTLE PROFESSIONALISM AWARD

American Pharmacists Association
Attn: Academy of Student Pharmacists
1100 15th Street, N.W., Suite 400
Washington, DC 20005
Toll-free: (800) 237-2742, ext. 7586   Fax: (202) 628-0443
E-mail: jathay@aphanet.org
Web: www.aphanet.org

Summary To recognize and reward pharmacy students who demonstrate outstanding performance in pharmacy administration and who submit outstanding essays.

Eligibility This program is open to pharmacy students in their senior year of an entry-level degree program who are nominated by the dean of their school or college. Nominees must have demonstrated exceptional service and commitment to the profession of pharmacy through involvement in professional organizations and other extracurricular learning opportunities. They must be members of the Academy of Student Pharmacists of the American Pharmacists Association (APhA-ASP). The students selected by their schools are then eligible to compete in an essay contest judged by the editors of leading pharmacy journals.

Financial data The winner of the essay contest receives a laminated plaque and a $2,000 scholarship to be applied toward continuing education in pharmacy.

Duration The awards are presented annually.

Additional information This program was originally established in the early 1980s and given its current format in 1995. It is sponsored by McNeil Consumer and Health Care.

Number awarded 1 scholarship winner is selected each year.

Deadline Nominations must be submitted by May of each year. Students must submit their essays by August.

[843]
MRC-SOT YOUNG INVESTIGATOR AWARD

Society of Toxicology-Midwest Regional Chapter
c/o Susan L. Schantz
University of Illinois at Urbana-Champaign
College of Veterinary Medicine
Department of Veterinary Biosciences
2001 South Lincoln Avenue
Urbana, IL 61802
(217) 333-6230   Fax: (217) 244-1652
E-mail: schantz@uiuc.edu
Web: www.toxicology.org/isot/rc/midwest/index.htm

Summary To provide financial assistance for research training in fields related to toxicology to undergraduate and graduate students at universities in the area served by the Midwest Regional Chapter of the Society of Toxicology (MRC-SOT).

Eligibility This program is open to students enrolled at universities in the MRC-SOT region, which covers Illinois, Wisconsin, and portions of eastern Iowa. Applicants must be either 1) undergraduates majoring in the life sciences, or 2) enrolled in a graduate degree program related to the field of toxicology (e.g., a biomedical, environmental, or nutritional program). They must be proposing to conduct research related to the toxicological sciences, including (but not limited to) regulatory toxicology, environmental toxicology, carcinogenesis, cellular and molecular toxicology, teratology, genetic toxicology, or immunotoxicology. Along with their application, they must include a statement describing how the proposed research project offers them an opportunity to develop research skills and knowledge leading to a research career in the toxicological sciences.

Financial data The grant is $1,500. Funds may be used at the discretion of the recipient for costs associated with toxicological training, education, and research.

Duration 1 year.

Number awarded 1 each year.

Deadline March of each year.

[844]
MWH FELLOWSHIP FOR ADVANCED WATER/WASTEWATER TREATMENT TECHNOLOGIES

National Water Research Institute
Attn: Fellowship Program
10500 Ellis Avenue
P.O. Box 20865
Fountain Valley, CA 92728-0865
(714) 378-3278   Fax: (714) 378-3375
E-mail: fellow@nwri-usa.org
Web: www.nwri-usa.org

Summary To provide funding to graduate students interested in conducting research on advanced water and wastewater technologies.

Eligibility This program is open to full-time graduate students interested in conducting research on the development of novel and innovative advanced water and wastewater treatment, disinfection, or oxidation technologies. These technologies should address the need to create new sources of water supply from impaired and nontraditional water sources. Research areas include, but are not limited to, engineering, physical and chemical sciences, biological sciences, health sciences, political sciences, economics, and planning and public policy that are related to water and/or water resources. Preference is given to doctoral candidates, but outstanding students in master's programs may be considered. Applicants must submit a letter of inquiry describing the importance of the research to them and the water community, how their research will contribute to water science in general, what they expect to accomplish, and how their research relates to the mission of the National Water Research Institute (NWRI) to create new sources of water through research and technology and to protect the freshwater and marine environments.

Financial data The grant is $10,000 per year.

Duration 2 years.

Additional information This fellowship is jointly sponsored by the NWRI and MWH, an environmental consulting firm based in Broomfield, Colorado.

Number awarded 1 each year.

Deadline February of each year.

[845]
NAPNAP FOUNDATION GRADUATE STUDENT RESEARCH AWARD

National Association of Pediatric Nurse Practitioners
Attn: NAPNAP Foundation
20 Brace Road, Suite 200
Cherry Hill, NJ 08034-2633
(856) 857-9700   Toll-free: (877) 662-7627
Fax: (856) 857-1600   E-mail: info@napnap.org
Web: www.napnap.org

Summary To provide funding to graduate student members of the National Association of Pediatric Nurse Practitioners (NAPNAP) who are interested in conducting research.

Eligibility This program is open to graduate student members of the association who are interested in conducting research related to pediatric nursing. The proposed research should deal with a significant problem regarding children and families.

Financial data The maximum grant is $1,000.

Duration 1 year.

Number awarded 1 each year.

Deadline March of each year.

[846]
NASA SPACE PHYSIOLOGY RESEARCH GRANTS

American College of Sports Medicine
Attn: Research Administration and Programs Office
401 West Michigan Street
P.O. Box 1440
Indianapolis, IN 46206-1440
(317) 637-9200, ext. 143   Fax: (317) 634-7817
E-mail: jsenior@acsm.org
Web: www.acsm.org

Summary   To provide funding for research to doctoral students who are members of the American College of Sports Medicine (ACSM).

Eligibility   This program is open to doctoral students enrolled full time in programs in sports medicine or exercise science. Applicants must be U.S. citizens and current members of ACSM interested in conducting research in the areas of exercise, weightlessness, and musculoskeletal physiology.

Financial data   The grant is $5,000 per year.

Duration   1 year.

Additional information   Funding for this program is provided by the U.S. National Aeronautics and Space Administration (NASA).

Number awarded   2 each year.

Deadline   January of each year.

[847]
NASN DIRECTED RESEARCH GRANTS

National Association of School Nurses
Attn: NASN Research Committee
163 U.S. Route 1
P.O. Box 1300
Scarborough, ME 04070-1300
(207) 883-2117   Toll-free: (877) NASN-4SN
Fax: (207) 883-2683   E-mail: nasn@nasn.org
Web: www.nasn.org

Summary   To provide funding to members of the National Association of School Nurses (NASN) who are interested in conducting research on specified school nursing issues.

Eligibility   This program is open to qualified professional school nurses who have been members of the association for at least 1 year. Applicants must be 1) engaged in the practice of school nursing, the education of school nurses, or the study of school nursing as a graduate or undergraduate student; or 2) retired from school nursing. They must be interested in conducting research on 1 of several topics that are selected annually by the association as research priorities. Recently, the topics were mental health issues for students and/or staff; chronic health conditions in students; contemporary and emergent health issues; and factors affecting student success. Selection is based on research question and purpose (5%), study aim and hypothesis (10%), background/review of literature/theoretical discussion (15%), methodology (35%), significance to school nursing (15%), qualifications of the researcher (15%), and overall quality of application (5%).

Financial data   Grants range up to $5,000 and average $2,500.

Duration   1 year.

Additional information   This program, originally called the Carol Costante Research Grant, began in 1998. Information is also available from NASN's western office, 1416 Park Street, Suite A, Castle Rock, CO 80109, (303) 663-2329, (866) 627-6767, Fax: (303) 663-0403.

Number awarded   1 to 3 each year.

Deadline   February of each year.

[848]
NATA DOCTORAL RESEARCH GRANTS

National Athletic Trainers' Association
Attn: Research and Education Foundation
2952 Stemmons Freeway, Suite 200
Dallas, TX 75247-6103
(214) 637-6282   Toll-free: (800) TRY-NATA, ext. 147
Fax: (214) 637-2206   E-mail: patsyb@nata.org
Web: www.natafoundation.org/research-progs.html

Summary   To provide funding for research to doctoral candidates who are members of the National Athletic Trainers' Association (NATA).

Eligibility   Applicants must be current certified members of the association and doctoral candidates at the institution where they are proposing to conduct research. The proposed research may involve basic science, clinical studies, sports injury epidemiology, or observational studies. Preference is given to research proposals in designated areas, recently, topical heat therapy.

Financial data   The grant is $2,500 per year.

Duration   1 year.

Additional information   Information is also available from Mark Hoffman, NATA Foundation Research Committee Chair, Oregon State University, Women's Building, Room 107B, Corvallis, OR 97331-3303, (541) 737-6787, Fax: (541) 737-2788, E-mail: mark.hoffman@oregonstate.edu.

Number awarded   Varies each year; recently, 4 of these grants were awarded.

Deadline   February of each year.

[849]
NATIONAL ASSOCIATION OF SCHOOL NURSES RESEARCH GRANTS

National Association of School Nurses
Attn: NASN Research Committee
163 U.S. Route 1
P.O. Box 1300
Scarborough, ME 04070-1300
(207) 883-2117   Toll-free: (877) NASN-4SN
Fax: (207) 883-2683   E-mail: nasn@nasn.org
Web: www.nasn.org

Summary   To provide funding to members of the National Association of School Nurses (NASN) who are interested in conducting research on a school nursing issue.

Eligibility   This program is open to qualified professional school nurses who have been members of the association for at least 1 year. Applicants must be 1) engaged in the practice of school nursing, the education of school nurses, or the study of school nursing as a graduate or undergraduate student; or 2) retired from school nursing. They must be interested in conducting a research project on any topic that has an impact on student health and well being. Selection is based on research question and purpose (5%), study aim and hypothesis (10%), background/review of literature/theoretical discussion (15%), methodology (35%), significance to school nursing (15%), qualifications of the researcher (15%), and overall quality of application (5%).

Financial data   Grants range up to $5,000 and average $2,500.

Duration   1 year.

Additional information   This program was established in 1997 by combining 3 prior programs: the Lillian Wald Research Award, established in 1982 for research impacting the health of children; the Pauline Fenelon Research Award, established in 1987 for research in school nurse practice issues; and the Lina Rogers Award, established in 1990 for research impacting school nursing services for students. Information is also available from NASN's western office, 1416 Park Street, Suite A, Castle Rock, CO 80109, (303) 663-2329, (866) 627-6767, Fax: (303) 663-0403.

Number awarded 1 or more each year.

Deadline February of each year.

[850]
NELL I. MONDY FELLOWSHIP

Sigma Delta Epsilon-Graduate Women in Science, Inc.
c/o Jennifer Ingram, Fellowships Coordinator
Duke University-Department of Medicine
Box 2641, 275 MSRB, Research Drive
Durham, NC 27710
(919) 668-1439   E-mail: fellowshipsquestions@gwis.org
Web: www.gwis.org/grants/default.htm

Summary To provide funding to women interested in conducting research in the United States or abroad in the natural sciences.

Eligibility The program is open to women in the United States and Canada who are doing graduate or postdoctoral work in the natural sciences (defined to include anthropology, computer sciences, environmental sciences, life sciences, mathematics, psychology, physical sciences, and statistics). Preference is given to students working in the areas of food science, nutrition, and toxicology. Applicants must give evidence of outstanding ability and promise in scientific research. They may be proposing to conduct research at an institution in the United States or abroad. Along with their application, they must submit a brief description of relevant personal factors, including financial need, that should be considered in the selection process. Applicants must either be members of Sigma Delta Epsilon–Graduate Women in Science or include a processing fee of $20 (the cost of a 1-year membership).

Financial data Grants range up to $3,000. The funds must be used for scientific research, including professional travel costs. They may not be used for tuition, child care, travel to professional meetings or to begin a new appointment, administrative overhead or indirect costs, personal computers, living allowances, or equipment of general use.

Duration 1 year; may be renewed in unusual circumstances, contingent upon receipt of an annual progress report.

Additional information This fellowship was first awarded in 2002.

Number awarded 1 each year.

Deadline January of each year.

[851]
NEVADA SPACE GRANT CONSORTIUM GRADUATE FELLOWSHIP PROGRAM

Nevada Space Grant Consortium
c/o University of Nevada at Reno
Mackay School of Mines Building, Room 308
MS 168
Reno, NV 89557
(775) 784-6261   Fax: (775) 327-2235
E-mail: nvsg@mines.unr.edu
Web: www.unr.edu/spacegrant

Summary To provide financial assistance for space-related study or research to graduate students at institutions that are members of the University and Community College System of Nevada (UCCSN) and participate in the Nevada Space Grant Consortium (NSGC).

Eligibility This program is open to graduate students at UCCSN member institutions. Applicants must be working on a degree in an aerospace-related field (including engineering, mathematics, physical and life sciences, and technology) that will prepare them for a career in aerospace science, technology, and related fields. They must be U.S. citizens, be enrolled full time (or accepted for full-time study), present a proposed study or research plan related to aerospace, include in the research or activity plan an extramural experience at a field center of the U.S. National Aeronautics and Space Administration (NASA), plan to be involved in NSGC outreach activities, not receive other federal funds, and intend to prepare for a career in a field of interest to NASA. Members of underrepresented groups (African Americans, Hispanics, American Indians, Pacific Islanders, people with physical disabilities, and women of all races) who have an interest in aerospace fields are encouraged to apply. Selection is based on the academic qualifications of the applicant, the quality of the proposed research program or plan of study and its relevant to NASA's aerospace science and technology program, the quality of the approach to achieving the objectives of the proposed utilization of a NASA center in carrying out the objectives of the program, the prospects for completion of the project within the allotted time, and the applicant's motivation for an aerospace career.

Financial data The grant is $22,500, including $16,000 as a stipend for the student and $6,500 for tuition and a student research and travel allowance.

Duration 12 months; may be renewed up to 24 additional months.

Additional information Funding for this program is provided by NASA.

Number awarded Varies each year; recently, 3 of these awards were granted.

Deadline March of each year.

[852]
NEW HAMPSHIRE SPACE GRANT CONSORTIUM PROJECT SUPPORT

New Hampshire Space Grant Consortium
c/o University of New Hampshire
Institute for the Study of Earth, Oceans, and Space
Morse Hall
39 College Road
Durham, NH 03824-3525
(603) 862-0094   Fax: (603) 862-1915
E-mail: nhspacegrant@unh.edu
Web: www.nhsgc.sr.unh.edu

Summary To provide financial assistance to students at member institutions of the New Hampshire Space Grant Consortium (NHSGC) who are interested in participating in space-related activities.

Eligibility This program is open to students at member institutions of the NHSGC. Applicants must be studying space physics, astrophysics, astronomy, or aspects of computer science, engineering, earth sciences, ocean sciences, atmospheric sciences, or life sciences that utilize space technology and/or adopt a planetary view of the global environment. U.S. citizenship is required. The New Hampshire Space Grant Consortium is a component of the U.S. National Aeronautics and Space Administration (NASA) Space Grant program, which encourages participation by women, underrepresented minorities, and persons with disabilities.

Financial data The amount of the award depends on the nature of the project.

Duration From 1 quarter to 1 year.

Additional information This program is funded by NASA. Currently, projects operating through this program include space grant fellowships at the University of New Hampshire, Agnes M. Lindsay Trust/NASA Challenge Scholars Initiative at the New Hampshire Community Technical College System, Presidential Scholars Research Assistantships at Dartmouth College, and Women in Science Internships at Dartmouth.

Number awarded Varies each year.

Deadline Each participating college or university sets its own deadline.

[853]
NORTH DAKOTA SPACE GRANT PROGRAM FELLOWSHIPS

North Dakota Space Grant Program
c/o University of North Dakota
Department of Space Studies
Clifford Hall, Fifth Floor
P.O. Box 9008
Grand Forks, ND 58202-9008
(701) 777-4856   Toll-free: (800) 828-4274
Fax: (701) 777-3711   E-mail: bieri@space.edu
Web: www.space.edu/spacegrant/fellowships.html

Summary To provide funding for space-related research to undergraduate and graduate students at public and tribal academic institutions in North Dakota.

Eligibility This program is open to undergraduate and graduate students at tribal or public 2-year and 4-year institutions of higher education in North Dakota who have a GPA of 3.0 or higher. U.S. citizenship is required. Applicants must be working on a degree in an area of science, technology, engineering, or mathematics (STEM) that is relevant to the interests of the U.S. National Aeronautics and Space Administration (NASA). They are required to conduct a science research project under the supervision of a faculty advisor. Acceptable majors include, but are not limited to, astronomy, atmospheric science, biology, chemistry, engineering, geology, mathematics, nursing, physics, and space studies. A goal of the program is to encourage members of underrepresented groups (women, minorities, and persons with disabilities) to enter STEM fields of study. Selection is based on academic excellence and relevance of the student's disciplines and interests to STEM.

Financial data The undergraduate stipend is $2,000 per semester. Graduate students receive a quarter-time appointment as a graduate research assistant (GRA); the GRA appointment must include a tuition waiver as a match.

Duration 1 semester; may be renewed for 1 additional semester.

Additional information This program is funded by NASA. Recipients are required to submit a 10- to 15-page paper on their research at the end of the semester.

Number awarded Varies each year.

Deadline September of each year for fall semester; November of each year for spring semester.

[854]
NOVA FOUNDATION RESEARCH GRANT

Nurses Organization of Veterans Affairs
Attn: NOVA Foundation
1726 M Street, N.W., Suite 1101
Washington, DC 20036
(202) 296-0888   Fax: (202) 833-1577
E-mail: nova@vanurse.org
Web: www.vanurse.org/researchgrant.html

Summary To provide funding to graduate students and nurses interested in conducting research related to PTSD among returning military personnel from Iraq or Afghanistan.

Eligibility Applicants must be interested in conducting a nursing research project related to PTSD among returning military personnel from Iraq and Afghanistan. Master's theses, doctoral dissertations, and pilot projects are considered.

Financial data The grant is $5,000.

Duration 1 year.

Additional information This program is offered in collaboration with the DAV Charitable Trust.

Number awarded 1 each year.

Deadline March of each year.

[855]
NOVO NORDISK PHARMACY PRACTICE DIABETES PROGRAM FOR PROFESSIONAL DEGREE PHARMACY STUDENTS

American Association of Colleges of Pharmacy
Attn: Director of Development
1426 Prince Street
Alexandria, VA 22314-2841
(703) 739-2330, ext. 1036   Fax: (703) 836-8982
E-mail: aconnelly@aacp.org
Web: www.aacp.org

Summary To provide funding to professional degree pharmacy students who wish to explore pharmacist-initiated treatments/interventions that could influence the management of diabetes.

Eligibility This program is open to students who are registered in a Pharm.D. degree program and have completed at least 2 years of college course work. Enrollees in dual degree programs (e.g., Pharm.D./M.S., Pharm.D./Ph.D., Pharm.D./M.B.A.) are ineligible. Applicants must be proposing to investigate the effect of pharmacist education, monitoring, interventions, or ancillary treatments on the management of persons with diabetes in the ambulatory/retail pharmacy practice environment. They must be teamed with a faculty mentor. U.S. citizenship or permanent resident status is required.

Financial data The grant is $5,000, including $4,500 for student stipend plus $500 for supplies or travel to a pharmacy association meeting.

Duration 1 year, beginning with the summer or fall semester.

Additional information Funding for this program is provided by Novo Nordisk Pharmaceuticals, Inc.

Number awarded 2 each year.

Deadline March of each year.

[856]
NP DOCTORAL DISSERTATION RESEARCH GRANT

American Academy of Nurse Practitioners
Attn: AANP Foundation
P.O. Box 10729
Glendale, AZ 85318-0729
(623) 376-9467   Fax: (623) 376-0369
E-mail: foundation@aanp.org
Web: www.aanpfoundation.org

Summary To provide funding to members of the American Academy of Nurse Practitioners (AANP) who wish to conduct research for a doctoral degree project.

Eligibility This program is open to current student and full members of the academy who are working on a doctoral degree and their dissertation research. Applicants must be a currently licensed, practicing nurse practitioner (NP) in the United States and the principal investigator on a research project that is to be used for their degree program. Their GPA in their doctoral program must be 3.75 or higher. The research must have an evidence-based and/or outcomes-based primary care focus relevant to health care provided by NPs within the United States.

Financial data The grant is $2,000. Funds must be used for the proposed research, not tuition expenses.

Duration 1 year.

Additional information The AANP Foundation was established in 1998. Recent corporate sponsors have included Ross Products Division of Abbott Laboratories. There is a $10 application fee.

Number awarded 1 or more each year.

Deadline April or October of each year.

[857]
NSCA GRADUATE RESEARCH GRANT

National Strength and Conditioning Association
Attn: Grants and Scholarships
1885 Bob Johnson Drive
Colorado Springs, CO 80906
(719) 632-6722, ext. 105   Toll-free: (800) 815-6826
Fax: (719) 632-6367   E-mail: nsca@nsca-lift.org
Web: www.nsca-lift.org/Foundation

Summary To provide funding for research related to strength and conditioning to graduate student members of the National Strength and Conditioning Association (NSCA).

Eligibility This program is open to graduate students who are members of the association studying in the field of strength and conditioning. Applicants must be proposing to conduct research under the supervision of a faculty member who will serve as a co-investigator in the study.

Financial data The maximum grant is $2,500 for master's degree students or $5,000 for doctoral candidates. Funds may not be used for overhead costs.

Additional information The NSCA is a nonprofit organization of strength and conditioning professionals, including coaches, athletic trainers, physical therapists, educators, researchers, and physicians.

Number awarded 1 or more each year.

Deadline March of each year.

[858]
NURSES CHARITABLE TRUST DISTRICT V GRANT

American Nurses Foundation
Attn: Nursing Research Grants Program
8515 Georgia Avenue, Suite 400
Silver Spring, MD 20910-3492
(301) 628-5298   Fax: (301) 628-5354
E-mail: anf@ana.org
Web: www.anfonline.org

Summary To provide funding to nurses interested in conducting research.

Eligibility This program is open to registered nurses who have earned a baccalaureate or higher degree. Applicants may be either beginning or experienced researchers. Proposed research may be for a master's thesis or doctoral dissertation if the project has been approved by the principal investigator's thesis or dissertation committee. There are no restrictions on the research topic.

Financial data The grant is $10,000. Funds may not be used as a salary for the principal investigator.

Duration 1 year.

Additional information This program was established in 2000 with funding provided by the Nurses Charitable Trust of District V, Florida Nurses Association. There is a $75 application fee.

Number awarded 1 each year.

Deadline April of each year.

[859]
NURSING EXCELLENCE FELLOWSHIP IN HEMOPHILIA

National Hemophilia Foundation
Attn: Manager of Healthcare Provider Programs
116 West 32nd Street, 11th Floor
New York, NY 10001
(212) 328-3745   Toll-free: (800) 42-HANDI, ext. 3745
Fax: (212) 328-3799   E-mail: mjohnson@hemophilia.org
Web: www.hemophilia.org

Summary To provide funding to registered nurses interested in conducting nursing research or clinical projects related to hemophilia.

Eligibility This program is open to registered nurses from an accredited nursing school enrolled in a graduate nursing program or practicing hemophilia nursing. Applicants must be interested in conducting a nursing research or a clinical project. Preference is given to applicants who are endorsed by a federally-funded hemophilia treatment center. Current topics of interest include, but are not limited to, the development of clinical pathways, measurable outcomes in bleeding disorders care, service utilization, epidemiology, patient and community education, rehabilitation, therapeutic modalities, psychosocial issues, women's health, liver disease, and HIV/AIDS. Selection is based on scientific merit and relevance to the research priorities of the National Hemophilia Foundation.

Financial data The grants is $13,500 per year.

Duration 1 year.

Number awarded 1 each year.

Deadline Letters of intent must be submitted by January of each year. Completed applications are due in March.

[860]
NWRI FELLOWSHIPS

National Water Research Institute
Attn: Fellowship Program
10500 Ellis Avenue
P.O. Box 20865
Fountain Valley, CA 92728-0865
(714) 378-3278   Fax: (714) 378-3375
E-mail: fellow@nwri-usa.org
Web: www.nwri-usa.org

Summary To provide funding to graduate students interested in conducting research on water science and technology.

Eligibility This program is open to full-time graduate students interested in conducting research in areas of interest to the National Water Research Institute (NWRI): water treatment technologies, water quality, water environmental chemistry, water policy and economics, public health and risk assessment, or water resources management. Research areas include, but are not limited to, engineering, physical and chemical sciences, biological sciences, health sciences, political sciences, economics, and planning and public policy that are related to water and/or water resources. Preference is given to doctoral candidates, but outstanding students in master's programs may be considered. Applicants must submit a letter of inquiry describing the importance of the research to them and the water community, how their research will contribute to water science in general, what they expect to accomplish, and how their research relates to the mission of the NWRI to create new sources of water through research and technology and to protect the freshwater and marine environments.

Financial data The grant is $10,000 per year.

Duration 1 year; may be renewed up to 2 additional years.

Number awarded Varies each year; recently, 4 of these grants were awarded.

Deadline February of each year.

[861]
PARKINSON'S DISEASE FOUNDATION SUMMER FELLOWSHIP PROGRAM

Parkinson's Disease Foundation
Attn: Director, Research and External Programs
1359 Broadway, Suite 1509
New York, NY 10018
(212) 923-4700   Toll-free: (800) 457-6676
Fax: (212) 923-4778   E-mail: info@pdf.org
Web: www.pdf.org/Research/fellowships.cfm

Summary To provide an opportunity for high school seniors, undergraduates, and medical students to work on a summer research project related to Parkinson's Disease.

Eligibility This program is open to high school seniors, undergraduates, and medical students. Applicants must be interested in engaging in summer laboratory work related to Parkinson's Disease under the supervision of an established investigator. Along with their application, they must submit a letter from the investigator affirming that he or she will make facilities available to the student and will guide the student's work.

Financial data The stipend is $3,000.

Duration 10 weeks during the summer.

Number awarded Varies each year.

Deadline February of each year.

[862]
PAUL CALABRESI MEDICAL STUDENT RESEARCH FELLOWSHIP

Pharmaceutical Research and Manufacturers of America
Attn: PhRMA Foundation
950 F Street, N.W., Suite 300
Washington, DC 20004
(202) 572-7756   Fax: (202) 572-7799
E-mail: foundation@phrma.org
Web: www.phrmafoundation.org

Summary To provide funding to medical and dental students who wish to conduct research in pharmacology or clinical pharmacology.

Eligibility This program is open to medical and dental students who have substantial interests in research and teaching careers in pharmacology or clinical pharmacology. Applicants must have completed at least 1 year of their program and be willing to interrupt their training in order to work full time on a research project in pharmacology or clinical pharmacology. They must be sponsored by the pharmacology or clinical pharmacology program where they wish to conduct their research project; that program may be affiliated with their medical or dental school or it may be at another institution. Students who are already in a training sequence leading to a research career and students already in an M.D./Ph.D. program are eligible to apply; awards are not made to a student in an M.D./Ph.D. program who is entering the last 2 years of medical school. Priority is given to applicants who project strong commitments to career in the field of clinical pharmacology. U.S. citizenship or permanent resident status is required.

Financial data The stipend is up to $1,500 per month; the maximum award is $18,000, even if the research continues more than 1 year.

Duration From 3 to 24 months.

Additional information This program began in 1974.

Number awarded Varies each year; recently, 2 of these fellowships were awarded.

Deadline August of each year.

[863]
PDA JOURNAL OF PHARMACEUTICAL SCIENCE AND TECHNOLOGY FELLOWSHIP

Parenteral Drug Association
Attn: Senior Vice President, Scientific and Regulatory Affairs
4350 East West Highway
Bethesda, MD 20814
(301) 656-5900   Fax: (301) 986-0296
E-mail: rice@pda.org
Web: www.pda.org/ssp

Summary To provide funding to doctoral candidates interested in conducting dissertation research related to pharmaceuticals.

Eligibility This program is open to doctoral candidates interested in conducting dissertation research relevant to the scientific foundations of pharmaceutical and biopharmaceutical product development, drug manufacturing, and quality assurance technologies. Applicants must submit a research proposal that includes hypothesis and specific aims, methods used to address each specific aim, experimental design and expected outcomes, scientific justifications for the research project, brief descriptions of relevant background literature and preliminary results, and proposed budget and timing.

Financial data The grant is $10,000. The majority of the funding is to be used for a stipend for the student, with the balance available for any tuition, travel, search, clerical help, or equipment needed to carry out the purposes of the award. No portion may be utilized or charged for overhead, indirect, or administrative costs.

Duration 12 months.

Additional information Manuscripts reporting on sponsored research are published in the *PDA Journal of Pharmaceutical Science and Technology.*

Number awarded Up to 4 each year.

Deadline March of each year.

---

[864]
PDEF PILOT RESEARCH GRANTS

Society of Nuclear Medicine
Attn: Committee on Awards
1850 Samuel Morse Drive
Reston, VA 20190-5316
(703) 708-9000, ext. 1255   Fax: (703) 708-9020
E-mail: grantinfo@snm.org
Web: www.snm.org

Summary To provide funding to members of the Society of Nuclear Medicine Technologist Section (SNMTS) interested in conducting research.

Eligibility This program is open to SNMTS members who have nuclear medicine technology degrees and are working in a clinical, educational, and/or research environment. Graduate students with nuclear medicine technology degrees who are undertaking or completing research projects as part of their degree requirements are also eligible. Full-time M.D. students and employees of for-profit companies not in a clinical or academic setting are ineligible. Applicants must be interested in 1) funding a pilot project that will provide preliminary data to be used in future research; 2) funding a new project that is complete in itself; or 3) supplementing other project support. Any area of research in clinical practice, education, or professional development is acceptable.

Financial data The grant is $10,000.

Duration 1 year.

Additional information This program is supported by corporate sponsors of the SNMTS Professional Development and Education Fund (PDEF).

Number awarded Up to 2 each year.

Deadline August of each year.

---

[865]
PETER K. NEW STUDENT PRIZE COMPETITION

Society for Applied Anthropology
P.O. Box 2436
Oklahoma City, OK 73101-2436
(405) 843-5113   Fax: (405) 843-8553
E-mail: info@sfaa.net
Web: www.sfaa.net/pknew/pknew.html

Summary To recognize and reward the best student research papers in applied social, health, or behavioral sciences.

Eligibility This competition is open to currently-enrolled undergraduate and graduate students in the applied social, health, and behavioral sciences. Applicants must not have already earned a doctoral degree (e.g., a person with an M.D. degree who is now registered as a student in a Ph.D. program is not eligible). Eligible students are invited to submit a manuscript that reports on research which, in large measure, has not been previously published. Research should be in the domain of health care or human services (broadly defined). The competition is limited to manuscripts that have a single author; multiple-authored papers are not eligible. The paper should be double spaced and must be less than 45 pages in length, including footnotes, tables, and appendices. Selection is based on originality, research design/method, clarity of analysis and presentation, and contribution to the social or behavioral sciences.

Financial data The winner receives $1,000 plus a $350 travel allowance to partially offset the cost of transportation and lodging at the society's annual meeting.

Duration The competition is held annually.

Additional information The winning paper is published in the society's journal, *Human Organization.* Applicants who transmit their manuscripts by fax must pay a fee for duplication. Manuscripts may not be submitted electronically. The winner must attend the society's annual meeting to present the paper.

Number awarded 2 each year.

Deadline December of each year.

---

[866]
PHILIPS MEDICAL SYSTEMS CLINICAL OUTCOMES GRANTS

American Association of Critical-Care Nurses
Attn: Research Department
101 Columbia
Aliso Viejo, CA 92656-4109
(949) 362-2050, ext. 321
Toll-free: (800) 394-5995, ext. 321   Fax: (949) 362-2020
E-mail: research@aacn.org
Web: www.aacn.org

Summary To provide funding to members of the American Association of Critical-Care Nurses (AACN) who wish to conduct research on outcomes or efficiencies in critical care.

Eligibility Registered nurses who are regular or affiliated members of the association and experienced researchers may apply for these grants. They must be proposing to conduct a research project focusing on improved outcomes and/or system efficiencies in the care of acute or critically ill individuals of any age in any clinical environment. Preference is given to proposals for hospital-based inquiry that focus of any of the following: intervention strategies addressing technology integration into patient care; use of computerized medical record systems in assessing patient outcomes and managing care; improving specific patient care outcomes (e.g., clinical, safety, financial); use of simulation in clinical education of nurses; or any of the 2006 National Patient Safety Goals issues by the Joint Commission on Accreditation of Healthcare Organizations. Funds may be sought for research required for an academic degree. Selection is based on scientific merit of the project; direct and/or indirect benefits to the care of critically/acutely ill patients; ability of the principal investigator to meet the required timeline to complete and present results; and adequacy of facilities and resources available to the principal investigator.

Financial data The grant is $10,000. Funds may be used to support direct project expenses, such as research assistants, secretarial support, equipment, supplies, and consultative assistance. They may not be used for salaries of the principle or co-investigators, travel to presentations, preparation of slides, presentation or publication of findings, or such educational expenses as tuition or books. Indirect costs are limited to 10% of direct costs.

Duration 3 years.

Additional information This program is supported by Philips Medical Systems.

Number awarded 3 each year.

Deadline December of each year.

[867]
PHILLIPS MEDICAL IMAGING AWARD

Society of Diagnostic Medical Sonography
Attn: SDMS Educational Foundation
2745 North Dallas Parkway, Suite 350
Plano, TX 75093-8730
(214) 473-8057   Toll-free: (800) 229-9506
Fax: (214) 473-8563   E-mail: foundation@sdms.org
Web: www.sdms.org/foundation/atl.asp

Summary To recognize and reward members of the Society of Diagnostic Medical Sonography (SDMS) who make outstanding contributions to research in sonography.

Eligibility This award is available to SDMS members, including undergraduate and graduate student members, who have conducted outstanding research on the use of contrast agents in sonography. Selection is based on innovation, originality, research results, feasibility, and impact on current imaging modalities.

Financial data The award is $1,000.

Duration The award is presented annually.

Additional information This award is sponsored by Philips Medical Systems.

Number awarded 1 each year.

Deadline April of each year.

[868]
PLUS ONE RESEARCH GRANT ON WELLNESS USING INTERNET TECHNOLOGY

American College of Sports Medicine
Attn: Research Administration and Programs Office
401 West Michigan Street
P.O. Box 1440
Indianapolis, IN 46206-1440
(317) 637-9200, ext. 143   Fax: (317) 634-7817
E-mail: jsenior@acsm.org
Web: www.acsm.org

Summary To provide financial assistance to graduate students who are interested in conducting research on physical activity and human performance.

Eligibility This program is open to graduate students enrolled full time in programs in sports medicine or exercise science. Applicants must be interested in conducting research in the area of physical activity and human performance. Emphasis is place on new and innovative approaches to wellness solutions and education using Internet technology.

Financial data The grant is $5,000.

Duration 1 year.

Deadline January of each year.

[869]
PRE-DOCTORAL ASSOCIATED HEALTH REHABILITATION RESEARCH FELLOWSHIP PROGRAM

Department of Veterans Affairs
Attn: Office of Academic Affiliations
810 Vermont Avenue, N.W., Room 475
Washington, DC 20420
(202) 357-4028   E-mail: Robert.zeiss@va.gov
Web: www.va.gov/oaa/residencies_fellowships.asp

Summary To provide funding to doctoral candidates interested in conducting research that is relevant to the needs of veterans with disabilities.

Eligibility This program is open to graduate students who have completed their doctoral course work in a rehabilitation health care profession and are prepared to work on a research dissertation related to the health care needs of veterans with disabilities. Students pursuing doctorates in rehabilitation health care professions, such as rehabilitation engineering, occupational therapy, physical therapy, audiology, speech-language pathology, nursing, psychology, and orientation and mobility are encouraged to apply. Areas of research priority include prosthetics; orthotics; mobility; orthopedics; amputations; spinal cord injury and other neurologic disorders; single or multiple impairments of vision, hearing and communications; traumatic brain injury; dementia and cognitive disorders; geriatric rehabilitation; chronic psychiatric disorders; and rehabilitation outcomes. Students in allopathic or osteopathic medical schools are not eligible. U.S. citizenship is required.

Financial data The grant is $25,000.

Duration 1 year, beginning October 1 of each year.

Additional information Recipients are encouraged to seek permanent employment within the VA system after completing their fellowship; however, there is no service obligation required following the program. Fellows must conduct their research on a full-time basis at a VA facility.

Number awarded Up to 6 each year.

Deadline May of each year.

[870]
PREDOCTORAL FELLOWSHIPS FOR STUDENTS IN NUTRITION RESEARCH

American Society for Nutrition
9650 Rockville Pike, Suite L-4500
Bethesda, MD 20814-3990
(301) 634-7050   Fax: (301) 634-7892
E-mail: sec@nutrition.org
Web: www.nutrition.org/awardsTC.htm

Summary To provide financial assistance to doctoral students interested in conducting research on nutrition.

Eligibility This program is open to graduate students working on a doctorate in nutrition. Applicants must submit a 1-page statement explaining the contribution of the proposed research to the knowledge of nutrition. Proposals are evaluated on the basis of significance, feasibility, communication and clarity, and overall scientific technical quality.

Financial data The grant is $5,000.

Duration 1 year.

Additional information These awards are sponsored by Gerber Foundation, Mars Inc., Kraft Foods, Inc., Cargill, McNeil Nutritionals, and Wyeth Consumer Healthcare.

Number awarded Varies each year. Recently, 6 of these fellowships were awarded (1 by each of the sponsors).

Deadline November of each year.

[871]
PREDOCTORAL RESEARCH FELLOWSHIPS IN AUTISM

National Alliance for Autism Research
Attn: Grants Administrator
99 Wall Street, Research Park
Princeton, NJ 08540
(609) 430-9160, ext. 23   Toll-free: (888) 777-NAAR
Fax: (609) 430-9163   E-mail: grantadmin@naar.org
Web: www.naar.org/research/research.asp

Summary To provide funding to doctoral candidates interested in a program of research training related to autism.

Eligibility This program is open to predoctoral students enrolled in a program leading to a research doctorate (e.g., Ph.D., Sc.D., M.D./Ph.D.) in a relevant academic department of a university or health/medical institution. Students must be interested in working on a dissertation related to autism. Relevant scientific disciplines include (but are not limited to) biochemistry, cellular physiology, clinically based studies, cognitive development, development biology and teratology, epidemiology, genetics, immunology, language, molecular biology, neuroanatomy, neuroimaging, pharmacology, structural biology, toxicology, and virology. The research training must be conducted with a mentor who submits the application and chooses the fellow. Selection of grantees is based on the quality and activity of the mentor's autism research programs, his or her experience with training graduate fellows, evidence of sufficient research support and adequate facilities to provide an appropriate training environment for a predoctoral fellow, quality and nature of the research plan, and presence of institutional research programs and/or clinical assets that enhance the richness of fellow training in the multidisciplinary complexity of autism spectrum disorder investigation.

Financial data Stipends range from $21,000 to $24,000 per year, depending upon the years of prior training. A research allowance of $4,000 is provided to partially cover fringe benefits, supplies, and travel. No indirect costs are covered.

Duration 2 years.

Additional information Fellows must devote at least 80% of their time to working on the project outlined in the research plan of the application. They may not simultaneously hold another named fellowship award.

Number awarded 1 or more each year.

Deadline Letters of intent must be submitted by March; the completed application is due in the following June.

[872]
PREDOCTORAL RESEARCH FELLOWSHIPS ON LANGUAGE AND COMMUNICATIONS IN INDIVIDUALS WITH AUTISM SPECTRUM DISORDERS

National Alliance for Autism Research
Attn: Grants Administrator
99 Wall Street, Research Park
Princeton, NJ 08540
(609) 430-9160, ext. 23   Toll-free: (888) 777-NAAR
Fax: (609) 430-9163   E-mail: grantadmin@naar.org
Web: www.naar.org/research/research.asp

Summary To provide funding to doctoral candidates interested in a program of research training in language and autism.

Eligibility This program is open to predoctoral students enrolled in a program leading to a research doctorate (e.g., Ph.D.,

Sc.D., M.D./Ph.D.) in a relevant academic department of a university or health/medical institution. Students must be interested in working on a dissertation related to autism and language. Relevant scientific disciplines include (but are not limited to) cognitive development, language, linguistics and augmentative communication strategies, child language development, speech-language pathology, pharmacology, psychology, and neuropsychology. The research training must be conducted with co-mentors, 1 with research expertise in communication and language and the other from the field of autism. Applications must be submitted by the co-mentors, who choose the fellow. Selection of grantees is based on the quality and activity of the mentors' autism research programs, their experience with training graduate fellows, evidence of sufficient research support and adequate facilities to provide an appropriate training environment for a predoctoral fellow, quality and nature of the research plan, and presence of institutional research programs and/or clinical assets that enhance the richness of fellow training in the multidisciplinary complexity of autism spectrum disorder investigation.

Financial data Stipends range from $21,000 to $24,000 per year, depending upon the years of prior training. A research allowance of $4,000 is provided to partially cover fringe benefits, supplies, and travel. No indirect costs are covered.

Duration 2 years.

Additional information Fellows must devote at least 80% of their time to working on the project outlined in the research plan of the application. They may not simultaneously hold another named fellowship award.

Number awarded 1 or more each year.

Deadline Letters of intent must be submitted by March; the completed application is due in the following June.

[873]
PREDOCTORAL RESEARCH TRAINING FELLOWSHIPS IN EPILEPSY

Epilepsy Foundation
Attn: Research Department
8301 Professional Place
Landover, MD 20785-2237
(301) 459-3700   Toll-free: (800) EFA-1000
Fax: (301) 577-2684   TDD: (800) 332-2070
E-mail: grants@efa.org
Web: www.epilepsyfoundation.org/research/grants.cfm

Summary To provide funding to doctoral candidates in designated fields for dissertation research on a topic related to epilepsy.

Eligibility This program is open to full-time graduate students working on a Ph.D. in biochemistry, genetics, neuroscience, nursing, pharmacology, pharmacy, physiology, or psychology. Applicants must be conducting dissertation research on a topic relevant to epilepsy under the guidance of a mentor with expertise in the area of epilepsy investigation. Applications from women, members of minority groups, and people with disabilities are especially encouraged. Selection is based on the relevance of the proposed work to epilepsy, the applicant's qualifications, the mentor's qualifications, the scientific quality of the proposed dissertation research, the quality of the training environment for research related to epilepsy, and the adequacy of the facility.

Financial data The grant is $20,000, consisting of $19,000 for a stipend and $1,000 to support travel to attend the annual meeting of the American Epilepsy Society.

Duration 1 year.

Additional information Support for this program, which began in 1998, is provided by many individuals, families, and corporations, especially the American Epilepsy Society, Abbott Laboratories, Ortho-McNeil Pharmaceutical, and Pfizer Inc.

Number awarded Varies each year; recently, 8 of these fellowships were awarded.

Deadline August of each year.

[874]
PROCTER & GAMBLE GRADUATE FELLOWSHIP AWARD

National Organization for the Professional Advancement of Black Chemists and Chemical Engineers
c/o Howard University
P.O. Box 77040
Washington, DC 20013
(202) 667-1699   Toll-free: (800) 776-1419
Fax: (267) 200-0156
Web: www.nobcche.org

Summary To provide funding to African American doctoral students for research in chemistry, chemical engineering, or life sciences.

Eligibility This program is open to African American candidates in a Ph.D. program for chemistry, chemical engineering, or life sciences. Applicants must submit 3 letters of recommendation, a resume, official transcripts for undergraduate and graduate study, a description of their proposed research, and a statement of their career objective. Preference is given to those who have completed at least 1 year of graduate study. U.S. citizenship is required.

Financial data The grant is $17,000.

Duration 1 year.

Additional information This program is sponsored by the Procter & Gamble Company. Information is also available from Dr. Marlon L. Walker, Awards and Scholarships Committee Chair, National Institute of Standards and Technology, 100 Bureau Drive, Gaithersburg, MD 20899-8372, (301) 975-5593, E-mail: marlon.walker@nist.gov.

Number awarded 1 each year.

Deadline January of each year.

[875]
P3 AWARD PROGRAM

Environmental Protection Agency
Attn: National Center for Environmental Research
Ariel Rios Building - 3500
1200 Pennsylvania Avenue, N.W.
Washington, DC 20460
(202) 343-9862   E-mail: barnwell.thomas@epa.gov
Web: es.epa.gov/ncer/P3

Summary To provide funding to teams of undergraduate and graduate students interested in conducting a research project related to environmental sustainability.

Eligibility This competition is open to teams of undergraduate and graduate students at U.S. colleges and universities who are interested in conducting a research project related to the 3 components of sustainability: people, prosperity, and the planet. Projects must address the causes, effects, extent, prevention, reduction, or elimination of air, water, or solid and hazardous waste pollution. Categories include agriculture (e.g., irrigation practices, reduction or elimination of pesticides); materials and chemicals (e.g., materials conservation, green engineering, green chemistry, biotechnology, recovery and reuse of materials); energy (e.g., reduction in air emissions, energy conservation); information technology (e.g., delivery of and access to environmental perfor-

mance, technical, educational, or public health information related environmental decision making); water (e.g., quality, quantity, conservation, availability, and access); or the built environment (e.g., environmental benefits through innovative green buildings, transportation, and mobility strategies, and smart growth as it results in reduced vehicle miles traveled or reduces storm water runoff). Student teams, with a faculty advisor (who serves as the principal investigator on the grant), submit designs for Phase I of the competition. Selection of grantees is based on the extent to which the proposed project achieves the outcomes of minimizing the use and generation of hazardous substances; utilizes resources and energy effectively and efficiently; and advances the goals of economic competitiveness, human health, and environmental protection for societal benefit. Recipients of Phase I grants are then invited to apply for additional funding through a Phase II grant.

Financial data Phase I grants are $10,000. Phase II grants are $75,000. Grants cover all direct and indirect costs; cost-sharing is not required.

Duration 1 year for Phase I and 1 additional year for Phase II.

Additional information This program began in 2004. It is supported by a large number of organizations from industry, the nonprofit sector, and the federal government.

Number awarded Varies each year. Recently, 42 Phase I grants were awarded, of which 10 were selected to receive Phase II grants.

Deadline February of each year.

[876]
RALPH PHILLIPS STUDENT RESEARCH AWARD

Academy of Operative Dentistry
c/o Nairn H.F. Wilson, Research Committee Chair
King's College, Guy's Tower, Floor 18
London SE1 1UL
England
44 20 7955 4343   Fax: 44 20 7955 8873
E-mail: nairn.wilson@kd.ac.uk
Web: www.operativedentistry.com/awards.html

Summary To provide funding to dental students interested in conducting research on operative dentistry.

Eligibility This program is open to dental students at all levels and in all countries. Applicants must be proposing to undertake research related to operative dentistry. They must submit a protocol outlining the background, aims, and hypothesis of the proposed research, the methodology to be employed, a time schedule, and the expected outcome of the study.

Financial data Grants up to $6,000 are available. Additional funding, up to $1,000, may be available to help pay the costs of attending the annual meeting of the International Association for Dental Research/American Association for Dental Research (IADR/AADR).

Additional information If an abstract of the research is accepted for presentation at the IADR/AADR annual meeting, funding is provided for the student to attend that meeting.

Number awarded 1 or more each year.

Deadline December of each year.

[877]
RALPH PHILLIPS STUDENT RESEARCH AWARD

Academy of Operative Dentistry
c/o Greg Smith, Secretary
P.O. Box 14996
Gainesville, FL 32604-2996
(352) 392-4341   E-mail: Greg679@cox.net
Web: www.operativedentistry.com/awards.html

Summary To provide funding to dental students interested in conducting research in operative dentistry.

Eligibility This program is open to predoctoral dental students interested in conducting research related to operative dentistry. Applications must be cosigned by a faculty member, should outline the proposed research, and must include a budget.

Financial data The grant is $6,000. If an abstract based on the research is accepted for presentation at the annual meeting of the American Association for Dental Research (AADR), additional travel funds up to $1,000 are made available to the awardee.

Number awarded 1 each year.

Deadline December of each year.

[878]
RAYMOND AND ROSALEE WEISS RESEARCH ENDOWMENT

American College of Sports Medicine
Attn: Research Administration and Programs Office
401 West Michigan Street
P.O. Box 1440
Indianapolis, IN 46206-1440
(317) 637-9200, ext. 143   Fax: (317) 634-7817
E-mail: jsenior@acsm.org
Web: www.acsm.org

Summary To provide funding for research to student members of the American College of Sports Medicine (ACSM).

Eligibility This program is open to graduate students who are current members of ACSM. Applicants must be interested in conducting research on the health benefits (physical, mental, and emotional) of physical activity and sports. Their proposal must involve applied rather than basic research, with the intent of applying the results to programs involving physical activity and sports. Priority is given to proposals studying the psychological and emotional benefits of physical activity.

Financial data The grant is $1,500 per year.

Duration 1 year.

Number awarded 1 each year.

Deadline January of each year.

[879]
RAYMOND H. STETSON SCHOLARSHIP IN PHONETICS AND SPEECH PRODUCTION

Acoustical Society of America
Attn: Office Manager
2 Huntington Quadrangle, Suite 1NO1
Melville, NY 11747-4502
(516) 576-2360   Fax: (516) 576-2377
E-mail: asa@aip.org
Web: asa.aip.org/fellowships.html

Summary To provide funding to members of the Acoustical Society of America who are conducting graduate research in phonetics and speech production.

Eligibility This program is open to society members conducting graduate research in the following preferential order: motor speech production (including motor coordination of speech organs, kinematics of speech articulation, aerodynamics of speech production, combined acoustic/kinematic modeling of speech); phonetics (including linguistic issues related to speech production, articulatory phonology, experimental phonology); and bio-developmental factors in speech (including neural function for speech communication, infant/child development for speech communication). Selection is based on the applicant's academic record, a 3-page personal statement on their career objectives, 2 letters of recommendation, a copy of a paper that demonstrates their ability to carry out and write up a research project, and the relevance of the research area to the program's purpose.

Financial data The grant is $3,000 per year.

Duration 1 year.

Additional information This program was established in 1998.

Number awarded 1 each year.

Deadline April of each year.

[880]
REHABILITATION NURSING FOUNDATION FELLOW RESEARCH GRANTS

Association of Rehabilitation Nurses
Attn: Rehabilitation Nursing Foundation
4700 West Lake Avenue
Glenview, IL 60025-1485
(847) 375-4710   Toll-free: (800) 229-7530
Fax: (877) 734-9384   E-mail: info@rehabnurse.org
Web: www.rehabnurse.org/research/researchgrants.hmtl

Summary To provide funding to graduate students and professionals interested in conducting research on topics related to rehabilitation nursing.

Eligibility The principal investigator for the research project must be a registered nurse who is active in rehabilitation or who has demonstrated interest in and significant contributions to rehabilitation nursing. Membership in the association is not required. Graduate students may apply. Research proposals that address the clinical, educational, or administrative dimensions of rehabilitation nursing are requested. Quantitative and qualitative research projects will be accepted for review.

Financial data Up to $20,000 for rehabilitation nursing research is available each year and may be awarded in the form of multiple grants.

Duration The project must be completed within 2 years.

Number awarded Up to 2 each year.

Deadline March of each year.

[881]
RICHARD G. OUELLETTE RESEARCH AWARD

American Association of Nurse Anesthetists
Attn: AANA Foundation
222 South Prospect Avenue
Park Ridge, IL 60068-4001
(847) 692-7050, ext. 1171   Fax: (847) 692-7137
E-mail: foundation@aana.com
Web: www.aana.com/foundation/default.asp

Summary To provide funding to student members of the American Association of Nurse Anesthetists who are interested in conducting research.

Eligibility This program is open to nurse anesthesia students in good academic standing who are members of the association. Applicants must be proposing a research project related to their field. Along with their application, they must submit a letter of support from their research advisor and a 100-word statement on how their research impacts nurse anesthesia practice and/or education. Preference is given to CRNAs.

Financial data Grants are currently limited to $1,000.

Duration 1 academic year.

Number awarded 1 each year.

Deadline April of each year.

[882]
RITA K. CHOW AND YAYE TOGASKI-BREITENBACH SCHOLAR AWARD

American Nurses Foundation
Attn: Nursing Research Grants Program
8515 Georgia Avenue, Suite 400
Silver Spring, MD 20910-3492
(301) 628-5298   Fax: (301) 628-5354
E-mail: anf@ana.org
Web: www.anfonline.org

Summary To provide funding to nurses interested in conducting research.

Eligibility This program is open to registered nurses who have earned a baccalaureate or higher degree. Applicants must be beginning researchers who have had no more than 3 research-based publications in refereed journals and have received, as a principal investigator, no more than $15,000 in extramural funding in any 1 research area. Proposed research may be for a master's thesis or doctoral dissertation if the project has been approved by the principal investigator's thesis or dissertation committee. There are no restrictions on the research topic.

Financial data The grant is $3,500. Funds may not be used as a salary for the principal investigator.

Duration 1 year.

Additional information There is a $75 application fee.

Number awarded 1 each year.

Deadline April of each year.

[883]
RNF NEW INVESTIGATOR RESEARCH GRANTS

Association of Rehabilitation Nurses
Attn: Rehabilitation Nursing Foundation
4700 West Lake Avenue
Glenview, IL 60025-1485
(847) 375-4710   Toll-free: (800) 229-7530
Fax: (877) 734-9384   E-mail: info@rehabnurse.org
Web: www.rehabnurse.org/research/researchgrants.hmtl

Summary To encourage nurses who are novice researchers to conduct research on topics related to rehabilitation nursing.

Eligibility This award is open to rehabilitation nurses who are interested in conducting research or graduate nursing students working on theses or dissertations. Applicants must not have conducted research at the doctoral level, must have a rehabilitation focus, and must not have had previous research funding of more than $5,000. Quantitative and qualitative research projects will be accepted for review. Membership in the association is not required.

Financial data The maximum grant is $10,000.

Duration The project must be completed within 2 years.

Number awarded 1 each year.

Deadline January of each year.

[884]
ROBERT O. GILBERT GRANT

International Society of Psychiatric-Mental Health Nurses
Attn: ISPN Foundation
2810 Crossroads Drive, Suite 3800
Madison, WI 53718
(608) 443-2463   Toll-free: (866) 330-7227
Fax: (608) 443-2474   E-mail: info@ispn-psych.org
Web: www.ispn-psych.org

Summary To provide funding to members of the International Society of Psychiatric-Mental Health Nurses (ISPN) who are interested in conducting research on mental illness, children, adolescents, and/or their families.

Eligibility This program is open to psychiatric nurses who 1) are active members of the association and 2) already have a master's or doctoral degree in nursing or are working on a master's or doctoral degree in nursing. Applicants must be interested in conducting research (qualitative or quantitative) that is intervention-outcome oriented or exploratory-descriptive. The research must deal with mental health or mental illness, children, adolescents, and/or their families. Proposals (no more than 5 single-spaced pages) must include: title and purpose, background and significance, hypotheses and research questions, methods, budget, timeline, and references.

Financial data The grant is $1,000.

Duration 1 year.

Additional information Recipients must submit a written summary or completed research to the foundation and a copy of the manuscript to the association's journal. They must acknowledge the support of ISPN in any published or presented manuscript that incorporates the funded research.

Number awarded 1 each year.

Deadline October of each year.

[885]
RONALD B. LINSKY FELLOWSHIP FOR OUTSTANDING WATER RESEARCH

National Water Research Institute
Attn: Fellowship Program
10500 Ellis Avenue
P.O. Box 20865
Fountain Valley, CA 92728-0865
(714) 378-3278   Fax: (714) 378-3375
E-mail: fellow@nwri-usa.org
Web: www.nwri-usa.org

Summary To provide funding to graduate students interested in conducting research on water science and technology.

Eligibility This program is open to full-time graduate students interested in conducting research in areas of interest to the National Water Research Institute (NWRI): water treatment technologies, water quality, water environmental chemistry, water policy and economics, public health and risk assessment, water resources management. Research areas include, but are not limited to, engineering, physical and chemical sciences, biological sciences, health sciences, political sciences, economics, and planning and public policy that are related to water and/or water resources. Preference is given to doctoral candidates, but outstanding students in master's programs may be considered. Applicants must submit a letter of inquiry describing the importance of the research to them and the water community, how their research will contribute to water science in general, what they expect to accomplish, and how their research relates to the mission of the NWRI to create new sources of water through research and technology and to protect the freshwater and marine environments. They must also submit a 1-page essay on their technical capabilities, interest in fields other than what they are studying, career goals, and where they hope to take their technical expertise and vision in the future.

Financial data The grant is $20,000 per year.

Duration 2 years.

Additional information This fellowship was first offered in 2007.

Number awarded 1 each year.

Deadline February of each year.

[886]
ROSIE WALL COMMUNITY SPIRIT GRANTS

American Dental Hygienists' Association
Attn: Institute for Oral Health
444 North Michigan Avenue, Suite 3400
Chicago, IL 60611
(312) 440-8918   Toll-free: (800) 243-2342, ext. 244
Fax: (312) 440-8929   E-mail: institute@adha.net
Web: www.adha.org

Summary To provide funding to dental hygienists and dental hygiene students who are interested in conducting a community service project.

Eligibility This program is open to licensed dental hygienists and to dental hygiene students, undergraduate or graduate, full-time or part-time. Applicants must be proposing to conduct a specific community health or research project. They must be able to demonstrate that the project is in harmony with the sponsor's mission and vision. The project should demonstrate its capacity to improve the public's overall health, including dental, medical, or mental health. U.S. citizenship and membership in the American Dental Hygienists' Association are required.

Financial data Grants range from $1,000 to $3,000.

Duration 1 year.

Number awarded 6 each year: 1 reserved for a student, 1 for an applicant from Hawaii, and 4 for applicants from the other 49 states.

Deadline February of each year.

[887]
ROYAL SOCIETY OF TROPICAL MEDICINE AND HYGIENE MEDICAL STUDENT ELECTIVE PRIZE

Royal Society of Tropical Medicine and Hygiene
Attn: The Administrator
50 Bedford Square
London WC1B 3DP
England
44 20 7580 2127   Fax: 44 20 7436 1389
E-mail: mail@rstmh.org
Web: www.rstmh.org

Summary To recognize and reward medical students from any country who have conducted outstanding research in a tropical or developing country.

Eligibility This prize is available to medical students of any nationality. Applicants must have conducted research in a tropical or developing country during an elective period and completed the project within the past 12 months. It must have contributed to knowledge or understanding of tropical diseases. Preference is given to projects that have been developed and carried out by the students themselves. Nominations must be submitted by the head of department, supervisor, or dean.

Financial data The prize is 500 English pounds.

Duration The prize is awarded annually.

Number awarded 1 each year.

Deadline Nominations must be submitted by December of each year.

[888]
RSNA RESEARCH MEDICAL STUDENT GRANTS

Radiological Society of North America
Attn: Research and Education Foundation
820 Jorie Boulevard
Oak Brook, IL 60523-2251
(630) 571-2670   Fax: (630) 571-7837
E-mail: R&Efoundation@rsna.org
Web: www.rsna.org

Summary To provide funding to medical students who are interested in participating in a research project supported by the Radiological Society of North America (RSNA).

Eligibility This program is open to full-time students enrolled in recognized North American medical schools. Applicants must be interested in conducting a research project in a department of radiology, nuclear medicine, or radiation oncology, but it does not need to be at their home institution. They may not have received grant or contract awards totaling $50,000 or more in a single calendar year as a principal investigator.

Financial data The grant is $3,000, which must be matched by the sponsoring department. Funds are intended as a stipend for the student and may not be used for non-personnel research expenses.

Duration Students are expected to complete the project within 3 months.

Number awarded Varies each year; recently, 10 of these grants were awarded.

Deadline Applications may be submitted at any time.

[889]
RUTH L. KIRSCHSTEIN NATIONAL RESEARCH SERVICE AWARDS FOR INDIVIDUAL PREDOCTORAL FELLOWS

National Institutes of Health
Division of Extramural Outreach and Information Resources
Attn: Grants Information
6701 Rockledge Drive, Suite 6095
Bethesda, MD 20892-7910
(301) 435-0714   Fax: (301) 480-0525
TTY: (301) 451-0088   E-mail: NIHTrain@mail.nih.gov
Web: www.nih.gov

Summary To provide financial assistance to students working on a graduate degree and preparing for a career in biomedical and behavioral research.

Eligibility This program is open to students enrolled in a Ph.D. or equivalent research degree program; a formally combined M.D./Ph.D. program; or other combined professional doctoral/research Ph.D. graduate program in the biomedical, behavioral, health, or clinical sciences. Students in health professional degree programs (e.g., M.D., D.O., D.D.S., D.V.M.) are not eligible. Applicants must be at the dissertation research stage of their doctoral program. They must be U.S. citizens, nationals, or permanent residents.

Financial data The fellowship provides an annual stipend of $20,772, a tuition and fee allowance (60% of costs up to $16,000 or 60% of costs up to $21,000 for dual degrees), and an institutional allowance of $4,200 for travel to scientific meetings and for laboratory and other training expenses.

Duration Up to 5 years.

Additional information These fellowships are offered by the following components of the National Institutes of Health (NIH): National Institute on Aging, National Institute on Alcohol Abuse and Alcoholism, National Institute on Deafness and Other Communication Disorders, National Institute on Drug Abuse, National Institute of Mental Health, and National Institute of Neurological Disorders and Stroke. Write for a list of names and telephone numbers of responsible officers at each component.

Number awarded Varies each year.

Deadline April, August, or December of each year.

[890]
RUTH L. KIRSCHSTEIN NATIONAL RESEARCH SERVICE AWARDS FOR INDIVIDUAL PREDOCTORAL MD/PHD FELLOWS

National Institutes of Health
Division of Extramural Outreach and Information Resources
Attn: Grants Information
6701 Rockledge Drive, Suite 6095
Bethesda, MD 20892-7910
(301) 435-0714   Fax: (301) 480-0525
TTY: (301) 451-0088   E-mail: NIHTrain@mail.nih.gov
Web: www.nih.gov

Summary To provide financial assistance to students working on a combined M.D./Ph.D. degree and preparing for a career in biomedical and behavioral research.

Eligibility This program is open to students enrolled in an accredited M.D./Ph.D. program at a medical school, accepted in a related Ph.D. scientific program, and supervised by a mentor in that scientific discipline. Applicants generally should be in the first 2 years of medical school, but they may be at any stage of medical school provided that they have at least 1 year of dissertation-stage research training remaining. They must be U.S. citizens, nationals, or permanent residents.

Financial data The fellowship provides an annual stipend of $20,772, a tuition and fee allowance (60% of costs up to $16,000 or 60% of costs up to $21,000 for dual degrees), and an institutional allowance of $4,200 for travel to scientific meetings and for laboratory and other training expenses.

Duration Up to 6 years.

Additional information These fellowships are offered by the following components of the National Institutes of Health (NIH): National Institute on Aging, National Institute on Alcohol Abuse and Alcoholism, National Institute on Deafness and Other Communication Disorders, National Institute on Drug Abuse, National Institute of Environmental Health Sciences, National Institute of Mental Health, and National Institute of Neurological Disorders and Stroke. Write for a list of names and telephone numbers of responsible officers at each component.

Number awarded Varies each year.

Deadline April, August, or December of each year.

[891]
RUTH L. KIRSCHSTEIN NRSA PROGRAM FOR NIGMS MARC PREDOCTORAL FELLOWSHIPS

National Institute of General Medical Sciences
Attn: Minority Access to Research Careers Branch
45 Center Drive, Room 2AS.37
Bethesda, MD 20892-6200
(301) 594-3900   Fax: (301) 480-2753
TTY: (301) 451-0088   E-mail: at21z@nih.gov
Web: www.nigms.nih.gov

Summary To provide financial assistance to minority doctoral students who are interested in preparing for a research career in the biomedical sciences.

Eligibility This program is open to students from minority groups underrepresented in the behavioral and biomedical sciences who are currently enrolled in a Ph.D. or equivalent research degree program, a combined M.D./Ph.D. program, or other combined professional and Ph.D. degree program in the behavioral or biomedical sciences, including mathematics. Support is not available to individuals enrolled in medical or other professional schools unless they are working on a degree combined with a Ph.D. Applicants must have graduated from an undergraduate program supported by the Minority Access to Research Careers (MARC) Branch of the National Institute of General Medical Sciences (NIGMS). Only U.S. citizens, nationals, and permanent residents are eligible.

Financial data The fellowship provides an annual stipend of $20,772, a tuition and fee allowance (60% of costs up to $16,000 or 60% of costs up to $21,000 for dual degrees), and an institutional allowance of $4,200 for travel to scientific meetings and for laboratory and other training expenses.

Duration Up to 5 years.

Additional information This program is part of the National Research Service Award program of the National Institutes of Health (NIH), named in honor of Ruth L. Kirschstein in 2002.

Deadline April, August, or December of each year.

[892]
SARNOFF FELLOWSHIP PROGRAM

Sarnoff Cardiovascular Research Foundation
Attn: Executive Director
731 G-2 Walker Road
Great Falls, VA 22066
(703) 759-7600   Toll-free: (888) 4-SARNOF
Fax: (703) 759-7838
E-mail: dboyd@SarnoffFoundation.org
Web: www.sarnoffendowment.org/fellowship.shtml

Summary To provide medical students with an opportunity to conduct cardiovascular research.

Eligibility This program is open to medical students who have completed their second or third year at a medical school in the United States. Students in M.D./Ph.D. programs are not eligible. Applicants must be proposing to conduct cardiovascular research at a U.S. institution, other than the medical school they attend, in conjunction with a faculty member at their school who will help them plan their research and select a preceptor at the institution where the research will be conducted. Prior research experience is not required. Applicants must submit 1) a 1-page personal statement describing their scholarly interests and career plans; and 2) a 3-page essay on a cardiovascular research topic of interest to them. The research essay is not intended to be a proposal of the research the applicant intends to conduct and should not include specific laboratory protocols or descriptions of experiments currently being performed by the applicant. Semifinalists are interviewed in Atlanta. Selection is based on the applicant's interest in a career in cardiovascular research, as documented by the personal statement; the quality of the applicant's research essay and ability to discuss the research topic with selection committee members; and the impact of the award on providing the applicant an opportunity for an intensive research experience.

Financial data Fellows receive an annual stipend of $25,000, an allowance of up to $2,000 for moving expenses, an allowance of up to $2,000 for travel costs associated with selecting a laboratory, funds to attend several professional conferences, and funds to help cover the cost of health insurance.

Duration 1 year, beginning in June. In exceptional circumstances, the fellowship may be renewed 1 additional year.

Additional information During the period of their research, fellows work with 3 mentors: the sponsor from their own medical school, the preceptor from the research institution, and a member of the Sarnoff Scientific Board who will also serve as an advisor throughout the fellowship. This program began in 1980.

Number awarded Up to 18 each year.

Deadline January of each year.

[893]
SAYRE MEMORIAL FUND SCHOLAR AWARD

American Nurses Foundation
Attn: Nursing Research Grants Program
8515 Georgia Avenue, Suite 400
Silver Spring, MD 20910-3492
(301) 628-5298   Fax: (301) 628-5354
E-mail: anf@ana.org
Web: www.anfonline.org

Summary To provide funding to nurses interested in conducting research.

Eligibility This program is open to registered nurses who have earned a baccalaureate or higher degree. Applicants must be beginning researchers who have had no more than 3 research-based publications in refereed journals and have received, as a principal investigator, no more than $15,000 in extramural funding in any 1 research area. They must be interested in conducting research that relates to the interaction between clinical practice and the role of those occupying leadership/management positions. Preference is given to studies examining that relationship in a community or managed care setting (as opposed to acute care). Proposed research may be for a master's thesis or doctoral dissertation if the project has been approved by the principal investigator's thesis or dissertation committee.

Financial data The grant is $3,500. Funds may not be used as a salary for the principal investigator.

Duration 1 year.

Additional information There is a $75 application fee.

Number awarded 1 each year.

Deadline April of each year.

[894]
SCHWARTZ AWARD

American College of Legal Medicine
Attn: Student Writing Competition
1111 North Plaza Drive, Suite 550
Schaumburg, IL 60173-4946
(847) 969-0283   Toll-free: (800) 433-9137
Fax: (847) 517-7229   E-mail: info@aclm.org
Web: www.aclm.org/resources/swc.asp

Summary To recognize and reward outstanding original papers on legal medicine written by medical students.

Eligibility This competition is open to currently-enrolled medical students in the United States or Canada. They must submit an original essay on legal medicine. Some examples: physician-patient relationship under managed care; informed consent and referral; medical records (privacy and confidentiality); emergency care; physician-assisted suicide. No paper that has been previously published in any form will be considered. Papers must contain only uncollaborated original work.

Financial data The prize is $1,000.

Duration The prize is given annually.

Additional information All papers submitted are considered for publication in the *Journal of Legal Medicine* or other medical legal publications.

Number awarded 1 each year.

Deadline January of each year.

[895]
SCIENCE GRADUATE STUDENT GRANT FUND

Foundation for Science and Disability, Inc.
c/o Dr. E.C. Keller, Jr., Treasurer
West Virginia University-Department of Biology
P.O. Box 6057
Morgantown, WV 26506-6057
(304) 293-5201, ext. 2513   Fax: (304) 293-6363
E-mail: ekeller@wvu.edu
Web: www.as.wvu.edu

Summary To provide supplemental grants to students with disabilities who are interested in working on a graduate degree in a science-related field.

Eligibility This program is open to 1) college seniors who have a disability and have been accepted to a graduate or professional school in the sciences, and 2) graduate science students who have a disability. Applicants must be U.S. citizens interested in working on a degree in an area of engineering, mathematics, medicine, science, or technology. Along with their application, they must submit an essay (about 250 words) describing professional goals and objectives, as well as the specific purpose for which the grant would be used. Selection is based on financial need, sincerity of purpose, and scholarship and/or research ability.

Financial data The grant is $1,000. Funds may be used for an assistive device or instrument, as financial support to work with a professor on an individual research project, or for some other special need.

Duration The award is granted annually.

Additional information The Foundation for Science and Disability, Inc. is an affiliate society of the American Association for the Advancement of Science. Information is also available from Richard Mankin, Science Student Grant Committee Chair, 503 N.W. 89th Street, Gainesville, FL 32607-1400, (352) 374-5774, Fax: (352) 374-5781, E-mail: rmankin@gainesville.usda.ufl.edu.

Number awarded Varies each year.

Deadline November of each year.

[896]
SCOTTISH RITE SCHIZOPHRENIA DISSERTATION RESEARCH FELLOWSHIP AWARDS

Ancient Accepted Scottish Rite of the Northern Masonic Jurisdiction
Attn: Scottish Rite Charities
33 Marrett Road
P.O. Box 519
Lexington, MA 02420-0519
(781) 465-3326   Toll-free: (800) 814-1432, ext. 3326
Fax: (781) 674-2102   E-mail: info@scottishritecharities.org
Web: www.scottishritecharities.org/page.asp?page=13

Summary To give support to a limited number of exceptionally promising graduate students at selected schools who are preparing their doctoral dissertations in fields of value to the study of schizophrenia.

Eligibility Eligible to submit proposals are graduate students working on a dissertation in 1 of the following fields: biochemistry, epidemiology, genetics, neuroanatomy, neurobiology, pharmacology, physiology, psychiatry, psychology, sociology, or related fields. Their dissertation must deal with some aspect of schizophrenia. Selection is based on: 1) potential of the candidate for genuinely creative work; 2) likelihood that the candidate's career will advance research on schizophrenia; 3) the educational and research training environment; and 4) the scientific merit of the proposed project.

Financial data The fellowship stipend is $15,000 per year.

Duration 1 year; may be renewed.

Additional information The fellowships are available at the following universities: Chicago Medical School, University of Cincinnati, Columbia University, Cornell University, Harvard University, Indiana University, University of Michigan, University of Pennsylvania, University of Pittsburgh, Ohio State University, University of Wisconsin, or Yale University. Recipients are expected to engage in dissertation research on a full-time basis and must submit 1 copy of their completed dissertation to the Scottish Rite Schizophrenia Research Program library.

Number awarded Up to 15 each year.

Deadline Schools set their own deadlines but must submit the names of their designees by May of each year.

[897]
SDMS GRADUATE RESEARCH AWARD

Society of Diagnostic Medical Sonography
Attn: SDMS Educational Foundation
2745 North Dallas Parkway, Suite 350
Plano, TX 75093-8730
(214) 473-8057   Toll-free: (800) 229-9506
Fax: (214) 473-8563   E-mail: foundation@sdms.org
Web: www.sdms.org/foundation/graduate.asp

Summary To provide funding to graduate student members of the Society of Diagnostic Medical Sonography (SDMS) interested in conducting research as part of the requirements for a graduate degree.

Eligibility This program is open to SDMS members who are working on a master's or doctoral degree. Applicants must submit a description of a research project they plan to conduct as part of the requirements for their degree.

Financial data The grant is $1,000.

Duration 1 year.

Number awarded 1 or more each year.

Deadline May of each year.

[898]
SIGMA DELTA EPSILON FELLOWSHIPS

Sigma Delta Epsilon-Graduate Women in Science, Inc.
c/o Jennifer Ingram, Fellowships Coordinator
Duke University-Department of Medicine
Box 2641, 275 MSRB, Research Drive
Durham, NC 27710
(919) 668-1439   E-mail: fellowshipsquestions@gwis.org
Web: www.gwis.org/grants/default.htm

Summary To provide funding to women interested in conducting research in the United States or abroad in the natural sciences.

Eligibility The program is open to women in the United States and Canada who are doing graduate or postdoctoral work in the natural sciences (defined to include anthropology, computer sciences, environmental sciences, life sciences, mathematics, psychology, physical sciences, and statistics). Applicants must give evidence of outstanding ability and promise in scientific research. They may be proposing to conduct research at an institution in the United States or abroad. Along with their application, they must submit a brief description of relevant personal factors, including financial need, that should be considered in the selection process. Applicants must either be members of Sigma Delta Epsilon–Graduate Women in Science or include a processing fee of $20 (the cost of a 1-year membership).

Financial data Grants recently ranged from $1,250 to $3,000. The funds must be used for scientific research, including professional travel. They may not be used for tuition, child care, travel to professional meetings or to begin a new appointment, administrative overhead or indirect costs, personal computers, living allowances, or equipment for general use.

Duration 1 year; may be renewed in unusual circumstances, contingent upon receipt of an annual progress report.

Additional information The highest scoring applicant receives the Adele Lewis Grant. The second-highest scoring applicant receives the Hartley Fellowship.

Number awarded Varies each year. Recently, 5 of these fellowships were awarded: 2 at $3,000, 2 at $2,000, and 1 at $1,250.

Deadline January of each year.

[899]
SIGMA THETA TAU CLINICAL CARE GRANT

American Association of Critical-Care Nurses
Attn: Research Department
101 Columbia
Aliso Viejo, CA 92656-4109
(949) 362-2050, ext. 321
Toll-free: (800) 394-5995, ext. 321   Fax: (949) 362-2020
E-mail: research@aacn.org
Web: www.aacn.org

Summary To provide funding to registered nurses who wish to conduct research directly related to the priorities of the American Association of Critical-Care Nurses (AACN).

Eligibility This program is open to registered nurses who propose to conduct research on a topic that the association has identified as a priority for critical care nursing: effective and appropriate use of technology to achieve optimal patient assessment, management, and/or outcomes; creating a healing, humane environment; processes and systems that foster the optimal contribution of critical care nurses; effective approaches to symptom management; and prevention and management of complications. The proposed research may be used to meet the requirements for an academic degree. Applicants must be a member of AACN and/or Sigma Theta Tau.

Financial data The grant is $10,000. Funds may be used to support direct project expenses, such as research assistants, secretarial support, equipment, supplies, and consultative assistance. They may not be used for salaries of the principle or co-investigators, travel to presentations, preparation of slides, presentation or publication of findings, or such educational expenses as tuition or books. Indirect costs are limited to 10% of direct costs.

Additional information This grant is co-sponsored by AACN and Sigma Theta Tau International.

Number awarded 1 each year.

Deadline September of each year.

[900]
SIGMA THETA TAU INTERNATIONAL/ASSOCIATION OF NURSES IN AIDS CARE GRANT

Sigma Theta Tau International
Attn: Research Department
550 West North Street
Indianapolis, IN 46202-3191
(317) 634-8171   Toll-free: (888) 634-7575
Fax: (317) 634-8188   E-mail: research@stti.iupui.edu
Web: www.nursingsociety.org/research/grant_anac.html

Summary To provide funding to nurses interested in conducting research related to AIDS.

Eligibility This program is open to registered nurses who have a master's degree and/or are enrolled in a doctoral program. Applicants must be interested in conducting clinically oriented HIV/AIDS research, including studies focused on HIV prevention, symptom management, and promotion of self-care and adherence. Proposals for pilot and/or developmental research may be submitted. Membership in either Sigma Theta Tau International or the Association of Nurses in AIDS Care is required; preference is given to applicants who are members of both organizations.

Financial data The maximum grant is $2,500.

Duration 1 year.

Additional information This program is sponsored jointly by Sigma Theta Tau International and the Association of Nurses in AIDS Care, 3538 Ridgewood Road, Akron, OH 44333, (330) 670-0101, (800) 260-6780, Fax: (330) 670-0109.

Deadline March of each year.

[901]
SOCIETY FOR THE SCIENTIFIC STUDY OF SEXUALITY STUDENT RESEARCH GRANTS

Society for the Scientific Study of Sexuality
Attn: Executive Director
P.O. Box 416
Allentown, PA 18105-0416
(610) 530-2483   Fax: (610) 530-2485
E-mail: thesociety@sexscience.org
Web: www.sexscience.org

Summary To provide funding for research to student members of the Society for the Scientific Study of Sexuality (SSSS).

Eligibility This program is open to graduate students interested in conducting research in the area of human sexuality. The proposed research can be for a master's thesis or doctoral disserta-

tion, but this is not a requirement. Applicants must be enrolled in a degree-granting program and student members of SSSS.

Financial data The grants are $1,000 each.

Duration The grants are offered annually.

Additional information Grant recipients must provide the society with 1 copy of a final report on the research 1 year after receipt of the grant.

Number awarded 3 each year: 1 in spring and 2 in fall.

Deadline January of each year for the spring award; August of each year for the fall awards.

[902]
SOCIETY OF TOXICOLOGY GRADUATE STUDENT FELLOWSHIP AWARDS

Society of Toxicology
Attn: Education Committee
1821 Michael Faraday Drive, Suite 300
Reston, VA 20190-5348
(703) 438-3115   Fax: (703) 438-3113
E-mail: sothq@toxicology.org
Web: www.toxicology.org/ai/af/awards.aspx

Summary To provide financial assistance to doctoral student members of the Society of Toxicology (SOT) engaged in dissertation research.

Eligibility This program is open to graduate student members of the society who have been advanced to candidacy for a Ph.D. in toxicology. Their research director must also be an SOT member. Along with their application, they must submit a description of their dissertation research, including its objectives, work already accomplished, work planned for the term of the fellowship, and relevance of the work to toxicology. Selection is based on originality of the dissertation topic, research productivity, importance and relevance to toxicology, scholastic achievement, and letters of recommendation.

Financial data The stipend is $16,000. Funds are paid to the recipient's university to be used for a stipend, tuition payment, or other education and research-related expenses, including travel.

Duration 1 year.

Additional information These fellowships have been awarded since 1979. They are currently sponsored by Novartis Pharmaceuticals Corporation.

Number awarded 1 each year.

Deadline October of each year.

[903]
SOUTHERN MEDICAL ASSOCIATION RESEARCH PROJECT FUND

Southern Medical Association
Attn: Research and Education Endowment Fund
35 Lakeshore Drive
P.O. Box 190088
Birmingham, AL 35219-0088
(205) 945-1840   Toll-free: (800) 423-4992, ext. 147
Fax: (205) 942-4454   E-mail: jfowler@sma.org
Web: www.sma.org

Summary To provide funding for small research projects to physicians and medical students in southern states.

Eligibility This program is open to 1) physicians in training and 2) medical students located at medical schools, medical centers, osteopathic schools, and affiliated hospitals. Established faculty investigators are not eligible. Applicants must be affiliated with an institution within the territorial boundaries of the association.

Financial data Grants up to $2,500 are available. Funds are to be used primarily for the purchase of expendable items but may be used to pay research assistants if deemed appropriate for the proposed research. Travel expenses are not covered.

Duration 1 year.

Additional information The association covers the states of Alabama, Arkansas, Florida, Georgia, Kentucky, Louisiana, Maryland, Mississippi, Missouri, North Carolina, Oklahoma, South Carolina, Tennessee, Texas, Virginia, West Virginia, and the District of Columbia.

Number awarded Varies each year; recently, 3 of these grants were awarded.

Deadline March of each year.

[904]
SOUTHERN REGIONAL EDUCATION BOARD DISSERTATION-YEAR FELLOWSHIP

Southern Regional Education Board
592 10th Street N.W.
Atlanta, GA 30318-5790
(404) 875-9211, ext. 269   Fax: (404) 872-1477
E-mail: doctoral.scholars@sreb.org
Web: www.sreb.org/programs/dsp/dspindex.asp

Summary To provide funding to minority students who wish to complete a doctoral dissertation while in residence at a university in the southern states.

Eligibility This program is open to U.S. citizens who are members of racial/ethnic minority groups (Native Americans, Hispanic Americans, Asian Americans, and African Americans) and have completed all requirements for a Ph.D. except the dissertation. Applicants must be in a position to write full time and must expect to complete their dissertation within the year of the fellowship. Eligibility is limited to individuals who plan to become full-time faculty members at a southern institution upon completion of their doctoral degree. It does not include students working on a professional degree (M.D., D.B.A., D.D.S., J.D., and D.V.M.) or doing graduate work leading to the Ed.D.

Financial data Fellows receive waiver of tuition and fees (in or out of state), a stipend of $15,000, and a small grant for research expenses.

Duration 1 year; nonrenewable.

Number awarded Varies each year.

Deadline March of each year.

[905]
STUDENT ESSAY COMPETITION IN HEALTHCARE MANAGEMENT

American College of Healthcare Executives
Attn: Associate Director, Division of Research and
    Development
One North Franklin Street, Suite 1700
Chicago, IL 60606-3529
(312) 424-9444   Fax: (312) 424-0023
E-mail: ache@ache.org
Web: www.ache.org/Faculty_Students/student_essay.cfm

Summary To recognize and reward undergraduate or graduate student members of the American College of Healthcare Executives (ACHE) who submit outstanding essays on health care administration.

Eligibility This competition is open to ACHE student associates or affiliates who are enrolled in an undergraduate or graduate program in health care management at an accredited college or university in the United States or Canada. Applicants must submit an essay, up to 15 pages in length, on a topic with a focus on such health management topics as strategic planning and policy; accountability of and/or relationships among board, medical staff, and executive management; financial management; human resources management; systems management; plant and facility management; comprehensive systems of services; quality assessment and assurance; professional, public, community, or interorganization relations; government relations or regulation; marketing; education; research; or law and ethics. Selection is based on significance of the subject to health care management, innovativeness in approach to the topic, thoroughness and precision in developing the subject, practical usefulness for guiding management action, and clarity and conciseness of expression.

Financial data The first-place winners in each division (undergraduate and graduate) receive $3,000 and their programs receive $1,000. The second-place winner receives $2,000 and third $1,000.

Duration The competition is held annually.

Additional information This program was established in 1989.

Number awarded 6 each year: 3 undergraduate and 3 graduate students.

Deadline December of each year.

[906]
STUDENT FELLOWSHIP AWARDS IN NUCLEAR MEDICINE

Society of Nuclear Medicine
Attn: Committee on Awards
1850 Samuel Morse Drive
Reston, VA 20190-5316
(703) 708-9000, ext. 1255   Fax: (703) 708-9020
E-mail: grantinfo@snm.org
Web: www.snm.org

Summary To enable undergraduate, graduate, and medical students to spend time assisting in clinical and basic research activities in nuclear medicine.

Eligibility This program is open to students enrolled in medical school, pharmacy school, or graduate school, and to undergraduates who demonstrate competence for nuclear medicine research. Applicants may be from any country, but they must be enrolled at an institution in the United States. They must submit detailed documentation of the proposed research project and letters of support from the nuclear medicine faculty advisor and 1 or 2 others.

Financial data The grant is $1,000 per month.

Duration Normally 3 months. Occasionally, 2-month awards may be granted.

Additional information Awards are granted with the expectation that exposure to research will serve as an incentive to consider a career in nuclear medicine. The 3 top-ranked applicants are designated Bradley-Alavi Fellows.

Number awarded Varies each year; recently, 7 of these fellowships were awarded.

Deadline November of each year.

[907]
STUDENT RESEARCH GRANT IN AUDIOLOGY

American Speech-Language-Hearing Foundation
Attn: Research Grants
10801 Rockville Pike
Rockville, MD 20852-3279
(301) 897-5700, ext. 4314   Toll-free: (800) 498-2071
Fax: (301) 571-0457   TTY: (800) 498-2071
E-mail: foundation@asha.org
Web: www.ashfoundation.org/grants/research_grants.cfm

Summary To provide funding to graduate students interested in conducting research in audiology.

Eligibility This program is open to master's and doctoral students in the field of communication sciences and disorders. Applicants must be proposing to conduct research in the area of clinical and/or rehabilitative audiology. Selection is based on the significance of the research and its potential impact on the clinical needs related to audiology (15%); clearly-stated project objectives (10%); merits of the design for answering the question (40%); management plan that clearly outlines the activities and timelines of the project (10%); adequate provision for evaluating the results (10%); facilities, resources, and subjects to which the applicant would have access (10%); and the ability of the applicant to complete the proposed research within 1 year (5%).

Financial data The grant is $2,000.

Duration 1 year.

Number awarded 1 each year.

Deadline June of each year.

[908]
STUDENT RESEARCH GRANT IN EARLY CHILDHOOD LANGUAGE DEVELOPMENT

American Speech-Language-Hearing Foundation
Attn: Research Grants
10801 Rockville Pike
Rockville, MD 20852-3279
(301) 897-5700   Toll-free: (800) 498-2071
Fax: (301) 571-0457   TTY: (800) 498-2071
E-mail: foundation@asha.org
Web: www.ashfoundation.org/grants/research_grants.cfm

Summary To provide funding to graduate students interested in conducting research in childhood language development.

Eligibility This program is open to master's or doctoral students in the field of communication sciences and disorders. The proposed research must be in the area of early childhood language development. Selection is based on the significance of the research and its potential impact on the clinical needs relevant to early childhood language development (15%); clearly-stated project objectives (10%); merits of the design for answering the question (40%); management plan that clearly outlines the activities and timelines of the project (10%); adequate provision for evaluating the results (10%); facilities, resources, and subjects to which the applicant would have access (10%); and the ability of the applicant to complete the proposed research within 1 year (5%).

Financial data The grant is $2,000.

Duration 1 year.

Number awarded 1 each year.

Deadline June of each year.

[909]
STUDENT WRITING COMPETITION IN BIOETHICS

American College of Legal Medicine
Attn: Student Writing Competition
1111 North Plaza Drive, Suite 550
Schaumburg, IL 60173-4946
(847) 969-0283   Toll-free: (800) 433-9137
Fax: (847) 517-7229   E-mail: info@aclm.org
Web: www.aclm.org

Summary To recognize and reward outstanding original papers on bioethics written by law or health professions students.

Eligibility This competition is open to currently-enrolled law and health professions students in the United States or Canada. They must submit an original essay on bioethics. Some examples: the implications of death and dying, reproductive rights, bioterrorism, patient-physician relationship, patient safety, public health, biological sciences, organ donation and allocation, biomedical and behavioral research, and medical genetics.

Financial data First prize is $1,000, second $500, and third $250. The first-prize winner also receives reimbursement of costs of travel and lodging to present the paper at the sponsor's annual meeting.

Duration The prizes are given annually.

Number awarded 3 each year.

Deadline January of each year.

[910]
SUMMER FELLOWSHIP IN ANGIOGENESIS RESEARCH

Angiogenesis Foundation
Attn: Fellowships Program
124 Mt. Auburn Street, Suite 200N
P.O. Box 382111
Cambridge, MA 02238-2111
(617) 576-5708   Fax: (617) 576-5808
E-mail: fellowships@angio.org
Web: www.angio.org/researcher/grant/grant.html

Summary To provide funding to medical and graduate students who are interested in participating in research related to angiogenesis during the summer.

Eligibility This program is open to students enrolled in accredited medical schools in the United States, working towards an M.D., Ph.D., or M.D./Ph.D. degree. Applicants must be interested in working on a research project involving scientific or clinical investigations that relate to angiogenesis and vascular proliferative disorders. They must arrange with a senior investigator who will accept them into the laboratory.

Financial data The stipend is $1,000.

Duration Summer months.

Number awarded 4 each year.

Deadline May of each year.

[911]
SUSAN G. KOMEN BREAST CANCER FOUNDATION DISSERTATION RESEARCH GRANTS

Susan G. Komen Breast Cancer Foundation
Attn: Grants Department
5005 LBJ Freeway, Suite 250
Dallas, TX 75244
(972) 855-1616   Toll-free: (888) 300-5582
Fax: (972) 855-1640   E-mail: grants@komen.org
Web: www.komen.org

Summary To provide funding for breast cancer research to doctoral students in the social and health sciences.

Eligibility This program is open to doctoral candidates in the health and social sciences who are interested in conducting dissertation research on breast health and breast cancer. Applicants must be enrolled in a Ph.D., Dr.P.H., Ed.D., Sc.D., D.S.N., or equivalent program for a doctoral degree that requires completion of a dissertation. They must have completed all pre-dissertation requirements at an accredited university in the United States (or a similarly recognized higher education institution in another country), be well advanced in the preparation of their dissertation proposal, and expect to complete their dissertation within 2 years. The programs may include the health professions (including health services management, medical sciences, nursing, nutrition, public health, rehabilitation), anthropology, education, mental health professions, psychology, sociology, or a related area. Applicants' dissertation supervisors must have a faculty appointment at the same institution as the candidate. U.S. citizenship or residency is not required.

Financial data The maximum grant is $15,000 per year.

Duration 2 years.

Number awarded Varies each year. Recently, 24 of these grants were awarded: 15 on the biology of breast cancer, 2 on cancer control, survivorship, and outcomes, 1 on early detections, diagnosis, and prognosis, 1 on etiology, and 5 on treatment.

Deadline August of each year.

[912]
TRANSCULTURAL NURSING RESEARCH AWARD

Transcultural Nursing Society
c/o Lisa A. Dobson
Madonna University
36600 Schoolcraft Road
Livonia, MI 48150-1173
Toll-free: (888) 432-5470   Fax: (734) 432-5463
Web: www.tcns.org

Summary To provide funding for doctoral or postdoctoral research to members of the Transcultural Nursing Society.

Eligibility This program is open to doctoral students in nursing and nurses who have received a doctoral degree within the past 3 years. Applicants must have been a member of the society for 2 out of the past 5 years. They must be interested in conducting a research project related to transcultural nursing.

Financial data The grant is $3,000.

Number awarded 1 each year.

Deadline October of each year.

[913]
ULTRASOUND CONTRAST IMAGING AWARD

Society of Diagnostic Medical Sonography
Attn: SDMS Educational Foundation
2745 North Dallas Parkway, Suite 350
Plano, TX 75093-8730
(214) 473-8057   Toll-free: (800) 229-9506
Fax: (214) 473-8563   E-mail: foundation@sdms.org
Web: www.sdms.org/foundation/bms.asp

Summary To recognize and reward members of the Society of Diagnostic Medical Sonography (SDMS) who make outstanding contributions to research on the use of contrast in ultrasound imaging.

Eligibility This award is available to SDMS members, including undergraduate and graduate student members, who have helped pioneer the use of contrast in ultrasound imaging. The research may have involved the use of contrast agents for both cardiovascular and general ultrasound application.

Financial data The award is $1,000.

Duration The award is presented annually.

Additional information This award is sponsored by Bristol-Myers Squibb Medical Imaging, Inc.

Number awarded 1 each year.

Deadline June of each year.

[914]
VA PREDOCTORAL NURSE FELLOWSHIP

Department of Veterans Affairs
Veterans Health Administration
Attn: Office of Academic Affiliations
810 Vermont Avenue, N.W., Room 475
Washington, DC 20420
(202) 273-8372   E-mail: Linda.Johnson@hq.med.va.gov
Web: www.va.gov/OAA

Summary To provide research funding to graduate students in nursing who have completed their advanced course work and are at the dissertation stage of their doctoral education.

Eligibility This fellowship is open to registered nurse doctoral candidates whose planned research has a clinical research focus and deals with topics that are relevant to the nursing care of adult or aging veterans. Dissertations studies that are considered relevant to the care of veterans are in such areas as geriatrics, primary care, rehabilitation, spinal cord injury, home health care, mental health and substance abuse. Applicants must be currently enrolled in an accredited doctoral program, have a master's degree in nursing or a master's degree in a field related to nursing and a baccalaureate degree in nursing, have successfully completed the required comprehensive examinations, have an approved dissertation proposal, be a U.S. citizen, have an active and current registration as a graduate professional nurse in a state, territory, or commonwealth of the United States, and be able to meet the credentialing and licensing requirements of the U.S. Department of Veterans Affairs (VA). They must be interested in working full time on their proposed dissertation research topic at a VA facility.

Financial data The award is $25,000 per year.

Duration 1 year; recipients may be reappointed for 1 additional year.

Additional information Awardees must agree to a 40-hour per week appointment at a VA facility, where they will conduct their dissertation research. Any expenses connected with the recipient's dissertation activities or research must be supported by funds other than provided in this program. Transportation to the

VA facility site and housing arrangements are the responsibility of the fellow.

Number awarded 2 each year.

Deadline June of each year.

[915]
VESALIUS TRUST STUDENT RESEARCH GRANTS

Vesalius Trust for Visual Communications in the Health
  Sciences
Attn: Wendy Hiller Gee, Student Grants and Scholarships
Krames-West Coast
1100 Grundy Lane
San Bruno, CA 94066
(650) 244-4320   E-mail: wendy.hillergee@krames.com
Web: www.vesaliustrust.org/scholarships.html

Summary To provide funding to students working on a research project in biocommunications.

Eligibility This program is open to undergraduate and graduate students who have completed at least 1 year of a biocommunications program in medical illustrating. Applicants must be interested in conducting a research project under the guidance of a faculty preceptor. Selection is based on the background and education of the applicant (20%); evaluation by the preceptor of the student's ability to complete the project and its potential contributions (10%); project concept and subject matter (30%); project design (20%); and production plan (20%).

Financial data Grant amounts vary each year.

Duration 1 year.

Additional information The top-ranked applicant receives the Alan Cole Scholarship. Other recipients whose projects show evidence of significant merit are designated Vesalian Scholarships.

Number awarded Varies each year. Recently, 19 of these grants were awarded, including 1 designated as the Alan Cole Scholarship and 5 designated as the Vesalian Scholarships.

Deadline November of each year.

[916]
VESSA NOTCHEV FELLOWSHIPS

Sigma Delta Epsilon-Graduate Women in Science, Inc.
c/o Jennifer Ingram, Fellowships Coordinator
Duke University-Department of Medicine
Box 2641, 275 MSRB, Research Drive
Durham, NC 27710
(919) 668-1439   E-mail: fellowshipsquestions@gwis.org
Web: www.gwis.org/grants/default.htm

Summary To provide funding to members of Sigma Delta Epsilon–Graduate Women in Science who are interested in conducting research in the United States or abroad in the natural sciences.

Eligibility The program is open to women in the United States and Canada who are doing graduate or postdoctoral work in the natural sciences (defined as anthropology, computer sciences, environmental sciences, life sciences, mathematics, psychology, physical sciences, and statistics). Applicants must give evidence of outstanding ability and promise in scientific research. They may be proposing to conduct research at any institution in the United States or abroad. Along with their application, they must submit a brief description of relevant personal factors, including financial need, that should be considered in the selection process. Applicants must either be members of Sigma Delta Epsilon–Graduate Women in Science or include a processing fee of $20 (the cost of a 1-year membership).

Financial data Grants range up to $1,000. The funds must be used for scientific research, including professional travel. They may not be used for tuition, child care, travel to professional meetings or to begin a new appointment, administrative overhead or indirect costs, personal computers, living allowances, or equipment for general use.

Duration 1 year; may be renewed in unusual circumstances, contingent upon receipt of an annual progress report.

Additional information This program was established in 1994.

Number awarded Varies each year; recently, 2 of these fellowships were awarded.

Deadline January of each year.

[917]
VIRENDA B. MAHESH AWARD OF EXCELLENCE IN ENDOCRINOLOGY

American Physiological Society
Attn: Membership Services Office
9650 Rockville Pike, Room 4407
Bethesda, MD 20814-3991
(301) 634-7171   Fax: (301) 634-7242
E-mail: members@the-aps.org
Web: www.the-aps.org/awards/section.htm

Summary To recognize and reward pre- and postdoctoral students who have conducted outstanding research in endocrinology.

Eligibility This program is open to graduate students and postdoctoral fellows who are the first author on an abstract submitted to an endocrinology and metabolism physiology section topic category at the Experimental Biology meeting. The award is presented to the author of the abstract in the area of endocrinology that is judged to be the best.

Financial data The award is $1,000 plus reimbursement of the advance registration fee for the meeting.

Duration The award is presented annually.

Number awarded 1 each year.

Deadline November of each year.

[918]
VIRGINIA HENDERSON CLINICAL RESEARCH GRANT

Sigma Theta Tau International
Attn: Research Department
550 West North Street
Indianapolis, IN 46202-3191
(317) 634-8171   Toll-free: (888) 634-7575
Fax: (317) 634-8188   E-mail: research@stti.iupui.edu
Web: www.nursingsociety.org/research/grant_vh.html

Summary To provide funding for clinically-oriented nursing research to members of Sigma Theta Tau International.

Eligibility This program is open to registered nurses actively involved in some aspect of health care delivery, education, or research in a clinical setting. Applicants must be members of the fraternity who have a master's or doctoral degree in nursing or are enrolled in a doctoral program. Selection is based on the quality of the proposed research, future potential of the applicant, appropriateness of the research budget, and feasibility of the time frame.

Financial data The maximum grant is $5,000.

Duration 1 year.

Number awarded 1 every other year.

Deadline November of odd-numbered years.

[919]
VIRGINIA KELLEY, CRNA SCHOLAR AWARD

American Nurses Foundation
Attn: Nursing Research Grants Program
8515 Georgia Avenue, Suite 400
Silver Spring, MD 20910-3492
(301) 628-5298   Fax: (301) 628-5354
E-mail: anf@ana.org
Web: www.anfonline.org

Summary To provide funding to nurses interested in conducting research on women's health.

Eligibility This program is open to registered nurses who have earned a baccalaureate or higher degree. Applicants must be beginning researchers who have had no more than 3 research-based publications in refereed journals and have received, as a principal investigator, no more than $15,000 in extramural funding in any 1 research area. They must be interested in conducting research on women's health. Proposed research may be for a master's thesis or doctoral dissertation if the project has been approved by the principal investigator's thesis or dissertation committee.

Financial data The grant is $3,500. Funds may not be used as a salary for the principal investigator.

Duration 1 year.

Additional information There is a $75 application fee.

Number awarded 1 each year.

Deadline April of each year.

[920]
VIRGINIA S. CLELAND, RN SCHOLAR AWARD

American Nurses Foundation
Attn: Nursing Research Grants Program
8515 Georgia Avenue, Suite 400
Silver Spring, MD 20910-3492
(301) 628-5298   Fax: (301) 628-5354
E-mail: anf@ana.org
Web: www.anfonline.org

Summary To provide funding to nurses interested in conducting research on health policy.

Eligibility This program is open to registered nurses who have earned a baccalaureate or higher degree. Applicants may be either beginning or experienced researchers. They must be interested in conducting research on nursing health policy. Proposed research may be for a master's thesis or doctoral dissertation if the project has been approved by the principal investigator's thesis or dissertation committee.

Financial data The grant is $3,500. Funds may not be used as a salary for the principal investigator.

Duration 1 year.

Additional information There is a $75 application fee.

Number awarded 1 each year.

Deadline April of each year.

[921]
VIRGINIA STONE, RN SCHOLAR AWARDS

American Nurses Foundation
Attn: Nursing Research Grants Program
8515 Georgia Avenue, Suite 400
Silver Spring, MD 20910-3492
(301) 628-5298   Fax: (301) 628-5354
E-mail: anf@ana.org
Web: www.anfonline.org

Summary To provide funding to nurses interested in conducting research on clinical gerontological issues.

Eligibility This program is open to registered nurses who have earned a baccalaureate or higher degree. Applicants must be experienced researchers who have had more than 3 research-based publications in refereed journals and have received, as a principal investigator, more than $15,000 in extramural funding in any 1 research area. They must be interested in conducting research that relates to clinical gerontological nursing issues. The proposed research may be for a master's thesis or doctoral dissertation if the project has been approved by the principal investigator's thesis or dissertation committee.

Financial data The grants are $20,000 or $10,000. Funds may not be used as a salary for the principal investigator.

Duration 1 year.

Additional information There is a $75 application fee.

Number awarded 2 each year: 1 at $20,000 and 1 at $10,000.

Deadline April of each year.

[922]
VISTAKON AWARDS OF EXCELLENCE IN CONTACT LENS PATIENT CARE

American Academy of Optometry
Attn: American Optometric Foundation
6110 Executive Boulevard, Suite 506
Rockville, MD 20852
(301) 984-4734, ext. 3007   Fax: (301) 984-4737
E-mail: laraf@aaoptom.org
Web: www.aaopt.org/aof/scholarship/index.asp

Summary To recognize and reward optometry students who demonstrate outstanding care for contact lens patients.

Eligibility This program is open to students in their fourth year of study at accredited colleges and schools of optometry. Candidates must have demonstrated knowledge of contact lenses as well as outstanding patient care as indicated by the skillful, considerate, and professional care of those patients entrusted to the student.

Financial data The award is $1,000.

Duration The awards are presented annually.

Additional information This program, established in 1993, is sponsored by the Vistakon Division of Johnson & Johnson Vision Care, Inc.

Number awarded 1 at each college or school of optometry.

Deadline April of each year.

[923]
WEATHERHEAD FELLOWSHIPS

School of American Research
Attn: Director of Academic Programs
660 Garcia Street
P.O. Box 2188
Santa Fe, NM 87504-2188
(505) 954-7201   E-mail: scholar@sarsf.org
Web: www.sarweb.org/scholars/description.htm

Summary To fund research residencies at the School of American Research in Santa Fe, New Mexico for pre- and postdoctoral scholars interested in the sciences or humanities.

Eligibility This program is open to scholars, either pre- or postdoctoral, who are interested in conducting research in the humanities or the sciences. Projects that are narrowly focused (geographically or theoretically) or that are primarily methodological seldom receive strong consideration. Topics addressed by recent resident scholars have included the following: social implications of hydraulic systems in early complex society, the symbolism of death and the afterlife in ancient central Mexico, and the politics of gender and identity in post-colonial India. Predoctoral applicants must be nominated by their department or degree-granting program (only 1 nominee will be considered per department). Applications must include: 6 copies of a proposal (no more than 4 pages in length), 6 copies of the applicant's curriculum vitae, and 3 letters of recommendation. Applications are evaluated on the basis of overall excellence and significance of the proposed project, in addition to such factors as clarity of presentation and the applicant's record of academic achievement. Preference is given to applicants whose field work or basic research and analysis are complete and who need time to write up their research.

Financial data The fellowship provides an apartment and office on the school's campus, a stipend up to $40,000, library assistance, and other benefits.

Duration 9 months, beginning in September.

Additional information Books written by recipients may be published by the School of American Research Press. Funding for this program is provided by the Weatherhead Foundation. Recipients are expected to reside at the school, in Santa Fe, for the tenure of the fellowship.

Number awarded 2 each year.

Deadline November of each year.

[924]
WENDELL J. KRIEG CORTICAL SCHOLAR PRIZE

Cajal Club
c/o Dr. Charles E. Ribak, Secretary/Treasurer
University of California at Irvine
Department of Anatomy and Neurobiology
Irvine, CA 92697-1275
(949) 824-5494   Fax: (949) 824-8549
E-mail: ribak@uci.edu
Web: cajalclub.org

Summary To recognize and reward outstanding predoctoral research on the cerebral cortex.

Eligibility This award is open to predoctoral students who are conducting research on the cerebral cortex and/or its connections. Nominations of candidates for this award should be accompanied by the following information: 1) 6 copies of a letter of nomination from a club member; 2) 6 copies of a brief statement by the candidate on how the receipt of this award would aid in obtaining career objectives; 3) 6 copies of the candidate's curriculum vitae; 4) 6 copies of the student's professional school aca-

demic record; and 5) 6 copies of up to 2 reprints and/or manuscripts describing the candidate's research (the candidate should be the primary author of these articles).

Financial data The prize is $1,000 plus $250 in travel funds to support attendance at the annual club meeting. An inscribed certificate is also presented to each winner.

Duration The prize is awarded annually.

Number awarded 1 each year.

Deadline September of each year.

[925]
WILLIAM AND CHARLOTTE CADBURY AWARD

National Medical Fellowships, Inc.
Attn: Scholarship Program
5 Hanover Square, 15th Floor
New York, NY 10004
(212) 483-8880   Fax: (212) 483-8897
E-mail: info@nmfonline.org
Web: www.nmf-online.org

Summary To recognize and reward underrepresented minority medical school students' outstanding academic achievement, leadership, and community service.

Eligibility This award is open to minority students enrolled in their senior year at an accredited U.S. medical school. For the purposes of this program, "minority" is defined as African American, Native Hawaiian, Alaska Native, American Indian, Mexican American, and mainland Puerto Rican. Candidates must be nominated by their medical school during the summer preceding their senior year. Selection is based on academic achievement, leadership, and community service.

Financial data This honor includes a certificate of merit and a $2,000 stipend.

Duration The award is presented annually.

Additional information This award was established in 1977.

Number awarded 1 each year.

Deadline Nominations must be submitted by July of each year.

[926]
WILLIAM B. BEAN STUDENT RESEARCH AWARD

American Osler Society
c/o Charles S. Bryan, Secretary-Treasurer
University of South Carolina School of Medicine
Two Medical Park, Suite 502
Columbia, SC 29203
(803) 540-1000   Fax: (803) 540-1079
E-mail: cbryan@gw.mp.sc.edu
Web: www.americanosler.org/awardspage.htm

Summary To provide financial support to graduate students interested in conducting research in the areas of medical history or medical humanities.

Eligibility This program is open to currently-enrolled students at approved schools of medicine in the United States or Canada. Applicants must be interested in conducting research in the broad areas of medical history and medical humanities. Along with their application, they must submit an abstract of the project, a goal statement, a statement of the background and relevance of the project, and a description of the methodology. In addition, the application must be accompanied by a letter from the proposed sponsor, outlining the sponsor's interest in the project and willingness to provide guidance during the fellowship period.

Financial data The grant is $1,500 (plus an additional $750 if the recipients are invited to present their research findings at the association's annual meeting).

Duration The grants are awarded annually.

Additional information Recipients may be invited to present a paper based on their findings at the annual meeting of the American Osler Society.

Number awarded 1 or more each year.

Deadline February of each year.

[927]
WILLIAM C. EZELL FELLOWSHIPS

American Academy of Optometry
Attn: American Optometric Foundation
6110 Executive Boulevard, Suite 506
Rockville, MD 20852
(301) 984-4734, ext. 3007　　　Fax: (301) 984-4737
E-mail: laraf@aaoptom.org
Web: www.aaopt.org/aof/scholarship/ezell/index.asp

Summary To provide financial assistance to students working on a graduate degree or conducting graduate research in optometric education.

Eligibility Students entering or continuing a full-time program of study and training in research that leads to a master's or doctoral degree relating to optometric education are eligible to apply.

Financial data The stipend is $8,000 per year. Funds are paid quarterly.

Duration 1 year; may be renewed for up to 2 additional years.

Additional information This program was established in 1949 in honor of the first president of the American Optometric Foundation. Sponsors of the program include Bausch & Lomb, CIBA Vision, Essilor, and Vistakon. Recipients are expected to attend school on a full-time basis (although other arrangements can be made).

Number awarded Varies; recently, 9 of these fellowships were awarded.

Deadline March of each year.

[928]
WILLIAM H. ROLLINS AWARD

American Academy of Oral and Maxillofacial Radiology
Attn: Executive Director
P.O. Box 1010
Evans, GA 30809-1010
(706) 721-2607　　　E-mail: mshrout@mail.mcq.edu
Web: www.aaomr.org/wh_rollins.htm

Summary To recognize and reward outstanding research projects completed by postgraduate students who are members of the American Academy of Oral and Maxillofacial Radiology.

Eligibility This award is open to students enrolled in graduate programs with an oral and maxillofacial radiology track. Applicants should be active or associate members of the academy or should have applied for membership. Applicants must have completed a project that involves research in some area of oral and maxillofacial radiology and should result in the eventual publication of a master's thesis or an article suitable for publication. Selection is based on originality, soundness of methodology, and significance of contribution of the research to the science of oral and maxillofacial radiology.

Financial data The award is $1,500.

Duration The award is presented annually.

Additional information Funding for this award is provided by Instrumentarium Imaging.

Number awarded 1 each year.

Deadline March of each year.

[929]
WILLIAM T. PORTER PHYSIOLOGY FELLOWSHIP AWARDS

American Physiological Society
Attn: Education Office
9650 Rockville Pike, Room 3111
Bethesda, MD 20814-3991
(301) 634-7132　　　Fax: (301) 634-7098
E-mail: education@the-aps.org
Web: www.the-aps.org

Summary To provide financial assistance to minorities interested in working on a doctoral degree in physiology.

Eligibility This program is open to U.S. citizens and permanent residents who are members of racial or ethnic minority groups (Hispanic or Latino, American Indian or Alaska Native, Asian, Black or African American, and Native Hawaiian or other Pacific Islander). Applicants must be currently enrolled in or accepted to a doctoral program in physiology at a university as full-time students. They must be planning a program of research training under the supervision of a qualified preceptor. Selection is based on the applicant's potential for success (academic record, statement of interest, previous awards and experiences, letters of recommendation); applicant's proposed training environment (including quality of preceptor); and applicant's research and training plan (clarity and quality).

Financial data The stipend is $20,772. No provision is made for a dependency allowance or tuition and fees.

Duration 1 year; may be renewed for 1 additional year and, in exceptional cases, for a third year.

Additional information This program is supported by the William Townsend Porter Foundation (formerly the Harvard Apparatus Foundation). The first Porter Fellowship was awarded in 1920. In 1966 and 1967, the American Physiological Society established the Porter Physiology Development Committee to award fellowships to minority students engaged in graduate study in physiology.

Number awarded Varies each year; recently, 8 of these fellowships were awarded.

Deadline January of each year.

[930]
WILLIAM TOWNSEND PORTER FELLOWSHIP FOR MINORITY INVESTIGATORS

Woods Hole Marine Biological Laboratory
Attn: Fellowship Coordinator
7 MBL Street
Woods Hole, MA 02543-1015
(508) 289-7441　　　Fax: (508) 457-1924
E-mail: skaufman@mbl.edu
Web: www.mbl.edu/research/fellowships.html

Summary To support underrepresented minority physiologists who wish to conduct research during the summer at the Woods Hole Marine Biological Laboratory (MBL).

Eligibility This program is open to young scientists (undergraduates, senior graduate students, and postdoctoral trainees) who are from an underrepresented minority group (African American, Hispanic American, or Native American), are U.S. citizens or permanent residents, and are interested in conducting research in the field of physiology with senior investigators at MBL.

Financial data Participants receive a stipend and a travel allowance. Recently, grants averaged $1,500.

Duration Summer months.

Additional information This fellowship was first awarded in 1921. Funding is provided by the Harvard Apparatus Foundation.

Number awarded Varies each year.

Deadline January of each year.

[931]
WILLY Z. SADEH GRADUATE STUDENT AWARD IN SPACE ENGINEERING AND SPACE SCIENCES

American Institute of Aeronautics and Astronautics
Attn: Student Programs Director
1801 Alexander Bell Drive, Suite 500
Reston, VA 20191-4344
(703) 264-7536   Toll-free: (800) 639-AIAA, ext. 536
Fax: (703) 264-7657   E-mail: stephenb@aiaa.org
Web: www.aiaa.org/content.cfm?pageid=227

Summary To provide funding for graduate research in space science and engineering.

Eligibility This program is open to graduate students who are specializing in space-based research at an accredited college or university anywhere in the world. Applicants must be enrolled full time in a graduate degree program that requires research in 1) space engineering pertaining to agricultural engineering, bioengineering, civil engineering and infrastructure, fluid dynamics, or geotechnical engineering; 2) space life sciences, encompassing agricultural sciences, biology, biosphere and life support sciences, food sciences and human nutrition, physiology, or plant sciences; or 3) space policy concerning economics, history, law, public policy, or science and technology. They must have a GPA of 3.3 or higher. Selection is based on student academic accomplishments, research record, letter of recommendation, and quality of the research proposal (content, methodology, originality, and practical application).

Financial data The grant is $5,000. The fellow also receives travel stipends to attend the AIAA Aerospace Sciences Meeting and the International Astronautical Federation Congress.

Duration 1 year; nonrenewable.

Additional information This program was instituted in 1999.

Number awarded 1 each year.

Deadline January of each year.

[932]
W.K. KELLOGG FOUNDATION DOCTORAL FELLOWSHIP IN HEALTH POLICY

National Medical Fellowships, Inc.
Attn: Scholarship Program
5 Hanover Square, 15th Floor
New York, NY 10004
(212) 483-8880   Fax: (212) 483-8897
E-mail: info@nmfonline.org
Web: www.nmf-online.org

Summary To provide financial assistance to minorities enrolled in a doctoral program in health policy research who are committed to working with underserved populations.

Eligibility This program is open to members of minority groups (African Americans, Native Americans, Asians, and Hispanics) enrolled in doctoral programs in public health, social policy, or health policy (Ph.D., Dr.P.H., or Sc.D.). Applicants must demon-

strate a willingness to complete relevant dissertation research and a commitment to work with underserved populations upon completion of the doctorate. They must include an essay of 500 to 1,000 words discussing their reasons for applying for a fellowship, their qualifications, how it will support their career plans, and which of 4 areas of focus (health policy, men's health, mental health, substance abuse) most interests them and why.

Financial data Fellowships cover tuition, fees, and a partial living stipend.

Duration Up to 5 years: 2 years to do the necessary course work and 3 years to complete the dissertation.

Additional information The program was created in 1998 with grant support from the W.K. Kellogg Foundation. Recently, it operated at 8 institutions: the RAND Graduate School, the Heller Graduate School at Brandeis University, the Joseph L. Mailman School of Public Health at Columbia University, the Harvard School of Public Health, the Johns Hopkins School of Hygiene and Public Health, the UCLA School of Public Health, the University of Michigan School of Public Health, and the University of Pennsylvania. Information is also available from the sponsor's Washington office at 1627 K Street, N.W., Suite 1200, Washington, DC 20006-1702, (202) 296-4431, Fax: (202) 293-1990.

Number awarded 5 each year.

Deadline June of each year.

[933]
YOUNG AMERICAN AWARDS

Boy Scouts of America
Attn: Learning for Life Division, S210
1325 West Walnut Hill Lane
P.O. Box 152079
Irving, TX 75015-2079
(972) 580-2418   Fax: (972) 580-2137
Web: www.learning-for-life.org

Summary To recognize and reward college and graduate students who demonstrate exceptional achievement and service.

Eligibility This program is open to students younger than 25 years of age who are currently enrolled in college or graduate school. Candidates must be nominated by a Boy Scout troop, Explorer post, Venturing crew, Learning for Life group, individual, or other community youth-serving organization that shares the same program objectives. Nominees must have 1) achieved exceptional excellence in 1 or more fields, such as art, athletics, business, community service, education, government, humanities, literature, mathematics, music, religion, or science; 2) be involved in service in their community, state, or country that adds to the quality of life; and 3) have maintained an above-average GPA. They must submit high school and college transcripts (graduate students need to submit only college transcripts) and at least 3 letters of recommendation. Nominations must be submitted to a local Boy Scout council, but nominees are not required to be a participant in a council unit or program.

Financial data The award is $5,000. Local councils may also provide awards to their nominees.

Duration The awards are presented annually.

Additional information These awards were first presented in 1968.

Number awarded 5 each year.

Deadline Applications must be submitted to the local council office by November of each year.

[934]
3D ULTRASOUND AWARD

Society of Diagnostic Medical Sonography
Attn: SDMS Educational Foundation
2745 North Dallas Parkway, Suite 350
Plano, TX 75093-8730
(214) 473-8057   Toll-free: (800) 229-9506
Fax: (214) 473-8563   E-mail: foundation@sdms.org
Web: www.sdms.org/foundation/medison.asp

Summary To recognize and reward members of the Society of Diagnostic Medical Sonography (SDMS) who make outstanding contributions to research in 3-dimensional ultrasound.

Eligibility This award is available to SDMS members, including undergraduate and graduate student members, who have conducted research related to 3D sonography. Acceptable submissions include new techniques, other innovations in the use of 3D sonography, or notable case studies and abstracts.

Financial data The award is $2,500.

Duration The award is presented annually.

Additional information This award is sponsored by Medison America, Inc.

Number awarded 1 each year.

Deadline May of each year.

Sponsoring Organization Index

The Sponsoring Organization Index makes it easy to identify agencies that offer the financial aid programs described in this book. In this index, the sponsoring organizations are listed alphabetically, word by word. In addition, we've used an alphabetical code (within parentheses) to help you identify the focus of the funding offered by the organizations: S = Study and Training; R = Research and Creative Activities. For example, if the name of a sponsoring organization is followed by (S) 241, a program sponsored by that organization is described in the Study/Training section, in entry 241. If that sponsoring organization's name is followed by another entry number—for example, (R) 990—the same or a different program sponsored by that organization is described in the Research/Creative Activities section, in entry 990. Remember: the numbers cited here refer to program entry numbers, not to page numbers in the book.

AABB, (R) 664
Abbott Endowment for Rheumatology Development., (R) 670–672
Abbott Laboratories, (S) 10, (R) 668, 678, 723, 741, 796, 873
Abbott Laboratories. Ross Products Division, (S) 37–39, (R) 856
Abbott Renal Care Group, (S) 1
Academia Resource Management, (R) 675
Academy for Educational Development, (S) 138
Academy of Natural Sciences of Philadelphia, (R) 812
Academy of Neonatal Nursing, (S) 4, 218
Academy of Operative Dentistry, (R) 781, 876–877
Academy of Osseointegration, (R) 806
Acoustical Society of America, (R) 879
Advanstar Medical Economics Nursing Group, (S) 445
Air Force Officers' Wives' Club of Washington, D.C., (S) 14
Alabama Department of Veterans Affairs, (S) 16
Alcavis International, Inc., (S) 18
Alcoa Foundation, (S) 19
Alexander Graham Bell Association for the Deaf, (S) 24, 152, 194, 207, 343, 362–363, 547, 628, 631
All-Ink.com, (S) 22
Allegiance Home Health Care, (S) 40
Alpha Chi, (S) 283, 320, 548
Alpha Epsilon Iota, (S) 26
Alpha Kappa Alpha Sorority, Inc., (S) 27–28
Alpha Mu Tau Fraternity, (S) 29, 80, 563
Alpha Omega Alpha Honor Medical Society, (R) 730, 797
Alpha Tau Delta, (S) 31
American Academy of Ambulatory Care Nursing, (S) 36, (R) 686
American Academy of Neurology, (R) 772, 836
American Academy of Nurse Practitioners, (S) 37–39, 143–144, 326, (R) 747, 856
American Academy of Nursing, (S) 119
American Academy of Optometry, (S) 64, 643, (R) 922, 927
American Academy of Oral and Maxillofacial Radiology, (S) 536, (R) 683, 736, 928

American Academy of Pediatric Dentistry, (R) 667
American Academy of Physician Assistants, (R) 811
American Action Fund for Blind Children and Adults, (S) 335
American Alliance for Health, Physical Education, Recreation and Dance, (S) 558
American Arab Nurses Association, (S) 40
American Art Therapy Association, Inc., (S) 41, 429, 539
American Association for Dental Research, (R) 665
American Association for Health Education, (S) 88, 146, 380, 640
American Association for Respiratory Care, (S) 449, 646
American Association for the History of Nursing, (R) 687
American Association of Colleges of Nursing, (S) 102, 423
American Association of Colleges of Osteopathic Medicine, (S) 578–579
American Association of Colleges of Pharmacy, (S) 10, (R) 855
American Association of Critical-Care Nurses, (S) 181, (R) 688, 738, 770, 833, 866, 899
American Association of Endodontists, (S) 197, (R) 769
American Association of Family and Consumer Sciences, (S) 415
American Association of Japanese University Women, (S) 42
American Association of Neuroscience Nurses, (S) 459
American Association of Nurse Anesthetists, (S) 43, 61, 137, 140–141, 223, 241, 311, 316, 323, 344, 447, 487, 496–497, 503, 553, (R) 666, 814, 881
American Association of Occupational Health Nurses, Inc., (S) 19, 44, 356, 404
American Association of Pharmaceutical Scientists, (S) 10, (R) 668
American Association of Public Health Dentistry, (S) 273
American Association of University Women, (S) 45, 213, (R) 669
American Brain Tumor Association, (R) 674
American Business Women's Association, (S) 559, 595
American Cancer Society, (S) 153–154, 398
American Chemical Society. Division of Medicinal Chemistry, (R) 750

American College of Healthcare Executives, (S) 17, 217, (R) 905
American College of Legal Medicine, (R) 802, 894, 909
American College of Medical Practice Executives, (S) 5, 86, 131, 251, 413, 490, 545–546, 638
American College of Nurse Practitioners, (S) 46
American College of Nurse–Midwives, (S) 47, 89, 633
American College of Rheumatology, (R) 670–672
American College of Sports Medicine, (S) 48, (R) 689–690, 729, 846, 868, 878
American Council of Pharmaceutical Education, (S) 10
American Council of the Blind, (S) 79, 212, 554
American Dental Association, (S) 6, 421, (R) 781
American Dental Education Association, (S) 134, 359, 584
American Dental Hygienists' Association, (S) 9, 20, 159, 293–294, 583, (R) 676, 813, 886
American Dental Society of Anesthesiology, Inc., (R) 677, 709
American Diabetes Association, (R) 691, 828
American Dietetic Association, (S) 49
American Epilepsy Society, (R) 723, 796, 873
American Ex–prisoners of War, Inc. Columbia River Chapter, (S) 510
American Foundation for Pharmaceutical Education, (S) 10, 330, 514, 543, (R) 668, 678
American Foundation for the Blind, (S) 148, 502, 556
American Gastroenterological Association, (R) 679–681
American Health Information Management Association, (S) 203, 215–216, 540, (R) 725, 774–775
American Hellenic Educational Progressive Association, (S) 169, 473, 495
American Holistic Nurses' Association, (S) 114
American Indian Graduate Center, (S) 50, 166, 226, 235, 243, 318, 564
American Indian Science and Engineering Society, (S) 83
American Institute of Aeronautics and Astronautics, (R) 931
American Institute of the History of Pharmacy, (R) 692
American Legion. Americanism and Children & Youth Division, (S) 185
American Legion. Illinois Auxiliary, (S) 416
American Lung Association, (R) 824
American Medical Association, (S) 33–34, 84, 319, 550, (R) 693
American Medical Women's Association Foundation, (S) 639, (R) 731, 785
American Membrane Technology Association, (R) 708
American Mensa Education and Research Foundation, (S) 309, 406
American Meteorological Society, (R) 694
American Nephrology Nurses' Association, (S) 1, 18, 58, 63, 300, 447, 477, 614, 634
American Nurses Association, (S) 121, (R) 739
American Nurses Credentialing Center, (R) 826
American Nurses Foundation, (R) 695, 711, 733, 743, 756–757, 766, 787, 801, 810, 816–817, 823, 827, 837, 858, 882, 893, 919–921
American Occupational Therapy Foundation, (S) 8, 301, 329, 383, 470, 488, 533, 552, 605, 655, (R) 696
American Optometric Association, (S) 176
American Organization of Nurse Executives, (S) 447, 566–567
American Osler Society, (R) 926
American Osteopathic Foundation, (S) 636, 647, (R) 712
American Otological Society Research Fund, (R) 697
American Parkinson Disease Association Inc., (R) 832
American Pediatric Society, (R) 698

American Pharmaceutical Association, (S) 10
American Pharmacists Association, (S) 598, (R) 789, 842
American Philosophical Society, (R) 699, 815
American Physical Therapy Association, (S) 219, 388–389, 422, (R) 776
American Physiological Society, (S) 650, (R) 917, 929
American Podiatric Medical Association, (S) 67
American Psychiatric Association, (R) 714, 840
American Psychological Association. Division 54, (R) 820
American Psychological Association. Minority Fellowship Program, (S) 276, 407–408, 529, 599
American Psychological Foundation, (S) 270, 377, (R) 767, 820
American Radio Relay League, (S) 381, 386, 463
American School Health Association, (R) 715
American Skin Association, (R) 700
American Society for Clinical Laboratory Science, (S) 80, (R) 685, 701–702
American Society for Clinical Laboratory Science. Pennsylvania, (S) 183
American Society for Clinical Laboratory Science. Wisconsin, (S) 635
American Society for Investigative Pathology, (R) 718
American Society for Nutrition, (R) 870
American Society for Quality, (S) 648
American Society of Crime Laboratory Directors, (S) 51
American Society of Extra–Corporeal Technology, Inc., (S) 297, 308, 384, 509, 519
American Society of Health–System Pharmacists, (S) 10, (R) 716–717
American Society of Hematology, (S) 52, (R) 703, 839
American Society of PeriAnesthesia Nurses, (S) 53, (R) 704–705
American Society of Podiatric Medical Assistants, (S) 661
American Society of Radiologic Technologists, (S) 188, 227, 281, 424, 582, (R) 706–707
American Society of Safety Engineers, (S) 122, 136, 214, 231, 239, 253, 298, 403, 611
American Society of Safety Engineers. Arizona Chapter, (S) 71
American Society of Safety Engineers. Craters of the Moon Chapter 88, (S) 569
American Speech–Language–Hearing Foundation, (S) 54–55, 327, 354, 462, (R) 907–908
American Therapeutic Recreation Association, (R) 724
American Water Ski Educational Foundation, (S) 433
Amgen Inc., (S) 58, 397, (R) 750
Ancient Accepted Scottish Rite of the Northern Masonic Jurisdiction, (R) 896
Ancient and Accepted Scottish Rite of Freemasonry, Southern Jurisdiction, (S) 577
Andrew W. Mellon Foundation, (R) 699
Angiogenesis Foundation, (R) 910
Anheuser–Busch Companies, Inc., (S) 97, (R) 727
Anthony J. Jannetti, Inc., (S) 218, 300, 445
Applied Measurement Professionals, Inc., (S) 449
ARC of Washington Trust Fund, (S) 69
Arizona Commission for Postsecondary Education, (S) 72
Arkansas Business and Professional Women, (S) 651
Arkansas Department of Higher Education, (S) 73–74
Arkansas Environmental Federation, (S) 345, 538
Armenian International Women's Association, (S) 12
Armenian Professional Society, (S) 76
Armenian Relief Society of Eastern U.S.A., Inc., (S) 349
Armenian Students' Association, (S) 77

Arthritis Foundation, (R) 751
Association for Women in Science, (R) 719, 821
Association of American Medical Colleges, (S) 271
Association of Black Cardiologists, Inc., (S) 175
Association of Nurses in AIDS Care, (S) 60, (R) 900
Association of periOperative Registered Nurses, (S) 65–66, 81, (R) 713
Association of Rehabilitation Nurses, (R) 835, 880, 883
Association of Schools of Public Health, (R) 732
Association of United Nurses, (S) 82
Association of University Programs in Health Administration, (S) 613
Association on American Indian Affairs, Inc., (S) 189, 574
AstraZeneca Pharmaceuticals, L.P., (S) 10, 499, 518, (R) 668, 678
Audio–Digest Foundation, (S) 84
Audiology Foundation of America, (S) 352, 516, 541, 572, 609
Autism Society of America, (R) 742
Auxiliary to the National Medical Association, (S) 25
Aventis Pharmaceuticals, Inc., (S) 10, 38, 499

Bamford–Lahey Children's Foundation, (S) 87, (R) 722
Bank of America Foundation, (S) 222
Bausch & Lomb, (S) 643, (R) 927
Big 12 Conference, (S) 173
Bill and Melinda Gates Foundation, (S) 226
Black Nurses' Association of Greater Washington, D.C. Area, Inc., (S) 208
Blinded Veterans Association, (S) 332
Blistex, Inc., (S) 10
Boomer Esiason Foundation, (S) 95
BostonWorks, (S) 96
Boy Scouts of America. Learning for Life Division, (R) 933
Bracco Diagnostics, Inc., (R) 726
Bristol–Myers Squibb Company, (S) 10, (R) 668, 678, 750
Bristol–Myers Squibb Medical Imaging, Inc., (R) 913
Bristol–Myers Squibb Oncology, (S) 610
Burroughs Wellcome Fund, (S) 10
Bush Foundation, (S) 99
Business and Professional Women of Virginia, (S) 98, 658
Business and Professional Women's Clubs of New York State, (S) 242
Business and Professional Women's Foundation, (S) 105

Cajal Club, (R) 924
California Adolescent Nutrition, Physical Education, and Culinary Arts Scholarships, (S) 103
California Association for Postsecondary Education and Disability, (S) 597, 649
California Breast Cancer Research Program, (S) 100, (R) 728
California Rural Indian Health Board, Inc., (S) 515
California Scottish Rite Foundation, (S) 101
California–Pacific United Methodist Foundation, (S) 157
The Camden Group, (S) 620
CampusRN, (S) 102
Caremark Rx, Inc., (S) 200
Cargill, Inc., (R) 870
Carrington Laboratories, (S) 177, (R) 762

Catching the Dream, (S) 409
CDC Foundation, (S) 68
Center for American Nurses, (R) 733
The Center for Reintegration, Inc., (S) 357
Central Association of Obstetricians and Gynecologists, (R) 734–735
CFIDS Association of America, (S) 38
Charles A. Dana Foundation, (S) 402, (R) 831
Chickasaw Foundation, (S) 182
Chinese American Physicians Society, (S) 104
Christian Connector, Inc., (S) 118
CIBA Vision, (S) 643, (R) 927
CNA Foundation, (S) 122
Colgate–Palmolive Company, (S) 85, 124, 162–163, 170, 421, 442, 453, (R) 721
Colin Higgins Foundation, (R) 740
College Hall of Fame, Inc., (S) 444, 622
College of Physicians of Philadelphia. Francis C. Wood Institute for the History of Medicine, (R) 777–778
Colorado Commission on Higher Education, (S) 126–127
Commission on Graduates of Foreign Nursing Schools, (R) 743
Community Foundation for Greater Atlanta, Inc., (S) 596
Community Foundation of Middle Tennessee, (S) 351
Congressional Black Caucus Foundation, Inc., (S) 115, 129
Connecticut Community College System, (S) 130
Consortium of Universities of the Washington Metropolitan Area, (R) 744
ConvaTec, (S) 657
Cosmos Club Foundation, (R) 744
Costco Wholesale, (S) 133
Council of Citizens with Low Vision International, (S) 107, 221
Council of Energy Resource Tribes, (S) 110
Council on Accreditation of Nurse Anesthesia Educational Programs, (S) 316
Covance Corporation, (R) 902
Cystic Fibrosis Foundation, (S) 642, (R) 745

Daiichi Pharmaceutical Corporation, (S) 37–39
DaimlerChrysler Corporation, (S) 136
Dan David Prize, (R) 746
Danish Sisterhood of America, (S) 91
Daughters of Penelope, (S) 92, 587
DAV Charitable Trust, (R) 854
David L. Jelinek Agency, LLC, (S) 487
Davis–Putter Scholarship Fund, (S) 139
Delaware Community Foundation, (S) 269
Delaware Higher Education Commission, (S) 145
Delaware State Bar Association, (S) 269
Delta Gamma Foundation, (S) 148
Delta Sigma Theta Sorority, Inc. Century City Alumnae Chapter, (S) 390
Dentsply International, (R) 665
Dermatology Nurses' Association, (S) 151, 224
Dermik Laboratories, (S) 151
Dolores Zohrab Liebmann Fund, (S) 155, (R) 752
Donald D. Hammill Foundation, (R) 753
Doris Duke Charitable Foundation, (R) 755
Dow Chemical Company, (R) 758
Drexel University College of Medicine, (R) 825

E-Z-EM Inc., (S) 281
Eastman Kodak Company, (R) 764
Educational Communications Scholarship Foundation, (S) 112
E.I. duPont de Nemours and Company, Inc., (R) 765
Eight and Forty, (S) 185
Elekta, (S) 188
Eli Lilly and Company, (S) 357, 518, (R) 750
Elizabeth Nash Foundation, (S) 191
Emergency Medicine Foundation, (R) 768
Emergency Nurses Association, (S) 195–196, 331, 405, 447, 498
Environmental Professionals' Organization of Connecticut, (S) 199
Epilepsy Foundation, (R) 723, 796, 873
Epsilon Sigma Alpha, (S) 201
Essilor, (S) 643, (R) 927
Ethel Louise Armstrong Foundation, (S) 186
Evangelical Lutheran Church in America, (S) 165
Exact Sciences, (S) 38

Far West Athletic Trainers' Association, (S) 206, 418
Fenwal Inc., (R) 664
Finlandia Foundation National, (S) 210
Finlandia Foundation. New York Metropolitan Chapter, (S) 174, (R) 761
Fitzgerald Health Education Association, (S) 38
Florida Council of periOperative Registered Nurses, (S) 120
Florida Education Fund, (S) 400
Florida Nurses Association, (R) 858
Ford Motor Company, (S) 214
Foundation for Amateur Radio, Inc., (S) 347, 660, 663
Foundation for Digestive Health and Nutrition, (R) 679–681
Foundation for Science and Disability, Inc., (S) 568, (R) 895
Foundation for the Carolinas, (S) 108
Fujisawa Healthcare, Inc., (S) 10

Galderma Laboratories, (S) 224
Gallaudet University Alumni Association, (S) 30, 245
Garden Club of America, (R) 710
Gay and Lesbian Medical Association. Lesbian Health Fund, (R) 818
GE Healthcare, (S) 227, (R) 771
Genentech BioOncology, (R) 839
General Dynamics, (S) 313
General Federation of Women's Clubs of Virginia, (S) 517
General Mills, Inc., (S) 115
General Nutrition Centers, Inc., (R) 788
Georgia Association of Homes and Services for Children, (S) 109
Gerber Companies Foundation, (R) 783, 870
GlaxoSmithKline, (S) 10, 89, 238, 499, 514, 518, (R) 665, 668, 678, 786
GN ReSound North America, (S) 541
Golden Key International Honour Society, (S) 240, (R) 809
Golf Course Superintendents Association of America, (S) 168
Grass Foundation, (R) 793
Greater Kanawha Valley Foundation, (S) 472
Grundy Foundation, (R) 699

H. Fletcher Brown Trust, (S) 247
Harlem Hospital School of Anesthesia Alumni, (S) 241, 311
Harold B. & Dorothy A. Snyder Scholarship Fund, (S) 250
Harry J. Bosworth Company, (S) 421
Hartford Foundation for Public Giving, (S) 220
Harvard Apparatus Foundation, (R) 930
Harvard University. John F. Kennedy School of Government, (R) 773
Hawai'i Community Foundation, (S) 132, 160, 167, 209, 254, 256, 277, 315, 346, 504, 621
Hawaii. Department of Hawaiian Home Lands, (S) 256
Hawaiian Civic Club of Honolulu, (S) 255
Health Careers Foundation, (S) 257
Health Monitor Network, (S) 38
Health Physics Society, (S) 259
Healthcare Information and Management Systems Society, (S) 261–262, 573
Healthcare Information and Management Systems Society. Colorado Chapter, (S) 116
Healthcare Information and Management Systems Society. Minnesota Chapter, (S) 419
Healthcare Information and Management Systems Society. National Capital Area Chapter, (S) 450
Heart of America Contact Lens Society, (S) 263
Helen Laidlaw Foundation, (S) 264
Hellenic Times Scholarship Fund, (S) 265
Hellenic University Club of New York, (R) 760
Helping Hands Foundation, (S) 266
Hemophilia Health Services, (S) 267
Hispanic College Fund, (S) 133
Hispanic Dental Association, (S) 124, 238, 532
Hispanic Scholarship Fund, (S) 125, 226
Hospice and Palliative Nurses Foundation, (R) 803
Howard Hughes Medical Institute, (S) 274, 280, (R) 799, 804

Idaho Association of Nurse Anesthetists, (S) 553
Illinois Hospital Association, (S) 285
Illinois Student Assistance Commission, (S) 286
Indiana Space Grant Consortium, (R) 807
Infusion Nursing Society, (S) 225
Ingenix Companies, (S) 216
Institute for Diversity in Healthcare Management, (S) 613
Institute of Food Technologists, (R) 782
Instrumentarium Imaging, (R) 928
International Alumnae of Delta Epsilon Sorority, (S) 284
International Dairy-Deli-Bakery Association, (S) 290
International Foundation for Ethical Research, (R) 790
International Order of Job's Daughters, (S) 244
International Order of the King's Daughters and Sons, (S) 258
International Society of Psychiatric-Mental Health Nurses, (R) 884
International Union of Electronic, Electrical, Salaried, Machine, and Furniture Workers, (S) 233
Iowa Academy of Family Physicians, (S) 557
Iowa Farm Bureau Federation, (S) 557
Iowa Space Grant Consortium, (S) 291
Isaac Comly Martindale Fund, (R) 699

Jack Kent Cooke Foundation, (S) 296
James Q. Cannon Memorial Endowment, (S) 299
Janssen Pharmaceutica Products, L.P., (S) 10
Japanese American Citizens League, (S) 2, 117, 171, 268, 368, 474, 537, 542
Japanese Medical Society of America, Inc., (S) 302
Japanese Women's Society Foundation, (S) 303
Joanna F. Reed Medical Scholarship Trust, (S) 312
John A. Hartford Foundation, (S) 119
John F. Steinman Fellowship Fund, (S) 317
Johnson & Johnson Long Term Care Business Group, (S) 432
Johnson & Johnson Medical, Inc., (S) 10, (R) 665
Johnson & Johnson Vision Care, Inc. Vistakon Division, (S) 643, (R) 922, 927
Josephine de Kármán Fellowship Trust, (S) 321
Journal of the National Medical Association, (S) 310

Kaiser Permanente School of Anesthesia, (S) 323
Kansas Board of Regents, (S) 328
Kansas Federation of Business & Professional Women's Clubs, Inc., (S) 193
Kappa Epsilon Pharmacy Fraternity, (S) 10, 330
Ke Ali'i Pauahi Foundation, (S) 149, 232, 255
Kentucky Department of Veterans Affairs, (S) 336
Kentucky Occupational Therapy Foundation, (S) 305
Kids' Chance of Indiana, Inc., (S) 338
Kids' Chance of South Carolina, (S) 339
Knights of Lithuania, (S) 340
Kosciuszko Foundation, (S) 172, 341
Kraft Foods, Inc., (R) 870
Kurzweil Foundation, (S) 79, 212, 554

League of United Latin American Citizens, (S) 364–366
Lebanese American Heritage Club, (S) 350
Leopold Schepp Foundation, (S) 353
Liberty Leadership Fund, (S) 356
Lincoln Community Foundation, (S) 358
Lincoln Foodservice Products Company, Inc., (R) 805
L'Oréal USA., (R) 821
Los Angeles Department of Water and Power, (S) 222
Los Angeles Hillel Council, (S) 361
Los Padres Foundation, (S) 237
Lupus Foundation of America, (R) 784
Luso–American Education Foundation, (S) 3

Maids of Athena, (S) 369
Maine. Bureau of Veterans' Services, (S) 374
Maine Community Foundation, (S) 135, 355, 375
Maine Dental Association, (S) 32
Maine Education Services, (S) 370–371
Maine Employers' Mutual Insurance Company, (S) 278
Maine. Legislative Information Office, (S) 370
Maine Osteopathic Association, (S) 90, 372–373
March of Dimes Birth Defects Foundation, (S) 378
Marian J. Wettrick Charitable Foundation, (S) 379
Mars Inc., (R) 870
Maryland Higher Education Commission, (S) 184, 392–395

Massachusetts Federation of Polish Women's Clubs, (S) 172
Massachusetts Hospital Association, (S) 96
Massachusetts Office of Student Financial Assistance, (S) 396
Mayday Fund, (S) 119
MC Strategies, Inc., (S) 216
McNeil Consumer and Health Care, (R) 842
McNeil Consumer and Specialty Pharmaceuticals, (S) 401, 518
McNeil Consumer Healthcare, (S) 615
McNeil Nutritionals, (R) 870
MedQuist Inc., (S) 216
Medtronic Cardiopulmonary, Inc., (S) 384
Medtronic Physio–Control Corporation, (S) 404–405, (R) 833
Mentor HealthCare, Inc., (R) 835
Merck Company Foundation, (S) 10
Metropolitan Life Foundation, (S) 410
Michigan Department of Treasury, (S) 412
Microcirculatory Society, (R) 720
Midwest Nursing Research Society, (R) 837
Midwestern Higher Education Commission, (S) 414
Military Order of the Purple Heart, (S) 417
Miss America Pageant, (S) 161
Missouri Botanical Garden, (R) 710
Monster Healthcare, (S) 423–424
MWH, (R) 844
Myasthenia Gravis Foundation of America, Inc., (R) 798

National Alliance for Autism Research, (S) 530–531, (R) 871–872
National AMBUCS, Inc., (S) 35
National Arab American Medical Association, (S) 430
National Association Directors of Nursing Administration in Long Term Care, (S) 483, 594
National Association for Campus Activities, (S) 555
National Association for the Advancement of Colored People, (S) 11
National Association of Chain Drug Stores, (S) 10, 512
National Association of Collegiate Directors of Athletics, (S) 431
National Association of Directors of Nursing Administration in Long Term Care, (S) 106, 432, 617
National Association of Health Services Executives, (S) 438
National Association of Hispanic Nurses, (S) 324, 439
National Association of Junior Auxiliaries, Inc., (S) 440
National Association of Orthopaedic Nurses, (S) 333
National Association of Pediatric Nurse Practitioners, (S) 187, 401, (R) 845
National Association of School Nurses, (S) 435, (R) 847, 849
National Association of University Women, (S) 441
National Association of University Women. Southwest Section, (S) 7
National Athletic Trainers' Association, (S) 436–437, (R) 822, 848
National Board for Respiratory Care, (S) 449
National Collegiate Athletic Association, (S) 451, 630
National Community Pharmacists Association, (S) 10, 304, 452, 641
National Consortium for Graduate Degrees for Minorities in Engineering and Science (GEM), (S) 228
National Dental Association, (S) 162–163, 170, 442, 453
National Environmental Health Association, (S) 457
National Federation of Republican Women, (S) 434
National Federation of the Blind, (S) 113, 204, 249, 272, 279, 306, 335, 342, 443

National Fish and Wildlife Foundation, (S) 97, (R) 727
National Football Foundation, (S) 444, 622
National Forty and Eight, (S) 229
National Gerontological Nurses Association, (S) 391
National Hemophilia Foundation, (S) 535, (R) 859
National Inventors Hall of Fame, (R) 741
National Medical Association, (S) 475, 500
National Medical Fellowships, Inc., (S) 282, 295, 310, 410, 475–476, 500, 656, (R) 779, 783, 925, 932
National Military Family Association, Inc., (S) 313
National Organization for Associate Degree Nursing, (S) 94
National Organization for the Professional Advancement of Black Chemists and Chemical Engineers, (R) 758, 764–765, 786, 874
National Science Foundation. Directorate for Education and Human Resources, (S) 481
National Society Daughters of the American Revolution, (S) 21, 164, 292
National Strength and Conditioning Association, (S) 111, 479–480, 525, (R) 788, 857
National Student Nurses' Association, (S) 445–447
National Water Research Institute, (R) 708, 844, 860, 885
National Wildlife Federation, (R) 794
Nebraska Space Grant Consortium, (S) 454
Nephrology Nursing Certification Commission, (S) 477
Nesbitt Medical Student Foundation, (S) 458
Nevada Space Grant Consortium, (S) 460, (R) 851
Nevada State Medical Association, (S) 461
New England Board of Higher Education, (S) 464
New Hampshire Charitable Foundation, (S) 465
New Hampshire Space Grant Consortium, (R) 852
New Jersey Commission on Higher Education, (S) 466
New Jersey Hospital Association, (S) 260
New Mexico Department of Veterans' Services, (S) 468
New Mexico Higher Education Department, (S) 467, 469
New York State Higher Education Services Corporation, (S) 471
Norfolk Foundation, (S) 211
North American Interfraternal Foundation., (S) 360, 387
North Carolina Nurses Association, (S) 385
North Carolina Rehabilitation Association, (S) 612
North Carolina State Education Assistance Authority, (S) 93
North Dakota Space Grant Program, (R) 853
North Georgia United Methodist Foundation, (S) 157
Northeastern Association of Forensic Scientists, (S) 234
Northstar Engineering Consultants, Inc., (S) 345
Northwest Osteopathic Medical Foundation, (S) 478
Novartis Oncology, (S) 397, 499
Novartis Pharmaceuticals Corporation, (S) 10, (R) 668, 678, 750, 902
Novo Nordisk Pharmaceuticals, Inc., (S) 10, 37, (R) 855
Nurse Practitioner Healthcare Foundation, (S) 482
Nurses Educational Funds, Inc., (S) 202, 367, 455–456
Nurses Organization of Veterans Affairs, (R) 854
Nursing Economic$ Foundation, (S) 484
Nursing Foundation of Rhode Island, (S) 485
Nursing Spectrum, (S) 566

Oak Ridge Institute for Science and Education, (S) 150, (R) 748, 800
Oak Ridge National Laboratory, (R) 800

Occupational Therapy Association of Oregon, (S) 486
Ohio Board of Regents, (S) 489
Ohio Environmental Health Association, (S) 230
Oklahoma United Methodist Foundation, (S) 157
Oncology Education Services, Inc., (S) 397
Oncology Nursing Certification Corporation, (S) 397
Oncology Nursing Society, (S) 62, 322, 397, 447, 491, 549, 610
Oregon Community Foundation, (S) 348, 510
Oregon Student Assistance Commission, (S) 348, 492–493, 510
Organization of Chinese Americans, Inc., (S) 226
Organon USA, (S) 38
Ortho Biotech Products, L.P., (S) 10
Ortho–McNeil Pharmaceutical Corporation, (S) 10, 47, (R) 723, 796, 873
Orthopaedic Research and Education Foundation, (R) 830
Oticon Foundation, (S) 572, 609

Pampers., (S) 378
Pampers Parenting Institute, (S) 324
Parenteral Drug Association, (R) 863
Parkinson's Disease Foundation, (R) 861
Patient Advocate Foundation, (S) 499
Paul and Daisy Soros Fellowships for New Americans, (S) 501
Pediatric Endocrinology Nursing Society, (S) 507
Pennsylvania Masonic Youth Foundation, (S) 506
Pennsylvania Medical Society, (S) 23, 198
P.E.O. Sisterhood, (S) 508
Perfusion.com, Inc., (R) 780
Pfizer Consumer Healthcare Group, (R) 665
Pfizer Inc., (S) 10, 62, 68, 499, 511, 518, 617, (R) 668, 678, 723, 750, 796, 873
Pharmaceutical Research and Manufacturers of America, (S) 526–528, (R) 862
Pharmaceutical Research and Manufacturers of America Foundation, (S) 10
Pharmacia Corporation, (S) 10
Phi Kappa Phi, (S) 513
Phi Lambda Sigma, (S) 514
Phi Sigma Pi, (S) 544, 551
Philadelphia General Hospital Training School for Nurses. Alumni Association, (R) 684
Philips Medical Systems, (R) 866–867
Phillips Fund, (R) 699
Phonak AG, (S) 516
Pisacano Leadership Foundation, (S) 520
Pittsburgh Foundation, (S) 334, 592
Point Foundation, (S) 521
Polonia Foundation of Ohio, (S) 522
Portuguese Foundation of Connecticut, (S) 523
Possible Woman Enterprises, (S) 524
Power Systems, Inc., (S) 525
Procter & Gamble Company, (S) 10, 134, 324, 421, 482, 532, (R) 665, 874, 902
Procter & Gamble Pharmaceuticals, (S) 518
Psi Iota Xi, (S) 54
Purdue Pharma L.P., (S) 518

Quest Medical, Inc., (S) 519

Radiological Society of North America, (R) 888
Redi–Tag Corporation, (S) 540
Research to Prevent Blindness, (R) 829
Rho Chi, (S) 543
Robert O. Gilbert Foundation, (R) 884
Roche Pharmaceuticals, (S) 518
Romanian Orthodox Episcopate of America, (S) 70
Rosalynn Carter Institute for Human Development, (S) 314, 399
Royal Society of Tropical Medicine and Hygiene, (R) 887
Ruth Jackson Orthopaedic Society, (R) 759

Salvadoran American Leadership and Educational Fund, (S) 222
Sanofi–Aventis Pharmaceuticals, Inc., (S) 397, (R) 750
Sanofi–Synthelabo, Inc., (S) 10
Sarnoff Cardiovascular Research Foundation, (R) 892
Schering Laboratories, (S) 10, (R) 668, 678
Schering–Plough Corporation, (S) 543
Schering–Plough Foundation, Inc., (S) 10
Scholarship Administrative Services, Inc., (S) 82
Scholarship America, (S) 465, 615, 618, 629
Scholarship Program Administrators, Inc., (S) 5, 86, 131, 251, 267, 413, 490, 545–546, 638
School Nutrition Association, (S) 123, (R) 805
School of American Research, (R) 923
Scudder Association, Inc., (S) 570
Seattle Foundation, (S) 158
Sertoma International, (S) 128
Seymour L. Kaplan Scholarship Foundation Fund, (S) 575
Shui Kuen and Allen Chin Foundation, (S) 581
Siemens, (S) 567
Siemens Medical Solutions USA, Inc., (S) 582
Sigma Alpha Iota Philanthropies, Inc., (S) 428
Sigma Delta Epsilon–Graduate Women in Science, Inc., (R) 850, 898, 916
Sigma Theta Tau International, (R) 754, 803, 899–900, 918
The Sisters of Perpetual Indulgence, Inc., (S) 585
Smithsonian Institution Libraries, (R) 749
Smithsonian Institution. Office of Research Training and Services, (R) 841
Society for Academic Emergency Medicine, (R) 768
Society for Applied Anthropology, (R) 865
Society for Epidemiologic Research, (R) 673
Society for Pediatric Research, (R) 698
Society for the Scientific Study of Sexuality, (R) 901
Society of Diagnostic Medical Sonography, (R) 726, 771, 795, 867, 897, 913, 934
Society of Gastroenterology Nurses and Associates, Inc., (S) 576
Society of Mexican American Engineers and Scientists, (S) 411
Society of Nuclear Medicine, (S) 505, (R) 864, 906
Society of Otorhinolaryngology and Head–Neck Nurses, Inc., (S) 586
Society of Toxicology, (S) 85, (R) 721, 902
Society of Toxicology. Midwest Regional Chapter, (R) 843
SonoSite Inc., (R) 795
South Carolina Department of Health and Environmental Control, (S) 624
South Carolina Nurses Foundation, Inc., (S) 624
Southeast Athletic Trainers Association, (S) 307, 571
Southern Medical Association, (S) 589, (R) 903
Southern Regional Education Board, (S) 590–591, (R) 904

Starkey Laboratories, Inc., (S) 645
State Student Assistance Commission of Indiana, (S) 287
State University System of Florida, (S) 147
Stokely–Van Camp, (R) 729
Sunstar Americas, (S) 421
Sunstar Butler, (S) 665
SuperCollege.com, (S) 600
Susan G. Komen Breast Cancer Foundation, (R) 911

Taylor J. Ertel Foster Children Foundation, (S) 602
Tennessee Chiropractic Association, (S) 351
Texas Amateur Athletic Federation, (S) 603
Texas Federation of Business and Professional Women's Foundation, Inc., (S) 420, (R) 838
Texas Higher Education Coordinating Board, (S) 604, 606–608
Texas Safety Foundation, (S) 231
Thomson Micromedex, (S) 567
Toro Company, (S) 168
Transcultural Nursing Society, (R) 912
Triad Hospitals, Inc., (S) 613
Turlock Social Club of California, (S) 474
Tyco Kendall Healthcare Products, (S) 614

UCB Pharma, Inc., (S) 337
Ukrainian Fraternal Association, (S) 205
United Daughters of the Confederacy, (S) 325, 376, 580
United Daughters of the Confederacy. Virginia Division, (S) 382
United Methodist Church. General Board of Global Ministries, (S) 156, 252, 275
United Methodist Church. General Board of Higher Education and Ministry, (S) 178–179, 236, 248, 616
United Methodist Higher Education Foundation, (S) 157, 448
United Negro College Fund, (S) 226
United States Patent and Trademark Office, (R) 741
University of Pennsylvania. Center for the Study of the History of Nursing, (R) 684, 819
U.S. Agency for Healthcare Research and Quality, (R) 792
U.S. Air Force, (S) 13
U.S. Air Force. Reserve Officers' Training Corps, (S) 15
U.S. Army. Human Resources Command, (S) 78
U.S. Army. Reserve Officers' Training Corps, (S) 142, 246
U.S. Centers for Disease Control and Prevention, (R) 732
U.S. Corporation for National and Community Service, (S) 56–57
U.S. Department of Education. Office of Special Education and Rehabilitative Services, (S) 593
U.S. Department of Homeland Security, (S) 150, (R) 748
U.S. Department of Veterans Affairs, (S) 425–427, 601, 627
U.S. Department of Veterans Affairs. Office of Academic Affiliations, (R) 869, 914
U.S. Environmental Protection Agency, (R) 875
U.S. National Aeronautics and Space Administration, (S) 291, 454, 460, (R) 807, 846, 851–853
U.S. National Institutes of Health, (S) 274, 561, (R) 799
U.S. National Institutes of Health. National Cancer Institute, (R) 791
U.S. National Institutes of Health. National Heart, Lung, and Blood, (R) 791

S–Study and Training

R–Research and Creative Activities

U.S. National Institutes of Health. National Institute of Allergy and Infectious Diseases, (R) 791
U.S. National Institutes of Health. National Institute of Dental and Craniofacial Research, (S) 288, (R) 808
U.S. National Institutes of Health. National Institute of Diabetes and Digestive and Kidney Diseases, (R) 791
U.S. National Institutes of Health. National Institute of Environmental Health Sciences, (R) 890
U.S. National Institutes of Health. National Institute of General Medical Sciences, (S) 562, (R) 891
U.S. National Institutes of Health. National Institute of Mental Health, (S) 276, 408, 529, 599, (R) 834, 889–890
U.S. National Institutes of Health. National Institute of Neurological Disorders and Stroke, (R) 889–890
U.S. National Institutes of Health. National Institute of Nursing Research, (S) 560, (R) 791
U.S. National Institutes of Health. National Institute on Aging, (R) 682, 889–890
U.S. National Institutes of Health. National Institute on Alcohol Abuse and Alcoholism, (R) 889–890
U.S. National Institutes of Health. National Institute on Deafness and Other Communication Disorders, (R) 889–890
U.S. National Institutes of Health. National Institute on Drug Abuse, (R) 763, 889–890
U.S. National Institutes of Health. Office of Intramural Training and Education, (R) 791
U.S. Navy. Naval Medical Education and Training Command, (S) 75
U.S. Substance Abuse and Mental Health Services Administration, (S) 121, 407, (R) 739, 840
USA Funds, (S) 618
Utah Golf Association, (S) 619

Vasa Order of America, (S) 192, 494
Vermont Student Assistance Corporation, (S) 190
Vesalius Trust for Visual Communications in the Health Sciences, (S) 289, (R) 915
Virginia Association for Health, Physical Education, Recreation, and Dance, (S) 623
Virginia Dental Hygienists' Association Foundation, (S) 20
Virginia Department of Veterans' Affairs, (S) 626
Virginia. State Council of Higher Education, (S) 625

Walman Optical Company, (S) 629
Warner–Lambert Company, (S) 359
Warner–Lambert Company. Parke–Davis Division, (S) 106
Washington Occupational Therapy Association, (S) 632
Watson Pharma, Inc., (S) 634
Weatherhead Foundation, (R) 923
Western Interstate Commission for Higher Education, (S) 534, 637
Wilderness Medical Society, (R) 737
William E. Docter Educational Fund, (S) 644
William Townsend Porter Foundation, (S) 650, (R) 929
Wisconsin Department of Veterans Affairs, (S) 652
Wisconsin Medical Society, (S) 59, 653–654
W.K. Kellogg Foundation, (S) 656, (R) 932
Women's Basketball Coaches Association, (S) 659

Woods Hole Marine Biological Laboratory, (R) 793, 930
Wound, Ostomy and Continence Nurses Society, (S) 177, 657, (R) 762
Wyeth Consumer Healthcare, (R) 870
Wyeth Pharmaceuticals, (S) 10, 518, 588, (R) 668, 678, 750

Young Ladies' Radio League, (S) 660

Zeta Phi Beta Sorority, Inc., (S) 565, 662
Zonta Club of Washington, D.C., (S) 180

10–10 International Net, Inc., (S) 663
3M Dental Products, (R) 665
3M Health Information Systems, (S) 216

Residency Index

Some programs listed in this book are restricted to residents of a particular state or region. Others are open to applicants wherever they may live. The Residency Index will help you pinpoint programs available only to residents in your area as well as programs that have no residency restrictions at all (these are listed under the term "United States"). To use this index, look up the geographic areas that apply to you (always check the listings under "United States"), jot down the entry numbers listed after the program purpose that interests you (study/training or research/creative activities), and use those numbers to find the program descriptions in the directory. To help you in your search, we've provided some "see also" references in each index entry. Remember: the numbers cited here refer to program entry numbers, not to page numbers in the book.

Africa: **Study and Training:** 43. See also Foreign countries; names of specific countries

Alabama: **Study and Training:** 16, 312, 440; **Research and Creative Activities:** 734–735. See also Southern states; United States; names of specific cities and counties

Alameda County, California: **Study and Training:** 410. See also California

Alaska: **Study and Training:** 386, 478, 534, 637–638. See also United States; names of specific cities

Albany, New York: **Study and Training:** 410. See also New York

American Samoa: **Study and Training:** 105. See also United States

Amsterdam, New York: **Study and Training:** 341. See also New York

Arizona: **Study and Training:** 7–8, 71–72, 239, 534, 569, 637–638; **Research and Creative Activities:** 734–735. See also United States; names of specific cities and counties

Arkansas: **Study and Training:** 73–74, 263, 345, 440, 538, 651; **Research and Creative Activities:** 734–735. See also Southern states; United States; names of specific cities and counties

Ashland County, Wisconsin: **Study and Training:** 99. See also Wisconsin

Atlanta, Georgia: **Study and Training:** 410. See also Georgia

Aurora, Illinois: **Study and Training:** 410. See also Illinois

Austin, Texas: **Study and Training:** 410. See also Texas

Australia: **Research and Creative Activities:** 809. See also Foreign countries

Bangor, Maine: **Study and Training:** 90. See also Maine

Barron County, Wisconsin: **Study and Training:** 99. See also Wisconsin

Bay County, Florida: **Study and Training:** 312. See also Florida

Bayfield County, Wisconsin: **Study and Training:** 99. See also Wisconsin

Bayonne, New Jersey: **Study and Training:** 341. See also New Jersey

Boston, Massachusetts: **Study and Training:** 410. See also Massachusetts

Buffalo County, Wisconsin: **Study and Training:** 99. See also Wisconsin

Burnett County, Wisconsin: **Study and Training:** 99. See also Wisconsin

Calhoun County, Florida: **Study and Training:** 312. See also Florida

California: **Study and Training:** 3, 7, 100–101, 103, 144, 361, 515, 597, 620, 638, 649; **Research and Creative Activities:** 728. See also United States; names of specific cities and counties

Canada: **Study and Training:** 17, 48, 52, 92, 176, 205, 217, 258, 266, 352, 397, 430, 494, 508, 516, 541, 572, 587, 609; **Research and Creative Activities:** 674, 677, 680–681, 689, 697–698, 703, 709, 720, 726, 737, 759, 771–772, 782, 795, 802, 809, 839, 850, 867, 888, 894, 897–898, 905, 909, 913, 916, 926, 934. See also Foreign countries

Chicago, Illinois: **Study and Training:** 410. See also Illinois

Chicopee, Massachusetts: **Study and Training:** 341. See also Massachusetts

Chippewa County, Wisconsin: **Study and Training:** 99. See also Wisconsin

Colorado: **Study and Training:** 7, 71, 116, 126–127, 173, 239, 534, 569, 637–638; **Research and Creative Activities:** 734–735. See also United States; names of specific cities and counties

Connecticut: **Study and Training:** 199, 220, 523, 555. See also New England states; United States; names of specific cities and counties

Connecticut, southern: **Study and Training:** 410. See also Connecticut

Cyprus: **Study and Training:** 92, 587. See also Foreign countries

Dallas, Texas: **Study and Training:** 410. See also Texas

Dayton, Ohio: **Study and Training:** 410. *See also* Ohio

DeKalb County, Illinois: **Study and Training:** 458. *See also* Illinois

Delaware: **Study and Training:** 145, 247, 269. *See also* Southern states; United States; names of specific cities and counties

Denver, Colorado: **Study and Training:** 410. *See also* Colorado

District of Columbia. *See* Washington, D.C.

Douglas County, Wisconsin: **Study and Training:** 99. *See also* Wisconsin

Dunn County, Wisconsin: **Study and Training:** 99. *See also* Wisconsin

Eau Claire County, Wisconsin: **Study and Training:** 99. *See also* Wisconsin

Escambia County, Florida: **Study and Training:** 312. *See also* Florida

Finland: **Study and Training:** 210. *See also* Foreign countries

Florence County, Wisconsin: **Study and Training:** 99. *See also* Wisconsin

Florida: **Study and Training:** 120, 144, 147, 440. *See also* Southern states; United States; names of specific cities and counties

Foreign countries: **Study and Training:** 240, 280, 321, 327, 606, 663; **Research and Creative Activities:** 692, 699, 719, 746, 781, 793, 804, 806, 812, 824, 864, 876, 887, 906, 911, 931. *See also* names of specific continents; names of specific countries

Forest County, Wisconsin: **Study and Training:** 99. *See also* Wisconsin

Fort Worth, Texas: **Study and Training:** 410. *See also* Texas

Georgia: **Study and Training:** 109, 131, 596. *See also* Southern states; United States; names of specific cities and counties

Greece: **Study and Training:** 92, 587. *See also* Foreign countries

Greenville, South Carolina: **Study and Training:** 410. *See also* South Carolina

Guam: **Study and Training:** 618. *See also* United States

Gulf County, Florida: **Study and Training:** 312. *See also* Florida

Harbor City, California. *See* Los Angeles, California

Hawaii: **Study and Training:** 7, 132, 144, 149, 160, 167, 209, 232, 254–255, 277, 303, 315, 346, 504, 534, 621, 637–638; **Research and Creative Activities:** 886. *See also* United States; names of specific cities and counties

Hollywood, California. *See* Los Angeles, California

Holmes County, Florida: **Study and Training:** 312. *See also* Florida

Houston, Texas: **Study and Training:** 410. *See also* Texas

Idaho: **Study and Training:** 71, 239, 386, 478, 534, 553, 569, 637–638; **Research and Creative Activities:** 734–735. *See also* United States; names of specific cities and counties

Illinois: **Study and Training:** 144, 263, 285–286, 413, 416, 458, 497; **Research and Creative Activities:** 734–735. *See also* Midwestern states; United States; names of specific cities and counties

Indiana: **Study and Training:** 287, 338, 413; **Research and Creative Activities:** 734–735, 807. *See also* Midwestern states; United States; names of specific cities and counties

Iosco County, Michigan: **Study and Training:** 264. *See also* Michigan

Iowa: **Study and Training:** 173, 263, 291, 413, 557; **Research and Creative Activities:** 734–735. *See also* Midwestern states; United States; names of specific cities and counties

Iron County, Wisconsin: **Study and Training:** 99. *See also* Wisconsin

Jackson County, Florida: **Study and Training:** 312. *See also* Florida

Kansas: **Study and Training:** 173, 193, 263, 328, 414; **Research and Creative Activities:** 734–735. *See also* Midwestern states; United States; names of specific cities and counties

Kentucky: **Study and Training:** 305, 336; **Research and Creative Activities:** 734–735. *See also* Southern states; United States; names of specific cities and counties

La Crosse County, Wisconsin: **Study and Training:** 99. *See also* Wisconsin

Latin America. *See* Mexico

Lincoln County, Wisconsin: **Study and Training:** 99. *See also* Wisconsin

Long Island, New York: **Study and Training:** 410. *See also* New York

Los Angeles, California: **Study and Training:** 410. *See also* California

Louisiana: **Study and Training:** 440; **Research and Creative Activities:** 734–735. *See also* Southern states; United States; names of specific cities and parishes

Maine: **Study and Training:** 32, 90, 135, 278, 355, 370–375, 555. *See also* New England states; United States; names of specific cities and counties

Malaysia: **Research and Creative Activities:** 809. *See also* Foreign countries

Marin County, California: **Study and Training:** 410. *See also* California

Maryland: **Study and Training:** 144, 184, 392–395. *See also* Southern states; United States; names of specific cities and counties

Maryland, regional: **Study and Training:** 14. *See also* Maryland

Massachusetts: **Study and Training:** 396, 555. *See also* New England states; United States; names of specific cities and counties

Mexico: **Study and Training:** 52, 266, 608; **Research and Creative Activities:** 703. *See also* Foreign countries

Miami, Florida: **Study and Training:** 410. *See also* Florida

Michigan: **Study and Training:** 264, 412–414; **Research and Creative Activities:** 734–735. *See also* Midwestern states; United States; names of specific cities and counties

Midwestern states: **Research and Creative Activities:** 837. *See also* United States; names of specific states

Minnesota: **Study and Training:** 99, 282, 413–414, 419; **Research and Creative Activities:** 734–735. *See also* Midwestern states; United States; names of specific cities and counties

Mississippi: **Study and Training:** 440; **Research and Creative Activities:** 734–735. *See also* Southern states; United States; names of specific cities and counties

Missouri: **Study and Training:** 173, 263, 414, 440; **Research and Creative Activities:** 734–735. *See also* Midwestern states; United States; names of specific cities and counties

Montana: **Study and Training:** 71, 239, 386, 478, 534, 569, 637–638; **Research and Creative Activities:** 734–735. *See also* United States; names of specific cities and counties

Nebraska: **Study and Training:** 173, 263, 358, 413–414, 454; **Research and Creative Activities:** 734–735. *See also* United States; Midwestern states; names of specific cities and counties

Nevada: **Study and Training:** 7, 71, 239, 460–461, 534, 569, 637–638; **Research and Creative Activities:** 734–735, 851. *See also* United States; names of specific cities

New England states: **Study and Training:** 463–464. *See also* United States; names of specific states

New Hampshire: **Study and Training:** 341, 383, 465, 555; **Research and Creative Activities:** 852. *See also* New England states; United States; names of specific cities and counties

New Jersey: **Study and Training:** 144, 250, 260, 466. *See also* United States; names of specific cities and counties

New Jersey, central: **Study and Training:** 410. *See also* New Jersey

New Jersey, northern: **Study and Training:** 410. *See also* New Jersey

New Mexico: **Study and Training:** 7, 71, 239, 467–469, 534, 569, 637–638; **Research and Creative Activities:** 734–735. *See also* United States; names of specific cities and counties

New York: **Study and Training:** 144, 242, 470–471. *See also* United States; names of specific cities and counties

New York County, New York. *See* New York, New York

New York, New York: **Study and Training:** 410. *See also* New York

New York, southern: **Study and Training:** 410. *See also* New York

New Zealand: **Research and Creative Activities:** 809. *See also* Foreign countries

North Carolina: **Study and Training:** 93, 108, 301, 385. *See also* Southern states; United States; names of specific cities and counties

North Dakota: **Study and Training:** 99, 413–414, 534, 637; **Research and Creative Activities:** 734–735, 853. *See also* Midwestern states; United States; names of specific cities

Ohio: **Study and Training:** 230, 413, 488–490, 522, 552; **Research and Creative Activities:** 734–735. *See also* Midwestern states; United States; names of specific cities and counties

Okaloosa County, Florida: **Study and Training:** 312. *See also* Florida

Oklahoma: **Study and Training:** 173, 263; **Research and Creative Activities:** 734–735. *See also* Southern states; United States; names of specific cities and counties

Oneida County, Wisconsin: **Study and Training:** 99. *See also* Wisconsin

Oregon: **Study and Training:** 348, 386, 478, 486, 492–493, 510, 534, 637–638. *See also* United States; names of specific cities and counties

Pennsylvania: **Study and Training:** 23, 183, 198, 379, 506, 602. *See also* United States; names of specific cities and counties

Pepin County, Wisconsin: **Study and Training:** 99. *See also* Wisconsin

Philadelphia, Pennsylvania: **Study and Training:** 410. *See also* Pennsylvania

Phoenix, Arizona: **Study and Training:** 410. *See also* Arizona

Pierce County, Wisconsin: **Study and Training:** 99. *See also* Wisconsin

Pittsburgh, Pennsylvania: **Study and Training:** 410. *See also* Pennsylvania

Polk County, Wisconsin: **Study and Training:** 99. *See also* Wisconsin

Price County, Wisconsin: **Study and Training:** 99. *See also* Wisconsin

Providence, Rhode Island: **Study and Training:** 410. *See also* Rhode Island

Puerto Rico: **Study and Training:** 75, 105, 125, 133, 267, 274, 618; **Research and Creative Activities:** 799. *See also* United States

Rensselaer, New York: **Study and Training:** 410. *See also* New York

Rhode Island: **Study and Training:** 485, 555. *See also* New England states; United States; names of specific cities

Rusk County, Wisconsin: **Study and Training:** 99. *See also* Wisconsin

Samoa. *See* American Samoa

San Francisco, California: **Study and Training:** 410. *See also* California

San Mateo County, California: **Study and Training:** 410. *See also* California

San Pedro, California. *See* Los Angeles, California

Santa Rosa County, Florida: **Study and Training:** 312. *See also* Florida

Sawyer County, Wisconsin: **Study and Training:** 99. *See also* Wisconsin

Scranton, Pennsylvania: **Study and Training:** 410. *See also* Pennsylvania

South Carolina: **Study and Training:** 108, 339, 624. *See also* Southern states; United States; names of specific cities and counties

South Dakota: **Study and Training:** 99, 413, 637; **Research and Creative Activities:** 734–735. *See also* Midwestern states; United States; names of specific cities and counties

Southern states: **Study and Training:** 590–591; **Research and Creative Activities:** 904. *See also* United States; names of specific states

St. Croix County, Wisconsin: **Study and Training:** 99. *See also* Wisconsin

St. Louis, Missouri: **Study and Training:** 410. *See also* Missouri

St. Petersburg, Florida: **Study and Training:** 410. *See also* Florida

Sweden: **Study and Training:** 494. *See also* Foreign countries

Tampa, Florida: **Study and Training:** 410. *See also* Florida

Taylor County, Wisconsin: **Study and Training:** 99. *See also* Wisconsin

Tennessee: **Study and Training:** 351, 440; **Research and Creative Activities:** 734–735. *See also* Southern states; United States; names of specific cities and counties

Texas: **Study and Training:** 144, 173, 231, 420, 440, 603–607; **Research and Creative Activities:** 734–735, 838. *See also* Southern states; United States; names of specific cities and counties

Trempealeau County, Wisconsin: **Study and Training:** 99. *See also* Wisconsin

Tulsa, Oklahoma: **Study and Training:** 410. *See also* Oklahoma

United States: **Study and Training:** 1–2, 4–6, 9–13, 15, 17–19, 21–22, 24–31, 33–70, 74–89, 91–92, 94–97, 102, 104–107, 110–115, 117–119, 121–126, 128–130, 134, 136–143, 146, 148–157, 159, 161–166, 168–172, 174–179, 181–182, 185–189, 191–192, 194–197, 200–207, 210, 212–219, 221–229, 231–238, 240–241, 243–246, 248–253, 256–259, 261–262, 265–268, 270–276, 279–281, 283–284, 288–290, 292–300, 302, 304, 306–311, 313–314, 316–327, 329–335, 337, 340–344, 347, 349–354, 356–357, 359–369, 376–378, 380–381, 384, 386–391, 397–411, 415, 417–419, 421–439, 441–453, 455–457, 459, 462–463, 473–477, 479–484, 487, 491, 494–503, 505, 507–514, 516, 518–521, 524–533, 535–537, 539–551, 553–554, 556–568, 570–589, 592–595, 598–601, 606, 609–618, 622, 627–631, 633–634, 636, 639–648, 650, 656–657, 659–663; **Research and Creative Activities:** 664–727, 729–733, 736–806, 808–836, 839–850, 854–903, 905–934. *See also* names of specific cities, counties, states, and regions

Utah: **Study and Training:** 71, 239, 534, 569, 619, 637–638; **Research and Creative Activities:** 734–735. *See also* United States; names of specific cities and counties

Utica, New York: **Study and Training:** 410. *See also* New York

Vermont: **Study and Training:** 190, 555. *See also* New England states; United States; names of specific cities and counties

Vilas County, Wisconsin: **Study and Training:** 99. *See also* Wisconsin

Virgin Islands: **Study and Training:** 105, 125, 618. *See also* United States

Virginia: **Study and Training:** 20, 98, 144, 211, 382, 517, 623, 625–626, 658. *See also* Southern states; United States; names of specific cities and counties

Virginia, regional: **Study and Training:** 14. *See also* Virginia

Walton County, Florida: **Study and Training:** 312. *See also* Florida

Warwick, Rhode Island: **Study and Training:** 410. *See also* Rhode Island

Washburn County, Wisconsin: **Study and Training:** 99. *See also* Wisconsin

Washington: **Study and Training:** 144, 158, 386, 478, 534, 632, 637–638. *See also* United States; names of specific cities and counties

Washington County, Florida: **Study and Training:** 312. *See also* Florida

Washington, D.C.: **Study and Training:** 14, 180, 208. *See also* Southern states; United States

West Virginia: **Study and Training:** 472, 490; **Research and Creative Activities:** 734–735. *See also* Southern states; United States; names of specific cities

Wilmington, California. *See* Los Angeles, California

Wisconsin: **Study and Training:** 59, 413, 635, 652–655; **Research and Creative Activities:** 734–735. *See also* Midwestern states; United States; names of specific cities and counties

Wyoming: **Study and Training:** 71, 239, 534, 569, 637–638; **Research and Creative Activities:** 734–735. *See also* United States; names of specific cities and counties

Tenability Index

Some programs listed in this book can be used only in specific cities, counties, states, or regions. Others may be used anywhere in the United States (or even abroad). The Tenability Index will help you locate funding that is restricted to a specific area as well as funding that has no tenability restrictions (these are listed under the term "United States"). To use this index, look up the geographic areas where you'd like to go (always check the listings under "United States"), jot down the entry numbers listed after the program purpose that interests you (study/training or research/creative activities), and use those numbers to find the program descriptions in the directory. To help you in your search, we've provided some "see also" references in each index entry. Remember: the numbers cited here refer to program entry numbers, not to page numbers in the book.

Alabama: **Study and Training:** 16, 307, 571, 589; **Research and Creative Activities:** 734–735, 903. *See also* Southern states; United States; names of specific cities and counties

Alameda County, California: **Study and Training:** 410. *See also* California

Alaska: **Study and Training:** 69, 386, 637–638. *See also* United States; names of specific cities

Albany, New York: **Study and Training:** 410. *See also* New York

American Samoa: **Study and Training:** 105. *See also* United States

Ames, Iowa: **Research and Creative Activities:** 791. *See also* Iowa

Ann Arbor, Michigan: **Study and Training:** 656; **Research and Creative Activities:** 896, 932. *See also* Michigan

Arizona: **Study and Training:** 8, 72, 534, 637–638; **Research and Creative Activities:** 734–735. *See also* United States; names of specific cities and counties

Arkansas: **Study and Training:** 74, 345, 538, 589; **Research and Creative Activities:** 734–735, 903. *See also* Southern states; United States; names of specific cities and counties

Arlington, Virginia: **Research and Creative Activities:** 744. *See also* Virginia

Atlanta, Georgia: **Study and Training:** 25, 68, 410. *See also* Georgia

Aurora, Illinois: **Study and Training:** 410. *See also* Illinois

Austin, Texas: **Study and Training:** 107, 410. *See also* Texas

Australia: **Research and Creative Activities:** 809. *See also* Foreign countries

Baltimore, Maryland: **Study and Training:** 656; **Research and Creative Activities:** 791, 932. *See also* Maryland

Baton Rouge, Louisiana: **Study and Training:** 73. *See also* Louisiana

Bethesda, Maryland: **Study and Training:** 274; **Research and Creative Activities:** 791, 799. *See also* Maryland

Birmingham, Alabama: **Study and Training:** 73. *See also* Alabama

Bloomington, Indiana: **Research and Creative Activities:** 896. *See also* Indiana

Boston, Massachusetts: **Study and Training:** 410, 656; **Research and Creative Activities:** 755, 791, 896, 932. *See also* Massachusetts

California: **Study and Training:** 42, 100–101, 103, 206, 361, 418, 534, 597, 638, 649; **Research and Creative Activities:** 728, 794. *See also* United States; names of specific cities and counties

Cambridge, Massachusetts: **Research and Creative Activities:** 773. *See also* Massachusetts

Canada: **Study and Training:** 17, 48, 52, 92, 176, 205, 217, 258, 266, 352, 397, 430, 508, 516, 541, 550, 572, 587, 609, 644; **Research and Creative Activities:** 674, 677, 679–681, 689, 697–698, 703, 709, 720, 726, 737, 759, 771–772, 782, 795, 802, 809, 839, 867, 888, 894, 897, 905, 909, 913, 926, 934. *See also* Foreign countries

Champaign, Illinois: **Research and Creative Activities:** 791. *See also* Illinois

Chapel Hill, North Carolina: **Research and Creative Activities:** 755, 791. *See also* North Carolina

Chesterfield, Missouri: **Study and Training:** 73. *See also* Missouri

Chicago, Illinois: **Study and Training:** 73, 341, 410; **Research and Creative Activities:** 896. *See also* Illinois

Cincinnati, Ohio: **Research and Creative Activities:** 896. *See also* Ohio

Cleveland, Ohio: **Study and Training:** 73. *See also* Ohio

College Park, Maryland: **Research and Creative Activities:** 744, 791. *See also* Maryland

Colorado: **Study and Training:** 126–127, 534, 637–638; **Research and Creative Activities:** 734–735. *See also* United States; names of specific cities and counties

Columbia, Missouri: **Study and Training:** 73. *See also* Missouri

Columbus, Ohio: **Research and Creative Activities:** 896. *See also* Ohio

Connecticut: **Study and Training:** 130, 234, 555. *See also* New England states; United States; names of specific cities and counties

Cyprus: **Study and Training:** 92, 587. *See also* Foreign countries

Dallas, Texas: **Study and Training:** 73, 410; **Research and Creative Activities:** 755. *See also* Texas

Davenport, Iowa: **Study and Training:** 73. *See also* Iowa

Dayton, Ohio: **Study and Training:** 410. *See also* Ohio

DeKalb, Illinois: **Study and Training:** 107. *See also* Illinois

Delaware: **Study and Training:** 145. *See also* Southern states; United States; names of specific cities and counties

Denmark: **Study and Training:** 91. *See also* Foreign countries

Denver, Colorado: **Study and Training:** 410. *See also* Colorado

Des Moines, Iowa: **Study and Training:** 73. *See also* Iowa

District of Columbia. *See* Washington, D.C.

East Lansing, Michigan: **Research and Creative Activities:** 791. *See also* Michigan

England: **Research and Creative Activities:** 791. *See also* Foreign countries

Finland: **Study and Training:** 174, 210; **Research and Creative Activities:** 761. *See also* Foreign countries

Florida: **Study and Training:** 120, 147, 307, 400, 571, 589; **Research and Creative Activities:** 794, 903. *See also* Southern states; United States; names of specific cities and counties

Foreign countries: **Study and Training:** 138, 240, 296, 481, 601; **Research and Creative Activities:** 710, 746, 751, 781, 850, 864, 876, 887, 898, 911, 916, 931. *See also* names of specific continents; names of specific countries

Fort Worth, Texas: **Study and Training:** 410. *See also* Texas

Georgia: **Study and Training:** 131, 307, 314, 571, 589; **Research and Creative Activities:** 903. *See also* Southern states; United States; names of specific cities and counties

Greece: **Study and Training:** 92, 587. *See also* Foreign countries

Greenville, South Carolina: **Study and Training:** 410. *See also* South Carolina

Guam: **Study and Training:** 206, 418, 618. *See also* United States

Harbor City, California. *See* Los Angeles, California

Hawaii: **Study and Training:** 132, 149, 160, 206, 209, 232, 254–255, 277, 315, 346, 418, 504, 534, 621, 637–638; **Research and Creative Activities:** 886. *See also* United States; names of specific cities and counties

Hollywood, California. *See* Los Angeles, California

Houston, Texas: **Study and Training:** 410. *See also* Texas

Idaho: **Study and Training:** 69, 386, 534, 637–638; **Research and Creative Activities:** 734–735. *See also* United States; names of specific cities and counties

Illinois: **Study and Training:** 286, 413, 416, 458, 497; **Research and Creative Activities:** 734–735, 843. *See also* Midwestern states; United States; names of specific cities and counties

Indiana: **Study and Training:** 287, 413; **Research and Creative Activities:** 734–735, 807. *See also* Midwestern states; United States; names of specific cities and counties

Iowa: **Study and Training:** 291, 413, 557; **Research and Creative Activities:** 734–735. *See also* Midwestern states; United States; names of specific cities and counties

Iowa City, Iowa: **Research and Creative Activities:** 755. *See also* Iowa

Iowa, eastern: **Research and Creative Activities:** 843. *See also* Iowa

Irving, Texas: **Study and Training:** 73. *See also* Texas

Ithaca, New York: **Research and Creative Activities:** 896. *See also* New York

Kalamazoo, Michigan: **Study and Training:** 107. *See also* Michigan

Kansas: **Study and Training:** 193, 328, 414; **Research and Creative Activities:** 734–735. *See also* Midwestern states; United States; names of specific cities and counties

Kansas City, Missouri: **Study and Training:** 73. *See also* Missouri

Kentucky: **Study and Training:** 305, 307, 336, 571, 589; **Research and Creative Activities:** 734–735, 903. *See also* Southern states; United States; names of specific cities and counties

Lancaster County, Pennsylvania: **Study and Training:** 317. *See also* Pennsylvania

Latin America. *See* Mexico

Long Island, New York: **Study and Training:** 410. *See also* New York

Los Angeles, California: **Study and Training:** 25, 410, 656; **Research and Creative Activities:** 932. *See also* California

Louisiana: **Study and Training:** 307, 571, 589; **Research and Creative Activities:** 734–735, 903. *See also* Southern states; United States; names of specific cities and parishes

Louisville, Kentucky: **Study and Training:** 73. *See also* Kentucky

Madison, Wisconsin: **Research and Creative Activities:** 896. *See also* Wisconsin

Maine: **Study and Training:** 90, 135, 234, 370–374, 555. *See also* New England states; United States; names of specific cities and counties

Malaysia: **Research and Creative Activities:** 809. *See also* Foreign countries

Marin County, California: **Study and Training:** 410. *See also* California

Maryland: **Study and Training:** 184, 392–395, 589; **Research and Creative Activities:** 903. *See also* Southern states; United States; names of specific cities and counties

Maryland, regional: **Study and Training:** 450. *See also* Maryland

Massachusetts: **Study and Training:** 234, 396, 555. *See also* New England states; United States; names of specific cities and counties

Memphis, Tennessee: **Study and Training:** 73. *See also* Tennessee

Mexico: **Study and Training:** 52, 266; **Research and Creative Activities:** 703. *See also* Foreign countries

Miami, Florida: **Study and Training:** 410. *See also* Florida

Miami Shores, Florida: **Study and Training:** 73. *See also* Florida

Michigan: **Study and Training:** 412–414; **Research and Creative Activities:** 734–735. *See also* Midwestern states; United States; names of specific cities and counties

Midwestern states: **Research and Creative Activities:** 837. *See also* United States; names of specific states

Minnesota: **Study and Training:** 413–414, 419; **Research and Creative Activities:** 734–735. *See also* Midwestern states; United States; names of specific cities and counties

Mississippi: **Study and Training:** 307, 571, 589; **Research and Creative Activities:** 734–735, 903. *See also* Southern states; United States; names of specific cities and counties

Missoula, Montana: **Research and Creative Activities:** 791. *See also* Montana

Missouri: **Study and Training:** 414, 589; **Research and Creative Activities:** 734–735, 903. *See also* Midwestern states; United States; names of specific cities and counties

Montana: **Study and Training:** 386, 534, 637–638; **Research and Creative Activities:** 734–735. *See also* United States; names of specific cities and counties

Nashville, Tennessee: **Study and Training:** 25, 73, 107. *See also* Tennessee

Nebraska: **Study and Training:** 413–414, 454; **Research and Creative Activities:** 734–735. *See also* United States; Midwestern states; names of specific cities and counties

Nevada: **Study and Training:** 206, 418, 460, 534, 637–638; **Research and Creative Activities:** 734–735, 851. *See also* United States; names of specific cities

New England states: **Study and Training:** 464; **Research and Creative Activities:** 794. *See also* United States; names of specific states

New Hampshire: **Study and Training:** 234, 465, 555; **Research and Creative Activities:** 852. *See also* New England states; United States; names of specific cities and counties

New Haven, Connecticut: **Research and Creative Activities:** 755, 896. *See also* Connecticut

New Jersey: **Study and Training:** 234, 466. *See also* United States; names of specific cities and counties

New Mexico: **Study and Training:** 467–469, 534, 637–638; **Research and Creative Activities:** 734–735. *See also* United States; names of specific cities and counties

New Orleans, Louisiana: **Study and Training:** 73. *See also* Louisiana

New York: **Study and Training:** 234, 242, 470–471; **Research and Creative Activities:** 794. *See also* United States; names of specific cities and counties

New York County, New York. *See* New York, New York

New York, New York: **Study and Training:** 73, 410, 656; **Research and Creative Activities:** 755, 791, 896, 932. *See also* New York

New Zealand: **Research and Creative Activities:** 809. *See also* Foreign countries

North Carolina: **Study and Training:** 93, 385, 589, 612; **Research and Creative Activities:** 903. *See also* Southern states; United States; names of specific cities and counties

North Dakota: **Study and Training:** 413–414, 534, 637; **Research and Creative Activities:** 734–735, 853. *See also* Midwestern states; United States; names of specific cities

Oak Ridge, Tennessee: **Research and Creative Activities:** 800. *See also* Tennessee

Ohio: **Study and Training:** 413, 488–489, 552; **Research and Creative Activities:** 734–735. *See also* Midwestern states; United States; names of specific cities and counties

Oklahoma: **Study and Training:** 589; **Research and Creative Activities:** 734–735, 903. *See also* Southern states; United States; names of specific cities and counties

Oklahoma City, Oklahoma: **Study and Training:** 73. *See also* Oklahoma

Oregon: **Study and Training:** 69, 386, 492–493, 534, 637–638. *See also* United States; names of specific cities and counties

Pasadena, Texas: **Study and Training:** 73. *See also* Texas

Pennsylvania: **Study and Training:** 23, 145, 198, 234, 379, 602. *See also* United States; names of specific cities and counties

Philadelphia, Pennsylvania: **Study and Training:** 107, 410, 656; **Research and Creative Activities:** 684, 699, 755, 777–778, 791, 812, 819, 825, 896, 932. *See also* Pennsylvania

Phoenix, Arizona: **Study and Training:** 410. *See also* Arizona

Pikeville, Kentucky: **Study and Training:** 73. *See also* Kentucky

Pittsburgh, Pennsylvania: **Study and Training:** 410; **Research and Creative Activities:** 791, 896. *See also* Pennsylvania

Polk City, Florida: **Study and Training:** 433. *See also* Florida

Portland, Oregon: **Research and Creative Activities:** 791. *See also* Oregon

Providence, Rhode Island: **Study and Training:** 410; **Research and Creative Activities:** 791. *See also* Rhode Island

Puerto Rico: **Study and Training:** 57, 75, 105, 125, 133, 267, 618. *See also* United States

Raleigh, North Carolina: **Research and Creative Activities:** 791. *See also* North Carolina

Rensselaer, New York: **Study and Training:** 410. *See also* New York

Rhode Island: **Study and Training:** 234, 485, 555. *See also* New England states; United States; names of specific cities

Salt Lake City, Utah: **Research and Creative Activities:** 791. *See also* Utah

Samoa. *See* American Samoa

San Francisco, California: **Study and Training:** 410; **Research and Creative Activities:** 755, 791. *See also* California

San Mateo County, California: **Study and Training:** 410. *See also* California

San Pedro, California. *See* Los Angeles, California

Santa Fe, New Mexico: **Research and Creative Activities:** 923. *See also* New Mexico

Santa Monica, California: **Study and Training:** 656; **Research and Creative Activities:** 932. *See also* California

Scranton, Pennsylvania: **Study and Training:** 410. *See also* Pennsylvania

South Carolina: **Study and Training:** 589; **Research and Creative Activities:** 903. *See also* Southern states; United States; names of specific cities and counties

South Dakota: **Study and Training:** 413, 637; **Research and Creative Activities:** 734–735. *See also* Midwestern states; United States; names of specific cities and counties

Southern states: **Study and Training:** 590–591; **Research and Creative Activities:** 904. *See also* United States; names of specific states

St. Louis, Missouri: **Study and Training:** 73, 410; **Research and Creative Activities:** 755. *See also* Missouri

St. Petersburg, Florida: **Study and Training:** 410. *See also* Florida

Starkville, Mississippi: **Study and Training:** 73. *See also* Mississippi

Stillwater, Oklahoma: **Study and Training:** 73. *See also* Oklahoma

Sweden: **Research and Creative Activities:** 791. *See also* Foreign countries

Tahlequah, Oklahoma: **Study and Training:** 73. *See also* Oklahoma

Tampa, Florida: **Study and Training:** 410. *See also* Florida

Tennessee: **Study and Training:** 307, 571, 589; **Research and Creative Activities:** 734–735, 903. *See also* Southern states; United States; names of specific cities and counties

Texas: **Study and Training:** 231, 420, 589, 603–608; **Research and Creative Activities:** 734–735, 838, 903. *See also* Southern states; United States; names of specific cities and counties

Tulsa, Oklahoma: **Study and Training:** 73, 410. *See also* Oklahoma

Tuskegee, Alabama: **Study and Training:** 73. *See also* Alabama

United States: **Study and Training:** 1–7, 9–15, 17–22, 24, 26–41, 43–67, 70–71, 75–92, 94–97, 99, 102, 104–106, 108–119, 121–125, 128–129, 132–134, 136–146, 148–179, 181–183, 185–192, 195–197, 199–205, 207–210, 212–233, 235–241, 243–273, 275–285, 288–290, 292–304, 306, 308–313, 315–327, 329–335, 337–344, 346–369, 372–378, 380–384, 386–392, 395, 397–399, 401–411, 415, 417, 421–449, 451–453, 455–459, 461–463, 465, 473–484, 486–487, 490–491, 494–516, 518–533, 535–537, 539–551, 553–554, 556, 558–570, 572–588, 592–596, 598–601, 603, 609–611, 613–618, 620–622, 624, 627–631, 633–636, 639–648, 650–651, 653, 656–657, 659–663; **Research and Creative Activities:** 664–683, 685–698, 700–727, 729–733, 736–743, 745–748, 750–754, 756–772, 774–776, 779–790, 792, 794–798, 801–806, 808–811, 813–818, 820–824, 826–836, 839–840, 842, 844–850, 854–886, 888–895, 897–902, 905–922, 924–929, 931–934. *See also* names of specific cities, counties, states, and regions

Urbana, Illinois. *See* Champaign, Illinois

Utah: **Study and Training:** 534, 619, 637–638; **Research and Creative Activities:** 734–735. *See also* United States; names of specific cities and counties

Utica, New York: **Study and Training:** 410. *See also* New York

Vermont: **Study and Training:** 234, 555. *See also* New England states; United States; names of specific cities and counties

Virgin Islands: **Study and Training:** 57, 105, 125, 618. *See also* United States

Virginia: **Study and Training:** 98, 211, 517, 589, 623, 625–626, 658; **Research and Creative Activities:** 903. *See also* Southern states; United States; names of specific cities and counties

Virginia, northern: **Study and Training:** 450. *See also* Virginia

Waltham, Massachusetts: **Study and Training:** 656; **Research and Creative Activities:** 932. *See also* Massachusetts

Warwick, Rhode Island: **Study and Training:** 410. *See also* Rhode Island

Washington: **Study and Training:** 69, 386, 534, 632, 637–638. *See also* United States; names of specific cities and counties

Washington, D.C.: **Study and Training:** 25, 180, 194, 450, 589; **Research and Creative Activities:** 744, 749, 791, 841, 903. *See also* Southern states; United States

West Virginia: **Study and Training:** 472, 589; **Research and Creative Activities:** 734–735, 903. *See also* Southern states; United States; names of specific cities

Wilmington, California. *See* Los Angeles, California

Wisconsin: **Study and Training:** 59, 413, 652–655; **Research and Creative Activities:** 734–735, 843. *See also* Midwestern states; United States; names of specific cities and counties

Woods Hole, Massachusetts: **Study and Training:** 529; **Research and Creative Activities:** 793, 930. *See also* Massachusetts

Wyoming: **Study and Training:** 534, 637–638; **Research and Creative Activities:** 734–735. *See also* United States; names of specific cities and counties

Subject Index

Use the Subject Index when you want to identify available funding programs in a particular subject area. To help you pinpoint your search, we've also included scores of "see" and "see also" references. In addition to looking for terms that represent your specific subject interest, be sure to check the "General programs" entry; many programs are listed there that can be used to support study, research, or other activities in *any* subject area (although the programs may be restricted in other ways). Remember: the numbers cited in this index refer to program entry numbers, not to page numbers in the book.

Acoustics: **Research and Creative Activities:** 879. *See also* General programs; Physics

Acquired Immunodeficiency Syndrome. *See* AIDS

Acting. *See* Performing arts

Actuarial sciences: **Study and Training:** 658. *See also* General programs; Statistics

Addiction. *See* Alcohol use and abuse; Drug use and abuse

Administration. *See* Business administration; Management; Nurses and nursing, administration; Public administration

Adolescents: **Study and Training:** 103, 440; **Research and Creative Activities:** 884. *See also* Child development; General programs

Aeronautical engineering. *See* Engineering, aeronautical

Aeronautics: **Research and Creative Activities:** 931. *See also* General programs; Physical sciences

Aerospace engineering. *See* Engineering, aerospace

Aerospace sciences. *See* Space sciences

Aged and aging: **Study and Training:** 303, 314, 399, 432, 483, 617; **Research and Creative Activities:** 682. *See also* General programs; Social sciences

Agriculture and agricultural sciences: **Study and Training:** 99, 150, 467, 513; **Research and Creative Activities:** 748. *See also* General programs

Agronomy: **Study and Training:** 619. *See also* Agriculture and agricultural sciences; General programs

AIDS: **Study and Training:** 60, 276; **Research and Creative Activities:** 693, 859, 900. *See also* Disabilities; General programs; Immunology; Medical sciences

Albanian language. *See* Language, Albanian

Alcohol use and abuse: **Study and Training:** 407, 599. *See also* Drug use and abuse; General programs; Health and health care

American history. *See* History, American

Amharic language. *See* Language, Amharic

Anatomy: **Research and Creative Activities:** 793, 896. *See also* General programs; Medical sciences; Physiology

Anesthesiology: **Research and Creative Activities:** 677. *See also* General programs; Medical sciences; Nurses and nursing, anesthesiology

Anesthetic nurses and nursing. *See* Nurses and nursing, anesthesiology

Anthropology: **Study and Training:** 138; **Research and Creative Activities:** 699, 719, 723, 850, 898, 911, 916. *See also* General programs; Social sciences

Arabic language. *See* Language, Arabic

Archaeology: **Research and Creative Activities:** 719. *See also* General programs; History; Social sciences

Architecture: **Study and Training:** 155, 279, 534; **Research and Creative Activities:** 752. *See also* General programs

Arithmetic. *See* Mathematics

Armenian language. *See* Language, Armenian

Art therapy: **Study and Training:** 41, 429, 539. *See also* General programs; Therapy

Arthritis: **Research and Creative Activities:** 670–672, 751. *See also* Disabilities; General programs; Health and health care; Medical sciences

Astronautics: **Research and Creative Activities:** 931. *See also* General programs; Space sciences

Astronomy: **Study and Training:** 481; **Research and Creative Activities:** 719, 852–853. *See also* General programs; Physical sciences

Astrophysics: **Research and Creative Activities:** 852. *See also* Astronomy; General programs

Athletic training: **Study and Training:** 48, 111, 160, 206, 307, 418, 436–437, 479–480, 525, 571; **Research and Creative Activities:** 689–690, 729, 822, 846, 848, 857, 868, 878. *See also* General programs

Atmospheric sciences: **Research and Creative Activities:** 694, 852–853. *See also* General programs; Physical sciences

Attorneys. *See* Law, general

Audiology: **Study and Training:** 35, 128, 352, 516, 541, 572, 609, 645; **Research and Creative Activities:** 869, 907. *See also* General programs; Health and health care; Medical sciences

Autism: **Study and Training:** 530–531; **Research and Creative Activities:** 742, 871–872. *See also* Disabilities; General programs

Automation. *See* Computer sciences; Information science; Technology

Aviation and space law: **Research and Creative Activities:** 931. *See also* General programs; Law, general

Azerbaijani language. *See* Language, Azeri

Azeri language. *See* Language, Azeri

Ballet. *See* Dance

Behavioral sciences: **Study and Training:** 561; **Research and Creative Activities:** 682, 723, 760, 763, 824, 834, 865, 889–890, 909. *See also* General programs; Social sciences; names of special behavioral sciences

Belarusian language. *See* Language, Belarusian

Biochemistry: **Research and Creative Activities:** 896. *See also* Biological sciences; Chemistry; General programs

Biological sciences: **Study and Training:** 150, 513; **Research and Creative Activities:** 748. *See also* General programs; Sciences; names of specific biological sciences

Biomedical engineering. *See* Engineering, biomedical

Biomedical sciences: **Study and Training:** 530, 561–562, 648; **Research and Creative Activities:** 682, 763, 791, 834, 843, 871, 889–891, 909. *See also* Biological sciences; General programs; Medical sciences

Blindness. *See* Visual impairments

Brain research. *See* Neuroscience

Brazilian language. *See* Language, Portuguese

Bulgarian language. *See* Language, Bulgarian

Burmese language. *See* Language, Burmese

Business administration: **Study and Training:** 5, 36, 86, 110, 123, 131, 138, 213, 216, 227, 251, 261, 290, 349, 400, 409, 413, 419, 490, 545–546, 638; **Research and Creative Activities:** 774–775. *See also* General programs; Management

Cancer: **Study and Training:** 62, 100, 154, 322, 397, 490–491, 549, 610; **Research and Creative Activities:** 674, 693, 700, 728, 911. *See also* Disabilities; General programs; Health and health care; Medical sciences

Cantonese language. *See* Language, Cantonese

Cardiac nurses and nursing. *See* Nurses and nursing, cardiology

Cardiology: **Study and Training:** 175, 405; **Research and Creative Activities:** 693, 833, 892. *See also* General programs; Medical sciences

Chemical engineering. *See* Engineering, chemical

Chemistry: **Study and Training:** 10, 51, 115, 199, 228, 247, 400, 481, 658; **Research and Creative Activities:** 699, 708, 719, 741, 750, 758, 764–765, 786, 844, 853, 860, 873–875, 885. *See also* Engineering, chemical; General programs; Physical sciences

Child development: **Study and Training:** 440; **Research and Creative Activities:** 767, 820, 884, 908. *See also* Adolescents; General programs

Chiropractic: **Study and Training:** 73, 351. *See also* General programs; Medical sciences

Civil engineering. *See* Engineering, civil

Colleges and universities. *See* Education, higher

Commerce. *See* Business administration

Communication disorders: **Study and Training:** 128. *See also* Disabilities; General programs

Communications: **Study and Training:** 54, 462, 531; **Research and Creative Activities:** 872, 915. *See also* General programs; Humanities

Community colleges. *See* Education, higher

Community services. *See* Social services

Computer engineering. *See* Engineering, computer

Computer sciences: **Study and Training:** 216, 228, 261, 400, 409, 419, 481, 502, 658; **Research and Creative Activities:** 719, 741, 774–775, 800, 821, 850, 852, 898, 916.

See also General programs; Information science; Libraries and librarianship; Mathematics; Technology

Computers. *See* Computer sciences

Conflict resolution. *See* Peace studies

Conservation. *See* Environmental sciences

Construction industry: **Study and Training:** 250. *See also* General programs

Continence. *See* Nurses and nursing, wound, ostomy and continence

Cooking. *See* Culinary arts

Counseling: **Study and Training:** 334, 440; **Research and Creative Activities:** 723. *See also* Behavioral sciences; General programs; Psychiatry; Psychology

Critical care nurses and nursing. *See* Nurses and nursing, critical care

Culinary arts: **Study and Training:** 103, 290. *See also* Food service industry; General programs

Cystic fibrosis: **Research and Creative Activities:** 745. *See also* Disabilities; General programs; Health and health care; Medical sciences

Czech language. *See* Language, Czech

Dance: **Study and Training:** 558, 623. *See also* General programs; Performing arts

Data entry. *See* Computer sciences

Deafness. *See* Hearing impairments

Death and dying: **Research and Creative Activities:** 909. *See also* Aged and aging; General programs; Health and health care

Demography. *See* Population studies

Dental hygiene: **Study and Training:** 9, 20, 134, 159, 238, 244, 293–294, 315, 442, 532, 583–584; **Research and Creative Activities:** 665, 676, 736, 813, 886. *See also* Dentistry; General programs

Dental laboratory technology: **Study and Training:** 532. *See also* Dental hygiene; General programs

Dentistry: **Study and Training:** 6, 13, 32, 73, 75, 78, 124, 162–163, 166, 170–171, 197, 238, 244, 247, 258, 273–274, 288, 315, 334, 359, 394, 421, 430, 442, 453, 532, 534, 536, 584, 591, 658; **Research and Creative Activities:** 665, 677, 683, 709, 715, 736, 769, 781, 799, 802, 806, 808, 876–877, 928. *See also* General programs; Health and health care; Medical sciences

Dentistry, pediatric: **Research and Creative Activities:** 667

Dermatology: **Research and Creative Activities:** 700. *See also* General programs; Medical sciences; Nurses and nursing, dermatology

Diabetes: **Research and Creative Activities:** 691, 828, 855. *See also* Disabilities; General programs; Health and health care; Medical sciences

Dietetics. *See* Nutrition

Disabilities: **Study and Training:** 79, 244, 314, 399; **Research and Creative Activities:** 753, 869. *See also* General programs; Rehabilitation; Therapy; names of specific disabilities

Disabilities, hearing. *See* Hearing impairments

Disabilities, visual. *See* Visual impairments

Disability law: **Study and Training:** 79. *See also* General programs; Law, general

Divinity. *See* Religion and religious activities

Documentaries. *See* Filmmaking

Drug use and abuse: **Study and Training:** 407, 599; **Research and Creative Activities:** 692, 763, 840. *See also* General programs; Health and health care

Earth sciences: **Study and Training:** 199, 228; **Research and Creative Activities:** 719, 800, 852. *See also* General programs; names of specific earth sciences
Eastern European history. *See* History, European
Ecology. *See* Environmental sciences
Economic planning. *See* Economics
Economics: **Study and Training:** 138, 349; **Research and Creative Activities:** 708, 719, 723, 844, 860, 885, 931. *See also* General programs; Social sciences
Education: **Study and Training:** 179, 216, 226, 409, 570, 590; **Research and Creative Activities:** 774–775, 911. *See also* General programs; specific types and levels of education
Education, health: **Study and Training:** 88, 146, 380, 640. *See also* Education; General programs; Health and health care
Education, higher: **Study and Training:** 584. *See also* Education; General programs
Education, physical: **Study and Training:** 103, 111, 115, 160, 479–480, 525, 558, 623; **Research and Creative Activities:** 857. *See also* Education; General programs
Education, special: **Study and Training:** 79, 148, 314, 440, 556. *See also* Disabilities; Education; General programs
Emergency nurses and nursing. *See* Nurses and nursing, emergency
Emotional disabilities. *See* Mental health
Engineering: **Study and Training:** 83, 110, 115, 138, 155, 226, 247, 250, 279, 347, 382, 400, 409, 411, 481, 502, 513, 547, 568, 590, 658; **Research and Creative Activities:** 675, 708, 719, 741, 752, 800, 821, 844, 860, 885, 895. *See also* General programs; Physical sciences; names of specific types of engineering
Engineering, aeronautical: **Research and Creative Activities:** 931. *See also* Engineering; General programs
Engineering, aerospace: **Study and Training:** 291, 460; **Research and Creative Activities:** 807, 851–853, 931. *See also* Engineering; General programs
Engineering, biomedical: **Study and Training:** 13, 280, 648, 658; **Research and Creative Activities:** 804, 931. *See also* Biomedical sciences; Engineering; General programs
Engineering, chemical: **Study and Training:** 199, 345, 538; **Research and Creative Activities:** 758, 764–765, 786, 874. *See also* Chemistry; Engineering; General programs
Engineering, civil: **Study and Training:** 199, 345, 538; **Research and Creative Activities:** 931. *See also* Engineering; General programs
Engineering, computer: **Study and Training:** 481. *See also* Computer sciences; Engineering; General programs
Engineering, environmental: **Study and Training:** 71, 122, 136, 214, 231, 239, 253, 298, 403, 569. *See also* Engineering; Environmental sciences; General programs
Engineering, fire protection: **Study and Training:** 611. *See also* Engineering; Fire science; General programs
Engineering, geological: **Research and Creative Activities:** 931. *See also* Engineering; General programs
Engineering, industrial: **Study and Training:** 71, 122, 136, 214, 231, 239, 253, 261, 298, 403, 419, 569. *See also* Engineering; General programs
Engineering, mechanical: **Study and Training:** 199. *See also* Engineering; General programs

English language. *See* Language, English
Enterostomal therapy nurses and nursing. *See* Nurses and nursing, wound, ostomy and continence
Environmental engineering. *See* Engineering, environmental
Environmental sciences: **Study and Training:** 71, 122, 136, 214, 231, 239, 253, 298, 403, 569, 611. *See also* General programs; Sciences
Epidemiology: **Study and Training:** 68, 274, 530; **Research and Creative Activities:** 673, 799, 824, 871, 896. *See also* General programs; Medical sciences
Epilepsy: **Research and Creative Activities:** 723, 796, 873. *See also* Disabilities; General programs; Health and health care; Medical sciences
Ethics: **Research and Creative Activities:** 797, 909. *See also* General programs; Humanities
Ethnic affairs. *See* Minority affairs
European history. *See* History, European
Exercise science. *See* Athletic training
Eye doctors. *See* Ophthalmology; Optometry
Eye problems. *See* Visual impairments

Family and consumer studies: **Study and Training:** 415. *See also* General programs; Social sciences
Farming. *See* Agriculture and agricultural sciences
Farsi language. *See* Language, Farsi
Feminist movement. *See* Women's studies and programs
Fiction: **Research and Creative Activities:** 797. *See also* General programs; Writers and writing
Filmmaking: **Study and Training:** 310. *See also* General programs
Fire protection engineering. *See* Engineering, fire protection
Fire science: **Study and Training:** 393, 611. *See also* General programs; Sciences
Food. *See* Culinary arts; Nutrition
Food service industry: **Study and Training:** 49. *See also* General programs
Foreign affairs. *See* International affairs
Foreign language. *See* Language and linguistics
Forensic science: **Study and Training:** 51, 234. *See also* General programs
Forestry management: **Study and Training:** 99. *See also* General programs; Management
French language. *See* Language, French

Gender. *See* Women's studies and programs
General programs: **Study and Training:** 2, 7, 11–12, 14–16, 22, 24, 27–28, 30, 42, 45, 50, 56–57, 70, 72, 74, 76–77, 91–92, 95, 105, 108–109, 112–113, 118, 125–127, 129–130, 139, 142, 145, 147, 149, 152, 155, 157, 169, 173, 178, 184, 186, 191, 194, 200–201, 204–205, 207, 210, 212, 221–222, 233, 236–237, 240, 242, 245–246, 248–249, 254–256, 265–268, 272, 277–278, 283–284, 286–287, 296, 306, 309, 313, 318, 320–321, 328, 332, 335–343, 350, 353, 355, 357, 360, 362–366, 368–371, 374–376, 381, 386–387, 390, 392, 395–396, 406, 412, 414, 416–417, 425–427, 431, 433–434, 441, 443–444, 448, 451, 454, 463–469, 471, 473–474, 489, 492–495, 499, 501, 506, 508, 510–511, 513, 517, 521, 523–524, 535, 537, 542, 544, 548, 551, 554–555, 559, 574, 577, 581, 585, 587–588, 593, 595, 597, 600–604, 606–607, 616, 618–619, 621–622, 625–628, 630–631, 637, 642, 644, 649, 651–652, 659–660, 662–663; **Research and Creative**

Activities: 669, 740, 744, 746, 752, 809, 815, 841, 904, 933. *See also* General programs

Genetics: **Study and Training:** 274, 280, 530; **Research and Creative Activities:** 699, 791, 799, 804, 871, 873, 896, 909. *See also* General programs; Medical sciences

Geological engineering. *See* Engineering, geological

Georgian language. *See* Language, Georgian

Geosciences. *See* Earth sciences

Geriatric nurses and nursing. *See* Nurses and nursing, geriatrics

Geriatrics. *See* Aged and aging

Gerontology. *See* Aged and aging

Golf course management. *See* Turfgrass science

Government. *See* Political science and politics; Public administration

Greek language. *See* Language, Greek

Guidance. *See* Counseling

Gynecology: **Research and Creative Activities:** 734–735. *See also* General programs; Medical sciences

Handicapped. *See* Disabilities

Health and health care: **Study and Training:** 5, 17, 19, 36, 44, 59, 68, 86, 115–116, 131–132, 156, 167, 174, 179, 183, 190, 193, 203, 215–217, 227, 230, 232, 235, 251–252, 257–262, 264, 275, 285, 299, 334, 345, 356, 400, 404, 413, 419, 432, 438, 450, 457, 483, 490, 515, 538, 540, 545–546, 558, 564–565, 573, 584, 613, 615, 617, 623, 638, 653; **Research and Creative Activities:** 708, 715–716, 725, 751, 761, 774–775, 792, 796, 800, 802, 816, 818, 824, 844, 860, 865, 885, 905, 909, 911. *See also* General programs; Medical sciences

Health education. *See* Education, health

Hearing impairments: **Study and Training:** 54–55, 327, 354, 440, 462; **Research and Creative Activities:** 907. *See also* Disabilities; General programs; Rehabilitation

Heart disease. *See* Cardiology

Hebrew. *See* Language, Hebrew

Hemophilia: **Research and Creative Activities:** 859. *See also* Disabilities; General programs; Health and health care; Medical sciences

Higher education. *See* Education, higher

Hindi language. *See* Language, Hindi

History: **Study and Training:** 138, 325, 349; **Research and Creative Activities:** 684, 692, 819, 825, 931. *See also* Archaeology; General programs; Humanities; Social sciences; specific types of history

History, American: **Research and Creative Activities:** 699. *See also* General programs; History

History, European: **Research and Creative Activities:** 699. *See also* General programs; History

History, nursing. *See* Nurses and nursing, history

History, science: **Research and Creative Activities:** 926. *See also* General programs; History; Sciences

Holistic health nurses and nursing. *See* Nurses and nursing, holistic health

Homeland security. *See* Security, national

Hospitals. *See* Health and health care

Human services. *See* Social services

Humanities: **Research and Creative Activities:** 790, 923, 926. *See also* General programs; names of specific humanities

Hungarian language. *See* Language, Hungarian

Illustrators and illustrations: **Study and Training:** 289; **Research and Creative Activities:** 915. *See also* General programs

Immunology: **Study and Training:** 183, 274, 280, 402, 530; **Research and Creative Activities:** 791, 799, 804, 831, 871. *See also* General programs; Medical sciences

Indonesian language. *See* Language, Indonesian

Industrial engineering. *See* Engineering, industrial

Industrial hygiene: **Study and Training:** 71, 122, 136, 214, 231, 239, 253, 298, 403, 569, 611. *See also* General programs; Health and health care

Information science: **Study and Training:** 116, 203, 215–216, 261–262, 419, 450, 481, 540, 573; **Research and Creative Activities:** 725, 774–775, 875. *See also* Computer sciences; General programs; Libraries and librarianship

Insurance. *See* Actuarial sciences

International affairs: **Study and Training:** 138, 349; **Research and Creative Activities:** 773. *See also* General programs; Political science and politics

International law: **Study and Training:** 138. *See also* General programs; Law, general

International relations. *See* International affairs

Inventors and inventions: **Research and Creative Activities:** 741. *See also* General programs; Technology

Japanese language. *See* Language, Japanese

Journalism: **Study and Training:** 310, 349; **Research and Creative Activities:** 790. *See also* Communications; General programs; Writers and writing; names of specific types of journalism

Junior colleges. *See* Education, higher

Jurisprudence. *See* Law, general

Kazakh language. *See* Language, Kazakh

Khmer language. *See* Language, Khmer

Kidney disease: **Study and Training:** 1, 18, 58, 63, 300, 477, 614, 634. *See also* Disabilities; General programs; Health and health care; Medical sciences

Kinesiology: **Study and Training:** 48, 160; **Research and Creative Activities:** 689. *See also* Anatomy; General programs; Physiology

Korean language. *See* Language, Korean

Kurdish language. *See* Language, Kurdish

Kyrgyz language. *See* Language, Kyrgyz

Language, Albanian: **Study and Training:** 138. *See also* General programs; Language and linguistics

Language, Amharic: **Study and Training:** 138. *See also* General programs; Language and linguistics

Language and linguistics: **Study and Training:** 54, 462, 531; **Research and Creative Activities:** 699, 719, 872, 908. *See also* General programs; Humanities; names of specific languages

Language, Arabic: **Study and Training:** 138. *See also* General programs; Language and linguistics

Language, Armenian: **Study and Training:** 138. *See also* General programs; Language and linguistics

Language, Azeri: **Study and Training:** 138. *See also* General programs; Language and linguistics

Language, Belarusian: **Study and Training**: 138. *See also* General programs; Language and linguistics

Language, Brazilian. *See* Language, Portuguese

Language, Bulgarian: **Study and Training**: 138. *See also* General programs; Language and linguistics

Language, Burmese: **Study and Training**: 138. *See also* General programs; Language and linguistics

Language, Cantonese: **Study and Training**: 138. *See also* General programs; Language and linguistics

Language, Czech: **Study and Training**: 138. *See also* General programs; Language and linguistics

Language, English: **Study and Training**: 513. *See also* General programs; Language and linguistics

Language, Farsi: **Study and Training**: 138. *See also* General programs; Language and linguistics

Language, French: **Study and Training**: 138. *See also* General programs; Language and linguistics

Language, Georgian: **Study and Training**: 138. *See also* General programs; Language and linguistics

Language, Greek: **Study and Training**: 513. *See also* General programs; Language and linguistics

Language, Hebrew: **Study and Training**: 138. *See also* General programs; Language and linguistics

Language, Hindi: **Study and Training**: 138. *See also* General programs; Language and linguistics

Language, Hungarian: **Study and Training**: 138. *See also* General programs; Language and linguistics

Language, Indonesian: **Study and Training**: 138. *See also* General programs; Language and linguistics

Language, Japanese: **Study and Training**: 138. *See also* General programs; Language and linguistics

Language, Kazakh: **Study and Training**: 138. *See also* General programs; Language and linguistics

Language, Khmer: **Study and Training**: 138. *See also* General programs; Language and linguistics

Language, Korean: **Study and Training**: 138. *See also* General programs; Language and linguistics

Language, Kurdish: **Study and Training**: 138. *See also* General programs; Language and linguistics

Language, Kyrgyz: **Study and Training**: 138. *See also* General programs; Language and linguistics

Language, Latin: **Study and Training**: 513. *See also* General programs; Language and linguistics

Language, Lingala: **Study and Training**: 138. *See also* General programs; Language and linguistics

Language, Macedonian: **Study and Training**: 138. *See also* General programs; Language and linguistics

Language, Malay: **Study and Training**: 138. *See also* General programs; Language and linguistics

Language, Mandarin: **Study and Training**: 138. *See also* General programs; Language and linguistics

Language, Mongolian: **Study and Training**: 138. *See also* General programs; Language and linguistics

Language, Myanmar. *See* Language, Burmese

Language, Polish: **Study and Training**: 138. *See also* General programs; Language and linguistics

Language, Portuguese: **Study and Training**: 138. *See also* General programs; Language and linguistics

Language, Romanian: **Study and Training**: 138. *See also* General programs; Language and linguistics

Language, Russian: **Study and Training**: 138. *See also* General programs; Language and linguistics

Language, Serbo–Croatian: **Study and Training**: 138. *See also* General programs; Language and linguistics

Language, Sinhala: **Study and Training**: 138. *See also* General programs; Language and linguistics

Language, Slovak: **Study and Training**: 138. *See also* General programs; Language and linguistics

Language, Slovene: **Study and Training**: 138. *See also* General programs; Language and linguistics

Language, Spanish: **Study and Training**: 138. *See also* General programs; Language and linguistics

Language, Swahili: **Study and Training**: 138. *See also* General programs; Language and linguistics

Language, Tagalog: **Study and Training**: 138. *See also* General programs; Language and linguistics

Language, Tajik: **Study and Training**: 138. *See also* General programs; Language and linguistics

Language, Tamil: **Study and Training**: 138. *See also* General programs; Language and linguistics

Language, Thai: **Study and Training**: 138. *See also* General programs; Language and linguistics

Language, Turkish: **Study and Training**: 138. *See also* General programs; Language and linguistics

Language, Turkmen: **Study and Training**: 138. *See also* General programs; Language and linguistics

Language, Uighar: **Study and Training**: 138. *See also* General programs; Language and linguistics

Language, Ukrainian: **Study and Training**: 138. *See also* General programs; Language and linguistics

Language, Urdu: **Study and Training**: 138. *See also* General programs; Language and linguistics

Language, Uzbek: **Study and Training**: 138. *See also* General programs; Language and linguistics

Language, Vietnamese: **Study and Training**: 138. *See also* General programs; Language and linguistics

Language, Yugoslavian. *See* Language, Macedonian; Language, Serbo–Croatian; Language, Slovene

Latin. *See* Language, Latin

Law, general: **Study and Training**: 98, 138, 155, 158, 213, 247, 279, 349, 394, 522; **Research and Creative Activities**: 752, 909. *See also* General programs; Social sciences; names of legal specialties

Lawyers. *See* Law, general

Legal studies and services. *See* Law, general

Leisure studies: **Study and Training**: 160. *See also* General programs

Librarians. *See* Libraries and librarianship

Libraries and librarianship: **Study and Training**: 226, 534. *See also* General programs; Information science; Social sciences

Life insurance. *See* Actuarial sciences

Life sciences. *See* Biological sciences

Lingala language. *See* Language, Lingala

Linguistics. *See* Language and linguistics

Long–term care nurses and nursing. *See* Nurses and nursing, long–term care

Lung disease: **Study and Training**: 185; **Research and Creative Activities**: 824. *See also* Disabilities; General programs; Health and health care; Medical sciences

Lung disease nurses and nursing. *See* Nurses and nursing, lung and respiratory disease

Macedonian language. *See* Language, Macedonian

Magazines. *See* Journalism

Malay language. *See* Language, Malay

Management: **Study and Training:** 5, 17, 86, 131, 203, 215–217, 227, 251, 413, 438, 450, 490, 540, 545–546, 613, 638; **Research and Creative Activities:** 725, 774–775, 905. *See also* General programs; Social sciences

Management, nurses and nursing. *See* Nurses and nursing, administration

Mandarin language. *See* Language, Mandarin

Marketing: **Study and Training:** 290. *See also* General programs

Mass communications. *See* Communications

Mathematics: **Study and Training:** 83, 110, 226, 228, 261, 291, 400, 409, 419, 460, 481, 568, 590, 658; **Research and Creative Activities:** 675, 719, 741, 800, 807, 821, 850–851, 853, 895, 898, 916. *See also* Computer sciences; General programs; Physical sciences; Statistics

Mechanical engineering. *See* Engineering, mechanical

Media. *See* Communications; names of specific media

Media specialists. *See* Libraries and librarianship

Medical sciences: **Study and Training:** 3, 13, 21, 23, 25–26, 33–34, 52, 59, 68, 75, 78, 83–84, 93, 98, 104, 111, 115, 117, 155, 158, 161, 164–165, 172, 174, 179–180, 192, 198, 211, 213, 220, 232, 235, 247, 258, 269, 271, 274, 279–280, 282, 285, 289, 292, 295, 302–303, 310, 312, 314, 319, 325, 334, 349, 358, 361, 379, 382, 394, 410, 420, 430, 458, 461, 472, 475–476, 479–480, 500, 505, 520, 522, 525, 534, 550, 557, 565, 568, 570, 575, 589, 591, 596, 639, 653–654, 658; **Research and Creative Activities:** 664, 679–681, 688, 693, 697, 699, 703, 710, 715, 730–731, 737, 741, 750, 752, 755, 760–761, 768, 777–779, 784–785, 790, 796–797, 799–800, 802, 804, 818, 825, 838–839, 857, 887, 892, 894–895, 903, 906, 909–911, 915, 925–926. *See also* General programs; Health and health care; Sciences; names of specific diseases; names of medical specialties

Medical technology: **Study and Training:** 29, 59, 80, 183, 257, 297, 308, 348, 384, 393, 424, 509, 519, 563, 635; **Research and Creative Activities:** 685, 701–702, 706–707, 726, 771, 795, 864, 867, 897, 913, 934. *See also* General programs; Medical sciences; Technology

Mental health: **Study and Training:** 121, 135, 407–408, 440; **Research and Creative Activities:** 739, 834, 911. *See also* General programs; Health and health care; Psychiatry

Mental health nurses and nursing. *See* Nurses and nursing, psychiatry/mental health

Mental retardation: **Study and Training:** 69, 440. *See also* General programs; Medical sciences

Meteorology: **Research and Creative Activities:** 694. *See also* Atmospheric sciences; General programs

Microcomputers. *See* Computer sciences

Microscopy. *See* Medical technology

Middle Eastern studies: **Research and Creative Activities:** 773. *See also* General programs; Humanities

Midwifery. *See* Nurses and nursing, midwifery

Minority affairs: **Study and Training:** 271, 276, 407–408, 599. *See also* General programs; names of specific ethnic minority groups

Missionary work. *See* Religion and religious activities

Mongolian language. *See* Language, Mongolian

Museums: **Research and Creative Activities:** 812. *See also* General programs; Libraries and librarianship

Music: **Study and Training:** 522. *See also* General programs; Humanities; Performing arts

Music therapy: **Study and Training:** 428. *See also* General programs; Music; Therapy

Myasthenia Gravis: **Research and Creative Activities:** 798. *See also* Disabilities; General programs; Health and health care; Medical sciences

Narcotics. *See* Drug use and abuse

National security. *See* Security, national

Neonatal and perinatal nurses and nursing. *See* Nurses and nursing, neonatal and perinatal

Nephrology. *See* Kidney disease

Nephrology nurses and nursing. *See* Nurses and nursing, nephrology

Neuroscience: **Study and Training:** 270, 274, 280, 377, 529–531; **Research and Creative Activities:** 674, 772, 791, 793, 799, 804, 836, 871–873, 896, 924. *See also* General programs; Medical sciences

Neuroscience nurses and nursing. *See* Nurses and nursing, neuroscience

Newspapers. *See* Journalism

Nonfiction: **Research and Creative Activities:** 664, 673, 677, 716, 797, 842, 865. *See also* General programs; Writers and writing

Nuclear science: **Research and Creative Activities:** 906. *See also* General programs; Physical sciences

Nurses and nursing, administration: **Study and Training:** 218, 484, 566–567; **Research and Creative Activities:** 893. *See also* General programs; Management; Nurses and nursing, general

Nurses and nursing, anesthesiology: **Study and Training:** 13, 43, 53, 61, 78, 137, 140–141, 223, 241, 311, 316, 323, 344, 447, 487, 496–497, 503, 553; **Research and Creative Activities:** 666, 704–705, 814, 881. *See also* Anesthesiology; General programs; Nurses and nursing, general

Nurses and nursing, cardiology: **Study and Training:** 405; **Research and Creative Activities:** 833. *See also* Cardiology; General programs; Nurses and nursing, general

Nurses and nursing, critical care: **Study and Training:** 181, 405, 447; **Research and Creative Activities:** 688, 738, 770, 833, 866, 899. *See also* General programs; Nurses and nursing, general

Nurses and nursing, dermatology: **Study and Training:** 151, 224. *See also* Dermatology; General programs; Nurses and nursing, general

Nurses and nursing, emergency: **Study and Training:** 195–196, 331, 405, 447, 498. *See also* General programs; Nurses and nursing, general

Nurses and nursing, general: **Study and Training:** 13, 31, 36–40, 46, 59–60, 82, 94, 96, 102, 115–116, 144, 187, 202, 208–209, 225, 229, 250, 257, 260, 264, 285, 314, 326, 348, 358, 367, 385, 394, 399–400, 405, 423, 439, 445–446, 455–456, 482, 485, 534, 560, 564, 570, 576, 580, 592, 620, 653; **Research and Creative Activities:** 686, 695, 711, 733, 743, 747, 754, 756–757, 766, 787, 791, 802, 810, 816–817, 823, 826–827, 837, 853–854, 856, 858–859, 882, 893, 900, 912, 914, 918–920. *See also* General programs; Health and health care; Medical sciences; names of specific nursing specialties

Nurses and nursing, geriatrics: **Study and Training:** 119, 143, 303, 391, 447, 483, 594; **Research and Creative Activities:** 921. *See also* Aged and aging; General programs; Nurses and nursing, general

Nurses and nursing, history: **Research and Creative Activities:** 684, 687, 819, 825. *See also* General programs; History, science; Nurses and nursing, general

Nurses and nursing, holistic health: **Study and Training:** 114. *See also* General programs; Health and health care; Nurses and nursing, general

Nurses and nursing, long–term care: **Study and Training:** 106, 432, 483, 594, 617. *See also* General programs; Nurses and nursing, general

Nurses and nursing, lung and respiratory disease: **Study and Training:** 185; **Research and Creative Activities:** 824. *See also* General programs; Nurses and nursing, general

Nurses and nursing, midwifery: **Study and Training:** 47, 89, 633. *See also* General programs; Nurses and nursing, general

Nurses and nursing, neonatal and perinatal: **Study and Training:** 4, 218, 378. *See also* General programs; Nurses and nursing, general; Nurses and nursing, pediatrics; Pediatrics

Nurses and nursing, nephrology: **Study and Training:** 1, 18, 58, 63, 300, 447, 477, 614, 634. *See also* General programs; Nurses and nursing, general

Nurses and nursing, neuroscience: **Study and Training:** 459; **Research and Creative Activities:** 723, 873. *See also* General programs; Neuroscience; Nurses and nursing, general

Nurses and nursing, occupational health: **Study and Training:** 19, 44, 71, 122, 136, 214, 231, 239, 253, 298, 356, 403–404, 569, 611. *See also* General programs; Nurses and nursing, general

Nurses and nursing, oncology: **Study and Training:** 62, 153, 322, 397–398, 447, 491, 549, 610; **Research and Creative Activities:** 810, 835, 911. *See also* Cancer; General programs; Nurses and nursing, general

Nurses and nursing, operating room: **Study and Training:** 65–66, 81, 120, 447; **Research and Creative Activities:** 713. *See also* General programs; Nurses and nursing, general

Nurses and nursing, orthopedics: **Study and Training:** 333, 447. *See also* General programs; Nurses and nursing, general; Orthopedics

Nurses and nursing, otorhinolaryngology and head–neck: **Study and Training:** 586. *See also* General programs; Nurses and nursing, general

Nurses and nursing, palliative care: **Research and Creative Activities:** 803. *See also* General programs; Nurses and nursing, general

Nurses and nursing, pediatrics: **Study and Training:** 187, 324, 378, 401, 507; **Research and Creative Activities:** 757, 845, 884. *See also* General programs; Nurses and nursing, general; Pediatrics

Nurses and nursing, psychiatry/mental health: **Study and Training:** 121, 135, 292; **Research and Creative Activities:** 739, 801, 884. *See also* General programs; Mental health; Nurses and nursing, general; Psychiatry

Nurses and nursing, public health: **Study and Training:** 624. *See also* General programs; Nurses and nursing, general; Public health

Nurses and nursing, rehabilitation: **Research and Creative Activities:** 835, 869, 880, 883. *See also* General programs; Nurses and nursing, general; Rehabilitation

Nurses and nursing, school health: **Study and Training:** 435; **Research and Creative Activities:** 715, 847, 849. *See also* General programs; Nurses and nursing, general; Nurses and nursing, pediatrics

Nurses and nursing, wound, ostomy and continence: **Study and Training:** 177, 657; **Research and Creative Activities:** 762. *See also* General programs; Nurses and nursing, general

Nutrition: **Study and Training:** 49, 103, 123, 257, 415; **Research and Creative Activities:** 681, 782–783, 788, 805, 843, 850, 870, 911, 931. *See also* General programs; Medical sciences

Obstetrics: **Research and Creative Activities:** 734–735. *See also* General programs; Medical sciences

Occupational health nurses and nursing. *See* Nurses and nursing, occupational health

Occupational safety: **Study and Training:** 71, 122, 136, 214, 231, 239, 253, 298, 403, 569, 611. *See also* General programs; Health and health care

Occupational therapy: **Study and Training:** 8, 35, 160, 257–258, 301, 305, 329, 346, 383, 470, 486, 488, 533–534, 552, 605, 632, 655; **Research and Creative Activities:** 696, 869. *See also* Counseling; General programs

Oncology. *See* Cancer

Oncology nurses and nursing. *See* Nurses and nursing, oncology

Opera. *See* Music

Operations research: **Study and Training:** 261, 419. *See also* General programs; Mathematics; Sciences

Ophthalmology: **Research and Creative Activities:** 829. *See also* General programs; Medical sciences

Optometry: **Study and Training:** 13, 64, 73, 75, 78, 176, 263, 534, 591, 629, 643; **Research and Creative Activities:** 922, 927. *See also* General programs; Medical sciences

Orthopedic nurses and nursing. *See* Nurses and nursing, orthopedics

Orthopedics: **Study and Training:** 333; **Research and Creative Activities:** 759, 830. *See also* General programs; Medical sciences

Osteopathy: **Study and Training:** 13, 23, 26, 73, 75, 78, 90, 198, 213, 247, 372–373, 420, 430, 478, 534, 578–579, 591, 636, 639, 647; **Research and Creative Activities:** 712, 731, 785, 838. *See also* General programs; Medical sciences

Ostomy. *See* Nurses and nursing, wound, ostomy and continence

Otorhinolaryngology and head–neck nurses and nursing. *See* Nurses and nursing, otorhinolaryngology and head–neck

Papermaking: **Research and Creative Activities:** 794. *See also* General programs

Parkinson's Disease: **Research and Creative Activities:** 832, 861. *See also* Disabilities; General programs; Health and health care; Medical sciences

Pathology: **Research and Creative Activities:** 718. *See also* General programs; Medical sciences

Peace studies: **Research and Creative Activities:** 773. *See also* General programs; Political science and politics

Pediatric nurses and nursing. *See* Nurses and nursing, pediatrics

Pediatrics: **Research and Creative Activities:** 698, 782–783. *See also* General programs; Medical sciences

Performing arts: **Study and Training:** 400. *See also* General programs; Humanities; names of specific performing arts

Perinatal nurses and nursing. *See* Nurses and nursing, neonatal and perinatal

Pharmaceutical sciences: **Study and Training:** 10, 13, 133, 182, 257–258, 280, 285, 304, 330, 394, 452, 472, 512, 514, 526–528, 530–531, 534, 543, 598, 641; **Research and Creative Activities:** 668, 678, 692, 716–717, 750, 789, 791, 802, 804, 842, 855, 862–863, 871–873, 896, 906. *See also* General programs; Medical sciences

Philology. *See* Language and linguistics

Philosophy: **Research and Creative Activities:** 719. *See also* General programs; Humanities

Physical education. *See* Education, physical

Physical sciences: **Study and Training:** 51, 83, 460, 502; **Research and Creative Activities:** 708, 800, 821, 844, 850–851, 860, 885, 898, 916. *See also* General programs; Sciences; names of specific physical sciences

Physical therapy: **Study and Training:** 35, 111, 160, 219, 257–258, 388–389, 422, 479–480, 504, 525, 534; **Research and Creative Activities:** 776, 857, 869. *See also* Disabilities; General programs; Health and health care; Rehabilitation

Physician assistant: **Study and Training:** 348, 518, 534, 653; **Research and Creative Activities:** 811. *See also* General programs; Health and health care; Medical sciences

Physics: **Study and Training:** 228, 259, 400, 481, 658; **Research and Creative Activities:** 699, 719, 741, 852–853. *See also* General programs; Mathematics; Physical sciences

Physiology: **Study and Training:** 280, 530, 650; **Research and Creative Activities:** 699, 720, 793, 804, 846, 871, 873, 896, 917, 929–931. *See also* General programs; Medical sciences

Podiatry: **Study and Training:** 67, 73, 534, 591, 661; **Research and Creative Activities:** 802. *See also* General programs; Medical sciences

Poisons. *See* Toxicology

Polar studies: **Research and Creative Activities:** 699. *See also* General programs

Polish language. *See* Language, Polish

Political science and politics: **Study and Training:** 97, 138, 349; **Research and Creative Activities:** 708, 719, 723, 727, 844, 860, 885. *See also* General programs; Public administration; Social sciences

Population studies: **Research and Creative Activities:** 719. *See also* General programs; Social sciences

Portuguese language. *See* Language, Portuguese

Presidents, U.S. *See* History, American

Press. *See* Journalism

Print journalism. *See* Journalism

Psychiatric nurses and nursing. *See* Nurses and nursing, psychiatry/mental health

Psychiatry: **Study and Training:** 121, 317, 550; **Research and Creative Activities:** 693, 714, 739, 840, 884, 896. *See also* Behavioral sciences; Counseling; General programs; Medical sciences; Psychology

Psychology: **Study and Training:** 78, 270, 276, 314, 317, 334, 377, 400, 408, 440, 481, 531, 599; **Research and Creative Activities:** 719, 723, 767, 790, 824, 850, 869, 872–873, 896, 898, 911, 916. *See also* Behavioral sciences; General programs; Psychiatry; Social sciences

Public administration: **Study and Training:** 97, 260, 314, 349, 656; **Research and Creative Activities:** 708, 727, 773, 844, 860, 885, 931–932. *See also* General programs; Management; Political science and politics; Social sciences

Public affairs. *See* Public administration

Public health: **Study and Training:** 5, 49, 68, 86, 103, 124, 131, 138, 162–163, 189, 216, 226, 230, 243, 251, 273, 293, 303, 348, 413, 453, 457, 490, 534, 545–546, 584, 608, 624, 638, 656; **Research and Creative Activities:** 732, 774–775, 802, 824, 860, 875, 885, 911, 932. *See also* General programs; Health and health care

Public policy. *See* Public administration

Public sector. *See* Public administration

Public service: **Study and Training:** 158, 349. *See also* General programs; Public administration; Social services

Radiology: **Study and Training:** 188, 227, 257, 281, 424, 536, 582; **Research and Creative Activities:** 683, 706–707, 736, 888, 928. *See also* General programs; Medical sciences

Recreational therapy: **Research and Creative Activities:** 724. *See also* General programs; Therapy

Reentry programs: **Study and Training:** 98, 257. *See also* General programs

Rehabilitation: **Study and Training:** 79, 148, 556, 612; **Research and Creative Activities:** 723, 835, 869, 880, 883. *See also* General programs; Health and health care; specific types of therapy

Religion and religious activities: **Study and Training:** 250, 570. *See also* General programs; Humanities; Philosophy

Respiratory disease nurses and nursing. *See* Nurses and nursing, lung and respiratory disease

Respiratory therapy: **Study and Training:** 257, 449, 646. *See also* General programs; Health and health care; Therapy

Restaurants. *See* Food service industry

Retardation. *See* Mental retardation

Risk management: **Study and Training:** 611. *See also* Actuarial sciences; Business administration; General programs

Romanian language. *See* Language, Romanian

Russian language. *See* Language, Russian

Safety studies: **Study and Training:** 71, 122, 136, 214, 231, 239, 253, 298, 403, 569, 611. *See also* Engineering; General programs

Schizophrenia: **Research and Creative Activities:** 896. *See also* General programs; Health and health care; Medical sciences

School health nurses and nursing. *See* Nurses and nursing, school health

Schools. *See* Education

Science, history. *See* History, science

Sciences: **Study and Training:** 99. *See also* General programs; names of specific sciences

Security, national: **Research and Creative Activities:** 773. *See also* General programs

Serbo–Croatian language. *See* Language, Serbo–Croatian

Sexuality: **Research and Creative Activities:** 901. *See also* General programs; Medical sciences; Social sciences

Sight impairments. *See* Visual impairments

Sinhala language. *See* Language, Sinhala

Skin disease. *See* Dermatology

Slovak language. *See* Language, Slovak

Slovene language. *See* Language, Slovene

Social sciences: **Study and Training:** 481; **Research and Creative Activities:** 682, 763, 824, 865. *See also* General programs; names of specific social sciences

Social services: **Study and Training:** 158, 570, 612; **Research and Creative Activities:** 865. *See also* General programs; Public service; Social work

Social work: **Study and Training:** 154, 179, 303, 314, 317, 334, 394, 596; **Research and Creative Activities:** 723. *See also* General programs; Social sciences

Sociology: **Study and Training:** 138; **Research and Creative Activities:** 719, 723, 824, 896, 911. *See also* General programs; Social sciences

Songs. *See* Music

Space law. *See* Aviation and space law

Space sciences: **Study and Training:** 291, 460; **Research and Creative Activities:** 807, 851–853, 931. *See also* General programs; Physical sciences

Spanish language. *See* Language, Spanish

Special education. *See* Education, special

Speech impairments: **Study and Training:** 54–55, 87, 327, 354, 462; **Research and Creative Activities:** 722. *See also* Communication disorders; Disabilities; General programs; Speech therapy

Speech pathology: **Study and Training:** 35, 101, 128, 257, 531; **Research and Creative Activities:** 791, 869, 872, 879. *See also* General programs; Medical sciences; Speech impairments; Speech therapy

Speech therapy: **Study and Training:** 54–55, 440, 462. *See also* General programs; Health and health care; Therapy; Speech impairments

Sports medicine: **Study and Training:** 48, 160; **Research and Creative Activities:** 689–690, 729, 846, 868, 878. *See also* General programs; Medical sciences

Stage design. *See* Performing arts

Statistics: **Study and Training:** 274; **Research and Creative Activities:** 799, 824, 850, 898, 916. *See also* General programs; Mathematics

Substance abuse. *See* Alcohol use and abuse; Drug use and abuse

Swahili language. *See* Language, Swahili

Tagalog language. *See* Language, Tagalog

Tajik language. *See* Language, Tajik

Tamil language. *See* Language, Tamil

Teaching. *See* Education

Technology: **Study and Training:** 203, 215, 291, 460, 540, 568, 658; **Research and Creative Activities:** 675, 699, 741, 749, 773, 800, 807, 851, 895. *See also* Computer sciences; General programs; Sciences

Teenagers. *See* Adolescents

Thai language. *See* Language, Thai

Theater. *See* Performing arts

Theology. *See* Religion and religious activities

Therapy: **Study and Training:** 35. *See also* General programs; Health and health care; names of specific types of therapy

Toxicology: **Study and Training:** 10, 85, 199, 528, 530; **Research and Creative Activities:** 721, 843, 850, 871, 902. *See also* General programs; Medical sciences

Transportation: **Research and Creative Activities:** 875. *See also* General programs; Space sciences

Tuberculosis. *See* Lung disease

Turfgrass science: **Study and Training:** 168. *See also* Biological sciences; General programs; Management

Turkish language. *See* Language, Turkish

Turkmen language. *See* Language, Turkmen

Uighar language. *See* Language, Uighar

Ukrainian language. *See* Language, Ukrainian

Universities. *See* Education, higher

Unrestricted programs. *See* General programs

Urdu language. *See* Language, Urdu

Uzbek language. *See* Language, Uzbek

Veterinary sciences: **Study and Training:** 150; **Research and Creative Activities:** 748. *See also* General programs; Sciences

Video. *See* Filmmaking

Vietnamese language. *See* Language, Vietnamese

Visual arts: **Study and Training:** 400. *See also* General programs; Humanities; names of specific visual arts

Visual impairments: **Study and Training:** 107, 148, 556; **Research and Creative Activities:** 829. *See also* Disabilities; General programs; Health and health care

Welfare. *See* Social services

Western European history. *See* History, European

Women's studies and programs: **Research and Creative Activities:** 777, 825, 919. *See also* General programs

Wound, ostomy and continence nurses and nursing. *See* Nurses and nursing, wound, ostomy and continence

Writers and writing: **Research and Creative Activities:** 664, 673, 677, 716, 731, 736, 780, 785, 797, 802, 842, 865, 894, 905, 909. *See also* General programs; specific types of writing

Youth. *See* Adolescents; Child development

Yugoslavian language. *See* Language, Macedonian; Language, Serbo–Croatian; Language, Slovene

Calendar Index

Since most financial aid programs have specific deadline dates, some may have already closed by the time you begin to look for funding. You can use the Calendar Index to identify which study or research programs are still open. To do that, go to the type of program that interests you, think about when you'll be able to complete your application forms, go to the appropriate months, jot down the entry numbers listed there, and use those numbers to find the program descriptions in the directory. Keep in mind that the numbers cited here refer to program entry numbers, not to page numbers in the book. Note: not all sponsoring organizations supplied deadline information to us, so not all programs are listed in this index.

Study and Training:

January: 8, 27–28, 36, 48, 59, 62, 100, 110, 119–120, 138, 150, 155, 172, 188, 201, 210, 213, 219, 226–227, 237, 240, 265, 274, 276, 280–281, 301, 309, 317, 320–321, 329, 334, 341, 345, 353, 357, 378, 381, 383, 386, 397–398, 400, 406–408, 415, 420, 424, 433, 440, 445–447, 457, 459, 463, 470, 478, 488, 491, 513–514, 518, 529, 533, 538, 543, 549, 552, 565, 582, 599, 605, 610, 630, 632, 650, 654–655, 662

February: 3, 10, 14, 49, 69, 79–80, 85, 91, 102, 106, 121, 132, 160, 167, 174, 178, 183, 192, 202, 206, 209, 211–212, 225, 230, 242, 254, 256, 259, 264, 268, 277, 283, 289, 302, 304, 315, 330, 346, 348, 367, 392, 394–395, 410, 412, 418, 432, 436–437, 451–452, 455–456, 472, 483, 489, 493–494, 504, 510–511, 515, 520–521, 524, 548, 554, 594, 617–618, 621, 641

March: 2, 11, 17, 23, 29, 43, 47, 52, 57, 61, 77, 87, 89, 98, 101, 103–104, 108, 111, 113–114, 117, 128, 133, 137, 139–141, 157, 165, 169, 171, 181, 204, 217, 223, 233, 241, 247–250, 257–258, 268–269, 271–272, 279, 282, 290–291, 303, 306, 311, 313–314, 316, 323, 325, 335, 342, 344, 349, 351, 364–366, 368, 376, 390, 409, 416–417, 419, 428, 443, 460, 462, 473–474, 479–480, 487, 495, 497, 503, 506–507, 516–517, 523, 525, 530–531, 536–537, 542, 553, 563, 577–580, 590, 596, 620, 633, 643, 651, 653, 658

April: 4–5, 12, 21, 24, 26, 30, 33, 35, 37–39, 51, 64, 70, 74, 82, 86, 90, 93, 96–97, 102, 105, 107, 109, 115, 123, 129, 131, 135, 143–145, 148, 152, 158, 164, 177, 194, 199, 203, 207, 215–216, 218, 220–221, 234, 236, 244–245, 251, 267, 278, 285, 288, 292, 296, 305, 310, 324, 326, 332, 334, 343, 347, 350, 352, 355, 362–363, 370–373, 375, 399, 409, 413, 439, 450, 454, 458, 465, 471, 475, 484, 490, 499–500, 502, 540, 544–547, 551, 556, 560–562, 588, 603, 615, 619, 628–629, 631, 636, 638–639, 647–648, 657, 660, 663

May: 31, 34, 50, 60, 65–67, 81, 84, 92, 112, 118, 149, 162–163, 166, 170, 176, 179, 182, 185–186, 195–196, 205, 232, 235, 243, 255, 270, 299, 312, 318–319, 331, 337, 358, 360, 377, 379, 382, 387, 391, 401, 405, 434, 441–442, 448, 451, 453, 482, 485, 496, 498, 535, 550, 559, 564, 587, 595, 612–613, 616, 661

June: 9, 20, 40–41, 46, 53–55, 74, 83, 85, 94, 102, 124, 156–157, 159, 161, 175, 187, 190, 200, 222, 238, 252, 275, 290, 293–294, 327, 340, 354, 385, 393, 429–430, 438, 449, 476, 515, 522, 532, 539, 557, 583, 586, 644–646, 656

July: 74, 184, 189, 238, 260, 266, 461, 532, 541, 572, 574, 576, 600, 609, 624–625

August: 75–76, 102, 110, 284, 288, 334, 361, 388, 507, 528, 560–562, 597, 649

September: 151, 168, 191, 198, 224, 290, 334, 401, 409, 423, 444, 466, 526–527, 555, 622–623

October: 1, 6, 18, 32, 37–39, 42, 57–58, 63, 85, 99, 102, 125, 144, 153–154, 177, 228, 261–263, 273, 300, 326, 333, 411, 421, 435, 477, 501, 505, 512, 534, 558, 573, 589, 614, 634, 657

November: 7, 19, 44, 71, 74, 88, 122, 134, 136, 146, 197, 214, 231, 239, 253, 295, 297–298, 308, 322, 356, 359, 380, 384, 389, 403–404, 422, 481, 508–509, 519, 568–569, 575, 584–585, 598, 611, 625, 635, 640

December: 22, 45, 68, 102, 180, 193, 208, 266, 288, 290, 307, 451, 560–562, 571, 581, 592

Any time: 16, 72, 78, 286, 426, 601, 627, 652

Research and Creative Activities:

January: 665, 668, 670–676, 678, 686, 689–692, 697–698, 704–705, 710, 717, 719, 728–729, 748, 750, 752, 758, 764–765, 776, 780, 782, 786, 791, 797, 799, 802, 804, 825, 828, 835, 838, 841, 846, 850, 859, 868, 874, 878, 883, 892, 894, 898, 901, 909, 916, 929–931

February: 682, 694, 696, 699, 706, 708, 714, 721, 723, 732, 739, 742, 749, 761, 768–769, 777–778, 796, 812, 830, 840, 844, 847–849, 860–861, 875, 885–886, 926

March: 679–681, 703, 707, 712–713, 722, 740, 746, 774–775, 784, 788, 790, 798, 803, 820, 839, 843, 845, 851, 854–855, 857, 863, 871–872, 880, 900, 903–904, 927–928

April: 683, 695, 711, 715, 727, 733–735, 743, 747, 756–757, 762–763, 766, 787, 792, 801, 805, 808, 810–811, 814–818, 822–823, 827, 834, 837, 856, 858, 867, 879, 881–882, 889–891, 893, 919–922

May: 666, 685, 687, 696, 701–702, 716, 726, 741, 753, 771, 785, 795, 809, 842, 869, 896–897, 910, 934

June: 664, 667, 704–705, 721, 724, 731, 736, 760, 813, 829, 833, 907–908, 913–914, 932

July: 779, 925

August: 696, 706, 751, 763, 769, 792, 808, 824, 834, 862, 864, 873, 889–891, 901, 911

September: 700, 707, 738, 770, 774–775, 794, 812, 818, 826, 841, 853, 899, 924

October: 682, 709, 713, 720–721, 725, 762, 772, 783, 789, 806, 821–822, 836, 856, 884, 902, 912

November: 669, 693, 696, 718, 744, 754, 759, 767, 853, 870, 895, 906, 915, 917–918, 923, 933

December: 677, 684, 688, 724, 730, 737, 763, 770, 773, 781, 792–793, 807–808, 819, 829, 832, 834, 865–866, 876–877, 887, 889–891, 905

Any time: 675, 745, 800, 888